# General Motors A-Cars Automotive Repair Manual

## by Larry Warren, Doug Dodge and John H Haynes

Member of the Guild of Motoring Writers

**Models covered:**
**General Motors A-cars**
1982 thru 1989

*Does not include diesel engine or 4-wheel drive information*

(9S5 – 829)                    ABCDE
FG

**Haynes Publishing Group**
Sparkford Nr Yeovil
Somerset BA22 7JJ England

**Haynes Publications, Inc**
861 Lawrence Drive
Newbury Park
California 91320 USA

## Acknowledgments

We are grateful for the help and cooperation of General Motors Corporation for assistance with technical information, certain illustrations and vehicle photos, and the Champion Spark Plug Company, who supplied the illustrations of various spark plug conditions.

© **Haynes Publishing Group 1986, 1987, 1989**

A book in the **Haynes Automotive Repair Manual Series**

**Printed by J.H. Haynes & Co., Ltd. Sparkford Nr. Yeovil, Somerset BA22 7JJ, England**

**ISBN 1 85010 612 6**

**Library of Congress Catalog Card Number 89-84583**

# Contents

**Introductory pages**
  Acknowledgements                                                        2
  About this manual                                                       5
  Introduction to the General Motors A-cars                               5
  Vehicle Identification numbers                                          8
  Buying parts                                                           10
  Maintenance techniques, tools and working facilities                   10
  Booster battery (jump) starting                                        17
  Jacking and towing                                                     17
  Automotive chemicals and lubricants                                    18
  Safety first!                                                          19
  Conversion factors                                                     20
  Troubleshooting                                                        21

**Chapter 1**
Tune-up and routine maintenance                                          28

**Chapter 2 Part A**
2.5L four-cylinder engine                                                56

**Chapter 2 Part B**
2.8L V6 engine                                                           70

**Chapter 2 Part C**
3.0L and 3.8L V6 engines                                                 85

**Chapter 2 Part D**
General engine overhaul procedures                                       96

**Chapter 3**
Cooling, heating and air conditioning systems                           117

**Chapter 4**
Fuel and exhaust systems                                                123

**Chapter 5**
Engine electrical systems                                               158

**Chapter 6**
Emissions control systems                                               170

**Chapter 7 Part A**
Manual transaxle                                                        188

**Chapter 7 Part B**
Automatic transaxle                                                     192

**Chapter 8**
Clutch and driveaxles                                                   196

**Chapter 9**
Brakes                                                                  206

**Chapter 10**
Suspension and steering systems                                         229

**Chapter 11**
Body                                                                    249

**Chapter 12**
Chassis electrical system                                               263

**Wiring diagrams**                                                278, 328

**Chapter 13 Supplement:**
**Revisions and information on 1986 and later models**                  290

**Index**                                                               342

1984 Chevrolet Celebrity Eurosport 2-door sedan

# About this manual

## Its purpose

The purpose of this manual is to help you get the best value from your vehicle. It can do so in several ways. It can help you decide what work must be done, even if you choose to have it done by a dealer service department or a repair shop; it provides information and procedures for routine maintenance and servicing; and it offers diagnostic and repair procedures to follow when trouble occurs.

It is hoped that you will use the manual to tackle the work yourself. For many simpler jobs, doing it yourself may be quicker than arranging an appointment to get the vehicle into a shop and making the trips to leave it and pick it up. More importantly, a lot of money can be saved by avoiding the expense the shop must pass on to you to cover its labor and overhead costs. An added benefit is the sense of satisfaction and accomplishment that you feel after having done the job yourself.

## Using the manual

The manual is divided into Chapters. Each Chapter is divided into numbered Sections, which are headed in bold type between horizontal lines. Each Section consists of consecutively numbered paragraphs.

The two types of illustrations used (figures and photographs), are referenced by a number preceding their caption. Figure reference numbers denote Chapter and numerical sequence within the Chapter; i.e. Fig. 3.4 means Chapter 3, figure number 4). Figure captions are followed by a Section number which ties the figure to a specific portion of the text. All photographs apply to the Chapter in which they appear and the reference number pinpoints the pertinent Section and paragraph; i.e., 3.2 means Section 3, paragraph 2.

Procedures, once described in the text, are not normally repeated. When it is necessary to refer to another Chapter, the reference will be given as Chapter and Section number i.e. Chapter 1/16). Cross references given without use of the word "Chapter" apply to Sections and/or paragraphs in the same Chapter. For example, "see Section 8" means in the same Chapter.

Reference to the left or right side of the vehicle is based on the assumption that one is sitting in the driver's seat, facing forward.

Even though extreme care has been taken during the preparation of this manual, neither the publisher nor the author can accept responsibility for any errors in, or omissions from, the information given.

**NOTE**

A **Note** provides information necessary to properly complete a procedure or information which will make the steps to be followed easier to understand.

**CAUTION**

A **Caution** indicates a special procedure or special steps which must be taken in the course of completing the procedure in which the **Caution** is found which are necessary to avoid damage to the assembly being worked on.

**WARNING**

A **Warning** indicates a special procedure or special steps which must be taken in the course of completing the procedure in which the **Warning** is found which are necessary to avoid injury to the person performing the procedure.

# Introduction to the General Motors A-cars

These models are available in 2-door and 4-door sedan and 4-door station wagon body styles and feature four coil suspension and front wheel drive.

The cross mounted four-cylinder or V6 engines are equipped with fuel injection or a conventional carburetor, depending on model. The engine drives the front wheels through a choice of either a 4-speed manual or a 3 or 4-speed automatic transaxle by way of unequal length driveaxles. The power assisted rack and pinion steering gear is mounted behind the engine.

The brakes are disc at the front and either disc or drum-type at the rear, with vacuum servo assist as standard equipment.

1983 Chevrolet Celebrity 4-door sedan

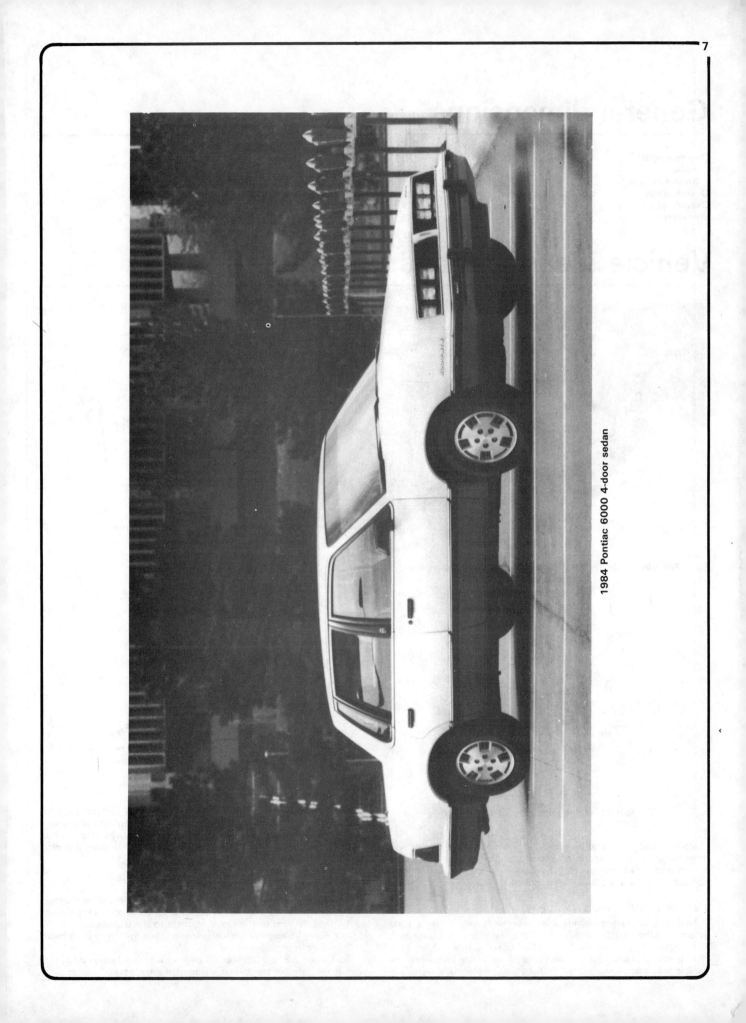

1984 Pontiac 6000 4-door sedan

# General dimensions

Overall length
  Sedan . . . . . . . . . . . . . . . . . . . . . . . . . . . . . . . . . . . . .   188 in
  Station wagon . . . . . . . . . . . . . . . . . . . . . . . . . . . .   190.8 in
Overall width . . . . . . . . . . . . . . . . . . . . . . . . . . . . . . .   68.2 in
Overall height . . . . . . . . . . . . . . . . . . . . . . . . . . . . . . .   54.8 in
Wheelbase . . . . . . . . . . . . . . . . . . . . . . . . . . . . . . . . .   104.9 in

# Vehicle identifications numbers

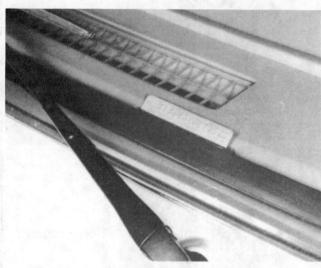

The VIN number is visible through the windshield on the drivers side

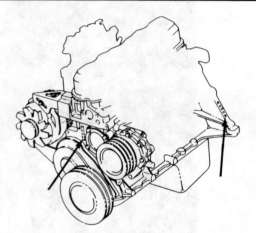

2.5 liter engine number locations (arrows)

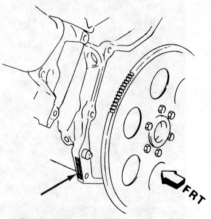

3.8 liter engine number location (arrow)

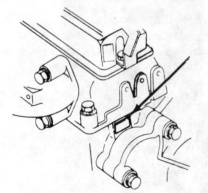

2.8 liter V6 engine number location (arrow)

Modifications are a continuing and unpublicized process in vehicle manufacturing. Since spare parts manuals and lists are compiled on a numerical basis, the individual vehicle numbers are essential to correctly identify the component required.

### Vehicle identification number (VIN)

This very important identification number is located on a plate attached to the top left corner of the dashboard of the vehicle (photo). The VIN also appears on the Vehicle Certificate of Title and Registration. It contains valuable information such as where and when the vehicle was manufactured, the model year and the body style.

### Body identification plate

This metal plate is located on the top side of the radiator support Like the VIN, it contains valuable information concerning the production of the vehicle as well as information about the way in which the vehicle is equipped. This plate is especially useful for matching the color and type of paint during repair work.

### Engine identification numbers

The engine VIN number on the 2.5 liter four-cylinder engine is either stamped on a pad at the front of the cylinder block above the timing cover or at the rear of the block adjacent to the transaxle.

On 2.8 liter V6 engines the VIN is found below the left cylinder head to the rear of the timing cover.

The VIN on 2.8 and 3.8 liter V6 engines is located on a pad at the rear of the cylinder block, just ahead of the transaxle.

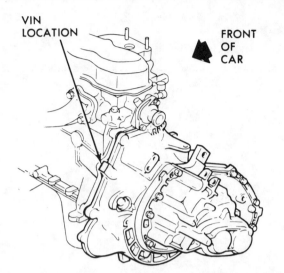

*Manual transaxle identification number location*

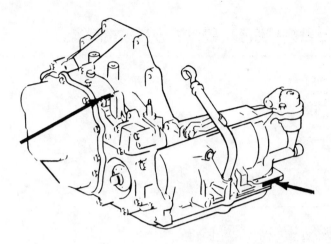

*Automatic transaxle identification number location*

**The Vehicle Emissions Control Information label is located in the engine compartment**

### Manual transaxle number

The 4-speed manual transaxle ID number is located on a pad on the forward side of the transaxle case.

### Automatic transaxle numbers

The VIN number is located on a flange pad at either the lower front edge near the dipstick or the top of the transaxle case. The model code is located at the top of the case.

### Alternator numbers

The alternator ID number is located on top of the drive end frame.

### Starter numbers

The starter ID number is stamped toward the rear of the outer case.

### Battery numbers

The battery ID number is located on the cell cover segment on top of the battery.

### Vehicle Emissions Control Information label

The Emissions Control Information label is attached to the suspension strut tower (photo).

# Buying parts

Replacement parts are available from many sources, which generally fall into one of two categories — authorized dealer parts departments and independent retail auto parts stores. Our advice concerning these parts is as follows:

*Authorized dealer parts department:* This is the best source for parts which are unique to your vehicle and not generally available elsewhere (i.e. major engine parts, transmission parts, trim pieces, etc.). It is also the only place you should buy parts if your vehicle is still under warranty, as non-factory parts may invalidate the warranty. To be sure of obtaining the correct parts, have your vehicle's engine and chassis numbers available and, if possible, take the old parts along for positive identification.

*Retail auto parts stores:* Good auto parts stores will stock frequently needed components which wear out relatively fast (i.e. clutch components, exhaust systems, brake parts, tune-up parts, etc.). These stores often supply new or reconditioned parts on an exchange basis, which can save a considerable amount of money. Discount auto parts stores are often very good places to buy materials and parts needed for general vehicle maintenance (i.e. oil, grease, filters, spark plugs, belts, touch up paint, bulbs, etc.). They also usually sell tools and general accessories, have convenient hours, charge lower prices, and can often be found not far from your home.

# Maintenance techniques, tools and working facilities

## Maintenance techniques

There are a number of techniques involved in maintenance and repair that will be referred to throughout this manual. Application of these techniques will enable the home mechanic to be more efficient, better organized and capable of performing the various tasks properly, which will ensure that the repair job is thorough and complete.

### Fasteners

Fasteners are nuts, bolts, studs and screws used to hold two or more parts together. There are a few things to keep in mind when working with fasteners. Almost all of them use a locking device of some type, either a lock washer, locknut, locking tab or thread adhesive. All threaded fasteners should be clean and straight, with undamaged threads and undamaged corners on the hex head where the wrench fits. Develop the habit of replacing all damaged nuts and bolts with new ones. Special locknuts with nylon or fiber inserts can only be used once. If they are removed, they lose their locking ability and must be replaced with new ones.

Rusted nuts and bolts should be treated with a penetrating fluid to ease removal and prevent breakage. Some mechanics use turpentine in a spout-type oil can, which works quite well. After applying the rust penetrant, let it "work" for a few minutes before trying to loosen the nut or bolt. Badly rusted fasteners may have to be chiseled or sawed off or removed with a special nut breaker, available at tool stores.

If a bolt or stud breaks off in an assembly, it can be drilled and removed with a special tool commonly available for this purpose. Most automotive machine shops can perform this task, as well as other repair procedures (such as repair of threaded holes that have been stripped out).

Flat washers and lock washers, when removed from an assembly, should always be replaced exactly as removed. Replace any damaged washers with new ones. Never use a lockwasher on any soft metal surface (such as aluminum), thin sheet metal or plastic.

## Fastener sizes

For a number of reasons, automobile manufacturers are making wider and wider use of metric fasteners. Therefore, it is important to be able to tell the difference between standard (sometimes called U.S., English or SAE) and metric hardware, since they cannot be interchanged.

All bolts, whether standard or metric, are sized according to diameter, thread pitch and length. For example a standard 1/2 - 13 x 1 bolt is 1/2 inch in diameter, has 13 threads per inch and is 1 inch long. An M12 — 1.75 x 25 metric bolt is 12 mm in diameter, has a thread pitch of 1.75 mm (the distance between threads) and is 25 mm long. The two bolts are nearly identical, and easily confused, but they are not interchangeable.

In addition to the differences in diameter, thread pitch and length, metric and standard bolts can also be distinguished by examining the bolt heads. To begin with, the distance across the flats on a standard bolt head is measured in inches, while the same dimension on a metric bolt is measured in millimeters (the same is true for nuts). As a result, a standard wrench should not be used on a metric bolt and a metric wrench should not be used on a standard bolt. Also, most standard bolts have slashes radiating out from the center of the head to denote the grade or strength of the bolt (which is an indication of the amount of torque that can be applied to it). The greater the number of slashes, the greater the strength of the bolt (grades 0 through 5 are commonly used on automobiles). Metric bolts have a property class (grade) number, rather than a slash, molded into their heads to indicate bolt strength. In this case, the higher the number, the stronger the bolt (property class numbers 8.8, 9.8 and 10.9 are commonly used on automobiles).

Strength markings can also be used to distinguish standard hex nuts from metric hex nuts. Many standard nuts have dots stamped into one side, while metric nuts are marked with a number. The greater the number of dots, or the higher the number, the greater the strength of the nut.

Metric studs are also marked on their ends according to property class (grade). Larger studs are numbered (the same as metric bolts),

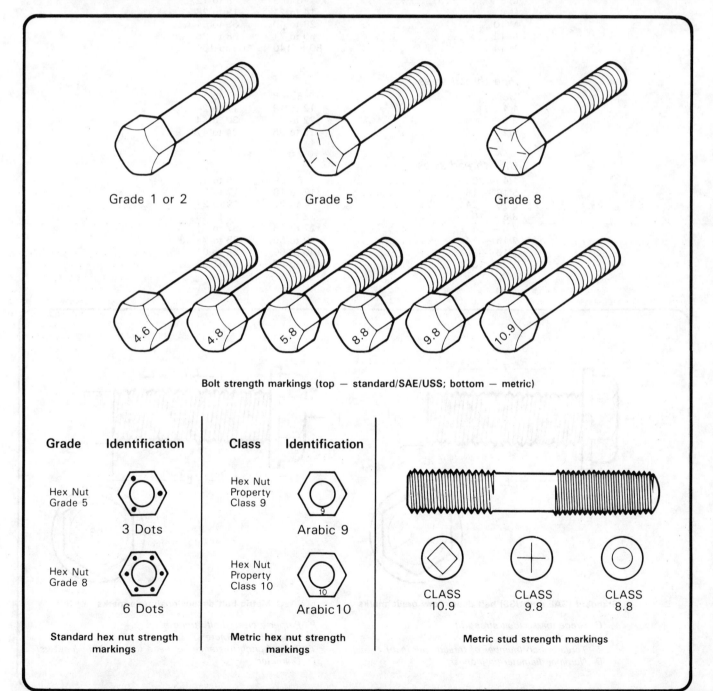

Grade 1 or 2          Grade 5          Grade 8

4.6   4.8   5.8   8.8   9.8   10.9

Bolt strength markings (top — standard/SAE/USS; bottom — metric)

| Grade | Identification |
|---|---|
| Hex Nut Grade 5 | 3 Dots |
| Hex Nut Grade 8 | 6 Dots |

Standard hex nut strength markings

| Class | Identification |
|---|---|
| Hex Nut Property Class 9 | Arabic 9 |
| Hex Nut Property Class 10 | Arabic 10 |

Metric hex nut strength markings

CLASS 10.9          CLASS 9.8          CLASS 8.8

Metric stud strength markings

while smaller studs carry a geometric code to denote grade.

It should be noted that many fasteners, especially Grades 0 through 2, have no distinguishing marks on them. When such is the case, the only way to determine whether it is standard or metric is to measure the thread pitch or compare it to a known fastener of the same size.

Standard fasteners are often referred to as SAE, as opposed to metric. However, it should be noted that SAE technically refers to a non-metric *fine thread* fastener only. Coarse thread non-metric fasteners are referred to as U.S.S. sizes.

Since fasteners of the same size (both standard and metric) may have different strength ratings, be sure to reinstall any bolts, studs or nuts removed from your vehicle in their original locations. Also, when replacing a fastener with a new one, make sure that the new one has a strength rating equal to or greater than the original.

## Tightening sequences and procedures

Most threaded fasteners should be tightened to a specific torque value (torque is a twisting force). Overtightening the fastener can weaken it and cause it to break, while undertightening can cause it to eventually come loose. Bolts, screws and studs, depending on the material they are made of and their thread diameters, have specific torque values (many of which are noted in the Specifications at the beginning of each Chapter). Be sure to follow the torque recommendations closely. For fasteners not assigned a specific torque, a general torque value chart is presented here as a guide. As was previously mentioned, the size and grade of a fastener determine the amount of torque that can safely be applied to it. The figures listed here are approximate for Grade 2 and Grade 3 fasteners (higher grades can tolerate higher torque values).

| Metric thread sizes | Ft-lb | Nm/m |
|---|---|---|
| M-6 | 6 to 9 | 9 to 12 |
| M-8 | 14 to 21 | 19 to 28 |
| M-10 | 28 to 40 | 38 to 54 |
| M-12 | 50 to 71 | 68 to 96 |
| M-14 | 80 to 140 | 109 to 154 |

| Pipe thread sizes | | |
|---|---|---|
| 1/8 | 5 to 8 | 7 to 10 |
| 1/4 | 12 to 18 | 17 to 24 |
| 3/8 | 22 to 33 | 30 to 44 |
| 1/2 | 25 to 35 | 34 to 47 |

| U.S. thread sizes | | |
|---|---|---|
| 1/4 — 20 | 6 to 9 | 9 to 12 |
| 5/16 — 18 | 12 to 18 | 17 to 24 |
| 5/16 — 24 | 14 to 20 | 19 to 27 |
| 3/8 — 16 | 22 to 32 | 30 to 43 |
| 3/8 — 24 | 27 to 38 | 37 to 51 |
| 7/16 — 14 | 40 to 55 | 55 to 74 |
| 7/16 — 20 | 40 to 60 | 55 to 81 |
| 1/2 — 13 | 55 to 80 | 75 to 108 |

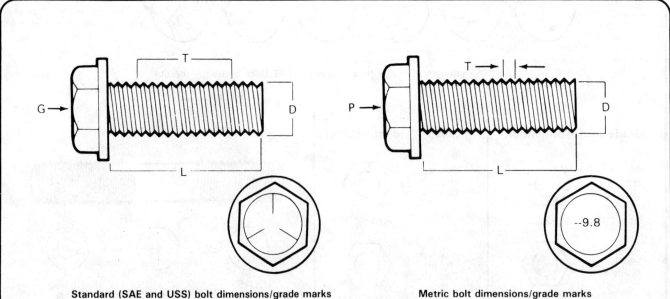

**Standard (SAE and USS) bolt dimensions/grade marks**

- G  Grade marks (bolt strength)
- L  Length (in inches)
- T  Thread pitch (number of threads per inch)
- D  Nominal diameter (in inches)

**Metric bolt dimensions/grade marks**

- P  Property class (bolt strength)
- L  Length (in millimeters)
- T  Thread pitch (distance between threads in millimeters)
- D  Diameter

Fasteners laid out in a pattern (i.e. cylinder head bolts, oil pan bolts, differential cover bolts, etc.) must be loosened or tightened in a sequence to avoid warping the component. This sequence will normally be shown in the appropriate Chapter. If a specific pattern is not given, the following procedures can be used to prevent warping. Initially, the bolts or nuts should be assembled finger-tight only. Next, they should be tightened one full turn each, in a crisscross or diagonal pattern. After each one has been tightened one full turn, return to the first one and tighten them all one-half turn, following the same pattern. Finally, tighten each of them one-quarter turn at a time until each fastener has been tightened to the proper torque. To loosen and remove the fasteners, the procedure would be reversed.

### Component disassembly

Component disassembly should be done with care and purpose to help ensure that the parts go back together properly. Always keep track of the sequence in which parts are removed. Make note of special characteristics or marks on parts that can be installed more than one way (such as a grooved thrust washer on a shaft). It is a good idea to lay the disassembled parts out on a clean surface in the order that they were removed. It may also be helpful to make sketches or take instant photos of components before removal.

When removing fasteners from a component, keep track of their locations. Sometimes threading a bolt back in a part, or putting the washers and nut back on a stud, can prevent mix-ups later. If nuts and bolts cannot be returned to their original locations, they should be kept in a compartmented box or a series of small boxes. A cupcake or muffin tin is ideal for this purpose, since each cavity can hold the bolts and nuts from a particular area (i.e. oil pan bolts, valve cover bolts, engine mount bolts, etc.). A pan of this type is especially helpful when working on assemblies with very small parts, such as the carburetor, alternator, valve train or interior dash and trim pieces. The cavities can be marked with paint or tape to identify the contents.

Whenever wiring looms, harnesses or connectors are separated, it's a good idea to identify the two halves with numbered pieces of masking tape so they can be easily reconnected.

### Gasket sealing surfaces

Throughout any vehicle, gaskets are used to seal the mating surfaces between two parts and keep lubricants, fluids, vacuum or pressure contained in an assembly.

Many times these gaskets are coated with a liquid or paste-type gasket sealing compound before assembly. Age, heat and pressure can sometimes cause the two parts to stick together so tightly that they are very difficult to separate. Often, the assembly can be loosened by striking it with a soft-faced hammer near the mating surfaces. A regular hammer can be used if a block of wood is placed between the hammer and the part. Do not hammer on cast parts or parts that could be easily damaged. With any particularly stubborn part, always recheck to make sure that every fastener has been removed.

Avoid using a screwdriver or bar to pry apart an assembly, as they can easily mar the gasket sealing surfaces of the parts (which must remain smooth). If prying is absolutely necessary, use an old broom

handle, but keep in mind that extra clean up will be necessary if the wood splinters.

After the parts are separated, the old gasket must be carefully scraped off and the gasket surfaces cleaned. Stubborn gasket material can be soaked with rust penetrant or treated with a special chemical to soften it so it can be easily scraped off. A scraper can be fashioned from a piece of copper tubing by flattening and sharpening one end. Copper is recommended because it is usually softer than the surfaces to be scraped, which reduces the chance of gouging the part. Some gaskets can be removed with a wire brush, but regardless of the method used, the mating surfaces must be left clean and smooth. If for some reason the gasket surface is gouged, then a gasket sealer thick enough to fill scratches will have to be used during reassembly of the components. For most applications, a non-drying (or semi-drying) gasket sealer should be used.

### Hose removal tips

**Caution:** *If the vehicle is equipped with air conditioning, do not disconnect any of the A/C hoses without first having the system depressurized by a dealer service department or an air conditioning specialist.*

Hose removal precautions closely parallel gasket removal precautions. Avoid scratching or gouging the surface that the hose mates against or the connection may leak. This is especially true for radiator hoses. Because of various chemical reactions, the rubber in hoses can bond itself to the metal spigot that the hose fits over. To remove a hose, first loosen the hose clamps that secure it to the spigot. Then, with slip-joint pliers, grab the hose at the clamp and rotate it around the spigot. Work it back and forth until it is completely free, then pull it off. Silicone or other lubricants will ease removal if they can be applied between the hose and the outside of the spigot. Apply the same lubricant to the inside of the hose and the outside of the spigot to simplify installation.

As a last resort (and if the hose is to be replaced with a new one anyway), the rubber can be slit with a knife and the hose peeled from the spigot. If this must be done, be careful that the metal connection is not damaged.

If a hose clamp is broken or damaged, do not reuse it. Wire-type clamps usually weaken with age, so it is a good idea to replace them with screw-type clamps whenever a hose is removed.

## Tools

A selection of good tools is a basic requirement for anyone who plans to maintain and repair his or her own vehicle. For the owner who has few tools, if any, the initial investment might seem high, but when compared to the spiraling costs of professional auto maintenance and repair, it is a wise one.

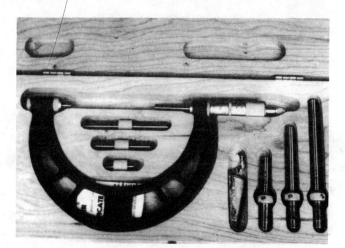

Dial caliper

Hand-operated vacuum pump

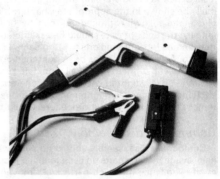

Timing light

Compression gauge with spark plug
hole adapter

Damper/steering wheel puller

General purpose puller

Hydraulic lifter removal tool

Valve spring compressor

Valve spring compressor

Ridge reamer

Piston ring groove cleaning tool

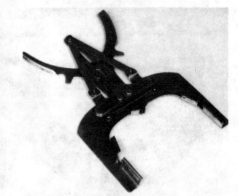

Ring removal/installation tool

Ring compressor

Cylinder hone

Brake hold-down spring tool

Brake cylinder hone

Clutch plate alignment tool

Tap and die set

To help the owner decide which tools are needed to perform the tasks detailed in this manual, the following tool lists are offered: maintenance and minor repair, repair/overhaul and special. The newcomer to practical mechanics should start off with the maintenance and minor repair tool kit, which is adequate for the simpler jobs performed on a vehicle. Then, as confidence and experience grow, the owner can tackle more difficult tasks, buying additional tools as they are needed. Eventually the basic kit will be expanded into the repair and overhaul tool set. Over a period of time, the experienced do-it-yourselfer will assemble a tool set complete enough for most repair and overhaul procedures and will add tools from the special category when it is felt that the expense is justified by the frequency of use.

## Maintenance and minor repair tool kit

The tools in this list should be considered the minimum required for performance of routine maintenance, servicing and minor repair work. We recommend the purchase of combination wrenches (box-end and open-end combined in one wrench); while more expensive than open end ones, they offer the advantages of both types of wrench.

*Combination wrench set (1/4-in to 1-in or 6 mm to 19 mm)*
*Adjustable wrench, 8-in*
*Spark plug wrench (with rubber insert)*
*Spark plug gap adjusting tool*
*Feeler gauge set*
*Brake bleeder wrench*
*Standard screwdriver (5/16-in x 6-in)*
*Phillips screwdriver (No. 2 x 6-in)*
*Combination pliers — 6-in*
*Hacksaw and assortment of blades*
*Tire pressure gauge*
*Grease gun*
*Oil can*
*Fine emery cloth*
*Wire brush*

*Battery post and cable cleaning tool*
*Oil filter wrench*
*Funnel (medium size)*
*Safety goggles*
*Jackstands (2)*
*Drain pan*

**Note:** *If basic tune-ups are going to be part of routine maintenance, it will be necessary to purchase a good quality stroboscopic timing light and combination tachometer/dwell meter. Although they are included in the list of special tools, it is mentioned here because they are absolutely necessary for tuning most vehicles properly.*

## Repair and overhaul tool set

These tools are essential for anyone who plans to perform major repairs and are in addition to those in the maintenance and minor repair tool kit. Included is a comprehensive set of sockets which, though expensive, are invaluable because of their versatility (especially when various extensions and drives are available). We recommend the 1/2-inch drive over the 3/8-inch drive. Although the larger drive is bulky and more expensive, it has the capacity of accepting a very wide range of large sockets (ideally, the mechanic would have a 3/8-inch drive set and a 1/2-inch drive set).

*Socket set(s)*
*Reversible ratchet*
*Extension — 10-in*
*Universal joint*
*Torque wrench (same size drive as sockets)*
*Ball peen hammer — 8 oz*
*Soft-faced hammer (plastic/rubber)*
*Standard screwdriver (1/4-in x 6-in)*
*Standard screwdriver (stubby — 5/16-in)*
*Phillips screwdriver (No. 3 x 8-in)*
*Phillips screwdriver (stubby — No. 2)*

*Pliers — vise grip*
*Pliers — lineman's*
*Pliers — needle nose*
*Pliers — snap-ring (internal and external)*
*Cold chisel — 1/2-in*
*Scribe*
*Scraper (made from flattened copper tubing)*
*Center punch*
*Pin punches (1/16, 1/8, 3/16-in)*
*Steel rule/straightedge — 12-in*
*Allen wrench set (1/8 to 3/8-in or 4 mm to 10 mm)*
*A selection of files*
*Wire brush (large)*
*Jackstands (second set)*
*Jack (scissor or hydraulic type)*

**Note:** *Another tool which is often useful is an electric drill motor (with a chuck capacity of 3/8-inch) and a set of good quality drill bits.*

### Special tools

The tools in this list include those which are not used regularly, are expensive to buy, or which need to be used in accordance with their manufacturer's instructions. Unless these tools will be used frequently, it is not very economical to purchase many of them. A consideration would be to split the cost and use between yourself and a friend or friends. In addition, most of these tools can be obtained from a tool rental shop on a temporary basis.

This list primarily contains only those tools and instruments widely available to the public, and not those special tools produced by the vehicle manufacturer for distribution to dealer service departments. Occasionally, references to the manufacturer's special tools are included in the text of this manual. Generally, an alternative method of doing the job without the special tool is offered. However, sometimes there is no alternative to their use. Where this is the case, and the tool cannot be purchased or borrowed, the work should be turned over to the dealer service department or an automotive repair shop.

*Valve spring compressor*
*Piston ring groove cleaning tool*
*Piston ring compressor*
*Piston ring installation tool*
*Cylinder compression gauge*
*Cylinder ridge reamer*
*Cylinder surfacing hone*
*Cylinder bore gauge*
*Micrometer(s) and/or dial calipers*
*Hydraulic lifter removal tool*
*Balljoint separator*
*Universal-type puller*
*Impact screwdriver*
*Dial indicator set*
*Stroboscopic timing light (inductive pick-up)*
*Hand operated vacuum/pressure pump*
*Tachometer/dwell meter*
*Universal electrical multimeter*
*Cable hoist*
*Brake spring removal and installation tools*
*Floor jack*

### Buying tools

For the do-it-yourselfer who is just starting to get involved in vehicle maintenance and repair, there are a number of options available when purchasing tools. If maintenance and minor repair is the extent of the work to be done, the purchase of individual tools is satisfactory. If,

on the other hand, extensive work is planned, it would be a good idea to purchase a modest tool set from one of the large retail chain stores. A set can usually be bought at a substantial savings over the individual tool prices (and they often come with a tool box). As additional tools are needed, add-on sets, individual tools and a larger tool box can be purchased to expand the tool selection. Building a tool set gradually allows the cost of the tools to be spread over a longer period of time and gives the mechanic the freedom to choose only those tools that will actually be used.

Tool stores will often be the only source of some of the special tools that are needed, but regardless of where tools are bought, try to avoid cheap ones (especially when buying screwdrivers and sockets) because they won't last very long. The expense involved in replacing cheap tools will eventually be greater than the initial cost of quality tools.

### Care and maintenance of tools

Good tools are expensive, so it makes sense to treat them with respect. Keep them clean and in usable condition and store them properly when not in use. Always wipe off any dirt, grease or metal chips before putting them away. Never leave tools lying around in the work area. Upon completion of a job, always check closely under the hood for tools that may have been left there (so they don't get lost during a test drive).

Some tools, such as screwdrivers, pliers, wrenches and sockets, can be hung on a panel mounted on the garage or workshop wall, while others should be kept in a tool box or tray. Measuring instruments, gauges, meters, etc. must be carefully stored where they cannot be damaged by weather or impact from other tools.

When tools are used with care and stored properly, they will last a very long time. Even with the best of care, tools will wear out if used frequently. When a tool is damaged or worn out, replace it; subsequent jobs will be safer and more enjoyable if you do.

## Working facilities

Not to be overlooked when discussing tools is the workshop. If anything more than routine maintenance is to be carried out, some sort of suitable work area is essential.

It is understood, and appreciated, that many home mechanics do not have a good workshop or garage available and end up removing an engine or doing major repairs outside. It is recommended, however, that the overhaul or repair be completed under the cover of a roof.

A clean, flat workbench or table of comfortable working height is an absolute necessity. The workbench should be equipped with a vise that has a jaw opening of at least four inches.

As mentioned previously, some clean, dry storage space is also required for tools, as well as the lubricants, fluids, cleaning solvents, etc. which soon become necessary.

Sometimes waste oil and fluids, drained from the engine or cooling system during normal maintenance or repairs, present a disposal problem. To avoid pouring them on the ground or into a sewage system, simply pour the used fluids into large containers, seal them with caps and take them to an authorized disposal site or recycling center. Plastic jugs (such as old antifreeze containers) are ideal for this purpose.

Always keep a supply of old newspapers and clean rags available. Old towels are excellent for mopping up spills. Many mechanics use rolls of paper towels for most work because they are readily available and disposable. To help keep the area under the vehicle clean, a large cardboard box can be cut open and flattened to protect the garage or shop floor.

Whenever working over a painted surface (such as when leaning over a fender to service something under the hood), always cover it with an old blanket or bedspread to protect the finish. Vinyl covered pads, made especially for this purpose, are available at auto parts stores.

# Booster battery (jump) starting

Certain precautions must be observed when using a booster battery to ''jump start'' a vehicle.

a) Before connecting the booster battery, make sure that the ignition switch is in the Off position.

b) Turn off the lights, heater and other electrical loads.

c) The eyes should be shielded; safety goggles are a good idea.

d) Make sure the booster battery is the same voltage as the dead one in the vehicle.

e) The two vehicles must not touch each other.

f) Make sure the transmission is in Neutral (manual transmission) or Park (automatic transmission).

g) If the booster battery is not a maintenance-free type, remove the vent caps and lay a cloth over the vent holes.

Connect the red jumper cable to the *positive* ( + ) terminals of each battery.

Connect one end of the black jumper cable to the *negative* (-) terminal of the booster battery. The other end of this cable should be connected to a good ground on the vehicle to be started, such as a bolt or bracket on the engine block. Use caution to insure that the cable will not come into contact with the fan, drivebelts or other moving parts of the engine.

Start the engine using the booster battery, then, with the engine running at idle speed, disconnect the jumper cables in the reverse order of connection.

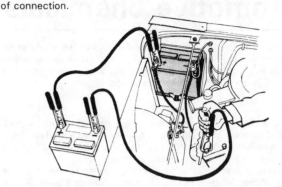

**Booster battery cable connections (note that the negative cable is *not* attached to the negative terminal of the dead battery)**

# Jacking and towing

## Jacking

The jack supplied with the vehicle should only be used for raising the vehicle when changing a tire or placing jackstands under the frame. **Caution:** *Never work under the vehicle or start the engine while this jack is being used as the only means of support.*

The vehicle should be on level ground with the wheels blocked and the transaxle in Park (automatic) or Reverse (manual). If the tire is to be changed, pry off the hub cap (if equipped) using the tapered end of the lug wrench. If the wheel is being replaced, loosen the wheel nuts one-half turn and leave them in place until the wheel is raised off the ground. Refer to Chapter 10 for the tire changing procedure.

Place the jack under the side of the vehicle in the indicated position and raise it until the jack head groove fits into the rocker flange notch. Operate the jack with a slow, smooth motion until the wheel is raised off the ground.

Lower the vehicle, remove the jack and tighten the nuts (if loosened or removed) in a criss-cross sequence by turning the wrench clockwise.

Replace the hub cap (if equipped) by placing it in position and using the heel of your hand or a rubber mallet to seat it.

## Towing

The vehicle can be towed with all four wheels on the ground, provided that speeds do not exceed 35 mph and the distance is not over 50 miles, otherwise transmission damage can result.

Towing equipment specifically designed for this purpose should be used and should be attached to the main structural members of the vehicle and not the bumper or brackets.

Safety is a major consideration when towing and all applicable state and local laws must be obeyed. A safety chain system must be used for all towing.

While towing, the parking brake should be released and the transmission should be in Neutral. The steering must be unlocked (ignition switch in the Off position). Remember that power steering and power brakes will not work with the engine off.

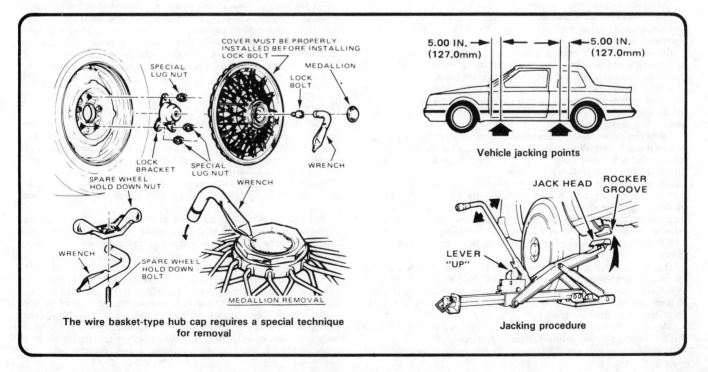

**The wire basket-type hub cap requires a special technique for removal**

**Jacking procedure**

# Automotive chemicals and lubricants

A number of automotive chemicals and lubricants are available for use during vehicle maintenance and repair. They include a wide variety of products ranging from cleaning solvents and degreasers to lubricants and protective sprays for rubber, plastic and vinyl.

## Cleaners

*Carburetor cleaner and choke cleaner* is a strong solvent for gum, varnish and carbon., Most carburetor cleaners leave a dry-type lubricant film which will not harden or gum up. Because of this film it is not recommended for use on electrical components.

*Brake system cleaner* is used to remove grease and brake fluid from the brake system where clean surfaces are absolutely necessary. It leaves no residue and often eliminates brake squeal caused by contaminants.

*Electrical cleaner* removes oxidation, corrosion and carbon deposits from electrical contacts, restoring full current flow. It can also be used to clean spark plugs, carburetor jets, voltage regulators and other parts where an oil free surface is desired.

*Demoisturants* remove water and moisture from electrical components such as alternators, voltage regulators, electrical connectors and fuse blocks. It is non-conductive, non-corrosive and non-flammable.

*Degreasers* are heavy-duty solvents used to remove grease from the outside of the engine and from chassis components. They can be sprayed or brushed on, and, depending on the type, are rinsed off either with water or solvent.

## Lubricants

*Motor oil* is the lubricant formulated for use in engines. It normally contains a wide variety of additives to prevent corrosion and reduce foaming and wear. Motor oil comes in various weights (viscosity ratings) from 5 to 80. The recommended weight of the oil depends on the season temperature and the demands on the engine. Light oil is used in cold climates and under light load conditions. Heavy oil is used in hot climates and where high loads are encountered. Multi-viscosity oils are designed to have characteristics of both light and heavy oils and are available in a number of weights from 5W-20 to 20W-50.

*Gear oil* is designed to be used in differentials, manual transmissions and transfer cases, as well as other areas where high friction, high-temperature lubrication is required.

*Chassis and wheel bearing grease* is a heavy grease used where increased loads and friction are encountered, such as for wheel bearings, balljoints, tie rod ends and universal joints.

*High temperature wheel bearing grease* is designed to withstand the extreme temperatures encountered by wheel bearings in disc brake equipped vehicles. It usually contains molybdenum disulfide (moly), which is a dry-type lubricant.

*White grease* is a heavy grease for metal to metal applications where water is a problem. White grease stays soft under both low and high temperatures (usually from -100°F to +190°F), and will not wash off or dilute in the presence of water.

*Assembly lube* is a special extreme pressure lubricant, usually containing moly, used to lubricate high load parts such as main and rod bearings and cam lobes for initial start-up of a new engine. The assembly lube lubricates the parts without being squeezed out or washed away until the engine oiling system begins to function.

*Silicone lubricants* are used to protect rubber, plastic, vinyl and nylon parts.

*Graphite lubricants* are used where oils cannot be used due to contamination problems, such as in locks. The dry graphite will lubricate metal parts while remaining uncontaminated by dirt, water, oil or acids. It is electrically conductive and will not foul electrical contacts in locks such as the ignition switch.

*Moly penetrants* loosen and lubricate frozen, rusted and corroded fasteners and prevent future rusting or freezing.

*Heat-sink grease* is a special electrically non-conductive grease that is used for mounting HEI ignition modules where it is essential that heat be transferred away from the module.

## Sealants

*RTV sealant* is one of the most widely used gasket compounds. Made from silicone, RTV is air curing, it seals, bonds, waterproofs, fills surface irregularities, remains flexible, doesn't shrink, is relatively easy to remove, and is used as a supplementary sealer with almost all low and medium temperature gaskets.

*Anaerobic sealant* is much like RTV in that it can be used either to seal gaskets or to form gaskets by itself. It remains flexible, is solvent resistant and fills surface imperfections. The difference between an anaerobic sealant and an RTV-type sealant is in the curing. RTV cures when exposed to air, while an anaerobic sealant cures only in the absence of air. This means that an anaerobic sealant cures only after the assembly of parts, sealing them together.

*Thread and pipe sealant* is used for sealing hydraulic and pneumatic fittings and vacuum lines. It is usually made from a teflon compound, and comes in a spray, a paint-on liquid and as a wrap-around tape.

## Chemicals

*Anti-seize compound* prevents seizing, galling, cold welding, rust and corrosion in fasteners. High temperature anti-seize, usually made with copper and graphite lubricants, is used for exhaust system and manifold bolts.

*Anaerobic locking compounds* are used to keep fasteners from vibrating or working loose, and cure only after installation, in the absence of air. Medium strength locking compound is used for small nuts, bolts and screws that you expect to be removing later. High strength locking compound is for large nuts, bolts and studs which you don't intend to be removing on a regular basis.

*Oil additives* range from viscosity index improvers to chemical treatments that claim to reduce internal engine friction. It should be noted that most oil manufacturers caution against using additives with their oils.

*Gas additives* perform several functions, depending on their chemical makeup. They usually contain solvents that help dissolve gum and varnish that build up on carburetor and intake parts. They also serve to break down carbon deposits that form on the inside surfaces of the combustion chambers. Some additives contain upper cylinder lubricants for valves and piston rings, and others chemicals to remove condensation from the gas tank.

## Other

*Brake fluid* is specially formulated hydraulic fluid that can withstand the heat and pressure encountered in brake systems. Care must be taken that this fluid does not come in contact with painted surfaces or plastics. An opened container should always be resealed to prevent contamination by water or dirt.

*Weatherstrip adhesive* is used to bond weatherstripping around doors, windows and trunk lids. It is sometimes used to attach trim pieces.

*Undercoating* is a petroleum-based tar-like substance that is designed to protect metal surfaces on the underside of the vehicle from corrosion. It also acts as a sound deadening agent by insulating the bottom of the vehicle.

*Waxes and polishes* are used to help protect painted and plated surfaces from the weather. Different types of paint may require the use of different types of wax and polish. Some polishes utilize a chemical or abrasive cleaner to help remove the top layer of oxidized (dull) paint on older vehicles. In recent years many non-wax polishes that contain a wide variety of chemicals such as polymers and silicones have been introduced. These non-wax polishes are usually easier to apply and last longer than conventional waxes and polishes.

# Safety first!

Regardless of how enthusiastic you may be about getting on with the job at hand, take the time to ensure that your safety is not jeopardized. A moment's lack of attention can result in an accident, as can failure to observe certain simple safety precautions. The possibility of an accident will always exist, and the following points should not be considered a comprehensive list of all dangers. Rather, they are intended to make you aware of the risks and to encourage a safety conscious approach to all work you carry out on your vehicle.

## Essential DOs and DON'Ts

**DON'T** rely on a jack when working under the vehicle. Always use approved jackstands to support the weight of the vehicle and place them under the recommended lift or support points.

**DON'T** attempt to loosen extremely tight fasteners (i.e. wheel lug nuts) while the vehicle is on a jack — it may fall.

**DON'T** start the engine without first making sure that the transmission is in Neutral (or Park where applicable) and the parking brake is set.

**DON'T** remove the radiator cap from a hot cooling system — let it cool or cover it with a cloth and release the pressure gradually.

**DON'T** attempt to drain the engine oil until you are sure it has cooled to the point that it will not burn you.

**DON'T** touch any part of the engine or exhaust system until it has cooled sufficiently to avoid burns.

**DON'T** siphon toxic liquids such as gasoline, antifreeze and brake fluid by mouth, or allow them to remain on your skin.

**DON'T** inhale brake lining dust — it is potentially hazardous (see *Asbestos* below)

**DON'T** allow spilled oil or grease to remain on the floor — wipe it up before someone slips on it.

**DON'T** use loose fitting wrenches or other tools which may slip and cause injury.

**DON'T** push on wrenches when loosening or tightening nuts or bolts. Always try to pull the wrench toward you. If the situation calls for pushing the wrench away, push with an open hand to avoid scraped knuckles if the wrench should slip.

**DON'T** attempt to lift a heavy component alone — get someone to help you.

**DON'T** rush or take unsafe shortcuts to finish a job.

**DON'T** allow children or animals in or around the vehicle while you are working on it.

**DO** wear eye protection when using power tools such as a drill, sander, bench grinder, etc. and when working under a vehicle.

**DO** keep loose clothing and long hair well out of the way of moving parts.

**DO** make sure that any hoist used has a safe working load rating adequate for the job.

**DO** get someone to check on you periodically when working alone on a vehicle.

**DO** carry out work in a logical sequence and make sure that everything is correctly assembled and tightened.

**DO** keep chemicals and fluids tightly capped and out of the reach of children and pets.

**DO** remember that your vehicle's safety affects that of yourself and others. If in doubt on any point, get professional advice.

## Asbestos

Certain friction, insulating, sealing, and other products — such as brake linings, brake bands, clutch linings, torque converters, gaskets, etc. — contain asbestos. *Extreme care must be taken to avoid inhalation of dust from such products since it is hazardous to health*. If in doubt, assume that they *do* contain asbestos.

## Fire

Remember at all times that gasoline is highly flammable. Never smoke or have any kind of open flame around when working on a vehicle. But the risk does not end there. A spark caused by an electrical short circuit, by two metal surfaces contacting each other, or even by static electricity built up in your body under certain conditions, can ignite gasoline vapors, which in a confined space are highly explosive. Do not, under any circumstances, use gasoline for cleaning parts. Use an approved safety solvent.

Always disconnect the battery ground (–) cable *at the battery* before working on any part of the fuel system or electrical system. Never risk spilling fuel on a hot engine or exhaust component.

It is strongly recommended that a fire extinguisher suitable for use on fuel and electrical fires be kept handy in the garage or workshop at all times. Never try to extinguish a fuel or electrical fire with water.

## Fumes

Certain fumes are highly toxic and can quickly cause unconsciousness and even death if inhaled to any extent. Gasoline vapor falls into this category, as do the vapors from some cleaning solvents. Any draining or pouring of such volatile fluids should be done in a well ventilated area.

When using cleaning fluids and solvents, read the instructions on the container carefully. Never use materials from unmarked containers.

Never run the engine in an enclosed space, such as a garage. Exhaust fumes contain carbon monoxide, which is extremely poisonous. If you need to run the engine, always do so in the open air, or at least have the rear of the vehicle outside the work area.

If you are fortunate enough to have the use of an inspection pit, never drain or pour gasoline and never run the engine while the vehicle is over the pit. The fumes, being heavier than air, will concentrate in the pit with possibly lethal results.

## The battery

Never create a spark or allow a bare light bulb near a battery. They normally give off a certain amount of hydrogen gas, which is highly explosive.

Always disconnect the battery ground (–) cable *at the battery* before working on the fuel or electrical systems.

If possible, loosen the filler caps or cover when charging the battery from an external source (this does not apply to sealed or maintenance-free batteries). Do not charge at an excessive rate or the battery may burst.

Take care when adding water to a non maintenance-free battery and when carrying a battery. The electrolyte, even when diluted, is very corrosive and should not be allowed to contact clothing or skin.

Always wear eye protection when cleaning the battery to prevent the caustic deposits from entering your eyes.

## Household current

When using an electric power tool, inspection light, etc., which operates on household current, always make sure that the tool is correctly connected to its plug and that, where necessary, it is properly grounded. Do not use such items in damp conditions and, again, do not create a spark or apply excessive heat in the vicinity of fuel or fuel vapor.

## Secondary ignition system voltage

A severe electric shock can result from touching certain parts of the ignition system (such as the spark plug wires) when the engine is running or being cranked, particularly if components are damp or the insulation is defective. In the case of an electronic ignition system, the secondary system voltage is much higher and could prove fatal.

# Conversion factors

### Length (distance)

| | | | | |
|---|---|---|---|---|
| Inches (in) | X 25.4 | = Millimetres (mm) | X 0.0394 | = Inches (in) |
| Feet (ft) | X 0.305 | = Metres (m) | X 3.281 | = Feet (ft) |
| Miles | X 1.609 | = Kilometres (km) | X 0.621 | = Miles |

### Volume (capacity)

| | | | | |
|---|---|---|---|---|
| Cubic inches (cu in; in³) | X 16.387 | = Cubic centimetres (cc; cm³) | X 0.061 | = Cubic inches (cu in; in³) |
| Imperial pints (Imp pt) | X 0.568 | = Litres (l) | X 1.76 | = Imperial pints (Imp pt) |
| Imperial quarts (Imp qt) | X 1.137 | = Litres (l) | X 0.88 | = Imperial quarts (Imp qt) |
| Imperial quarts (Imp qt) | X 1.201 | = US quarts (US qt) | X 0.833 | = Imperial quarts (Imp qt) |
| US quarts (US qt) | X 0.946 | = Litres (l) | X 1.057 | = US quarts (US qt) |
| Imperial gallons (Imp gal) | X 4.546 | = Litres (l) | X 0.22 | = Imperial gallons (Imp gal) |
| Imperial gallons (Imp gal) | X 1.201 | = US gallons (US gal) | X 0.833 | = Imperial gallons (Imp gal) |
| US gallons (US gal) | X 3.785 | = Litres (l) | X 0.264 | = US gallons (US gal) |

### Mass (weight)

| | | | | |
|---|---|---|---|---|
| Ounces (oz) | X 28.35 | = Grams (g) | X 0.035 | = Ounces (oz) |
| Pounds (lb) | X 0.454 | = Kilograms (kg) | X 2.205 | = Pounds (lb) |

### Force

| | | | | |
|---|---|---|---|---|
| Ounces-force (ozf; oz) | X 0.278 | = Newtons (N) | X 3.6 | = Ounces-force (ozf; oz) |
| Pounds-force (lbf; lb) | X 4.448 | = Newtons (N) | X 0.225 | = Pounds-force (lbf; lb) |
| Newtons (N) | X 0.1 | = Kilograms-force (kgf; kg) | X 9.81 | = Newtons (N) |

### Pressure

| | | | | |
|---|---|---|---|---|
| Pounds-force per square inch (psi; lbf/in²; lb/in²) | X 0.070 | = Kilograms-force per square centimetre (kgf/cm²; kg/cm²) | X 14.223 | = Pounds-force per square inch (psi; lbf/in²; lb/in²) |
| Pounds-force per square inch (psi; lbf/in²; lb/in²) | X 0.068 | = Atmospheres (atm) | X 14.696 | = Pounds-force per square inch (psi; lbf/in²; lb/in²) |
| Pounds-force per square inch (psi; lbf/in²; lb/in²) | X 0.069 | = Bars | X 14.5 | = Pounds-force per square inch (psi; lbf/in²; lb/in²) |
| Pounds-force per square inch (psi; lbf/in²; lb/in²) | X 6.895 | = Kilopascals (kPa) | X 0.145 | = Pounds-force per square inch (psi; lbf/in²; lb/in²) |
| Kilopascals (kPa) | X 0.01 | = Kilograms-force per square centimetre (kgf/cm²; kg/cm²) | X 98.1 | = Kilopascals (kPa) |
| Millibar (mbar) | X 100 | = Pascals (Pa) | X 0.01 | = Millibar (mbar) |
| Millibar (mbar) | X 0.0145 | = Pounds-force per square inch (psi; lbf/in²; lb/in²) | X 68.947 | = Millibar (mbar) |
| Millibar (mbar) | X 0.75 | = Millimetres of mercury (mmHg) | X 1.333 | = Millibar (mbar) |
| Millibar (mbar) | X 0.401 | = Inches of water (inH₂O) | X 2.491 | = Millibar (mbar) |
| Millimetres of mercury (mmHg) | X 0.535 | = Inches of water (inH₂O) | X 1.868 | = Millimetres of mercury (mmHg) |
| Inches of water (inH₂O) | X 0.036 | = Pounds-force per square inch (psi; lbf/in²; lb/in²) | X 27.68 | = Inches of water (inH₂O) |

### Torque (moment of force)

| | | | | |
|---|---|---|---|---|
| Pounds-force inches (lbf in; lb in) | X 1.152 | = Kilograms-force centimetre (kgf cm; kg cm) | X 0.868 | = Pounds-force inches (lbf in; lb in) |
| Pounds-force inches (lbf in; lb in) | X 0.113 | = Newton metres (Nm) | X 8.85 | = Pounds-force inches (lbf in; lb in) |
| Pounds-force inches (lbf in; lb in) | X 0.083 | = Pounds-force feet (lbf ft; lb ft) | X 12 | = Pounds-force inches (lbf in; lb in) |
| Pounds-force feet (lbf ft; lb ft) | X 0.138 | = Kilograms-force metres (kgf m; kg m) | X 7.233 | = Pounds-force feet (lbf ft; lb ft) |
| Pounds-force feet (lbf ft; lb ft) | X 1.356 | = Newton metres (Nm) | X 0.738 | = Pounds-force feet (lbf ft; lb ft) |
| Newton metres (Nm) | X 0.102 | = Kilograms-force metres (kgf m; kg m) | X 9.804 | = Newton metres (Nm) |

### Power

| | | | | |
|---|---|---|---|---|
| Horsepower (hp) | X 745.7 | = Watts (W) | X 0.0013 | = Horsepower (hp) |

### Velocity (speed)

| | | | | |
|---|---|---|---|---|
| Miles per hour (miles/hr; mph) | X 1.609 | = Kilometres per hour (km/hr; kph) | X 0.621 | = Miles per hour (miles/hr; mph) |

### Fuel consumption*

| | | | | |
|---|---|---|---|---|
| Miles per gallon, Imperial (mpg) | X 0.354 | = Kilometres per litre (km/l) | X 2.825 | = Miles per gallon, Imperial (mpg) |
| Miles per gallon, US (mpg) | X 0.425 | = Kilometres per litre (km/l) | X 2.352 | = Miles per gallon, US (mpg) |

### Temperature

Degrees Fahrenheit = (°C x 1.8) + 32          Degrees Celsius (Degrees Centigrade; °C) = (°F - 32) x 0.56

*It is common practice to convert from miles per gallon (mpg) to litres/100 kilometres (l/100km), where mpg (Imperial) x l/100 km = 282 and mpg (US) x l/100 km = 235

# Troubleshooting

**Contents**

| Symptom | Section |
|---|---|
| **Engine** | |
| Engine backfires | 15 |
| Engine diesels (continues to run) after switching off | 17 |
| Engine hard to start when cold | 4 |
| Engine hard to start when hot | 5 |
| Engine lacks power | 14 |
| Engine lopes while idling or idles erratically | 8 |
| Engine misses at idle speed | 9 |
| Engine misses throughout driving speed range | 10 |
| Engine misses when horn is operated (1982 4-cylinder models) | 11 |
| Engine mount or floor pan vibration or moan during low speed driving (1982 4-cylinder models) | 12 |
| Engine rotates but will not start | 2 |
| Engine stalls | 13 |
| Engine starts but stops immediately | 7 |
| Engine will not rotate when attempting to start | 1 |
| Pinging or knocking engine sounds during acceleration or uphill | 16 |
| Starter motor noisy or excessively rough in engagement | 6 |
| Starter motor operates without rotating engine | 3 |
| **Engine electrical system** | |
| Battery will not hold a charge | 18 |
| "Check engine" light comes on | 21 |
| Ignition light fails to come on when key is turned on | 20 |
| Ignition light fails to go out | 19 |
| **Fuel system** | |
| Excessive fuel consumption | 22 |
| Fuel leakage and/or fuel odor | 23 |
| **Cooling system** | |
| Coolant loss | 28 |
| External coolant leakage | 26 |
| Internal coolant leakage | 27 |
| Overcooling | 25 |
| Overheating | 24 |
| Poor coolant circulation | 29 |
| **Clutch** | |
| Clutch slips (engine speed increases with no increase in vehicle speed) | 31 |
| Clutch pedal stays on floor when disengaged | 35 |
| Fails to release (pedal pressed to the floor — shift lever does not move freely in and out of Reverse) | 30 |
| Grabbing (chattering) as clutch is engaged | 32 |
| Squeal or rumble with clutch fully disengaged (pedal depressed) | 34 |
| Squeal or rumble with clutch fully engaged (pedal released) | 33 |

| Symptom | Section |
|---|---|
| **Manual transaxle** | |
| Difficulty in engaging gears | 40 |
| Noisy in all gears | 37 |
| Noisy in Neutral with engine running | 36 |
| Noisy in one particular gear | 38 |
| Oil leakage | 41 |
| Slips out of high gear | 39 |
| **Automatic transaxle** | |
| Foaming transaxle fluid (1982 models only) | 46 |
| Fluid leakage | 47 |
| General shift mechanism problems | 42 |
| Transaxle slips, shifts rough, is noisy or has no drive in forward or reverse gears | 44 |
| Transaxle starts in 2nd gear only (1982 models) | 45 |
| Transaxle will not downshift with accelerator pedal pressed to the floor | 43 |
| **Driveaxles** | |
| Clicking noise in turns | 48 |
| Knock or clunk when accelerating from a coast | 49 |
| Shudder or vibration during acceleration | 50 |
| **Brakes** | |
| Brake pedal feels spongy when depressed | 55 |
| Brake pedal pulsates during brake application | 58 |
| Excessive brake pedal travel | 54 |
| Excessive effort required to stop vehicle | 56 |
| Noise (high-pitched squeal without the brakes applied) | 53 |
| Pedal travels to the floor with little resistance | 57 |
| Vehicle pulls to one side during braking | 52 |
| **Rear axle** | |
| Noise | 51 |
| **Suspension and steering systems** | |
| Excessive pitching and/or rolling around corners or during braking | 61 |
| Excessive play in steering | 63 |
| Excessive tire wear (not specific to one area) | 65 |
| Excessive tire wear on inside edge | 67 |
| Excessive tire wear on outside edge | 66 |
| Excessively stiff steering | 62 |
| Lack of power assistance | 64 |
| Shimmy, shake or vibration | 60 |
| Tire tread worn in one place | 68 |
| Vehicle pulls to one side | 59 |

This section provides an easy reference guide to the more common problems which may occur during the operation of your vehicle. These problems and possible causes are grouped under various components or systems; i.e. Engine, Cooling system, etc., and also refer to the Chapter and/or Section which deals with the problem.

Remember that successful troubleshooting is not a mysterious "black art" practiced only by professional mechanics; it's simply the result of a bit of knowledge combined with an intelligent, systematic approach to the problem. Always work by a process of elimination, starting with the simplest solution and working through to the most complex — and never overlook the obvious. Anyone can forget to fill the gas tank or leave the lights on overnight, so don't assume that you are above such oversights.

Finally, always get clear in your mind why a problem has occurred and take steps to ensure that it doesn't happen again. If the electrical system fails because of a poor connection, check all other connections in the system to make sure that they don't fail as well; if a particular fuse continues to blow, find out why — don't just go on replacing fuses. Remember, failure of a small component can often be indicative of potential failure or incorrect functioning of a more important component or system.

## *Engine*

### 1  Engine will not rotate when attempting to start

1    Battery terminal connections loose or corroded. Check the cable terminals at the battery; tighten the cable or remove corrosion as necessary.
2    Battery discharged or faulty. If the cable connections are clean and tight on the battery posts, turn the key to the On position and switch on the headlights and/or windshield wipers. If they fail to function, the battery is discharged.
3    Automatic transmission not completely engaged in Park or clutch not completely depressed.
4    Broken, loose or disconnected wiring in the starting circuit. Inspect all wiring and connectors at the battery, starter solenoid and ignition switch.
5    Starter motor pinion jammed in flywheel ring gear. If manual transmission, place transmission in gear and rock the vehicle to manually turn the engine. Remove starter and inspect pinion and flywheel at earliest convenience.
6    Starter solenoid faulty (Chapter 5).
7    Starter motor faulty (Chapter 5).
8    Ignition switch faulty (Chapter 12).

### 2  Engine rotates but will not start

1    Fuel tank empty.
2    Battery discharged (engine rotates slowly). Check the operation of electrical components as described in previous Section.
3    Battery terminal connections loose or corroded. See previous Section.
4    Carburetor flooded and/or fuel level in carburetor incorrect. This will usually be accompanied by a strong fuel odor from under the hood. Wait a few minutes, depress the accelerator pedal all the way to the floor and attempt to start the engine.
5    Choke control inoperative (Chapter 1).
6    Fuel not reaching carburetor. With ignition switch in Off position, open hood, remove the top plate of air cleaner assembly and observe the top of the carburetor (manually move the choke plate back if necessary). Have an assistant depress the accelerator pedal and check that fuel spurts into the carburetor. If not, check the fuel filter (Chapter 1), fuel lines and fuel pump (Chapter 4).
7    Fuel injector or fuel pump faulty (fuel injected vehicles) (Chapter 4).
8    Excessive moisture on, or damage to, ignition components (Chapter 5).
9    Worn, faulty or incorrectly gapped spark plugs (Chapter 1).
10   Broken, loose or disconnected wiring in the starting circuit (see previous Section).
11   Distributor loose, causing ignition timing to change. Turn the distributor as necessary to start engine, then set ignition timing as soon as possible (Chapter 1).
12   Broken, loose or disconnected wires at the ignition coil or faulty coil (Chapter 5).

### 3  Starter motor operates without rotating engine

1    Starter pinion sticking. Remove the starter (Chapter 5) and inspect.
2    Starter pinion or flywheel teeth worn or broken. Remove the cover at the rear of the engine and inspect.

### 4  Engine hard to start when cold

1    Battery discharged or low. Check as described in Section 1.
2    Choke control inoperative or out of adjustment (Chapter 4).
3    Carburetor flooded (see Section 2).
4    Fuel supply not reaching the carburetor (see Section 2).
5    Carburetor/fuel injection system in need of overhaul (Chapter 4).
6    Distributor rotor carbon tracked and/or mechanical advance mechanism rusted (Chapter 5).

### 5  Engine hard to start when hot

1    Choke sticking in the closed position (Chapter 1).
2    Carburetor flooded (see Section 2).
3    Air filter clogged (Chapter 1).
4    Fuel not reaching the carburetor (see Section 2).
5    On 1982 4-cylinder models, a General Motors technical service bulletin has been issued. Take the vehicle to your dealer and inform him of the problem.

### 6  Starter motor noisy or excessively rough in engagement

1    Pinion or flywheel gear teeth worn or broken. Remove the cover at the rear of the engine (if so equipped) and inspect.
2    Starter motor mounting bolts loose or missing.

### 7  Engine starts but stops immediately

1    Loose or faulty electrical connections at distributor, coil or alternator.
2    Insufficient fuel reaching the carburetor/fuel injector(s). Disconnect the fuel line at the carburetor/fuel injector(s) and remove the filter (Chapter 1). Place a container under the disconnected fuel line. Observe the flow of fuel from the line. If little or none at all, check for blockage in the lines and/or replace the fuel pump (Chapter 4).
3    Vacuum leak at the gasket surfaces of the intake manifold and/or carburetor/fuel injection unit(s). Make sure that all mounting bolts (nuts) are tightened securely and that all vacuum hoses connected to the carburetor/fuel injection unit(s) and manifold are positioned properly and in good condition.

### 8  Engine lopes while idling or idles erratically

1    Vacuum leakage. Check mounting bolts (nuts) at the carburetor/fuel injection unit(s) and intake manifold for tightness. Make sure that all vacuum hoses are connected and in good condition. Use a stethoscope or a length of fuel hose held against your ear to listen for vacuum leaks while the engine is running. A hissing sound will be heard. A soapy water solution will also detect leaks. Check the carburetor/fuel injector and intake manifold gasket surfaces.
2    Leaking EGR valve or plugged PCV valve (see Chapters 1 and 6).
3    Air filter clogged (Chapter 1).
4    Fuel pump not delivering sufficient fuel to the carburetor/fuel

injector (see Section 7).
5 Carburetor out of adjustment (Chapter 4).
6 Leaking head gasket. If this is suspected, take the vehicle to a repair shop or dealer where the engine can be pressure checked.
7 Timing chain and/or gears worn (Chapter 2).
8 Camshaft lobes worn (Chapter 2).
9 On 1982 models with 2.8 liter V6 engines, a General Motors dealer technical service bulletin concerning this has been issued. Take the vehicle to your dealer and inform him of the problem.

**9  Engine misses at idle speed**

1 Spark plugs worn or not gapped properly (Chapter 1).
2 Faulty spark plug wires (Chapter 1).
3 Choke not operating properly (Chapter 1).

**10  Engine misses throughout driving speed range**

1 Fuel filter clogged and/or impurities in the fuel system (Chapter 1). Also check fuel output at the carburetor/fuel injector (see Section 7).
2 Faulty or incorrectly gapped spark plugs (Chapter 1).
3 Incorrect ignition timing (Chapter 1).
4 Check for cracked distributor cap, disconnected distributor wires and damaged distributor components (Chapter 1).
5 Leaking spark plug wires (Chapter 1).
6 Faulty emissions system components (Chapter 6).
7 Low or uneven cylinder compression pressures. Remove spark plugs and test compression with gauge (Chapter 1).
8 Weak or faulty ignition system (Chapter 5).
9 Vacuum leaks at carburetor/fuel injection unit(s), intake manifold or vacuum hoses (see Section 8).

**11  Engine misses when horn is operated (1982 four-cylinder models)**

A General Motors dealer technical service bulletin concerning this problem has been issued. Take the vehicle to your dealer and inform him of the problem.

**12  Engine mount or floor pan vibration or "moan" during low speed driving (1982 4-cylinder models)**

A General Motors dealer technical service bulletin concerning this problem has been issued. Take the vehicle to your dealer and inform him of the problem.

**13  Engine stalls**

1 Idle speed incorrect (Chapter 1).
2 Fuel filter clogged and/or water and impurities in the fuel system (Chapter 1).
3 Choke improperly adjusted or sticking (Chapter 1).
4 Distributor components damp or damaged (Chapter 5).
5 Faulty emissions system components (Chapter 6).
6 Faulty or incorrectly gapped spark plugs (Chapter 1). Also check spark plug wires (Chapter 1).
7 Vacuum leak at the carburetor/fuel injection unit(s), intake manifold or vacuum hoses. Check as described in Section 8.
8 Valve clearances incorrectly set (Chapter 2).

**14  Engine lacks power**

1 Incorrect ignition timing (Chapter 1).
2 Excessive play in distributor shaft. At the same time, check for

worn rotor, faulty distributor cap, wires, etc. (Chapters 1 and 5).
3 Faulty or incorrectly gapped spark plugs (Chapter 1).
4 Carburetor/fuel injection unit not adjusted properly or excessively worn (Chapter 4).
5 Faulty coil (Chapter 5).
6 Brakes binding (Chapter 1).
7 Automatic transmission fluid level incorrect (Chapter 1).
8 Clutch slipping (Chapter 8).
9 Fuel filter clogged and/or impurities in the fuel system (Chapter 1).
10 Emissions control system not functioning properly (Chapter 6).
11 Use of substandard fuel. Fill tank with proper octane fuel.
12 Low or uneven cylinder compression pressures. Test with compression tester, which will detect leaking valves and/or blown head gasket (Chapter 1).

**15  Engine backfires**

1 Emissions system not functioning properly (Chapter 6).
2 Ignition timing incorrect (Chapter 1).
3 Faulty secondary ignition system (cracked spark plug insulator, faulty plug wires, distributor cap and/or rotor) (Chapters 1 and 5).
4 Carburetor/fuel injection unit in need of adjustment or worn excessively (Chapter 4).
5 Vacuum leak at carburetor/fuel injection unit(s), intake manifold or vacuum hoses. Check as described in Section 8.
6 Valve clearances incorrectly set, and/or valves sticking (Chapter 2).

**16  Pinging or knocking engine sounds during acceleration or uphill**

1 Incorrect grade of fuel. Fill tank with fuel of the proper octane rating.
2 Ignition timing incorrect (Chapter 1).
3 Carburetor/fuel injection unit in need of adjustment (Chapter 4).
4 Improper spark plugs. Check plug type against Emissions Control Information label located in engine compartment. Also check plugs and wires for damage (Chapter 1).
5 Worn or damaged distributor components (Chapter 5).
6 Faulty emissions system (Chapter 6).
7 Vacuum leak. Check as described in Section 8.
8 On 1982 models with a 1.8 liter engine, 2-barrel carburetor and cruise control, but no air conditioning, a General Motors dealer service bulletin concerning this problem has been issued. Take the vehicle to your dealer and inform him of the problem.

**17  Engine diesels (continues to run) after switching off**

1 Idle speed too high (Chapter 1).
2 Electrical solenoid at side of carburetor not functioning properly (not all models, see Chapter 4).
3 Ignition timing incorrectly adjusted (Chapter 1).
4 Thermo-controlled air cleaner heat valve not operating properly (Chapter 6).
5 Excessive engine operating temperature. Probable causes of this are malfunctioning thermostat, clogged radiator, faulty water pump (Chapter 3).

*Engine electrical system*

**18  Battery will not hold a charge**

1 Alternator drivebelt defective or not adjusted properly (Chapter 1).
2 Electrolyte level low or battery discharged (Chapter 1).
3 Battery terminals loose or corroded (Chapter 1).
4 Alternator not charging properly (Chapter 5).
5 Loose, broken or faulty wiring in the charging circuit (Chapter 5).
6 Short in vehicle wiring causing a continual drain on battery.
7 Battery defective internally.

## 19  Ignition light fails to go out

1   Fault in alternator or charging circuit (Chapter 5).
2   Alternator drivebelt defective or not properly adjusted (Chapter 1).

## 20  Ignition light fails to come on when key is turned on

1   Warning light bulb defective (Chapter 12).
2   Alternator faulty (Chapter 5).
3   Fault in the printed circuit, dash wiring or bulb holder (Chapter 12).

## 21  "Check engine" light comes on

See Chapter 6.

## Fuel system

## 22  Excessive fuel consumption

1   Dirty or clogged air filter element (Chapter 1).
2   Incorrectly set ignition timing (Chapter 1).
3   Choke sticking or improperly adjusted (Chapter 1).
4   Emissions system not functioning properly (not all vehicles, see Chapter 6).
5   Carburetor idle speed and/or mixture not adjusted properly (Chapter 1).
6   Carburetor/fuel injection internal parts excessively worn or damaged (Chapter 4).
7   Low tire pressure or incorrect tire size (Chapter 1).

## 23  Fuel leakage and/or fuel odor

1   Leak in a fuel feed or vent line (Chapter 4).
2   Tank overfilled. Fill only to automatic shut-off.
3   Emissions system filter clogged (Chapter 1).
4   Vapor leaks from system lines (Chapter 4).
5   Carburetor/fuel injection internal parts excessively worn or out of adjustment (Chapter 4).

## Cooling system

## 24  Overheating

1   Insufficient coolant in system (Chapter 1).
2   Water pump drivebelt defective or not adjusted properly (Chapter 1).
3   Radiator core blocked or radiator grille dirty and restricted (Chapter 3).
4   Thermostat faulty (Chapter 3).
5   Fan blades broken or cracked (Chapter 3).
6   Radiator cap not maintaining proper pressure. Have cap pressure tested by gas station or repair shop.
7   Ignition timing incorrect (Chapter 1).

## 25  Overcooling

1   Thermostat faulty (Chapter 3).
2   Inaccurate temperature gauge (Chapter 12)

## 26  External coolant leakage

1   Deteriorated or damaged hoses or loose clamps. Replace hoses and/or tighten clamps at hose connections (Chapter 1).
2   Water pump seals defective. If this is the case, water will drip from the "weep" hole in the water pump body (Chapter 1).
3   Leakage from radiator core or header tank. This will require the radiator to be professionally repaired (see Chapter 3 for removal procedures).
4   Engine drain plugs or water jacket core plugs leaking (see Chapter 2).

## 27  Internal coolant leakage

**Note:** *Internal coolant leaks can usually be detected by examining the oil. Check the dipstick and inside of the rocker arm cover for water deposits and an oil consistency like that of a milkshake.*
1   Leaking cylinder head gasket. Have the cooling system pressure tested.
2   Cracked cylinder bore or cylinder head. Dismantle engine and inspect (Chapter 2).

## 28  Coolant loss

1   Too much coolant in system (Chapter 1).
2   Coolant boiling away due to overheating (see Section 24).
3   Internal or external leakage (see Sections 26 and 27).
4   Faulty radiator cap. Have the cap pressure tested.
5   On 1982 models with 3.0 liter V6 engines, a General Motors dealer technical service bulletin concerning this problem has been issued. Take the vehicle to your dealer and inform him of the problem.

## 29  Poor coolant circulation

1   Inoperative water pump. A quick test is to pinch the top radiator hose closed with your hand while the engine is idling, then let it loose. You should feel the surge of coolant if the pump is working properly (Chapter 1).
2   Restriction in cooling system. Drain, flush and refill the system (Chapter 1). If necessary, remove the radiator (Chapter 3) and have it reverse flushed.
3   Water pump drivebelt defective or not adjusted properly (Chapter 1).
4   Thermostat sticking (Chapter 3).

## Clutch

## 30  Fails to release (pedal pressed to the floor — shift lever does not move freely in and out of Reverse)

1   Improper linkage free play adjustment (Chapter 8).
2   Clutch fork off ball stud.
3   Clutch plate warped or damaged (Chapter 8).

## 31  Clutch slips (engine speed increases with no increase in vehicle speed)

1   Linkage out of adjustment (Chapter 8).
2   Clutch plate oil soaked or lining worn. Remove clutch (Chapter 8) and inspect.
3   Clutch plate not seated. It may take 30 or 40 normal starts for a new one to seat.

## 32 Grabbing (chattering) as clutch is engaged

1 Oil on clutch plate lining. Remove (Chapter 8) and inspect. Correct any leakage source.
2 Worn or loose engine or transmission mounts. These units move slightly when clutch is released. Inspect mounts and bolts.
3 Worn splines on clutch plate hub. Remove clutch components (Chapter 8) and inspect.
4 Warped pressure plate or flywheel. Remove clutch components and inspect.

## 33 Squeal or rumble with clutch fully engaged (pedal released)

1 Improper adjustment; no free play (Chapter 1).
2 Release bearing binding on transmission bearing retainer. Remove clutch components (Chapter 8) and check bearing. Remove any burrs or nicks, clean and relubricate before reinstallation.
3 Weak linkage return spring. Replace the spring.

## 34 Squeal or rumble with clutch fully disengaged (pedal depressed)

1 Worn, defective or broken release bearing (Chapter 8).
2 Worn or broken pressure plate springs (or diaphragm fingers) (Chapter 8).

## 35 Clutch pedal stays on floor when disengaged

1 Bind in linkage or release bearing. Inspect linkage or remove clutch components as necessary.
2 Linkage springs being over-extended. Adjust linkage for proper free play. Make sure proper pedal stop (bumper) is installed.

## Manual transaxle

## 36 Noisy in Neutral with engine running

1 Input shaft bearing worn.
2 Damaged main drive gear bearing.
3 Worn countershaft bearings.
4 Worn or damaged countershaft end play shims.

## 37 Noisy in all gears

1 Any of the above causes, and/or:
2 Insufficient lubricant (see checking procedures in Chapter 1).

## 38 Noisy in one particular gear

1 Worn, damaged or chipped gear teeth for that particular gear.
2 Worn or damaged synchronizer for that particular gear.

## 39 Slips out of high gear

1 Transaxle loose on clutch housing (Chapter 7).
2 Shift rods interfering with engine mounts or clutch lever (Chapter 7).
3 Shift rods not working freely (Chapter 7).
4 Damaged mainshaft pilot bearing.
5 Dirt between transaxle case and engine or misalignment of transaxle (Chapter 7).
6 Worn or improperly adjusted linkage (Chapter 7).

## 40 Difficulty in engaging gears

1 Clutch not releasing completely (see clutch adjustment in Chapter 8).
2 Loose, damaged or out-of-adjustment shift linkage. Make a thorough inspection, replacing parts as necessary (Chapter 7).

## 41 Oil leakage

1 Excessive amount of lubricant in transaxle (see Chapter 1 for correct checking procedures). Drain lubricant as required.
2 Side cover loose or gasket damaged.
3 Rear oil seal or speedometer oil seal in need of replacement (Chapter 7).

## Automatic transaxle

**Note:** *Due to the complexity of the automatic transaxle, it is difficult for the home mechanic to properly diagnose and service this component. For problems other than the following, the vehicle should be taken to a dealer or reputable mechanic.*

## 42 General shift mechanism problems

1 Chapter 7 deals with checking and adjusting the shift linkage on automatic transaxles. Common problems which may be attributed to poorly adjusted linkage are:
*Engine starting in gears other than Park or Neutral.*
*Indicator on shifter pointing to a gear other than the one actually being used.*
*Vehicle moves when in Park.*
2 Refer to Chapter 7 to adjust the linkage.

## 43 Transaxle will not downshift with accelerator pedal pressed to the floor

Chapter 7 deals with adjusting the throttle valve (TV) cable to enable the transaxle to downshift properly.

## 44 Transaxle slips, shifts rough, is noisy or has no drive in forward or reverse gears

1 There are many probable causes for the above problems, but the home mechanic should be concerned with only one possibility — fluid level.
2 Before taking the vehicle to a repair shop, check the level and condition of the fluid as described in Chapter 1. Correct fluid level as necessary or change the fluid and filter if needed. If the problem persists, have a professional diagnose the probable cause.

## 45 Transaxle starts out in 2nd gear only (1982 models)

A General Motors dealer technical service bulletin concerning this problem has been issued. Take the vehicle to your dealer and inform him of the problem.

## 46 Foaming transaxle fluid (1982 models only)

A general motors dealer technical service bulletin concerning this problem has been issued. Take the vehicle to your dealer and inform him of the problem.

### 47  Fluid leakage

1   Automatic transaxle fluid is a deep red color. Fluid leaks should not be confused with engine oil, which can easily be blown by air flow to the transaxle.
2   To pinpoint a leak, first remove all built-up dirt and grime from around the transaxle. Degreasing agents and/or steam cleaning will achieve this. With the underside clean, drive the vehicle at low speeds so air flow will not blow the leak far from its source. Raise the vehicle and determine where the leak is coming from. Common areas of leakage are:
   a) Pan: Tighten mounting bolts and/or replace pan gasket as necessary (see Chapters 1 and 7).
   b) Filler pipe: Replace the rubber seal where pipe enters transaxle case.
   c) Transaxle oil lines: Tighten connectors where lines enter transaxle case and/or replace lines.
   d) Vent pipe: Transaxle overfilled and/or water in fluid (see checking procedures, Chapter 1).
   e) Speedometer connector: Replace the O-ring where speedometer cable enters transaxle case (Chapter 7).

## Driveaxles

### 48  Clicking noise in turns

1   Worn or damaged outboard joint. Check for cut or damaged seals. Repair as necessary (Chapter 8).

### 49  Knock or clunk when accelerating from a coast

1   Worn or damaged inboard joint. Check for cut or damaged seals. Repair as necessary (Chapter 8)

### 50  Shudder or vibration during acceleration

1   Excessive joint angle. Have checked and correct as necessary (Chapter 8).
2   Worn or damaged inboard or outboard joints. Repair or replace as necessary (Chapter 8).
3   Sticking inboard joint assembly. Correct or replace as necessary (Chapter 8).

## Rear axle

### 51  Noise

1   Road noise. No corrective procedures available.
2   Tire noise. Inspect tires and check tire pressures (Chapter 1).
3   Rear wheel bearings loose, worn or damaged (Chapter 10).

## Brakes

**Note:** *Before assuming that a brake problem exists, make sure that the tires are in good condition and inflated properly (see Chapter 1), that the front end alignment is correct and that the vehicle is not loaded with weight in an unequal manner.*

### 52  Vehicle pulls to one side during braking

1   Defective, damaged or oil contaminated disc brake pads on one side. Inspect as described in Chapter 9.

2   Excessive wear of brake pad material or disc on one side. Inspect and correct as necessary.
3   Loose or disconnected front suspension components. Inspect and tighten all bolts to the specified torque (Chapter 10).
4   Defective caliper assembly. Remove caliper and inspect for stuck piston or other damage (Chapter 9).

### 53  Noise (high-pitched squeal without the brakes applied)

Disc brake pads worn out. The noise comes from the wear sensor rubbing against the disc (does not apply to all vehicles). Replace pads with new ones immediately (Chapter 9).

### 54  Excessive brake pedal travel

1   Partial brake system failure. Inspect entire system (Chapter 9) and correct as required.
2   Insufficient fluid in master cylinder. Check (Chapter 1), add fluid and bleed system if necessary (Chapter 9).
3 ·  Rear brakes not adjusting properly. Make a series of starts and stops while the vehicle is in Reverse. If this does not correct the situation, remove drums and inspect self-adjusters (Chapter 9).

### 55  Brake pedal feels spongy when depressed

1   Air in hydraulic lines. Bleed the brake system (Chapter 9).
2   Faulty flexible hoses. Inspect all system hoses and lines. Replace parts as necessary.
3   Master cylinder mounting bolts/nuts loose.
4   Master cylinder defective (Chapter 9).

### 56  Excessive effort required to stop vehicle

1   Power brake booster not operating properly (Chapter 9).
2   Excessively worn linings or pads. Inspect and replace if necessary (Chapter 9).
3   One or more caliper pistons or wheel cylinders seized or sticking. Inspect and rebuild as required (Chapter 9).
4   Brake linings or pads contaminated with oil or grease. Inspect and replace as required (Chapter 9).
5   New pads or shoes installed and not yet seated. It will take a while for the new material to seat against the drum (or rotor).

### 57  Pedal travels to the floor with little resistance

Little or no fluid in the master cylinder reservoir caused by leaking wheel cylinder(s), leaking caliper piston(s), loose, damaged or disconnected brake lines. Inspect entire system and correct as necessary.

### 58  Brake pedal pulsates during brake application  .

1   Wheel bearings not adjusted properly or in need of replacement (Chapter 1).
2   Caliper not sliding properly due to improper installation or obstructions. Remove and inspect (Chapter 9).
3   Rotor defective. Remove the rotor (Chapter 9) and check for excessive lateral runout and parallelism. Have the rotor resurfaced or replace it with a new one.
4   On 1982 models only, a General Motors dealer technical service bulletin concerning this problem has been issued. Take the vehicle to your dealer and inform him of the problem.

*Suspension and steering systems*

### 59   Vehicle pulls to one side

1   Tire pressures uneven (Chapter 1).
2   Defective tire (Chapter 1).
3   Excessive wear in suspension or steering components (Chapter 10).
4   Front end in need of alignment.
5   Front brakes dragging. Inspect brakes as described in Chapter 9.

### 60   Shimmy, shake or vibration

1   Tire or wheel out-of-balance or out-of-round. Have professionally balanced.
2   Loose, worn or out-of-adjustment wheel bearings (Chapters 1 and 8).
3   Shock absorbers and/or suspension components worn or damaged (Chapter 10).

### 61   Excessive pitching and/or rolling around corners or during braking

1   Defective shock absorbers. Replace as a set (Chapter 10).
2   Broken or weak springs and/or suspension components. Inspect as described in Chapter 10.

### 62   Excessively stiff steering

1   Lack of fluid in power steering fluid reservoir (Chapter 1).
2   Incorrect tire pressures (Chapter 1).
3   Lack of lubrication at steering joints (Chapter 1).
4   Front end out of alignment.
5   See also section titled *Lack of power assistance.*

### 63   Excessive play in steering

1   Loose front wheel bearings (Chapter 1).
2   Excessive wear in suspension or steering components (Chapter 10).
3   Steering gearbox out of adjustment (Chapter 10).

### 64   Lack of power assistance

1   Steering pump drivebelt faulty or not adjusted properly (Chapter 1).
2   Fluid level low (Chapter 1).
3   Hoses or lines restricted. Inspect and replace parts as necessary.
4   Air in power steering system. Bleed system (Chapter 10).

### 65   Excessive tire wear (not specific to one area)

1   Incorrect tire pressures (Chapter 1).
2   Tires out of balance. Have professionally balanced.
3   Wheels damaged. Inspect and replace as necessary.
4   Suspension or steering components excessively worn (Chapter 10).

### 66   Excessive tire wear on outside edge

1   Inflation pressures incorrect (Chapter 1).
2   Excessive speed in turns.
3   Front end alignment incorrect (excessive toe-in). Have professionally aligned.
4   Suspension arm bent or twisted (Chapter 10).

### 67   Excessive tire wear on inside edge

1   Inflation pressures incorrect (Chapter 1).
2   Front end alignment incorrect (toe-out). Have professionally aligned.
3   Loose or damaged steering components (Chapter 10).

### 68   Tire tread worn in one place

1   Tires out of balance.
2   Damaged or buckled wheel. Inspect and replace if necessary.
3   Defective tire (Chapter 1).

# Chapter 1   Tune-up and routine maintenance

*Refer to Chapter 13 for Specifications and information applicable to 1986 and later models*

## Contents

Air filter and PCV filter replacement .................... 29
Automatic transaxle fluid change ..................... 28
Battery check and maintenance ..................... 5
Brake check .................................... 13
Carburetor choke check ......................... 14
Carburetor/throttle body injection (TBI) mounting torque
   check .................................... 20
Chassis lubrication .............................. 10
Check engine light ......................... See Chapter 6
Clutch pedal adjustment ......................... 24
Compression check ............................. 38
Cooling system check ........................... 7
Cooling system servicing (draining, flushing and refilling) .... 26
Drivebelt check and adjustment ..................... 6
Early Fuel Evaporation (EFE) system check .......... 37
Engine idle speed check and adjustment ............ 15
Engine oil and filter change ....................... 16
Evaporative Emissions Control System (EECS) check ....... 33
Exhaust Gas Recirculation (EGR) valve check .......... 32
Exhaust system check ........................... 11
Fluid level checks .............................. 4

Fuel filter replacement ........................... 18
Fuel system check .............................. 17
Ignition timing check and adjustment ................ 34
Introduction and routine maintenance schedule ........ 1
Oxygen sensor replacement ..................... 30
Positive Crankcase Ventilation (PCV) valve — checking and
   replacement ................................ 31
Manual transaxle oil change ...................... 25
Spark plug replacement ......................... 35
Spark plug wires, distributor cap and rotor check and
   replacement ................................ 36
Suspension and steering check .................... 12
Thermo-controlled Air Cleaner (THERMAC) check ....... 20
Throttle linkage check and adjustment ............... 19
Tire and tire pressure checks ..................... 3
Tire rotation .................................. 23
Transaxle output shaft seal and driveaxle boot check ...... 22
Tune-up sequence ............................. 2
Underhood hose check and replacement ............. 8
Wheel bearing check ........................... 27
Wiper blade inspection and replacement ............. 9

## Specifications

### *Recommended lubricants, fluids and capacities*

| | |
|---|---|
| Engine oil type ............................ | Grade SF, SG, SF/SG/CC or CD |
| Engine oil viscosity | |
|   40° to 100° plus F (4° to 38° plus C) ............. | SAE 30 |
|   20° to 100° plus F (-7° to 38° plus C) ............. | SAE 20W-20, 20W-40, 20W-50 |
|   10° to 100' plus F (-14° to 38° plus C) ............ | SAE 15W-40 |
|   0° to 100° plus F (-18° to 38° plus C) ............. | SAE 10W-30, 10W-40 |
|   0° to 60° F (-18° to 17° plus C) ............. | SAE 10W |
|   Below -20° to 60° F (below -30° to 17° C) ......... | SAE 5W-30 (may be used up to 100°F/38° C) |
|   Below -20° F to 20° F (below -30° to -7° C) ......... | SAE 5W-20 (not to be used for continuous high speed driving) |
| Engine oil capacity (including filter) .................... | 4 qts |
| Cooling system capacity | |
|   Including heater ............................ | 7.3 qts |
|   Not including heater ......................... | 6.9 qts |
| Coolant type ................................ | Ethylene glycol base antifreeze and water |
| Manual transaxle oil type | |
|   Above 0° (-18° C) ........................... | API GL-5 SAE 80W-90 or 90W gear oil |
|   Below 0° F (-18° C) .......................... | Dexron II ATF |
| Manual transaxle oil capacity* .................... | 3.5 qts |
| Automatic transaxle fluid type .................... | Dexron II ATF |
| Automatic transaxle fluid capacity* .................... | 6 qts |
| Brake fluid type ............................. | DOT 3 or 4 |
| Power steering fluid type ....................... | GM power steering fluid (no. 1050017) |
| Rear wheel bearing lubricant .................... | NLGI No. 2 lithium base wheel bearing grease |

*Capacity is approximate for refill after draining for routine maintenance. Actual capacity should be measured on the transaxle dipstick as discussed in Section 4*

## General engine

| | |
|---|---|
| Radiator cap opening pressure | 15 psi |
| Thermostat | |
|     Starts to open | 188° to 193° F |
|     Fully open | 212° F |
| Engine idle speed* | |
|     Automatic transaxle | 700 rpm |
|     Manual tranaxle | 750 rpm |
| Valve clearance | 0.012 in |
| Engine compression pressure | Lowest reading should not be less than 70% of the highest cylinder reading with no cylinder below 100 psi |
| Drivebelt deflection | |
|     Type 1 alternator and power steering pump | 0.24 to 0.47 in |
|     Type 2 alternator and power steering pump | 0.16 to 0.28 in |
|     Type 2 air conditioner | 0.24 to 0.47 in |
|     Type 3 | 0.16 to 0.28 in |

*\* Refer to the Emission Control label in the engine compartment and follow the information on the label if it differs from that shown here.*

## Ignition system

| | |
|---|---|
| Distributor direction of rotation | Clockwise |
| Firing order | |
|     2.5L four-cylinder engine | 1-3-4-2 |
|     2.8L V6 engine | 1-2-3-4-5-6 |
|     3.0L and 3.8L V6 engines | 1-6-5-4-3-2 |
| Spark plug type* | |
|     NGK | BPR-5ES, BPR-6ES |
|     Motorcraft | AGR-32, AGR-22 |
| Spark plug gap* | 0.045 to 0.060 in |
| Ignition timing (BTDC)* | 6° |

*\* Refer to the Emission Control Label in the engine compartment and follow the information on the label if it differs from that shown here.*

## Brakes

| | |
|---|---|
| Pad and shoe lining minimum thickness | 0.04 in |

| **Torque specifications** | **Ft-lbs** |
|---|---|
| Rocker arm cover bolt | 2 to 3 |
| Spark plugs | 10.8 to 16.6 |
| Cylinder head bolts | 69 to 72 |
| Rear wheel bearing hub nut preload | 20 to 30 |
| Automatic transaxle drain plug | 12 |
| Wheel lug nuts | 65 to 87 |
| Carburetor mounting nuts | 10 |
| TBI mounting nuts | 13 |

### 1  Introduction and routine maintenance

This Chapter was designed to help the home mechanic maintain his or her vehicle for peak performance, economy, safety and long life.

On the following pages you will find a maintenance schedule, along with Sections which deal specifically with each item on the schedule. Included are visual checks, adjustments and component replacement.

Servicing your vehicle using the time/mileage maintenance schedule and the sequenced Sections will give you a planned program of maintenance. Keep in mind that it is a full plan, and maintaining only a few items at the specified intervals will not give you the same results.

You will find as you service your vehicle that many of the procedures can, and should, be grouped together, due to the nature of the job at hand. Examples of this are as follows:

If the vehicle is raised for chassis lubrication, for example, it is an ideal time to check the exhaust system, suspension, steering and fuel system.

If the tires and wheels are removed, as during a routine tire rotation, check the brakes and wheel bearings at the same time.

If you must borrow or rent a torque wrench it is a good idea to service the spark plugs and check the carburetor or TBI mounting torque all in the same day to save time and money.

The first step of the maintenance plan is to prepare yourself before the actual work begins. Read through the appropriate Sections for all work that is to be performed. Gather together all the necessary parts and tools. If it appears that you could have a problem during a particular job, don't hesitate to seek advice from your local parts man or dealer service department.

### Routine maintenance intervals

The following recommendations are given with the assumption that the vehicle owner will be doing the maintenance or service work, as opposed to having it done by a dealer service department. The following are factory maintenance recommendations. The owner interested in keeping his or her vehicle in peak conditions at all times may wish to perform these operations more often. This can also enhance the resale value of the vehicle, and we encourage such owner initiative.

When the vehicle is new it should be serviced by a factory authorized dealer service department to protect the factory warranty. In many cases the initial maintenance check is done at no cost to the owner. **Note:** *The following maintenance intervals are recommended by the manufacturer. In the interest of vehicle longevity, we recommend shorter intervals on certain operations, such as fluid and filter replacement.*

---

**Every 250 miles or weekly, whichever comes first**

---

Check the engine oil level (Sec 4)
Check the engine coolant level (Sec 4)
Check the windshield washer fluid level (Sec 4)
Check the tires and tire pressures (Sec 3)
Check the automatic transaxle fluid level (Sec 4)

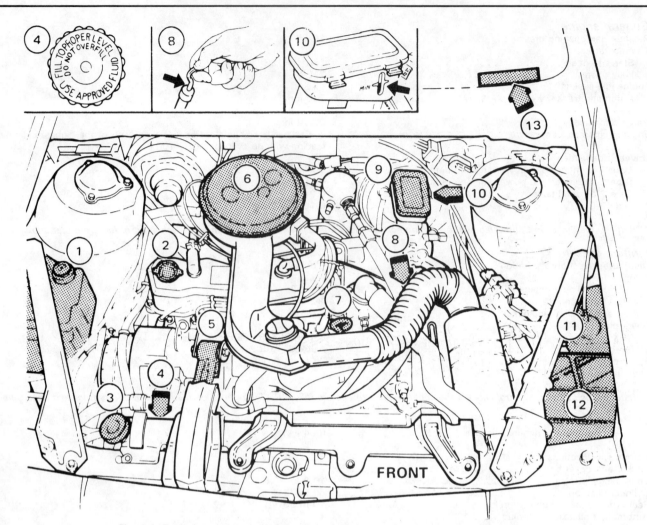

**Fig. 1.1  Typical engine compartment component layout (2.5 liter 4-cylinder engine)**

1  *Coolant reservoir (Sec 4)*
2  *Engine oil fill cap (Sec 4)*
3  *Radiator cap (Sec 4)*
4  *Power steering reservoir (Sec 4)*

5  *Engine mounting bracket (ground attachment for jump starting)*
6  *Air cleaner (Sec 29)*
7  *Engine oil dipstick (Sec 4)*
8  *Automatic transaxle dipstick (Sec 4)*

9  *Brake master cylinder fluid reservoir (Sec 4)*
10  *Brake fluid level checking window (Sec 4)*
11  *Windshield washer fluid reservoir (Sec 4)*
12  *Battery (Sec 5)*
13  *VIN number*

---

**Every 5000 miles or 5 months, whichever comes first**

Adjust the clutch pedal (Sec 24)

---

**Every 6000 miles or 6 months, whichever comes first**

Check the power steering fluid level (Sec 4)
Change the engine oil and oil filter (Sec 16)
Check the tightness of the carburetor or TBI mounting bolts (Sec 21)
Check and lubricate the chassis components (Sec 10)
Check the cooling system (Sec 7)
Check and replace (if necessary) the underhood hoses (Sec 8)
Check the exhaust system (Sec 11)
Check the steering and suspension components (Sec 12)
Check and adjust (if necessary) the engine drivebelts (Sec 6)
Check the brake master cylinder fluid level (Sec 4)
Check the manual transaxle oil level (Sec 4)
Check the output shaft seals and driveaxle boots (Sec 22)
Check the disk brake pads (Sec 13)
Check the brake system (Sec 13)
Check and service the battery (Sec 5)

Check and replace (if necessary) the windshield wiper blades (Sec 9)
Check the operation of the choke (Sec 14)
Check and adjust (if necessary) the engine idle speed (Sec 15)

---

**Every 12000 miles or 12 months, whichever comes first**

Check the drum brake linings (Sec 13)
Check the parking brake (Sec 13)
Rotate the tires (Sec 23)
Check the Thermo-controlled air cleaner (THERMAC) for proper operation (Sec 20)
Check the fuel system components (Sec 17)
Replace the fuel filter (Sec 18)
Check the throttle linkage (Sec 19)

---

**Every 15000 miles or 15 months, whichever comes first**

Change the automatic transaxle fluid and filter (if driven primarily in heavy city traffic, in hot climate regions, in hilly or mountainous areas or if used for frequent trailer pulling (Sec 28)

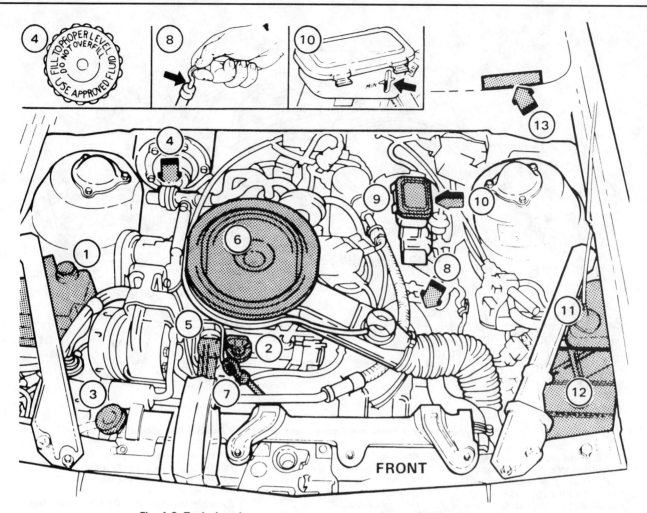

**Fig. 1.2 Typical engine compartment component layout (2.8 liter V6 engine)**

1  Coolant reservoir (Sec 4)
2  Engine oil fill cap (Sec 4)
3  Radiator cap (Sec 4)
4  Power steering reservoir (Sec 4)

5  Engine mounting bracket (ground attachment for jump starting)
6  Air cleaner (Sec 29)
7  Engine oil level dipstick (Sec 4)
8  Automatic transaxle dipstick (Sec 4)

9   Brake master cylinder fluid reservoir (Sec 4)
10  Brake fluid level checking window (Sec 4)
11  Windshield washer fluid reservoir (Sec 4)
12  Battery (Sec 5)
13  VIN number location

---

**Every 24000 miles or 24 months, whichever comes first**

Check the EGR system (Sec 32)
Check and adjust (if necessary) the ignition timing (Sec 34)
Check the EECS emissions system and replace the canister filter (Sec 33)
Check the engine compression (Sec 37)

**Every 30000 miles or 30 months, whichever comes first**

Change the automatic transaxle fluid and filter (Sec 28)
Drain, flush and refill the cooling system (Sec 26)
Check the operation of the EGR valve (Sec 32)
Inspect and replace (if necessary) the PCV valve (Sec 31)
Replace the air filter and PCV valve filter (Sec 29)
Replace the spark plugs (Sec 35)
Inspect and replace (if necessary) the spark plug wires, distributor cap and rotor (Sec 36)
Inspect the fuel system hoses, lines and filler cap (Sec 17)
Inspect and clean (if necessary) the EGR valve (3.0 and 3.8 liter engines) (Chapter 6)
Check the oxygen sensor (Chapter 6) and replace if necessary (Sec 30)

**Every 48000 miles or 48 months, whichever comes first**

Drain and refill the automatic transaxle (Sec 25)

---

**2   Tune-up sequence**

The term *tune-up* is loosely used for any general operation that puts the engine back in its proper running condition. A tune-up is not a specific operation, but rather a combination of individual operations, such as replacing the spark plugs, adjusting the idle speed, setting the ignition timing, etc.

If, from the time the vehicle is new, the routine maintenance schedule (Section 1) is followed closely and frequent checks are made of fluid levels and high wear items, as suggested throughout this manual, the engine will be kept in relatively good running condition and the need for additional tune-ups will be minimized.

More likely than not, however, there will be times when the engine is running poorly due to lack of regular maintenance. This is even more likely if a used vehicle, which has not received regular and frequent maintenance checks, is purchased. In such cases an engine tune-up will be needed outside of the regular routine maintenance intervals.

The following series of operations are those most often needed to bring a poor running engine back into a proper state of tune.

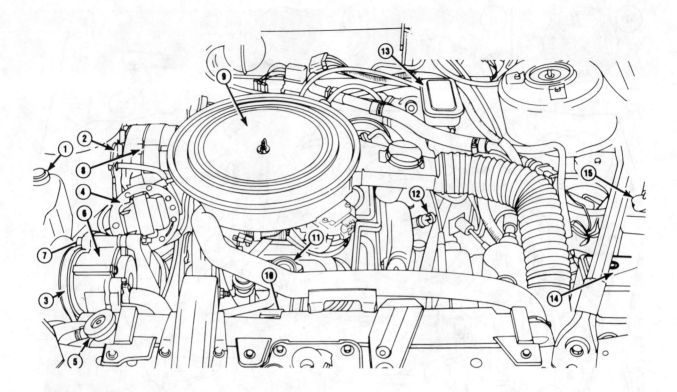

Fig. 1.3 Typical engine compartment component layout (3.0 and 3.8 liter engine)

| | | |
|---|---|---|
| 1 Coolant reservoir (Sec 4) | 6 AIR pump (Sec 32) | 11 Oil filler cap (Sec 4) |
| 2 Alternator drivebelt (Sec 6) | 7 Power steering drivebelt (Sec 6) | 12 Transaxle dipstick (Sec 4) |
| 3 AIR pump drivebelt (Sec 6) | 8 Alternator (Sec 6) | 13 Master cylinder reservoir (Sec 4) |
| 4 Distributor (Sec 36) | 9 Air cleaner (Sec 29) | 14 Battery (Sec 5) |
| 5 Radiator cap (Sec 4) | 10 Oil dipstick (Sec 4) | 15 Windshield washer fluid reservoir (Sec 4) |

## Minor tune-up

Clean, inspect and test battery (Sec 5)
Check all engine-related fluids (Sec 4)
Check engine compression (Sec 37)
Check and adjust drivebelts (Sec 6)
Replace spark plugs (Sec 35)
Inspect distributor cap and rotor (Sec 36)
Inspect spark plug wires and coil wire (Sec 36)
Check and adjust idle speed (Sec 15)
Check and adjust timing (Sec 34)
Check and adjust fuel/air mixture (see underhood VECI label)
Replace fuel filter (Sec 18)
Check PCV valve (Sec 31)
Check cooling system (Sec 7)

## Major tune-up

(Check the above operations plus those listed below)
Check EGR system (Chapter 6)
Check ignition system (Chapter 5)
Check charging system (Chapter 5)
Check fuel system (Sec 17)

## 3  Tire and tire pressure checks

1    Periodically inspecting the tires may not only prevent you from being stranded with a flat tire, but can also give you clues as to possible problems with the steering and suspension systems before major damage occurs.
2    Proper tire inflation adds miles to the lifespan of the tires, allows the vehicle to achieve maximum miles per gallon figures and contributes to the overall quality of the ride.
3    When inspecting the tires, first check the wear of the tread. Irregularities in the tread pattern (cupping, flat spots, more wear on one side than the other) are indications of front end alignment and/or balance problems. If any of these conditions are noted, take the vehicle to a reputable repair shop to correct the problem.
4    Check the tread area for cuts and punctures. Many times a nail or tack will embed itself in the tire tread and yet the tire will hold air pressure. In most cases, a repair shop or gas station can repair the punctured tire.
5    It is also important to check the sidewalls of the tires, both inside and outside. Check for deteriorated rubber, cuts, and punctures. Also inspect the inboard side of the tire for signs of brake fluid leakage, indicating that a thorough brake inspection is needed immediately.
6    Incorrect tire pressure cannot be determined merely by looking at the tire. This is especially true for radial tires. A tire pressure gauge must be used (photo). If you do not have a reliable gauge it is a good idea to purchase one and keep it in the glovebox. Built-in pressure gauges at gas stations are often inaccurate.
7    Always check tire inflation when the tires are cold. Cold, in this case, means the vehicle has not been driven more than one mile after sitting for three hours or more. It is normal for the pressure to increase four to eight pounds when the tires are hot.
8    Unscrew the valve stem cap and press the gauge firmly onto the valve stem. Observe the reading on the gauge and compare the figure to the recommended tire pressure listed on the tire placard. The tire placard is usually attached to the driver's door.
9    Check all tires and add air as necessary to bring them up to the recommended pressure levels. Do not forget the spare tire. Be sure to reinstall the valve caps, which will keep dirt and moisture out of the valve stem mechanism.

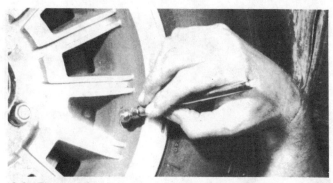

3.6 The use of an accurate tire pressure gauge is essential for long tire life

## 4 Fluid level checks

1    There are a number of components on a vehicle which rely on the use of fluids to perform their job. During normal operation of the vehicle these fluids are used up and must be replenished before damage occurs. See *Recommended lubricants and fluids* at the beginning of this Chapter for the specific fluid to be used when addition is required. When checking fluid levels it is important to have the vehicle on a level surface.

### Engine oil
2    The engine oil level is checked with a dipstick, which is located at the side of the engine block. The dipstick travels through a tube and into the oil pan.
3    Preferably the oil level should be checked before the vehicle has been driven, or about 15 minutes after the engine has been shut off. If the oil is checked immediately after driving the vehicle, some of the oil will remain in the upper engine components, producing an inaccurate reading on the dipstick.
4    Pull the dipstick from the tube and wipe the oil from the end with a clean rag. Insert the clean dipstick all the way back into the oil pan (photo) and pull it out again. Observe the oil at the end of the dipstick. At its highest point, the level should be between the Add and Full marks (photo).
5    It takes one quart of oil to raise the level from the Add mark to the Full mark on the dipstick. Do not allow the level to drop below the add mark as engine damage due to oil starvation may occur. On the other hand, do not overfill the engine by adding oil above the full mark, since this may result in oil-fouled spark plugs, oil leaks or oil seal failures.
6    Oil is added to the engine after removing a twist-off cap located on the rocker arm cover or through a raised tube near the front of the engine. The cap should be marked *Engine Oil* or *Oil*. An oil can spout or funnel will help reduce spills.
7    Checking the oil level can also be an important preventative maintenance step. If you find the oil level dropping abnormally, it is an indication of oil leakage or internal engine wear which should be corrected. If there are water droplets in the oil, or if the oil looks like chocolate milk, component failure is indicated and the engine should be checked immediately. The condition of the oil can also be checked along with the level. With the dipstick removed from the engine, take your thumb and index finger and wipe the oil up the dipstick, looking for small dirt or metal particles which will cling to the dipstick. This is an indication that the oil should be drained and fresh oil added (Section 16).

### Engine coolant
8    All vehicles covered by this manual are equipped with a pressurized coolant recovery system. A white coolant reservoir attached to the inner fender panel is connected by a hose to the radiator cap. As the engine heats up during operation the expanding coolant is forced from the radiator, through the connecting tube and into the reservoir. As the engine cools the coolant is automatically drawn back into the radiator to keep the level correct.
9.    The coolant level should be checked when the engine is hot. Observe the level of fluid in the reservoir, which should be at or near the Full Hot mark (photo). If the system is completely cool you can also check the level in the radiator by removing the cap.

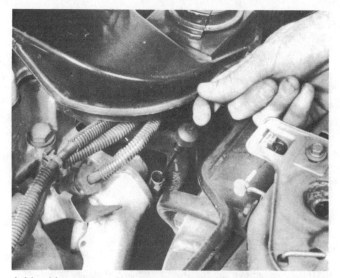

4.4A   After wiping off the engine oil dipstick, make sure it is reinserted all the way before withdrawing it for the oil level check

4.4B   The oil level should appear between the Add and Full marks; do not overfill the crankcase

4.9   The engine coolant level should appear near the Full Hot mark with the engine at normal operating temperature

4.10  Never remove the radiator cap while the engine is hot. The cap is removed by pushing down and rotating (arrows)

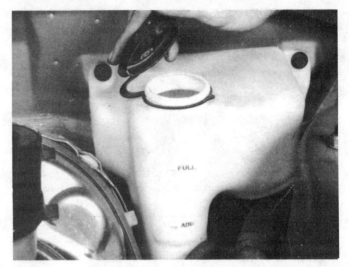

4.15  The windshield washer fluid level should be kept between the Full and Add marks

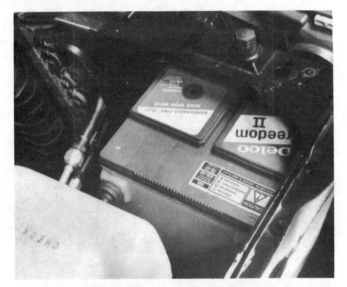

4.17  This type of battery never requires adding water, but normal maintenance should be performed

10  **Caution:** *Under no circumstances should the radiator cap or the coolant recovery reservoir cap be removed when the system is hot. Escaping steam and scalding liquid could cause serious personal injury.* In the case of the radiator, wait until the system has cooled completely, then wrap a thick cloth around the cap and turn it to the first stop (photo). If any steam escapes, wait until the system has cooled further, then remove the cap. The coolant recovery cap may be removed after it is apparent that no further boiling is occurring in the recovery tank.

11  If only a small amount of coolant is required to bring the system up to the proper level, regular water can be used. However, to maintain the proper antifreeze/water mixture in the system, both should be mixed together to replenish a low level. High-quality antifreeze offering protection to -20 °F should be mixed with water in the proportion specified on the container. Do not allow antifreeze to come in contact with your skin or painted surfaces of the vehicle. Flush contacted areas immediately with plenty of water.

12  Coolant should be added to the reservoir until it reaches the Full Cold mark.

13  As the coolant level is checked, note the condition of the coolant. It should be relatively clear. If it is brown or a rust color, the system should be drained, flushed and refilled (Section 26).

14  If the cooling system requires repeated additions to maintain the proper level, have the radiator cap checked for proper sealing. Also check for leaks in the system (cracked hoses, loose hose connections, leaking gaskets, etc.).

### Windshield washer fluid

15  Fluid for the windshield washer system is located in a plastic reservoir located next to the coolant reservoir (photo). The reservoir should be kept no more than 2/3-full to allow for expansion should the fluid freeze. The use of a windshield washer fluid addition, available at auto parts stores, will help lower the freezing point of the fluid and will result in better cleaning of the windshield surface. Do not use antifreeze because it will cause damage to the vehicle's paint.

16  To prevent icing in cold weather, warm the windshield with the defroster before using the washer.

### Battery electrolyte

17  All vehicles with which this manual is concerned are equipped with a *Freedom* battery which is permanently sealed (except for vent holes) and has no filler caps (photo). Water does not have to be added to these batteries.

### Brake fluid

18  The brake master cylinder is mounted on the firewall (manual brake models) or on the front of the power booster unit (power brake models) in the engine compartment.

19  The master cylinder reservoir incorporates a window which allows checking the fluid level without removal of the reservoir cover. The

4.19  The brake fluid level can be checked without removing the cap

4.21  Be careful not to spill brake fluid on painted surfaces

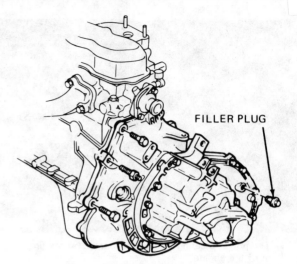

**Fig. 1.4  Manual transaxle filler plug location (Sec 4)**

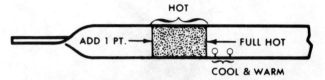

**Fig. 1.5  The automatic transaxle level should be kept within the marked areas, depending on whether the fluid is hot or cool when checked (Sec 4)**

level should be maintained at 1/4-inch below the lowest edge of each reservoir (photo).

20  If a low level is indicated, be sure to wipe the top of the reservoir cover with a clean rag to prevent contamination of the brake system before lifting the cover.

21  When adding fluid, pour it carefully into the reservoir, taking care not to spill any onto surrounding painted surfaces (photo). Be sure the specified fluid is used, since mixing different types of brake fluid can cause damage to the system. See *Recommended lubricants and fluids* or your owner's manual.

22  At this time the fluid and cylinder can be inspected for contamination. Normally the brake system will not need periodic draining and refilling, but if rust deposits, dirt particles or water droplets are seen in the fluid the system should be dismantled, drained and refilled with fresh fluid.

23  After filling the reservoir to the proper level, make sure the lid is properly seated to prevent fluid leakage and/or system pressure loss.

24  The brake fluid in the master cylinder will drop slightly as the brake shoes or pads at each wheel wear down during normal operation. If the master cylinder requires repeated replenishing to keep it at the proper level, this is an indication of leakage in the brake system, which should be corrected immediately. Check all brake lines and connections, along with the wheel cylinders and booster (see Section 13 for more information).

25  If, upon checking the master cylinder fluid level, you discover one or both reservoirs empty or nearly empty, the brake system should be bled (Chapter 9).

### Manual transaxle oil

26  Manual transaxles do not have a dipstick. The fluid level is checked with the engine cold by removing a plug in the side of the transaxle case. Locate the plug and use a rag to clean the plug and the area around it, then remove the plug.

27  If oil immediately starts leaking out, thread the plug back into the transaxle. The oil level is correct. If there is no leakage, completely remove the plug and place your little finger inside the hole. The oil level should be just at the bottom of the plug hole.

28  If the transaxle needs more oil, use a syringe to squeeze the appropriate lubricant into the plug hole until the proper level is reached.

29  Thread the plug back into the transaxle and tighten it securely.

30  Drive the vehicle a short distance, then check for leaks around the plug.

### Automatic transaxle fluid

31  The level of the automatic transaxle fluid should be carefully maintained. Low fluid level can lead to slipping or loss of drive, while overfilling can cause foaming and loss of fluid.

32  With the parking brake set, start the engine, then move the shift lever through all the gear ranges, ending in Park. The fluid level must be checked with the vehicle level and the engine running at idle. **Note:** *Incorrect fluid level readings will result if the vehicle has just been driven at high speeds for an extended period, in hot weather in city traffic, or if it's been pulling a trailer. If any of these conditions apply, wait*

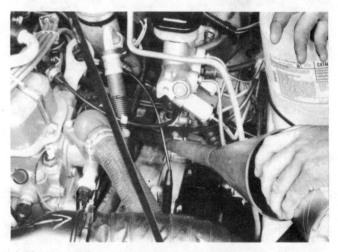

4.40  Using a funnel to add fluid to the automatic transaxle

*until the fluid has cooled (about 30 minutes).*

33  With the transaxle at normal operating temperature, remove the dipstick, located on the left side of the engine compartment.

34  Wipe the fluid from the dipstick with a clean rag and push it back into the filler tube until the cap seats.

35  Carefully touch the end of the dipstick to determine the temperature of the fluid. It may be cool, warm or hot.

36  Wipe the fluid from the dipstick with a clean rag and push the dipstick back into the filler tube until the cap seats.

37  Pull the dipstick out and note the fluid level.

38  If the fluid felt cool or warm, the level should be between the dimples above the Full mark.

39  If the fluid felt hot, the level should be in the crosshatched area near the Full mark.

40  Add just enough of the recommended fluid to fill the transmission to the proper level (photo). It takes about one pint to raise the level from the Add mark to the Full mark with a hot transaxle, so add the

4.43   The power steering reservoir is located on the firewall or on the front of the engine

4.47   Checking of the power steering fluid level is done with the engine at normal operating temperature (the level should be near the Full Hot mark)

5.1   Eye and hand protection, baking soda, petroleum jelly and tools required for battery maintenance

5.4   Unlike older model batteries, the cable terminals are on the side of Freedom-type batteries

fluid a little at a time and keep checking the level until it is correct.
41  The condition of the fluid should also be checked. If the fluid is a dark reddish-brown color, or if the fluid has a burned smell, the trans-axle fluid should be changed. If you are in doubt about the condition of the fluid, purchase some new fluid and compare the two for color and smell.

## Power steering fluid
42  Unlike manual steering, the power steering system relies on fluid which may, over a period of time, require replenishing.
43  The fluid reservoir for the power steering pump will either be located near the front of the engine or on the engine compartment firewall (photo).
44  For the check, the front wheels should be pointed straight ahead and the engine should be off.
45  Use a clean rag to wipe off the reservoir cap and the area around the cap. This will help prevent any foreign matter from entering the reservoir during the check.
46  Warm the engine to normal operating temperature.
47  Remove the dipstick, wipe it off with a clean rag, reinsert it, then withdraw it and read the fluid level (photo). The level should be between the Add and Full Hot marks.
48  If additional fluid is required, pour the specified type directly into the reservoir, using a funnel to prevent spills.
49  If the reservoir requires frequent fluid additions, all power steering hoses, hose connections and the power steering pump should be checked for leaks.

## 5   Battery check and maintenance

1   Tools and materials required for battery maintenance include eye and hand protection, baking soda, petroleum jelly, a battery cable puller and cable/terminal post cleaning tools (photo).
2   A sealed *Freedom* battery is standard equipment on all vehicles with which this manual is concerned. Although this type of battery has many advantages over the older, capped cell type, and never re-quires the addition of water, it should nevertheless be routinely main-tained according to the procedures which follow. **Warning:** *Hydrogen gas in small quantities is present in the area of the two small side vents on sealed batteries, so keep lighted tobacco and open flames or sparks away from them.*
3   The external condition of the battery should be monitored periodically for damage such as a cracked case or cover.
4   Check the tightness of the battery cable clamps to ensure good electrical connections (photo). Check the entire length of each cable for cracks and frayed conductors.
5   If corrosion (visible as white, fluffy deposits) is evident, remove the cables from the terminals, clean them with a battery brush and reinstall the cables. Corrosion can be kept to a minimum by applying a layer of petroleum jelly or grease to the terminals and cable clamps after they are assembled.
6   Make sure that the rubber protector (if so equipped) over the positive terminal is not torn or missing. It should completely cover the terminal.
7   Check to see that the battery carrier is in good condition and that the hold-down clamp bolts are tight. If the battery is removed from the carrier make sure that no parts remain in the bottom of the carrier when the battery is reinstalled (photo). When reinstalling the hold-down clamp bolts do not overtighten them.

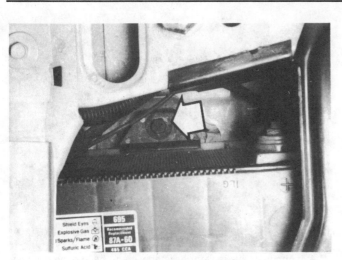

5.7  Use a socket extension to reach the battery hold-down bolt

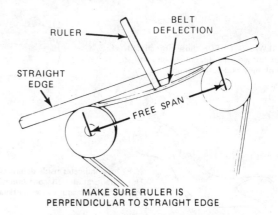

Fig. 1.6  Drivebelt tension can be checked with a straightedge and ruler (Sec 6)

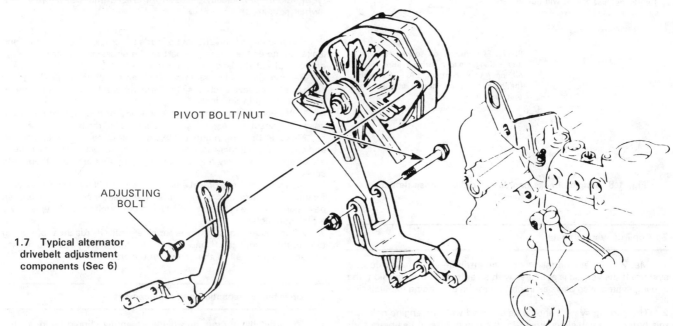

1.7  Typical alternator drivebelt adjustment components (Sec 6)

8    Corrosion on the hold-down components, battery case and surrounding areas may be removed with a solution of water and baking soda, but take care to prevent any corrosion from coming in contact with your eyes, skin or clothes, as it contains acid. Protective gloves should be worn. Thoroughly wash all cleaned areas with plain water.
9    Any metal parts of the vehicle damaged by corrosion cleaned as outlined above, dried, coated with a zinc-based primer, then painted.
10  Further information on the battery, charging and jump-starting can be found in Chapter 5 and at the front of this manual.

## 6  Drivebelt check and adjustment

1    The drivebelts, or V-belts as they are often called, are located at the front of the engine and play an important role in the overall operation of the vehicle and its components. Due to their function and material make-up, the belts are prone to failure after a period of time and should be inspected and adjusted periodically to prevent major engine damage.
2    The number of belts used on a particular vehicle depends on the accessories installed. Drivebelts are used to turn the generator/alternator, power steering pump, water pump and air-conditioning compressor. Depending on the pulley arrangement, more than one of these components may be driven by a single belt.
3    With the engine off, open the hood and locate the various belts at the front of the engine. Using your fingers (and a flashlight, if

necessary), move along the belts checking for cracks and separation of the belt plies. Also check for fraying and glazing, which gives the belt a shiny appearance. Both sides of the belt should be inspected, which means you will have to twist the belt to check the underside.
4    The tension of each belt is checked by pushing on the belt at a distance halfway between the pulleys. Push firmly with your thumb and see how much the belt moves (deflects). A rule of thumb is that if the distance from pulley center to pulley center is between 7 and 11 inches, the belt should deflect 1/4-inch. If the belt travels between pulleys spaced 12 to 16 inches apart, the belt should deflect 1/2-inch.
5    If it is necessary to adjust the belt tension, either to make the belt tighter or looser, it is done by moving the belt-driven accessory on the bracket.
6    For each component there will be an adjusting bolt and a pivot bolt. Both bolts must be loosened slightly to enable you to move the component.
7    After the two bolts have been loosened, move the component away from the engine to tighten the belt or toward the engine to loosen the belt. Hold the accessory in position and check the belt tension. If it is correct, tighten the two bolts until just snug, then recheck the tension. If the tension is all right, tighten the bolts.
8    It will often be necessary to use some sort of pry bar to move the accessory while the belt is adjusted. If this must be done to gain the proper leverage, be very careful not to damage the component being moved or the part being pried against.

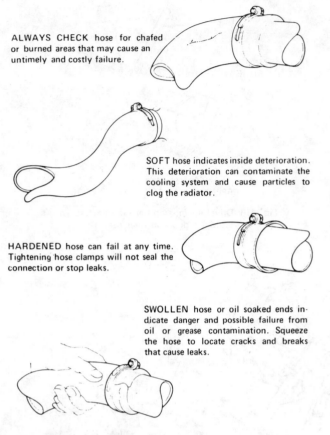

ALWAYS CHECK hose for chafed or burned areas that may cause an untimely and costly failure.

SOFT hose indicates inside deterioration. This deterioration can contaminate the cooling system and cause particles to clog the radiator.

HARDENED hose can fail at any time. Tightening hose clamps will not seal the connection or stop leaks.

SWOLLEN hose or oil soaked ends indicate danger and possible failure from oil or grease contamination. Squeeze the hose to locate cracks and breaks that cause leaks.

**Fig. 1.8 Simple checks can detect radiator hose defects (Sec 7)**

7.4    Although this radiator hose appears to be in good condition, it should be periodically checked for cracks (more easily revealed when squeezed)

## 7   Cooling system check

1    Many major engine failures can be attributed to a faulty cooling system. If the vehicle is equipped with an automatic transmission, the cooling system also plays an important role in prolonging transmission life.
2    The cooling system should be checked with the engine cold. Do this before the vehicle is driven for the day or after it has been shut off for at least three hours.
3    Remove the radiator cap and thoroughly clean the cap, inside and out, with clean water. Also clean the filler neck on the radiator. All traces of corrosion should be removed.
4    Carefully check the upper and lower radiator hoses and the smaller diameter heater hoses. Inspect each hose along its entire length, replacing any hose which is cracked, swollen or shows signs of deterioration. Cracks may become more apparent if the hose is squeezed (photo).
5    Make sure that all hose connections are tight. A leak in the cooling system will usually show up as white or rust colored deposits on the areas near the leak.
6    Use compressed air or a soft brush to remove bugs, leaves, etc. from the front of the radiator or air-conditioning condenser. Be careful not to damage the delicate cooling fins or cut yourself on them.
7    Finally, have the cap and system pressure tested. If you do not have a pressure tester, most gas stations and repair shops will do this for a minimal change.

## 8   Underhood hose check and replacement

**Caution:** *Replacement of air-conditioner hoses must be left to a dealer or air-conditioning specialist who can depressurize the system and perform the work safely.*
1    The high temperatures present under the hood can cause deterioration of rubber and plastic hoses.

2    Periodic inspection should be made for cracks, loose clamps and leaks. Some of the hoses are part of the emissions control systems and can affect the engine's performance.
3    Remove the air cleaner if necessary and trace the entire length of each hose. Squeeze each hose to check for cracks and look for swelling, discoloration and leaks.
4    If the vehicle has considerable mileage or if one or more of the hoses is suspect, it is a good idea to replace all of the hoses at one time.
5    Measure the length and inside diameter of each hose and obtain and cut the replacement to size. Since original equipment hose clamps are often good for only one use it is a good idea to replace them with screw-type clamps.
6    Replace each hose one at a time to eliminate the possibility of confusion. Hoses attached to the heater and radiator contain coolant, so newspapers or rags should be kept handy to catch the spills when they are disconnected.
7    After installation, run the engine until it reaches operating temperature, shut it off and check for leaks. After the engine has cooled, retighten all of the screw-type clamps.

## 9   Wiper blade inspection and replacement

1    The windshield wiper and blade assembly should be inspected periodically for damage, loose components and cracked or worn blade elements.
2    Road film can build up on the wiper blades and affect their efficiency, so they should be washed regularly with a mild detergent solution.
3    The action of the wiping mechanism can loosen the bolts, nuts and fasteners so they should be checked and tightened, as necessary, at the same time the wiper blades are checked.
4    If the wiper blade elements are cracked, worn or warped, they should be replaced with new ones.
5    Remove the wiper blade by raising the wiper arm and pushing the bottom of the blade towards the glass to disengage the arm from the blade. Lift the blade and remove it as shown in the accompanying illustration.
6    Install the blade by inserting the pronged end of the arm into the blade slots and pulling the bottom of the blade towards the arm to lock it in place.

## 10   Chassis lubrication

1    A grease gun and a cartridge filled with the proper grease (see *Recommended fluids and lubricants*) are usually the only equipment necessary to lubricate the chassis components. In some chassis locations plugs may be installed rather than grease fittings, in which case grease fittings will have to be installed.

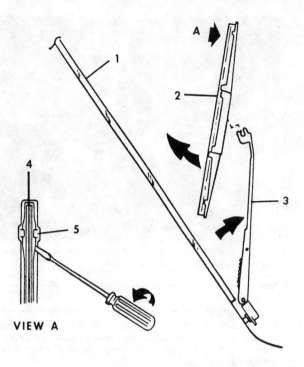

**Fig. 1.9  Details of windshield wiper blade replacement (Sec 9)**

| | |
|---|---|
| 1  *Glass* | 4  *Element* |
| 2  *Wiper blade* | 5  *Housing tab* |
| 3  *Wiper arm* | |

2    Refer to the accompanying illustration which shows where the various grease fittings are located. Look under the vehicle to find these components and determine if grease fittings or solid plugs are installed. If there are plugs, remove them and thread grease fittings into the component. A GM dealer or auto parts store will be able to supply replacement fittings. Straight, as well as angled, fittings are available.

3    For easier access under the vehicle raise it with a jack and place jackstands under the frame. Make sure the vehicle is securely supported by the stands.

4    Before proceeding pump a little of the grease out of the nozzle of the grease gun to remove any dirt from the end of the gun. Wipe the nozzle clean with a rag.

5    With the grease gun, plenty of clean rags and the diagram, crawl under the vehicle and begin lubricating the components.

6    Wipe the grease fitting nipple clean and push the nozzle firmly over the fitting nipple. Pump the trigger on the grease gun to force grease into the component. **Note:** *The upper steering arm joins (one for each front wheel) should be lubricated until the rubber reservoir is firm to the touch. Do not pump too much grease into these fittings as it could rupture the reservoir.* On the lower suspension fittings, continue pumping grease into the nipple until grease seeps out of the joint between the two components. If the grease seeps out around the grease gun nozzle, the nipple is clogged or the nozzle is not seated on the fitting nipple. Resecure the gun nozzle to the fitting and try again. If necessary, replace the fitting.

7    Wipe the excess grease from the components and the grease fitting. Follow the same procedures for the remaining fittings.

8    While you are under the vehicle clean and lubricate the parking brake cable, the cable guides and levers. This can be done by smearing some of the chassis grease onto the cable and its related parts with your fingers. Place a few drops of light engine oil on the transmission shift linkage rods and swivels.

9    Lower the vehicle for the remaining lubrication procedures.

10   Open the hood and apply chassis grease to the hood latch mechanism (photo). If the hood has an inside release, have an assistant pull the release knob as you lubricate the cable at the latch.

11   Lubricate all the hinges (door, hood, hatch) with a few drops of light engine oil.

12   The key lock cylinders can be lubricated with spray-on graphite dry lubricant, which is available at auto parts stores.

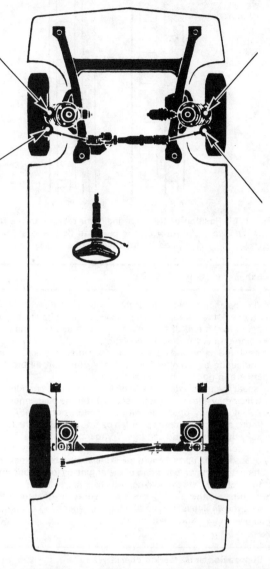

**Fig. 1.10  Chassis grease fitting locations (arrows) (Sec 10)**

10.10   Multi-purpose grease is used to lubricate the hood latch mechanism

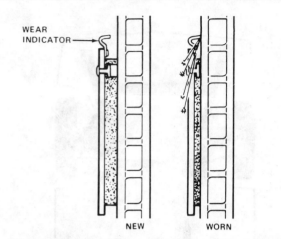

Fig. 1.11 Position of the wear indicator relative to the face of the disc brake rotor on the new pad (left) and a worn pad (right) (Sec 13)

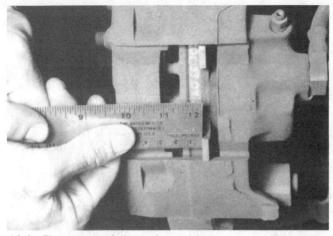

13.6   The amount of disc pad material remaining can be checked by looking through the hole in the caliper

## 11   Exhaust system check

1   With the engine cold (at least three hours after the vehicle has been driven), check the complete exhaust system from its starting point at the engine to the end of the tailpipe. This should be done on a hoist where unrestricted access is available.
2   Check the pipes and connections for signs of leakage and corrosion, indicating a potential failure. Make sure that all brackets and hangers are in good condition and tight.
3   Inspect the underside of the body for holes, corrosion, open seams, etc., which may allow exhaust gases to enter the passenger compartment. Seal all body openings with silicone or body putty.
4   Rattles and other noises can often be traced to the exhaust system, especially the mounts and hangers. Try to move the pipes, muffler and catalytic converter. If the components can come in contact with the body or suspension parts, secure the exhaust system with new mounts.
5   Check the running condition of the engine by inspecting inside the end of the tailpipe. The exhaust deposits here are an indication of engine state-of-tune. If the pipe is black and sooty or coated with white deposits, the engine is in need of a tune-up, including a thorough carburetor inspection and adjustment.

## 12   Suspension and steering check

1   Whenever the front of the vehicle is raised for service visually check the suspension and steering components for wear.
2   Indications of a fault in these systems are excessive play in the steering wheel before the front wheels react, excessive sway around corners, body movement over rough roads or binding at some point as the steering wheel is turned.
3   Before the vehicle is raised for inspection, test the shock absorbers by pushing down to rock the vehicle at each corner. If you push down and the vehicle does not come back to a level position within one or two bounces, the shocks/struts are worn and must be replaced. As this is done, check for squeaks and noises coming from the suspension components. Information on suspension components can be found in Chapter 10.
4   Raise the front of the vehicle and support it securely on jackstands placed under the frame rails. Because of the work to be done, make sure the vehicle cannot fall from the stands.
5   Check the wheel bearings (see Section 27).
6   Crawl under the vehicle and check for loose bolts, broken or disconnected parts and deteriorated rubber bushings on all suspension and steering components. Look for grease or fluid leaking from the steering box. Check the power steering hoses and connections for leaks. Check the balljoints for wear.
7   Have an assistant turn the steering wheel from side-to-side and check the steering components for free movement, chafing and binding. If the steering does not react with the movement of the steering wheel, try to determine where the slack is located.

## 13   Brake check

**Note:** *For detailed photographs of the brake system refer to Chapter 9.*
1   The brakes should be inspected every time the wheels are removed or whenever a defect is suspected. Indications of a potential brake system defect are:
   a)   The vehicle pulls to one side when the brake pedal is depressed.
   b)   Noises coming from the brakes when they are applied.
   c)   Excessive brake pedal travel.
   d)   Pulsating pedal.
   e)   Leakage of fluid, usually seen on the inside of the tire or wheel.

### Disc brakes

2   Both front and rear disc brakes (if the rear is so equipped) can be visually checked without removing any parts except the wheels.
3   Raise the vehicle and place it securely on jackstands. Remove the wheels (see *Jacking and towing* at the front of the manual, if necessary).
4   The disc brake calipers, which contain the pads, are now visible. There is an outer pad and an inner pad in each caliper. All pads should be inspected.
5   The inner pads on the front wheels are equipped with a wear sensor. This is a small, bent piece of metal which is visible from the inboard side of the brake caliper. When the pads wear to the danger limit the mental sensor rubs against the rotor and makes a screeching sound.
6   Check the pad thickness by looking at each end of the caliper and through the inspection hole in the caliper body (photo). If the wear sensor clip is very close to the rotor, or if the lining material is 1/16-inch or less in thickness, the pads should be replaced. Keep in mind that the lining material is riveted or bonded to a metal backing shoe and the metal portion is not included in this measurement.
7   Remove the pads for further inspection or replacement if you are in doubt as to the quality of the pad.
8   Before installing the wheels, check for leakage around the brake hose connections leading to the caliper and damage (cracking, splitting, etc.) to the brake hose. Replace the hose or fittings as necessary, referring to Chapter 9.
9   Check the condition of the rotor. Look for scoring, gouging and burned spots. If these conditions exist the hub/rotor assembly should be removed for servicing (Chapter 9).

### Drum brakes — rear (if so equipped)

10   Using a scribe or chalk, mark the drum and hub so the drum can be reinstalled in the same position on the hub.
11   Remove and discard the retaining clip and pull the brake drum off the axle and brake assembly. If this proves difficult, make sure the parking brake is released, then squirt some penetrating oil around the center hub area. Allow the oil to soak in and try to pull the drum off again. If the drum still cannot be pulled off, the brake shoes will have to be adjusted in. This is done by first removing the lanced knock-out in the backing plate with a hammer and chisel. With the lanced area punched in, pull the self-adjusting lever off the star wheel and use a small

screwdriver to turn the wheel, which will move the shoes away from the drum.

12 With the drum removed, carefully brush away any accumulations of dirt and dust. **Warning:** *Do not blow the dust out with compressed air. Do not inhale any of the dust, as it contains asbestos and is harmful to your health.*

13 Note the thickness of the lining material on the brake shoes. If the material is worn to within 1/16-inch of the recessed rivets or metal backing, the shoes should be replaced. If the linings look worn, but you are unable to determine their exact thickness, compare them with a new set at an auto parts store. The shoes should also be replaced if they are cracked, glazed (shiny surface) or contaminated with brake fluid.

14 Check to see that all the brake assembly springs are connected and in good condition.

15 Check the brake components for signs of fluid leakage. Carefully pry back the rubber cups on the wheel cylinder, located at the top of the brake backing plate. Any leakage is an indication that the wheel cylinders should be overhauled immediately (Chapter 9). Also check the hoses and connections for signs of leakage.

16 Wipe the inside of the drum with a clean rag and denatured alcohol. Again, be careful not to breathe the asbestos dust.

17 Check the inside of the drum for cracks, scores, deep scratches and hard spots, which will appear as small discolored areas. If imperfections cannot be removed with fine emery cloth the drum must be taken to a machine shop for resurfacing.

18 After the inspection process, if all parts are found to be in good condition, reinstall the brake drum. Install the wheel and lower the vehicle to the ground.

*Parking brake*

19 The easiest way to check the operation of the parking brake is to park the vehicle on a steep hill with the parking brake set and the transmission in Neutral. If the parking brake cannot prevent the vehicle from rolling, it is in need of adjustment (see Chapter 9).

---

### 14 Carburetor choke check

1 The choke only operates when the engine is cold, so this check should be performed before the engine has been started for the day.

2 Open the hood and remove the top plate of the air cleaner assembly. It is held in place by a wing nut. If any vacuum hoses must be disconnected make sure you tag them to insure reinstallation in their original positions. Place the top plate and nut aside, out of the way of moving engine components.

3 Look at the top of the carburetor at the center of the air cleaner housing. You will notice a flat plate at the carburetor opening.

4 Have an assistant press the accelerator pedal to the floor. The plate should close completely. Start the engine while you observe the plate at the carburetor. **Caution:** *Do not position your face directly over the carburetor. The engine could backfire and cause serious burns.* When the engine starts the choke plate should open slightly.

5 Allow the engine to continue running at an idle speed. Every thirty seconds depress the throttle slightly. As the engine warms up to operating temperature the plate should slowly open, allowing more air to enter through the top of the carburetor.

6 After a few minutes the choke plate should be all the way open to the vertical position.

7 You will notice that the engine speed corresponds with the plate opening. With the plate completely closed, the engine should run at a fast idle. As the plate opens, the engine speed will decrease.

8 If a malfunction is detected during the above checks, refer to Chapter 4 for specific information related to adjusting and servicing choke components.

---

### 15 Engine idle speed check and adjustment

1 The engine idle speed is adjustable on some models and should be checked at the scheduled maintenance interval.

2 On those vehicles with provisions for idle speed adjustment, the specifications for such adjustments are shown on the vehicle Emissions Control Information label. However, the adjustments must be made using calibrated test equipment. The adjustments should therefore be made by a dealer or automotive repair facility.

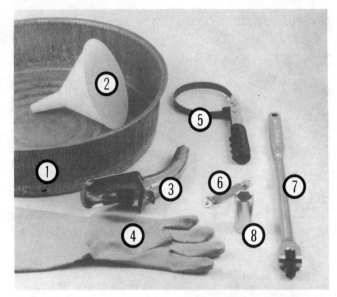

16.3  Typical oil change tools

| | | | |
|---|---|---|---|
| 1 | Drain pan | 5 | Filter wrench |
| 2 | Funnel | 6 | Can opener |
| 3 | Oil can spout | 7 | Breaker bar |
| 4 | Rubber gloves | 8 | Socket (6-point) |

---

### 16 Engine oil and filter change

1 Frequent oil changes may be the best form of preventative maintenance available to the home mechanic. When engine oil ages, it becomes diluted and contaminated, which leads to premature engine wear.

2 Although some sources recommend oil filter changes every other oil change, we feel that the minimal cost of an oil filter and the relative ease with which it is installed dictate that a new filter be used whenever the oil is changed.

3 The tools necessary for a oil and filter change are a wrench to fit the drain plug at the bottom of the oil pan, an oil filter wrench to remove the old filter, a container with at least a six-quart capacity to drain the old oil into and a funnel or oil can spout to help pour fresh oil into the engine (photo).

4 In addition, you should have plenty of clean rags and newspapers handy to mop up any spills. Access to the underside of the vehicle is greatly improved if the vehicle can be lifted on a hoist, driven onto ramps or supported by jackstands. **Warning:** *Do not work under a vehicle which is supported only by a bumper, hydraulic or scissors-type jack.*

5 If this is your first oil change on the vehicle, it is a good idea to crawl underneath and familiarize yourself with the locations of the oil drain plug and the oil filter. The engine and exhaust components will be hot during the actual work, so it is a good idea to figure out any potential problems before becoming involved with the procedure.

6 Allow the engine to warm up to normal operating temperature. If the new oil or any tools are needed, use this warm-up time to gather everything necessary for the job. The correct type of oil to buy for your application can be found in *Recommended lubricants and fluids* at the beginning of this manual.

7 With the engine oil warm (warm engine oil will drain better and more built-up sludge will be removed with the oil), raise and support the vehicle. Make sure it is firmly supported.

8 Move all necessary tools, rags and newspapers under the vehicle. Position the drain pan under the drain plug. Keep in mind that the oil will initially flow from the pan with some force, so place the pan accordingly.

9 Being careful not to touch any of the hot exhaust components, use the wrench to remove the drain plug near the bottom of the oil pan. Depending on how hot the oil has become, you may want to wear gloves while unscrewing the plug the final few turns.

10 Allow the old oil to drain into the pan. It may be necessary to reposi-

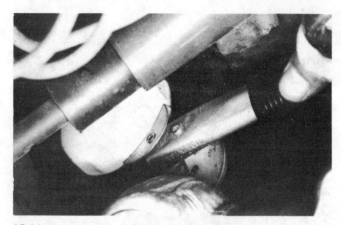

16.14   A strap-type oil filter wrench works well in hard-to-reach locations

16.23   Oil is added through a filler opening in the rocker arm cover

17.5   With today's sophisticated emissions systems, it is essential that the seal in the gas tank cap be checked regularly

tion the pan as the oil flow slows to a trickle.

11   After all the oil has drained wipe off the drain plug with a clean rag. Small metal particles may cling to the plug and would immediately contaminate the new oil.

12   Clean the area around the drain plug opening and reinstall the plug. Tighten the plug securely with the wrench.

13   Move the drain pan into position under the oil filter.

14   Use the filter wrench to loosen the oil filter. Chain or metal band-type filter wrenches may distort the filter canister, but this is of no concern as the filter will be discarded (photo).

15   Sometimes the oil filter is on so tight it cannot be loosened, or is positioned in an area which is inaccessible with a filter wrench. As a last resort you can punch a metal bar or long screwdriver directly through the sides of the canister and use it as a T-bar to turn the filter. If this becomes necessary be prepared for oil to spurt out of the canister as it is punctured.

16   Completely unscrew the old filter. Be careful, it is full of oil. Empty the filter into the drain pan.

17   Compare the old filter with the new one to make sure they are the same type.

18   Use a clean rag to remove all oil, dirt and sludge from the area where the oil filter mounts to the engine. Check the old filter to make sure the rubber gasket is not stuck to the engine mounting surface. If the gasket is stuck to the engine remove it.

19   Open one of the cans of oil and fill the filter half-full. Apply a light coat of oil around the full circumference of the rubber gasket of the oil filter.

20   Attach the filter to the engine following the tightening directions printed on the filter canister or packing box. Most filter manufacturers recommend against using a filter wrench due to the possibility of over-tightening and damage to the seal.

21   Remove all tools, rags, etc. from under the vehicle, being careful not to spill the oil in the drain pan, then lower the vehicle.

22   Move to the engine compartment and locate the oil filler cap on the engine.

23   If an oil can spout is used, push the spout into the top of the oil can and pour the fresh oil through the filler opening. A funnel may also be used (photo).

24   Pour three quarts of fresh oil into the engine. Wait a few minutes to allow the oil to drain into the pan, then check the level on the oil dipstick (see Section 4 if necessary). If the oil level is at or near the lower Add mark, start the engine and allow the new oil to circulate.

25   Run the engine for one minute then shut it off. Immediately look under the vehicle and check for leaks at the oil pan drain plug and around the oil filter. If either is leaking, tighten with a bit more force.

26   With the new oil circulated and the filter now completely full, recheck the level on the dipstick and add enough oil to bring the level to the Full mark on the dipstick.

27   During the first few trips after an oil change, make it a point to check frequently for leaks and proper oil level.

28   The old oil drained from the engine cannot be reused in its present state and should be disposed of. Oil reclamation centers, auto repair shops and gas stations will normally accept the oil, which can be refined and used again. After the oil has cooled, it can be drained into a suitable container (capped plastic jugs, topped bottles, milk cartons, etc.) for transport to one of these disposal sites.

## 17   Fuel system check

**Caution:** *There are certain precautions to take when inspecting or servicing the fuel system components. Work in a well-ventilated area and do not allow open flames (cigarettes, appliance pilot lights, etc.) to get near the work area. Mop up spills immediately and do not store fuel-soaked rags where they could ignite.*

1   If your vehicle is equipped with fuel injection, refer to the fuel injection pressure relief procedure (Chapter 4) before servicing any component of the fuel system. Also, remove the fuel tank cap to relieve the pressure in the tank.

2   The fuel system is under a small amount of pressure, so before any fuel lines are disconnected for servicing be prepared to catch the fuel as it spurts out. Plug all disconnected fuel lines immediately after disconnection to prevent the tank from emptying itself.

3   The fuel system is most easily checked with the vehicle raised on a hoist so the components underneath the vehicle are readily visible and accessible.

4   If the smell of gasoline is noticed while driving or after the vehicle has been in the sun, the system should be thoroughly inspected immediately.

5   Remove the gas filler cap and check for damage, corrosion and an unbroken sealing imprint on the gasket (photo). Replace the cap with a new one if necessary.

6   With the vehicle raised, inspect the gas tank and filler neck for punctures, cracks or other damage. The connection between the filler

neck and the tank is especially critical. Sometimes a rubber filler neck will leak due to loose clamps or deteriorated rubber, problems a home mechanic can usually rectify. **Warning:** *Do not, under any circumstances, try to repair a fuel tank yourself (except rubber components) unless you have had considerable experience. A welding torch or any open flame can easily cause the fuel vapors to explode if the proper precautions are not taken.*

7    Check all rubber hoses and metal lines leading away from the fuel tank. Check for loose connections, deteriorated hoses, crimped lines and other damage. Follow the lines to the front of the vehicle, carefully inspecting them all the way. Repair or replace damaged sections as necessary.

8    If a fuel odor is still evident after the inspection, refer to Section 33.

---

## 18  Fuel filter replacement

---

### *Carburetor-equipped models*

1    On these models the fuel filter is located inside the fuel inlet at the carburetor. It is made of pleated paper and cannot be cleaned or reused.

2    This job should be done with the engine cold (after sitting at least three hours). The necessary tools include open-end wrenches to fit the fuel line nuts. Flare nut wrenches, which wrap around the nut, should be used, if available, to prevent damage to the fittings, which are generally made of brass or aluminum. In addition, you will have to obtain a replacement filter. Make sure it is for your specific vehicle and engine. You will also need some clean rags.

3    Remove the air cleaner assembly. If vacuum hoses must be disconnected, be sure to note their positions and/or tag them so they can be reinstalled correctly.

4    Follow the fuel line from the fuel pump to the point where it enters the carburetor. The fuel pump is located low on the engine, at the left front. In most cases the fuel line will be metal all the way from the fuel pump to the carburetor.

5    Place some rags under the fuel inlet fittings to catch spilled fuel as the fittings are disconnected. Remove the fuel tank cap to relieve the pressure in the tank.

6    With the proper size wrench, hold the large nut immediately next to the carburetor body. Loosen the fitting at the end of the metal fuel line. A flare nut wrench on this fitting will help prevent slipping and possible damage. Make sure the larger nut next to the carburetor is held securely while the fuel line is disconnected.

7    After the fuel line is disconnected, move it aside for better access to the inlet filter nut. Do not crimp the fuel line.

8    Unscrew the fuel inlet filter nut which was previously held steady. As this fitting is drawn away from the carburetor body, be careful not to lose the thin washer-type gasket or the spring located behind the fuel filter.

9    Compare the old filter with the new one to make sure they are the same length and design.

10   Reinstall the spring in the carburetor body.

11   Place the new filter in position. The filter will have a rubber gasket and a check valve at one end, which should point away from the carburetor.

12   Install a new washer-type gasket on the fuel inlet filter nut. A gasket is usually supplied with the new filter. Tighten the nut in the carburetor. Make sure it is not cross-threaded. Tighten it securely. If a torque wrench is available, tighten it to 18 ft-lbs. Do not overtighten it, as the hole can strip easily, causing fuel leaks.

13   Hold the fuel inlet nut securely with a wrench while the fuel line is connected. Again, be careful not to cross-thread the connector. Tighten the fitting securely.

14   Plug the vacuum hose which leads to the air cleaner snorkel motor so the engine can be started.

15   Start the engine and check carefully for leaks. If the fuel line connector leaks, disconnect it using the above procedures and check for stripped or damaged threads. If the fuel line connector has stripped threads, remove the entire line and have a repair shop install a new fitting. If the threads look all right, purchase some thread sealing tape and wrap the connector threads with it. Reinstall and tighten it securely. Inlet repair kits are available at most auto parts stores to overcome leaking at the fuel inlet filter nut.

16   Reinstall the air cleaner assembly, connecting the hoses in their original positions.

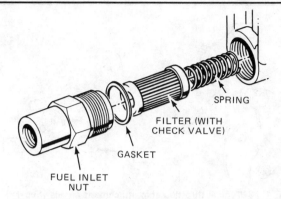

**Fig. 1.12  Carburetor mounted fuel filter component layout (Sec 18)**

SPRING
FILTER (WITH CHECK VALVE)
GASKET
FUEL INLET NUT

**Fig. 1.13  Typical engine mounted fuel filter used with TBI (Sec 18)**

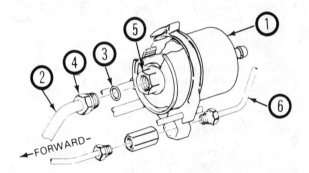

**Fig. 1.14  Details of multi-port fuel injection in-line fuel filter replacement (Sec 18)**

1   Fuel filter
2   Fuel feed line
3   O-ring (must be in this pipe prior to installation)
4   Fuel line fitting
5   Filter fitting
6   Brake pipe

### *Fuel-injected models*

**Warning:** *Refer to the fuel injection pressure relief procedure in Chapter 4 before performing this procedure.*

17   Fuel-injected engines employ a stainless steel in-line fuel filter. On four-cylinder engines it is located at the left rear of the engine, clamped to the cylinder head. On V6 models the filter is attached to the frame rail or on the rear crossmember in the engine compartment.

18   With the engine cold, place a container under the fuel filter.

19   Remove any bolts attaching the fuel filter bracket to the engine.

20   Remove the line from the top of the filter.

21   Unclamp and remove the fuel line from the bottom of the filter and remove the filter.

22   Install the new filter by reversing the removal procedure. Do not overtighten the fitting at the top of the fuel filter. If a torque wrench is available, tighten the fitting to 18 ft-lbs.

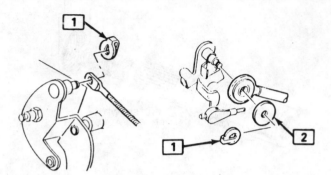

**Fig. 1.15  Typical throttle cable attachment details (Sec 19)**

1  Retainer                    2  Washer

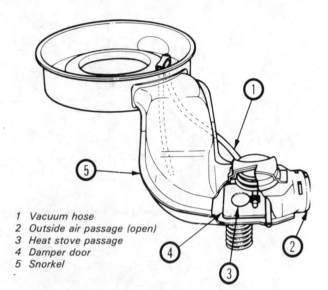

1  Vacuum hose
2  Outside air passage (open)
3  Heat stove passage
4  Damper door
5  Snorkel

**Fig. 1.17  THERMAC assembly (fuel injected engine) shown
with the snorkel open (Sec 20)**

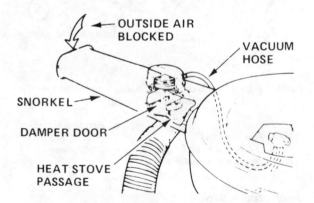

**Fig. 1.18  THERMAC assembly shown with the snorkel
passage (damper door) closed (Sec 20)**

### 19  Throttle linkage check and adjustment

1   The throttle linkage is a cable type and although there are no
adjustments to the linkage itself, periodic maintenance is necessary
to assure its proper function.
2   Remove the air cleaner (refer to Chapter 2) so the entire linkage
is visible.
3   Check the entire length of the cable to make sure that it is not
binding.

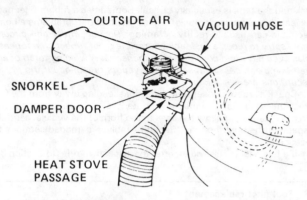

**Fig. 1.16  THERMAC assembly shown with the snorkel
passage (damper door) open (Sec 20)**

4   Check all the nylon bushings for wear, replacing them with new
ones as necessary.
5   Lubricate the cable mechanisms with engine oil at the pivot points,
but do not lubricate the cable itself.

### 20  Carburetor/throttle body injection (TBI) mounting torque check

1   The carburetor/TBI is attached to the top of the intake manifold
by four nuts. These fasteners can sometimes work loose from vibration and temperature changes during normal engine operation and cause
a vacuum leak.
2   To properly tighten the mounting nuts a torque wrench is
necessary. If you do not own one, they can usually be rented on a
daily basis.
3   Remove the air cleaner assembly, tagging each hose to be disconnected with a piece of numbered tape to make reassembly easier.
4   Locate the mounting nuts at the base of the carburetor/TBI. Decide
what special tools or adapters will be necessary, if any, to tighten the
fasteners with a socket and the torque wrench.
5   Tighten the nuts to the specified torque. Do not overtighten them,
as the threads could strip.
6   If you suspect that a vacuum leak exists at the bottom of the carburetor, obtain a length of hose about the diameter of fuel hose. Start
the engine and place one end of the hose next to your ear as you
probe around the base of the carburetor with the other end. You will
hear a hissing sound if a leak exists.
7   If, after the nuts are properly tightened, a vacuum leak still
exists, the carburetor/TBI must be removed and a new gasket installed.
See Chapter 4 for more information.
8   After tightening the fasteners, reinstall the air cleaner and return
all hoses to their original positions.

### 21  Thermostatically controlled air cleaner (THERMAC) check

1   All engines are equipped with a thermostatically controlled air
cleaner which draws air to the carburetor from different locations,
depending upon engine temperature.
2   This is a visual check. If access is limited, a small mirror may have
to be used.
3   Open the hood and locate the damper door inside the air cleaner
assembly. It will be located inside the long snorkel of the metal air
cleaner housing.
4   If there is a flexible air duct attached to the end of the snorkel,
leading to an area behind the grille, disconnect it at the snorkel. This
will enable you to look through the end of the snorkel and see the
damper inside.
5   The check should be done when the engine is cold. Start the engine
and look through the snorkel at the damper, which should move to
a closed position. With the damper closed, air cannot enter through
the end of the snorkel, but instead enters the air cleaner through the
flexible duct attached to the exhaust manifold and the heat stove
passage.

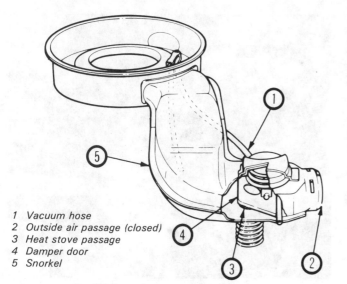

1 Vacuum hose
2 Outside air passage (closed)
3 Heat stove passage
4 Damper door
5 Snorkel

**Fig. 1.19 THERMAC assembly (fuel injected engine) shown with the snorkel passage closed (Sec 20)**

6    As the engine warms up to operating temperature, the damper should open to allow air through the snorkel end. Depending on ambient temperature, this may take 10 to 15 minutes. To speed up this check you can reconnect the snorkel air duct, drive the vehicle, then check to see if the damper is completely open.
7    If the thermo-controlled air cleaner is not operating properly see Chapter 6 for more information.

## 22   Transaxle output shaft seal and driveaxle boot check

1    At the recommended intervals the transaxle output shaft seals and driveaxle boots should be inspected for leaks and damage.
2    Raise the front of the vehicle and support it securely on jackstands.
3    Check the transaxle output shaft seals located where the driveaxles exit from the transaxle. It may be necessary to clean this area before inspection. If there is any oil leaking from either of the driveaxle/transaxle junctions, the output shaft seals must be replaced. Refer to Chapter 7.
4    The driveaxle boots prevent dirt, water and other foreign material from entering and damaging the constant velocity (CV) joints. Inspect the condition of all four boots (two on each axleshaft). Clean the boots using soap and water as oil or grease will cause the boot material to deteriorate prematurely. If there is any damage or evidence of leaking lubricant they must be replaced as described in Chapter 8 (photo). Check the tightness of the boot clamps. If they are loose and can't be tightened, the clamp must be replaced.

## 23   Tire rotation

1    The tires should be rotated at the specified intervals and whenever uneven wear is noticed. With the vehicle raised and the tires removed, you can also check the brakes (Section 13) and the wheel bearings (Section 27).
2    Refer to the accompanying illustration of the *preferred* and *optional* tire rotation patterns. Do not include *Temporary Use Only* spare tires in the rotation sequence. The optional X-rotation procedure is acceptable when required for more uniform tire wear.
3    Refer to the information in *Jacking and towing* at the front of this manual for the proper procedures to follow when raising the vehicle and changing a tire. If the brakes are to be checked, do not apply the parking brake as stated. Make sure the tires are blocked to prevent the vehicle from rolling.
4    Preferably, the entire vehicle should be raised at the same time. This can be done on a hoist or by jacking up each corner and then lowering the vehicle onto jackstands placed under the frame rails. Always

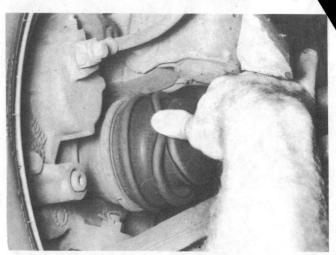

**22.4   Check the drive axle boot to make sure it is not cracked or loose**

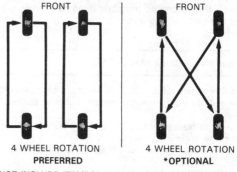

FRONT                              FRONT

4 WHEEL ROTATION              4 WHEEL ROTATION
**PREFERRED**                    **\*OPTIONAL**

DO NOT INCLUDE 'TEMPORARY USE ONLY' SPARE TIRE IN ROTATION

\*THE OPTIONAL 'X' ROTATION PATTERN FOR RADIALS IS ACCEPTABLE WHEN REQUIRED FOR MORE UNIFORM TIRE WEAR

**Fig. 1.20  Tire rotation diagram (Sec 23)**

**24.2   Pull the clutch pedal back to the stop, then depress it slowly to adjust the freeplay**

use four jackstands and make sure the vehicle is firmly supported.
5    After rotation, check and adjust the the tire pressures as necessary and be sure to check the lug nut tightness.

## 24   Clutch pedal adjustment

1    At the specified interval the clutch pedal must be adjusted to maintain a constant tension on the clutch self-adjusting mechanism cable.
2    Grasp the pedal and pull it up to the rubber stop and then depress the pedal slowly (photo). Note: *Do not pull up on the pedal after it stops or the clutch linkage could be damaged.*

28.7  Begin the automatic transaxle drain pan removal by loosening the bolts at one end

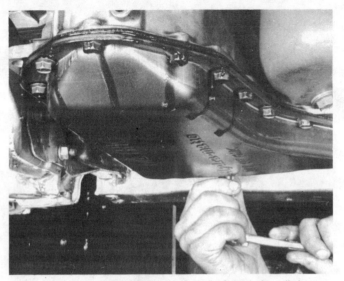

28.8  Work around the pan, loosening all of the bolts a little at a time

## 25  Manual transaxle oil change

1    Raise the vehicle and support it securely on jackstands.
2    Move a drain pan, rags, newspapers and wrenches under the transaxle.
3    Remove the transaxle drain plug at the bottom of the case and allow the oil to drain into the pan.
4    After the oil has drained completely, reinstall the plug and tighten it securely.
5    Remove the fill plug in the side of the transaxle case. Using a hand pump, syringe or funnel, fill the transaxle with the correct amount of the specified lubricant. Reinstall the fill plug and tighten it securely.
6    Lower the vehicle.

## 26  Cooling system servicing (draining, flushing and refilling)

1    Periodically the cooling system should be drained, flushed and refilled to replenish the antifreeze mixture and prevent formation of rust and corrosion, which can impair the performance of the cooling system and cause engine damage.
2    At the same time the cooling system is serviced, all hoses and the radiator cap should be inspected and, if necessary, replaced (see Section 7).
3    Since antifreeze is a corrosive and poisonous solution, be careful not to spill any of the coolant mixture on the vehicle's paint or your skin. If this happens, rinse immediately with plenty of clean water. Consult your local authorities about the dumping of antifreeze before draining the cooling system. In many areas reclamation centers have been set up to collect automobile oil and drained antifreeze/water mixtures, rather than allowing them to be added to the sewage system.
4    With the engine cold, remove the radiator cap.
5    Move a large container under the radiator to catch the coolant as it is drained.
6    Drain the radiator. Most models are equipped with a drain plug at the bottom. If this drain has excessive corrosion and cannot be turned easily, or if the radiator is not equipped with a drain, disconnect the lower radiator hose to allow the coolant to drain. Be careful that none of the solution is splashed on your skin or into your eyes.
7    If accessible, remove the two engine drain plugs. There is usually one plug on each side of the engine about halfway back, on the lower edge near the oil pan rail. These will allow the coolant to drain from the engine itself.
8    Disconnect the hose from the coolant reservoir and remove the reservoir. Flush it out with clean water.
9    Place a garden hose in the radiator filler neck and flush the system until the water runs clear at all drain points.

10   In severe cases of contamination or clogging of the radiator, remove it (see Chapter 3) and reverse flush it. This involves inserting the hose in the bottom radiator outlet to allow the clear water to run against the normal flow, draining through the top. A radiator repair shop should be consulted if further cleaning or repair is necessary.
11   When the coolant is regularly drained and the system refilled with the correct antifreeze/water mixture, there should be no need to use chemical cleaners or descalers.
12   To refill the system reconnect the radiator hoses and install the drain plugs securely in the engine. Special thread-sealing tape, available at auto parts stores, should be used on the drain plugs. Install the reservoir and the overflow hose where applicable.
13   Fill the radiator to the base of the filler neck and then add more coolant to the reservoir until it reaches the Full Cold mark.
14   Run the engine until normal operating temperature is reached and, with the engine idling, add coolant to the Full Hot level. Install the radiator and reservoir caps.
15   Always refill the system with a mixture of high quality antifreeze and water in the proportion called for on the antifreeze container or in your owner's manual. Chapter 3 also contains information on antifreeze mixtures.
16   Keep a close watch on the coolant level and the various cooling system hoses during the first few miles of driving. Tighten the hose clamps and add more coolant as necessary.

## 27  Wheel bearing check

1    With the vehicle securely supported on jackstands, spin the wheels and check for noise, rolling resistance and free play. Grasp the top of the tire with one hand and the bottom of the tire with the other. Move the tire in and out. If it moves more than 0.005 inch, the bearings should be checked and, if necessary, replaced.
2    The wheel bearings on these models are of the sealed type which cannot be serviced and must be replaced with new ones if a fault develops. Refer to Chapter 10 for the proper procedure.

## 28  Automatic transaxle fluid change

1    At the specified time intervals the transaxle fluid should be changed and the filter replaced.
2    Since there is no drain plug, the transaxle oil pan must be removed to drain the fluid. Before beginning work, purchase the specified transmission fluid (see *Recommended Fluids* at the front of this Chapter), and a new filter.
3    Other tools necessary for this job include jackstands to support

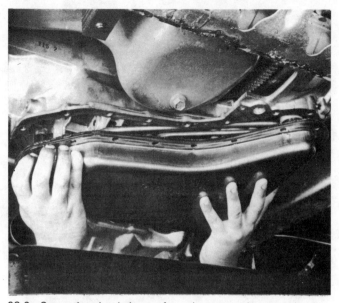

28.9   Separating the drain pan from the automatic transaxle

28.11   Removing the automatic transaxle filter

the vehicle in a raised position, a drain pan capable of holding at least 8 pints, newspapers and clean rags.

4    The fluid should be drained immediately after the vehicle has been driven. This will remove any built-up sediment better than if the fluid were cold. Because of this, it may be wise to wear protective gloves. Fluid temperature can exceed 350° in a hot transaxle.

5    After the vehicle has been driven to warm up the fluid, raise it and place it on jackstands for access underneath.

6    Move the necessary equipment under the vehicle, being careful not to touch any of the hot exhaust components.

7    Place the drain pan under the transaxle oil pan and loosen, but do not remove, the bolts at one end of the pan (photo).

8    Moving around the pan, loosen all the bolts a little at a time. Be sure the drain pan is in position, as fluid will begin dripping out (photo). Continue in this manner until all of the bolts are removed except for one at each of the corners.

9    While supporting the pan, remove the remaining bolts and lower the pan (photo). If necessary, use a screwdriver to break the gasket seal, but be careful not to damage the pan or transaxle gasket surfaces. Drain the remaining fluid into the drain pan. As this is done check the fluid for metal particles, which may be an indication of internal failure.

10   Now visible at the bottom of the transaxle is the filter/strainer.

11   Remove the filter and O-ring seal (photo).

12   Thoroughly clean the transaxle oil pan with solvent. Check for metal filings or foreign material. Dry with compressed air if available. It is important that all remaining gasket material be removed from the oil pan mounting flange. Use a gasket scraper or putty knife for this.

13   Clean the filter mounting surface on the valve body. Again, this surface should be smooth and free of any leftover gasket material.

14   Install the new filter with a new O-ring seal.

15   Press the new gasket into place on the pan, making sure all bolt holes line up.

16   Lift the pan up to the bottom of the transaxle and install the mounting bolts. Tighten the bolts in a diagonal pattern working around the pan. Using a torque wrench tighten the bolts to the specified torque.

17   Lower the vehicle.

18   Open the hood and remove the transaxle fluid dipstick.

19   Add the specified amount and type of fluid to the transaxle through the filler tube. Use a funnel to prevent spills. It is best to add a little fluid at a time, continually checking the level with the dipstick. Allow the fluid time to drain into the pan.

20   With the selector lever in Park, apply the parking brake and start the engine without depressing the accelerator pedal (if possible). Do not race the engine — run at slow idle only.

21   With the engine idling, check the level on the dipstick. Look under the vehicle for leaks around the transaxle oil pan mating surface.

22   Check the fluid level to make sure it is just below the Add mark

29.4   Removing the air filter element

on the dipstick. Do no allow the fluid level to go above this point as the transaxle would then be overfilled, necessitating the removal of the pan to drain excess fluid.

23   Push the dipstick firmly back into its tube and drive the vehicle far enough to reach normal operating temperature in the transmission. This should take approximately 15 miles of highway driving, slightly less in the city. Park the vehicle on a level surface and check the fluid level on the dipstick with the engine idling and the transaxle in Park. The level should now be at the *F* mark on the dipstick. If not, add more fluid to bring the level up to this point. Again, do not overfill.

## 29   Air filter and PCV filter replacement

1    At the specified intervals, the air filter and PCV filter should be replaced with new ones. A thorough program of preventative maintenance would call for the two filters to be inspected between changes.

2    The air filter is located inside the air cleaner housing on the top of the engine. The filter is replaced by removing the wing nut at the top of the air cleaner assembly and lifting off the top plate.

3    While the top plate is off, be careful not to drop anything down into the carburetor.

4    Lift the air filter element out of the housing (photo).

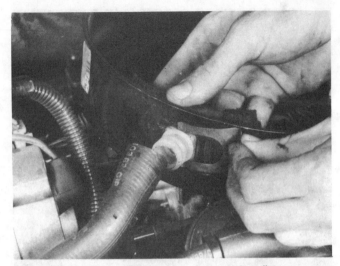

29.9A   Removing the PCV filter housing retaining clip

29.9B   Removing the PCV filter

30.1   The oxygen sensor (arrow) threads into the exhaust manifold

5    Wipe out the inside of the air cleaner housing with a clean rag.
6    Place the new filter into the air cleaner housing. Make sure it seats properly in the bottom of the housing.
7    The PCV filter is also located inside the air cleaner housing. Remove the top plate and air filter as described previously, then locate the PCV filter on the side of the housing.
9    Remove the PCV filter housing clip and remove the PCV filter (photos).
10   Install a new PCV filter and the air filter.
11   Install the top plate and any hoses which were disconnected.

## 30   Oxygen sensor replacement

**Note:** *Special care must be taken when handling the sensitive oxygen sensor:*
    a)   The oxygen sensor has a permanently attached pigtail and connector, which should not be removed from the sensor. Damage or removal of the pigtail or connector can adversely affect its operation.
    b)   Grease, dirt and other contaminants should be kept away from the electrical connector and the louvered end of the sensor.
    c)   Do not use cleaning solvents of any kind on the oxygen sensor.
    d)   Do not drop or roughly handle the sensor.
    e)   The silicone boot must be installed in the correct position to prevent the boot from being melted and to allow the sensor to operate properly.

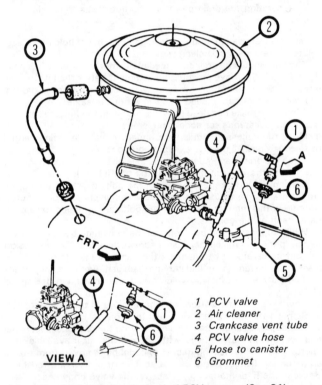

1   PCV valve
2   Air cleaner
3   Crankcase vent tube
4   PCV valve hose
5   Hose to canister
6   Grommet

**Fig. 1.21  Details of a typical PCV system (Sec 31)**

1    The sensor is located in the exhaust manifold or exhaust pipe and is accessible from under the vehicle or in the engine compartment (photo).
2    Since the oxygen sensor may be difficult to remove with the engine cold, begin by operating the engine until it has warmed to at least 120 °F (48 °C).
3    Disconnect the electrical wire from the oxygen sensor.
4    Note the position of the silicone boot and carefully back out the oxygen sensor from the exhaust manifold. Be advised that excessive force may damage the threads. Inspect the oxygen sensor for damage.
5    A special anti-seize compound must be used on the threads of the oxygen sensor to aid in future removal. New or service sensors will have this compound already applied, but if for any reason an oxygen sensor is removed and then reinstalled, the threads must be coated before reinstallation.
6    Install the sensor and tighten it to 30 ft-lbs.
7    Connect the electrical wire.

31.2   Removing the PCV valve from the rocker arm cover

32.2A   The diaphragm, located under the EGR valve, should be checked for free movement

32.2B   Check the EGR valve by pressing on the diaphragm from underneath (valve removed for clarity)

## 31  Positive Crankcase Ventilation (PCV) valve — checking and replacement

1    The PCV valve is located in the rocker arm cover. A hose runs from the valve to the carburetor or intake manifold.
2    Pull the valve (with hose attached) from the rubber grommet in the rocker arm cover (photo).
3    Start the engine and bring it to normal operating temperature.
4    Place your finger over the end of the valve. If the engine speed drops, the valve is working properly. If the speed doesn't drop the valve is faulty and should be replaced with a new one.
5    To replace the valve, pull it from the end of the hose, noting its installed position and direction.
6    When purchasing a replacement PCV valve, make sure it is for your particular vehicle, model year and engine size. Compare the old valve with the new one to make sure they are the same.
6    Push the valve into the end of the hose until it is seated.
7    Inspect the rubber grommet for damage and replace it with a new one if necessary.
8    Push the PCV valve and hose securely into position.
9    More information on the PCV system can be found in Chapter 6.

## 32  Exhaust Gas Recirculation (EGR) valve check

1    The EGR valve is located on the intake manifold, adjacent to the carburetor or TBI unit. Most problems in the emissions system are due

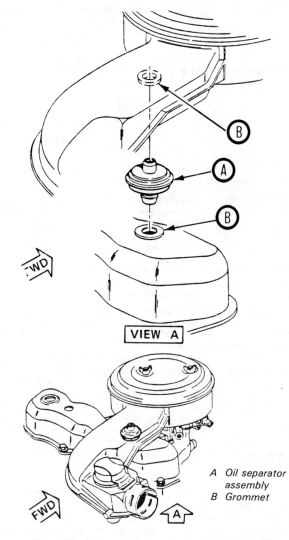

A  Oil separator assembly
B  Grommet

Fig. 1.22 Oil separator installation details (Sec 31)

to a stuck or corroded EGR valve.
2    With the engine cold to prevent burns, reach under the EGR valve and manually push on the diaphragm. Using moderate pressure, you should be able to press the diaphragm up and down inside the housing (photos).

33.2   The EECS canister is located at the front corner of the engine compartment

**Fig. 1.23  Location of a typical timing mark plate (Sec 34)**

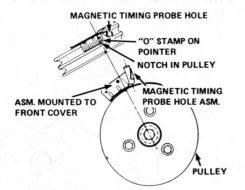

**Fig. 1.24  Location of the magnetic timing probe hole incorporated on some engines (Sec 34)**

3   If the diaphragm does not move or moves only with much effort, replace the EGR valve with a new one. If in doubt about the condition of the valve, compare the free movement of your EGR valve with a new valve.

4   Refer to Chapter 6 for more information on the EGR system.

### 33   Evaporative emissions control system check

1   The function of the Evaporative Emissions Control System is to capture fuel vapors from the tank and carburetor before they can escape into the atmosphere, store them in a charcoal canister and then burn them during normal engine operation.

2   The most common symptom of a fault in the evaporative emissions system is a strong fuel odor in the engine compartment. If a fuel odor is detected, inspect the charcoal canister, located on the engine compartment firewall, and system hoses (photo).

3   A simple check of system operation is to place your hand under the canister with the engine at normal operating temperature and slowly increase engine speed. If air can be felt being sucked into the bottom of the canister the system is operating properly.

4   The evaporative emissions control system is explained in more detail in Chapter 6.

### 34   Ignition timing check and adjustment

**Note:** *It is imperative that the procedures included on the Vehicle Emissions Control Information label be followed when adjusting the ignition timing. The label will include all information concerning preliminary steps to be performed before adjusting the timing, as well as the timing specifications. Two different methods of timing are used. The conventional method and, on some four-cylinder models, the averaging method. The VECI label will tell you which method is used with your engine.*

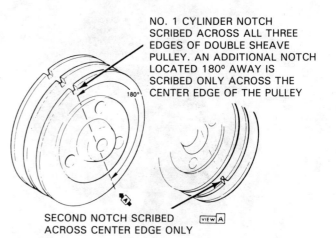

NO. 1 CYLINDER NOTCH SCRIBED ACROSS ALL THREE EDGES OF DOUBLE SHEAVE PULLEY. AN ADDITIONAL NOTCH LOCATED 180° AWAY IS SCRIBED ONLY ACROSS THE CENTER EDGE OF THE PULLEY

SECOND NOTCH SCRIBED ACROSS CENTER EDGE ONLY

**Fig. 1.25  Engines which use the averaging timing adjustment method have special crankshaft pulleys (Sec 34)**

1   Locate the VECI label under the hood and read through and perform all preliminary instructions concerning ignition timing.

2   Locate the timing mark pointer plate located beside the crankshaft pulley. The *T* mark represents top dead center (TDC). The pointer plate will be marked in either one or two-degree increments and should have the proper timing mark for your particular vehicle noted. If not, count back from the *T* mark the correct number of degrees BTDC, as noted on the VECI label, and mark the plate.

3   Locate the notch on the crankshaft balancer or pulley and mark it with chalk or a dab of paint so it will be visible under the timing light.

4   Start the engine, warm it up to the normal operating temperature and shut it off. Turn off all lights and other electrical loads.

5   With the ignition off, connect the pick-up lead of the timing light to the number one spark plug. Use either a jumper lead between the wire and plug or an inductive-type pick-up. Do not pierce the wire or attempt to insert a wire between the boot and wire. Connect the timing light power leads according to the manufacturer's instructions.

6   Start the engine, aim the timing light at the timing mark by the crankshaft pulley and note which timing mark the notch on the pulley is lining up with.

7   If the notch is not lining up with the correct mark, loosen the distributor hold-down bolt and rotate the distributor until the notch is lined up with the correct timing mark.

8   Retighten the hold-down bolt and recheck the timing.

9   Turn off the engine and disconnect the timing light. Reconnect the number one spark plug wire, if removed, and any other components which were disconnected.

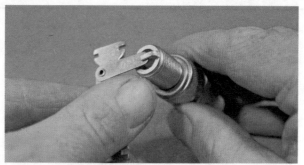

**Measuring plug gap.** A feeler gauge of the correct size (see ignition system specifications) should have a slight 'drag' when slid between the electrodes. Adjust gap if necessary

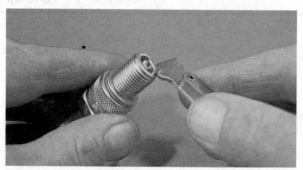

**Adjusting plug gap.** The plug gap is adjusted by bending the ground electrode inwards, or outwards, as necessary until the correct clearance is obtained. Note the use of the correct tool

**Normal.** Gray brown deposits, lightly coated core nose. Gap increasing by around 0.001 in (0.025 mm) per 1000 miles (1600 km). Plugs ideally suited to engine, and engine in good condition

**Carbon fouling.** Dry, black, sooty deposits. Will cause weak spark and eventually misfire. Fault: over-rich fuel mixture. Check: carburetor mixture settings, float level and jet sizes; choke operation and cleanliness of air filter. Plugs can be re-used after cleaning

**Oil fouling.** Wet, oily deposits. Will cause weak spark and eventually misfire. Fault: worn bores/piston rings or valve guides; sometimes occurs (temporarily) during running-in period. Plugs can be re-used after thorough cleaning

**Overheating.** Electrodes have glazed appearance, core nose very white – few deposits. Fault: plug overheating. Check: plug value, ignition timing, fuel octane rating (too low) and fuel mixture (too weak). Discard plugs and cure fault immediately.

**Electrode damage.** Electrodes burned away; core nose has burned, glazed appearance. Fault: pre-ignition. Check: as for 'Overheating' but may be more severe. Discard plugs and remedy fault before piston or valve damage occurs

**Split core nose (may appear initially as a crack).** Damage is self-evident, but cracks will only show after cleaning. Fault: pre-ignition or wrong gap-setting technique. Check: ignition timing, cooling system, fuel octane rating (too low) and fuel mixture (too weak). Discard plugs, rectify fault immediately

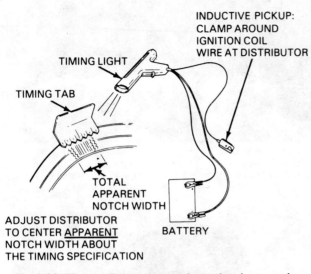

Fig. 1.26 Timing adjustment procedure using the averaging method (Sec 34)

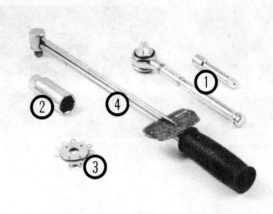

35.1   Tools required for spark plug replacement

1   Ratchet/extension       3   Spark plug gap tool
2   Spark plug socket        4   Torque wrench

35.10   A length of 3/16-inch i.d. rubber hose eases the job of installing a spark plug in difficult to reach areas

## Averaging method

10   The averaging method is used to bring the timing of each cylinder into alignment with the base timing specification. Models using the averaging method have a double-notched crankshaft pulley with the notch for the number one cylinder scribed across all three edges of the pulley. Another notch, scribed across only the center section of the pulley, is located 180° away, as shown in the accompanying illustration. The coil wire, instead of the number one spark plug wire, is used to trigger the timing light. Because the trigger signal is picked up at the coil wire, each spark firing causes a flash from the timing light. This makes the timing notch appear to *jiggle*, since each firing is indicated. Adjustment is accomplished by centering the total apparent notch width over the specified timing mark.

11   On electronic spark timing equipped models disconnect the four terminal EST plug at the distributor so the engine will operate in the bypass timing mode.

12   Connect the timing light, following the manufacturer's instructions. Be very careful not to tangle the wires in moving engine parts.

13   Clamp the timing light inductive pickup around the high tension coil wire as shown in the accompanying illustration. Peel back the protective plastic on the wire when installing the timing light inductive pickup.

14   Loosen the distributor clamp nut sufficiently to allow the distributor to be rotated for adjustment.

15   Start the engine, aim the timing light at the timing tab and, if necessary, rotate the distributor to center the notch width over the specified mark. Remember that a slight jiggling of the pulley notch is normal.

16   Shut the engine off and tighten the distributor clamp nut, taking care not to move the distributor.

17   Recheck the timing and repeat the adjustment if necessary.

18   Plug in the EST connector, replace the plastic cover on the coil wire and remove the timing light. **Note:** *On some models it will be necessary to remove and replace the ECM '1' fuse to clear the trouble code memory.*

## 35   Spark plug replacement

1   In most cases, tools necessary for a spark plug replacement include a plug wrench or spark plug socket which fits onto a ratchet wrench (this special socket will be insulated inside to protect the porcelain insulator) and a wire-type feeler gauge to check and adjust the spark plug gap (photo).

2   The spark plugs are located on each side of V6 engines and on the front (radiator) side of four-cylinder engines.

3   The best procedure to follow when replacing the spark plugs is to purchase the new spark plugs beforehand, adjust them to the proper gap and then replace each plug one at a time. When buying the new spark plugs, it is important to obtain the correct plugs for your specific engine. This information can be found on the Vehicle Emissions Control Information label, located under the hood, or in the owner's manual. If differences exist between these sources, purchase the spark plug type specified on the Emissions Control label because the information was printed for your specific engine.

4   With the new spark plugs at hand, allow the engine to cool completely before attempting plug removal. During this time, each of the new spark plugs can be inspected for defects and the gaps can be checked.

5   The gap is checked by inserting the proper thickness gauge between the electrodes at the tip of the plug. The gap between the electrodes should be the same as that given in the specifications or on the Emissions Control label. The wire should just touch each of the electrodes. If the gap is incorrect, use the notched adjuster on the feeler gauge body to bend the curved side electrode slightly until the proper gap is achieved. If the side electrode is not exactly over the center electrode, use the notched adjuster to align the two. Check for cracks in the porcelain insulator, indicating the spark plug should not be used.

6   With the engine cool, remove the spark plug wire from one spark plug. Do this by grabbing the boot at the end of the wire, not the wire itself. Sometimes it is necessary to use a twisting motion while the boot and plug wire are pulled free.

7   If compressed air is available, use it to blow any dirt or foreign material away from the spark plug area. A common bicycle pump will also work. The idea here is to eliminate the possibility of material falling into the cylinder as the spark plug is removed.

8   Place the spark plug wrench or socket over the plug and remove it from the engine by turning in a counterclockwise direction.

9   Compare the spark plug with those shown in the accompanying color photos to get an indication of the overall running condition of the engine.

10   Due to the angle at which the spark plugs must be installed on most engines, installation will be simplified by inserting the plug wire terminal of the new spark plug into a 3/16-inch i.d. rubber hose 12-inches long (photo). This procedure serves two purposes. The rub-

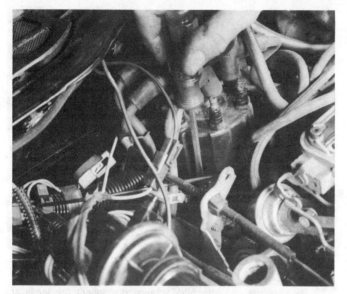

36.3  Releasing the distributor cap hold-down latches (spark plug wire ring removed for clarity)

36.4  Inspect the distributor cap for cracks and carbon tracks and the contacts (arrow) for corrosion and damage

36.6  Removing the rotor

36.7  Close-up of metal contact on this rotor reveals normal wear pattern

ber hose gives you flexibility for establishing the proper angle of plug insertion in the head and, should the threads be improperly aligned, the rubber hose will slip on the spark plug when it meets resistance, preventing cross-threading into the head.

11  After installing the plug to the limit of the hose grip, tighten it with the sprocket. It is a good idea to use a torque wrench for this to insure that the plug is seated correctly. The correct torque figure is included in the specifications.

12  Before pushing the spark plug wire onto the end of the plug, inspect it following the procedures outlined in Section 36.

13  Attach the plug wire to the new spark plug, again using a twisting motion on the boot until it is firmly seated on the spark plug. Make sure the wire is routed away from the exhaust manifold.

14  Follow the above procedure for the remaining spark plugs, replacing them one at a time to prevent mixing up the spark plug wires.

## 36  Spark plug wires, distributor cap and rotor check and replacement

1  Begin this procedure by making a visual check of the spark plug wires while the engine is running. In a darkened garage (make sure

there is ventilation) start the engine and observe each plug wire. Be careful not to come into contact with any moving engine parts. If there is a break in the wire, you will see arcing or a small spark at the damaged area. If arcing is noticed, make a note to obtain new wires, then allow the engine to cool and check the distributor cap and rotor.

2  Disconnect the negative cable from the battery. At the distributor, disconnect the ECM connector and the coil connector (coil-in-cap models) or coil wire (models with a separately mounted coil).

3  Remove the distributor cap by placing a screwdriver on the slotted head of each latch. Press down on the latch and turn it 90° to release the hooked end at the bottom (photo). On some engines, due to restricted working room, a stubby screwdriver will work best. With all latches disengaged, separate the cap from the distributor with the spark plug wires still attached.

4  Inspect the cap for cracks and other damage. Closely examine the contacts on the inside of the cap for excessive corrosion (photo). Slight scoring is normal. Deposits on the contacts may be removed with a small file.

5  If the inspection reveals damage to the cap, make a note to obtain a replacement for your particular engine, then examine the rotor.

6  The rotor is visible, with the cap removed, at the top of the distributor shaft. It is held in place by two screws. Remove the screws and the rotor (photo).

7  Inspect the rotor for cracks and other damage. Carefully check the condition of the metal contact at the top of the rotor for excessive burning and pitting (photo). On coil-in-cap models, also check the top of the rotor for carbon tracks. This is a sign of moisture contamination due to a leaking seal between the distributor cap and the coil. The

36.17A  Removing the spark plug wire retaining ring clip from the top of the distributor cap

36.17B  Removing the plug wire retainer from the cap

rotor and seal should be replaced with new ones if carbon tracks are visible.

8    If it is determined that a new rotor is required, make a note to that effect. If the rotor and cap are in good condition, reinstall them at this time. Be sure to apply a small dab of silicone lubricant to the contacts inside the cap before installing it. Note that the rotor has two raised pegs on the bottom and that it has a wide slot and a narrow slot. Make sure that the slots are correctly aligned and that the pegs are firmly seated with the rotor is installed.

9    If the cap must be replaced, do not reinstall it. Leave it off the distributor with the wires still connected.

10  If the spark plug wires are being replaced, now is the time to obtain a new set, along with a new cap and rotor as determined in the checks above. Purchase a wire set for your particular engine, pre-cut to the proper size, with the rubber boots already installed.

11  If the spark plug wires passed the check in Step 1, they should be checked further as follows.

12  Examine the wires one at a time to avoid mixing them up.

13  Disconnect the plug wire from the spark plug. A removal tool can be used for this, or you can grab the rubber boot, twist slightly and then pull the wire free. Do not pull on the wire itself, only on the rubber boot.

14  Inspect inside the boot for corrosion, which will look like a white crusty powder. Some models use a conductive white silicone lubricant, which should not be mistaken for corrosion.

15  Push the wire and boot back onto the end of the spark plug. It should be a tight fit on the plug end. If not, remove the wire and use pliers to carefully crimp the metal connector inside the wire boot until the fit is snug.

16  Using a clean rag, clean the entire length of the wire. Remove all built-up dirt and grease. As this is done, check for burns, cracks and any other form of damage. Bend the wires in several places to ensure that the conductive wire inside has not hardened.

17  The wires should be checked at the distributor cap in the same manner. On·four-cylinder engines, remove the wire from the cap by pulling on the boot, again examining the wires one at a time, and reinstalling each one after examination. Apply new silicone lubricant before installation. On V6 engines, the distributor boots are connected to a circular retaining ring attached to the distributor cap. Release the locking tabs, turn the ring upside down and check all wire boots at the same time (photos).

18  If the wires appear to be in good condition, reinstall the retaining ring (some models) and make sure that all wires are secure at both ends. If the cap and rotor are also in good condition, the check is finished. Reconnect the wires at the distributor and the battery.

19  If it was determined that new wires are required, obtain them at this time, along with a new cap and rotor if so determined by the checks above.

20  If a new cab is being installed on a coil-in-cap type distributor, the coil and cover from the cap being replaced should be transferred to the new cap.

21  Remove the three coil attaching screws and lift off the cover.

22  Remove the coil attaching screws, disconnect the leads and separate the coil from the distributor.

23  Attach the new coil to the cap by reversing Steps 21 and 22. Use a new seal between the coil and cap and be sure to lubricate the seal with multi-purpose grease.

24  Attach the rotor to the distributor. Make sure that the carbon brush is properly installed in the cap, as a side gap between the carbon brush and the rotor will cause rotor burn-through and/or damage to the distributor cap.

25  If new wires are being installed, replace them one at a time. **Note:** *It is important to replace wires one at a time, noting the routing as each wire is removed and installed, to maintain the correct firing order and to prevent cross-firing.*

26  Attach the cap to the distributor, reconnecting all wires disconnected earlier, then reconnect the battery cable.

### 37   Early Fuel Evaporation (EFE) system check

1    The EFE system is designed to recirculate exhaust gases to help preheat the induction system, thereby improving cold engine driveability and, by reducing the time that the choke is closed, reducing exhaust emissions levels. There are two basic types of EFE systems. The first is a valve in the exhaust system, between the exhaust manifold and the exhaust pipe, which is called a vacuum servo type. The second type is an electrically heated unit located between the carburetor base and the intake manifold. The procedures which follow in this Section are concerned only with the first type. If you have the electrically heated type, refer to Chapter 6 for more information.

2    Locate the EFE actuator, which is bolted to the exhaust manifold.

3    With the engine cold, have an assistant start it. Observe the movement of the actuator link. It should immediately be drawn into the diaphragm, closing the valve.

4    If the valve does not close it could be seized. Shut off the engine and apply penetrating oil to the shaft at the pivot points in the valve assembly, allow it to work, then restart the engine and observe the actuator link. If it still does not close, disconnect the vacuum hose at the actuator.

5    Hold your thumb over the disconnected hose. If vacuum is felt, test the actuator and valve as follows.

6    Attach a piece of hose to the actuator vacuum outlet, apply vacuum to the hose, then quickly place your thumb over it. If the actuator holds vacuum, it is operating correctly and the valve is defective. Refer to Chapter 6 and replace the valve assembly.

7    If the actuator does not hold vacuum, the actuator diaphragm is defective. Refer to Chapter 6 and replace the actuator.

8    If no vacuum was felt at the disconnected vacuum source hose in Step 5, either the hose is crimped or plugged, or the EFE solenoid is not functioning properly.

9    Check the hose for cracks and restrictions and replace it as necessary. Because of its interrelationship with the ECM, the solenoid

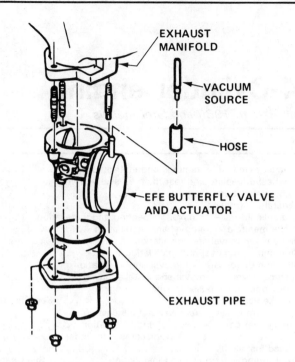

Fig. 1.27  Components of a typical valve-actuated EFE system (Sec 37)

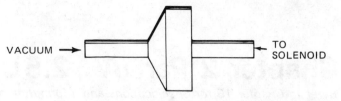

Fig. 1.28  EFE check valve (Sec 37)

38.4   Using a compression gauge to check cylinder compression

must be tested by a dealer service department.

10  With the hose again connected to the EFE actuator, continue to warm up the engine until it reaches normal operating temperature.

11  Make sure that the actuating link has moved the valve to the open position.

12  If the valve does not open, remove the hose from the actuator. If the valve opens, there is no air bleed for the valve actuator diaphragm, the electrical solenoid plunger is stuck in the cold mode or the engine is not reaching proper operating temperature. Refer to Chapter 6 to replace the actuator diaphragm. If the engine is not reaching proper operating temperature, check the thermostat (refer to Chapter 3). If the valve does not open with the hose removed from the actuator, it may be stuck closed by corrosion.

13  Check the EFE check valve located in the vacuum hose between the carburetor and the EFE solenoid.

14  Remove the check valve from the hose and apply vacuum to the tapered end. Air should flow freely through the valve.

15  Vacuum applied to the other (squared off) end of the valve should not flow through and should not leak down for at least one minute.

16  If the check valve fails either test, replace it with a new one.

## 38  Compression check

1  A compression check will tell you what mechanical condition the engine is in. Specifically, it can tell you if the compression is down due to leakage caused by worn piston rings, defective valves and seats or a blown head gasket.

2  Begin by cleaning the area around the spark plugs before you remove them. This will keep dirt from falling into the cylinders while you are performing the compression test.

3  Disconnect the coil wire from the distributor. Block the throttle and choke valves open.

4  With the compression gauge in the number one spark plug hole, crank the engine over at least four compression strokes and observe

the gauge. The compression should build up quickly. (photo). Low compression on the first stroke, which does not build up during successive strokes, indicates leaking valves, a blown head gasket or a cracked head. Record the highest gauge reading obtained.

5  Repeat the procedure for the remaining cylinders. The lowest compression reading should not be less than 70% of the highest reading. No reading should be less than 100 lbs.

6  Pour a couple of teaspoons of engine oil (a squirt can works great for this) into each cylinder, through the spark plug hole, and repeat the test.

7  If the compression increases after the oil is added, the piston rings are worn. If the compression does not increase significantly, the leakage is occurring at the valves or head gasket. Leakage past the valves may be caused by burned valve seats or faces or warped, cracked or bent valves.

8  If two adjacent cylinders have equally low compression, there is a strong possibility that the head gasket between them is blown. The appearance of coolant in the combustion chambers or the crankcase would verify this condition.

9  If the compression is higher than normal, the combustion chambers are probably coated with carbon deposits. If that it the case, the cylinder head(s) should be removed and decarbonized.

10  If compression is down or varies greatly between cylinders, it would be a good idea to have a leak-down test performed by an automotive repair shop. This test will pinpoint exactly where the leakage is occurring and how severe it is.

# Chapter 2 Part A   2.5L 4-Cylinder engine

*Refer to Chapter 13 for Specifications and information applicable to 1986 and later models*

## Contents

| | |
|---|---|
| Air filter | See Chapter 1 |
| Camshaft — removal and installation | 14 |
| Check engine light | See Chapter 6 |
| Compression check | See Chapter 1 |
| Crankshaft pulley hub and oil seal — removal and installation | 12 |
| Cylinder head — removal and installation | 7 |
| Drivebelt check and adjustment | See Chapter 1 |
| Engine (automatic transaxle models) — removal and installation | 17 |
| Engine (manual transaxle models) — removal and installation | 18 |
| Engine and transaxle mounts — replacement with engine in vehicle | 16 |
| Engine oil and filter change | See Chapter 1 |
| Engine oil level check | See Chapter 1 |
| Engine overhaul — general information | See Chapter 2D |
| Engine removal — methods and installation | See Chapter 2D |
| Exhaust manifold — removal and installation | 6 |
| Flywheel/driveplate and rear main oil seal — removal and installation | 15 |
| General information | 1 |
| Hydraulic lifters — removal, inspection and installation | 8 |
| Intake manifold — removal and installation | 5 |
| Oil pan — removal and installation | 10 |
| Oil pump — removal and installation | 11 |
| Oil pump driveshaft — removal and installation | 9 |
| Pushrod cover — removal and installation | 3 |
| Repair operations possible with the engine in the vehicle | See Chapter 2D |
| Rocker arm cover — removal and installation | 2 |
| Timing gear cover — removal and installation | 13 |
| Valve train components — replacement (cylinder head installed) | 4 |
| Water pump — removal and installation | See Chapter 3 |

## Specifications

| Torque specifications | Ft-lbs |
|---|---|
| Main bearing cap bolt | 70 |
| Connecting rod nut | 32 |
| Oil pan bolt | 7.4 |
| Oil pan drain plug | 25 |
| Oil screen support bolt | 37 |
| Oil pump-to-block bolt | 22 |
| Oil pump cover bolt | 10 |
| Pushrod cover bolt | 7.4 |
| Harmonic balancer bolt | 200 |
| Automatic transaxle driveplate-to-crankshaft bolt | 63 |
| Manual transaxle flywheel-to-crankshaft bolt | 70 |
| TBI assembly-to-manifold bolt or nut | 13 |
| Intake manifold-to-cylinder head bolt | 29 |
| Exhaust manifold-to-cylinder head bolt | 44 |
| Fuel pump-to-engine block bolt | 18 |
| Distributor clamp bolt | 20 |
| EGR valve-to-manifold bolt | 20 |
| Water outlet housing bolt | 20 |
| Thermostat housing bolt | 20 |
| Water pump-to-engine block bolt | 20 |
| Timing cover bolt | 7.4 |
| Fan and pulley-to-water pump bolt | 18 |
| Radiator hose clamps | 17 |
| Rocker arm bolt | 20 |
| Cylinder head bolt | 85 |
| Rocker arm cover bolt | 6 |
| Camshaft thrust plate bolt | 7 |

## 1   General information

The forward sections in this part of Chapter 2 are devoted to invehicle repair procedures for the 2.5 liter 4-cylinder engine. The latter sections contain the removal and installation procedures for this engine. Information concerning engine block and cylinder head servicing can be found in Part D of this Chapter.

The repair procedures are based on the assumption that the engine is still installed in the vehicle. Therefore, if this information is being used during a complete engine overhaul, with the engine already out of the vehicle and on a stand, many of the steps included here will not apply.

The specifications included apply only to the engine and procedures found here. For specifications regarding engines other than the 2.5 liter 4-cylinder engine, see Part B or C, whichever applies. Part D contains the specifications necessary for engine block and cylinder head rebuilding.

## 2   Rocker arm cover — removal and installation

1   Remove the air cleaner assembly, tagging each hose as it is disconnected with a piece of numbered tape to simplify installation.
2   Disconnect the throttle cable from the fuel injection assembly, making careful note of the exact locations of the cable components and hardware to ensure correct reinstallation.
3   Remove the PCV valve from the rocker arm cover.
4   Remove the spark plug wires from the spark plugs, refering to the removal technique described in Chapter 1, then remove the wires and retaining clips from the rocker arm cover. Be sure to label each wire before removal to ensure that all wires are reinstalled correctly.
5   Loosen the fuel injection mounting nuts and bolts to provide clearance for removal of the EGR valve, then remove the EGR valve.
6   Remove the rocker arm cover bolts (photo).
7   Remove the rocker arm cover. **Note:** *If the cover sticks to the cylinder head, use a block of wood and a hammer to dislodge it. If the cover still will not come loose, pry on it carefully, but do not distort the sealing flange surface.*
8   Prior to reinstallation of the cover clean all dirt, oil and old gasket material from the sealing surfaces of the cover and cylinder head with a scraper and degreaser.
9   Apply a continuous 3/16-inch (5 mm) diameter bead of RTV-type sealant to the sealing flange of the cover. Be sure to apply the sealant inboard of the bolt holes.
10  Place the rocker arm cover on the cylinder head while the sealant is still wet and install the mounting bolts. Tighten the bolts a little at a time to the specified torque.
11  Complete the installation by reversing the removal procedure.

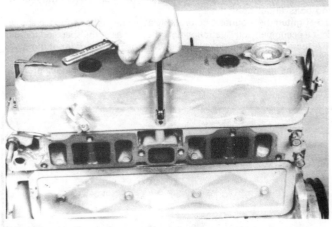

2.6   Remove the rocker arm cover bolts

## 3   Pushrod cover — removal and installation

1   Rotate the steering shaft until the gear stub shaft clamp bolt is accessible. Remove the bolt and disconnect the shaft from the stub.
2   Raise the vehicle and support it securely on jackstands.
3   Remove the two rear engine support cradle bolts.
4   Remove the two exhaust pipe flex joint bolts. Lower the support cradle between four and six inches for access to the pushrod cover bolts.
5   Remove the pushrod cover bolts and lift off the cover. If the gasket seal is difficult to break, tap on the cover gently with a rubber hammer. Do not pry on the cover.
6   Using a scraper and degreaser, clean the sealing surfaces on the cover and engine block to remove all oil and old gasket material.
7   Prior to installation of the cover apply a continuous 3/16-inch (5 mm) bead of RTV-type sealant to the mounting flange of the pushrod cover.
8   With the sealant still wet, place the cover in position on the block and install the cover bolts. Tighten the bolts gradually, following a crisscross pattern, to the specified torque.
9   Install the cradle and exhaust pipe, lower the vehicle and reconnect the steering shaft.

## 4   Valve train components — replacement (cylinder head installed)

1   Remove the rocker arm cover as described in Section 2.
2   If only a pushrod is to be replaced, loosen the rocker bolt enough to allow the rocker arm to be rotated away from the pushrod. Pull the pushrod out of the hole in the cylinder head. If the rocker arm is to be removed, remove the rocker bolt and pivot and lift off the rocker arm.
3   If a valve spring is to be removed, remove the spark plug from the affected cylinder.
4   There are two methods that will allow the valve to remain in place while the valve spring is removed. If you have access to compressed air, install an air hose adapter (GM part number J-22794) in the spark plug hole. These adapters are also available at most parts stores, and some compression gauges come with a quick-connect hose which doubles as an adapter for this procedure. When air pressure is applied to the adapter the valves will be held in place by the pressure.
5   If you do not have access to compressed air, bring the piston of the affected cylinder to slightly before top dead center (TDC) on the compression stroke. Feed a long piece of 1/4-inch nylon cord in through the spark plug hole until it fills the combustion chamber. Be sure to leave the end of the cord hanging out of the spark plug hole so it can be removed easily. Rotate the crankshaft with a wrench (in the normal direction of rotation) until slight resistance is felt.
6   Install a puller-type valve spring compressor over the valve spring, making sure the arms lock firmly under the lower spring coils.
7   Tighten the valve spring compressor just enough to remove the

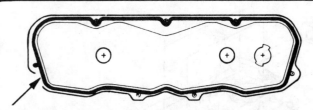

Fig. 2A.1   Apply a continuous 3/16-inch bead of RTV-type sealant (arrow) to the rocker arm cover flange (make sure it is applied to the inside of the bolt holes as shown) (Sec 2)

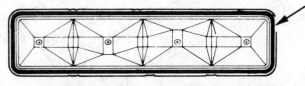

Fig. 2A.2   Apply a continuous 3/16-inch bead of RTV-type sealant (arrow) to the pushrod cover flange (Sec 3)

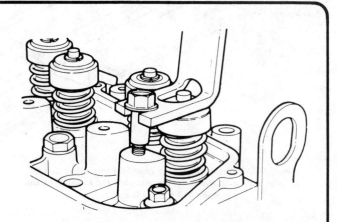

Fig. 2A.3   A valve spring compressor is used to compress the valve springs and remove the spring keepers (Sec 4)

spring keepers, then release the pressure on the tool. If, after the spring is compressed, the valve spring retainer will not release from the keepers, squirt the retainers with penetrating oil and tap the top of the spring compressor lightly with a hammer.

8    Remove the valve spring compressor, retainer, cup shield, O-ring seal, spring, spring damper (if so equipped) and valve stem oil seal (if so equipped).

9    Inspection procedures for valve train components are covered in Section 8 and in Chapter 2, Part D.

10   Installation of the valve train components is the reverse of the removal procedure. Always use new valve stem oil seals whenever the spring keepers have been disturbed. Prior to installing the rocker arms, coat the bearing surfaces of the arms and rocker arm pivots with moly-base grease or engine assembly lube. The engine valve mechanisms require no special valve lash adjustment. Simply tighten the rocker arm bolts to the specified torque.

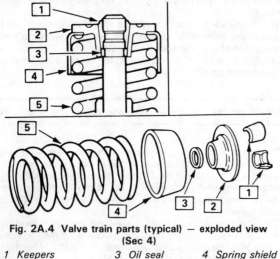

**Fig. 2A.4  Valve train parts (typical) — exploded view (Sec 4)**

| | | |
|---|---|---|
| 1  Keepers | 3  Oil seal | 4  Spring shield |
| 2  Retainer | | 5  Spring |

## 5   Intake manifold — removal and installation

1    Disconnect the cable from the negative battery terminal.

2    Remove the air cleaner assembly, tagging each hose as it is disconnected with a piece of numbered tape to simplify reinstallation.

3    Remove the PCV valve and hose.

4    Drain the cooling system (refer to Chapter 1).

5    Label and disconnect the fuel line, vacuum lines and electrical leads from the fuel injection assembly. When disconnecting the fuel line be prepared to catch some fuel, then plug the fuel line to prevent contamination.

6    Disconnect the fuel injection throttle linkage, making careful note of how it is installed.

7    Disconnect the cruise control linkage (if so equipped).

8    Disconnect the coil wire, remove the two retaining screws and one bolt, then remove the coil.

9    Remove the coolant hoses from the manifold.

10   Remove the manifold retaining bolts and separate the manifold from the cylinder head. Do not pry between the manifold and head, as damage to the gasket sealing surfaces may result.

11   Remove the manifold gasket.

12   If the intake manifold is to be replaced with another, transfer all components still attached to the old manifold to the new one.

13   Before installing the manifold, clean the cylinder head and manifold gasket surfaces. All gasket material and sealing compound must be removed prior to installation.

14   Apply a thin bead of RTV-type sealant to the intake manifold and cylinder head mating surfaces. Make certain that the sealant will not spread into the air or coolant passages when the manifold is installed.

15   Place a new intake manifold gasket on the manifold, hold the manifold in position against the cylinder head and install the mounting bolts finger tight.

16   Tighten the mounting bolts a little at a time in the sequence shown in the accompanying illustration until they are all at the specified torque.

17   Install the remaining components in the reverse order of removal.

18   Fill the radiator with coolant, start the engine and check for leaks. Adjust the ignition timing and idle speed as necessary (Chapter 1).

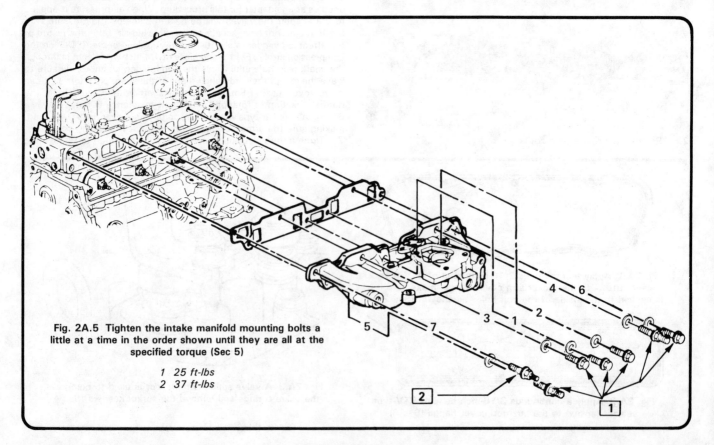

**Fig. 2A.5  Tighten the intake manifold mounting bolts a little at a time in the order shown until they are all at the specified torque (Sec 5)**

1   25 ft-lbs
2   37 ft-lbs

## 6   Exhaust manifold — removal and installation

1   If the vehicle is equipped with air-conditioning, carefully examine the routing of the hoses and the mounting of the compressor. You may be able to remove the exhaust manifold without disconnecting the system. If you are in doubt, take the vehicle to a GM dealer or automotive repair shop to have the system depressurized. **Caution:** *Do not, under any circumstances, disconnect any air-conditioning system lines while the system is under pressure.*
2   Remove the cable from the negative battery terminal.
3   Remove the air cleaner assembly, tagging each hose as it is disconnected with a piece of numbered tape to simplify reinstallation.
4   Disconnect and remove the torque strut located between the engine mount bracket and cylinder head.
5   Raise the vehicle and support it securely on jackstands.
6   Remove the oxygen sensor.
7   Label the four spark plug wires, then disconnect them and secure them out of the way.
8   Disconnect the exhaust pipe from the exhaust manifold. You may have to apply penetrating oil to the fastener threads, as they are usually corroded. The exhaust pipe can be hung from the frame with a piece of wire.
9   Remove the exhaust manifold end bolts first, then remove the center bolts and separate the exhaust manifold from the engine.
10   Remove the exhaust manifold gasket.
11   Before installing the manifold, clean the gasket mating surfaces on the cylinder head and manifold. All leftover gasket material and carbon deposits must be removed.
12   Place a new exhaust manifold gasket in position on the cylinder head, then place the manifold in position and install the mounting bolts finger tight.
13   Tighten the mounting bolts a little at a time in the sequence shown in the accompanying illustration until all of the bolts are at the specified torque.
14   Lower the vehicle.
15   Install the remaining components in the reverse order of removal, using new gaskets wherever one has been removed.
16   Start the engine and check for exhaust leaks between the manifold and cylinder head and between the manifold and exhaust pipe.

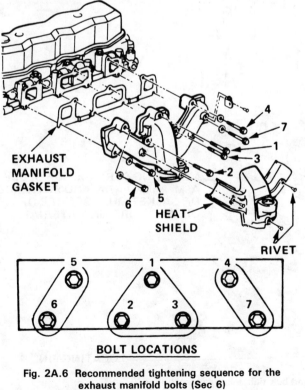

**Fig. 2A.6 Recommended tightening sequence for the exhaust manifold bolts (Sec 6)**

*Bolts 3, 4 and 5 — 37 ft-lbs*
*Bolts 1, 2, 6 and 7 — 16 ft-lbs*

## 7   Cylinder head — removal and installation

### Removal

1   Drain the cooling system (Chapter 1) and remove the air cleaner assembly.
2   Remove the intake manifold as described in Section 5.
3   Remove the exhaust manifold as described in Section 6.
4   Remove the bolts that secure the alternator bracket to the cylinder head.
5   If so equipped, unbolt the air conditioner compressor and swing it out of the way for clearance. **Caution:** *Do not disconnect any of the air-conditioning lines unless the system has been depressurized by a dealer or repair shop, because personal injury may occur.*
6   Disconnect all electrical and vacuum lines from the cylinder head. Be sure to label the lines to simplify reinstallation.
7   Remove the upper radiator hose.
8   Disconnect the spark plug wires and remove the spark plugs. Be sure to label the plug wires to simplify reinstallation.
9   Remove the rocker arm cover. To break the gasket seal it may be necessary to strike the cover with your hand or a rubber hammer. Do not pry between the sealing surfaces. Refer to Section 2 if necessary.
10   When disassembling the valve mechanisms, keep all of the components separate so they can be reinstalled in their original positions. A cardboard box or rack, numbered to correspond to the engine cylinders, can be used for this purpose.
11   Remove each of the rocker arm nuts and separate the rocker arms and pivots from the cylinder head (photo).
12   Remove the pushrods (photo).

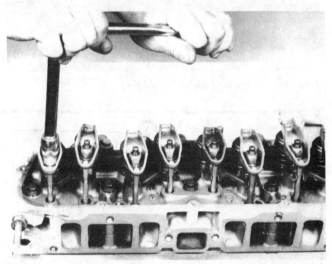

7.11   Remove the rocker arm nuts

7.12   Remove the pushrods

13 If the ignition coil is mounted separately from the distributor, disconnect the wires and remove the coil.

14 Loosen each of the cylinder head mounting bolts one turn at a time until they can be removed (photo). Note the length and position of each bolt to ensure correct reinstallation.

15 Lift the head off of the engine. If it is stuck to the engine block, do not attempt to pry it free, as you could damage the sealing surfaces. Instead, use a hammer and block of wood to tap the head and break the gasket seal. Place the head on a block of wood to prevent damage to the gasket surface.

16 Remove the cylinder head gasket.

17 Refer to Chapter 2D for cylinder head disassembly and valve service procedures.

*Installation*

18 If a new cylinder head is being installed, transfer all external parts from the old cylinder head to the new one.

19 Thoroughly clean the gasket surfaces on the cylinder head and the engine block. Do not gouge or otherwise damage the gasket surfaces.

20 To get the proper torque readings, the threads of the head bolts must be clean. This also applies to the threaded holes in the engine block. Run a tap through the holes to ensure that they are clean.

21 Place the gasket in position over the engine block dowel pins.

22 Carefully lower the cylinder head onto the engine, over the dowel pins and the gasket.

23 Coat the threads of each cylinder head bolt and the point at which the head and the bolt meet with sealing compound and install the bolts finger tight (photo). Do not tighten any of the bolts at this time.

24 Tighten each of the bolts a little at a time in the sequence shown in the accompanying illustration. Continue tightening in this sequence until the proper torque reading is obtained. As a final check, work around the head in a front-to-rear sequence to make sure none of the bolts have been left out of the sequence.

25 The remaining installation steps are the reverse of removal.

7.14   Loosen the cylinder head mounting bolts

7.23   The cylinder head mounting bolts should be coated with sealant (arrows) before installation

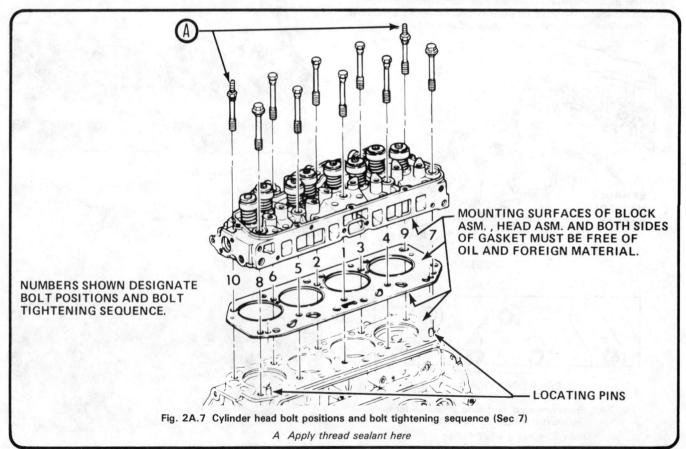

NUMBERS SHOWN DESIGNATE BOLT POSITIONS AND BOLT TIGHTENING SEQUENCE.

MOUNTING SURFACES OF BLOCK ASM., HEAD ASM. AND BOTH SIDES OF GASKET MUST BE FREE OF OIL AND FOREIGN MATERIAL.

LOCATING PINS

**Fig. 2A.7  Cylinder head bolt positions and bolt tightening sequence (Sec 7)**

*A  Apply thread sealant here*

## 8  Hydraulic lifters — removal, inspection and installation

1    A noisy valve lifter can be isolated when the engine is idling. Place a length of hose or tubing near the position of each valve while listening at the other end of the tube. Another method is to remove the rocker arm cover and, with the engine idling, place a finger on each of the valve spring retainers, one at a time. If a valve lifter is defective, it will be evident from the shock felt at the retainer as the valve seats.

2    The most likely cause of a noisy valve lifter is a piece of dirt trapped between the plunger and the lifter body.

3    Remove the rocker arm cover as described in Section 2.

4    Remove the intake manifold as described in Section 5.

5    Remove the pushrod cover as described in Section 3.

6    Loosen the rocker arm bolt and rotate the rocker arm away from the pushrod.

7    Remove the pushrod.

8    To remove the lifter, a special hydraulic lifter removal tool should be used (photo) or a scribe can be positioned at the top of the lifter and used to force the lifter up and out of the bore. Do not use pliers or other tools on the outside of the lifter body, because they will damage the finished surface and render the lifter useless.

9    The lifters should be kept in order for reinstallation in their original positions.

10   To dismantle a valve lifter, hold the plunger down with a pushrod and extract the retainer ring with a small screwdriver.

11   Remove the pushrod seat and the metering valve.

12   Remove the plunger, ball check valve and plunger spring. The ball check valve and spring are removed by prying them out with a small screwdriver.

13   Clean the lifter components with solvent and dry them with compressed air. Examine the internal components for wear and check the ball carefully for flat spots. **Note:** *Refer to Chapter 2, Part D, for additional lifter and camshaft inspection procedures.*

14   If the lifters are worn they must be replaced with new ones and the camshaft must be replaced as well (see Chapter 2, Part D). If the lifters were contaminated with dirt, they can be reinstalled — they may operate normally.

15   Reassembly should be done in the following manner:

  a) Place the ball check valve on the small hole in the bottom of the plunger.

  b) Insert the ball check spring into the seat in the valve retainer and place the retainer over the ball so that the spring rests on the ball. Using a small screwdriver, carefully press the retainer into position in the plunger.

  c) Place the plunger spring over the ball retainer, invert the lifter body and slide it over the spring and plunger. Make sure the oil holes in the body and plunger line up.

8.8   Remove the hydraulic lifters with a special tool

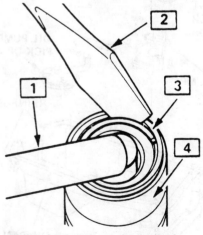

**Fig. 2A.8 Remove the pushrod
seat retainer from the lifter (Sec 8)**

| | |
|---|---|
| 1  Pushrod | 3  Retainer ring |
| 2  Screwdriver | 4  Lifter body |

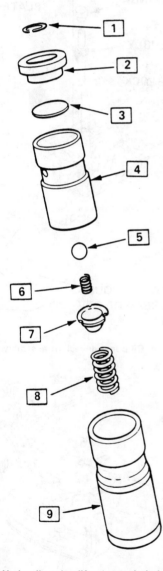

**Fig. 2A.9 Hydraulic valve lifter — exploded view (Sec 8)**

| | |
|---|---|
| 1  Retainer ring | 6  Ball check valve spring |
| 2  Pushrod seat |    (not on all lifters) |
| 3  Rocker feed metering valve | 7  Ball check valve retainer |
| 4  Plunger | 8  Plunger spring |
| 5  Ball check valve | 9  Lifter body |

d) Fill the assembly with 10-weight oil. Place the metering valve and pushrod seat in position, press down on the seat with a pushrod and install the retainer ring.

16  When installing the lifters, make sure they are replaced in their original bores. Coat them with moly-base grease or engine assembly lube.

17  The remaining installation steps are the reverse of removal.

---

**9  Oil pump driveshaft — removal and installation**

1   Rotate the steering shaft until the clamp bolt is accessible, remove the bolt and disconnect the shaft from the steering gear stub shaft (Chapter 10).

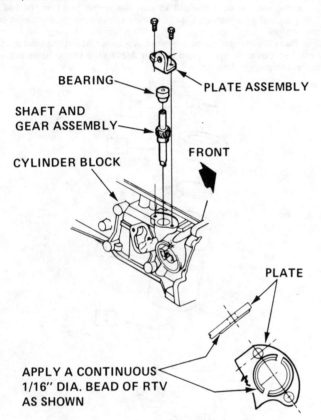

APPLY A CONTINUOUS 1/16'' DIA. BEAD OF RTV AS SHOWN

Fig. 2A.10  Oil pump driveshaft assembly (Sec 9)

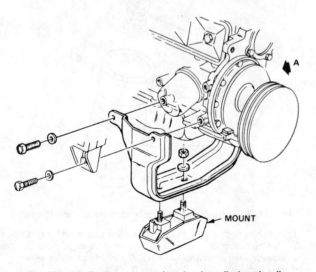

Fig. 2A.11  Engine support bracket installation details (Sec 10)

2   Raise the vehicle and support it securely on jackstands.

3   Support the engine.

4   Remove the two rear engine cradle bolts and lower the cradle for access.

5   Remove the oil filter.

6   Remove the oil pump driveshaft cover plate bolts.

7   Remove the bushing.

8   Remove the shaft and gear assembly.

9   Thoroughly clean the sealing surfaces on the engine block and cover plate.

10  Inspect the gear teeth to see if they are chipped or cracked.

11  Install the oil pump driveshaft in the block and turn it until it engages with the camshaft drive gear in the oil pump body.

12  Apply a 1/16-inch (1.5 mm) diameter bead of RTV-type sealant to the cover plate so that it completely seals around the oil pump driveshaft hole in the block, as shown in the accompanying illustration.

13  Install the cover plate mounting bolts and tighten them to the specified torque.

14  Complete the installation by reversing the removal procedure.

---

**10  Oil pan — removal and installation**

1   Disconnect the cable from the negative battery terminal.

2   Raise the vehicle, place it securely on jackstands and drain the engine oil. Refer to Chapter 1 if necessary.

3   Remove the cradle-to-front engine mount nuts.

4   Disconnect the exhaust pipe at the exhaust manifold and the rear transaxle mount.

5   Disconnect the starter and remove the flywheel inspection cover.

6   Remove the upper alternator bracket.

7   Support the engine with a hoist.

8   Remove the lower alternator bracket and engine support bracket.

9   Remove the oil pan bolts and separate the oil pan from the block.

10  Clean the pan with solvent and remove all old sealant and gasket material from the block and pan sealing surfaces.

11  Install the rear pan oil seal in the groove in the rear main bearing cap and apply a small quantity of RTV-type sealant to the depressions where the seal meets the block.

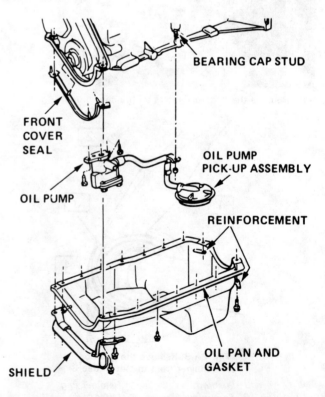

Fig. 2A.12  Oil pan and oil pump details (Sec 10)

12  Install the front pan oil seal on the timing cover, pressing the tips into the holes in the cover (photo).

13  Using a light coat of grease as a retainer, install the pan side gaskets. Apply a 1/8-inch diameter by 1/4-inch long bead of RTV-type sealant at the parting lines of the front seal and side gaskets.

14  Attach the oil pan to the block. The bolts that secure the pan to the timing cover should be installed last. They are installed at an angle into holes which will line up as the rest of the pan bolts are tightened.

15  After all bolts are installed, tighten them to the specified torque. Use a criss-cross pattern and work up to the final torque in three or four steps.

16  The remaining steps are the reverse of the removal procedure.

## 11  Oil pump — removal and installation

1  Remove the oil pan (refer to Section 10).

2  Remove the two oil pump flange mounting bolts and the nut from the main bearing cap bolt (photo).

3  Lift out the oil pump and screen as an assembly.

4  To install the pump, align the shaft so it mates with the oil pump driveshaft tang, then install the pump on the block, over the oil pump

driveshaft lower bushing. No gasket is used. The oil pump should slide easily into place. If not, remove it and relocate the slot.

5  Install the mounting bolts and nut and tighten them to the specified torque.

6  Reinstall the oil pan (refer to Section 10).

## 12  Crankshaft pulley hub and front oil seal — removal and installation

1  Remove the cable from the negative battery terminal.

2  Loosen the accessory drivebelt tension adjusting bolts, as necessary, and remove the drivebelts. Tag each belt as it is removed to simplify reinstallation.

3  Remove the right front inner fender splash shield.

4  With the parking brake applied and the shifter in Park (automatic) or in gear (manual) to prevent the engine from turning over, remove the crank hub bolt (photo). A breaker bar will probably be necessary, since the bolt is very tight.

5  Mark the position of the pulley in relation to the hub. Remove the bolts and separate the pulley from the hub.

6  Using a puller, remove the hub from the crankshaft (photo).

7  Carefully pry the oil seal out of the front cover with a large

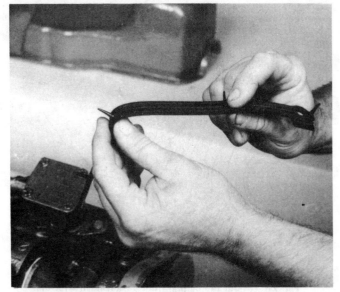

10.12   During installation, the rubber tips on the front oil pan gasket should be pressed into the holes in the timing gear cover

11.2   Remove the oil pump flange mounting bolts

12.4   Remove the crankshaft hub bolt

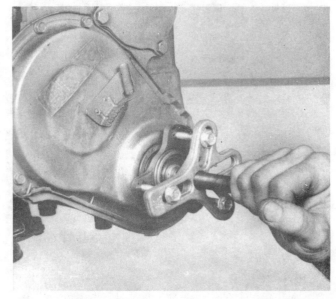

12.6   Use a puller to remove the hub from the crankshaft

screwdriver. Be careful not to distort the cover.

8   Install the new seal with the helical lip toward the rear of the engine. Drive the seal into place using a seal installation tool or a large socket. If there is enough room, a block of wood and hammer can also be used.

9   Apply a thin layer of multi-purpose grease to the seal contact surface of the hub.

10  Position the pulley hub on the crankshaft and slide it through the seal until it bottoms against the crankshaft gear. Note that the slot in the hub must be aligned with the Woodruff key in the end of the crankshaft. The hub-to-crankshaft bolt can also be used to press the hub into position (photo).

11  Install the crank pulley on the hub, noting the alignment marks made during removal. The pulley-to-hub bolts should be coated with thread locking compound whenever they are removed and installed.

12  Tighten the hub-to-crankshaft bolt to the specified torque.

13  The remaining installation steps are the reverse of removal. Tighten the drivebelts to the proper tension (refer to Chapter 1).

## 13   Timing gear cover — removal and installation

1   Remove the crankshaft pulley hub as described in Section 12.

2   Remove the lower alternator bracket.

12.10   Use the pulley hub bolt to press the hub onto the crankshaft

3   Remove the front engine mount-to-cradle nuts.

4   Raise the engine sufficiently with a jack to allow removal of the engine support bracket and mount assembly.

5   Remove the mounting bracket-to-engine block bolts and remove the support bracket and mount as an assembly.

6   Remove the oil pan-to-timing gear cover bolts.

7   Remove the timing cover-to-block bolts (photo).

8   Using a sharp knife, cut the oil pan front gasket flush with the engine block at both sides.

9   Remove the cover and the attached portion of the oil pan gasket.

10  Remove the cover gasket.

11  Using a scraper and degreaser, remove all dirt and old gasket material from the sealing surfaces of the timing gear cover, engine block and oil pan.

12  Remove the front oil seal by carefully prying it out of the timing gear cover with a large screwdriver. Do not distort the cover.

13  Install the new seal with the helical lip toward the inside of the cover. Drive the seal into place using a seal installation tool or a large socket and hammer. A block of wood will also work (photo).

14  Prior to installing the cover, install a new front oil pan gasket. Cut the ends off of the gasket, as shown in the accompanying illustration, and attach it to the cover by pressing the rubber tips into the holes provided.

15  Apply a thin coat of RTV-type gasket sealant to the timing gear cover gasket and place it in position on the cover.

16  Apply a bead of RTV-type sealant to the joint between the oil pan and engine block.

17  Insert the hub through the cover seal and place the cover in position on the block as the hub slides onto the crankshaft.

18  Install the oil pan-to-cover bolts and partially tighten them.

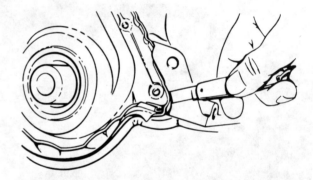

**Fig. 2A.13  Cut the oil pan front gasket flush with the engine block (Sec 13)**

13.7   Remove the timing gear cover mounting bolts

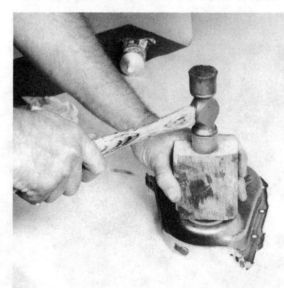

13.13   Use a block of wood to install the oil seal

19  Install the bolts that secure the cover to the block, then tighten all of the mounting bolts to the specified torque.
20  Complete the installation by reversing the removal procedure.

## 14   Camshaft — removal and installation

**Note:** *Before removing the camshaft, refer to Chapter 2, Part D (Section 15), and measure the lobe lift.*

1  Remove engine as described in Section 17 or 18 and install it on an engine stand.
2  Remove the rocker arm cover.
3  Drain the oil from the crankcase (refer to Chapter 1).
4  Loosen the rocker arm bolts and pivot the rocker arms away from the pushrods.
5  Remove the distributor and fuel pump (refer to the appropriate Chapter).
6  Remove the alternator and lower bracket and the front engine mount bracket assembly.
7  Remove the oil pump driveshaft assembly (refer to Section 9).
8  Remove the spark plugs (refer to Chapter 1).
9  Remove the pushrod cover and gasket (refer to Section 3), then remove the pushrods.

10  Remove the valve lifters (refer to Section 8).
11  Remove the crankshaft hub (refer to Section 12).
12  Remove the timing gear cover (refer to Section 13).
13  Working through the holes in the camshaft gear, remove the two camshaft thrust plate screws (photo).
14  Supporting the camshaft carefully to prevent damage to the bearings, remove the camshaft and gear assembly by pulling it out through the front of the engine.
15  Refer to Chapter 2, Part D, for the camshaft inspection procedures.
16  If the gear must be removed from the camshaft, it must be pressed off. If you do not have access to a press, take it to your dealer or an automotive machine shop. The thrust plate must be positioned so that the Woodruff key in the shaft does not damage it when the shaft is pressed off.
17  If the gear has been removed, it must be pressed back on prior to installation of the camshaft.

   a) Support the camshaft in an arbor press by placing press plate adaptors behind the front journal.
   b) Place the gear spacer ring and the thrust plate over the end of the shaft.
   c) Install the Woodruff key in the shaft keyway.
   d) Position the camshaft gear and press it onto the shaft until it bottoms against the gear spacer ring.
   e) Use a feeler gauge to check the end clearance of the thrust plate. It should be 0.0015 to 0.0050-inch. If the clearance is less than 0.0015-inch, the spacer ring should be replaced. If the clearance is more than 0.0050-inch the thrust plate should be replaced.

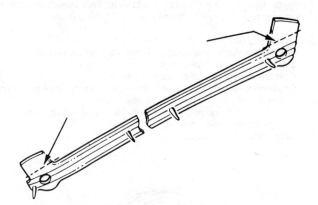

Fig. 2A.14  Cut the oil pan front gasket as shown before installing it (Sec 13)

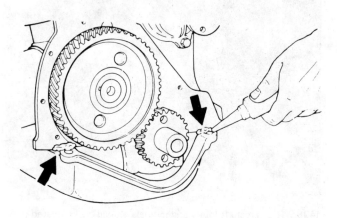

Fig. 2A.15  Apply RTV-type sealant at the joints (arrows) between the oil pan and the engine block (Sec 13)

14.13   Remove the camshaft thrust plate screws

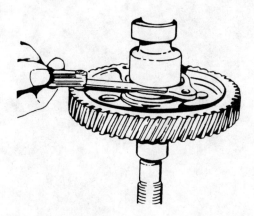

Fig. 2A.16  Use a feeler gauge to check the thrust plate end clearance (Sec 14)

18  Prior to installing the camshaft, coat each of the lobes and journals with engine assembly lube or moly-base grease (photo).
19  Slide the camshaft into the engine block. Again, be extra careful not to damage the bearings.
20  Position the camshaft and crankshaft gears so that the valve timing marks line up (photo). With the shafts in this position, the engine is in the number four cylinder firing position.
21  Install the camshaft thrust plate mounting screws and tighten them to the specified torque.
22  Complete the installation by reversing the removal procedure. When installing the distributor, be sure to rotate the engine 360° to the number one cylinder firing position (see Chapter 5).

### 15  Flywheel/driveplate and rear main bearing oil seal — removal and installation

1  The rear main bearing oil seal can be replaced without removal of the oil pan or crankshaft.

14.18   The camshaft lobes and journals should be lubricated prior to installing the camshaft in the block

14.20   The camshaft and crankshaft gears must be positioned so that the timing marks (arrows) line up

2  Refer to Chapter 7, follow all precautionary notes and remove the transaxle.
3  If equipped with a manual transmission, remove the pressure plate and clutch disc.
4  Remove the flywheel or driveplate mounting bolts and separate it from the crankshaft.
5  Using a screwdriver or pry bar, carefully remove the oil seal from the block.
6  Using solvent, thoroughly clean the block-to-seal mating surfaces, then dry them with compressed air.
7  Apply a light coat of engine oil to the outside surface of the new seal.
8  Using your fingertips, press the new seal evenly into position in the block.
9  Install the flywheel or driveplate and tighten the bolts to the specified torque.
10  If equipped with a manual transaxle, reinstall the clutch disc and pressure plate.
11  Reinstall the transaxle as described in Chapter 7.

### 16  Engine and transaxle mounts — replacement with engine in vehicle

1  If the rubber mounts have become hard, split or separated from the metal backing, they must be replaced. This operation may be carried out with the engine/transaxle still in the vehicle.

*Engine mounts*
2  Raise the vehicle and support it securely on jackstands.
3  Support the engine with a jack.
4  Remove the mount-to-chassis cradle nuts.
5  On air conditioning equipped models, remove the forward torque reaction rod bolts at the radiator support panel.
6  Remove the two upper mount-to-engine support bracket nuts and lift the mount from the vehicle.
7  Installation is the reverse of removal.

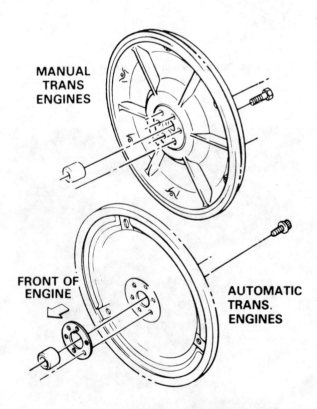

MANUAL TRANS ENGINES

FRONT OF ENGINE

AUTOMATIC TRANS. ENGINES

**Fig. 2A.17  Manual transaxle flywheel and automatic transaxle driveplate installation details (Sec 15)**

### Forward transaxle mounts

8    Raise the vehicle and support it securely on jackstands.
9    Support the transaxle with a jack.
10   Remove the mount-to-cradle nuts.
11   Remove the mount-to-transaxle support bracket nut and lift the mount from the vehicle.
12   Install the new mount and tighten the nut.
13   Install the mount-to-chassis nuts.
14   Remove the jack supporting the transaxle and lower the vehicle.

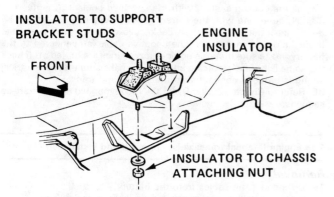

**Fig. 2A.18   Engine mount installation details (Sec 16)**

### Rear transaxle mounts

15   Raise the vehicle and support it securely on jackstands.
16   Place a jackstand under the rear cradle, remove the bolts and lower the cradle.
17   Remove the upper mount bolts and the cradle-to-mount nuts.
18   Raise the engine with a jack sufficiently to allow removal of the mount.
19   Install the new mount and install the upper mount bolts.
20   Remove the jack supporting the engine.
21   Raise the cradle into position and install the bolts.
22   Install the lower mount-to-cradle nuts.
23   Lower the vehicle.

---

**17   Engine (automatic transaxle models) — removal and installation**

### Removal

1    Disconnect the cable from the negative battery terminal.
2    Disconnect the underhood light electrical connector (if equipped) and unbolt the assembly from the hood.
3    Remove the hood (Chapter 12).
4    Drain the radiator.
5    Remove the air cleaner and preheat tube assembly.
6    Unplug the engine harness connector.
7    Mark all vacuum hoses for ease of installation and disconnect them.
8    Disconnect the throttle and transaxle linkage at the intake manifold and TBI assembly.
9    Remove the upper radiator hose.

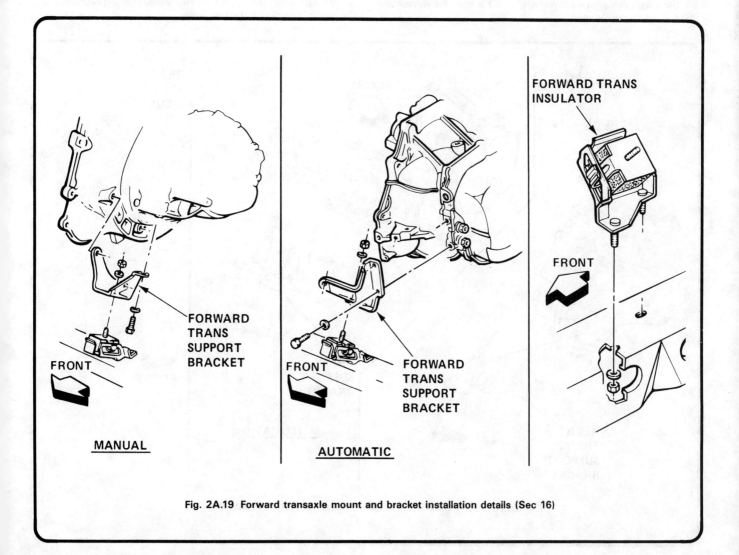

**Fig. 2A.19   Forward transaxle mount and bracket installation details (Sec 16)**

10 If so equipped, remove the air conditioning compressor and brackets and lay them to one side. **Caution:** *Do not disconnect any of the air conditioning lines unless the system has been depressurized by a dealer service department or air conditioning technician, as personal injury may occur. Disconnection of the lines should not be necessary in this case.*
11 Remove the front engine strut assembly.
12 Disconnect the heater hose from the intake manifold.
13 Remove all but the two upper transaxle-to-engine bolts.
14 Remove the front engine mount-to-cradle nuts.
15 Remove the front exhaust pipe.
16 Remove the driveplate inspection cover and the starter motor.
17 Remove the converter-to-driveplate bolts. It will be necessary to turn the crankshaft to bring each of the bolts into view. Use a wrench on the large bolt at the front of the crankshaft to rotate the converter and driveplate. Mark the relative position of the converter and driveplate with a scribe so it can be reinstalled in the same position. Engage a long screwdriver in the teeth of the driveplate to prevent movement as the bolts are loosened.
18 Remove the power steering pump and bracket and lay them to one side.
19 Remove the heater hose and lower radiator hose.
20 Remove the two rear transaxle support bracket bolts.
21 Disconnect the fuel line at the filter.
22 Place a jack under the transaxle, using a block of wood to protect the pan and raise the engine and transaxle assembly until the front mount studs clear the cradle.
23 Connect a suitable lifting device to the engine and raise it until all slack is out of the chains.
24 Remove the two remaining transaxle bolts.
25 Slide the engine forward you raise it, lift it from the vehicle and install it on an engine stand.

*Installation*
26 Lower the engine into the vehicle while guiding it into alignment with the transaxle bellhousing.
27 With the engine weight still supported by the lifting device, install two upper bellhousing bolts. Do not completely lower the engine weight until the jack is removed from the transaxle.
28 Remove the jack from the transaxle, lower the engine into the chassis mounts and remove the lifting device.
29 Raise the vehicle and support it securely on jackstands.
30 Install the front mount-to-chassis nuts.
31 The remainder of installation is the reverse of removal.
32 Fill the cooling system with the specified coolant (Chapter 1).
33 Fill the engine with the correct grade of engine oil (Chapter 1).
34 Connect the positive battery cable, followed by the negative cable. If sparks or arcing occur as the negative cable is connected to the battery, make sure that all electrical accessories are turned off (check the dome light first). If arcing still occurs, make sure that all electrical wiring is properly connected to the engine and transaxle.
35 Refer to Chapter 2, Part D, for the recommended engine start-up sequence.

---

**18   Engine (Manual transaxle) — removal and installation**

*Removal*
1 Disconnect the cables from the battery.
2 Raise the vehicle and support it securely on jackstands.
3 Remove the front mount-to-cradle nuts and the forward exhaust pipe.
4 With the wires still connected, remove the starter motor and swing the whole assembly out of the way.

Fig. 2A.20 Rear transaxle mount and bracket installation details (Sec 16)

5 Remove the flywheel inspection cover and lower the vehicle.
6 Remove the bellhousing bolts.
7 Remove the forward torque reaction rod.
8 If so equipped, remove the air conditioning compressor and brackets and lay them to one side. **Caution:** *Do not disconnect any of the air conditioning lines unless the system has been depressurized by a dealer service department or air conditioning technician, as personal injury may occur. Disconnection of the lines should not be necessary in this case.*
9 Disconnect the EVAP hoses at the canister.
10 Remove the power steering hose on models so equipped.
11 Remove the heater blower motor.
12 Disconnect the throttle cable.
13 Drain the cooling system (Chapter 1).
14 Unplug the engine electrical harness at the bulkhead connector.
15 Connect a suitable lifting device to the engine.
16 Make sure that all the wires and hoses have been disconnected from the engine and that all accessories have enough clearance.
17 Raise the engine hoist until all slack is out of the chains, disconnect the fuel line and remove the heater hose from the intake manifold.
18 Carefully lift the engine from the vehicle.

## Installation

19 Lower the engine into the engine compartment and connect the heater hose and fuel line.
20 Install the four upper bellhousing bolts.
21 Raise the vehicle and support it securely on jackstands.
22 Install the two lower bellhousing bolts and the front mount-to-cradle nuts.
23 Install the flywheel inspection cover and the exhaust pipe.
24 Install the starter motor assembly.
25 Lower the vehicle.
26 Install the heater blower motor and connect the engine electrical harness.
27 Install the power steering hose and connect the EVAP hoses to the canister.
28 Install the heater and radiator hoses.
29 Install the torque reaction rod.
30 Install the air cleaner assembly.
31 Fill the cooling system with the specified coolant mixture (Chapter 1).
32 Fill the engine with the correct grade of engine oil (Chapter 1).
33 Check the transaxle fluid level, adding fluid as necessary.
34 Connect the battery cables, positive battery cable first, followed by the negative cable. If sparks or arcing occur as the negative cable is connected to the battery, make sure that all electrical accessories are turned off (check the dome light first). If arcing still occurs, make sure that all electrical wiring is properly connected to the engine and transmission.
35 Refer to Chapter 2D for the recommended engine start-up sequence.

# Chapter 2 Part B  2.8L V6 engine

*Refer to Chapter 13 for Specifications and information applicable to 1986 and later models*

## Contents

| | | | |
|---|---|---|---|
| Air filter — replacement | See Chapter 1 | General information | 1 |
| Camshaft — removal and installation | 16 | Hydraulic lifters — removal, inspection and installation | 5 |
| Check engine light | See Chapter 6 | Intake manifold — removal and installation | 4 |
| Crankcase front cover — removal and installation | 13 | Oil pan — removal and installation | 9 |
| Compression check | See Chapter 1 | Oil pump — removal and installation | 10 |
| Cylinder heads — removal and installation | 8 | Rear main bearing oil seal — replacement (engine | |
| Drivebelt check and adjustment | See Chapter 1 | in vehicle) | 11 |
| Engine — removal and installation | 18 | Rocker arm covers — removal and installation | 2 |
| Engine mounts — replacement with engine in vehicle | 17 | Spark plug replacement | See Chapter 1 |
| Engine oil and filter change | See Chapter 1 | Timing chain and sprockets — inspection, removal and | |
| Engine overhaul — general information | See Chapter 2D | installation | 15 |
| Engine removal — methods and precautions | See Chapter 2D | Valve lash — adjustment | 6 |
| Engine repairs possible with the engine in the | | Valve train components — replacement (cylinder head | |
| vehicle | See Chapter 2D | installed) | 3 |
| Exhaust manifolds — removal and installation | 7 | Vibration damper — removal and installation | 12 |
| Front cover oil seal — replacement | 14 | Water pump — removal and installation | See Chapter 3 |

## Specifications

| Torque specifications | Ft-lbs |
|---|---|
| Camshaft sprocket bolts | 18 |
| Clutch or driveplate cover bolts | 15 |
| Rear camshaft cover bolts | 7 |
| Cylinder head bolts | 68 |
| Connecting rod cap nuts | 37 |
| Crankshaft pulley bolts | 25 |
| Crankshaft damper bolt | 75 |
| Distributor hold-down bolt | 25 |
| Driveplate-to-torque converter bolts | 30 |
| EGR valve mounting bolts | 15 |
| Engine mounting bracket bolts | 80 |
| Engine strut bracket bolt | 35 |
| Engine strut assembly nut and bolt | 35 |
| Exhaust manifold mounting bolts | 25 |
| Flywheel mounting bolts | 50 |
| Front cover mounting bolts (small) | 15 |
| Front cover mounting bolts (large) | 25 |
| Fuel pump mounting bolts | 15 |
| Intake manifold mounting bolts | 23 |
| Main bearing cap bolts | 70 |
| Oil filter | 15 |
| Oil filter connector | 29 |
| Oil pan mounting bolts (small) | 7 |
| Oil pan mounting bolts (large) | 18 |
| Oil pump mounting bolt | 30 |
| Oil pump cover bolts | 8 |
| Oil pressure switch | 5 |
| Oil drain plug | 18 |
| Rear lifting bracket bolt | 25 |
| Rocker arm cover bolts | 8 |
| Rocker arm studs | 45 |
| Spark plugs | 12 |
| Starter motor mounting bolts | 32 |
| Timing chain tensioner bolts | 15 |
| Water outlet housing bolts | 25 |
| Water pump mounting bolts (small) | 7 |
| Water pump mounting bolts (medium) | 15 |
| Water pump mounting bolts (large) | 25 |
| Water pump pulley bolt | 15 |

## 1   General information

The forward Sections in this Part of Chapter 2 are devoted to in vehicle repair procedures for the 2.8 liter V6 engine. The latter Sections in this Part of Chapter 2 involve removal and installation procedures. All information concerning engine block and cylinder head servicing can be found in Part D of this Chapter.

The repair procedures are based on the assumption that the engine is still installed in the vehicle. Therefore, if this information is being used during a complete engine overhaul — with the engine already out of the vehicle and on a stand — many of the steps included here will not apply.

The Specifications included in this Part of Chapter 2 apply only to the engine and procedures found here. For specifications regarding engines other than the 2.8 liter V6, see Part A or C, whichever applies. Part D of Chapter 2 contains the specifications necessary for engine block and cylinder head rebuilding procedures.

## 2   Rocker arm covers — removal and installation

**Note:** *Refer to the illustrations in Section 18.*

### Right side
1    Disconnect the cable from the negative battery terminal.
2    Remove the air cleaner assembly, tagging each hose to be disconnected with a piece of numbered tape to simplify reinstallation.
3    Disconnect the wires and hoses which would interfere with the removal of the rocker arm covers, tagging them as they are disconnected.
4    On automatic transaxle equipped models, disconnect the throttle valve (TV) cable from the carburetor.
5    Remove the bolts retaining the air management valve.
6    Disconnect the carburetor controls at the carburetor, then remove them from the support bracket.
7    Remove the carburetor (Chapter 4).
8    Remove the rocker arm cover bolts (photo).
9    Remove the rocker arm cover. **Note:** *If the cover sticks to the cylinder head, use a block of wood and a rubber hammer to dislodge it. If the cover still will not come loose, pry on it carefully, but do not distort the sealing flange surface.*
10   Before reinstalling the cover, clean all dirt, oil and old gasket material from the sealing surfaces of the cover and cylinder head with a scraper and degreaser.

11   Apply a continuous 3/16-inch (5 mm) diameter bead of RTV-type sealant to the flange of the cover. Be sure to apply the sealant inboard of the bolt holes.
12   Place the rocker arm cover on the cylinder head while the sealant is still wet and install the mounting bolts. Tighten the bolts a little at a time to the specified torque.
13   Complete the installation by reversing the removal procedure.

### Left side
14   Disconnect the cable from the negative battery terminal.
15   Disconnect the hoses at the PCV valve and label them.
16   Remove the air cleaner assembly, tagging each hose to be disconnected with a piece of numbered tape to simplify reinstallation.
17   Disconnect all other wires and hoses that would interfere with the removal of the rocker arm cover, tagging them as they are disconnected.
18   Remove the front engine support strut and bracket.
19   Remove the rocker arm cover bolts.
20   Disconnect the fuel line at the carburetor, plugging the fitting at the carburetor and the disconnected fuel line to prevent leakage and contamination.
21   Refer to Paragraphs 8 through 13 in this Section.

## 3   Valve train components — replacement (cylinder head installed)

1    Remove the rocker arm cover(s) as described in Section 2.
2    If only the pushrod is to be replaced, loosen the rocker nut enough to allow the rocker arm to be rotated away from the pushrod. Pull the pushrod out of the hole in the cylinder head.
3    If the rocker arm is to be removed, remove the rocker arm nut and pivot and lift off the rocker arm.
4    If the valve spring is to be removed, remove the spark plug from the affected cylinder.
5    There are two methods that will hold the valve in place while the valve spring is removed. If you have access to compressed air, install an air hose adapter (GM part number J-22794) in the spark plug hole. This adapter is also available at most parts stores. When air pressure is applied to the adapter, the valves will be held in place by the pressure.
6    If you do not have access to compressed air, bring the piston of the affected cylinder to just before top dead center (TDC) on the compression stroke. Feed a long piece of 1/4-inch nylon cord in through the spark plug hole until it fills the combustion chamber. Be sure to leave the end of the cord hanging out of the spark plug hole so it can be removed easily. Rotate the crankshaft with a wrench (in the normal direction of rotation) until slight resistance is felt.

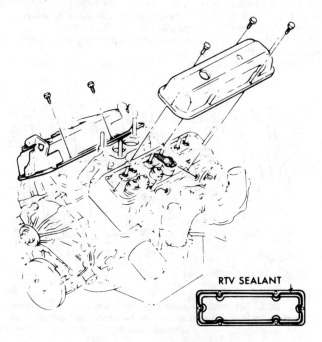

**Fig. 2B.1  Rocker arm cover installation details (Sec 2)**

RTV SEALANT

2.8   Remove the rocker arm cover bolts

7    Reinstall the rocker arm nut (without the rocker arm).
8    Insert the slotted end of a valve spring compression tool under the nut and compress the spring just enough to remove the spring keepers, then release the pressure on the tool.
9    Remove the retainer, cup shield, O-ring seal, spring, spring damper (if so equipped) and valve stem oil seal (if so equipped).
10   The rocker arm studs may be replaced by simply removing the damaged one and replacing it with a new one. Be sure to reinstall the pushrod guide (if so equipped) under the stud nut and tighten the nut to the specified torque.
11   Inspection procedures for the hydraulic lifters are detailed in Section 5. Procedures regarding other valve train components are detailed in Chapter 2, Part D.
12   Installation of the valve train components is the reverse of the removal procedure. Always use new valve stem oil seals whenever the spring keepers have been disturbed. Before installing the rocker arms, coat the bearing surfaces of the arms and pivots with moly-base grease or engine assembly lube. Be sure to adjust the valve lash as detailed in Section 6.

### 4   Intake manifold — removal and installation

1    If the vehicle is equipped with air conditioning, carefully examine the routing of the hoses and the mounting of the compressor. You may be able to remove the intake manifold without disconnecting the system. If you are in doubt, take the vehicle to a dealer or refrigeration specialist to have the system depressurized. Do not, under any circumstances, disconnect the hoses while the system is under pressure.
2    Disconnect the cable from the negative battery terminal.
3    Drain the coolant from the radiator (Chapter 1).
4    Remove the air cleaner assembly, tagging each hose to be disconnected with a piece of numbered tape to simplify reinstallation.
5    Label and disconnect all electrical wires and vacuum hoses at the carburetor.
6    Disconnect the fuel line at the carburetor. Be prepared to catch some fuel, then plug the fuel line to prevent contamination.
7    Disconnect the throttle cable, making careful note of how it was installed.
8    Disconnect the spark plug wires at the spark plugs, referring to the removal technique described in Chapter 1.

4.23   Use a large screwdriver or pry bar to break the manifold gasket seal

9    Disconnect the wires at the coil, again using numbered pieces of tape to label them.
10   Remove the distributor cap and the attached spark plug wires (refer to Chapter 5).
11   Remove the distributor (refer to Chapter 5).
12   Remove the power brake pipe and bracket.
13   Move the power brake tube/hose aside so it will not interfere with the removal of the manifold.
14   Remove the solenoid/hose bracket.
15   Remove the mounting bolts from the left rocker arm cover, then remove the cover.
16   Remove the AIR pump and bracket.
17   Remove the bolts from the right rocker arm cover, then remove the cover.
18   Remove the upper radiator hose from the manifold.
19   Disconnect the heater hose at the manifold.
20   Make sure that all wires, vacuum hoses and coolant hoses that would interfere with manifold removal have been disconnected.
21   If the manifold is to be replaced with a new one, the external components remaining on the manifold must be removed for transfer to the new manifold. These components may be removed either before or after the manifold has been separated from the engine. On most models these components include:
     Carburetor choke assembly and carburetor studs or bolts (Refer to Chapter 4 for details)
     Coolant switch
     EGR valve (use a new gasket when installing)
     Emissions system TVS valve
22   Remove the manifold mounting bolts.
23   Separate the manifold from the engine by prying with a suitable bar (do not pry between the mating surfaces) or tapping the manifold with a hammer and wooden block to loosen it (photo).
24   If a new manifold is being installed, transfer the external components from the old manifold to the new one.
25   Before installing the manifold, place clean, lint-free rags in the engine cavity and clean the engine block, cylinder head and manifold gasket surfaces. All gasket material and sealant must be removed prior to installation. Remove all dirt and gasket remnants from the engine cavity.
26   Clean the gasket sealing surfaces with degreaser, then apply a 3/16-inch (5 mm) diameter bead of RTV-type sealant to the engine block end ridges only (see Fig. 2B.3).
27   Install the new intake gaskets on the cylinder heads. Notice that the gaskets are marked *Right* and *Left*. Be sure to use the correct gasket on each cylinder head.
28   Hold the gaskets in place by extending the bead of RTV 1/4-inch onto the gasket ends. The new gaskets will have to be cut, as illustrated, so they can be installed behind the pushrods.
29   Carefully lower the intake manifold into position, making sure that you do not disturb the gaskets.
30   Install the intake manifold mounting bolts and tighten them

Fig. 2B.2   The intake manifold gasket must be cut as shown before installing it so the top can be positioned behind the pushrods (Sec 4)

following the sequence illustrated. Tighten the bolts a little at a time until they are all at the specified torque.

31 Install the remaining components in the reverse order of removal.

32 Fill the radiator with coolant, start the engine and check for leaks. Adjust the ignition timing and idle speed as necessary (refer to Chapter 1).

## 5   Hydraulic lifters — removal, inspection and installation

1   A noisy hydraulic lifter can be isolated while the engine is idling. Place a length of hose or tubing near the position of each valve while listening at the other end of the tube. Another method is to remove the rocker arm cover and, with the engine idling, place a finger on each of the valve spring retainers, one at a time. If a valve lifter is defective, it will be evident from the shock felt at the retainer as the valve seats.

2   Assuming that adjustment is correct, the most likely cause of a noisy valve lifter is a piece of dirt trapped between the plunger and the lifter body.

3   Remove the rocker arm covers as described in Section 2.

4   Remove the intake manifold as described in Section 4.

5   Loosen the rocker arm nut and rotate the rocker arm away from the pushrod.

6   Remove the pushrod.

7   To remove the lifter, a special hydraulic lifter removal tool should be used, or a scribe can be positioned at the top of the lifter and used to force the lifter up. Do not use pliers or other tools on the outside of the lifter body, as they will damage the finished surface and render the lifter useless.

8   The lifters should be kept in order for reinstallation in their original positions (photo).

9   To dismantle a valve lifter, hold the plunger down with a pushrod and extract the retainer ring with a small screwdriver.

10  Remove the pushrod seat and metering valve.

11  Remove the plunger, ball check valve and plunger spring. The ball

check valve and spring are removed by prying them out with a small screwdriver.

12  Clean the lifter components with solvent and dry them with compressed air. Examine the internal components for wear and check the ball carefully for flat spots. Some later models use a roller-type lifter which uses roller at the point where the lifter contacts the camshaft. Inspect the roller to make sure it turns freely and that its surface is free of damage. Refer to Chapter 2, Part D, for additional lifter and camshaft inspection procedures.

13  If the lifters are worn they must be replaced with new ones and the camshaft must be replaced as well (see Chapter 2, Part D). If the lifters were contaminated with dirt, they can be reinstalled — they may operate normally.

14  Reassembly should be done in the following manner:

   a) Place the ball check valve on the small hole in the bottom of the plunger.

   b) Insert the ball check valve spring into the seat in the retainer and place the retainer over the ball so that the spring rests on the ball. Using a small screwdriver, carefully press the retainer into position in the plunger.

   c) Place the plunger spring over the ball retainer, invert the lifter body and slide it over the spring and plunger. Make sure the oil holes in the body and plunger line up.

   d) Fill the assembly with 10-weight oil. Place the metering valve and pushrod seat in position, press down on the seat with a pushrod and install the retainer ring.

15  When installing the lifters, make sure they are replaced in their original bores. Coat them with moly-base grease or engine assembly lube.

16  The remaining installation steps are the reverse of removal.

## 6   Valve lash — adjustment

1   Disconnect the cable from the negative battery terminal.

2   If the rocker arm covers are still on the engine, refer to Section 2 and remove them.

3   If the valve train components have been serviced just prior to this procedure, make sure that the components are completely reassembled.

4   Rotate the crankshaft until the number one piston is at top dead center (TDC) on the compression stroke. To make sure that you do not mix up the TDC positions of the number one and four pistons, check the position of the rotor in the distributor to see which terminal it is pointing at. Another method is to place your fingers on the number one rocker arms as the timing marks line up at the crankshaft pulley. If the rocker arms are not moving, the number one piston is at TDC. If they move as the timing marks line up, the number four piston is at TDC.

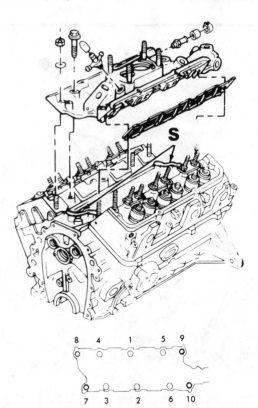

**Fig. 2B.3  Intake manifold installation details and mounting bolt tightening sequence (Sec 4)**

*S Sealant application area*

5.8   As the lifters are removed from the engine block, they should be stored separately to ensure reinstallation in their original positions

5   Back off the rocker arm nut until play is felt at the pushrod, then turn it back in until all play is removed. This can be determined by rotating the pushrod while tightening the nut. Just when drag is felt at the pushrod, all lash has been removed. Now turn the nut an additional 1-1/2 turns.
6   Adjust the number one, five and six cylinder intake valves and the number one, two and three cylinder exhaust valves, with the crankshaft in this position, using the method just described.
7   Rotate the crankshaft until the number four piston is at TDC on the compression stroke and adjust the number two, three and four cylinder intake valves and the number four, five and six cylinder exhaust valves.
8   Refer to Section 2 and install the rocker arm covers.

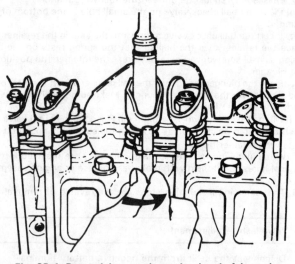

Fig. 2B.4 Determining at what point drag is felt on the pushrod by turning it as the nut is tightened (Sec 6)

### 7  Exhaust manifolds — removal and installation

*Right side*
1   Remove the cable from the negative battery terminal.
2   Remove the air cleaner assembly.
3   Disconnect the air injection reactor (AIR) bracket.
4   Raise the front of the vehicle and support it securely on jackstands. Block the rear wheels to keep the vehicle from rolling.
5   Remove the bolts attaching the exhaust pipe to the exhaust manifold, then separate the pipe from the manifold.
6   Remove the jackstands and lower the vehicle.
7   Disconnect the oxygen sensor pigtail electrical connector.
8   Disconnect the air management hose at the check valve.
9   Disconnect the spark plug wires from the spark plugs, labeling them as they are disconnected to simplify installation.
10   Remove the exhaust manifold mounting bolts and separate the manifold from the engine.
11   Installation is the reverse of the removal procedure. Before installing the manifold, be sure to thoroughly clean the mating surfaces on the manifold and cylinder head.

*Left side*
12   Disconnect the cable from the negative battery terminal.
13   Remove the air cleaner assembly, labeling all hoses.
14   Disconnect the crossover pipe.
15   Remove the bolts retaining the exhaust pipe to the manifold, then disconnect the pipe from the manifold.
16   Remove the four bolts and one nut accessible at the rear of the manifold.
17   Disconnect and label any wires that will interfere with the removal of the manifold.
18   Remove the remaining manifold bolts and separate the manifold and heat shield from the engine.
19   Installation is the reverse of the removal procedure. Be sure to thoroughly clean the cylinder head and manifold surfaces before installing the manifold.

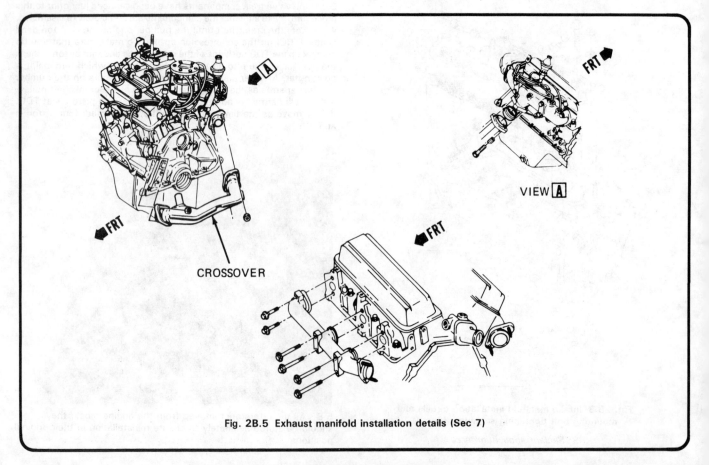

Fig. 2B.5 Exhaust manifold installation details (Sec 7)

## 8  Cylinder heads — removal and installation

### Left side

1   Raise the vehicle and place it securely on jackstands.
2   Locate the engine block drain plugs, remove them and drain the coolant.
3   Remove the jackstands and lower the vehicle.
4   Remove the intake manifold (refer to Section 4).
5   Remove the exhaust crossover pipe.
6   Remove the alternator and bracket and the air injection reactor (AIR) pump and brackets.
7   Remove the oil dipstick tube assembly from the side of the engine.
8   Loosen the rocker arm nuts enough to allow removal of the pushrods, then remove the pushrods (photos).
9   Loosen the head bolts in a sequence opposite to the one used for tightening (see accompanying illustration).
10  Remove the cylinder head. To break the gasket seal, insert a bar into one of the exhaust ports, then carefully lift on the tool (photo).
11  If a new cylinder head is being installed, transfer the various com-

ponents, such as the manifold, brackets and coolant temperature sensor, from the old head. Before installing the new head the gasket surfaces of both the head and the engine block must be clean and free of nicks and scratches. Also, the threads in the block and on the head bolts must be completely clean, as any dirt or sealant in the threads will affect bolt torque.
12  Place the gasket in position over the locating dowels, with the note *This Side Up* visible.
13  Position the cylinder head over the gasket.
14  Coat the cylinder head bolts with an appropriate sealer (GM part number 1052080, or equivalent) and install the bolts.
15  Tighten the bolts in the proper sequence (see the accompanying illustration) to the specified torque. Work up to the final torque in three steps.
16  Install the pushrods, making sure the lower ends are in the lifter seats, place the rocker arm ends over the pushrods and loosely install the rocker arm nuts.
17  The remaining installation steps are the reverse of those for removal. Before installing the rocker arm covers, adjust the valve lash (refer to Section 6).

8.8A   Loosen the rocker arm adjusting nuts

8.8B   When removing the pushrods, be sure to store them separately to ensure reinstallation in their original positions

8.10   Use a wrench handle to break the gasket seal on the cylinder head

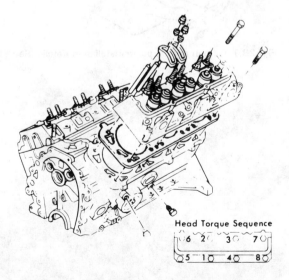

Fig. 2B.6 Recommended tightening sequence for the cylinder head mounting bolts (Sec 8)

Head Torque Sequence

## Right side

18  Raise the vehicle and place it securely on jackstands.
19  Locate the engine block drain plugs (the plug on the left side is just above the oil filter) and drain the coolant from the block.
20  Disconnect the exhaust pipe from the exhaust manifold.
21  Remove the jackstands and lower the vehicle.
22  Remove the emissions system air management valve and hose.
23  Remove the cruise control servo bracket (if equipped).
24  Remove the intake manifold (Section 4).
25  Disconnect the exhaust crossover.
26  Loosen the rocker arm nuts sufficiently to allow removal of the pushrods, then remove the pushrods.
27  Loosen the head bolts in a sequence opposite to the one used for tightening (see accompanying illustration).
28  Remove the cylinder head. To break the gasket seal, insert a bar into one of the exhaust ports, then carefully lift on the tool.
29  To install the head, refer to Steps 11 through 17.

## 9   Oil pan — removal and installation

1  Disconnect the cable from the negative battery terminal.
2  Raise the vehicle and support it on jackstands.
3  Drain the engine oil.
4  If equipped with an automatic transmission, remove the converter shroud.

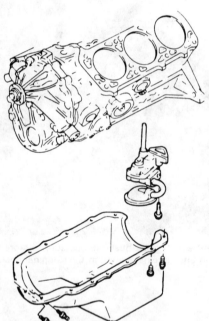

Fig. 2B.7 Oil pan and oil pump installation details (Sec 9)

10.2   Remove the oil pump-to-rear main bearing cap bolt

5  If equipped with a manual transmission, remove the flywheel cover.
6  Remove the starter (refer to Chapter 5).
7  Support the engine with a hoist.
8  Remove the engine mount bracket-to-engine bolts.
9  Remove the oil pan bolts. Note the different sizes used and their locations.
10  Raise the engine and remove the oil pan.
11  Before installing the pan, make sure that the sealing surfaces on the pan, block and front cover are clean and free of oil. If the old pan is being reinstalled, make sure that all sealant has been removed from the pan sealing flange and from the blind attaching holes.
12  With all the sealing surfaces clean, place a 1/8-inch bead of RTV type sealant on the oil pan sealing flange.
13  Lift the pan into position and install all bolts finger tight. There is no specific order for torquing the bolts, but it is a good idea to tighten the end bolts first.
14  Lower the front of the engine onto the mount and install the retaining nuts. Tighten the nuts to the specified torque.
15  Follow the removal steps in reverse order. Fill the crankcase with the correct grade and quantity of oil, start the engine and check for leaks.
16  Most of the above steps will not be required if the engine has been removed from the vehicle. The pan can simply be unbolted and removed, cleaned and installed as indicated.

## 10   Oil pump — removal and installation

1  Remove the oil pan (refer to Section 9).
2  Remove the pump-to-rear main bearing cap bolt and separate the pump and extension shaft from the engine (photo).
3  To install the pump, move it into position and align the top end of the hexagonal extension shaft with the hexagonal socket in the lower end of the distributor drive gear. The distributor drives the oil pump, so it is essential that this alignment is correct.
4  Install the oil pump-to-rear main bearing cap bolt and tighten it to the specified torque.
5  Reinstall the oil pan.

## 11   Rear main bearing oil seal — replacement (engine in vehicle)

### 1982 and 1983 engines

**Note:** *Special tools, as noted in the Steps which follow, are required for this procedure. They are available from your dealer or may, in some cases, be rented from an auto parts store or tool rental shop.*
1  Although the crankshaft must be removed to install a new seal, the upper portion of the seal can be repaired with the crankshaft in place.
2  Remove the oil pan and oil pump (Sections 9 and 10).
3  Using GM tool J-29114-2, drive the old seal gently back into the groove, packing it tight. It will pack in to a depth of 1/4 to 3/4-inch.

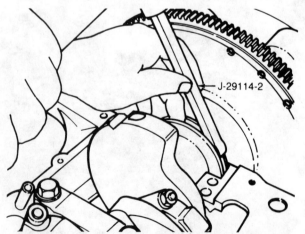

Fig. 2B.8 Using a packing tool to pack the old rear main bearing oil seal into the groove — 1982 and 1983 engines (Sec 11)

4    Repeat the procedure on the other end of the seal.
5    Measure the amount that the seal was driven up into the groove on one side and add 1/16-inch. Remove the old seal from the main bearing cap. Use the main bearing cap as a fixture and cut off a piece of the old seal to the predetermined length. Repeat this process for the other side.
6    Install the guide tool J-29114-1 on the block.
7    Using the packing tool J-29114-2, work the short pieces of the previously cut seal into the guide tool J-29114-1 and pack them into the block groove on each side. The guide and packing tools have been machined to provide a built-in stop. Use of oil on the seal pieces will ease installation.
8    Remove the guide tool.
9    Install a new seal in the main bearing cap.
10   Apply a thin, even coat of anaerobic-type gasket sealant to the areas of the rear main bearing cap indicated in the illustration in Chapter 2, Part D (Section 21). **Caution:** *Do not get any sealant on the bearing or seal faces.*
11   Tighten the rear main bearing cap bolts to the specified torque.
12   Install the oil pump and oil pan.

*1984 and 1985 engines*
13   Always service both halves of the rear main oil seal. While replacement of this seal is much easier with the engine removed from the

vehicle, the job can be done with the engine in place.
14   Remove the oil pan and oil pump as described previously in this Chapter.
15   Remove the rear main bearing cap from the engine.
16   Using a screwdriver, pry the lower half of the oil seal from the bearing cap.
17   To remove the upper half of the seal, use a small hammer and a brass pin punch to roll the seal around the crankshaft journal. Tap one end of the seal with the hammer and punch (be careful not to strike the crankshaft) until the other end of the seal protrudes enough to pull it out with pliers.
18   Remove all sealant and foreign material from the main bearing cap. Do not use an abrasive cleaner for this.
19   Inspect the components for nicks, scratches and burrs at all sealing surfaces. Remove any defects with a fine file or deburring tool.
20   Apply a very thin coat of RTV-type gasket sealant to the outer surface of the upper seal as shown in the accompanying illustration. Do not get any sealant on the seal lips.
21   Included in the purchase of the rear main oil seal should be a small plastic installation tool. If not, a tool may be fashioned from an old feeler gauge blade (refer to the accompanying illustration).
22   With the upper half of the seal positioned so that the seal lip faces toward the front of the engine and the small dust lip faces toward the flywheel, install the seal by rolling it around the crankshaft using the installation tool as a *shoehorn* for protection.

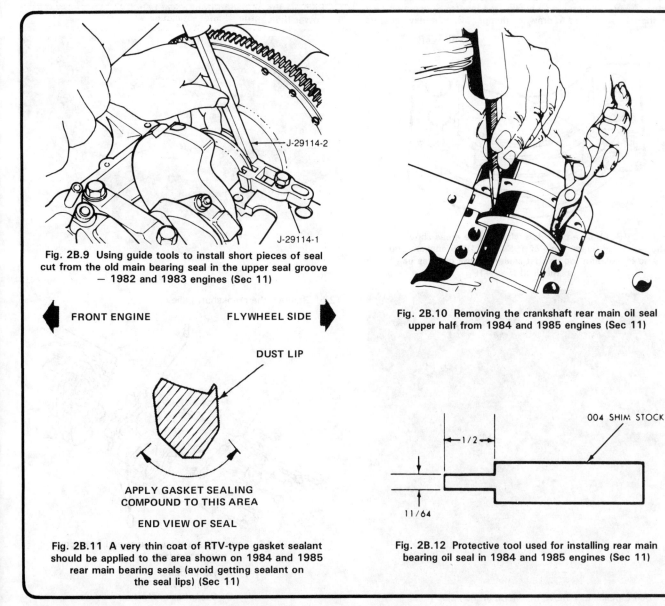

**Fig. 2B.9  Using guide tools to install short pieces of seal cut from the old main bearing seal in the upper seal groove — 1982 and 1983 engines (Sec 11)**

FRONT ENGINE                    FLYWHEEL SIDE

DUST LIP

APPLY GASKET SEALING COMPOUND TO THIS AREA

END VIEW OF SEAL

**Fig. 2B.11  A very thin coat of RTV-type gasket sealant should be applied to the area shown on 1984 and 1985 rear main bearing seals (avoid getting sealant on the seal lips) (Sec 11)**

**Fig. 2B.10  Removing the crankshaft rear main oil seal upper half from 1984 and 1985 engines (Sec 11)**

004 SHIM STOCK

1/2

11/64

**Fig. 2B.12  Protective tool used for installing rear main bearing oil seal in 1984 and 1985 engines (Sec 11)**

23  Apply sealing compound as described in Step 20 to the other half of the seal and install it in the bearing cap.
24  Apply a 1/32-inch bead of anaerobic sealant to the cap between the rear main oil seal end and oil pan rear seal groove. Be sure to keep the sealant off the rear main oil seal and bearing and out of the drain slot.
25  Just before installing the cap, apply a light coat of moly-based grease or engine assembly lube to the crankshaft surface that will contact the seal.
26  Install the rear main bearing cap and tighten the bolts to the specified torque.
27  Install the oil pump and oil pan.

## 12   Vibration damper — removal and installation

1   Disconnect the negative cable at the battery.
2   Loosen the accessory drivebelt adjusting bolts as necessary, then remove the drivebelts, tagging each one as it is removed to simplify reinstallation.
3   Raise the vehicle and support it securely on jackstands.
4   Remove the inner fender splash shield for access.
5   Remove the accessory drivebelt pulley (photo).
6   Remove the bolts from the crankshaft pulley. A screwdriver can be used to lock the starter ring gear on the flywheel. Remove the pulley.
7   Attach a puller to the damper. Draw the damper off the crankshaft, being careful not to drop it as it breaks free (photo). A common gear puller should not be used to draw the damper off, as it may separate

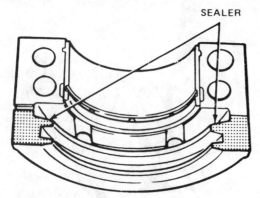

Fig. 2B.13  Apply anaerobic sealant to the areas shown on the rear main bearing cap of 1984 and 1985 engines prior to installation (do not get sealant in the grooves or on the seal) (Sec 11)

12.7   Use a puller to remove the vibration damper

the outer portion of the damper from the hub. Use only a puller which bolts to the hub.
8   Before installing the damper, coat the front cover seal area on the damper with moly-base grease.
9   Place the damper in position over the key on the crankshaft. Make sure the damper keyway lines up with the key.
10  Using a damper installation tool (GM no. J-23523 or equivalent), push the damper onto the crankshaft. The special tool distributes the pressure evenly around the hub.
11  Remove the installation tool and install the damper retaining bolt. Tighten the bolt to the specified torque.
12  Follow the removal procedure in the reverse order for the remaining components.
13  Adjust the drivebelts (refer to Chapter 1).

## 13   Crankcase front cover — removal and installation

1   If equipped with air conditioning, remove the compressor, mounting bracket and air injection reactor (AIR) pump and bracket. Do not disconnect any of the air conditioning system hoses without having the system depressurized by a GM dealer or air conditioning technician.
2   Remove the water pump as described in Chapter 3.
3   Raise the vehicle and support it securely on jackstands.
4   Remove the vibration damper as described in Section 12.
5   Remove the oil pan-to-front cover bolts.
6   Lower the vehicle.

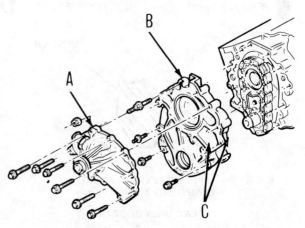

12.5   Remove the crankshaft pulley

Fig. 2B.14  Details of the water pump and front cover orientation (Sec 13)

A  Water pump
B  Front cover
C  Gasket or sealant

7   Remove the front cover mounting bolts and separate the cover from the engine.

8   Clean all oil, dirt and old gasket material from the sealing surfaces of the front cover and block. Replace the front cover oil seal as described in Section 14.

9   On models which do not use a gasket, apply a continuous 3/32-inch (2 mm) bead of RTV-type sealant to both mating surfaces of the front cover. Apply RTV-type sealant to the cover-to-oil pan area. Also apply sealant to the areas surrounding the coolant passages. On models which use a gasket, apply a 7/64-inch (3 mm) bead of RTV-type sealant to the oil pan contact surface of the cover as shown in the accompanying illustration.

10   Place the front cover in position on the engine block and install the mounting bolts. Tighten the bolts to the specified torque within five minutes.

11   The remaining installation procedures are the reverse of removal.

---

## 14   Front cover oil seal — replacement

### With front cover installed on engine

1   With the vibration damper removed (Section 12), pry the old seal out of the crankcase front cover with a large screwdriver. Be careful not to damage the surface of the crankshaft.

2   Place the new seal in position with the open end of the seal (seal lip) toward the inside of the cover.

3   Drive the seal into the cover until it is seated. GM tool J-23042 is available for this purpose. These tools are designed to exert even pressure around the entire circumference of the seal as it is hammered into place. A section of large-diameter pipe or a large socket can also be used.

4   Be careful not to distort the front cover.

### With front cover removed from engine

5   This method is preferred, as the cover can be supported while the old seal is removed and the new one is installed.

6   Remove the crankcase front cover (refer to Section 13).

7   Using a large screwdriver, pry the old seal out of the front cover. Alternatively, support the cover and drive the seal out from the rear (photo). Be careful not to damage the cover.

8   With the front of the cover facing up, place the new seal in position with the open end of the seal toward the inside of the cover.

9   Using a wooden block and hammer, drive the new seal into the cover until it is completely seated (photo).

10   If the cover was removed, install it by reversing the removal procedure.

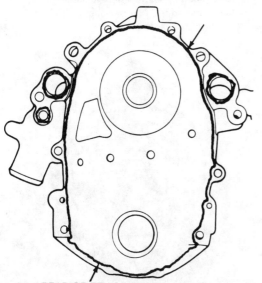

3mm BEAD OF RTV SEALANT

Fig. 2B.15  Sealant application on non-gasket timing cover installation (Sec 13)

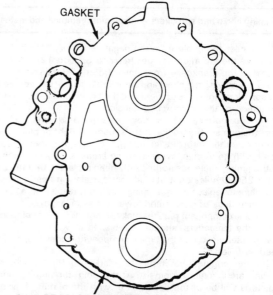

GASKET

3mm BEAD OF RTV SEALANT

Fig. 2B.16  RTV-type sealant application on a timing cover which uses a gasket (Sec 13)

14.7   Drive the seal out of the front cover

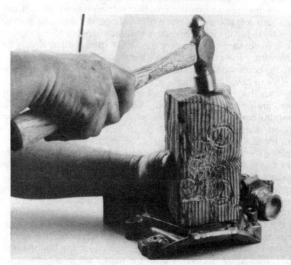

14.9   Install the front cover oil seal with a wood block and hammer

Fig. 2B.17  Timing chain and sprocket installation details
(Sec 15)

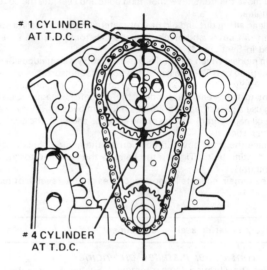

# 1 CYLINDER
AT T.D.C.

# 4 CYLINDER
AT T.D.C.

Fig. 2B.18  Proper alignment of the camshaft and
crankshaft timing marks (Sec 15)

## 15  Timing chain and sprockets — inspection, removal and installation

1   Disconnect the cable from the negative battery terminal.
2   Remove the vibration damper (refer to Section 12).
3   Remove the crankcase front cover (refer to Section 13).
4   Before removing the chain and sprockets, visually inspect the teeth on the sprockets for signs of wear and the chain for looseness. Check the condition of the timing chain tensioners.
5   If either or both sprockets show any signs of wear (edges on the teeth of the camshaft sprocket not ''square'', bright or blue areas on the teeth of either sprocket, chipping, pitting, etc.), they should be replaced with new ones. Wear in these areas is very common.
6   If the timing chain has not recently been replaced, or if the engine has over 25000 miles on it, it is almost certainly in need of replacement. Failure to replace a worn timing chain may result in erratic engine performance, loss of power and lowered gas mileage.
7   If any one component requires replacement, all related components, including the tensioners, should be replaced as well.
8   If it is determined that the timing components require replacement, proceed as follows.
9   Turn the engine over until the marks on the camshaft and crankshaft are in exact alignment. At this point the number one and four pistons will be at top dead center with the number four piston in the firing position (verify by checking the position of the rotor in the distributor). Do not attempt to remove either sprocket or the timing chain until this is done and do not turn the crankshaft or camshaft after the sprockets and chain are removed.
10  Remove the three camshaft sprocket retaining bolts and lift the camshaft sprocket and timing chain off the front of the engine. It may be necessary to tap the sprocket with a soft-face hammer to dislodge it.
11  If it is necessary to remove the crankshaft sprocket, it can be withdrawn from the crankshaft with a puller.
12  Push the crankshaft sprocket onto the nose of the crankshaft, aligning it with the key, until it seats against the shoulder.
13  Lubricate the thrust (rear) surface of the camshaft sprocket with moly-base grease or engine assembly lube (photo). Install the timing chain over the camshaft sprocket with slack in the chain hanging down over the crankshaft sprocket.
14  With the timing marks aligned, slip the chain over the crankshaft sprocket and then draw the camshaft sprocket into place with the three retaining bolts. Do not hammer or attempt to drive the camshaft sprocket into place, as it could dislodge the Welch plug at the rear of the engine.
15  With the chain and both sprockets in place, check again to ensure that the timing marks on the two sprockets are properly aligned. If not, remove the timing chain and cam sprocket, turn the camshaft enough to change the chain position on the crankshaft sprocket one tooth, reinstall the chain and camshaft sprocket and check the timing mark alignment. Repeat as necessary until the marks are in alignment.
16  Lubricate the chain with engine oil and install the remaining components in the reverse order of removal.

15.13   Lubricate the thrust surface of the camshaft sprocket

## 16  Camshaft — removal and installation

**Note:** Before removing the camshaft, refer to Chapter 2, Part D (Section 15), and measure the lobe lift.
1   Remove the engine from the vehicle (Section 18).
2   Remove the valve lifters (refer to Section 5).
3   Remove the crankcase front cover (refer to Section 13).
4   Remove the fuel pump and pushrod (refer to Chapter 4).
5   Remove the timing chain and sprocket (refer to Section 15).
6   Install a long bolt in one of the camshaft bolt holes to be used as a handle and support for the camshaft.
7   Carefully draw the camshaft out of the engine block. Do this very slowly to avoid damage to the camshaft bearings as the lobes pass over the bearing surfaces. Always support the camshaft with one hand near the engine block (photo).
8   Refer to Chapter 2, Part D, for the camshaft inspection procedures.
9   Prior to installing the camshaft, coat each of the lobes and journals with engine assembly lube or moly-base grease (photo).
10  Slide the camshaft into the engine block, again taking care not to damage the bearings (photo).

16.7   Remove the camshaft from the engine block (be very careful not to damage the cam bearings as the shaft is withdrawn)

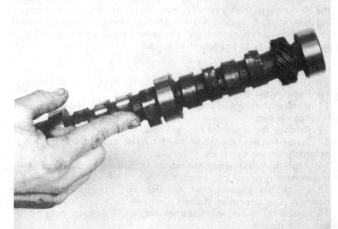

16.9   Be sure to apply engine assembly lube or moly-base grease to the cam lobes and bearing journals before installing the camshaft

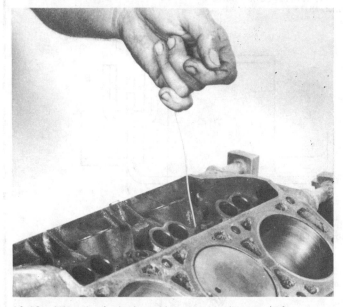

16.10   A length of wire is used to support the camshaft, preventing damage to the bearings from the cam lobes as it is passed through the bearings during installation

11   Install the camshaft sprocket and timing chain as described in Section 15.
12   Install the remaining components in the reverse order of removal by referring to the appropriate Chapter or Section.
13   Adjust the valve lash (refer to Section 6).

## 17   Engine mounts — replacement with engine in vehicle

1   If the mounts have become hard, split or separated from the metal backing, they must be replaced. This operation may be carried out with the engine/transaxle still in the vehicle.

### Engine mount
2   Remove the engine mount retaining nuts from below the cradle mounting bracket.
3   Raise the engine slightly, using a hoist or a jack with a wood block under the oil pan, then remove the mount-to-engine bracket nuts and remove the mount. The engine should be raised only enough to provide clearance.
4   Install the new mount and lower the engine into place. Install the nuts and tighten them to the specified torque.

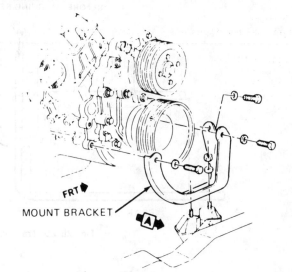

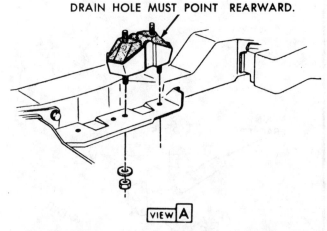

Fig. 2B.19  Front engine mount installation details (Sec 17)

### Rear mount
5   Remove the crossmember-to-mount bolts, then raise the transmission slightly with a jack.
6   Remove the mount-to-transmission bolts, followed by the mount.
7   Install the new mount, lower the transmission and align the crossmember-to-mount bolts.

8    Tighten all the bolts to the specified torque. After installation, check the alignment of the transaxle mounts by referring to the accompanying illustration. If window *A* is not located properly, loosen the mount-to-cradle retaining nuts, allow the mount to reposition itself, then tighten the nuts to the specified torque.

### Front transaxle mount

9    Lift the transaxle sufficiently to take the weight off the mounts.
10   Remove the crossmember-to-mount nuts.
11   Remove the bracket-to-transaxle bolts and remove the mount and bracket assembly.
12   Remove the mount-to-bracket nuts.
13   Install the new mount on the transaxle bracket and the mount assembly on the transaxle.
14   Align the crossmember-to-transaxle studs with the holes as the transaxle is lowered into position.
15   Check the alignment of the transaxle mounts, adjusting as necessary, as described in Step 9.
16   Install the mount-to-crossmember nuts. Tighten nuts to the specified torque.

### Rear transaxle mount

17   Remove the crossmember-to-mount nuts.
18   Remove the mount-to-transaxle bracket nut.
19   Remove the left rear cradle-to-body mount nuts.
20   Pry the cradle down and block it in position with 2 by 4 wood block.
21   Raise the transaxle with a jack and remove the mount.
22   Install the mount with the stud through the transaxle bracket. Install the nut finger tight.
23   Align the crossmember-to-mount studs with the holes as the transaxle is lowered.
24   Install the cradle-to-body mount bolt and tighten to the specified torque.
25   Install the mount-to-crossmember nuts and tighten to the specified torque.

### Engine strut

26   Remove the strut-to-bracket bolts and lift the bracket out of the bracket and radiator support.
27   Place the strut in position and install the bolts. Tighten the bolts to the specified torque.

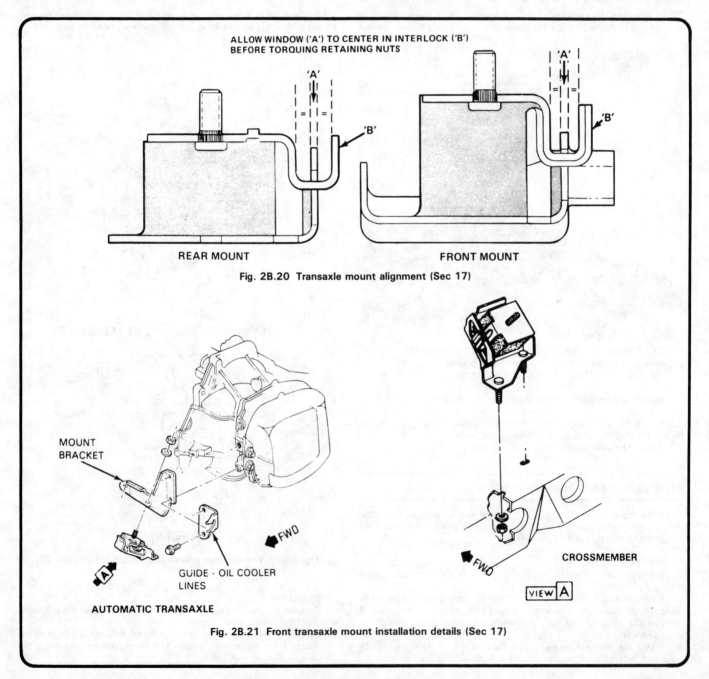

**ALLOW WINDOW ('A') TO CENTER IN INTERLOCK ('B') BEFORE TORQUING RETAINING NUTS**

REAR MOUNT

FRONT MOUNT

**Fig. 2B.20  Transaxle mount alignment (Sec 17)**

MOUNT BRACKET

FWD

GUIDE - OIL COOLER LINES

AUTOMATIC TRANSAXLE

CROSSMEMBER

FWD

VIEW A

**Fig. 2B.21  Front transaxle mount installation details (Sec 17)**

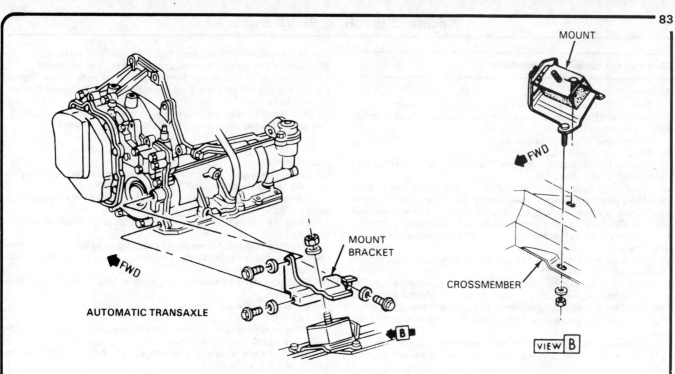

**Fig. 2B.22  Rear transaxle mount installation details (Sec 17)**

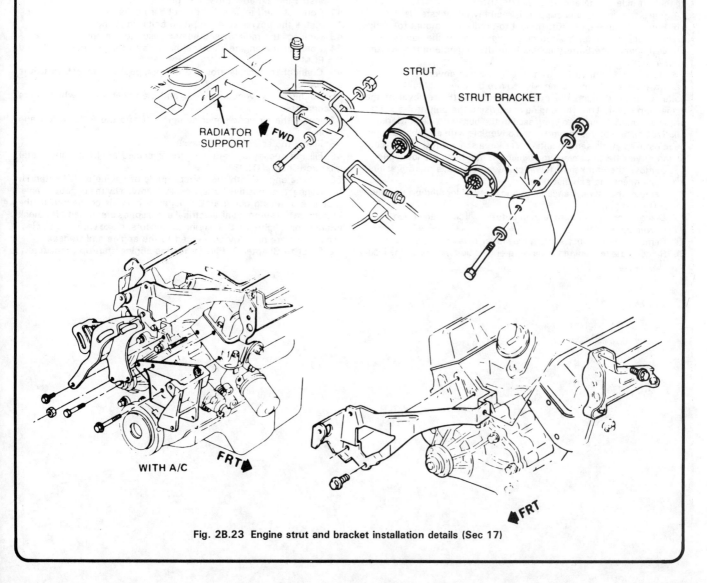

**Fig. 2B.23  Engine strut and bracket installation details (Sec 17)**

## 18  Engine — removal and installation

### Removal

1   Disconnect the cable from the negative battery terminal.
2   Disconnect the hoses at the air cleaner. Carefully label them as they are removed to simplify installation.
3   Remove the air cleaner assembly.
4   Drain the cooling system.
5   Remove the engine strut bracket from the radiator bracket and swing it out of the way.
6   On air conditioning equipped models, remove the air injection reactor (AIR) pump and bracket, followed by the air conditioning compressor and bracket. Lay the compressor aside with the hoses still attached. **Caution:** *Do not attempt to disconnect the air conditioning system hoses — the refrigerant in the system can cause serious injuries and respiratory irritation.*
7   Disconnect the vacuum hoses which are connected to non-engine components.
8   Disconnect the accelerator cable and (if equipped) detent cable.
9   Unplug the engine electrical harness from the electronic control module (ECM) and pull the connector through the front of the dash.
10  Disconnect the engine electrical harness at the left side of the dash panel.
11  Disconnect the radiator hoses and heater hoses from the engine.
12  Remove the power steering pump and bracket assembly (if so equipped).
13  Disconnect and plug the fuel lines at the rubber hose connections at the left side of the engine compartment.
14  Raise the vehicle and support it securely on jackstands.
15  Remove the engine front mount-to-cradle and mount-to-cradle bracket retaining nuts, located on the right side of the vehicle.
16  Disconnect the battery cables from the engine and remove the starter motor.
17  Unbolt and remove the transaxle inspection cover.
18  On automatic transaxle models, remove the converter-to-driveplate bolts, working through the opening gained by the removal of the inspection cover. Turn the engine over, using the bolt at the center of the vibration damper, to bring each of the bolts into view. Mark the relative position of the converter and driveplate with a scribe so it can be reinstalled in the same position. Wedge a screwdriver in the teeth of the driveplate to prevent movement as the bolts are loosened.
19  Remove the crankshaft lower pulley and remove the drivebelts.
20  Disconnect the exhaust pipe.
21  Remove the lower transaxle-to-engine bolt, located on the back side of the engine.
22  Disconnect the power steering cutoff switch (if equipped).
23  Lower the vehicle.
24  Remove the exhaust system crossover pipe.
25  Remove the remaining transaxle-to-engine bolts, marking the location of the ground stud for installation in the same position.
26  Support the transaxle extension with a jack or jackstand.
27  Attach a hoist and lifting chains to the lifting eyes on the engine.
28  Lift the engine from the engine compartment and mount it on an engine stand.
29  Refer to the appropriate Sections of this Chapter and Chapter 2, Part D, for further disassembly and rebuilding alternatives.

### Installation

30  Lower the engine into the engine compartment, align the engine with the transaxle and install the attaching bolts.
31  Remove the lifting device, raise the vehicle and support it securely on jackstands.
32  Install the engine front mount retaining nuts to the cradle and engine bracket.
33  Place the power steering pump and bracket assembly in position on the engine and install the lower adjusting nut finger tight. Connect the cutoff switch.
34  Install the lower transaxle-to-engine bolt, located on the back side of the engine.
35  Install the exhaust pipe.
36  Install the crankshaft pulley.
37  On automatic transaxle models, install the converter to driveplate bolts and install the inspection cover.
38  Install the starter motor and connect the battery cables at the starter and transaxle bolts.
39  Lower the vehicle.
40  Install the exhaust crossover pipe.
41  Connect the fuel lines to the rubber hoses.
42  Install the power steering pump bolts finger tight.
43  Connect the radiator and heater hoses to the engine.
44  Connect the engine electrical harness to the junction block and the ECM.
45  Connect the accelerator and (if equipped) detent cables to the carburetor.
46  Connect any vacuum hoses and electrical wires which were disconnected.
47  Install the air conditioner compressor and the AIR bracket and pump.
48  Install the engine strut bracket.
49  Fill the cooling system with the specified antifreeze and water mixture (Chapter 1).
50  Fill the engine with the correct grade of engine oil (Chapter 1).
51  Connect the positive battery cable, followed by the negative cable. If sparks or arcing occur as the negative cable is connected to the battery, make sure that all electrical accessories are turned off (check interior dome lights first). If arcing still occurs, make sure that all electrical wires are properly connected to the engine and transaxle.
52  Refer to Chapter 2, Part D, for the engine start-up procedure.

# Chapter 2 Part C  3.0L and 3.8L V6 engines

*Refer to Chapter 13 for Specifications and information applicable to 1986 and later models*

## Contents

| | |
|---|---|
| Air filter replacement . . . . . . . . . . . . . . . . . . . . . . | See Chapter 1 |
| Camshaft — removal and installation . . . . . . . . . . . . . . | 12 |
| Check Engine light. . . . . . . . . . . . . . . . . . . . . . . | See Chapter 6 |
| Compression check . . . . . . . . . . . . . . . . . . . . . . | See Chapter 1 |
| Crankshaft balancer — removal and installation . . . . . . . . . | 10 |
| Cylinder head — removal and installation . . . . . . . . . . . . | 6 |
| Drivebelt check and adjustment . . . . . . . . . . . | See Chapter 1 |
| Engine — removal and installation . . . . . . . . . . . . . . . . | 19 |
| Engine and transaxle mounts — replacement with engine in vehicle . . . . . . . . . . . . . . . . . . . . . . | 18 |
| Engine oil and filter change . . . . . . . . . . . . . . | See Chapter 1 |
| Engine oil level check . . . . . . . . . . . . . . . . . . . | See Chapter 1 |
| Engine overhaul — general information . . . . . . . . | See Chapter 2D |
| Engine removal — methods and installation . . . . | See Chapter 2D |
| Exhaust manifold — removal and installation . . . . . . . . . . . | 5 |
| Front crankshaft oil seal — replacement . . . . . . . . . . . . . | 11 |
| General information . . . . . . . . . . . . . . . . . . . . . . | 1 |

| | |
|---|---|
| Hydraulic lifters — removal, inspection and installation . . . . . | 7 |
| Intake manifold — removal and installation . . . . . . . . . . . . | 4 |
| Oil pan — removal and installation . . . . . . . . . . . . . . . . | 13 |
| Oil pump cover and gears — removal and installation . . . . . . | 14 |
| Oil pump and screen assembly — removal and installation . . . | 15 |
| Rear main bearing cap oil seal — replacement (engine in vehicle) . . . . . . . . . . . . . . . . . . . . . . . . . . . . . . . | 16 |
| Rear main bearing upper oil seal — repair (engine in vehicle) . . . . . . . . . . . . . . . . . . . . . . . . . . . . . . . | 17 |
| Repair operations possible with the engine in the vehicle . . . . . . . . . . . . . . . . . . . . . . | See Chapter 2D |
| Rocker arm cover — removal and installation . . . . . . . . . . . | 2 |
| Timing chain cover — removal and installation . . . . . . . . . | 8 |
| Timing chain and sprockets — removal and installation . . . . . | 9 |
| Valve train components — replacement (cylinder head installed . . . . . . . . . . . . . . . . . . . . . . . . . . . . . | 3 |
| Water pump — removal and installation . . . . . . . | See Chapter 3 |

## Specifications

## Oil pump service limits

| | |
|---|---|
| Gear length . . . . . . . . . . . . . . . . . . . . . . . . . . . . . . . | 0.8835 to 0.8720 in |
| Gear diameter . . . . . . . . . . . . . . . . . . . . . . . . . . . . . | 1.666 to 1.664 in |
| Gear pocket depth . . . . . . . . . . . . . . . . . . . . . . . . . . | 0.8697 to 0.8677 in |
| Gear pocket diameter . . . . . . . . . . . . . . . . . . . . . . . . | 1.674 to 1.671 in |
| Gear lash . . . . . . . . . . . . . . . . . . . . . . . . . . . . . . . . | 0.0015 to 0.003 in |
| Side clearance . . . . . . . . . . . . . . . . . . . . . . . . . . . . . | 0.003 to 0.005 in |
| End clearance. . . . . . . . . . . . . . . . . . . . . . . . . . . . . . | 0.002 to 0.006 in |
| Cover flatness . . . . . . . . . . . . . . . . . . . . . . . . . . . . . | 0.001 in |

## Torque specifications

| | Ft-lbs |
|---|---|
| Spark plug . . . . . . . . . . . . . . . . . . . . . . . . . . . . . | 15 |
| Crankshaft bearing cap bolts . . . . . . . . . . . . . . . . . . | 100 |
| Crankshaft balancer bolt . . . . . . . . . . . . . . . . . . . . . | 200 to 225 |
| Connecting rod bolts . . . . . . . . . . . . . . . . . . . . . . . | 40 |
| Cylinder head bolts. . . . . . . . . . . . . . . . . . . . . . . . | 80 |
| Cylinder block drain bolt . . . . . . . . . . . . . . . . . . . . | 22 |
| Water pump pulley-to-balancer bolt . . . . . . . . . . . . . . | 20 |
| Driveplate or flywheel-to-crankshaft bolt . . . . . . . . . . . | 60 |
| Oil pan bolts . . . . . . . . . . . . . . . . . . . . . . . . . . . . | 14 |
| Oil pan drain plug . . . . . . . . . . . . . . . . . . . . . . . . . | 30 |
| Oil pump | |
|     Cover-to-timing chain cover bolt. . . . . . . . . . . . . . | 10 |
|     Pressure regulator retainer bolt . . . . . . . . . . . . . . | 35 |
|     Pump housing-to-cylinder block bolt . . . . . . . . . . . . | 8 |
| Timing chain cover bolt . . . . . . . . . . . . . . . . . . . . . | 30 |
| Water pump cover-to-timing chain cover bolt . . . . . . . . . | 7 |
| Water pump pulley bolt . . . . . . . . . . . . . . . . . . . . . | 20 |
| Intake manifold-to-cylinder head bolts . . . . . . . . . . . . | 45 |
| Exhaust manifold-to-cylinder head bolts. . . . . . . . . . . . | 25 |
| Engine mount-to-bracket bolt . . . . . . . . . . . . . . . . . | 41 |
| Engine mount bracket-to-cylinder block bolt . . . . . . . . . | 81 |
| Timing chain sprocket bolts . . . . . . . . . . . . . . . . . . | 20 |
| Rocker arm cover-to-cylinder head bolt . . . . . . . . . . . . | 4 |
| Rocker arm shaft bolt . . . . . . . . . . . . . . . . . . . . . . | 30 |
| Alternator bracket-to-cylinder head bolt . . . . . . . . . . . | 35 |
| Alternator adjusting bracket-to-water pump bolt . . . . . . . | 20 |
| Distributor hold-down clamp bolt . . . . . . . . . . . . . . . | 13 |
| Lower flywheel cover bolt . . . . . . . . . . . . . . . . . . . . | 4 |
| Transaxle-to-cylinder block . . . . . . . . . . . . . . . . . . | 35 |
| Timing chain dampener bolt . . . . . . . . . . . . . . . . . . | 12 |

## 1 General information

The forward Sections in this Part of Chapter 2 are devoted to in vehicle repair procedures for the 3.0 and 3.8 liter V6 engine. The latter Sections in this Part of Chapter 2 involve the removal and installation procedures for this engine. All information concerning engine block and cylinder head servicing can be found in Part D of this Chapter.

The repair procedures are based on the assumption that the engine is still installed in the vehicle. Therefore, if this information is being used during a complete engine overhaul with the engine already out of the vehicle and on a stand, many of the steps included here will not apply.

The Specifications included in this Part of Chapter 2 apply only to the engine and procedures found here. For specifications regarding engines other than the 3.0 and 3.8 V6 engine, see Part A or B, whichever applies. Part D of Chapter 2 contains the specifications necessary for engine block and cylinder head rebuilding.

## 2 Rocker arm cover — removal and installation

1   Remove the air cleaner assembly, tagging each hose to be disconnected with a piece of numbered tape to simplify installation.
2   Disconnect the negative battery cable.
3   On the right side rocker arm cover, remove the PCV pipe, the hot air tube and any emissions system hoses or electrical leads which will interfere with removal.
4   Remove the spark plug wires from the spark plugs (refer to the removal technique described in Chapter 1), then remove the wires and retaining clips from the rocker arm cover. Be sure to label each wire before removal to ensure that all wires are reinstalled correctly.
5   Remove any accessory mounting brackets which would interfere with rocker arm cover removal.
6   Remove the rocker arm cover bolts.
7   Remove the rocker arm cover. **Note:** *If the cover sticks to the cylinder head, use a block of wood and a hammer to dislodge it. If the cover still will not come loose, pry on it carefully, but do not distort the sealing flange surface.*
8   Prior to installation of the cover, clean all dirt, oil and old gasket material from the sealing surfaces of the cover and cylinder head with a scraper and degreaser.
9   To install, place the rocker arm cover in position, using new gasket, and install the retaining bolts. Tighten the bolts a little at a time to the specified torque.
10   Complete the installation by reversing the removal procedure.

## 3 Valve train components — replacement (cylinder head installed)

1   Remove the rocker arm cover(s) as described in Section 2.
2   Remove the retaining bolts and lift the rocker arm shaft assembly from the cylinder head. Pull the pushrods out of the holes in the cylinder head. If a rocker arm is to be removed, use pliers to remove the nylon retainer and slide the rocker arm off the shaft. The rocker arms are stamped right (*R*) or left (*L*) and must be kept in the proper order for installation in their original positions.
3   If the valve spring is to be removed, remove the spark plug from the affected cylinder.
4   There are two methods that will hold the valve closed while the valve spring is removed. If you have access to compressed air, install an air hose adapter (GM part number J-22794) in the spark plug hole.

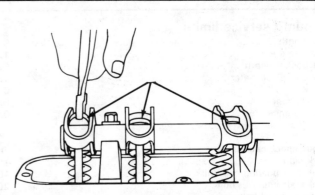

Fig. 2C.2 Remove the plastic rocker arm retainers (arrows) using pliers (Sec 3)

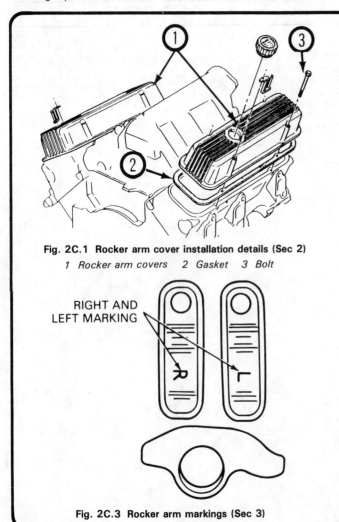

**Fig. 2C.1 Rocker arm cover installation details (Sec 2)**

*1 Rocker arm covers   2 Gasket   3 Bolt*

RIGHT AND LEFT MARKING

**Fig. 2C.3 Rocker arm markings (Sec 3)**

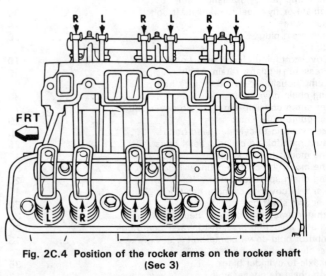

**Fig. 2C.4 Position of the rocker arms on the rocker shaft (Sec 3)**

These adapters are also available at most parts stores. When air pressure is applied to the adapter, the valves will be held in place by the pressure.

5   If you do not have access to compressed air, bring the piston to just before top dead center (TDC) on the compression stroke. Feed a long piece of 1/4-inch nylon cord in through the spark plug hole until it fills the combustion chamber. Be sure to leave the end of the cord hanging out of the spark plug hole so it can be removed easily. Rotate the crankshaft with a wrench in the normal direction of rotation until slight resistance is felt.

6   Insert a valve spring compressing tool such as GM tool J-8062 under the bolt head and compress the spring just enough to remove the valve keys, then release the pressure on the tool.

7   Remove the valve cap, spring, and valve stem oil seal (if so equipped).

8   Inspection procedures for valve train components are covered in Section 8 and in Chapter 2, Part D.

9   Installation of the valve train components is the reverse of the removal procedure. Always use new valve stem oil seals whenever the spring keepers have been disturbed. Prior to installing the rocker arms, coat the bearing surfaces of the arms and rocker arm shafts with moly-base grease or engine assembly lube. The engine valve mechanisms require no special valve lash adjustment. Simply tighten the rocker arm bolts to the specified torque.

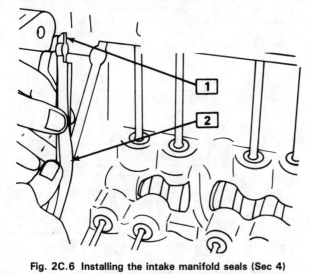

**Fig. 2C.5  Remove the valve spring keys with a compressor tool (Sec 3)**

## 4   Intake manifold — removal and installation

1   Disconnect the cable from the negative battery terminal.

2   Remove the air cleaner assembly, tagging each hose to be disconnected with a piece of numbered tape to simplify reinstallation.

3   Drain the cooling system (refer to Chapter 1).

4   Disconnect the upper radiator hose and heater hose at the manifold.

5   Label and disconnect the fuel line, vacuum lines and electrical leads. When disconnecting the fuel line, be prepared to catch some fuel, then plug the fuel line to prevent contamination.

6   Disconnect the throttle linkage, making careful note of how it is installed.

7   Disconnect the cruise control linkage (if so equipped).

8   On models so equipped, remove the distributor cap and rotor for access to the Torx head bolt on the left side of the manifold.

9   Remove the manifold retaining bolts and separate the manifold from the cylinder head. Do not pry between the manifold and head, as damage to the gasket sealing surfaces may result.

10  Remove the manifold gasket.

11  If the intake manifold is to be replaced with another, transfer all components still attached to the old manifold to the new one.

12  Before installing the manifold, clean the cylinder head and manifold gasket surfaces. All gasket material and sealing compound must be removed prior to installation.

13  Place the new intake manifold gasket and seals in position at the front and rear cylinder block rails, making sure the pointed end of the seal fits snugly against both the head and block. Apply RTV-type sealer to the ends of the seals before installation.

14  Place the manifold in position and install the mounting bolts finger tight, starting with the center bolts (bolts 1 and 2 in the accompanying illustration).

15  Tighten the mounting bolts a little at a time in the sequence shown in the illustration until they are all at the specified torque.

16  Install the remaining components in the reverse order of removal.

17  Fill the radiator with coolant, start the engine and check for leaks.

18  Adjust the ignition timing and idle speed as necessary (Chapter 1).

## 5   Exhaust manifold — removal and installation

1   If the vehicle is equipped with air conditioning, carefully examine the routing of the hoses and the mounting of the compressor. You may be able to remove the exhaust manifold without disconnecting the system. If you are in doubt, take the vehicle to a GM dealer or automotive repair shop to have the system depressurized. **Caution:** *Do not, under any circumstances, disconnect any air-conditioning system lines while the system is under pressure.*

2   Remove the cable from the negative battery terminal.

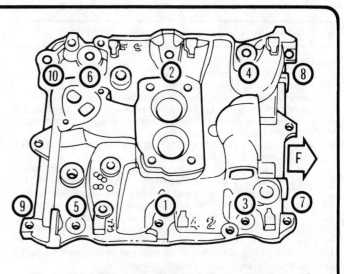

**Fig. 2C.6  Installing the intake manifold seals (Sec 4)**

*1  RTV-type sealant application area        2  Seal*

**Fig. 2C.7  Intake manifold bolt tightening sequence (Sec 4)**

## Right manifold

3   Disconnect the steering intermediate shaft from the rack and pinion stub shaft.
4   Raise the vehicle and support it securely on jackstands.
5   From under the vehicle, remove the two exhaust pipe-to-manifold bolts. You may have to apply penetrating oil to the fastener threads, as they are usually corroded.
6   Lower the vehicle.
7   Remove the upper engine support strut and support the cradle crossmember with a jack. Raise the jack sufficiently to begin raising the vehicle.
8   Remove the two body mount bolts and cushions.
9   Thread the body mount bolts and retainers at least three turns into the cage nuts so the bolts will restrain cradle movement.
10  Slowly lower the jack until the crossmember is in contact with the body mount bolt retainers. Watch carefully as the jack is lowered to make sure there is no interference with any of the hoses, pipes, lines and cables.
11  Remove the alternator and disconnect the power steering pump from the cylinder head and exhaust manifold.
12  Unbolt the exhaust manifold at the crossover pipe.
13  Remove the heat shield (if equipped).
14  Remove the six retaining bolts, separate the exhaust manifold from the cylinder head and lift it from the vehicle.
15  Before installing the exhaust manifold, clean the mating surfaces on the cylinder head and manifold. All old gasket material must be removed.
16  Place the manifold in position and install the bolts finger tight.
17  Tighten the mounting bolts a little at a time until all of the bolts are at the specified torque.
18  Install the remaining components in the reverse order of removal.
19  Start the engine and check for exhaust leaks between the manifold and cylinder head and between the manifold and exhaust pipe.

## Left manifold

20  Under the vehicle, remove the two crossover pipe-to-manifold retaining nuts
21  Remove the upper engine support between the radiator support and the exhaust manifold.
22  Disconnect the oxygen sensor.
23  Remove the heat shield (if equipped).
24  Unbolt and remove the exhaust manifold.
25  Clean and inspect the mating surfaces on the cylinder head and manifold. All gasket material must be removed.
26  Place the manifold in position and install the bolts finger tight.
27  Tighten the bolts a little at a time until all the bolts are at the specified torque.
28  Install the remaining components in the reverse order of removal.
29  Start the engine and check for exhaust leaks between the manifold and exhaust pipe.

---

**6   Cylinder head — removal and installation**

## Removal

1   Disconnect the negative cable at the battery.
2   Remove the air cleaner assembly.
3   Remove the intake manifold as described in Section 4.
4   When removing the left cylinder head, remove the dipstick, the air and vacuum pumps and mounting brackets and move them out of the way with hoses still attached.
5   When removing the right cylinder head, remove the alternator and disconnect the power steering pump and brackets.
6   If so equipped, unbolt the air conditioner compressor and swing it out of the way for clearance. **Caution:** *Do not disconnect any of the air conditioning lines unless the system has been depressurized by a dealer or repair shop, because personal injury may occur. Disconnection of the lines should not be necessary in this case.*
7   Disconnect all electrical and vacuum lines from the cylinder head. Be sure to label the lines to simplify reinstallation.
8   Disconnect the spark plug wires and remove the spark plugs. Be sure to label the plug wires to simplify reinstallation.
9   Remove the exhaust manifold bolts from the cylinder head being removed (Section 5).
10  Remove the rocker arm cover. To break the gasket seal it may be

necessary to strike the cover with your hand or a rubber hammer. Do not pry between the sealing surfaces. Refer to Section 2 if necessary.
11  When disassembling the valve mechanisms, keep all of the components in order so they can be reinstalled in their original positions. A cardboard box or rack, numbered to correspond to the engine cylinders, can be used for this purpose.
12  Remove retaining bolts and separate the rocker arm shafts or pedestals from the cylinder head.
13  Remove the pushrods.
14  If the ignition coil is mounted separately from the distributor, disconnect the wires and remove the coil.
15  Loosen each of the cylinder head mounting bolts one turn at a time until they can be removed. Note the length and position of each bolt to ensure correct reinstallation.
16  Lift the head off of the engine. If it is stuck to the engine block, do not attempt to pry it free, as you could damage the sealing surfaces. Instead, use a hammer and block of wood to tap the head and break the gasket seal. Place the head on a block of wood to prevent damage to the gasket surface.
17  Remove the cylinder head gasket.
18  Refer to Chapter 2D for cylinder head disassembly and valve service procedures.

## Installation

19  If a new cylinder head is being installed, transfer all external parts from the old cylinder head to the new one.
20  If not already done, thoroughly clean the gasket surfaces on the cylinder head and the engine block. Do not gouge or otherwise damage the gasket surfaces.
21  To get the proper torque readings the threads of the head bolts must be clean. This also applies to the threaded holes in the engine block. Run a tap through the holes to ensure that they are clean.
22  Place the gasket in position, bead side down, over the engine block dowel pins.
23  Carefully lower the cylinder head onto the engine, over the dowel pins and the gasket.
24  Coat the threads of each cylinder head bolt and the point at which the head and the bolt meet with a sealing compound and install the bolts finger tight. Do not tighten any of the bolts at this time.
25  Tighten each of the bolts a little at a time in the sequence shown in the accompanying illustration. Continue tightening in this sequence until the proper torque reading is obtained. As a final check, work around the head in a front-to-rear sequence to make sure none of the bolts have been left out of the sequence.
26  The remaining installation steps are the reverse of removal.

---

**7   Hydraulic lifters — removal, inspection and installation**

1   A noisy valve lifter can be isolated when the engine is idling. Place a length of hose or tubing near the position of each valve while listening at the other end of the tube. Another method is to remove the rocker arm cover and, with the engine idling, place a finger on each of the valve spring retainers, one at a time. If a valve lifter is defective, it will be evident from the shock felt at the retainer as the valve seats.

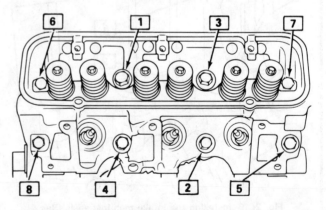

Fig. 2C.8 Cylinder head bolt tightening sequence (Sec 6)

2   The most likely cause of a noisy valve lifter is a piece of dirt trapped between the plunger and the lifter body.

3   Remove the rocker arm cover as described in Section 2.

4   Remove the intake manifold as described in Section 4.

5   Remove the rocker arm shaft assemblies.

6   Remove the pushrod.

7   To remove the lifter, a special hydraulic lifter removal tool should be used, or a scribe can be positioned at the top of the lifter and used to force the lifter up and out of the bore. Do not use pliers or other tools on the outside of the lifter body. They will damage the finished surface and render the lifter useless.

8   The lifters should be kept in order for reinstallation in their original positions.

9   To dismantle a valve lifter, hold the plunger down with a pushrod and extract the retainer ring with a small screwdriver.

10  Remove the pushrod seat and the metering valve.

11  Remove the plunger, ball check valve and plunger spring. The ball check valve and spring are removed by prying them out with a small screwdriver.

12  Clean the lifter components with solvent and dry them with compressed air. Examine the internal components for wear and check the ball carefully for flat spots. **Note:** *Refer to Chapter 2, Part D, for additional lifter and camshaft inspection procedures.*

13  If the lifters are worn, they must be replaced with new ones and the camshaft must be replaced as well (see Chapter 2, Part D). If the lifters are contaminated with dirt, they can be cleaned and reinstalled — they may operate normally.

14  Reassembly should be done in the following manner:

  a) Place the ball check valve on the small hole in the bottom of the plunger.

  b) Insert the ball check spring into the seat in the valve retainer and place the retainer over the ball so that the spring rests on the ball. Using a small screwdriver, carefully press the retainer into position in the plunger.

  c) Place the plunger spring over the ball retainer, invert the lifter body and slide it over the spring and plunger. Make sure the oil holes in the body and plunger line up.

  d) Fill the assembly with 10-weight oil. Place the metering valve and pushrod seat in position, press down on the seat with a pushrod and install the retainer ring.

15  When installing the lifters, make sure thay are replaced in their original bores. Coat them with moly-base grease or engine assembly lube.

16  The remaining installation steps are the reverse of removal.

## 8  Timing chain cover — removal and installation

1   Disconnect the negative cable at the battery.

2   Drain the radiator (Chapter 1).

3   Remove the upper and lower radiator hoses and the heater return hose.

4   Support the engine with a jack and remove the two nuts at the cradle.

5   Remove the water pump drive belt and pulley.

6   Remove the alternator and mounting bracket.

7   Remove the distributor or crankshaft sensor (Chapter 5). **Note:** *If the timing chain and sprockets are to be moved or disturbed, note the position of the distributor rotor so that it can be reinstalled in the same position.*

8   Remove the front clamp from the coolant bypass hose.

9   Remove the crankshaft balancer assembly (Section 10).

10  Remove the timing chain cover-to-engine block bolts.

11  Remove the timing chain-to-oil pan bolts.

12  Separate the cover from the front of the engine.

13  Using a scraper and degreaser, remove all dirt and old gasket material from the sealing surfaces of the timing chain cover, engine block and oil pan.

14  Using a punch and hammer, drive out the old oil seal and shedder. Drive from the front toward the rear of the timing chain cover.

15  Replace the front oil seal with a new one unless it is in obviously good condition (Section 11).

16  The oil pump cover must be removed and the cavity packed with petroleum jelly as described in Section 14 before installation.

17  Using new gaskets, place the timing chain cover in position on the engine, making sure the oil pump drive is securely engaged with the distributor gear.

18  Install the attaching bolts with thread sealant applied to the threads and tighten to the specified torque.

19  The remainder of installation is the reverse of removal.

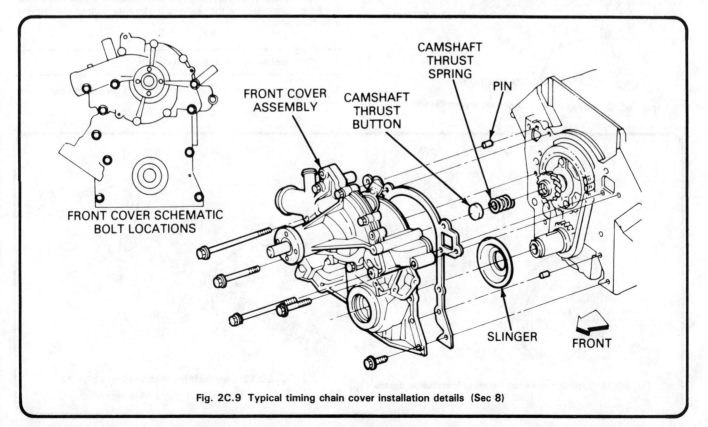

**Fig. 2C.9 Typical timing chain cover installation details (Sec 8)**

## 9   Timing chain and sprockets — removal and installation

1   Remove the timing chain cover (Section 8).
2   The timing chain should be replaced with a new one if the total in and out movement of the chain exceeds one inch. Failure to replace the timing chain may result in erratic engine performance, loss of power and lowered gas mileage.
3   Temporarily install the front crankshaft balancer bolt and turn the bolt to align the timing marks on the crankshaft and camshaft sprockets at their closest positions. Use a sharp blow on the end of the wrench to remove the crankshaft balancer bolt so that the timing marks are not moved.
4   Remove the crankshaft oil slinger (if equipped).
5   Remove the camshaft sprocket bolts.
6   Use two large screwdrivers to alternately pry first the camshaft sprocket and then the crankshaft sprocket forward and remove the camshaft sprocket and timing chain.
7   Remove the crankshaft sprocket.
8   Clean the timing chain, sprockets, distributor drive gear and fuel pump eccentric in solvent.
9   Inspect the components for wear or damage. Signs of wear to the sprockets are teeth that are not square, bright or blue areas on the teeth of either sprocket and chipping or pitting.
10   If the pistons have not been moved, go to Step 11.
11   If the pistons have been moved, rotate the crankshaft until the number one piston is at top dead center. Turn the camshaft until, with

the sprocket temporarily installed, the timing mark is straight down. Remove the sprocket.
12   Assemble the timing chain on the sprockets and then slide the sprocket and chain assembly onto the shafts with the timing marks in their closest together position and aligned with the sprocket hubs.
13   Install the oil slinger (if equipped) with the large part of the cone to the front of the engine.
14   Install the camshaft sprocket bolts and tighten to the specified torque.
15   Install the camshaft thrust button and spring.
16   Install the timing chain cover.

## 10   Crankshaft balancer — removal and installation

1   Disconnect the negative cable from the battery.
2   On some models it will be necessary to remove the steering shaft pinch bolt and separate the shaft from the steering gear.
3   Remove the engine support strut.
4   Place a jack under the front cradle crossmember and raise it until it begins to raise the vehicle.
5   Remove the two body mount bolts and cushions.
6   Thread the body mount bolts and retainers into the cage nuts a minimum of three turns to restrain the cradle.
7   Remove the right front wheel and the right side splash shield.
8   Remove the drivebelts.
9   Remove the bolt, washer and balancer assembly.
10   Installation is the reverse of removal.

## 11   Front crankshaft oil seal — replacement

1   Remove the timing chain cover (Section 8).
2   Drive the old oil seal and shedder out of the timing chain cover toward the rear of the cover, using a hammer and punch.
3   Coil the new packing around the seal opening so that the ends are at the top.
4   Use a hammer and suitable size punch to drive the shedder into place over the seal. Stake the shedder in place in at least three locations.
5   Size the new seal by rotating a hammer handle or similar tool around the full circumference of the seal until the balancer hub can be inserted into the opening.

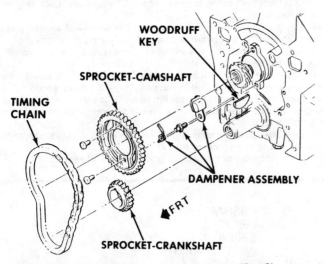

**WOODRUFF KEY**
**SPROCKET-CAMSHAFT**
**TIMING CHAIN**
**DAMPENER ASSEMBLY**
**FRT**
**SPROCKET-CRANKSHAFT**

Fig. 2C.10  Timing chain component layout (Sec 9)

## 12   Camshaft — removal and installation

1   The camshaft can only be removed with the engine out of the vehicle (Section 21).

Fig. 2C.11  Typical crankshaft balancer installation details (Sec 10)

Fig. 2C.12  Camshaft installation details (Sec 12)
1 Camshaft     2 Bearings

2   Remove the intake manifold (Section 4).
3   Remove the rocker arm cover (Section 2) and rocker arm assembly (Section 3) and lifters (Section 7).
4   Remove the timing chain cover (Section 8) and timing chain and sprockets (Section 9).
5   Align the camshaft and crankshaft sprocket timing marks at their closest positions.
6   Supporting the camshaft carefully to prevent damage to the bearings, remove the camshaft by pulling it out of through the front of the engine.
7   Refer to Chapter 2, Part D, for the camshaft inspection process.
8   Prior to installing the camshaft, coat each of the lobes and journals with engine assembly lube or moly-base grease.
9   Slide the camshaft into the engine block. Again, be careful not to damage the bearings.
10  The remainder of installation is a reversal of removal.

**13  Oil pan — removal and installation**

1   Disconnect the cable from the negative battery terminal.
2   Raise the vehicle, place it securely on jackstands and drain the engine oil (refer to Chapter 1 if necessary).
3   Remove the flywheel inspection cover.
4   Remove the oil pan bolts and separate the oil pan from the block.
5   Clean the pan with solvent and remove all old sealant and gasket material from the block and pan sealing surfaces.

6   Some models use a gasket while other use RTV-type sealant to seal the oil pan. On models which use a gasket, always use a new gasket whenever the oil pan has been removed. On models which use RTV-type sealant, apply a 1/8-inch diameter bead of the sealant to the contact surfaces of the oil pan flange inboard of the bolt holes.
7   Place the oil pan in position on the block and install the oil pan bolts.
8   After all bolts are installed, tighten them to the specified torque. Use a criss-cross pattern and work up to the final torque in three or four steps.
9   The remaining steps are the reverse of the removal procedure.

**14  Oil pump cover and gears — removal and inspection and installation**

*Removal*
1   Remove the oil filter.
2   Remove the oil pump cover-to-timing chain cover attaching bolts.
3   Lift out the cover, oil pump drive and driven gears as an assembly.
4   Do not attempt to remove the oil filter bypass valve and spring, as they are staked in place.

*Inspection*
5   Clean all components thoroughly in solvent.
6   Inspect all components for wear and scoring and the bypass valve for. cracks, nicks and warping.
7   Measure the oil pump gears as shown in the accompanying illustration.

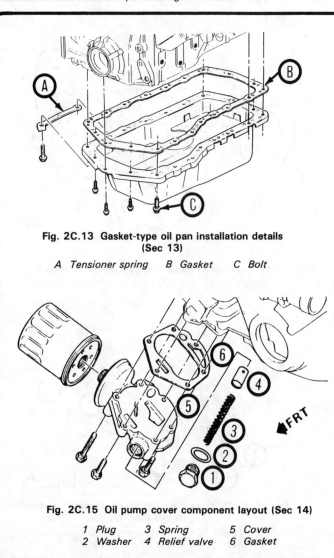

**Fig. 2C.13 Gasket-type oil pan installation details (Sec 13)**

*A Tensioner spring   B Gasket   C Bolt*

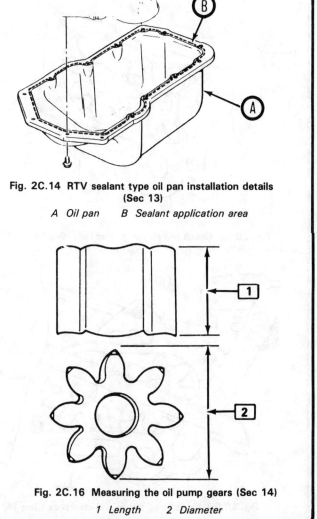

**Fig. 2C.14 RTV sealant type oil pan installation details (Sec 13)**

*A Oil pan   B Sealant application area*

**Fig. 2C.15 Oil pump cover component layout (Sec 14)**

*1 Plug   3 Spring   5 Cover*
*2 Washer   4 Relief valve   6 Gasket*

**Fig. 2C.16 Measuring the oil pump gears (Sec 14)**

*1 Length   2 Diameter*

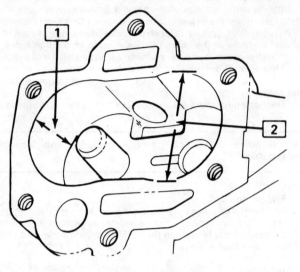

**Fig. 2C.17 Oil pump gear pocket measurement (Sec 14)**

*1 Depth          2 Diameter*

8    Measure the gear pocket as shown in the illustration.
9    Install the oil pump gears and shaft in the oil pump body section of the timing chain cover.
10   Measure the gear lash and side clearance at several points as shown in the illustrations.
11   Place a ruler over the gears and measure the clearance between the ruler edge and gasket surface as shown in the accompanying illustration.
12   Check the pump cover flatness by placing a ruler across the face and measuring with a feeler gauge between the ruler edge and cover surface.
13   Compare the measurements to specifications, replacing any worn or damaged components with new ones.

*Installation*
14   Remove the gears and pack the pump cavity with petroleum jelly.
15   Install the gears so that petroleum jelly is forced into every cavity. Failure to follow this procedure could cause the pump to "lose it's prime" when the engine is started, causing damage to the engine.
16   Install the cover, using a new gasket, and install the oil filter.

---

**15   Oil pump and screen assembly — removal and installation**

1    Remove the oil pan (Section 13).
2    Unbolt the oil pump and screen assembly and remove it from the engine.

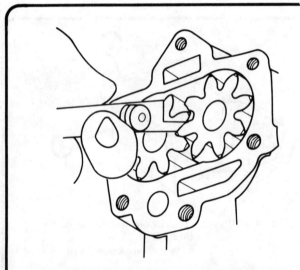

**Fig. 2C.18 Check the oil pump gear lash (Sec 14)**

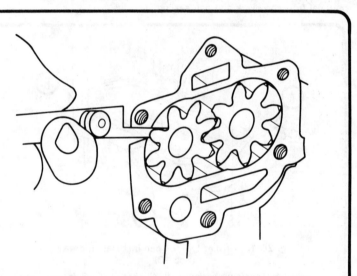

**Fig. 2C.19 Measure oil pump side gear clearance (Sec 14)**

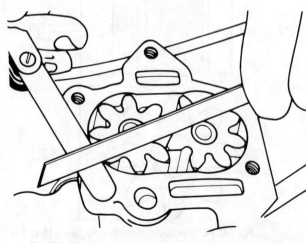

**Fig. 2C.20 Measure oil pump end clearance (Sec 14)**

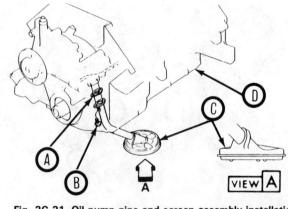

**Fig. 2C.21 Oil pump pipe and screen assembly installation details (Sec 15)**

*A Gasket          C Oil pump screen assembly*
*B Bolt            D Cylinder block*

3   Clean the screen and housing assembly thoroughly in solvent and dry with compressed air, if available.
4   Make sure the mating surfaces of the pipe flange and the engine block are clean and free of nicks and install the pump and screen assembly, using a new gasket. Install the retaining bolts and tighten them to the specified torque.

### 16   Rear main bearing cap oil seal — replacement (engine in vehicle)

1   Braided fabric seals inserted into grooves in the engine cylinder block and main bearing cap are used to seal against oil leakage around the crankshaft. The upper rear main bearing oil seal can be replaced only with the crankshaft removed (Chapter 2, Part D) but it can be repaired with the crankshaft in place. The main bearing cap oil seal can be replaced with the engine in the vehicle as described in Section 19.
2   Remove the oil pan (Section 13).
3   Remove the rear main bearing cap.
4   Carefully remove the oil seal from the main bearing cap.
5   Place a new seal in the groove with both ends projecting above the parting surface of the cap.
6   Use the handle of a hammer or similar tool to force the seal into the groove by rubbing down until the seal projects above the groove not more than 1/16-inch. Cut the ends of the seal flush with the surface of the cap with a single-edge razor blade.

7   Soak the neoprene seals which go into the grooves in the bearing cap in light oil or kerosene for one or two minutes.
8   Install the neoprene seals in the groove between the bearing cap and the crankcase. The seals are slightly undersize and swell in the presence of heat and oil. They are slightly longer than the groove in the bearing cap and must not be cut to fit.
9   Apply a small amount of RTV-type sealant at the joint where the bearing cap meets the crankcase to help eliminate oil leakage. A very thin coat is all that is necessary.
10  Install the bearing cap in the crankcase. Force the seals up into the bearing cap with a blunt instrument to be sure of a good seal at the upper parting line between the cap and case. Install the bolts and tighten to the specified torque.
11  Install the oil pan and bolts and tighten the bolts to the specified torque.

### 17   Rear main bearing upper oil seal — repair (engine in vehicle)

1   Although the crankshaft must be removed to install a new braided fabric seal, the upper seal can be repaired with the crankshaft in place.
2   Remove the oil pan.
3   Using GM tool J-21156-2, drive the old seal gently back into its groove, packing it tight. It will pack in to a depth of between 1/4-inch and 3/4-inch.
4   Repeat the procedure on the other end of the seal.

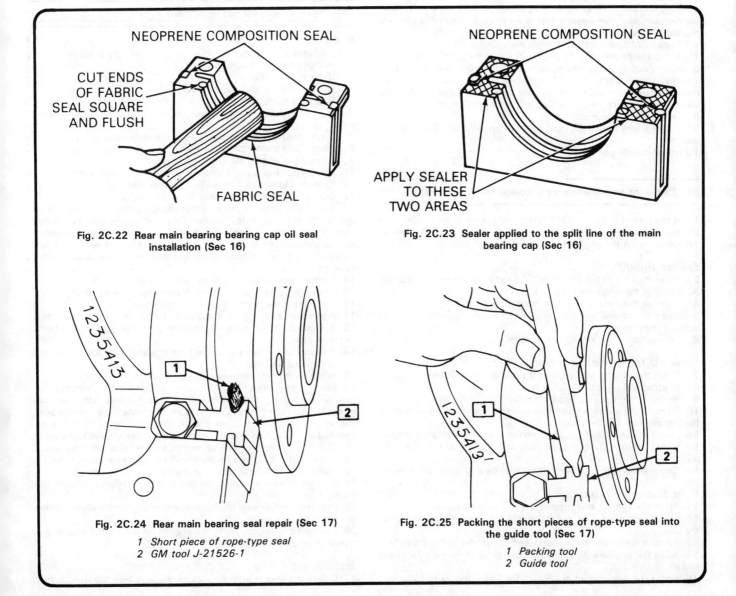

**Fig. 2C.22  Rear main bearing bearing cap oil seal installation (Sec 16)**

**Fig. 2C.23  Sealer applied to the split line of the main bearing cap (Sec 16)**

**Fig. 2C.24  Rear main bearing seal repair (Sec 17)**

1  Short piece of rope-type seal
2  GM tool J-21526-1

**Fig. 2C.25  Packing the short pieces of rope-type seal into the guide tool (Sec 17)**

1  Packing tool
2  Guide tool

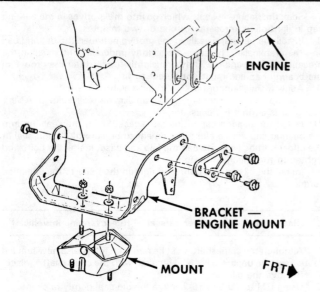

Fig. 2C.26 Engine mount installation details (Sec 18)

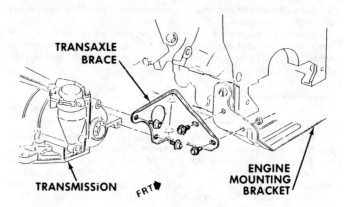

Fig. 2C.27 Transaxle-to-engine bracket istallation details (Sec 18)

5    Measure the amount that the seal was driven up in the groove on one side and add 1/16-inch. Remove the old seal from the main bearing cap. Use the main bearing cap as a fixture and cut off a piece of the old seal to the predetermined length.
6    Install GM tool J-21526-1 onto the cylinder block.
7    Using the packing tool (J-21256-2), work the short pieces of the previously cut seal into the guide tool (J-21256-1) and pack them into the cylinder block groove. The guide and packing tools have been machined to provide a built-in stop. Repeat this procedure on both sides. Using oil on the pieces of packing will ease installation.
8    Remove the guide tool.
9    Install a new seal in the main bearing cap (Section 18) and install the cap.
10   Install the oil pan.

## 18    Engine and transaxle mounts — replacement with engine in vehicle

1    If the rubber mounts have become hard, split or separated from the metal backing, they must be replaced. This operation may be carried out with the engine/transaxle still in the vehicle.

### Engine mounts
2    Raise the front of the vehicle and support it securely on jackstands.
3    Support the engine with a jack.
4    Remove the mount-to-engine mount bracket nuts.
5    Raise the engine slightly, remove the mount-to-frame nuts and remove the mount.
6    Installation is the reverse of removal.

### Forward transaxle mount
7    Raise the vehicle and support it securely on jackstands.
8    Support the transaxle with a jack.
9    Remove the mount-to-cradle nuts.
10   Remove the mount-to-transaxle support bracket nut and remove the mount from the vehicle.
11   Install the new mount and tighten the nut to the specified torque.
12   Install the mount-to-chassis nuts and tighten to the specified torque.
13   Remove the jack supporting the transaxle and lower the vehicle.

### Rear transaxle mounts
14   Raise the vehicle and support it securely on jackstands.
15   Place a jackstand under the rear cradle, remove the bolts and lower the cradle.
16   Remove the upper mount bolts and the cradle-to-mount nuts.
17   Raise the engine with a jack sufficiently to allow removal of the mount.
18   Install the new mount and install the upper mount bolts.

19   Remove the jack supporting the engine.
20   Raise the cradle into position and install the bolts.
21   Install the lower mount-to-cradle nuts.
22   Lower the vehicle.

## 19    Engine — removal and installation

### Removal
1    Disconnect the cable from the negative battery terminal.
2    Remove the hood (Chapter 11).
3    Drain the radiator.
4    Remove the air cleaner assembly.
5    Unplug the engine harness connector.
6    Mark all vacuum hoses for ease of reinstallation, then disconnect them.
7    Disconnect the detent cable from the carburetor lever.
8    Disconnect the throttle linkage.
9    Unplug the engine electrical connector.
10   Disconnect the ground strap at the engine forward strut.
11   Remove the radiator hoses from the engine.
12   Disconnect the heater hoses from the engine.
13   If equipped, remove the air conditioning compressor and brackets and lay them to one side. **Caution:** *Do not disconnect any of the air conditioning lines unless the system has been depressurized by a dealer service department or air conditioning technician, as personal injury may occur. Disconnection of the lines should not be necessary in this case.*
14   Remove power steering pump and bracket.
15   Raise the vehicle and support it securely on jackstands.
16   Disconnect the exhaust pipe from the manifold.
17   Disconnect and plug the fuel lines at the rubber hose connections.
18   Remove the front mount-to-cradle retaining nuts on the right side of the vehicle.
19   Disconnect the battery cables from the engine at the starter and transaxle housing bolt.
20   Remove the driveplate inspection cover.
21   Remove the converter-to-driveplate bolts. It will be necessary to turn the crankshaft to bring each of the bolts into view. Use a wrench on the large bolt at the front of the crankshaft. Mark the relative position of the converter and driveplate with a scribe so it can be re-installed in the same position. Engage a long screwdriver in the teeth of the driveplate to prevent movement as the bolts are loosened.
22   Remove the transaxle-to-engine block support bracket bolts.
23   Lower the vehicle support the transaxle with a jack.
24   Remove the engine strut bracket from the radiator support and swing it rearward.
25   Remove the transaxle-to-engine bolts, noting the installation of the ground stud location.
26   Connect a lifting device to the engine, lift it from the vehicle and mount it on an engine stand.

### Installation
27   Lower the engine into the vehicle, making sure the front mount

studs are properly located in the cradle on the right side of the vehicle.

28  With the engine weight still supported by the lifting device, align the transaxle with the engine block and install attaching bolts. Tighten the bolts to the specified torque.

29  Remove the lifting device from the engine.

30  If equipped, install the air conditioning compressor on the mounting bracket.

31  Raise the vehicle, support it securely on jackstands and install the transaxle-to-engine block support bracket bolts. Install the front mount-to-chassis nuts.

32  The remainder of installation is the reverse of removal.

33  Fill the cooling system with the specified coolant (Chapter 1).

34  Fill the engine with the correct grade of engine oil (Chapter 1).

35  Connect the positive battery cable, followed by the negative cable. If sparks or arcing occur as the negative cable is connected to the battery, make sure that all electrical accessories are turned off (check the dome light first). If arcing still occurs, make sure that all electrical wiring is properly connected to the engine and transaxle.

36  Refer to Chapter 2, Part D, for the recommended engine start-up sequence.

# Chapter 2 Part D
# General engine overhaul procedures

*Refer to Chapter 13 for Specifications and information applicable to 1986 and later models*

## Contents

Camshaft, lifters and bearings — inspection and bearing
   replacement ................................... 15
Crankshaft — inspection ........................... 17
Crankshaft — installation and main bearing oil clearance
   check ......................................... 21
Crankshaft — removal ............................. 12
Cylinder head — cleaning and inspection ............. 8
Cylinder head — disassembly ....................... 7
Cylinder head — reassembly ........................ 10
Engine block — cleaning ........................... 13
Engine block — inspection ......................... 14
Engine overhaul — disassembly sequence ............ 6
Engine overhaul — general information .............. 3
Engine overhaul — reassembly sequence ............. 23

Engine rebuilding alternatives ...................... 4
Engine removal — methods and precautions .......... 5
General information .............................. 1
Initial start-up and break-in after overhaul ........... 25
Main and connecting rod bearings — inspection ....... 18
Piston/connecting rod assembly — inspection ........ 16
Piston/connecting rod assembly — installation and bearing
   oil clearance check ............................. 22
Piston/connecting rod assembly — removal ........... 11
Piston rings — installation ......................... 19
Pre-oiling engine after overhaul (2.8 liter engines only) ...... 24
Rear main oil seal (V6 engines only) — installation ..... 20
Repair operations possible with the engine in vehicle ....... 2
Valves — servicing ............................... 9

## Specifications

### 2.5 liter four-cylinder engine
Oil pressure ............................................. 36 to 41 psi at 2000 rpm

#### Valves and related components
Valve face angle......................................... 45°
Valve seat angle......................................... 46°
Valve stem diameter
   Intake ............................................. 0.3425 to 0.3418 in (8.6995 to 8.6817 mm)
   Exhaust ........................................... 0.3418 to 0.3425 in (8.6817 to 8.6995 mm)
Stem-to-guide clearance
   Intake and top exhaust ............................. 0.0010 to 0.0027 in (0.0254 to 0.0686 mm)
   Bottom exhaust .................................... 0.0020 to 0.0037 in (0.0508 to 0.0939 mm)
Valve seat width
   Intake ............................................. 0.0353 to 0.0747 in (0.897 to 1.897 mm)
   Exhaust ........................................... 0.058 to 0.097 in (1.468 to 2.468 mm)
Valve spring installed height ............................. 1.69 in (42.93 mm)
Valve spring pressure and length (intake and exhaust)
   Valve closed ....................................... 1.66 in at 76 to 86 lbs.
   Valve open ........................................ 1.254 in at 122 to 180 lbs.
Pushrod length .......................................... 9.754 in (242.316 mm)

#### Crankshaft and connecting rods
Crankshaft end play ..................................... 0.0035 to 0.0085 in 0.0889 to 0.2159 mm)
Connecting rod end play (side clearance) ................. 0.006 to 0.022 in (0.1524 to 0.5588 mm)
Main bearing journal diameter ........................... 2.300 in (59.182 mm)
Main bearing oil clearance .............................. 0.0005 to 0.0026 in (0.0127 to 0.05588 mm)
Connecting rod bearing journal diameter ................. 2.000 in (50.8 mm)
Connecting rod bearing oil clearance .................... 0.0005 to 0.0026 in (0.0127 to 0.0660 mm)
Crankshaft journal taper/out-of-round limit .............. 0.0005 in (0.0127 mm)

#### Engine block
Cylinder bore diameter .................................. 4.000 in (101.6 mm)
Out-of-round limit ...................................... 0.0014 in (0.0356 mm)
Taper limit ............................................. 0.0005 in (0.0127 mm)

## Pistons and rings
Compression ring side clearance . . . . . . . . . . . . . . . . . . . . . 0.0030 in (0.0381 mm)
Piston diameter . . . . . . . . . . . . . . . . . . . . . . . . . . . . . . . . . 3.9971 to 3.9975 in (101.526 to 101.536 mm)
Piston-to-bore clearance
    Top . . . . . . . . . . . . . . . . . . . . . . . . . . . . . . . . . . . . . . . . 0.0025 to 0.0033 in (0.0635 to 0.0838 mm)
    Bottom . . . . . . . . . . . . . . . . . . . . . . . . . . . . . . . . . . . . . 0.0017 to 0.0041 in (0.043 to 0.104 mm)
Piston pin diameter . . . . . . . . . . . . . . . . . . . . . . . . . . . . . . 0.938 to 0.942 in (23.825 to 23.927 mm)
Pin-to-piston clearance . . . . . . . . . . . . . . . . . . . . . . . . . . . Loose; 0.003 to 0.005 in (0.076 to 0.127 mm)
Pin-to-rod clearance . . . . . . . . . . . . . . . . . . . . . . . . . . . . . Press fit
Piston ring end gap
    Top ring . . . . . . . . . . . . . . . . . . . . . . . . . . . . . . . . . . . . . 0.010 to 0.025 in (0.254 to 0.635 mm)
    Second ring . . . . . . . . . . . . . . . . . . . . . . . . . . . . . . . . . . 0.009 to 0.019 in (0.2286 to 0.4826 mm)
    Oil ring . . . . . . . . . . . . . . . . . . . . . . . . . . . . . . . . . . . . . . 0.015 to 0.055 in (0.381 to 1.397 mm)

## Camshaft
Lobe lift (intake and exhaust) . . . . . . . . . . . . . . . . . . . . . . 0.406 in (10.3124 mm)
Bearing journal diameter . . . . . . . . . . . . . . . . . . . . . . . . . . 1.869 in (47.4726 mm)
Bearing oil clearance . . . . . . . . . . . . . . . . . . . . . . . . . . . . . 0.0007 to 0.0027 in (0.0178 to 0.0685 mm)
Camshaft end play . . . . . . . . . . . . . . . . . . . . . . . . . . . . . . . 0.0015 to 0.0050 in (0.0381 to 0.127 mm)
Cylinder numbers . . . . . . . . . . . . . . . . . . . . . . . . . . . . . . . . 1-2-3-4 (front-to-rear)
Firing order . . . . . . . . . . . . . . . . . . . . . . . . . . . . . . . . . . . . 1-3-2-4

**Torque specifications**  **Ft-lbs**
Rocker arm nuts/bolts . . . . . . . . . . . . . . . . . . . . . . . . . . . . 20
Main bearing cap bolts . . . . . . . . . . . . . . . . . . . . . . . . . . . . 70
Connecting rod cap nuts . . . . . . . . . . . . . . . . . . . . . . . . . . 32
Cylinder head bolts . . . . . . . . . . . . . . . . . . . . . . . . . . . . . . 85
Oil pump driveshaft retainer plate bolts . . . . . . . . . . . . . . 10

# 2.8 liter V6 engine

## Valves and related components
Valve face angle . . . . . . . . . . . . . . . . . . . . . . . . . . . . . . . . 45°
Valve seat angle . . . . . . . . . . . . . . . . . . . . . . . . . . . . . . . . 46°
Valve seat runout . . . . . . . . . . . . . . . . . . . . . . . . . . . . . . . 0.002 in (0.05 mm) maximum
Stem-to-guide clearance . . . . . . . . . . . . . . . . . . . . . . . . . 0.001 to 0.0028 in (0.026 to 0.068 mm)
Valve seat width
    Intake . . . . . . . . . . . . . . . . . . . . . . . . . . . . . . . . . . . . . . . 0.049 to 0.059 in (1.25 to 1.50 mm)
    Exhaust . . . . . . . . . . . . . . . . . . . . . . . . . . . . . . . . . . . . . . 0.063 to 0.075 in (1.60 to 1.90 mm)
Valve spring installed height . . . . . . . . . . . . . . . . . . . . . . . 1.57 in (40.0 mm)
Valve spring free length . . . . . . . . . . . . . . . . . . . . . . . . . . 1.91 in (48.5 mm)
Valve spring pressure and length (intake and exhaust)
    Valve closed . . . . . . . . . . . . . . . . . . . . . . . . . . . . . . . . . . 1.57 in at 87.9 lbs.
    Valve open . . . . . . . . . . . . . . . . . . . . . . . . . . . . . . . . . . . 1.18 in at 194.9 lbs.

## Crankshaft and connecting rods
Crankshaft end play . . . . . . . . . . . . . . . . . . . . . . . . . . . . . 0.002 to 0.007 in (0.05 to 0.17 mm)
Connecting rod end play (side clearance) . . . . . . . . . . . . . 0.006 to 0.017 in (0.16 to 0.44 mm)
Main bearing journal diameter . . . . . . . . . . . . . . . . . . . . . . 2.4937 to 2.4946 in (63.340 to 63.364 mm)
Main bearing oil clearance . . . . . . . . . . . . . . . . . . . . . . . . 0.0017 to 0.0030 in (0.044 to 0.076 mm)
Connecting rod bearing journal diameter . . . . . . . . . . . . . 1.9983 to 1.9994 in (50.758 to 50.784 mm)
Connecting rod bearing oil clearance . . . . . . . . . . . . . . . . 0.0012 to 0.0037 in (0.035 to 0.095 mm)
Crankshaft journal taper/out-of-round limit . . . . . . . . . . . . 0.0002 in (0.005 mm)

## Engine block
Cylinder bore diameter . . . . . . . . . . . . . . . . . . . . . . . . . . . 3.504 to 3.507 in (88.992 to 89.070 mm)
Out-of-round limit . . . . . . . . . . . . . . . . . . . . . . . . . . . . . . . 0.0008 in (0.02 mm)
Taper limit . . . . . . . . . . . . . . . . . . . . . . . . . . . . . . . . . . . . 0.0008 in (0.02 mm)
Pistons and rings
Compression ring side clearance
    Top ring . . . . . . . . . . . . . . . . . . . . . . . . . . . . . . . . . . . . . 0.0019 to 0.0028 in (0.048 to 0.070 mm)
    Second ring . . . . . . . . . . . . . . . . . . . . . . . . . . . . . . . . . . 0.0016 to 0.0037 in (0.040 to 0.095 mm)
Oil ring side clearance . . . . . . . . . . . . . . . . . . . . . . . . . . . 0.0078 in (0.199 mm)
Piston-to-bore clearance
    Carburetor . . . . . . . . . . . . . . . . . . . . . . . . . . . . . . . . . . . 0.0006 to 0.0017 in (0.017 to 0.043 mm)
    Fuel injection . . . . . . . . . . . . . . . . . . . . . . . . . . . . . . . . . 0.0019 to 0.0022 in (0.048 to 0.055 mm)
Piston pin diameter . . . . . . . . . . . . . . . . . . . . . . . . . . . . . . 0.90526 to 0.90557 in (22.994 to 23.002 mm)
Pin-to-piston clearance . . . . . . . . . . . . . . . . . . . . . . . . . . . 0.00026 to 0.00036 in (0.0065 to 0.0091 mm)
Pin-to-rod clearance . . . . . . . . . . . . . . . . . . . . . . . . . . . . . 0.00074 to 0.00203 in (0.0187 to 0.0515 mm)
Piston ring end gap
    Top ring . . . . . . . . . . . . . . . . . . . . . . . . . . . . . . . . . . . . . 0.0098 to 0.0196 in (0.25 to 0.50 mm)
    Second ring . . . . . . . . . . . . . . . . . . . . . . . . . . . . . . . . . . 0.0098 to 0.0196 in (0.25 to 0.50 mm)
    Oil ring . . . . . . . . . . . . . . . . . . . . . . . . . . . . . . . . . . . . . . 0.020 to 0.055 in (0.51 to 1.40 mm)

## Camshaft

| | |
|---|---|
| Lobe lift | |
|     Intake . . . . . . . . . . . . . . . . . . . . . . . . . . . . . . . . . . . . . . . | 0.231 in (5.87 mm) |
|     Exhaust . . . . . . . . . . . . . . . . . . . . . . . . . . . . . . . . . . . . . . . | 0.262 in (6.67 mm) |
| Bearing journal diameter . . . . . . . . . . . . . . . . . . . . . . . . . . . | 1.868 to 1.870 in (47.44 to 47.49 mm) |
| Bearing oil clearance . . . . . . . . . . . . . . . . . . . . . . . . . . . . . . . | 0.001 to 0.004 in (0.026 to 0.101 mm) |
| Cylinder numbers | |
|     Right bank . . . . . . . . . . . . . . . . . . . . . . . . . . . . . . . . . . . . . | 1-3-5 (front-to-rear) |
|     Left bank . . . . . . . . . . . . . . . . . . . . . . . . . . . . . . . . . . . . . . | 2-4-6 (front-to-rear) |

| **Torque specifications** | **Ft-lbs** |
|---|---|
| Rocker arm nuts/bolts . . . . . . . . . . . . . . . . . . . . . . . . . . . . . . | 45 |
| Main bearing cap bolts . . . . . . . . . . . . . . . . . . . . . . . . . . . . . . | 70 |
| Connecting rod cap nuts . . . . . . . . . . . . . . . . . . . . . . . . . . . . | 37 |
| Cylinder head bolts . . . . . . . . . . . . . . . . . . . . . . . . . . . . . . . . | 68 |

# 3.0 and 3.8 liter V6 engine

## Valves and related components

| | |
|---|---|
| Valve lifter diameter . . . . . . . . . . . . . . . . . . . . . . . . . . . . . . . . | 0.8420 to 0.8427 in (21.3868 to 21.4046 mm) |
| Valve lifter clearance in crankcase . . . . . . . . . . . . . . . . . . . | 0.0008 to 0.0025 in (0.0203 to 0.0635 mm) |
| Intake valve | |
|     Head diameter . . . . . . . . . . . . . . . . . . . . . . . . . . . . . . . . . | 1.715 to 1.705 in (43.561 to 43.307 mm) |
|     Face angle . . . . . . . . . . . . . . . . . . . . . . . . . . . . . . . . . . . . | 45° |
|     Seat angle . . . . . . . . . . . . . . . . . . . . . . . . . . . . . . . . . . . . | 46° |
|     Seat width . . . . . . . . . . . . . . . . . . . . . . . . . . . . . . . . . . . . | 0.062 in (1.57 mm) |
|     Seat runout limit . . . . . . . . . . . . . . . . . . . . . . . . . . . . . . . | 0.002 in (0.05 mm) |
|     Stem diameter . . . . . . . . . . . . . . . . . . . . . . . . . . . . . . . . . | 0.3412 to 0.3401 in (8.666 to 8.638 mm) |
|     Clearance in guide . . . . . . . . . . . . . . . . . . . . . . . . . . . . . . | 0.0015 to 0.0035 in (0.038 to 0.089 mm) |
| Exhaust valve | |
|     Head diameter . . . . . . . . . . . . . . . . . . . . . . . . . . . . . . . . . | 1.505 to 1.495 in (38.227 to 37.973 mm) |
|     Face angle . . . . . . . . . . . . . . . . . . . . . . . . . . . . . . . . . . . . | 45° |
|     Seat angle . . . . . . . . . . . . . . . . . . . . . . . . . . . . . . . . . . . . | 46° |
|     Seat width . . . . . . . . . . . . . . . . . . . . . . . . . . . . . . . . . . . . | 0.074 to 0.104 in (1.905 to 2.642 mm) |
|     Seat runout limits . . . . . . . . . . . . . . . . . . . . . . . . . . . . . . | 0.002 in (0.05 mm) |
|     Stem diameter . . . . . . . . . . . . . . . . . . . . . . . . . . . . . . . . . | 0.3412 to 0.3405 in (8.666 to 8.649 mm) |
|     Clearance in guide . . . . . . . . . . . . . . . . . . . . . . . . . . . . . . | 0.0015 to 0.0032 in (0.038 to 0.081 mm) |
| Valve springs | |
|     Free length . . . . . . . . . . . . . . . . . . . . . . . . . . . . . . . . . . . . | 2.03 in (51.56 mm) |
|     Valve spring pressure | |
|         Closed . . . . . . . . . . . . . . . . . . . . . . . . . . . . . . . . . . . . | 59 to 69 lbs at 1.73 in (262 to 307 Nm at 43.66 mm) |
|         Open . . . . . . . . . . . . . . . . . . . . . . . . . . . . . . . . . . . . . . | 176 to 190 lbs at 1.34 in (783 to 845 Nm at 34.04 mm) |

## Crankshaft and connecting rods

| | |
|---|---|
| Crankshaft end play at thrust bearing . . . . . . . . . . . . . . . . | 0.003 to 0.011 in (0.762 to 0.2794 mm) |
| Connecting rod journal diameter . . . . . . . . . . . . . . . . . . . . . | 2.2487 to 2.2495 in (57.1169 to 57.1373 mm) |
| Connecting rod journal runout and taper limits . . . . . . . . . . | 0.0005 in (0.013 mm) |
| Connecting rod bearing clearance . . . . . . . . . . . . . . . . . . . . | 0.0005 to 0.0026 in (0.013 to 0.06 mm) |
| Connecting rod bearing side clearance . . . . . . . . . . . . . . . . | 0.005 to 0.026 in (0.13 to 0.66 mm) |
| Main bearing journal diameter . . . . . . . . . . . . . . . . . . . . . . . | 2.4995 in (63.4873 mm) |
| Main bearing-to-journal clearance . . . . . . . . . . . . . . . . . . . | 0.0003 to 0.0018 in (0.0076 to 0.0457 mm) |
| Main bearing overall length | |
|     Number 1 . . . . . . . . . . . . . . . . . . . . . . . . . . . . . . . . . . . . . | 0.864 in (21.9456 mm) |
|     Number 2 . . . . . . . . . . . . . . . . . . . . . . . . . . . . . . . . . . . . . | 1.057 in (26.8478 mm) |
|     Number 3 . . . . . . . . . . . . . . . . . . . . . . . . . . . . . . . . . . . . . | 0.864 in (21.9456 mm) |
|     Number 4 . . . . . . . . . . . . . . . . . . . . . . . . . . . . . . . . . . . . . | 0.864 in (21.9456 mm) |

## Engine block

| | |
|---|---|
| Cylinder bore diameter . . . . . . . . . . . . . . . . . . . . . . . . . . . . . | 3.80 in (96.5 mm) |
| Out-of-round limit . . . . . . . . . . . . . . . . . . . . . . . . . . . . . . . . . | 0.0005 in (0.013 mm) |
| Taper limit . . . . . . . . . . . . . . . . . . . . . . . . . . . . . . . . . . . . . . . | 0.0005 in (0.013 mm) |

## Pistons and rings

| | |
|---|---|
| Piston clearance limits | |
|     Top land . . . . . . . . . . . . . . . . . . . . . . . . . . . . . . . . . . . . . . | 0.046 to 0.056 in (1.168 to 1.422 mm) |
|     Skirt top . . . . . . . . . . . . . . . . . . . . . . . . . . . . . . . . . . . . . . | 0.0008 to 0.0020 in (0.203 to 0.508 mm) |
|     Skirt bottom . . . . . . . . . . . . . . . . . . . . . . . . . . . . . . . . . . . | 0.0013 to 0.0035 in (0.033 to 0.0889 mm) |
| Ring groove depth | |
|     Number 1 and 2 compression rings . . . . . . . . . . . . . . . . . | 0.184 to 0.194 in (4.724 to 4.928 mm) |
|     Oil ring . . . . . . . . . . . . . . . . . . . . . . . . . . . . . . . . . . . . . . . | 0.188 to 0.196 in (4.7752 to 4.9927 mm) |
| Ring width | |
|     Number 1 and 2 compression rings . . . . . . . . . . . . . . . . . | 0.077 to 0.078 in (1.955 to 1.981 mm) |
|     Oil ring . . . . . . . . . . . . . . . . . . . . . . . . . . . . . . . . . . . . . . . | 0.183 to 0.189 in (4.648 to 4.80 mm) |

| | |
|---|---|
| Piston ring end gap | |
| Top and second ring . . . . . . . . . . . . . . . . . . . . . . | 0.013 to 0.023 in (0.33 to 0.58 mm) |
| Oil ring . . . . . . . . . . . . . . . . . . . . . . . . . . . . | 0.015 to 0.035 in (0.38 to 0.89 mm) |
| Piston ring side clearance | |
| Top and second ring . . . . . . . . . . . . . . . . . . . . . | 0.003 to 0.005 in (0.08 to 0.13 mm) |
| Oil ring . . . . . . . . . . . . . . . . . . . . . . . . . . . | 0.0035 in (0.09 mm) |
| Piston-to-bore clearance | |
| Top . . . . . . . . . . . . . . . . . . . . . . . . . . . . . . | 0.001 to 0.002 in (0.02 to 0.05 mm) |
| Bottom . . . . . . . . . . . . . . . . . . . . . . . . . . . . | 0.0015 to 0.035 in (0.04 to 0.09 mm) |
| Piston pin diameter . . . . . . . . . . . . . . . . . . . . . . . | 0.9391 to 0.9394 in (23.85 to 23.86 mm) |
| Pin-to-rod clearance . . . . . . . . . . . . . . . . . . . . . . | 0.00075 to 0.00125 in (0.019 to 0.032 mm) |
| Pin-to-rod clearance . . . . . . . . . . . . . . . . . . . . . . | 0.0004 to 0.0007 in (0.010 to 0.018 mm) |

### Camshaft

| | |
|---|---|
| Bearing journal diameter . . . . . . . . . . . . . . . . . . . . . | 1.785 to 1.7886 in (45.339 to 45.364 mm) |
| Journal clearance in bearings . . . . . . . . . . . . . . . . . . | 0.0005 to 0.0025 in (0.013 to 0.0645 mm) |
| Cylinder numbers | |
| Right bank . . . . . . . . . . . . . . . . . . . . . . . . . . | 2-4-6 (front-to-rear) |
| Left bank . . . . . . . . . . . . . . . . . . . . . . . . . . | 1-3-5 (front-to-rear) |
| Firing order . . . . . . . . . . . . . . . . . . . . . . . . . . . | 1-6-5-4-3-2 |

| Torque specifications | Ft-lbs |
|---|---|
| Spark plugs . . . . . . . . . . . . . . . . . . . . . . . . . . . | 5 |
| Crankshaft bearing cap bolts . . . . . . . . . . . . . . . . . . | 100 |
| Crankshaft balancer bolt . . . . . . . . . . . . . . . . . . . . . | 200 to 225 |
| Connecting rod bolts . . . . . . . . . . . . . . . . . . . . . . | 40 |
| Cylinder head bolts . . . . . . . . . . . . . . . . . . . . . . . | 80 |
| Cylinder block drain bolt . . . . . . . . . . . . . . . . . . . . | 22 |
| Driveplate or flywheel-to-crankshaft bolt . . . . . . . . . . . . | 60 |
| Oil pump | |
| Cover-to-timing chain cover bolt . . . . . . . . . . . . . . . | 10 |
| Pressure regulator retainer bolt . . . . . . . . . . . . . . . | 35 |
| Pump and screen housing-to-cylinder | |
| block bolt . . . . . . . . . . . . . . . . . . . . . . . . . . | 8 |
| Timing chain cover bolt . . . . . . . . . . . . . . . . . . . . . | 30 |
| Rocker arm shaft bolt . . . . . . . . . . . . . . . . . . . . . . | 30 |

## 1   General information

Included in this portion of Chapter 2 are the general overhaul procedures for the cylinder head and internal engine components. The information ranges from advice concerning preparation for an overhaul and the purchase of replacement parts to detailed, step-by-step procedures covering removal and installation of internal engine components and the inspection of parts.

The following Sections have been written based on the assumption that the engine has been removed from the vehicle. For information concerning in-vehicle engine repair, as well as removal and installation of the external components necessary for the overhaul, see Part A, B or C of Chapter 2 (depending on engine type) and Section 2 of this Part.

The specifications included here are only those necessary for the inspection and overhaul procedures which follow. Refer to Part A, B or C for additional specifications related to the various engines covered in this manual.

## 2   Repair operations possible with the engine in the vehicle

Many major repair operations can be accomplished without removing the engine from the vehicle.

It is a good idea to clean the engine compartment and the exterior of the engine with some type of pressure washer before any work is begun. A clean engine will make the job easier and will prevent the possibility of getting dirt into internal areas of the engine.

Remove the hood (Chapter 11) and cover the fenders to provide as much working room as possible and to prevent damage to the painted surfaces.

If oil or coolant leaks develop, indicating a need for gasket or seal replacement, the repairs can generally be made with the engine in the vehicle. The oil pan gasket, the cylinder head gasket, intake and exhaust manifold gaskets, timing cover gaskets and the front crankshaft oil seal are accessible with the engine in place.

Exterior engine components, such as the water pump, the starter motor, the alternator, the distributor, the fuel pump and the carburetor or TBI, as well as the intake and exhaust manifolds, are quite easily removed for repair with the engine in place.

Since the cylinder heads can be removed without pulling the engine, valve component servicing can also be accomplished with the engine in the vehicle.

Replacement of, repairs to or inspection of the timing sprockets and chain and the oil pump are all possible with the engine in place.

In extreme cases caused by a lack of necessary equipment, repair or replacement of piston rings, pistons, connecting rods and rod bearings and reconditioning of the cylinder bores is possible with the engine in the vehicle. However, this practice is not recommended because of the cleaning and preparation work that must be done to the components involved.

Detailed removal, inspection, repair and installation procedures for the above mentioned components can be found in the appropriate Part of Chapter 2 or the other Chapters in this manual.

## 3   Engine overhaul — general information

It is not always easy to determine when, or if, an engine should be completely overhauled, as a number of factors must be considered.

High mileage is not necessarily an indication that an overhaul is needed, while low mileage does not preclude the need for an overhaul. Frequency of servicing is probably the most important consideration. An engine that has had regular and frequent oil and filter changes, as well as other required maintenance, will most likely give many thousands of miles of reliable service. Conversely, a neglected engine may require an overhaul very early in its life.

Excessive oil consumption is an indication that piston rings and/or valve guides are in need of attention. Make sure, however, that oil leaks are not responsible before deciding that the rings and guides are bad. Have a cylinder compression or leak-down test performed by an experienced tune-up mechanic to determine the extent of the work required.

If the engine is making obvious knocking or rumbling noises, the connecting rod and/or main bearings are probably at fault. Check the oil pressure with a gauge, installed in place of the oil pressure sending unit, and compare it to the Specifications. If it is extremely low, the bearings and/or oil pump are probably worn out.

Loss of power, rough running, excessive valve train noise and high fuel consumption rates may also point to the need for an overhaul, especially if they are all present at the same time. If a complete tune-up does not remedy the situation, major mechanical work is the only solution.

An engine overhaul involves restoring the internal parts to the specifications of a new engine. During an overhaul, the piston rings are replaced and the cylinder walls are reconditioned (rebored or honed). If a rebore is done, new pistons are also required. The main and connecting rod bearings are replaced with new ones and, if necessary, the crankshaft may be reground to restore the journals. Generally, the valves are serviced as well, since they are usually in less-than-perfect condition at this point. While the engine is being overhauled other components, such as the carburetor, distributor, starter and alternator can be rebuilt as well. The end result should be a like-new engine that will give many trouble-free miles.

Before beginning the engine overhaul, read through the entire procedure to familiarize yourself with the scope and requirements of the job. Overhauling an engine is not difficult, but it is time consuming. Plan on the vehicle being tied up for a minimum of two weeks, especially if parts must be taken to an automotive machine shop for repair or reconditioning. Check on availability of parts and make sure that any necessary special tools and equipment are obtained in advance. Most work can be done with typical hand tools, although a number of precision measuring tools are required for inspecting parts to determine if they must be replaced. Often an automotive machine shop will handle the inspection of parts and offer advice concerning reconditioning and replacement. **Note:** *Always wait until the engine has been completely disassembled and all components, especially the engine block, have been inspected before deciding what service and repair operations must be performed by an automotive machine shop.* Since the block's condition will be the major factor to consider when determining whether to overhaul the original engine or buy a rebuilt one, never purchase parts or have machine work done on other components until the block has been thoroughly inspected. As a general rule, time is the primary cost of an overhaul, so it does not pay to install worn or sub-standard parts.

As a final note, to ensure maximum life and minimum trouble from a rebuilt engine, everything must be assembled with care in a spotlessly clean environment.

## 4   Engine rebuilding alternatives

The do-it-yourselfer is faced with a number of options when performing an engine overhaul. The decision to replace the engine block, piston/connecting rod assemblies and crankshaft depends on a number of factors, with the primary consideration being the condition of the block. Other considerations are cost, access to machine shop facilities, parts availability, time required to complete the project and experience.

Some of the rebuilding alternatives include:

**Individual parts** — If the inspection procedures reveal that the engine block and most engine components are in reusable condition, purchasing individual parts may be the most economical alternative. The block, crankshaft and piston/connecting rod assemblies should all be inspected carefully. Even if the block shows little wear, the cylinder bores should receive a finish hone; a job for an automotive machine shop.

**Master kit (crankshaft kit)** — This rebuild package usually consists of a reground crankshaft and a matched set of pistons and connecting rods. The pistons will already be installed on the connecting rods. These kits are commonly available for standard cylinder bores, as well as for engine blocks which have been bored to a regular oversize.

**Short block** — A short block consists of an engine block with a crankshaft and piston/connecting rod assemblies already installed. All new bearings are incorporated and all clearances will be correct. Depending on where the short block is purchased, a guarantee may be included. The existing camshaft, valve train components, cylinder head and external parts can be bolted to the short block with little or

no machine shop work necessary.

**Long block** — A long block consists of a short block plus an oil pump, oil pan, cylinder head, rocker arm cover, camshaft and valve train components, timing sprockets and chain and timing chain cover. All components are installed with new bearings, seals and gaskets incorporated throughout. The installation of manifolds and external parts is all that is necessary. Some form of guarantee is usually included with the purchase.

Give careful thought to which alternative is best for you and discuss the situation with local automotive machine shops, auto parts dealers or dealership parts men before ordering or purchasing replacement parts.

## 5   Engine removal — methods and precautions

If it has been decided that an engine must be removed for overhaul or major repair work, certain preliminary steps should be taken.

Locating a suitable work area is extremely important. A shop is, of course, the most desirable place to work. Adequate work space, along with storage space for the vehicle, is very important. If a shop or garage is not available, at the very least a flat, level, clean work surface made of concrete or asphalt is required.

Cleaning the engine compartment and engine prior to removal will help keep tools clean and organized.

An engine hoist or A-frame will also be necessary. Make sure that the equipment is rated in excess of the combined weight of the engine and its accessories. Safety is of primary importance, considering the potential hazards involved in lifting the engine out of the vehicle.

If the engine is being removed by a novice, a helper should be available. Advice and aid from someone more experienced would also be helpful. There are many instances when one person cannot simultaneously perform all of the operations required when lifting the engine out of the vehicle.

Plan the operation ahead of time. Arrange for or obtain all the tools and equipment you will need prior to beginning the job. Some of the equipment necessary to perform engine removal and installation safely and with relative ease are, in addition to an engine hoist, a heavy duty floor jack, complete sets of wrenches and sockets as described in the front of this manual, wooden blocks and plenty of rags and cleaning solvent for mopping up the inevitable spills. If the hoist is to be rented, make sure that you arrange for it in advance and perform beforehand all of the operations possible without it. This will save you money and time.

Plan for the vehicle to be out of use for a considerable amount of time. A machine shop will be required to perform some of the work which the do-it-yourselfer cannot accomplish due to a lack of special equipment. These shops often have a busy schedule, so it would be wise to consult them before removing the engine in order to accurately estimate the amount of time required to rebuild or repair components that may need work.

Always use extreme caution when removing and installing the engine. Serious injury can result from careless actions. Plan ahead. Take your time and a job of this nature, although major, can be accomplished successfully.

## 6   Engine overhaul disassembly sequence

1    It is much easier to disassemble and work on the engine if it is mounted on a portable engine stand. These stands can often be rented for a reasonable fee from an equipment rental yard. Before the engine is mounted on a stand, the flywheel/driveplate should be removed from the engine (refer to Chapter 8).

2    If a stand is not available, it is possible to disassemble the engine with it blocked up on a sturdy workbench or on the floor. Be careful not to tip or drop the engine when working without a stand.

3    If you are going to obtain a rebuilt engine, all external components must come off your old engine to be transferred to the replacement engine, just as they will if you are doing a complete engine overhaul yourself. These include:

Alternator and brackets
Emissions control components
Distributor, spark plug wires and spark plugs

Thermostat and housing cover
Water pump
Carburetor/fuel injection components
Intake and exhaust manifolds
Oil filter
Fuel pump
Engine mounts
Flywheel or driveplate

**Note:** *When removing the external components from the engine, pay close attention to details that may be helpful or important during installation. Note the installed position of gaskets, seals, spacers, pins, washers, bolts and other small items.*

4    If you are obtaining a short block, which consists of the engine block, crankshaft, pistons and connecting rods all assembled, then the cylinder head, oil pan and oil pump will have to be removed as well. See *Engine rebuilding alternatives* for additional information regarding the different possibilities to be considered.

5    If you are planning a complete overhaul, the engine must be disassembled and the components removed in the following order:
Rocker arm cover
Cylinder head and pushrods
Valve lifters
Timing chain cover
Timing chain/sprockets/gears
Camshaft
Oil pan
Oil pump
Piston/connecting rod assemblies
Crankshaft

6    Before beginning the disassembly and overhaul procedures, make sure the following items are available:
Common hand tools
Small cardboard boxes or plastic bags for storing parts
Gasket scraper
Ridge reamer
Vibration damper puller
Micrometers
Small hole gauges
Telescoping gauges
Dial indicator set
Valve spring compressor
Cylinder surfacing hone
Piston ring groove cleaning tool
Electric drill motor
Tap and die set
Wire brushes
Cleaning solvent

## 7    Cylinder head – disassembly

**Note:** *New and rebuilt cylinder heads are commonly available for most engines at dealerships and auto parts stores. Due to the fact that some specialized tools are necessary for the disassembly and inspection procedures, and replacement parts may not be readily available, it may be more practical and economical for the home mechanic to purchase a replacement head rather than taking the time to disassemble, inspect and recondition the original head.*

1    Cylinder head disassembly involves removal of the intake and exhaust valves and their related components. If they are still in place, remove the nuts or bolts and pivot balls, then separate the rocker arms and/or shaft from the cylinder head. Label the parts or store them separately so they can be reinstalled in their original locations.

2    Before the valves are removed, arrange to label and store them, along with their related components, so they can be kept separate and reinstalled in the same valve guides. On 2.5 liter four-cylinder and 2.8 liter V6 engines, measure the valve spring installed height for each valve and compare it to the Specifications. If it is greater than specified, the valve seats and valve faces need attention.

3    Compress the valve spring with a spring compressor and remove the keepers (photo). Carefully release the valve spring compressor and remove the retainer, the shield (if so equipped), the springs, the valve guide seal and/or O-ring seal, any spring seat shims and the valve from the head. If the valve binds in the guide (won't pull through), push it back into the head and deburr the area around the keeper groove with

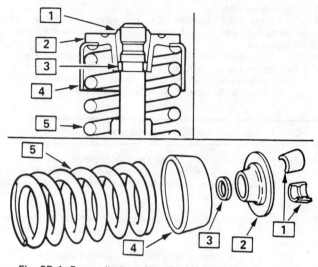

**Fig. 2D.1 Four-cylinder engine valve components — note the location of the valve stem seals (Sec 7)**

| | |
|---|---|
| 1   Keepers | 4   Shield |
| 2   Retainer | 5   Spring |
| 3   Valve stem O-ring seal | |

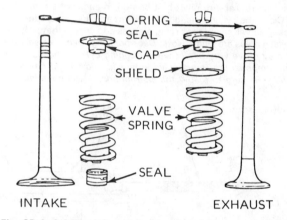

**Fig. 2D.2  2.8 liter V6 engine valve components — note the valve stem seal locations (Sec 7)**

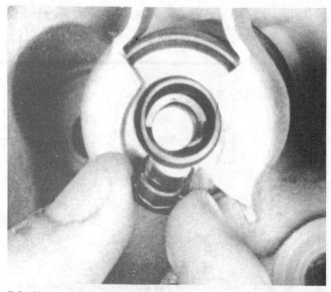

7.3   Use a valve spring compressor to compress the springs, then remove the keepers from the valve stem

a fine file or whetstone.

4   Repeat the procedure for the remaining valves. Remember to keep together all the parts for each valve so they can be reinstalled in the same locations.

5   Once the valves have been removed and safely stored, the head should be thoroughly cleaned and inspected. If a complete engine overhaul is being done, finish the engine disassembly procedures before beginning the cylinder head cleaning and inspection process.

## 8   Cylinder head — cleaning and inspection

1   Thorough cleaning of the cylinder head and related valve train components, followed by a detailed inspection, will enable you to decide how much valve service work must be done during the engine overhaul.

### Cleaning

2   Scrape away all traces of old gasket material and sealing compound from the head gasket, intake manifold and exhaust manifold sealing surfaces.

3   Remove any built-up scale around the coolant passages.

4   Run a stiff wire brush through the oil holes to remove any deposits that may have formed in them.

5   It is a good idea to run a tap into each of the threaded holes to remove any corrosion and thread sealant that may be present. If compressed air is available, use it to clear the holes of the debris produced by this operation.

6   Clean the exhaust and intake manifold stud threads with a die. Clean the rocker arm pivot bolt or stud threads with a wire brush.

7   Clean the cylinder head with solvent and dry it thoroughly. Compressed air will speed the drying process and ensure that all holes and recessed areas are clean. **Note:** *Decarbonizing chemicals are available and may prove very useful when cleaning cylinder heads and valve train components. They are very caustic and should be used with caution. Be sure to follow the instructions on the container.*

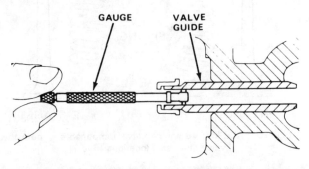

**Fig. 2D.3  Use a small hole gauge to determine the inside diameter of the valve guides (the gauge is then measured with a micrometer) (Sec 8)**

8   Clean the rocker arms, pivot balls and pushrods with solvent and dry them thoroughly. Compressed air will speed the drying process and can be used to clean out the oil passages.

9   Clean all the valve springs, keepers, retainers, shields and spring seat shims with solvent and dry them thoroughly. Do the components from one valve at a time to avoid mixing up the parts.

10  Scrape off any heavy deposits that may have formed on the valves, then use a motorized wire brush to remove deposits from the valve heads and stems. Again, make sure the valves do not get mixed up.

### Inspection

#### Cylinder head

11  Inspect the head very carefully for cracks, evidence of coolant leakage or other damage. If cracks are found, a new cylinder head should be obtained.

12  Using a straightedge and feeler gauge, check the head gasket mating surface for warpage. If the warpage exceeds 0.006-inch over the length of the head, it can be resurfaced at an automotive machine shop.

13  Examine the valve seats in each of the combustion chambers. If they are pitted, cracked or burned, the head will require valve service that is beyond the scope of the home mechanic.

14  Measure the inside diameter of the valve guides (at both ends and the center of each guide) with a small hole gauge and a 0-to-1-inch micrometer. Record the measurements for future reference. These measurements, along with the valve stem diameter measurements, will enable you to compute the valve stem-to-guide clearances. These clearances, when compared to the Specifications, will be one factor that will determine the extent of valve service work required. The guides are measured at the ends and at the center to determine if they are worn in a bellmouth pattern (more wear at the ends). If they are, guide reconditioning or replacement is necessary. As an alternative, use a dial indicator to measure the lateral movement of each valve stem with the valve in the guide and approximately 1/16-inch off the seat (see the accompanying illustration).

#### Rocker arm components

15  Check the rocker arm faces, where they contact the pushrod ends and valve stems, for pits, wear and rough spots. Check the pivot contact areas as well.

16  Inspect the pushrod ends for scuffing and excessive wear. Roll the pushrod on a flat surface, such as a piece of glass, to determine if it is bent.

17  Any damaged or excessively worn parts must be replaced with new ones.

#### Valves

18  Carefully inspect each valve face for cracks, pits and burned spots. Check the valve stem and neck for cracks. Rotate the valve and check for any obvious indication that it is bent. Check the end of the stem for pits and excessive wear. The presence of any of these conditions indicates the need for valve service by a properly equipped shop.

19  Measure the width of the valve margin on each valve and compare it to Specifications. Any valve with a margin narrower than specified will have to be replaced with a new one.

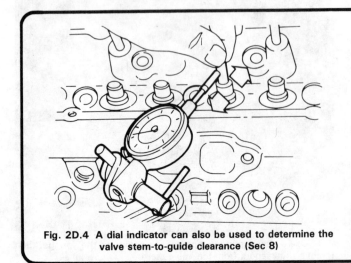

**Fig. 2D.4  A dial indicator can also be used to determine the valve stem-to-guide clearance (Sec 8)**

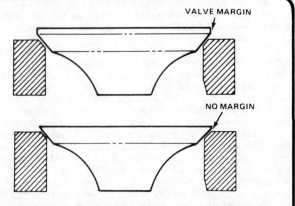

**Fig. 2D.5  The margin width on each valve must be as specified (if no margin exists, the valve must be replaced) (Sec 8)**

20  Measure the valve stem diameter (photo). **Note:** *The exhaust valves used in the 2.5 liter four-cylinder engine have tapered stems and are approximately 0.001-inch larger at the tip end than at the head end.* By subtracting the stem diameter from the corresponding valve guide diameter, the valve stem-to-guide clearance is obtained. Compare the results to the Specifications. If the stem-to-guide clearance is greater than specified, the guides will have to be reconditioned and new valves may have to be installed, depending on the condition of the old valves.

### Valve components

21  Check each valve spring for wear on the ends and pits. Measure the free length (photo) and compare it to the Specifications. Any springs that are shorter than specified have sagged and should not be reused. Stand the spring on a flat surface and check it for squareness (photo).

22  Check the spring retainers and keepers for obvious wear and cracks. Any questionable parts should be replaced with new ones, as extensive damage will occur in the event of failure during engine operation.

23  If the inspection process indicates that the valve components are in generally poor condition and worn beyond the limits specified, which is usually the case in an engine that is being overhauled, reassemble the valves in the cylinder head and refer to Section 9 for valve servicing recommendations.

24  If the inspection turns up no excessively worn parts, and if the valve faces and seats are in good condition, the valve train components can be reinstalled in the cylinder head without major servicing. Refer to the appropriate Section for cylinder head reassembly procedures.

## 9  Valves — servicing

1  Because of the complex nature of the job and the special tools and equipment needed, servicing of the valves, the valve seats and the valve guides (commonly known as a *valve job*) is best left to a professional.

2  The home mechanic can remove and disassemble the head, do the initial cleaning and inspection, then reassemble and deliver the head to a dealer service department or an automotive machine shop for the actual valve servicing.

3  The dealer service department, or automotive machine shop, will remove the valves and springs, recondition or replace the valves and valve seats, recondition the valve guides, check and replace the valve springs, spring retainers and keepers (as necessary), replace the valve

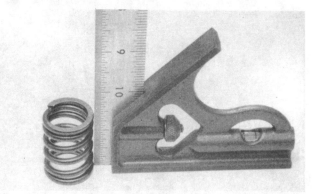

8.20  Measure the valve stem diameter at three points

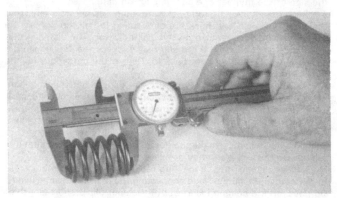

8.21A  Measure the free length of each valve spring with a dial or vernier caliper

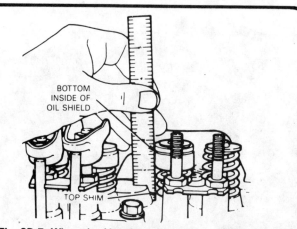

8.21B  Check each valve spring for squareness

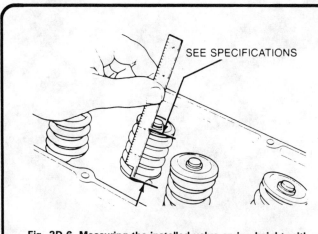

**Fig. 2D.6  Measuring the installed valve spring height with a steel rule (V6 engine intake valves only) (Sec 9)**

SEE SPECIFICATIONS

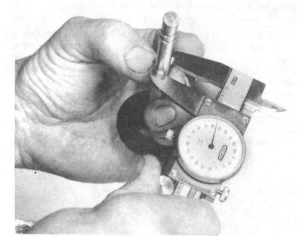

BOTTOM INSIDE OF OIL SHIELD

TOP SHIM

**Fig. 2D.7  When checking the valve spring height on 2.8 liter V6 engine exhaust valves and all four-cylinder engine valves, the measurement is made up to the bottom inside surface of the oil shield (Sec 9)**

seals with new ones, reassemble the valve components and make sure the installed spring height is correct. The cylinder head gasket surface will also be resurfaced if it is warped.

4    After the valve job has been performed by a professional, the head will be in like-new condition. When the head is returned, be sure to clean it again to remove any metal particles and abrasive grit that may still be present from the valve service or head resurfacing operations. Use compressed air, if available, to blow out all the oil holes and passages.

## 10   Cylinder head — reassembly

1    Regardless of whether or not the head was sent to an automotive repair shop for valve servicing, make sure it is clean before beginning reassembly.

2    If the head was sent out for valve servicing, the valves and related components will already be in place. Begin the reassembly procedure with Step 6.

3    Install new seals on each of the valve guides. Using a hammer and a deep socket, gently tap each seal into place until it is properly seated on the guide. Do not twist or cock the seals during installation or they will not seal properly on the valve stems.

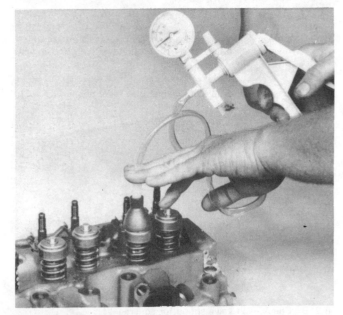

10.7   Checking the valve stem seals for leakage

4    Install the valves, taking care not to damage the new valve stem oil seals, drop the valve spring shim(s) around the valve guide boss and set the valve spring, cap and retainer in place.

5    Compress the spring with a valve compressor tool and install the valve locks. Release the compressor tool, making sure the locks are seated properly in the valve stem upper groove. If necessary, grease can be used to hold the locks in place while the compressor tool is released.

6    Double-check the installed valve spring height. If it was correct before reassembly it should still be within the specified limits. If it is not, install an additional valve spring seat shims (available from your dealer) to bring the height to within the specified limit.

7    Check the valve stem O-ring seals with a vacuum pump and adapter (photo). A properly installed oil seal should not leak.

8    Install the rocker arms and tighten the nuts to the specified torque. Be sure to lubricate the ball pivots with moly-base grease or engine assembly lube.

## 11   Piston/connecting rod assembly — removal

1    Prior to removal of the piston/connecting rod assemblies, the engine should be positioned upright.

2    Using a ridge reamer, completely remove the ridge at the top of each cylinder. Follow the manufacturer's instructions provided with the ridge reaming tool (photo). Failure to remove the ridge before attempting to remove the piston/connecting rod assemblies will result in piston breakage.

3    After the cylinder wear ridges have been removed, turn the engine upside-down.

4    Before the connecting rods are removed, check the end play. Mount a dial indicator with its stem in line with the crankshaft and touching the side of the number one connecting rod cap.

5    Push the connecting rod backward, as far as possible, and zero the dial indicator. Next, push the connecting rod all the way to the front and check the reading on the dial indicator. The distance that it moves is the end play. If the end play exceeds the service limit, a new connecting rod will be required. Repeat the procedure for the remaining connecting rods.

6    An alternative method is to slip feeler gauges between the connecting rod and the crankshaft throw until the play is removed (photo). The end play is then equal to the total thickness of the feeler gauges.

7    Check the connecting rods and connecting rod caps for identification marks. If they are not plainly marked, identify each rod and cap, using a small punch to make the appropriate number of indentations to indicate the cylinders they are associated with.

8    Loosen each of the connecting rod cap nuts approximately 1/2 turn. Remove the number one connecting rod cap and bearing insert. Do not drop the bearing insert out of the cap. Slip a short length of plastic or rubber hose over each connecting rod cap bolt to protect

11.2   A special tool is required to remove the ridge from the top of each cylinder (do it before removing the piston)

11.6   Checking connecting rod end play with a feeler gauge

the crankshaft journal and cylinder wall when the piston is removed (photo) and push the connecting rod/piston assembly out through the top of the engine. Use a wooden tool to push on the upper bearing insert in the connecting rod. If resistance is felt, double-check to make sure that all of the ridge was removed from the cylinder.

9    Repeat the procedure for the remaining cylinders. After removal, reassemble the connecting rod caps and bearing inserts in their respective connecting rods and install the cap nuts finger tight. Leaving the old bearing inserts in place until reassembly will help prevent the connecting rod bearing surfaces from being accidentally nicked or gouged.

## 12   Crankshaft — removal

1    Before the crankshaft is removed check the end play. Mount a dial indicator with the stem in line with the crankshaft and just touching one of the crank throws (see the accompanying illustration).
2    Push the crankshaft all the way to the rear and zero the dial indicator. Next, pry the crankshaft to the front as far as possible and check the reading on the dial indicator. The distance that it moves is the end play. If it is greater than specified, check the crankshaft thrust surfaces for wear. If no wear is apparent, new main bearings should correct the end play.
3    If a dial indicator is not available, feeler gauges can be used. Gently pry or push the crankshaft all the way to the front of the engine. Slip feeler gauges between the crankshaft and the front face of the thrust main bearing (photo) to determine the clearance, which is equivalent

to crankshaft end play. On 1985 2.8 liter engines, check the end play at the number three main bearing as shown in the accompanying illustration.
4    Loosen each of the main bearing cap bolts 1/4-turn at a time, until they can be removed by hand. Check the main bearing caps to see if they are marked as to their locations. They are usually numbered consecutively from the front of the engine to the rear. If they are not, mark them with number stamping dies or a centerpunch (photo). Most

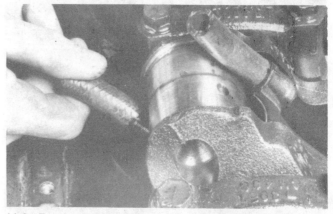

11.8   To prevent damage to the crankshaft journals and cylinder walls, slip sections of hose over the rod bolts before removing the pistons

12.3   Checking crankshaft end play with a feeler gauge

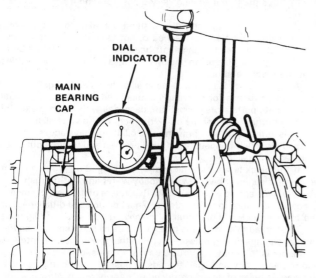

Fig. 2D.8  Checking crankshaft end play with a dial indicator (Sec 12)

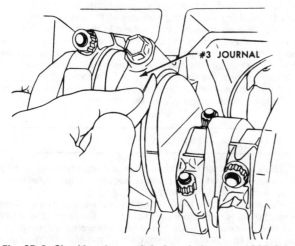

Fig. 2D.9  Checking the crankshaft end play on a 1985 2.8 liter V6 at the number three journal (Sec 12)

12.4   Mark the bearing caps with a centerpunch before removing them

13.1A   A hammer and large punch can be used to drive the soft plugs into the block

13.1B   Using pliers to remove a soft plug from the block

which cylinder they removed from and whether they were in the cap or the block, then set them aside.
4    Remove the threaded oil gallery plugs from the front and back of the block.
5    If the engine is extremely dirty it should be taken to an automotive machine shop to be steam cleaned or hot tanked. Any bearings left in the block, such as the camshaft bearings, will be damaged by the cleaning process, so plan on having new ones installed while the block is at the machine shop.
6    After the block is returned, clean all oil holes and oil galleries one more time. Brushes for cleaning oil holes and galleries are available at most auto parts stores. Flush the passages with warm water until the water runs clear, dry the block thoroughly and wipe all machined surfaces with a light, rust preventative oil. If you have access to compressed air, use it to speed the drying process and to blow out all the oil holes and galleries.
7    If the block is not extremely dirty or sludged up, you can do an adequate cleaning job with warm soapy water and a stiff brush. Take plenty of time and do a thorough job. Regardless of the cleaning method used, be very sure to thoroughly clean all oil holes and galleries, dry the block completely and coat all machined surfaces with light oil.
8    The threaded holes in the block must be clean to ensure accurate torque readings during reassembly. Run the proper size tap into each of the holes to remove any rust, corrosion, thread sealant or sludge and to restore any damaged threads. If possible, use compressed air to clear the holes of debris produced by this operation. Now is a good time to thoroughly clean the threads on the head bolts and the main bearing cap bolts as well.
9    Reinstall the main bearing caps and tighten the bolts finger tight.
10   After coating the sealing surfaces of the new soft plugs with a good quality gasket sealer, install them in the engine block (photo). Make sure they are driven in straight and seated properly or leakage could result. Special tools are available for this purpose, but equally good results can be obtained using a socket with an outside diameter that will just slip into the soft plug and a hammer.
11   If the engine is not going to be reassembled right away, cover it with a large plastic trash bag to keep it clean.

13.10   A large socket on an extension can be used to force the new soft plugs into their bores

main bearing caps have a cast-in arrow, which points to the front of the engine.
5    Gently tap the caps with a soft-face hammer, then separate them from the engine block. If necessary, use the main bearing cap bolts as levers to remove the caps. Try not to drop the bearing insert if it comes out with the cap.
6    Carefully lift the crankshaft out of the engine. It is a good idea to have an assistant available, since the crankshaft is quite heavy. With the bearing inserts in place in the engine block and in the main bearing caps, return the caps to their respective locations on the engine block and tighten the bolts finger tight.

## 13   Engine block — cleaning

1    Remove the soft plugs from the engine block. To do this, knock the plugs into the block, using a hammer and punch, then grasp them with large pliers and pull them back through the holes (photos).
2    Using a gasket scraper, remove all traces of gasket material from the engine block. Be very careful not to nick or gouge the gasket sealing surfaces.
3    Remove the main bearing caps and separate the bearing inserts from the caps and the engine block. Tag the bearings according to

## 14   Engine block — inspection

1    Thoroughly clean the engine block as described in Section 13 and double-check to make sure that the ridge at the top of each cylinder has been completely removed.
2    Visually check the block for cracks, rust and corrosion. Look for stripped threads in the threaded holes. It is also a good idea to have the block checked for hidden cracks by an automotive machine shop that has the special equipment to do this type of work. If defects are found, have the block repaired, if possible, or replaced.
3    Check the cylinder bores for scuffing and scoring.

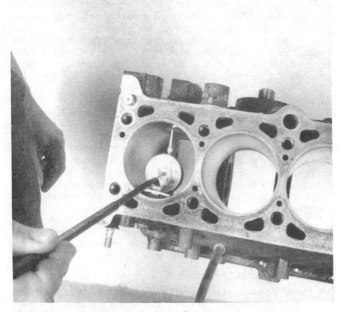

14.4   Measuring the cylinder bore diameter

14.7   Honing a cylinder with a surfacing hone

4   Using the appropriate precision measuring tools, measure each cylinder's diameter at the top (just under the ridge), center and bottom of the cylinder bore, parallel to the crankshaft axis (photo). Next, measure each cylinder's diameter at the same three locations across the crankshaft axis. Compare the results to the Specifications. If the cylinder walls are badly scuffed or scored, or if they are out-of-round or tapered beyond the limits given in the Specifications, have the engine block rebored and honed at an automotive machine shop. If a rebore is done, oversize pistons and rings will be required.

5   If the cylinders are in reasonably good condition and not worn to the outside of the limits, and if the piston-to-cylinder clearances can be maintained properly, then they do not have to be rebored. Honing is all that is necessary.

6   Before honing the cylinders, install the main bearing caps, without the bearings, and tighten the bolts to the specified torque.

7   To perform the honing operation you will need the proper size flexible hone (with fine stones), plenty of light oil or honing oil, some rags and an electric drill motor. Mount the hone in the drill motor, compress the stones and slip the hone into the first cylinder (photo).

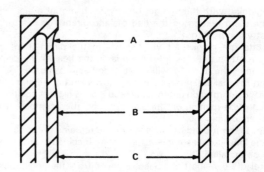

Fig. 2D.10   Measure the diameter of each cylinder just under the wear ridge (A), at the center (B) and at the bottom (C) (Sec 14)

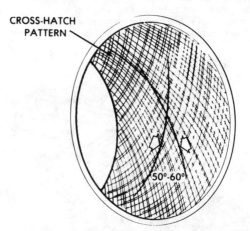

Fig. 2D.11   The cylinder hone should leave a crosshatch pattern with the lines intersecting at a 60° angle (Sec 14)

Lubricate the cylinder thoroughly, turn on the drill and move the hone up and down in the cylinder at a pace which will produce a fine crosshatch pattern on the cylinder walls, with the crosshatch lines intersecting at approximately a 60° angle. Be sure to use plenty of lubricant and do not take off any more material than is absolutely necessary to produce the desired finish. Do not withdraw the hone from the cylinder while it is running. Instead, shut off the drill and continue moving the hone up and down in the cylinder until it comes to a complete stop, then compress the stones and withdraw the hone. Wipe the oil out of the cylinder and repeat the procedure on the remaining cylinders. If you do not have the tools or do not desire to perform the honing operation, most automotive machine shops will do it for a reasonable fee.

8   After the honing job is complete, chamfer the top edges of the cylinder bores with a small file so the rings will not catch when the pistons are installed.

9   The entire engine block must be thoroughly washed again with warm, soapy water to remove all traces of the abrasive grit produced during the honing operation. Be sure to run a brush through all oil holes and galleries and flush them with running water. After rinsing, dry the block and apply a coat of light rust preventative oil to all machined surfaces. Wrap the block in a plastic trash bag to keep it clean and set it aside until reassembly.

## 15   Camshaft, lifters and bearings — inspection and bearing replacement

### Camshaft

1   The most critical camshaft inspection procedure on 2.5 liter four-cylinder and 2.8 liter V6 engines is lobe lift measurement, which must be done before the engine is disassembled.

2   Remove the rocker arm cover, then remove the nuts and separate the rocker arms and ball pivots from the cylinder head.

3　Beginning with the number one cylinder, mount a dial indicator with the stem resting on the end of, and directly in line with, the exhaust valve pushrod.

4　Rotate the crankshaft very slowly in the direction of normal running rotation until the lifter stem is on the heel of the cam lobe. At this point the pushrod will be at its lowest position.

5　Zero the dial indicator, then very slowly rotate the crankshaft in the direction of rotation until the pushrod is at its highest position. Note and record the reading on the dial indicator, then compare it to the lobe lift specifications.

6　Repeat the procedure for each of the remaining valves.

7　If the lobe lift measurements are not as specified, a new camshaft should be installed.

8　After the camshaft has been removed from the engine, cleaned with solvent and dried, inspect the bearing journals for uneven wear, pitting or evidence of seizure. If the journals are damaged, the bearing inserts in the block are probably damaged as well. Both the camshaft and bearings will have to be replaced with new ones. Measure the inside diameter of each camshaft bearing and record the results. Take two measurements, 90° apart, at each bearing.

9　Measure the bearing journals with a micrometer (photo) to determine if they are excessively worn or out-of-round. If they are more than 0.001-inch out-of-round, the camshaft should be replaced with a new one. Subtract the bearing journal diameter(s) from the corresponding bearing inside diameter measurement to obtain the clearance. If it is excessive, new bearings must be installed.

10　Check the camshaft lobes for heat discoloration, score marks, chipped areas, pitting or uneven wear. If the lobes are in good condition and if the lobe lift measurements (Steps 1 through 7) are as specified, the camshaft can be reused.

### Lifters

11　Clean the lifters with solvent and dry them thoroughly without mixing them up.

12　Check each lifter wall, pushrod seat and foot for scuffing, score marks or uneven wear. Each lifter foot (the surface that rides on the cam lobe) must be slightly convex — if they are concave (photo), the lifters and camshaft must be replaced with new ones. If the lifter walls are damaged or worn (which is not very likely), inspect the lifter bores in the engine block as well. If the pushrod seats are worn, check the pushrod ends.

13　If new lifters are being installed, a new camshaft must also be installed. If a new camshaft is installed, then use new lifters as well. Never install used lifters unless the original camshaft is used and the lifters can be installed in their original locations.

### Bearing replacement

14　Camshaft bearing replacement requires special tools and expertise that place it outside the scope of the do-it-yourselfer. Take the block to an automotive machine shop to ensure that the job is done correctly.

### 16　Piston/connecting rod assembly — inspection

1　Before the inspection process can be carried out, the piston/connecting rod assemblies must be cleaned and the original piston rings removed from the pistons. **Note:** *Always use new piston rings when the engine is reassembled.*

2　Using a piston ring installation tool, carefully remove the rings from the pistons. Do not nick or gouge the pistons in the process.

3　Scrape all traces of carbon from the top (or crown) of the piston. A hand-held wire brush or a piece of fine emery cloth can be used once the majority of the deposits have been scraped away. Do not, under any circumstances, use a wire brush mounted in a drill motor to remove deposits from the pistons. The piston material is soft and will be eroded away by the wire brush.

Fig. 2D.12　A dial indicator can be mounted as shown to check the camshaft lobe lift (Sec 15)

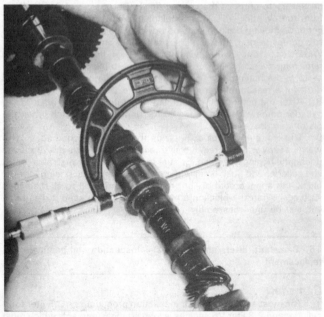

15.9　The camshaft bearing journal diameter is subtracted from the bearing inside diameter to obtain the oil clearance, which must be as specified

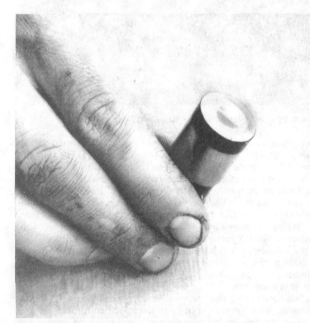

15.12　If the bottom of any lifter is worn concave, scratched or galled, they should all be replaced with new ones

4   Use a piston ring groove cleaning tool to remove any carbon deposits from the ring grooves. If a tool is not available, a piece broken off an old ring will do the job. Be very careful to remove only the carbon deposits. Do not remove any metal and do not nick or scratch the sides of the ring grooves (photo).

5   Once the deposits have been removed, clean the piston/rod assemblies with solvent and dry them thoroughly. Make sure that the oil return holes in the back sides of the ring grooves are clear.

6   If the pistons are not damaged or worn excessively, and if the engine block is not rebored, new pistons will not be necessary. Normal piston wear appears as even vertical wear on the piston thrust surfaces and slight looseness of the top ring in its groove. New piston rings, on the other hand, should always be used when an engine is rebuilt.

7   Carefully inspect each piston for cracks around the skirt, at the pin bosses and at the ring lands.

8   Look for scoring and scuffing on the thrust faces of the skirt, holes in the piston crown and burned areas at the edge of the crown. If the skirt is scored or scuffed, the engine may have been suffering from overheating or abnormal combustion, which caused excessively high operating temperatures. The cooling and lubrication systems should be checked thoroughly. A hole in the piston crown is an indication that abnormal combustion (preignition) was occurring. Burned areas at the edge of the piston crown are usually evidence of spark knock (detonation). If any of the above problems exist, the causes must be corrected or the damage will occur again.

9   Corrosion of the piston (evidenced by pitting) indicates that coolant is leaking into the combustion chamber or the crankcase. Again, the cause must be corrected or the problem may persist in the rebuilt engine.

10   Measure the piston ring side clearance by laying a new piston ring in each ring groove and slipping a feeler gauge between the ring and the edge of the ring groove (photo). Check the clearance at four locations around each groove. Be sure to use the correct ring for each groove; they are different. If the side clearance is greater than specified, new pistons will have to be used.

11   Check the piston-to-bore clearance by measuring the bore (see Section 14) and the piston diameter. Make sure that the pistons and bores are correctly matched. Measure the piston across the skirt (photo). Subtract the piston diameter from the bore diameter to obtain the clearance. If it is greater than specified, the block will have to be rebored and new pistons and rings installed. Check the piston-to-rod clearance by twisting the piston and rod in opposite directions. Any noticeable play indicates that there is excessive wear, which must be corrected. The piston/connecting rod assemblies should be taken to an automotive machine shop to have new piston pins installed and the pistons and connecting rods rebored.

12   If the pistons must be removed from the connecting rods, such as when new pistons must be installed, or if the piston pins have too much play in them, they should be taken to an automotive machine shop. While they are there have the connecting rods checked for bend and twist, as automotive machine shops have special equipment for this purpose. Unless new pistons or connecting rods must be installed, do not disassemble the pistons from the connecting rods.

13   Check the connecting rods for cracks and other damage. Temporarily remove the rod caps, lift out the old bearing inserts, wipe the rod and cap bearing surfaces clean and inspect them for nicks, gouges or scratches. After checking the rods, replace the old bearings, slip the caps into place and tighten the nuts finger tight.

## 17   Crankshaft — inspection

1   Clean the crankshaft with solvent and dry it thoroughly. Be sure to clean the oil holes with a stiff brush and flush them with solvent. Check the main and connecting rod bearing journals for uneven wear, scoring, pitting or cracks. Check the remainder of the crankshaft for cracks and damage.

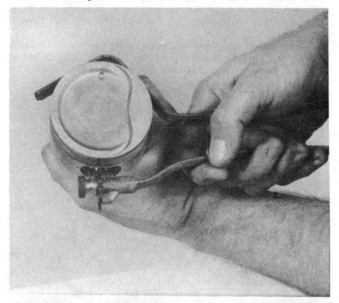

16.4   Cleaning the piston ring grooves with a piston ring groove cleaning tool

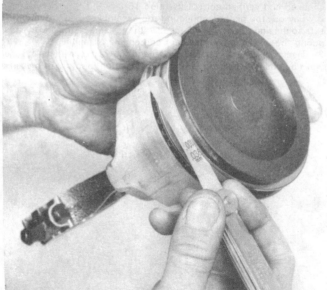

16.10   Checking the piston ring side clearance with a feeler gauge

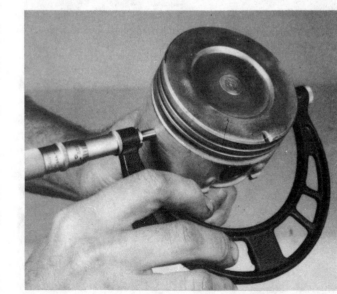

6.11   Measure the piston diameter directly in line with the piston pin hole

2    Using a micrometer, measure the diameter of the main and connecting rod journals (photo) and compare the results to the Specifications. By measuring the diameter at a number of points around the journal's circumference you will be able to determine whether or not the journal is out of round. Take the measurement at each end of the journal, near the crank counterweights, to determine whether the journal is tapered.

3    If the crankshaft journals are damaged, tapered, out of round or worn beyond the limits given in the Specifications, have the crankshaft reground by a reputable automotive machine shop. Be sure to use the correct undersize bearing inserts if the crankshaft is reconditioned.

## 18    Main and connecting rod bearings — inspection

1    Even though the main and connecting rod bearings should be replaced with new ones during the engine overhaul, the old bearings should be retained for close examination, as they may reveal valuable information about the condition of the engine.

2    Bearing failure occurs primarily because of lack of lubrication, the presence of dirt or other foreign particles, overloading the engine and corrosion. Regardless of the cause of bearing failure, it must be corrected before the engine is reassembled to prevent it from happening again.

3    When examining the bearings, remove them from the engine block, the main bearing caps, the connecting rods and the rod caps and lay them out on a clean surface in the same general position as their loca-

17.2    Measure the diameter of each crankshaft journal at several points to detect taper and out-of-round conditions

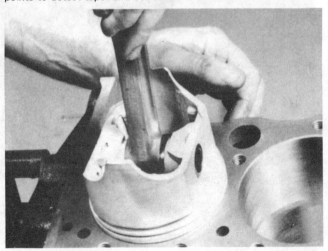

19.3A    Use the piston to square up the ring in the cylinder prior to checking the ring end gap

tion in the engine. This will enable you to match any bearing problems with the corresponding crankshaft journal.

4    Dirt and other foreign particles get into the engine in a variety of ways. It may be left in the engine during assembly, or it may pass through filters or breathers. It may get into the oil, and from there into the bearings. Metal chips from machining operations and normal engine wear are often present. Abrasives are sometimes left in engine components after reconditioning, especially when parts are not thoroughly cleaned using the proper cleaning methods. Whatever the source, these foreign objects often end up embedded in the soft bearing material and are easily recognized. Large particles will not embed in the bearing and will score or gouge the bearing and shaft. The best prevention for this cause of bearing failure is to clean all parts thoroughly and keep everything spotlessly clean during engine assembly. Frequent and regular engine oil and filter changes are also recommended.

5    Lack of lubrication (or lubrication breakdown) has a number of interrelated causes. Excessive heat (which thins the oil), overloading (which squeezes the oil from the bearing face) and oil leakage or throwoff (from excessive bearing clearances, worn oil pump or high engine speeds) all contribute to lubrication breakdown. Blocked oil passages, which usually are the result of misaligned oil holes in a bearing shell, will also oil-starve a bearing and destroy it. When lack of lubrication is the cause of bearing failure, the bearing material is wiped or extruded from the steel backing of the bearing. Temperatures may increase to the point where the steel backing turns blue from overheating.

6    Driving habits can have a definite effect on bearing life. Full-throttle, low-speed operation (or *lugging* the engine) puts very high loads on bearings, which tends to squeeze out the oil film. These loads cause the bearings to flex, which produces fine cracks in the bearing face (fatigue failure). Eventually the bearing material will loosen in pieces and tear away from the steel backing. Short-trip driving leads to corrosion of bearings because insufficient engine heat is produced to drive off the condensed water and corrosive gases. These products collect in the engine oil, forming acid and sludge. As the oil is carried to the engine bearings, the acid attacks and corrodes the bearing material.

7    Incorrect bearing installation during engine assembly will lead to bearing failure as well. Tight fitting bearings leave insufficient bearing oil clearance and will result in oil starvation. Dirt or foreign particles trapped behind a bearing insert result in high spots on the bearing which can lead to failure.

## 19    Piston rings — installation

1    Before installing the new piston rings, the ring end gaps must be checked. It is assumed that the piston ring side clearance has been checked and verified correct (Section 16).

2    Lay out the piston/connecting rod assemblies and the new ring sets so the ring sets will be matched with the same piston and cylinder during the end gap measurement and engine assembly.

3    Insert the top ring into the cylinder and square it up with the cylinder walls by pushing it in with the top of the piston (photo). To measure

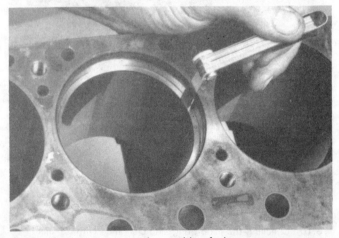

19.3B    Measure the ring end gap with a feeler gauge

the end gap, slip a feeler gauge between the ends of the ring (photo). Compare the measurement to the Specifications.

4   If the gap is larger or smaller than specified, double-check to make sure that you have the correct rings before proceeding.

5   If the gap is too small, it must be enlarged or the ring ends may come in contact with each other during engine operation, which can cause serious damage to the engine. The end gap can be increased by filing the ring ends very carefully with a fine file. Mount the file in a vise equipped with soft jaws, slip the ring over the file with the ends contacting the file face and slowly move the ring to remove material from the ends. When performing this operation, file only from the outside in.

6   Excess end gap is not critical unless it is greater than 0.040-inch (1 mm). Again, double-check to make sure you have the correct rings for your engine.

7   Repeat the procedure for the rest of the rings. Remember to keep rings, pistons and cylinders matched up.

8   Once the ring end gaps have been checked, the rings can be installed on the pistons.

9   The oil control ring (lowest one on the piston) is installed first. It is composed of three separate components. Slip the spacer/expander into the groove (photo), then install the lower side rail. Do not use a piston ring installation tool on the oil ring side rails, as they may be damaged. Instead, place one end of the side rail into the groove between the spacer/expander and the ring land, hold it firmly in place and slide a finger around the piston while pushing the rail into the groove

(photo). Next, install the upper side rail in the same manner.

10   After the three oil ring components have been installed, check to make sure that both the upper and lower side rails can be turned smoothly in the ring groove.

11   The number two (middle) ring is installed next. It should be stamped with a mark so it can be readily distinguished from the top ring. **Note:** *Always follow the instructions printed on the ring package or box — different manufacturers may require different approaches.* Do not mix up the top and middle rings, as they have different cross sections.

12   Use a piston ring installation tool and make sure that the identification mark is facing the top of the piston, then slip the ring into the middle groove on the piston (photo). Do not expand the ring any more than is necessary to slide it over the piston.

13   Install the number one (top) ring in the same manner. Make sure the identifying mark is facing up.

14   Repeat the procedure for the remaining pistons and rings. Be careful not to confuse the number one and number two rings.

---

### 20   Rear main oil seal (V6 engines only) — installation

*Rope-type seal*

1   Lay one seal section on edge in the seal groove in the block and push it into place with your thumbs. Both ends of the seal should extend out of the block slightly (photo).

19.9A   Installing the spacer/expander in the oil control ring groove

19.9B   Do not use a piston ring tool when installing the oil ring side rails

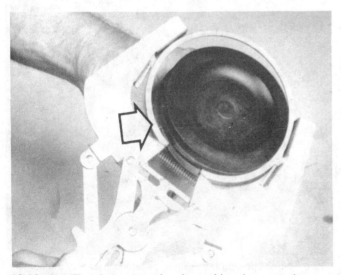

19.12   Installing the compression rings with a ring expander — the mark (arrow) must face up

20.1   When correctly installed, the ends of the rope-type seal should extend out of the block

20.2   Seat the seal in the groove, but do not depress it below the bearing surface (the seal must contact the crankshaft journal)

20.3A   Trim the ends flush with the block, . . .

20.4   Lubricate the seal with assembly lube or moly-base grease

2    Seat it in the groove by rolling a large socket or piece of bar stock along the entire length of the seal (photo). As an alternative, push the seal very carefully into place with a wooden hammer handle.

3    Once you are satisfied that the seal is completely seated in the groove, trim off the excess on the ends with a single-edge razor blade or razor knife. The seal ends must be flush with the block-to-cap mating surfaces (photos). Make sure that no seal fibers get caught between the block and cap.

4    Repeat the entire procedure to install the other half of the seal in the bearing cap. Apply a thin film of engine assembly lube to the edge of the seal where it contacts the crankshaft (photo).

5    On 3.0 and 3.8 liter V6 engines install the neoprene seals in the bearing cap groove as shown in the accompanying illustration. These seals are slightly undersize, but swell in the presence of oil and heat so that after the engine is run they will seal effectively. The seals are also slightly longer than the bearing cap grooves, but must not be cut to length. Soak the seals for two minutes in kerosene or light oil prior to installation.

6    During final installation of the crankshaft, after the main bearing oil clearances have been checked with Plastigage as described in Section 21, apply a thin, even film of anaerobic-type gasket sealant to the areas of the rear main bearing cap indicated in the accompanying illustration (photo). **Caution:** *Do not get any sealant on the bearing or seal faces.*

20.3B   . . . but leave the inner edge (arrow) protruding slightly

20.6   When applying the sealant, be sure it gets into the corner and onto the vertical cap-to-block mating surface or oil leaks will result

*Neoprene lip-type seal*

7   Inspect the bearing cap and engine block mating surfaces and seal grooves for nicks, burrs and scratches. Remove any defects with a fine file or deburring tool.

8   Install one seal section in the block with the lip facing the front of the engine. Leave one end protruding from the block 3/8-inch and make sure it is completely seated. **Note:** *Apply a very thin coat of RTV-type gasket sealant to the outer surface of the seal as shown in the accompanying illustration. Do not get any sealant on the seal lips.*

9   Repeat the procedure to install the remaining seal half in the rear main bearing cap. In this case, leave the opposite end of the seal protruding from the cap the same distance the block seal is protruding from the block.

10   Prior to final installation of the crankshaft lubricate the seal lips with moly-base grease or engine assembly lube.

---

### 21   Crankshaft — installation and main bearing oil clearance check

1   Crankshaft installation is generally one of the first steps in engine reassembly. It is assumed at this point that the engine block and crankshaft have been cleaned, inspected and repaired or reconditioned.

2   Position the engine with the bottom facing up.

3   Remove the main bearing cap bolts and lift out the caps. Lay them out in the proper order to help ensure that they are installed correctly.

4   If they are still in place, remove the old bearing inserts from the block and the main bearing caps. Wipe the main bearing surfaces of the block and caps with a clean, lint-free cloth. They must be kept spotlessly clean.

5   Clean the back sides of the new main bearing inserts and lay one

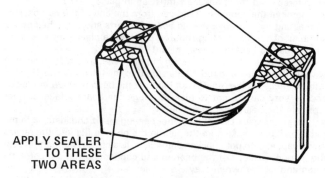

## NEOPRENE COMPOSITION SEAL

**APPLY SEALER TO THESE TWO AREAS**

Fig. 2D.13  3.0 and 3.8 liter V6 engine neoprene rear main bearing seal and sealer installation (Sec 20)

bearing half in each main bearing saddle in the block. Lay the other bearing half from each bearing set in the corresponding main bearing cap. Make sure the tab on the bearing insert fits into the recess in the block or cap. Do not hammer the bearing into place and do not nick or gouge the bearing faces. No lubrication should be used at this time.

6   The flanged thrust bearing must be installed in the number three cap and saddle on V6 engines and the number five cap and saddle on four cylinder engines.

7   Clean the faces of the bearings in the block and the crankshaft main bearing journals with a clean, lint-free cloth. Check or clean the oil holes in the crankshaft, as any dirt here can go only one way — straight through the new bearings.

8   Once you are certain that the crankshaft is clean, carefully lay it in position (an assistant would be very helpful here) in the main bearings.

9   Before the crankshaft can be permanently installed, the main bearing oil clearance must be checked.

10   Trim several pieces of the appropriate size of Plastigage slightly shorter than the width of the main bearings and place one piece on each crankshaft main bearing journal, parallel with the journal axis.

11   Clean the faces of the bearings in the caps and install the caps in their respective positions (do not mix them up) with the arrows pointing toward the front of the engine. Do not disturb the Plastigage.

12   Starting with the center main and working out toward the ends, tighten the main bearing cap bolts, in three steps, to the specified torque. Do not rotate the crankshaft at any time during this operation.

13   Remove the bolts and carefully lift off the main bearing caps. Keep them in order. Do not disturb the Plastigage or rotate the crankshaft. If any of the main bearing caps are difficult to remove, tap them gently from side-to-side with a soft-face hammer to loosen them.

14   Compare the width of the crushed Plastigage on each journal to the scale printed on the Plastigage container to obtain the main bearing oil clearance. Check the Specifications to make sure it is correct.

15   If the clearance is not correct, double-check to make sure you have the right size bearing inserts. Also, make sure that no dirt or oil is between the bearing inserts and the main bearing caps or the block when the clearance was measured.

16   Carefully scrape all traces of the Plastigage material off the main bearing journals and the bearing faces. Do not nick or scratch the bearing faces.

17   Carefully lift the crankshaft out of the engine. Clean the bearing faces in the block, then apply a thin, uniform layer of moly-base grease or engine assembly lube to each of the bearing surfaces. Be sure to coat the thrust flange faces as well as the journal face of the thrust bearing.

18   Lubricate the rear main bearing oil seal where it contacts the crankshaft with moly-base grease or engine assembly lube. Note that on four-cylinder engines the oil seal is installed after the crankshaft is in place.

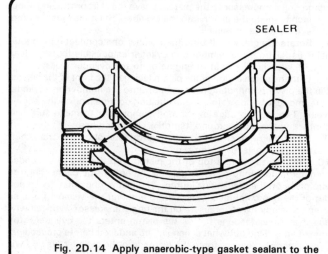

SEALER

Fig. 2D.14  Apply anaerobic-type gasket sealant to the shaded areas of the rear main bearing cap (2.8 liter V6 engine) (Sec 20)

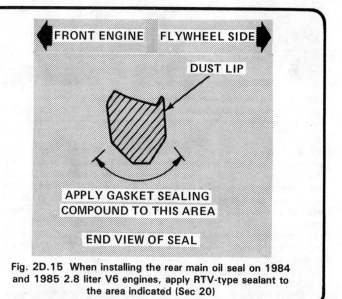

**FRONT ENGINE     FLYWHEEL SIDE**

**DUST LIP**

**APPLY GASKET SEALING COMPOUND TO THIS AREA**

**END VIEW OF SEAL**

Fig. 2D.15  When installing the rear main oil seal on 1984 and 1985 2.8 liter V6 engines, apply RTV-type sealant to the area indicated (Sec 20)

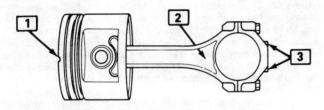

**Fig. 2D.16  Piston and connecting rod assembly installation
(3.0 and 3.8 liter V6 engines) (Sec 22)**

    *1  Piston notch faces toward the
       front of the engine*
**Left bank**
    *2  On assemblies number 1, 3 and 5,
       the two bosses on the rod (not
       shown) face toward the rear of
       the engine*
    *3  The chamfered corners on the rod
       cap face toward the front of the
       engine*
**Right bank**
    *2  Number 2, 4 and 6 assemblies —
       the bosses (not shown) face
       toward the front of the engine*
    *3  The chamfered rod cap corners
       face toward the rear of the engine*

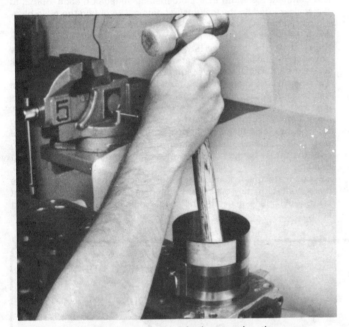

**22.10  If resistance is encountered when tapping the
piston/connecting rod assembly into the block, stop immediately
and make sure the rings are fully compressed**

19  If you are working on a V6 engine, refer to Section 20 and apply
anaerobic-type gasket sealant to the rear main bearing cap as described
there. Make sure the crankshaft journals are clean, then lay the
crankshaft back in place in the block. Clean the faces of the bearings
in the caps, then apply a thin, uniform layer of moly-base grease to
each of the bearing faces. Install the caps in their respective positions
with the arrows pointing toward the front of the engine. Install the
bolts and tighten them to the specified torque, starting with the center
main and working out toward the ends. Work up to the final torque
in three steps.
20  Rotate the crankshaft a number of times by hand and check for
any obvious binding.
21  Check the crankshaft end play with a feeler gauge or a dial indicator
as described in Section 12.

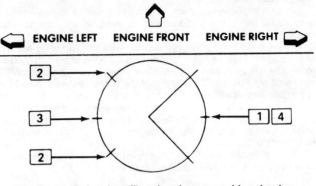

**Fig. 2D.17  Before installing the pistons, position the ring
end gaps as shown here (Sec 22)**

    *1   Oil ring spacer gap*
    *2   Oil ring rail gaps*
    *3   Second compression ring gap*
    *4   Top compression ring gap*

**22   Piston/connecting rod assembly — installation and bearing oil
clearance check**

1    Before installing the piston/connecting rod assemblies the cylinder
walls must be perfectly clean, the top edge of each cylinder must be
chamfered, and the crankshaft must be in place.
2    Remove the connecting rod cap from the end of the number one
connecting rod. Remove the old bearing inserts and wipe the bearing
surfaces of the connecting rod and cap with a clean, lint-free cloth
(they must be kept spotlessly clean).
3    Clean the back side of the new upper bearing half, then lay it in
place in the connecting rod. Make sure that the tab on the bearing fits
into the recess in the rod. Do not hammer the bearing insert into place
and be very careful not to nick or gouge the bearing face. Do not
lubricate the bearing at this time.
4    Clean the back side of the other bearing insert and install it in the
rod cap. Again, make sure the tab on the bearing fits into the recess
in the cap, and do not apply any lubricant. It is critically important that
the mating surfaces of the bearing and connecting rod are perfectly
clean and oil-free when they are assembled.
5    Position the piston ring gaps as shown in the accompanying illustrations, then slip a section of plastic or rubber hose over the connecting
rod cap bolts.
6    Lubricate the piston and rings with clean engine oil and attach a
piston ring compressor to the piston. Leave the skirt protruding about
1/4-inch to guide the piston into the cylinder. The rings must be compressed as far as possible.
7    Rotate the crankshaft until the number one connecting rod journal is as far from the number one cylinder as possible (bottom dead
center), and apply a coat of engine oil to the cylinder walls.
8    With the notch on top of the piston facing to the front of the engine,
slip the piston/connecting rod assembly into the number one cylinder
bore and rest the bottom edge of the ring compressor on the engine
block. Tap the top edge of the ring compressor to make sure it is
contacting the block around its entire circumference.
9    Clean the number one connecting rod journal on the crankshaft
and the bearing faces in the rod.
10  Carefully tap on the top of the piston with the end of a wooden
hammer handle (photo) while guiding the end of the connecting rod
into place on the crankshaft journal. The piston rings may try to pop
out of the ring compressor just before entering the cylinder bore, so
keep some downward pressure on the ring compressor. Work slowly,
and if any resistance is felt as the piston enters the cylinder, stop
immediately. Find out what is hanging up and fix it before proceeding.
Do not, for any reason, force the piston into the cylinder, as you will
break a ring and/or the piston.
11  Once the piston/connecting rod assembly is installed, the connecting rod bearing oil clearance must be checked before the rod cap is
permanently bolted in place.

22.12  Position the Plastigage strip on the bearing journal, parallel to the journal axis

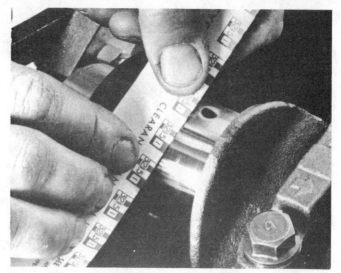

22.14  The crushed Plastigage is compared to the scale printed on the container to obtain the bearing oil clearance

12  Cut a piece of the the appropriate size Plastigage slightly shorter than the width of the connecting rod bearing and lay it in place on the number one connecting rod journal, parallel with the journal axis. It must not cross the oil hole in the journal (photo).

13  Clean the connecting rod cap bearing face, remove the protective hoses from the connecting rod bolts and install the rod cap in place. Make sure the mating mark on the cap is on the same side as the mark on the connecting rod. Install the nuts and tighten them to the specified torque, working up to it in three steps. Do not rotate the crankshaft at any time during this operation.

14  Remove the rod cap, being careful not to disturb the Plastigage. Compare the width of the crushed Plastigage to the scale printed on the Plastigage container to obtain the oil clearance (photo). Compare it to the Specifications to make sure the clearance is correct. If the clearance is not correct, double-check to make sure that you have the correct size bearing inserts. Also, recheck the crankshaft connecting rod journal diameter and make sure that no dirt or oil was between the bearing inserts and the connecting rod or cap when the clearance was measured.

15  Carefully scrape all traces of the Plastigage material off the rod journal and bearing face. Be very careful not to scratch the bearing — use your fingernail or a piece of hardwood. Make sure the bearing faces are perfectly clean, then apply a uniform layer of moly-base grease or engine assembly lube to both of them. You will have to push the piston into the cylinder to expose the face of the bearing insert in the connecting rod. Be sure to slip the protective hoses over the rod bolts first.

16  Slide the connecting rod back into place on the journal, remove the protective hoses from the rod cap bolts, install the rod cap and tighten the nuts to the specified torque. Again, work up to the torque in three steps.

17  Repeat the entire procedure for the remaining piston/connecting rod assemblies. Keep the back sides of the bearing inserts and the inside of the connecting rod and cap perfectly clean when assembling them. Make sure you have the correct piston for the cylinder and that the notch on the piston faces to the front of the engine when the piston is installed. Remember, use plenty of oil to lubricate the piston before installing the ring compressor. Also, when installing the rod caps for the final time, be sure to lubricate the bearing faces adequately.

18  After all the piston/connecting rod assemblies have been properly installed, rotate the crankshaft a number of times by hand and check for any obvious binding.

19  As a final step, the connecting rod end play must be checked. Refer to Section 11 for this procedure. Compare the measured end play to the Specifications to make sure it is correct.

## 23  Engine overhaul — reassembly sequence

1  Before beginning engine reassembly, make sure you have all the necessary new parts, gaskets and seals as well as the following items on hand:

*Common hand tools*
*A 1/2-inch drive torque wrench*
*Piston ring installation tool*
*Piston ring compressor*
*Short lengths of rubber hose to fit over rod bolts*
*Plastigage*
*Feeler gauges*
*A fine-tooth file*
*New engine oil*
*Engine assembly lube or moly-base grease*
*RTV-type gasket sealant*
*Anaerobic-type gasket sealant*
*Thread locking compound*

2  In order to save time and avoid problems, engine reassembly must be done in the following order.

*Rear main oil seal (V6 engines only)*
*Crankshaft and main bearings*
*Piston rings*
*Piston/connecting rod assemblies*
*Oil pump*
*Oil pan*
*Camshaft*
*Timing chain/sprockets or gears*
*Timing chain/gear cover*
*Valve lifters*
*Cylinder head(s) and pushrods*
*Intake and exhaust manifolds*
*Oil filter*
*Pre-oil the engine (2.8 liter V6 engines only — Section 24)*
*Rocker arm cover(s)*
*Fuel pump*
*Water pump*
*Rear main oil seal (four-cylinder engines only)*
*Flywheel/driveplate*
*Carburetor/fuel injection components*
*Thermostat and housing cover*
*Distributor, spark plug wires and spark plugs*
*Emissions control components*
*Alternator*

## 24  Pre-oiling engine after overhaul (2.8 liter V6 engines only)

1  After an overhaul it is a good idea to pre-oil the engine before it is installed and initially started. This will reveal any problems with the lubrication system at a time when corrections can be made easily and without major engine damage. Pre-oiling the engine will also allow the parts to be lubricated thoroughly in a normal fashion, but without the

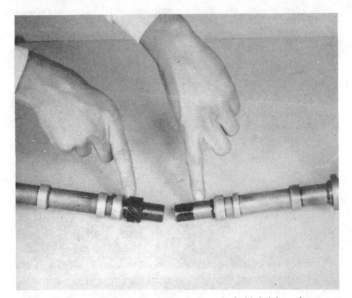

24.3  The pre-oiling modified distributor shaft (right) has the gear and advance weights ground off

24.4   A drill motor connected to the modified distributor drives the oil pump

24.5   Oil will spurt out of the holes in the rocker arms if the lubrication system is functioning properly

heavy loads associated with the combustion process placed upon them.

2    The engine should be assembled completely with the exception of the distributor and the rocker arm covers.

3    A modified distributor will be needed for this procedure. This pre-oil tool is a distributor body with the bottom gear ground off and the advance weight assembly removed from the top of the shaft (photo).

4    Place the pre-oiler into the distributor shaft access hole at the rear of the intake manifold and make sure the bottom of the shaft mates with the oil pump. Clamp the modified distributor into place just as you would an ordinary distributor. Now attach an electric drill motor to the top of the shaft (photo).

5    With the oil filter installed, all oil ways plugged (oil-pressure sending unit at rear of block) and the crankcase full of oil as shown on the dipstick, rotate the pre-oiler with the drill. Make sure the rotation is in a *clockwise* direction. Soon, oil should start to flow from the rocker arms, signifying that the oil pump and lubrication system are functioning

properly. It may take two or three minutes for oil to flow to all of the rocker arms (photo). Allow the oil to circulate through the engine for a few minutes, then shut off the drill motor.

6    Check for oil leaks at the filter and all gasket and seal locations.

7    Remove the pre-oil tool, then install the distributor and rocker arm covers.

## 25   Initial start-up and break-in after overhaul

1    Once the engine has been properly installed in the vehicle, double check the engine oil and coolant levels.

2    With the spark plugs out of the engine and the coil high tension lead grounded to the engine block, crank the engine over until oil pressure registers on the gauge (if so equipped) or until the oil light goes off.

3    Install the spark plugs, hook up the plug wires and the coil high tension lead.

4    Make sure the carburetor choke plate is closed, then start the engine. It may take a few moments for the gasoline to reach the carburetor, but the engine should start without a great deal of effort.

5    As soon as the engine starts it should be set at a fast idle to ensure proper oil circulation and allowed to warm up to normal operating temperature. While the engine is warming up, make a thorough check for oil and coolant leaks.

6    Shut the engine off and recheck the engine oil and coolant levels. Restart the engine and check the ignition timing and the engine idle speed (refer to Chapter 1). Make any necessary adjustments.

7    Drive the vehicle to an area with minimum traffic, accelerate at full throttle from 30 to 50 mph, then allow the vehicle to slow to 30 mph with the throttle closed. Repeat the procedure 10 or 12 times. This will load the piston rings and cause them to seat properly against the cylinder walls. Check again for oil and coolant leaks.

8    Drive the vehicle gently for the first 500 miles (no sustained high speeds) and keep a constant check on the oil level. It is not unusual for an engine to use oil during the break-in period.

9    At approximately 500 to 600 miles, change the oil and filter, retorque the cylinder head bolts and recheck the valve clearances (if applicable).

10  For the next few hundred miles, drive the vehicle normally. Do not either pamper it or abuse it.

11  After 2000 miles, change the oil and filter again and consider the engine fully broken in.

# Chapter 3
# Cooling, heating and air conditioning systems

*Refer to Chapter 13 for Specifications and information applicable to 1986 and later models*

## Contents

Air conditioning system — servicing .................. 10
Antifreeze — general information ................... 2
Coolant level check ...................... See Chapter 1
Coolant temperature sending unit — check and replacement 9
Cooling system check .................... See Chapter 1
Cooling system servicing ................. See Chapter 1
Fan — removal and installation .................... 6

General information ........................... 1
Radiator — removal, servicing and installation ........... 5
Thermostat — check ........................... 4
Thermostat — replacement ...................... 3
Water pump — check ........................... 7
Water pump — removal and installation .............. 8

## Specifications

Radiator cap pressure cap rating ........................ 15 psi
Thermostat rating................................. 195°F

| Torque specifications | Ft-lbs |
| --- | --- |
| Fan assembly-to-radiator support bolts ............... | 7 |
| Transaxle oil cooler fittings ...................... | 20 |
| Radiator-to-support bolts ........................ | 7 |
| Coolant recovery reservoir bolts ................... | 7 |
| Thermostat housing bolts ........................ | 20 |
| Water pump-to-block bolts | |
| 2.5 liter L4 engine ......................... | 20 |
| 2.8 liter V6 engine ......................... | 22 |
| 3.0 and 3.8 liter V6 engine ................... | 22 |
| Water pump-to-timing chain cover bolts | |
| 2.8 liter V6.............................. | 7 |
| 3.0 and 3.8 liter V6 ........................ | 7 |
| Water pump pulley bolts | |
| 2.8 liter V6.............................. | 15 |
| 3.0 and 3.8 liter V6 ........................ | 7 |

## 1  General information

The cooling system consists of either a cross or parallel flow radiator, an engine driven water pump and thermostat-controlled coolant flow.

The fan is driven by an electric motor which is mounted in the radiator shroud and is activated by a temperature switch. **Caution:** *The fan can start even when the engine is Off as long as the ignition switch is On. The battery negative cable should be disconnected whenever you are working in the vicinity of the fan.*

The water pump is mounted on the front of the engine and is driven by a belt from the crankshaft pulley.

The heater utilizes the heat produced by the engine, which is absorbed by the coolant to warm the vehicle interior. It is manually controlled by the driver or passenger.

Air conditioning is available as an option on these vehicles. The air conditioning system is located in the engine compartment and the compressor is driven by the crankshaft pulley by way of a drivebelt.

## 2  Antifreeze — general information

**Caution:** *Do not allow antifreeze to come in contact with your skin or painted surfaces of the vehicle. Flush contacted areas immediately with plenty of water. Antifreeze can be fatal to children and pets. They like it because it is sweet. Just a few licks can cause death. Wipe up garage floor and drip pan coolant spills immediately. Keep antifreeze containers covered and repair leaks in your cooling system immediately.*

The cooling system should be filled with a water/ethylene glycol based antifreeze solution which will prevent freezing down to at least -20°F. It also provides protection against corrosion and increases the coolant boiling point.

The cooling system should be drained, flushed and refilled at least every other year (see Chapter 1). The use of antifreeze solutions for periods of longer than two years is likely to cause damage and encourage the formation of rust and scale in the system.

Before adding antifreeze to the system, check all hose connections and retorque the cylinder head bolts, because antifreeze tends to search out and leak through very minute openings.

The exact mixture of antifreeze-to-water which you should use depends on the relative weather conditions. The mixture should contain at least 50 percent antifreeze, but should never contain more than 70 percent antifreeze.

## 3  Thermostat — replacement

**Caution:** *The engine must be completely cool before beginning this procedure. Also, when working in the vicinity of the electric fan, disconnect the negative battery cable from the battery to prevent the fan from coming on accidentally.*

## Four-cylinder engine

1   Refer to the Caution in Section 2.
2   Disconnect the cable from the negative battery terminal (if not done previously).
3   Drain the cooling system until the level is below the thermostat by opening the petcock at the bottom of the radiator. Close the petcock when enough coolant has drained.
4   Remove the upper radiator hose from the water outlet housing.
5   Remove the two housing bolts and separate the housing from the engine (photo).
6   Remove the thermostat from the thermostat housing.
7   Before installing the thermostat, clean the gasket sealing surfaces on the water outlet and thermostat housing (photo).
8   To install the thermostat, place it in the housing, install a new gasket, install the water outlet and tighten the water outlet bolts to the specified torque (photo).
9   Install the upper radiator hose.
10  Fill the cooling system with the proper antifreeze/water mixture (refer to Chapter 1).
11  Reconnect the battery cable and start the engine.
12  Run the engine with the radiator cap removed until the upper radiator hose is hot (thermostat open).
13  With the engine idling, add coolant to the radiator until the level reaches the bottom of the filler neck.
14  Install the radiator cap, making sure the arrows on the cap line up with the radiator overflow tube.

## V6 engines

15  Refer to the Caution in Section 2.

16  Disconnect the cable from the negative battery terminal.
17  Remove the air cleaner, tagging all hoses as they are removed to simplify installation.
18  Drain the cooling system until the level is below the thermostat (refer to Step 3).
19  Disconnect the upper radiator hose from the thermostat housing.
20  Remove the thermostat housing bolts and separate the housing from the engine. On models so equipped, the cruise control vacuum modulator will have to be disconnected first, as it is attached to the housing. Also, some model vehicles may have temperature sending switches installed in the thermostat housing. If so, disconnect each of the vacuum hoses from the switch (noting their installed positions) and then unscrew the switch from the housing.
21  After separating the thermostat housing from the engine, the thermostat will be visible and can be lifted out. Note how the thermostat is positioned in the recess, as it must be replaced in the same position.
22  Before installation, use a gasket scraper or putty knife to carefully remove all traces of the old gasket from the thermostat housing and the engine sealing surface. Do not allow the gasket pieces to drop down into the intake manifold.
23  Apply a 1/8-inch bead of RTV-type sealant to the sealing surface on the engine and place the thermostat into the recess (photo).
24  Immediately place the thermostat housing with sealant and a new gasket into position and tighten the bolts to the specified torque.
25  Where applicable, install the cruise control vacuum modulator/or the temperature sending switches and vacuum hoses.
26  Connect the upper radiator hose and tighten the hose clamp securely.
27  Reinstall the air cleaner.
28  To complete the installation, refer to Steps 10 through 14.

3.5   Remove the four-cylinder engine thermostat housing

3.7   Clean the thermostat housing with a scraper. Not all models use a gasket

3.8   When installing the thermostat, make sure the power element (arrow) is pointed down as shown

3.23   Installing the 2.8 liter V6 engine thermostat

## 4  Thermostat — check

1    The best way to check the operation of the thermostat is with it removed from the engine. In most cases, if the thermostat is suspect, it is more economical to simply buy and install a replacement thermostat, as they are not very costly.
2    To check, first remove the thermostat as described in Section 3.
3    Inspect the thermostat for excessive corrosion and damage. Replace it with a new one if either of these conditions is noted.
4    Place the thermostat in hot water, 25 degrees above the temperature stamped on the thermostat. When submerged in the water, which should be agitated thoroughly, the valve should open all the way.
5    Remove the thermostat, using a piece of bent wire, and place it in water which is 10 degrees below the temperature on the thermostat, or about 185 degrees. At this temperature, the thermostat valve should close completely.
6    Reinstall the thermostat if it operates properly. If it does not, purchase a new thermostat of the same temperature rating.

## 5  Radiator — removal, servicing and installation

**Caution:** *The engine must be completely cool before beginning this procedure. Also, when working in the vicinity of the electric fan, disconnect the negative battery cable from the battery to prevent the fan from coming on accidentally.*
1    Refer to the Caution in Section 2.
2    Disconnect the cable from the negative battery terminal (if not done previously).
3    Drain the radiator (refer to Chapter 1, if necessary).
4    Disconnect the engine forward strut bracket from the radiator, loosen the bolt and swing the bracket rearward.
5    Disconnect the forward headlamp harness from the frame and unplug the fan connector.
6    Remove the fan assembly.

7    Scribe a line around the hood latch on the radiator support to mark its location and remove the latch.
8    Remove the radiator hoses from the radiator, disconnect the coolant recovery hose, and on automatic transaxle models, disconnect and plug the cooler lines.
9    Remove the radiator attaching bolts and clamps and lift the radiator from the engine compartment. On air conditioning equipped models, lift the drivers side of the radiator first, so the radiator neck will clear the compressor.
10   Carefully examine the radiator for evidence of leaks and damage. It is recommended that any necessary repairs be performed by a radiator repair shop.
11   With the radiator removed, brush accumulations of insects and leaves from the fins and examine and replace, if necessary, any hoses or clamps which have deteriorated.
12   The radiator can be flushed as described in Chapter 1.
13   Replace the radiator cap with a new one of the same rating, or if the cap is comparatively new, have it tested by a service station.
14   If you are installing a new radiator, transfer the fittings from the old unit to the new one.
15   Installation is the reverse of removal. When setting the radiator in the chassis, make sure that it seats securely in the lower rubber mounting pads.
16   After installing the radiator, refill it with the proper coolant mixture (refer to Chapter 1), then start the engine and check for leaks.

## 6  Fan — removal and installation

**Caution:** *The engine must be completely cool before beginning this procedure. Also, when working in the vicinity of the electric fan, disconnect the negative battery cable from the battery to prevent the fan from coming on accidentally.*
1    Remove the fan frame-to-radiator bolts.
2    Lift the retaining tabs and unplug the fan connector.
3    Lift the fan assembly from the engine compartment.
4    To install, plug in the electrical connector, place the fan assembly

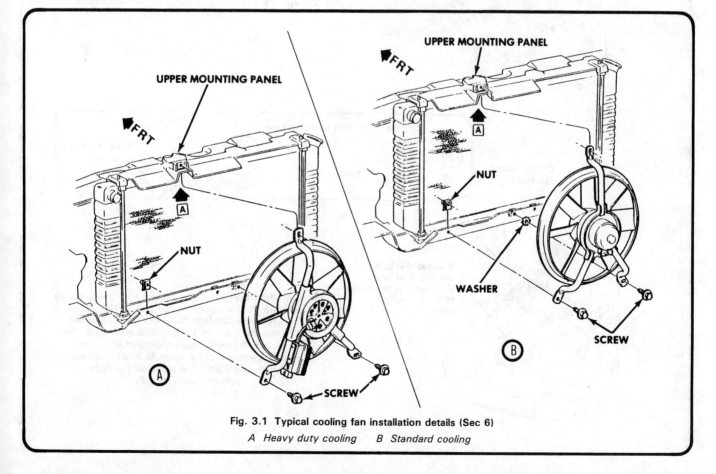

**Fig. 3.1  Typical cooling fan installation details (Sec 6)**
*A  Heavy duty cooling     B  Standard cooling*

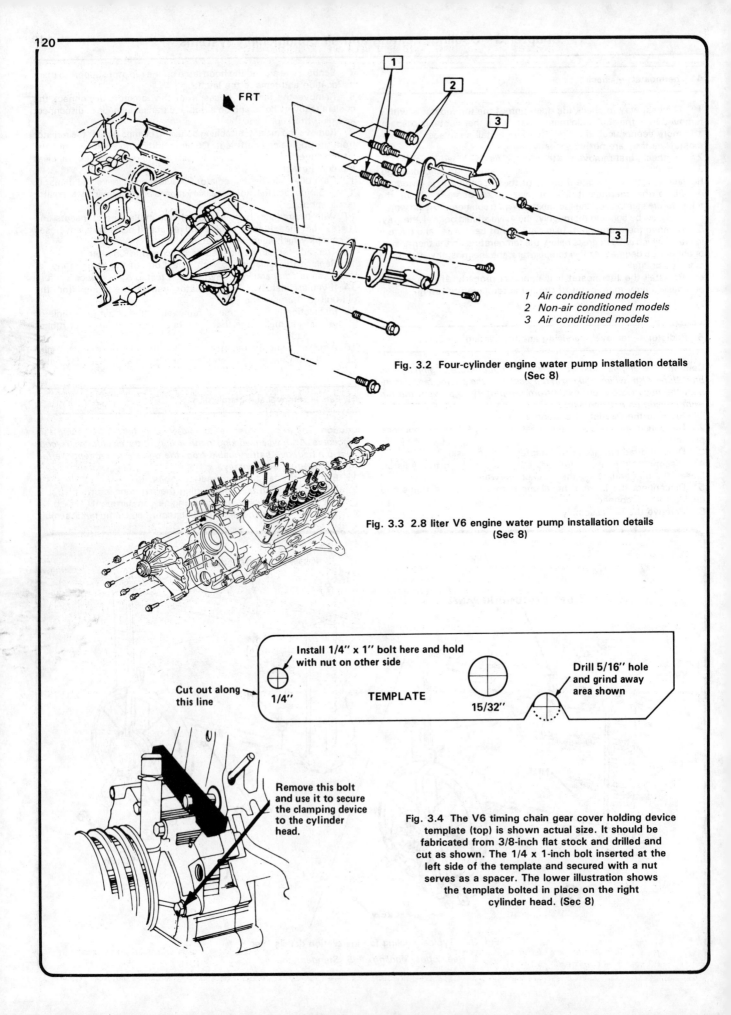

FRT

1  Air conditioned models
2  Non-air conditioned models
3  Air conditioned models

**Fig. 3.2  Four-cylinder engine water pump installation details (Sec 8)**

**Fig. 3.3  2.8 liter V6 engine water pump installation details (Sec 8)**

Install 1/4'' x 1'' bolt here and hold with nut on other side

Cut out along this line

1/4''

TEMPLATE

15/32''

Drill 5/16'' hole and grind away area shown

Remove this bolt and use it to secure the clamping device to the cylinder head.

**Fig. 3.4  The V6 timing chain gear cover holding device template (top) is shown actual size. It should be fabricated from 3/8-inch flat stock and drilled and cut as shown. The 1/4 x 1-inch bolt inserted at the left side of the template and secured with a nut serves as a spacer. The lower illustration shows the template bolted in place on the right cylinder head. (Sec 8)**

in position and install the retaining bolts.

5   Connect the negative battery cable and check for proper operation as the engine warms up to operating temperature.

## 7   Water pump — check

1   A failure in the water pump can cause overheating and serious engine damage, as a defective pump will not circulate coolant through the engine.

2   There are three ways to check the operation of the water pump while it is still installed on the engine. If the pump is defective, it should be replaced with a new or rebuilt unit.

3   With the engine at normal operating temperature, squeeze the upper radiator hose. If the water pump is working properly, a pressure surge will be felt as the hose is released.

4   Water pumps are equipped with *weep* or vent holes. If a pump seal failure occurs, small amounts of coolant will leak from the weep holes. In most cases it will be necessary to use a flashlight from under the vehicle to see evidence of leakage from this point on the pump body.

5   If the water pump shaft bearings fail, there may be a squealing sound emitted from the front of the engine while it is running. Shaft wear can be felt if the water pump pulley is forced up and down. Do not mistake drivebelt slippage, which also causes a squealing sound, for water pump failure.

## 8   Water pump — removal and installation

**Caution:** *The engine must be completely cool before beginning this procedure. Also, when working in the vicinity of the electric fan, disconnect the negative battery cable from the battery to prevent the fan from coming on accidentally.*

1   Refer to the Caution in Section 2.

2   Drain the cooling system (refer to Chapter 1, if necessary).

3   Remove the accessory drivebelts, alternator, air conditioning compressor and other components which could interfere with removal.

4   Disconnect the all hoses from the water pump.

5   **Note:** *On 2.8 liter V6 engines, care must be taken when removing the water pump bolts because they pass through the timing chain cover. Removal of the bolts can break the case seal and allow coolant to enter the crankcase. To prevent this, before removing the water pump, secure the timing chain cover to the block with a clamping device shown in the accompanying illustration (photo).*

6   On four-cylinder 2.5 liter and 2.8 liter V6 engines, remove the retaining bolts and lift the water pump from the engine.

7   On 3.0 and 3.8 liter engines, remove the two nuts from the right front engine mount at the cradle and raise the engine with a jack for access.

8   Remove the water pump pulley bolts and the pulley.

9   Remove the water pump bolts and lift the pump from the engine.

10   If installing a new or rebuilt pump, transfer the pulley from the old unit to the new one.

11   On all models, make sure all sealing surfaces are clean of any foreign material.

12   On 2.5 liter four-cylinder engines, place a 1/8-inch bead of RTV-type sealant on the pump sealing surface. While the sealant is still wet, install the pump, tighten the mounting bolts to the specified torque and connect the water hoses.

13   On 2.8 liter V6 engines, apply a 3/32-inch bead of anaerobic-type sealant on the water pump sealing surfaces as shown in the accompanying illustration.

14   Coat the threads of the retaining bolts with RTV-type sealant to prevent leaks and install the water pump. Tighten the bolts to the specified torque.

15   On 3.0 and 3.8 liter V6 engines, install the water pump, using a new gasket, and tighten the bolts to the specified torque. Install the pulley, lower the engine and install the engine mount-to-cradle nuts.

16   On all models, install the hoses, drivebelts and other components which were removed for access.

17   Refill the cooling system with a 50/50 solution of water and the specified coolant (Chapter 1).

18   Connect the battery negative cable, start the engine and run it until normal operating temperature is reached, then check for leaks.

8.6   On 2.8 liter V6 engines in which stud C goes through both the timing cover and the water pump, remove the water pump mounting bolts (arrows) after using bolt A to attach the tool mentioned to the right cylinder head at hole B

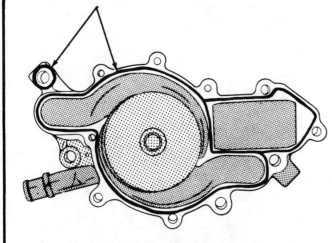

Fig. 3.5  2.8 liter engine water pump anaerobic sealant application (arrows) (Sec 8)

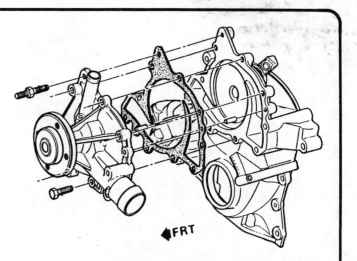

Fig. 3.6  3.0 and 3.8 liter engine water pump installation details (Sec 8)

## 9   Coolant temperature sending unit — check and replacement

1    The coolant temperature indicator system is composed of a light mounted in the instrument panel and a coolant temperature sending unit located in a water passage, usually in the cylinder head or engine block. If a temperature gauge is included in the instrument cluster, the temperature sending unit is replaced by a transducer.

2    **Caution:** *Since the ignition key will be in the On position for some of the diagnostic steps, be especially careful to stay clear of the electric fan blades.*

3    If overheating occurs, check the coolant level in the system and then make sure that the wiring between the light or gauge and the sending unit is secure.

4    When the ignition switch is turned on and the starter motor is turning, the indicator light should be on (overheated engine indication). If the light is not on, the bulb may be burned out, the ignition switch may be faulty or the circuit may be open.

5    As soon as the engine starts, the light should go out and remain out unless the engine overheats. Failure of the light to go out may be due to grounded wiring between the light and the sending unit, a defective sending unit or a faulty ignition switch.

6    If the sending unit is to be replaced, it is simply unscrewed and a replacement installed. Make sure that the engine is cool before removing the defective sending unit. There will be some coolant loss, so check the level after the replacement has been installed.

## 10   Air conditioning system — servicing

**Caution:** *The air conditioning system is under high pressure. Do not disassemble any portion of the system (hoses, compressor, line fittings, etc.) without having the system depressurized by a dealer or repair facility.*

1    Regularly inspect the condenser fins, located ahead of the radiator, and brush away leaves and bugs.

2    Clean the evaporator drain tubes.

3    Check the condition of the system hoses. If there is any sign of deterioration or hardening, have them replaced by a dealer or competent repair facility.

4    At the recommended intervals, check and adjust the compressor drivebelt as described in Chapter 1.

5    Because of the special tools, equipment and skills required to service air conditioning systems, and the differences between the various systems that may be installed on vehicles, major air conditioning servicing procedures cannot be covered in this manual.

# Chapter 4  Fuel and exhaust systems

*Refer to Chapter 13 for Specifications and information applicable to 1986 and later models*

## Contents

Carburetor — removal and installation . . . . . . . . . . . . . . .   7
Carburetor (E2ME/E2MC) — overhaul . . . . . . . . . . . . . . .   9
Carburetor (E2SE) — overhaul . . . . . . . . . . . . . . . . . . .   8
Electronic fuel injection (EFI) — general information . . . . . . .  10
Engine idle speed check and adjustment . . . . . . .   See Chapter 1
Exhaust system check . . . . . . . . . . . . . . . .   See Chapter 1
Exhaust system components — removal and installation . . . .  19
Fuel filter replacement . . . . . . . . . . . . . . . . .   See Chapter 1
Fuel injection pressure relief procedure . . . . . . . . . . . . . . .  11
Fuel line -- repair and replacement . . . . . . . . . . . . . . . . . .   4
Fuel pressure regulator — removal and installation . . . . . . . .  14
Fuel pump — check . . . . . . . . . . . . . . . . . . . . . . . . . . . .   2
Fuel pump (carbureted models) — removal and installation . . .   3

Fuel pump (injected models) — removal and installation . . . . .  12
Fuel system check . . . . . . . . . . . . . . . . . . . . .   See Chapter 1
Fuel tank — removal and installation . . . . . . . . . . . . . . . . .   5
Fuel tank — repair . . . . . . . . . . . . . . . . . . . . . . . . . . . . .   6
General information  . . . . . . . . . . . . . . . . . . . . . . . . . . . .   1
Idle air control (IAC) — removal and installation . . . . . . . . . .  13
Injector (TBI) — removal and installation . . . . . . . . . . . . . . .  15
Multi-port Fuel Injection (MFI) — check and repair . . . . . . . . .  18
Thermo-controlled air cleaner — check . . . . . . . .   See Chapter 1
Throttle body injection (TBI) — overhaul . . . . . . . . . . . . . . .  17
Throttle body injection (TBI) — removal and installation . . . . .  16
Throttle linkage check . . . . . . . . . . . . . . . . . . . .   See Chapter 1

## Specifications

### *Carburetor specifications — 1982 models*
#### E2ME and E2SE

| | |
|---|---|
| **Float adjustment** | |
| 17082196  . . . . . . . . . . . . . . . . . . . . . . . . . . . . . . . . . . . | 5/16-in |
| 17082316  . . . . . . . . . . . . . . . . . . . . . . . . . . . . . . . . . . . | 1/4-in |
| 17082317 | |
| 17082320 | |
| 17082321 | |
| 17082640 | |
| 17082641 | |
| 17082642 | |
| **Fast idle cam (choke rod)** | |
| 17082196  . . . . . . . . . . . . . . . . . . . . . . . . . . . . . . . . . . . | 18° |
| 17082317  . . . . . . . . . . . . . . . . . . . . . . . . . . . . . . . . . . . | 27° |
| 17082317 | |
| 17082640 | |
| 17082641 | |
| 17082320  . . . . . . . . . . . . . . . . . . . . . . . . . . . . . . . . . . . | 25° |
| 17082321 | |
| 17082640 | |
| **Primary vacuum break adjustment** | |
| 17082196  . . . . . . . . . . . . . . . . . . . . . . . . . . . . . . . . . . . | 21° |
| 17082316  . . . . . . . . . . . . . . . . . . . . . . . . . . . . . . . . . . . | 26° |
| 17082640 | |
| 17082317  . . . . . . . . . . . . . . . . . . . . . . . . . . . . . . . . . . . | 29° |
| 17082321 | |
| 17082641 | |
| 17082320  . . . . . . . . . . . . . . . . . . . . . . . . . . . . . . . . . . . | 30° |
| 17082642 | |
| **Air valve rod link adjustment (all)**  . . . . . . . . . . . . . . . . . . . | 10° |
| **Secondary vacuum break adjustment** | |
| 17082196  . . . . . . . . . . . . . . . . . . . . . . . . . . . . . . . . . . . | 19° |
| 17082316  . . . . . . . . . . . . . . . . . . . . . . . . . . . . . . . . . . . | 34° |
| 17082640 | |
| 17082317  . . . . . . . . . . . . . . . . . . . . . . . . . . . . . . . . . . . | 35° |
| 17082320 | |
| 17082321 | |
| 17082641 | |
| 17082642 | |

**Carburetor specifications — 1982 (continued)**

Unloader adjustment
    17082196 ............................................ 27°
    17082320 ............................................ 33°
    17082642
    17082316 ............................................ 35°
    17082317
    17082321
    17082640
    17082641
Lean mixture screw adjustment
    17082196 ............................................ 4-1/8 turns
    17082316 ............................................ 2-1/2 turns
    17082317
    17082320
    17082321
    17082640
    17082641
    17082642
Idle air bleed valve (all) ............................ 5-1/8 turns preset
Idle mixture needle
    17082196 ............................................ 1-3/4 turns preset
    17082316 ............................................ 4 turns preset
    17082317
    17082320
    17082321
    17082640
    17082641
    17082642

## Carburetor specifications — 1983

**E2ME**
Float adjustment (all) ............................ 5/16-in
Fast idle cam (choke rod) adjustment
    17083190 ............................................ 18°
    17083192
    17083193 ............................................ 17°
    17083194
Primary vacuum break adjustment
    17083190 ............................................ 28°
    17083192
    17083193 ............................................ 23°
    17083194 ............................................ 27'
Secondary vacuum break adjustment
    17083190 ............................................ 24°
    17083192
    17083193 ............................................ 28°
    17083194
Unloader adjustment
    17083190 ............................................ 32°
    17093191
    17083193 ............................................ 27°
    17083194 ............................................ 35°
Lean mixture screw adjustment using gauge (all) ......... 1.305 in
Rich mixture screw adjustment (all) .................. 1/8-in
Idle mixture screw preset adjustment (all) .............. 3 turns
Idle bleed screw adjustment using gauge (all) ........... 1.756 in
Choke coil lever adjustment using gauge (all) ........... 0.1206 in

**E2SE**
Float adjustment
    17082356 ............................................ 13/32-in
    17083357
    17083358
    17083359
    17083368 ............................................ 1/8-in
    17083370
    17083450
    17083451
    17083452
    17083453
    17083454
    17083455
    17083456

```
17083631  . . . . . . . . . . . . . . . . . . . . . . . . . . . . . . . .    1/4-in
17083632
17083633
17083634
17083635
17083636
17083650  . . . . . . . . . . . . . . . . . . . . . . . . . . . . . . . .    1/8-in
```

Fast idle cam (choke rod) adjustment
```
17083356  . . . . . . . . . . . . . . . . . . . . . . . . . . . . . . . .    22°
17083357
17083359
17083368
17083370
17083450  . . . . . . . . . . . . . . . . . . . . . . . . . . . . . . . .    28°
17083451
17083452
17083453
17083454
17083455
17083456
17083630
17083631
17083632
17083633
17083634
17083635
17083636
17083650
```

Primary vacuum break adjustment
```
17083356  . . . . . . . . . . . . . . . . . . . . . . . . . . . . . . . .    25°
17083357
17083358
17083359
17083368
17083370
17083450  . . . . . . . . . . . . . . . . . . . . . . . . . . . . . . . .    27°
17083451
17083452
17083453
17083454
17083455
17083456
17083630
17083631
17083632
17083633
17083634
17083635
17083636
17083650
```

Air valve rod link (all)  . . . . . . . . . . . . . . . . . . . . . . . . . . . .    1°
Air valve spring
```
17083356  . . . . . . . . . . . . . . . . . . . . . . . . . . . . . . . .    1 turn
17083357
17083358
17083359
17083368
17083370
17083450
17083451
17083452
17083453
17083454
17083455
17083456
17083630
17083631
17083632
17083633
17083634
17083635
17083636
```

Secondary vacuum break adjustment (all)  . . . . . . . . . . . . . .    35°
Unloader adjustment
```
17083356  . . . . . . . . . . . . . . . . . . . . . . . . . . . . . . . .    30°
17083357
```

**Carburetor specifications — 1983 (continued)**

| | |
|---|---|
| 17083358 ................................................. | 30° |
| 17083359 | |
| 17083368 | |
| 17083370 | |
| 17083450 ................................................. | 45° |
| 17083451 | |
| 17083452 | |
| 17083453 | |
| 17083454 | |
| 17083455 | |
| 17083456 | |
| 17083630 | |
| 17083631 | |
| 17083632 | |
| 17083633 | |
| 17083634 | |
| 17083635 | |
| 17083636 | |
| 17083650 | |
| Choke coil lever (all) .............................. | 0.085 in |

## *Carburetor specifications — 1984*

**E2ME**

| | |
|---|---|
| Float adjustment | |
| 17082130 ................................................. | 3/8-in |
| 17082132 | |
| 17084191 ................................................. | 5/16-in |
| 17084193 | |
| 17084194 | |
| 17084195 | |
| Lean mixture screw adjustment using gauge (all) .......... | 1.304 in |
| Rich mixture screw adjustment ........................ | 1/8-in |
| Idle mixture needle adjustment | |
| 17082130 ................................................. | 1-1/4 turns |
| 17082132 | |
| 17084191 ................................................. | Preset 3 turns, final adjustment on vehicle |
| 17084193 | |
| 17084194 | |
| 17084195 | |
| Choke coil lever adjustment using gauge (all) ............ | 0.120 in |
| Choke link cam adjustment | |
| 17084191 ................................................. | 18° |
| 17082130 ................................................. | 20° |
| 17082132 | |
| 17084193 ................................................. | 17° |
| 17084194 | |
| 17084195 | |
| Primary vacuum break adjustment | |
| 17084191 ................................................. | 28° |
| 17082130 ................................................. | 27° |
| 17082132 | |
| 17084193 | |
| 17084194 | |
| 17084195 | |
| Secondary vacuum break adjustment | |
| 17082132 ................................................. | 24° |
| 17084191 ................................................. | 25° |
| Unloader adjustment | |
| 17082130 ................................................. | 38° |
| 17082132 ................................................. | 32° |
| 17084192 ................................................. | 35° |
| 17084193 | |

**E2SE**

| | |
|---|---|
| Float adjustment | |
| 17084356 ................................................. | 9/32-in |
| 17084357 | |
| 17084358 | |
| 17084359 | |
| 17084632 | |
| 17084633 | |
| 17084635 | |
| 17084636 | |
| 17072683 | |

```
17074812 ....................................  9/32-in
17084356
17084357
17084358
17084359
17084368 ....................................  1/8-in
17084370
17084430 ....................................  11/32-in
17084431
17084434
17084435
17084452 ....................................  5/32-in
17084453
17084455
17084456
17084458
17084532
17085534
17084535
17084537
17084538
17084540
17084542
```

Fast idle cam (choke rod) adjustment
```
17084356 ....................................  22°
17084357
17084358
17084359
17084368
17084370
17084430 ....................................  15°
17084431
17084434
17084435
17084452 ....................................  28°
17084453
17084455
17084456
17084458
17084532
17084632
17084633
17084635
17084636
17084538
17084540
17084542
17072683
17074812
```

Primary vacuum break adjustment
```
17084356 ....................................  25°
17084357
17084358
17084368
17084370
17084452
17084453
17084455
17084456
17084458
17082683
17074812
17084356
17084357
17084358
17084359
17084368
17084370
17084452
17084453
17084455
17084456
17084458
17084532
17084534
17084535
```

**Carburetor specifications — 1984 (continued)**
| | |
|---|---|
| 17084537 .................................... | 25° |
| 17084538 | |
| 17084540 | |
| 17084542 | |
| 17084632 | |
| 17084633 | |
| 17084635 | |
| 17084636 | |

**Air valve rod link adjustment (all)** ..................... 1°

**Air valve spring adjustment**
| | |
|---|---|
| 17084356 ................................. | 3/4 turn |
| 17084357 | |
| 17084358 | |
| 17084359 | |
| 17084368 | |
| 17084370 | |
| 17084452 ................................. | 1/2 turn |
| 17084453 | |
| 17084455 | |
| 17084456 | |
| 17084458 | |
| 17084532 | |
| 17084632 | |
| 17084633 | |
| 17084634 | |
| 17084635 | |
| 17084537 | |
| 17084538 | |
| 17084540 | |
| 17084542 | |
| 17084430 ................................. | 1 turn |
| 17084431 | |
| 17084434 | |
| 17084435 | |

**Secondary vacuum break adjustment**
| | |
|---|---|
| 17084356 ................................. | 30° |
| 17084357 | |
| 17084358 | |
| 17084359 | |
| 17084368 | |
| 17084370 | |
| 17084430 ................................. | 38° |
| 17084431 | |
| 17084434 | |
| 17084435 | |
| 17084452 ................................. | 35° |
| 17084453 | |
| 17084455 | |
| 17084456 | |
| 17084458 | |
| 17084532 | |
| 17084632 | |
| 17084635 | |
| 17084636 | |
| 17072683 | |
| 17074812 | |
| 17084534 | |
| 17084537 | |
| 17084538 | |
| 17084540 | |
| 17084542 | |
| 17084633 | |

**Unloader adjustment**
| | |
|---|---|
| 17084356 ................................. | 30° |
| 17084357 | |
| 17084358 | |
| 17084359 | |
| 17084368 | |
| 17084370 | |
| 17084430 ................................. | 42° |
| 17084431 | |
| 17084434 | |
| 17084435 | |
| 17084452 ................................. | 45° |
| 17084453 | |

| | |
|---|---|
| 17084455 . . . . . . . . . . . . . . . . . . . . . . . . . . . . . . . . . . | 45° |
| 17084456 | |
| 17084458 | |
| 17084532 | |
| 17084632 | |
| 17084633 | |
| 17084635 | |
| 17084636 | |
| 17072683 | |
| 17074812 | |
| 17084534 | |
| 17084535 | |
| 17084537 | |
| 17084538 | |
| 17084540 | |
| 17084542 | |
| Lean mixture screw adjustment (all) . . . . . . . . . . . . . . . . . | 2-1/2 turns |
| Idle mixture screw adjustment (all) . . . . . . . . . . . . . . . . . | 4 turns |
| Choke coil lever adjustment (all) . . . . . . . . . . . . . . . . . . . . | 0.085 in |

## Carburetor specifications — 1985

### E2ME

| | |
|---|---|
| Float adjustment | |
| 17085190 . . . . . . . . . . . . . . . . . . . . . . . . . . . . . . . . . . | 5/16-in |
| 17085192 . . . . . . . . . . . . . . . . . . . . . . . . . . . . . . . . . . | 11/32-in |
| 17085194 | |
| Lean mixture screw adjustment with gauge (all) . . . . . . . . . | 1.304 in |
| Idle mixture screw adjustment (all) . . . . . . . . . . . . . . . . . | Preset 3 turns, final adjustment on vehicle |
| Choke lever adjustment with gauge (all) . . . . . . . . . . . . . . | 0.120 in |
| Fast idle cam (choke rod) | |
| 17085190 . . . . . . . . . . . . . . . . . . . . . . . . . . . . . . . . . . | 18° |
| 17085192 . . . . . . . . . . . . . . . . . . . . . . . . . . . . . . . . . . | 17° |
| 17085194 | |
| Primary vacuum break adjustment | |
| 17085190 . . . . . . . . . . . . . . . . . . . . . . . . . . . . . . . . . . | 28° |
| 17085192 . . . . . . . . . . . . . . . . . . . . . . . . . . . . . . . . . . | 27° |
| 17085194 | |
| Secondary vacuum break adjustment | |
| 17085190 . . . . . . . . . . . . . . . . . . . . . . . . . . . . . . . . . . | 32° |
| 17085192 . . . . . . . . . . . . . . . . . . . . . . . . . . . . . . . . . . | 35° |
| 17085194 | |

### E2SE

| | |
|---|---|
| Float adjustment | |
| 17084534 . . . . . . . . . . . . . . . . . . . . . . . . . . . . . . . . . . | 5/32-in |
| 17084535 | |
| 17084540 | |
| 17085542 | |
| 17085453 | |
| 17085458 | |
| 17084542 . . . . . . . . . . . . . . . . . . . . . . . . . . . . . . . . . . | 1/8-in |
| 17085368 | |
| 17085370 | |
| 17085356 . . . . . . . . . . . . . . . . . . . . . . . . . . . . . . . . . . | 9/32-in |
| 17085357 | |
| 17085358 | |
| 17085359 | |
| 17085369 | |
| 17085371 | |
| Fast idle cam (choke rod) adjustment | |
| 17084534 . . . . . . . . . . . . . . . . . . . . . . . . . . . . . . . . . . | 28° |
| 17084535 | |
| 17084540 | |
| 17084542 | |
| 17085452 | |
| 17085453 | |
| 17085458 | |
| 17085356 . . . . . . . . . . . . . . . . . . . . . . . . . . . . . . . . . . | 22° |
| 17085357 | |
| 17085358 | |
| 17085359 | |
| 17085359 | |
| 17085368 | |
| 17085369 | |
| 17085370 | |
| 17085371 | |

**Carburetor specifications — 1985 (continued)**

Primary vacuum break adjustment (all) . . . . . . . . . . . . . . . . . .          25°
Air valve rod link adjustment (all) . . . . . . . . . . . . . . . . . . . .          1°
Air valve spring adjustment
    17085356 . . . . . . . . . . . . . . . . . . . . . . . . . . . . . . . . .          1 turn
    17085357
    17085358
    17085359
    17085368
    17085370
    17085371
    17084534 . . . . . . . . . . . . . . . . . . . . . . . . . . . . . . . . .          1/2 turn
    17084535
    17084540
    17084542
    17085452
    17085453
    17085458
Secondary vacuum break adjustment
    17085356 . . . . . . . . . . . . . . . . . . . . . . . . . . . . . . . . .          30°
    17085357
    17085359
    17085368
    17085369
    17085370
    17085371
    17084534 . . . . . . . . . . . . . . . . . . . . . . . . . . . . . . . . .          35°
    17084535
    17084540
    17084542
    17085452
    17085453
    17085458
Unloader adjustment
    17085356 . . . . . . . . . . . . . . . . . . . . . . . . . . . . . . . . .          30°
    17085357
    17085358
    17085359
    17085368
    17085369
    17085370
    17085371
    17084534 . . . . . . . . . . . . . . . . . . . . . . . . . . . . . . . . .          45°
    17084535
    17084540
    17084542
    17085452
    17085453
    17085458
    17084633
    17084635
    17084636
    17084430 . . . . . . . . . . . . . . . . . . . . . . . . . . . . . . . . .          26°
    17084431
    17084434
    17084435
Lean mixture screw (all) . . . . . . . . . . . . . . . . . . . . . . . . . .          2-1/2 turns
Idle mixture screw (all) . . . . . . . . . . . . . . . . . . . . . . . . . . .          4 turns

**Torque specifications**          **Ft-lbs**
Carburetor retaining bolts . . . . . . . . . . . . . . . . . . . . . . . . .          14 to 16
Carburetor stud . . . . . . . . . . . . . . . . . . . . . . . . . . . . . . . .          2 to 3
Exhaust pipe-to-manifold nuts . . . . . . . . . . . . . . . . . . . . . .          15 to 22
Exhaust crossover pipe-to-manifold nuts . . . . . . . . . . . . . .          15
Early Fuel Evaporation (EFE) heater nuts . . . . . . . . . . . . . .          4 to 12
Intermediate exhaust pipe-to-bracket . . . . . . . . . . . . . . . . .          15 to 25
Idle Air Control assembly-to-throttle body . . . . . . . . . . . . .          13
Muffler exhaust pipe clamp . . . . . . . . . . . . . . . . . . . . . . . .          7 to 14
TBI fuel return line . . . . . . . . . . . . . . . . . . . . . . . . . . . . . .          17
TBI throttle body attaching screws . . . . . . . . . . . . . . . . . .          17
TBI-to-manifold . . . . . . . . . . . . . . . . . . . . . . . . . . . . . . . .          24
Fuel meter body screws . . . . . . . . . . . . . . . . . . . . . . . . . .          3
Fuel feed and return nuts . . . . . . . . . . . . . . . . . . . . . . . . .          21
Fuel meter cover screws . . . . . . . . . . . . . . . . . . . . . . . . . .          2.2
Fuel pump retaining nuts (carbureted engines) . . . . . . . . . . .          15 to 22

### 1  General information

The fuel system consists of a rear mounted fuel tank, a mechanically operated fuel pump (carburetor-equipped engines) or an electrically operated fuel pump (fuel-injected engines), a carburetor or fuel injection assembly and an air cleaner.

The exhaust system includes a catalytic converter, muffler, related emissions equipment and associated pipes and hardware.

### 2  Fuel pump — check

**Warning:** *Gasoline is extremely flammable, so extra precautions must be taken when working on any part of the fuel system. Do not smoke or allow open flames or bare light bulbs near the work area. Also, do not work in a garage if a natural gas-type appliance with a pilot light is present.*

1  On carburetor-equipped engines, the fuel pump is located either on the rear (firewall) side of four-cylinder models or low on the front (radiator) side of V6 engines.
2  The fuel pump for fuel injected models is located in the fuel tank.
3  Both types of fuel pumps are sealed and no repairs are possible. However, on carburetor-equipped models, the fuel pump can be inspected and tested on the vehicle as follows.
4  Make sure there is fuel in the fuel tank.
5  With the engine running, check for leaks at all gasoline line connections between the fuel tank and the carburetor. Tighten any loose connections. Inspect all hoses for flat spots and kinks which would restrict the fuel flow. Air leaks or restrictions on the suction side of the fuel pump will greatly affect pump output.
6  Check for leaks at the fuel pump diaphragm flange.
7  Disconnect the high energy ignition (HEI) connector at the distributor, then disconnect the fuel inlet line from the carburetor and place it in a metal container.
8  Crank the engine a few revolutions and make sure that well defined spurts of fuel are ejected from the open end of the line. If not, the fuel line is clogged or the fuel pump is defective.
9  Disconnect the fuel line at both ends and blow through it with compressed air. If the fuel line is not clogged, replace the fuel pump.

### 3  Fuel pump (carbureted models) — removal and installation

**Warning:** *Gasoline is extremely flammable, so extra precautions must be taken when working on any part of the fuel system. Do not smoke or allow open flames or bare light bulbs near the work area. Also, do not work in a garage if a natural gas-type appliance with a pilot light is present.*

1  Disconnect the cable from the negative battery terminal.
2  Remove the fuel inlet and outlet lines. Use two wrenches to prevent damage to the pump and connections (photo).
3  Remove the fuel pump shield (if equipped), mounting bolts, the pump and the gasket.

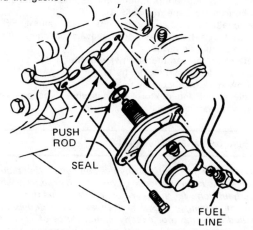

**Fig. 4.1  2.8 liter V6 fuel pump installation details (Sec 3)**

4  Install the pump using a new gasket. Use gasket sealant on the screw threads.
5  Connect the fuel lines, start the engine and check for leaks.

### 4  Fuel line — repair and replacement

**Warning:** *Gasoline is extremely flammable, so extra precautions must be taken when working on any part of the fuel system. Do not smoke or allow open flames or bare light bulbs near the work area. Also, do not work in a garage if a natural gas-type appliance with a pilot light is present.*

**Note:** *Before starting this procedure on fuel injected models, the fuel system pressure must be relieved as outlined in Section 11.*

#### *Fuel injected models*

1  Because the fuel lines on these models are under high pressure, they must always be replaced with original equipment or equivalent parts.
2  O-rings are used at screw fittings and these should be inspected for cuts and damage whenever the fittings are disconnected. Always tighten the fittings to the specified torque, using a backup wrench.

#### *Carbureted models*

3  If a section of metal fuel line must be replaced, only welded, seamless steel tubing should be used, since copper or aluminum does not have enough durability to withstand normal operating vibrations.
4  If only one section of a metal fuel line is damaged, it can be cut out and replaced with a piece of rubber hose. Be sure to use only reinforced fuel resistant hose, identified by the word *Fluroelastomer* on the hose. The inside diameter of the hose should match the outside diameter of the metal line. The rubber hose should be cut four inches longer than the section it's replacing, so there are two inches of overlap between the rubber and metal line at either end of the section. Hose clamps should be used to secure both ends of the repaired section.
5  If a section of metal line longer than six inches is being removed, use a combination of metal tubing and rubber hose so the hose lengths will be no longer than ten inches.
6  Never use rubber hose within four inches of any part of the exhaust system or within ten inches of the catalytic converter.
7  When replacing clamps, make sure the replacement clamp is identical to the one being replaced, as different clamps are used depending on location.

### 5  Fuel tank — removal and installation

**Warning:** *Gasoline is extremely flammable, so extra precautions must be taken when working on any part of the fuel system. Do not smoke or allow open flames or bare light bulbs near the work area. Also, do not work in a garage if a natural gas-type appliance with a pilot light is present. While performing any work on the fuel tank it is advisable to have a CO-2 fire extinguisher on hand and to wear safety glasses.*

3.2  Remove the fuel pump (hold the inside fitting with one wrench while turning the outside fitting with another) (2.8 liter V6 shown)

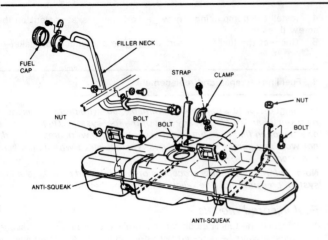

7.3   Remove the fuel line fitting

15   Installation is the reverse of the removal procedure. Replace the O-ring whenever the tank is removed.

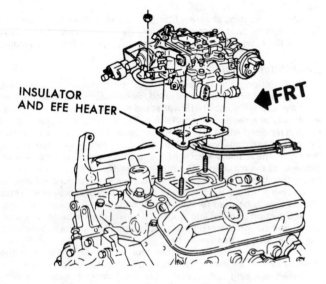

INSULATOR AND EFE HEATER

◄FRT

Note: *Before starting this procedure on fuel injected models, the fuel system pressure must be relieved as outlined in Section 11.*
1   Raise the rear of the vehicle and support it on jackstands.
2   Remove the cable from the negative battery terminal.
3   Disconnect the fuel feed line at the pump.
4   Drain all fuel from the tank into a clean container. Since there are no drain plugs on the tank, siphon the fuel through the filler neck or drain the fuel through the fuel line running to the carburetor or fuel injection unit. Do not start the siphoning process with your mouth because serious personal injury could result.
5   Remove the ground wire screw.
6   Disconnect the fuel fill and vapor return lines.
7   Disconnect the fuel pressure and fuel return hoses at the point where the rubber lines connect with the steel lines.
8   Remove the heat shield located between the exhaust pipe and the forward end of the fuel tank.
9   Disconnect the fuel gauge wire (fuel gauge/fuel pump wire on fuel injected models). Note: *The wiring harness on the fuel pump/gauge sending assembly is an integral, permanent part of the sending assembly. Do not pry up on the cover connector. Make the disconnection at the body wiring harness.*
10   While the tank is supported by an assistant or a floor jack, remove the two rear support strap bolts
11   Lower the tank sufficiently to allow disconnection of the tank electrical leads.
12   Remove the tank from the vehicle.
13   **Caution:** *Never perform any repair work involving heat or flame on the tank until it has been purged of gas and vapors. All repair work should be performed by a professional (see the following Section).*
14   Before reinstalling the tank make sure that all traces of dirt and corrosion are cleaned from it. A coat of rust preventative paint is recommended. If the tank is rusted internally, however, it should be replaced with a new one.

## 6   Fuel tank — repair

1   Any repairs to the fuel tank or filler neck should be carried out by a professional who has experience in this critical and potentially dangerous work. Even after cleaning and flushing of the fuel system, explosive fumes can remain and ignite during repair of the tank.
2   If the fuel tank is removed from the vehicle, it should not be placed in an area where sparks or open flames could ignite the fumes coming out of the tank. Be especially careful inside garages where a natural gas-type appliance is located, because the pilot light could cause an explosion.

## 7   Carburetor — removal and installation

**Warning:** *Gasoline is extremely flammable, so extra precautions must be taken when working on any part of the fuel system. Do not smoke or allow open flames or bare light bulbs near the work area. Also, do not work in a garage if a natural gas type appliance with a pilot light is present.*
1   Remove the fuel tank cap to relieve the pressure in the tank.
2   Detach the cable from the negative battery terminal, then remove the air cleaner.
3   Disconnect the fuel and vacuum lines from the carburetor, noting their locations (photo).
4   Disconnect the accelerator linkage and cruise control linkage (if so equipped).
5   Disconnect the throttle linkage and downshift cable (automatic transaxle).
6   Remove all hoses and wires, making very careful note of how they are attached. Tags or coded pieces of tape will help.
7   Remove the carburetor mounting nuts and/or bolts and separate the carburetor from the manifold.
8   Remove the gasket and/or Early Fuel Evaporation (EFE) insulator.
9   Installation is the reverse of the removal procedure, but the following points should be noted:
   a)   By filling the carburetor bowl with fuel, the initial start-up will be easier and less drain on the battery.
   b)   New gaskets should be used.
   c)   Idle speed and mixture settings should be checked and, if necessary, adjusted.

## 8   Carburetor (E2SE) — overhaul

Note: *Carburetor overhaul is an involved procedure that requires some experience. The home mechanic without much experience should have the overhaul done by a dealer service department or repair shop. Because of running production changes, some details of the unit overhauled here may not exactly match those of your carburetor, although the home mechanic with previous experience should be able to detect the differences and modify the procedure.*

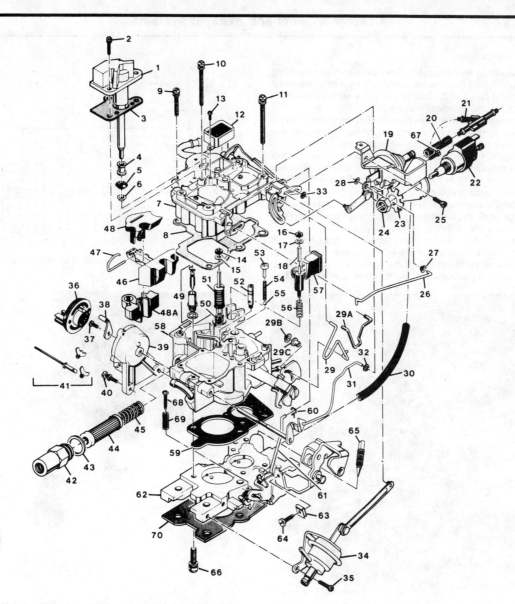

**Fig. 4.4 E2SE carburetor — exploded view (Sec 8)**

| | | | | | | | |
|---|---|---|---|---|---|---|---|
| 1 | Mixture control solenoid | 26 | Air valve link | 47 | Float hinge pin |
| 2 | Solenoid attaching screw | 27 | Air valve link bushing | 48 | Float bowl upper insert |
| 3 | Solenoid gasket | 28 | Air valve link retainer | 48A | Float bowl lower insert |
| 4 | Solenoid spacer | 29A | Fast idle cam link | 49 | Needle and seat assembly |
| 5 | Seal | 29B | Retainer link | 50 | Pump return spring |
| 6 | Seal retainer | 29C | Link bushing | 51 | Pump plunger assembly |
| 7 | Air horn assembly | 30 | Vacuum break hose | 52 | Primary metering jet assembly |
| 8 | Gasket | 31 | Intermediate choke | 53 | Pump discharge ball retainer |
| 9 | Short air horn screw | | shaft/lever/link assembly | 54 | Pump discharge spring |
| 10 | Long air horn screw | 32 | Intermediate choke link bushing | 55 | Pump discharge ball |
| 11 | Large air horn screw | 33 | Intermediate choke link retainer | 56 | TPS adjusting spring |
| 12 | Vent stack and screen assembly | 34 | Secondary vacuum break and | 57 | Throttle Position Sensor (TPS) |
| 13 | Vent stack attaching screw | | link assembly | 58 | Float bowl assembly |
| 14 | Pump stem seal | 35 | Screw | 59 | Gasket |
| 15 | Pump stem seal retainer | 36 | Electric choke cover and | 60 | Pump link retainer |
| 16 | TPS plunger seal | | coil assembly | 61 | Pump link |
| 17 | Seal retainer | 37 | Choke coil lever attaching screw | 62 | Throttle body assembly |
| 18 | TPS actuator plunger | 38 | Coke coil lever assembly | 63 | Cam screw clip |
| 19 | Choke primary vacuum break | 39 | Choke housing | 64 | Fast idle cam screw |
| | and bracket assembly | 40 | Choke housing attaching screw | 65 | Idle needle and spring assembly |
| 20 | Primary vacuum break hose | 41 | Choke cover retainer | 66 | Screw |
| 21 | Vacuum break tee | 42 | Fuel inlet nut | 67 | Vacuum break bracket |
| 22 | Idle speed solenoid | 43 | Inlet nut gasket | | attaching screw |
| 23 | Idle speed solenoid retainer | 44 | Inlet filter | 68 | Idle stop screw |
| 24 | Idle speed solenoid attaching nut | 45 | Fuel filter spring | 69 | Idle stop screw spring |
| 25 | Vacuum break attaching screw | 46 | Float and lever assembly | 70 | Gasket |

## Disassembly

1   Before disassembling the carburetor, purchase a carburetor rebuild kit for your particular model. The model number will be found on a metal tag at the side of the carburetor. This kit will have all the necessary replacement parts for the overhaul procedure.

2   It will be necessary to have a relatively large, clean workbench to lay out all of the parts as they are removed. Many of the parts are very small and can be lost easily if the work space is cluttered.

3   Carburetor disassembly is illustrated in the following step-by-step photo sequence to make the operation as easy as possible. Work slowly through the procedure and if at any point you feel the reassembly of a certain component may prove confusing, stop and make a rough sketch or apply identification marks. The time to think about reassembling the carburetor is when it is being taken apart. The disassembly photo sequence begins with photo 8.3/1.

4   The final step in disassembly involves the idle mixture needle. It is recessed in the throttle body and sealed with a hardened steel plug. The plug should not be removed unless the needle requires replacement or normal cleaning procedures fail to clean the idle mixture

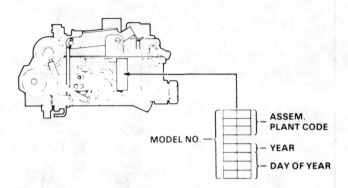

Fig. 4.5  Location of the carburetor identification tag (Sec 8)

8.3/1   Remove the gasket from the top of the air horn

8.3/2   Remove the fuel inlet nut, fuel filter and spring

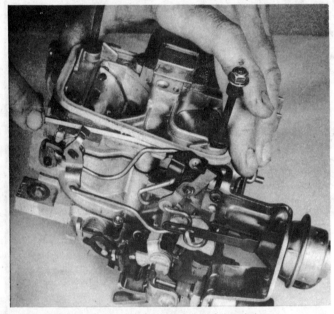

8.3/3   Remove the pump lever attaching screw

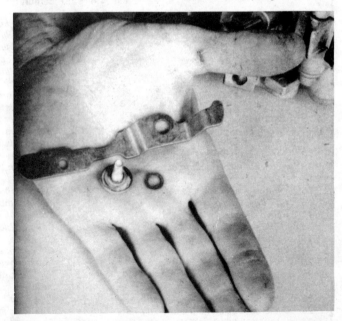

8.3/4   Disconnect the pump rod from the pump lever and remove the pump lever

8.3/5   Disconnect the primary vacuum break diaphragm hose from the throttle body

8.3/6   Remove the screws that retain the idle speed solenoid/vacuum break diaphragm bracket

8.3/7   Lift off the idle speed solenoid/vacuum break diaphragm assembly and disconnect the air valve link from the vacuum break plunger (repeat this step for the secondary vacuum break assembly, disconnecting the link from the slot in the choke lever)

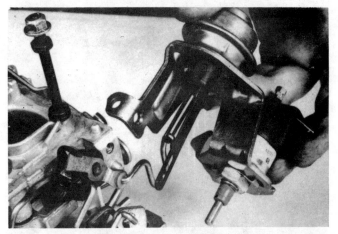

8.3/8   Disconnect the vacuum break and air valve links from the levers (it is not necessary to disconnect the links from the vacuum break plungers unless either of the rods or vacuum break units are being replaced)

8.3/9   Pry off the clip retaining the intermediate choke link to the choke lever and separate the link from the lever

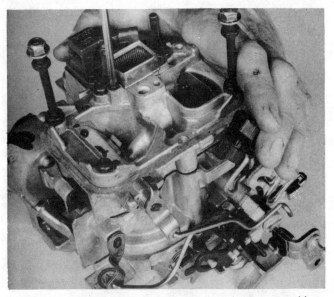

8.3/10   Remove the screws retaining the vent/screen assembly to the air horn and lift off the assembly

8.3/11   Remove the screws retaining the mixture control solenoid and, using a slight twisting motion, lift the solenoid out of the air horn

8.3/12   Remove the screws securing the air horn to the float bowl, noting their various lengths and positions to simplify installation

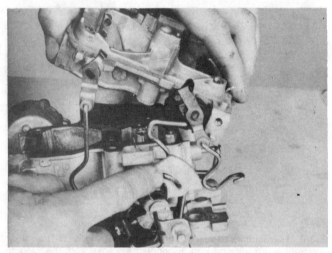

8.3/13   Rotate the fast idle cam up, lift off the air horn and disconnect the fast idle cam link from the fast idle cam

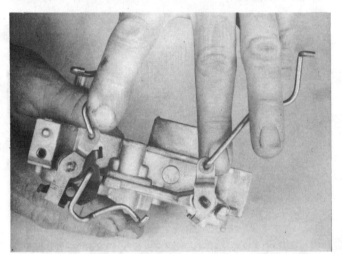

8.3/14   The links attached to the air horn need not be removed unless their replacement or removal is required to service other components

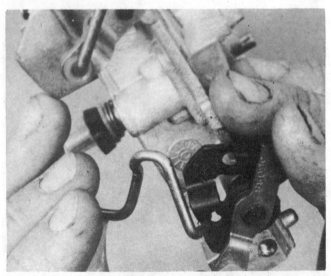

8.3/15   Disengage the fast idle cam link from the choke lever and save the bushing for reassembly

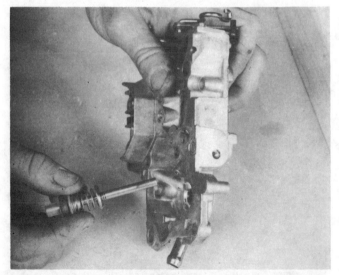

8.3/16   Remove the pump plunger from the air horn or the pump well in the float bowl (for throttle position sensor (TPS) equipped carburetors, refer to the exploded-view drawing at this time and remove the TPS)

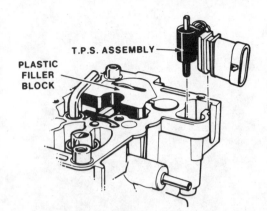

Fig. 4.6  To remove the E2SE carburetor TPS, push up from the bottom of the electrical connector and remove the TPS and connector assembly from the float bowl. Remove the spring from the bottom of the float bowl (Sec 8)

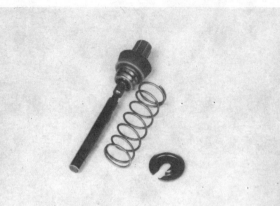

8.3/17  Compress the pump plunger spring and separate the spring retainer clip and spring from the piston

8.3/18  Remove the air horn gasket from the float bowl

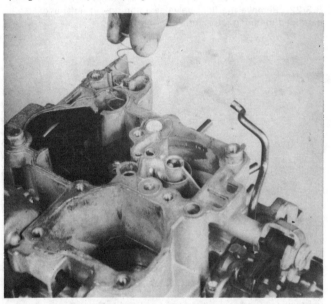

8.3/19  Remove the pump return spring from the pump well

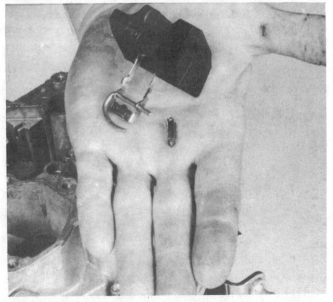

8.3/20  Remove the plastic filler block that covers the float valve

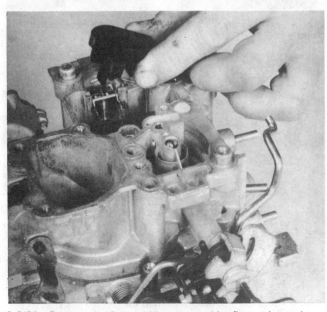

8.3/21  Remove the float and lever assembly, float valve and stabilizing spring (if used) by pulling up on the hinge pin

8.3/22  Remove the float valve seat and gasket (left) and extended metering jet (right) from the float bowl

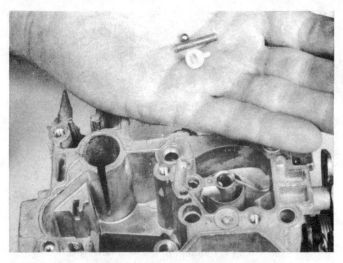

8.3/23  Using needle-nose pliers, pull out the white plastic retainer and remove the pump discharge spring and check ball (do not pry on the retainer to remove it)

8.3/24  Remove the screws retaining the choke housing to the throttle body

8.3/25  Remove the screws retaining the float bowl to the throttle body

8.3/26  Separate the float bowl from the throttle body

8.3/27  Carefully file the head off the pop rivets retaining the choke cover to the choke housing, remove the cover and tap out the remainder of the rivets

8.3/28   Remove the choke coil lever screw and lift out the lever

8.3/29   Remove the intermediate shaft and lever assembly by sliding it out of the lever side of the float bowl (for further procedures, refer to Step 4 in the text)

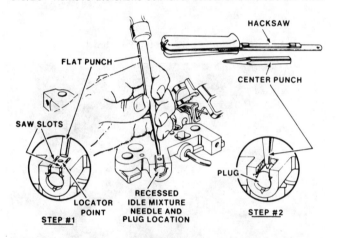

Fig. 4.7  E2SE carburetor idle mixture needle removal details (Sec 8)

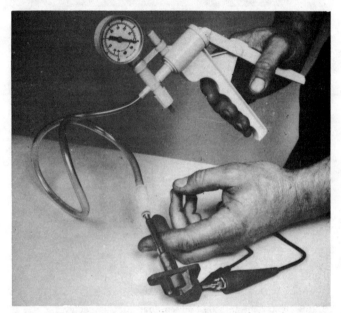

8.22   Attach a hand vacuum pump to the end of the mixture control solenoid

passages. If the idle mixture needle must be removed, refer to the accompanying illustration and proceed as follows.

5    Secure the throttle body in a vise so it is inverted with the manifold side up. Use blocks of wood to cushion the throttle body.

6    Locate the idle mixture needle and plug. It should be marked by an indented locator point on the underside of the throttle body. Using a hacksaw, make two parallel cuts in the throttle body on either side of the locator mark. The cuts should be deep enough to touch the steel plug, but should not extend more than 1/8-inch beyond the locator point.

7    Position a flat punch at a point near the ends of the saw marks. Holding it at a 45° angle, drive it into the throttle body until the casting breaks away, exposing the steel plug.

8    Use a center punch to make an indentation in the steel plug. Holding it at a 45° angle, drive the plug from the throttle body casting. **Note:** *If the plug breaks apart, be sure to remove all of the pieces.*

9    Use a 3/16-inch deep socket to remove the idle mixture needle and spring from the throttle body.

### Cleaning and inspection

10   Clean the air horn, float bowl, throttle body and related components with solvent and blow them out with compressed air. A can of compressed air can be used if an air compressor is not available. Do not use a piece of wire for cleaning the jets and passages.

11   The idle speed solenoid, mixture control solenoid, Throttle Position Sensor, electric choke, pump plunger, diaphragm, plastic filler block and other electrical, rubber and plastic parts should not be immersed in carburetor cleaner because they will harden, swell or distort.

12   Make sure all fuel passages, jets and other metering components are free of burrs and dirt.

13   Inspect the upper and lower surfaces of the air horn, float bowl

and throttle body for damage. Be sure all material has been removed.

14   Inspect all lever holes and plastic bushings for excessive wear and an out-of-round condition and replace them if necessary.

15   Inspect the float valve and seat for dirt, deep wear grooves and scoring and replace it if necessary.

16   Inspect the float valve pull clip for proper installation and adjust it if necessary.

17   Inspect the float, float arms and hinge pin for distortion and binding and correct or replace as necessary.

18   Inspect the rubber cup on the pump plunger for excessive wear and cracks.

19   Check the choke valve and linkage for excessive wear, binding and distortion and correct or replace as necessary.

20   Inspect the choke vacuum diaphragm for leaks and replace if necessary.

21   Check the choke valve for freedom of movement.

22   Check the mixture control solenoid in the following manner.

  a) Connect one end of a jumper wire to either end of the solenoid connector and the other end to the positive terminal of the battery.

  b) Connect another jumper wire between the other terminal of the solenoid connector and the negative terminal of the battery.

  c) Remove the rubber seal and retainer from the end of the solenoid stem and attach a hand vacuum pump to it (photo).

8.25    Install the gasket on the bottom of the float bowl

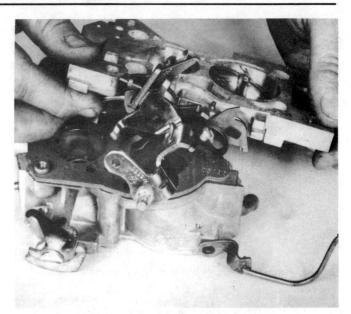

8.26A    Mount the throttle body on the float bowl

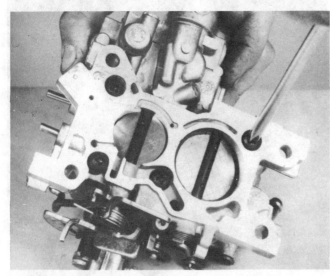

8.26B    Install the throttle body-to-float attaching screws

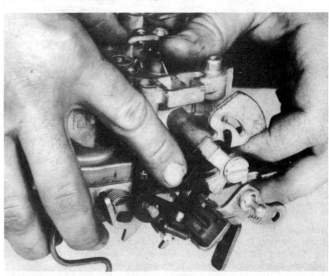

8.27    Check the engagement of the lockout tang in the secondary lockout lever

8.28A    Attach the choke housing to the throttle body

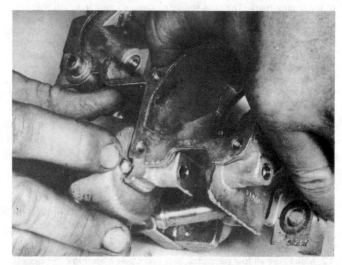

8.28B    The lug at the rear of the choke housing should sit in the bowl recess

d) With the solenoid fully energized (lean position), apply at least 25 in-Hg of vacuum and time the leak-down rate from 20 to 15 in-Hg. The leak down rate should not exceed 5 in-Hg in five seconds. If leakage exceeds that amount, replace the solenoid.

e) To check if the solenoid is sticking in the down position, again apply about 25 in-Hg of vacuum to it, then disconnect the jumper lead to the battery and watch the pump gauge reading. It should fall to zero in less than one second.

### Reassembly

23 Before reassembling the carburetor, compare all old and new gaskets back-to-back to make sure they match perfectly. Check especially that all the necessary holes are present and in the proper positions in the new gaskets.

24 If the idle mixture needle and spring have been removed, reinstall them by lightly seating the needle, then back it off three turns. This will provide a preliminary idle mixture adjustment. Final idle mixture adjustment must be made on the vehicle. Proper adjustment must be done using special emission sensing equipment, making it impractical for the home mechanic. To have the mixture settings checked or readjusted, take your vehicle to a GM dealer or other qualified mechanic with the proper equipment.

25 Install a new gasket on the bottom of the float bowl (photo).

26 Mount the throttle body on the float bowl so it is properly installed over the locating dowels on the bowl (photo), reinstall the screws and tighten them evenly and securely (photo). Be sure that the steps on the fast idle cam face toward the fast idle screw on the throttle lever when installed.

27 Inspect the linkage to make sure that the lockout tang properly engages in the slot of the secondary lockout lever and that the linkage moves freely without binding (photo).

28 Attach the choke housing to the throttle body, making sure the locating lug on the rear of the housing sits in the recess in the float bowl (photos).

29 Install the intermediate choke shaft and lever assembly in the float bowl by pushing it through from the throttle lever side.

30 Position the intermediate choke lever in the up position and install the thermostatic coil lever on the end sticking into the choke housing. The coil lever is properly aligned when the coil pick-up tang is in the 12 o'clock position (photo). Install the screw in the end of the intermediate shaft to secure the coil lever.

31 Three self-tapping screws supplied in the overhaul kit are used in place of the original pop rivets to secure the choke cover and coil assembly to the choke housing. Thread the screws into the housing, making sure they start easily and are properly aligned (photo), then remove them.

32 Place the fast idle screw on the highest step of the fast idle cam, then install the choke cover on the housing, aligning the notch in the cover with the raised casting projection on the housing cover flange (photo). When installing the cover, be sure the coil pick-up tang engages

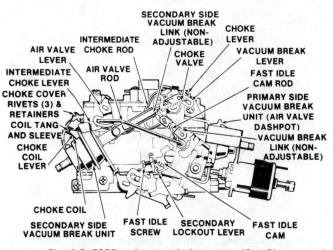

Fig. 4.8 E2SE carburetor choke system (Sec 8)

8.30 Install the thermostatic coil lever so it is in the 12 o'clock position when the intermediate choke lever is facing up

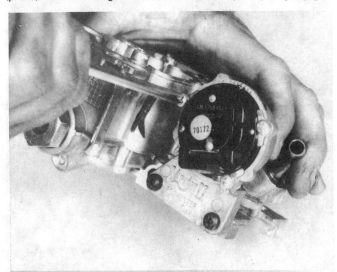

8.31 The choke cover is reinstalled with the self tapping screws supplied in the overhaul kit

8.32 Be sure the notch in the choke cover is aligned with the raised casting projection on the housing cover flange

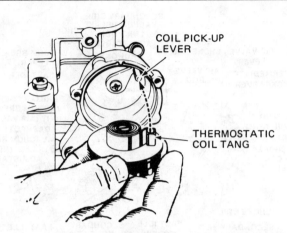

Fig. 4.9  Details of the choke housing assembly (Sec 8)

COIL PICK-UP LEVER

THERMOSTATIC COIL TANG

the inside choke lever. **Note:** *The thermostatic coil tang is formed so that it will completely encircle the coil pick-up lever. Make sure the lever is inside of the tang when installing the cover (refer to the accompanying illustration).*

33  With the choke cover in place, install the self-tapping screws and tighten them securely.

34  Install the pump discharge check ball and spring in the passage next to the float chamber, then place a new plastic retainer in the hole so that its end engages the spring and tap it lightly into place until the retainer top is flush with the bowl surface.

35  Install the main metering jet in the bottom of the float chamber (photo).

36  Install the float valve seat assembly and gasket (photo).

37  To make float level adjustments easier, bend the float arm up slightly at the notch before installing the float (photo).

38  Install the float valve onto the float arm by sliding the lever under the pull clip. The correct installation of the pull clip is shown in the accompanying illustrations. Install the float pin in the float lever (photo).

8.35  Install the main metering jet

8.36  Install the float valve seat assembly

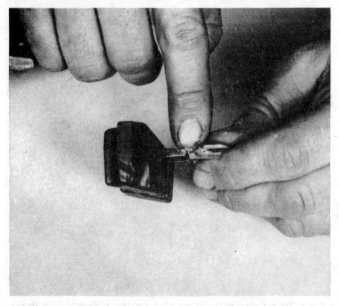

8.37  Prior to installation, bend the float arm up slightly at the point shown

8.38  Install the float retaining pin in the float lever

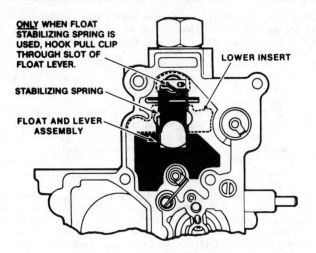

Fig. 4.10  Correct installation of the pull clip on E2SE floats with a stabilizing spring (Sec 8)

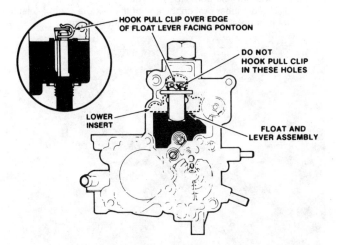

Fig. 4.11  Correct installation of the pull clip on E2SE floats without a stabilizing spring (Sec 8)

Install the float assembly by aligning the valve and seat and the float retaining pin and locating channels in the float bowl.

39  To adjust the float level, hold the float pin firmly in place, push down on the float arm at the outer end, against the top of the float valve, and see if the top of the float is the specified distance from the float bowl surface (photo). Bend the float arm as necessary to achieve the proper measurement by pushing down on the pontoon. See the Specifications for the proper float measurement for your vehicle. Check the float level visually following adjustment.

40  Install the plastic filler block over the float valve so that it is flush with the float bowl surface (photo).

41  If the carburetor is equipped with a Throttle Position Sensor, install the TPS return spring in the bottom of the well in the float bowl. Then install the TPS and connector assembly by aligning the groove in the electrical connector with the slot in the float bowl. When properly installed, the assembly should sit below the float bowl surface.

42  Install a new air horn gasket on the float bowl (photo).

8.39  Measure the float level

8.40  Install the plastic float block

8.42  Install a new air horn gasket on the float bowl

8.43   Install the pump return spring in the pump well

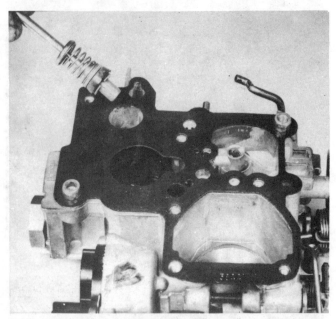

8.44   Install the pump plunger in the pump well

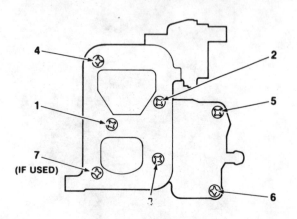

Fig. 4.12 Recommended E2SE carburetor air horn screw
tightening sequence (Sec 8)

43   Install the pump return spring in the pump well (photo).
44   Reassemble the pump plunger assembly, lubricate the plunger cap with a thin coat of engine oil and install the pump plunger in the pump well (photo).
45   If used, remove the old pump plunger seal and retainer and the old TPS plunger seal and retainer from the air horn. Install new seals and retainers in both locations and lightly stake both seal retainers in three places other than the original staking locations.
46   Install the fast idle cam rod in the lower hole of the choke lever.
47   If so equipped, apply a light coat of silicone grease or engine oil to the TPS plunger and push it through the seal in the air horn so that about one-half of the plunger extends above the seal.
48   Before installing the air horn, apply a light coat of silicone grease or engine oil to the pump plunger stem to aid in slipping it through the seal in the air horn.
49   Rotate the fast idle cam to the Up position so it can be engaged with the lower end of the fast idle cam rod (photo). While holding down on the pump plunger assembly, carefully lower the air horn onto the float bowl and guide the pump plunger stem through the seal.
50   Install the air horn retaining screws and washers, making sure the different length screws are inserted into their respective holes, then tighten them in the sequence illustrated.
51   If so equipped, install a new seal in the recess of the float bowl and attach the hot idle compensator valve.
52   Install a new rubber seal on the end of the mixture control solenoid stem until it is up against the boss on the stem (photo).

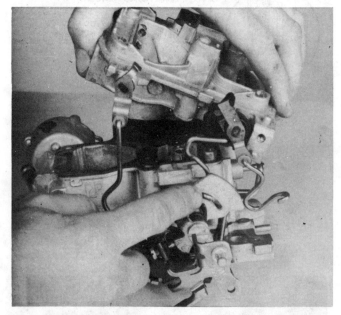

8.49   Engage the fast idle cam link in the fast idle cam prior to installation of the air horn

8.52   Attach a new rubber seal to the end of the mixture control solenoid

53  Using a 3/16-inch socket and a hammer (photo), drive the retainer over the mixture control solenoid stem just far enough to retain the rubber seal, while leaving a slight clearance between them for seal expansion.

54  Apply a light coat of engine oil to the rubber seal and, using a new gasket, install the mixture control solenoid in the air horn. Use a slight twisting motion while installing the solenoid to help the rubber seal slip into the recess.

55  Install the vent/screen assembly on the air horn.

56  Install a plastic bushing in the hole in the choke lever, with the small end facing out, then, with the intermediate choke lever at the 12 o'clock position, install the intermediate choke rod in the bushing. Install a new retaining clip on the end of the rod. Use a broad flat-blade screwdriver and a 3/16-inch socket as shown in the photo. Make sure the clip is not seated tightly against the bushing and that the linkage moves freely.

57  Reattach the primary and secondary vacuum break links and install the vacuum break and idle speed solenoid assemblies (photo).

58  Engage the pump rod with the pump rod lever (photo), install a new retaining clip on the pump rod and install the pump lever on the air horn with the washer between the lever and the air horn (photo).

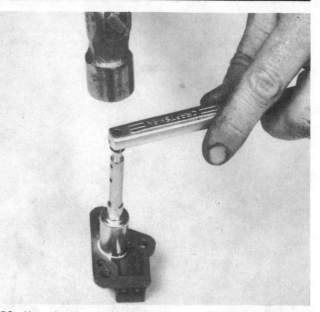

8.53  Use a hammer and hollow tool to tap the seal retainer onto the mixture control solenoid stem

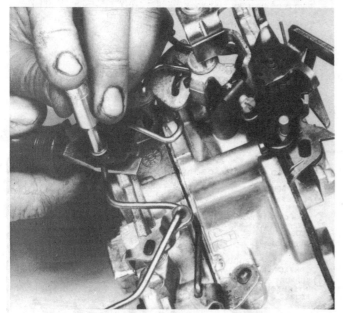

8.56  Attach a retaining clip to the intermediate choke rod to secure it to the choke lever

8.57  Install the idle speed solenoid/vacuum break diaphragm assembly

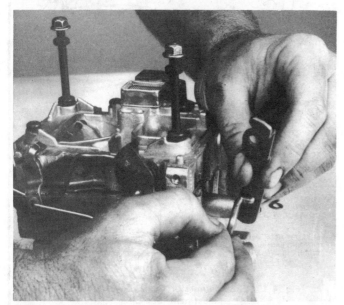

8.58A  Engage the pump with the pump rod lever

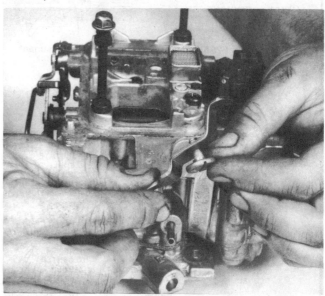

8.58B  Insert the pump rod mounting screw through the pump rod prior to installation

59 Reconnect the vacuum break hoses.
60 Install the fuel filter with the hole facing toward the inlet nut.
61 Place a new gasket on the inlet nut and install and tighten it securely. Take care not to over tighten the nut, as it could damage the gasket, leading to a fuel leak.

62 Install a new gasket on the top of the air horn (photo).
63 Check that all linkage hook-ups have been made and that they do not bind.
64 For external linkage adjustment procedures, refer to the accompanying illustrations.

8.62   Install a new gasket on top of the air horn

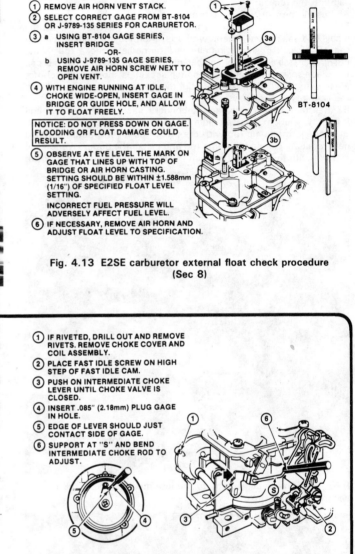

① REMOVE AIR HORN VENT STACK.
② SELECT CORRECT GAGE FROM BT-8104 OR J-9789-135 SERIES FOR CARBURETOR.
③ a USING BT-8104 GAGE SERIES, INSERT BRIDGE
      -OR-
   b USING J-9789-135 GAGE SERIES, REMOVE AIR HORN SCREW NEXT TO OPEN VENT.
④ WITH ENGINE RUNNING AT IDLE, CHOKE WIDE-OPEN, INSERT GAGE IN BRIDGE OR GUIDE HOLE, AND ALLOW IT TO FLOAT FREELY.

NOTICE: DO NOT PRESS DOWN ON GAGE. FLOODING OR FLOAT DAMAGE COULD RESULT.

⑤ OBSERVE AT EYE LEVEL THE MARK ON GAGE THAT LINES UP WITH TOP OF BRIDGE OR AIR HORN CASTING. SETTING SHOULD BE WITHIN ±1.588mm (1/16") OF SPECIFIED FLOAT LEVEL SETTING.

   INCORRECT FUEL PRESSURE WILL ADVERSELY AFFECT FUEL LEVEL.

⑥ IF NECESSARY, REMOVE AIR HORN AND ADJUST FLOAT LEVEL TO SPECIFICATION.

Fig. 4.13  E2SE carburetor external float check procedure (Sec 8)

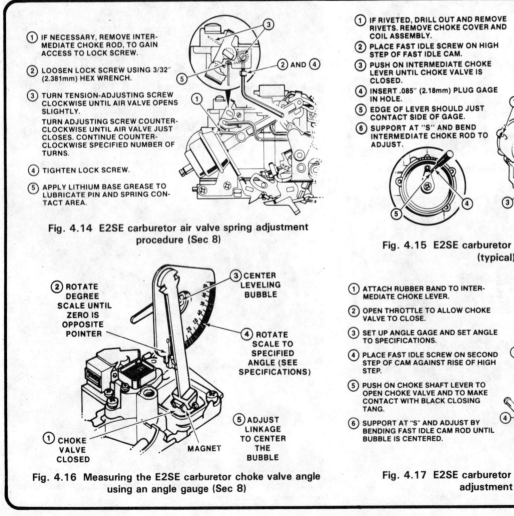

① IF NECESSARY, REMOVE INTERMEDIATE CHOKE ROD, TO GAIN ACCESS TO LOCK SCREW.
② LOOSEN LOCK SCREW USING 3/32" (2.381mm) HEX WRENCH.
③ TURN TENSION-ADJUSTING SCREW CLOCKWISE UNTIL AIR VALVE OPENS SLIGHTLY.
   TURN ADJUSTING SCREW COUNTER-CLOCKWISE UNTIL AIR VALVE JUST CLOSES. CONTINUE COUNTER-CLOCKWISE SPECIFIED NUMBER OF TURNS.
④ TIGHTEN LOCK SCREW.
⑤ APPLY LITHIUM BASE GREASE TO LUBRICATE PIN AND SPRING CONTACT AREA.

Fig. 4.14  E2SE carburetor air valve spring adjustment procedure (Sec 8)

① IF RIVETED, DRILL OUT AND REMOVE RIVETS. REMOVE CHOKE COVER AND COIL ASSEMBLY.
② PLACE FAST IDLE SCREW ON HIGH STEP OF FAST IDLE CAM.
③ PUSH ON INTERMEDIATE CHOKE LEVER UNTIL CHOKE VALVE IS CLOSED.
④ INSERT .085" (2.18mm) PLUG GAGE IN HOLE.
⑤ EDGE OF LEVER SHOULD JUST CONTACT SIDE OF GAGE.
⑥ SUPPORT AT "S" AND BEND INTERMEDIATE CHOKE ROD TO ADJUST.

Fig. 4.15  E2SE carburetor choke coil lever adjustment (typical) (Sec 8)

② ROTATE DEGREE SCALE UNTIL ZERO IS OPPOSITE POINTER
③ CENTER LEVELING BUBBLE
④ ROTATE SCALE TO SPECIFIED ANGLE (SEE SPECIFICATIONS)
⑤ ADJUST LINKAGE TO CENTER THE BUBBLE
① CHOKE VALVE CLOSED
MAGNET

Fig. 4.16  Measuring the E2SE carburetor choke valve angle using an angle gauge (Sec 8)

① ATTACH RUBBER BAND TO INTERMEDIATE CHOKE LEVER.
② OPEN THROTTLE TO ALLOW CHOKE VALVE TO CLOSE.
③ SET UP ANGLE GAGE AND SET ANGLE TO SPECIFICATIONS.
④ PLACE FAST IDLE SCREW ON SECOND STEP OF CAM AGAINST RISE OF HIGH STEP.
⑤ PUSH ON CHOKE SHAFT LEVER TO OPEN CHOKE VALVE AND TO MAKE CONTACT WITH BLACK CLOSING TANG.
⑥ SUPPORT AT "S" AND ADJUST BY BENDING FAST IDLE CAM ROD UNTIL BUBBLE IS CENTERED.

FAST IDLE CAM

Fig. 4.17  E2SE carburetor choke rod fast idle cam adjustment (Sec 8)

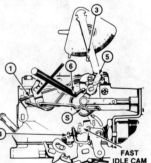

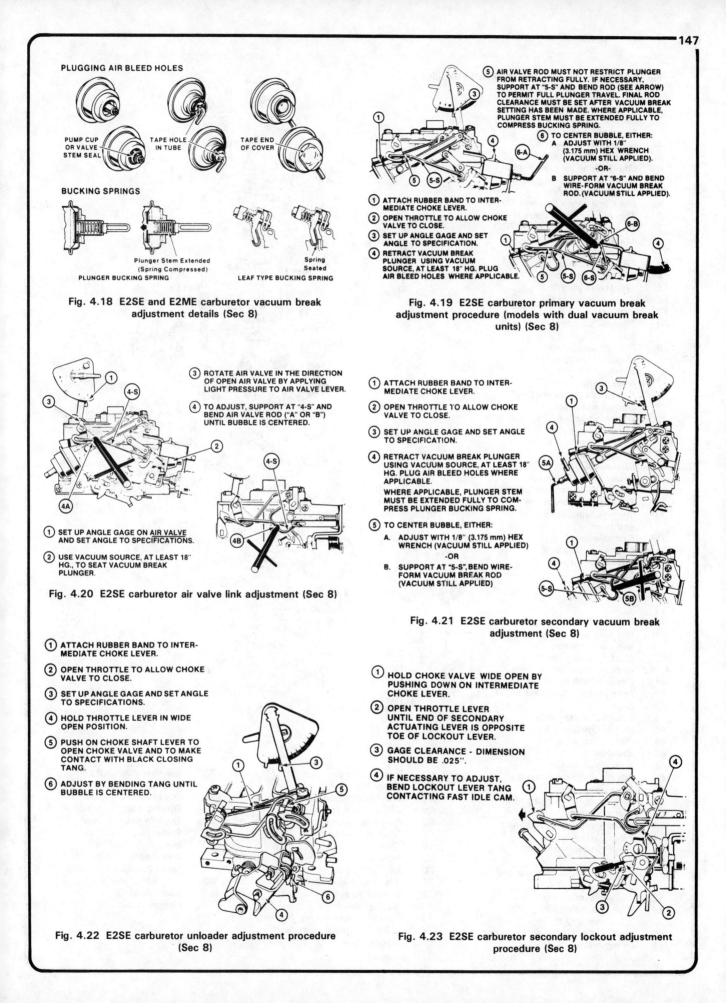

**PLUGGING AIR BLEED HOLES**

PUMP CUP OR VALVE STEM SEAL

TAPE HOLE IN TUBE

TAPE END OF COVER

**BUCKING SPRINGS**

Plunger Stem Extended (Spring Compressed)

PLUNGER BUCKING SPRING

Spring Seated

LEAF TYPE BUCKING SPRING

**Fig. 4.18 E2SE and E2ME carburetor vacuum break adjustment details (Sec 8)**

⑤ AIR VALVE ROD MUST NOT RESTRICT PLUNGER FROM RETRACTING FULLY. IF NECESSARY, SUPPORT AT "5-S" AND BEND ROD (SEE ARROW) TO PERMIT FULL PLUNGER TRAVEL. FINAL ROD CLEARANCE MUST BE SET AFTER VACUUM BREAK SETTING HAS BEEN MADE. WHERE APPLICABLE, PLUNGER STEM MUST BE EXTENDED FULLY TO COMPRESS BUCKING SPRING.

⑥ TO CENTER BUBBLE, EITHER:
A ADJUST WITH 1/8" (3.175 mm) HEX WRENCH (VACUUM STILL APPLIED).
-OR-
B SUPPORT AT "6-S" AND BEND WIRE-FORM VACUUM BREAK ROD. (VACUUM STILL APPLIED).

① ATTACH RUBBER BAND TO INTERMEDIATE CHOKE LEVER.
② OPEN THROTTLE TO ALLOW CHOKE VALVE TO CLOSE.
③ SET UP ANGLE GAGE AND SET ANGLE TO SPECIFICATION.
④ RETRACT VACUUM BREAK PLUNGER USING VACUUM SOURCE, AT LEAST 18" HG. PLUG AIR BLEED HOLES WHERE APPLICABLE.

**Fig. 4.19 E2SE carburetor primary vacuum break adjustment procedure (models with dual vacuum break units) (Sec 8)**

③ ROTATE AIR VALVE IN THE DIRECTION OF OPEN AIR VALVE BY APPLYING LIGHT PRESSURE TO AIR VALVE LEVER.
④ TO ADJUST, SUPPORT AT "4-S" AND BEND AIR VALVE ROD ("A" OR "B") UNTIL BUBBLE IS CENTERED.

① SET UP ANGLE GAGE ON AIR VALVE AND SET ANGLE TO SPECIFICATIONS.
② USE VACUUM SOURCE, AT LEAST 18" HG., TO SEAT VACUUM BREAK PLUNGER.

**Fig. 4.20 E2SE carburetor air valve link adjustment (Sec 8)**

① ATTACH RUBBER BAND TO INTERMEDIATE CHOKE LEVER.
② OPEN THROTTLE TO ALLOW CHOKE VALVE TO CLOSE.
③ SET UP ANGLE GAGE AND SET ANGLE TO SPECIFICATIONS.
④ RETRACT VACUUM BREAK PLUNGER USING VACUUM SOURCE, AT LEAST 18" HG. PLUG AIR BLEED HOLES WHERE APPLICABLE.
WHERE APPLICABLE, PLUNGER STEM MUST BE EXTENDED FULLY TO COMPRESS PLUNGER BUCKING SPRING.
⑤ TO CENTER BUBBLE, EITHER:
A. ADJUST WITH 1/8" (3.175 mm) HEX WRENCH (VACUUM STILL APPLIED) -OR-
B. SUPPORT AT "5-S", BEND WIRE-FORM VACUUM BREAK ROD (VACUUM STILL APPLIED)

**Fig. 4.21 E2SE carburetor secondary vacuum break adjustment (Sec 8)**

① ATTACH RUBBER BAND TO INTERMEDIATE CHOKE LEVER.
② OPEN THROTTLE TO ALLOW CHOKE VALVE TO CLOSE.
③ SET UP ANGLE GAGE AND SET ANGLE TO SPECIFICATIONS.
④ HOLD THROTTLE LEVER IN WIDE OPEN POSITION.
⑤ PUSH ON CHOKE SHAFT LEVER TO OPEN CHOKE VALVE AND TO MAKE CONTACT WITH BLACK CLOSING TANG.
⑥ ADJUST BY BENDING TANG UNTIL BUBBLE IS CENTERED.

**Fig. 4.22 E2SE carburetor unloader adjustment procedure (Sec 8)**

① HOLD CHOKE VALVE WIDE OPEN BY PUSHING DOWN ON INTERMEDIATE CHOKE LEVER.
② OPEN THROTTLE LEVER UNTIL END OF SECONDARY ACTUATING LEVER IS OPPOSITE TOE OF LOCKOUT LEVER.
③ GAGE CLEARANCE - DIMENSION SHOULD BE .025".
④ IF NECESSARY TO ADJUST, BEND LOCKOUT LEVER TANG CONTACTING FAST IDLE CAM.

**Fig. 4.23 E2SE carburetor secondary lockout adjustment procedure (Sec 8)**

**Fig. 4.24 E2ME carburetor — exploded view (Sec 9)**

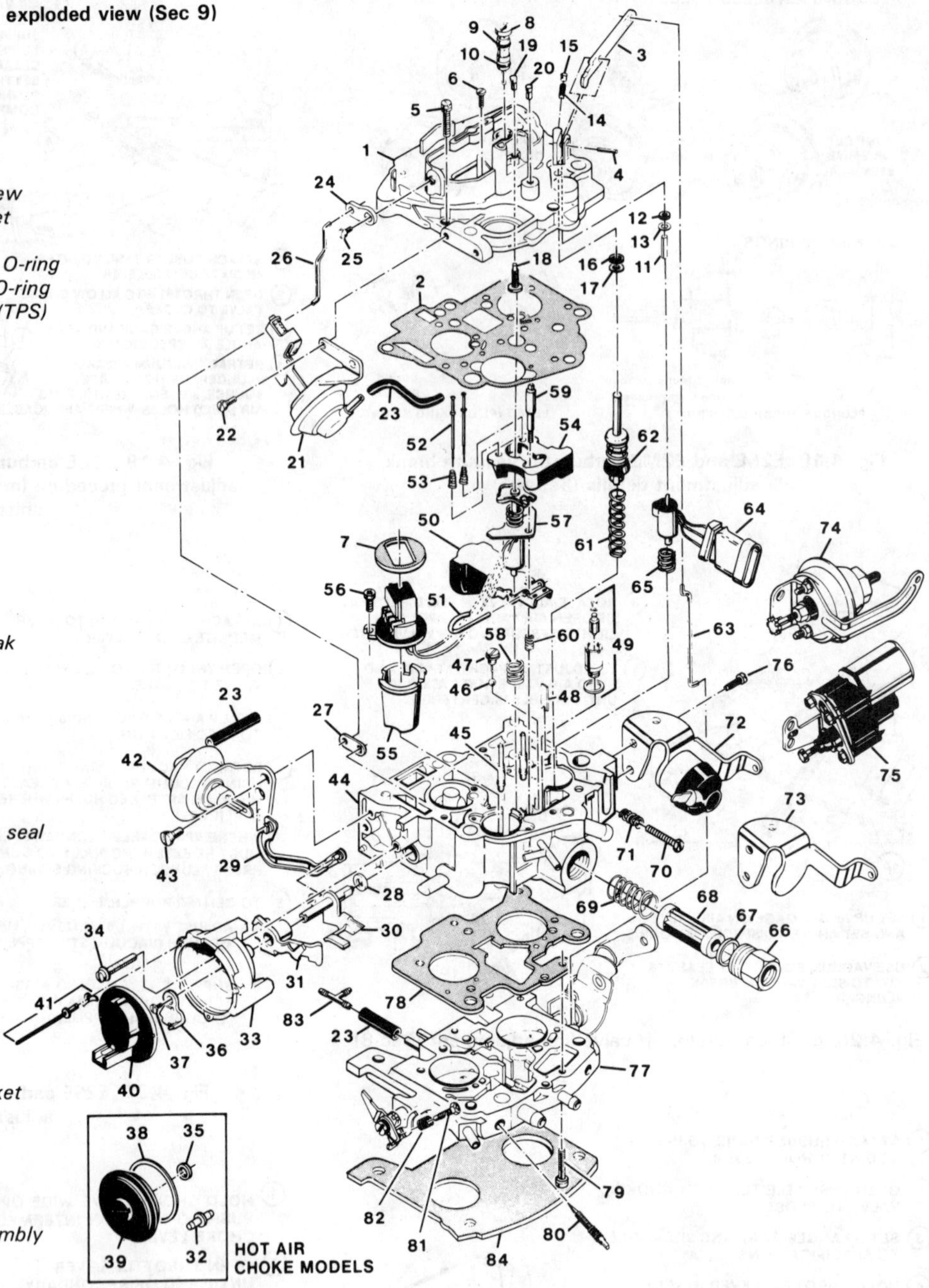

1　Air horn assembly
2　Gasket
3　Pump actuating lever
4　Pump lever hinge roll pin
5　Short air horn screw
6　Countersunk air horn screw
7　Solenoid connector gasket
8　Idle air bleed valve
9　Thick idle air bleed valve O-ring
10　Thin idle air bleed valve O-ring
11　Throttle Position Sensor (TPS) actuator plunger
12　TPS plunger seal
13　TPS seal retainer
14　TPS adjusting screw
15　TPS screw plug
16　Pump plunger seal
17　Retainer
18　Solenoid plunger screw (rich stop)
19　Plunger stop screw plug (rich stop)
20　Solenoid adjusting plug (lean mixture)
21　Front choke vacuum break control and bracket
22　Attaching screw
23　Vacuum hose
24　Upper choke rod lever
25　Choke lever screw
26　Choke rod
27　Lower choke rod lever
28　Intermediate choke shaft seal
29　Rear vacuum break link
30　Intermediate choke shaft and lever
31　Fast idle cam
32　Choke housing seal
33　Choke housing kit
34　Screw
35　Seal
36　Choke coil lever
37　Screw
38　Hot air choke cover gasket
39　Hot air choke cover and coil assembly
40　Electric choke cover and coil assembly
41　Cover attaching kit
42　Rear vacuum break assembly
43　Screw
44　Float bowl assembly
45　Primary metering jet
46　Pump discharge ball
47　Retainer
48　Pump well baffle
49　Needle and seat assembly
50　Float assembly
51　Float assembly hinge pin
52　Primary metering rod
53　Primary metering rod spring
54　Float bowl insert
55　Bowl cavity insert
56　Screw
57　Mixture control solenoid and plunger assembly
58　Solenoid tension spring
59　Solenoid adjusting (lean mixture) screw
60　Solenoid adjusting screw spring
61　Pump return spring
62　Pump assembly
63　Pump link
64　Throttle Position Sensor (TPS)
65　TPS tension spring
66　Fuel inlet filter nut
67　Filter nut gasket
68　Filter
69　Filter spring
70　Idle stop screw
71　Idle stop screw spring
72　Idle speed solenoid and bracket assembly
73　Throttle return spring bracket
74　Idle load compensator and bracket assembly
75　Idle speed control and bracket assembly
76　Bracket attaching screw
77　Throttle body assembly
78　Throttle body gasket
79　Screw
80　Idle needle and spring assemblies
81　Fast idle adjusting screw
82　Fast idle screw spring
83　Vacuum hose tee
84　Flange gasket

HOT AIR CHOKE MODELS

## 9  Carburetor (E2ME/E2MC) — overhaul

1    When a carburetor develops faults after considerable mileage, it is usually more economical to replace the complete unit, rather than to completely dismantle it and replace individual components. If it is decided to rebuild the unit, first obtain a repair kit which will contain all the necessary gaskets and other needed items, and proceed in the following sequence.

2    Remove the screws holding the wide-open throttle switch and idle solenoid and bracket assembly to the float bowl. Do not immerse these parts in carburetor cleaner.

3    Remove the upper choke lever from the end of the shaft by removing the retaining screw and rotating the lever.

4    Remove the choke rod from the lower lever inside the float bowl casting. Do this by holding the lever outward and twisting the rod counterclockwise.

5    Use a drift to drive the pump lever pivot pin inward until the lever can be removed from the air horn. Note the position of the accelerator pump rod in the lever and then remove the pump lever from the pump rod.

6    Remove the vacuum break hose from the tube on the float bowl.

7    Remove the nine air horn attaching screws. Two of them are countersunk near the center of the carburetor. Lift the air horn straight up and off the float bowl.

8    From the air horn assembly, remove the vacuum break control with its bracket. Do not immerse this in carburetor cleaner.

9    Remove the pump plunger stem seal by inverting the air horn and using a small screwdriver to remove the staking. Remove and discard the retainer and seal.

10   The air horn assembly includes an idle air bleed valve which is preset at the factory. The air valve and seals should not be removed from the air horn unless replacement is necessary. The air horn assembly should not be immersed or cleaned in carburetor cleaner in the normal manner as this may damage the O-rings which seal the idle air bleed valve.

11   Holding down on the pump plunger stem, raise the corner of the air horn gasket still attached to the float bowl and remove the pump plunger from its well.

12   Remove the solenoid metering rod plunger by lifting straight up.

13   Remove the rubber seal from around the mixture control solenoid plunger.

14   Remove the air horn gasket from the float bowl.

15   Remove the pump return spring from the well.

16   Remove the plastic filler block from the float valve.

17   Carefully lift out each metering rod assembly. Make sure the return spring comes with the assembly.

18   Remove the mixture control solenoid from the float bowl. Do this by first removing the two attaching screws. Do not remove the solenoid connector at this time. Turn the mixture control screw counterclockwise and remove the screw. Carefully lift the solenoid and connector assembly from the float bowl. The solenoid and connector are serviced as an assembly only.

19   Remove the plastic insert from the cavity in the float bowl under the solenoid connector.

20   Remove the solenoid screw tension spring next to the float hanger clip.

21   Remove the float assembly and float needle by pulling up on the retaining clip. Remove the needle and seat.

22   Remove the large mixture control solenoid spring from the bottom of the float bowl.

23   Remove the main metering jets, if necessary.

24   Remove the pump discharge check ball retainer and the check ball.

25   Remove the pump well fill slot baffle, if necessary for replacement.

26   Remove the rear vacuum break control, along with its attaching bracket. Do not immerse this in carburetor cleaner.

27   The non-adjustable choke used on some E2ME models is designed to be a permanent fixture. Rivets are used to secure the cover. If disassembly is necessary, follow the overhaul instructions for the E2SE, as the choke mechanisms are the same.

28   Remove the fuel inlet nut, gasket, check valve filter assembly and spring from the float bowl.

29   Remove the four throttle body attaching screws and remove the throttle body assembly.

30   Remove the pump rod from the throttle lever by rotating the rod until the tang aligns with the slot in the lever.

31   Do not remove the plugs covering the idle mixture needles unless they must be replaced, which is not common in a standard overhaul procedure.

32   Clean all metal parts in cold solvent. do not immerse rubber parts, plastic parts, the vacuum break assembly, wide-open throttle switch, solenoid or air horn assembly. Do not probe the jets to clean them. Blow through them with compressed air. Inspect all components for cracks, distortion, wear and other damage. Replace parts as necessary. Discard all gaskets and the fuel filter.

33   Assembly is essentially the reverse of the removal procedure, but the following points should be noted:

   a) To make the float level adjustment, hold the float retaining clip firmly in place and push down lightly on the float arm. Measure from the top of the float bowl casting (without gasket) to the top of the float about 3/16 in back from the toe. Bend the float arm as necessary for adjustment as shown in the accompanying illustration.

   b) Tighten the nine air horn attaching screws securely in the sequence shown in the accompanying illustration.

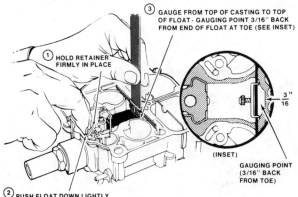

③ GAUGE FROM TOP OF CASTING TO TOP OF FLOAT - GAUGING POINT 3/16" BACK FROM END OF FLOAT AT TOE (SEE INSET)

① HOLD RETAINER FIRMLY IN PLACE

3/16

(INSET)

GAUGING POINT (3/16" BACK FROM TOE)

② PUSH FLOAT DOWN LIGHTLY AGAINST NEEDLE

④ REMOVE FLOAT AND BEND FLOAT ARM UP OR DOWN AT NOTCH, TO ADJUST.

⑤ ON CCC CARBURETORS, IF FLOAT LEVEL VARIES OVER ±1/16" FROM SPECIFICATIONS, ADJUST FLOAT AS FOLLOWS:

LEVEL TOO HIGH - HOLD RETAINER FIRMLY IN PLACE ( ① AND ② ) AND PUSH DOWN ON CENTER OF FLOAT PONTOON TO OBTAIN CORRECT SETTING.

LEVEL TOO LOW - LIFT OUT METERING RODS. REMOVE SOLENOID CONNECTOR SCREW. TURN LEAN MIXTURE SOLENOID SCREW CLOCKWISE COUNTING NUMBER OF TURNS UNTIL SCREW IS BOTTOMED LIGHTLY IN FLOAT BOWL. RECORD NUMBER OF TURNS COUNTED. TURN SCREW COUNTERCLOCKWISE AND REMOVE SCREW. LIFT SOLENOID AND CONNECTOR FROM FLOAT BOWL. REMOVE FLOAT AND BEND FLOAT ARM UP TO ADJUST. VISUALLY CHECK FLOAT ALIGNMENT AFTER ADJUSTING. REVERSE PROCEDURE TO RE-INSTALL PARTS REMOVED, MAKING SURE SOLENOID LEAN MIXTURE SCREW IS BACKED OUT OF FLOAT BOWL EXACTLY THE SAME NUMBER OF TURNS COUNTED AT DISASSEMBLY.

**Fig. 4.25  E2ME carburetor initial float level adjustment (Sec 9)**

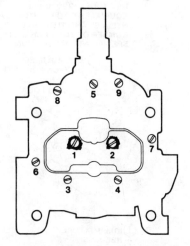

**Fig. 4.26  E2ME carburetor recommended air horn screw tightening sequence (Sec 9)**

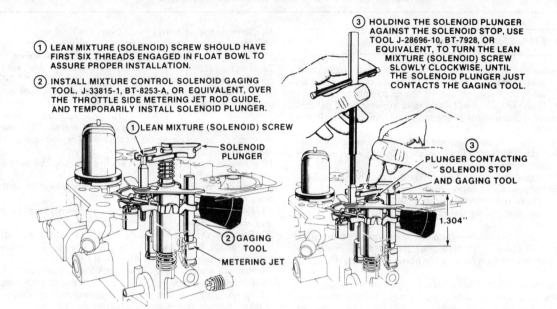

① LEAN MIXTURE (SOLENOID) SCREW SHOULD HAVE FIRST SIX THREADS ENGAGED IN FLOAT BOWL TO ASSURE PROPER INSTALLATION.

② INSTALL MIXTURE CONTROL SOLENOID GAGING TOOL, J-33815-1, BT-8253-A, OR EQUIVALENT, OVER THE THROTTLE SIDE METERING JET ROD GUIDE, AND TEMPORARILY INSTALL SOLENOID PLUNGER.

③ HOLDING THE SOLENOID PLUNGER AGAINST THE SOLENOID STOP, USE TOOL J-28696-10, BT-7928, OR EQUIVALENT, TO TURN THE LEAN MIXTURE (SOLENOID) SCREW SLOWLY CLOCKWISE, UNTIL THE SOLENOID PLUNGER JUST CONTACTS THE GAGING TOOL.

① LEAN MIXTURE (SOLENOID) SCREW

SOLENOID PLUNGER

② GAGING TOOL

METERING JET

③ PLUNGER CONTACTING SOLENOID STOP AND GAGING TOOL

1.304"

Fig. 4.27  E2ME carburetor lean mixture stop screw bench adjustment (Sec 9)

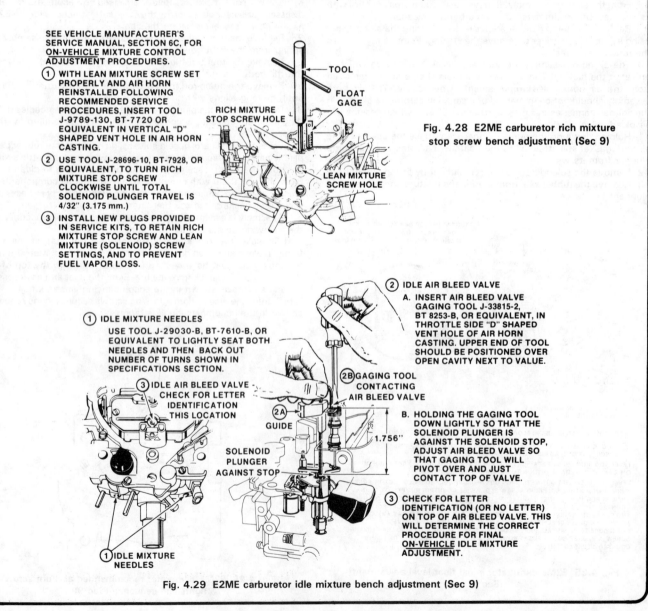

SEE VEHICLE MANUFACTURER'S SERVICE MANUAL, SECTION 6C, FOR ON-VEHICLE MIXTURE CONTROL ADJUSTMENT PROCEDURES.

① WITH LEAN MIXTURE SCREW SET PROPERLY AND AIR HORN REINSTALLED FOLLOWING RECOMMENDED SERVICE PROCEDURES, INSERT TOOL J-9789-130, BT-7720 OR EQUIVALENT IN VERTICAL "D" SHAPED VENT HOLE IN AIR HORN CASTING.

② USE TOOL J-28696-10, BT-7928, OR EQUIVALENT, TO TURN RICH MIXTURE STOP SCREW CLOCKWISE UNTIL TOTAL SOLENOID PLUNGER TRAVEL IS 4/32" (3.175 mm.)

③ INSTALL NEW PLUGS PROVIDED IN SERVICE KITS, TO RETAIN RICH MIXTURE STOP SCREW AND LEAN MIXTURE (SOLENOID) SCREW SETTINGS, AND TO PREVENT FUEL VAPOR LOSS.

TOOL

FLOAT GAGE

RICH MIXTURE STOP SCREW HOLE

LEAN MIXTURE SCREW HOLE

Fig. 4.28  E2ME carburetor rich mixture stop screw bench adjustment (Sec 9)

① IDLE MIXTURE NEEDLES

USE TOOL J-29030-B, BT-7610-B, OR EQUIVALENT TO LIGHTLY SEAT BOTH NEEDLES AND THEN BACK OUT NUMBER OF TURNS SHOWN IN SPECIFICATIONS SECTION.

③ IDLE AIR BLEED VALVE CHECK FOR LETTER IDENTIFICATION THIS LOCATION

② IDLE AIR BLEED VALVE

A. INSERT AIR BLEED VALVE GAGING TOOL J-33815-2, BT 8253-B, OR EQUIVALENT, IN THROTTLE SIDE "D" SHAPED VENT HOLE OF AIR HORN CASTING. UPPER END OF TOOL SHOULD BE POSITIONED OVER OPEN CAVITY NEXT TO VALUE.

②B GAGING TOOL CONTACTING AIR BLEED VALVE

②A GUIDE

B. HOLDING THE GAGING TOOL DOWN LIGHTLY SO THAT THE SOLENOID PLUNGER IS AGAINST THE SOLENOID STOP, ADJUST AIR BLEED VALVE SO THAT GAGING TOOL WILL PIVOT OVER AND JUST CONTACT TOP OF VALVE.

SOLENOID PLUNGER AGAINST STOP

1.756"

① IDLE MIXTURE NEEDLES

③ CHECK FOR LETTER IDENTIFICATION (OR NO LETTER) ON TOP OF AIR BLEED VALVE. THIS WILL DETERMINE THE CORRECT PROCEDURE FOR FINAL ON-VEHICLE IDLE MIXTURE ADJUSTMENT.

Fig. 4.29  E2ME carburetor idle mixture bench adjustment (Sec 9)

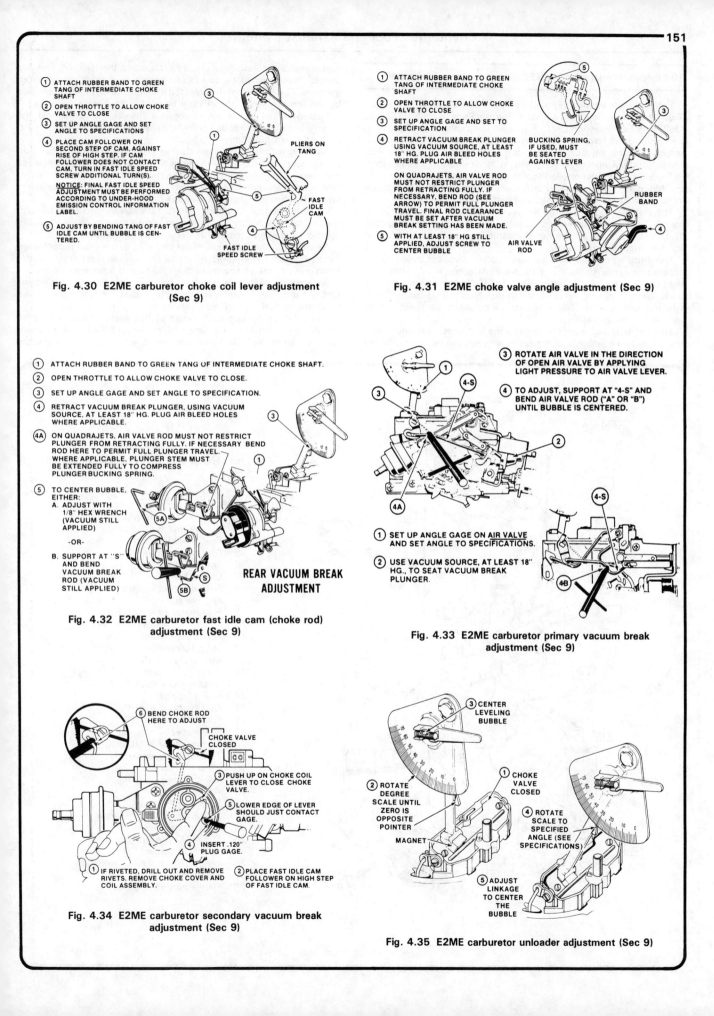

① ATTACH RUBBER BAND TO GREEN TANG OF INTERMEDIATE CHOKE SHAFT
② OPEN THROTTLE TO ALLOW CHOKE VALVE TO CLOSE
③ SET UP ANGLE GAGE AND SET ANGLE TO SPECIFICATIONS
④ PLACE CAM FOLLOWER ON SECOND STEP OF CAM, AGAINST RISE OF HIGH STEP. IF CAM FOLLOWER DOES NOT CONTACT CAM, TURN IN FAST IDLE SPEED SCREW ADDITIONAL TURN(S).
NOTICE: FINAL FAST IDLE SPEED ADJUSTMENT MUST BE PERFORMED ACCORDING TO UNDER-HOOD EMISSION CONTROL INFORMATION LABEL.
⑤ ADJUST BY BENDING TANG OF FAST IDLE CAM UNTIL BUBBLE IS CENTERED.

PLIERS ON TANG
FAST IDLE CAM
FAST IDLE SPEED SCREW

**Fig. 4.30  E2ME carburetor choke coil lever adjustment (Sec 9)**

① ATTACH RUBBER BAND TO GREEN TANG OF INTERMEDIATE CHOKE SHAFT
② OPEN THROTTLE TO ALLOW CHOKE VALVE TO CLOSE
③ SET UP ANGLE GAGE AND SET TO SPECIFICATION
④ RETRACT VACUUM BREAK PLUNGER USING VACUUM SOURCE, AT LEAST 18" HG. PLUG AIR BLEED HOLES WHERE APPLICABLE.

ON QUADRAJETS, AIR VALVE ROD MUST NOT RESTRICT PLUNGER FROM RETRACTING FULLY. IF NECESSARY, BEND ROD (SEE ARROW) TO PERMIT FULL PLUNGER TRAVEL. FINAL ROD CLEARANCE MUST BE SET AFTER VACUUM BREAK SETTING HAS BEEN MADE.
⑤ WITH AT LEAST 18" HG STILL APPLIED, ADJUST SCREW TO CENTER BUBBLE

BUCKING SPRING, IF USED, MUST BE SEATED AGAINST LEVER
RUBBER BAND
AIR VALVE ROD

**Fig. 4.31  E2ME choke valve angle adjustment (Sec 9)**

① ATTACH RUBBER BAND TO GREEN TANG OF INTERMEDIATE CHOKE SHAFT.
② OPEN THROTTLE TO ALLOW CHOKE VALVE TO CLOSE.
③ SET UP ANGLE GAGE AND SET ANGLE TO SPECIFICATION.
④ RETRACT VACUUM BREAK PLUNGER, USING VACUUM SOURCE, AT LEAST 18" HG. PLUG AIR BLEED HOLES WHERE APPLICABLE.
④A ON QUADRAJETS, AIR VALVE ROD MUST NOT RESTRICT PLUNGER FROM RETRACTING FULLY. IF NECESSARY BEND ROD HERE TO PERMIT FULL PLUNGER TRAVEL. WHERE APPLICABLE, PLUNGER STEM MUST BE EXTENDED FULLY TO COMPRESS PLUNGER BUCKING SPRING.
⑤ TO CENTER BUBBLE. EITHER:
A. ADJUST WITH 1/8" HEX WRENCH (VACUUM STILL APPLIED)
-OR-
B. SUPPORT AT "S" AND BEND VACUUM BREAK ROD (VACUUM STILL APPLIED)

**REAR VACUUM BREAK ADJUSTMENT**

**Fig. 4.32  E2ME carburetor fast idle cam (choke rod) adjustment (Sec 9)**

③ ROTATE AIR VALVE IN THE DIRECTION OF OPEN AIR VALVE BY APPLYING LIGHT PRESSURE TO AIR VALVE LEVER.
④ TO ADJUST, SUPPORT AT "4-S" AND BEND AIR VALVE ROD ("A" OR "B") UNTIL BUBBLE IS CENTERED.

① SET UP ANGLE GAGE ON AIR VALVE AND SET ANGLE TO SPECIFICATIONS.
② USE VACUUM SOURCE, AT LEAST 18" HG., TO SEAT VACUUM BREAK PLUNGER.

**Fig. 4.33  E2ME carburetor primary vacuum break adjustment (Sec 9)**

⑥ BEND CHOKE ROD HERE TO ADJUST
CHOKE VALVE CLOSED
③ PUSH UP ON CHOKE COIL LEVER TO CLOSE CHOKE VALVE.
⑤ LOWER EDGE OF LEVER SHOULD JUST CONTACT GAGE.
④ INSERT .120" PLUG GAGE.
① IF RIVETED, DRILL OUT AND REMOVE RIVETS. REMOVE CHOKE COVER AND COIL ASSEMBLY.
② PLACE FAST IDLE CAM FOLLOWER ON HIGH STEP OF FAST IDLE CAM.

**Fig. 4.34  E2ME carburetor secondary vacuum break adjustment (Sec 9)**

③ CENTER LEVELING BUBBLE
② ROTATE DEGREE SCALE UNTIL ZERO IS OPPOSITE POINTER
MAGNET
① CHOKE VALVE CLOSED
④ ROTATE SCALE TO SPECIFIED ANGLE (SEE SPECIFICATIONS)
⑤ ADJUST LINKAGE TO CENTER THE BUBBLE

**Fig. 4.35  E2ME carburetor unloader adjustment (Sec 9)**

## 10  Electronic Fuel Injection (EFI) system — general information

Some models employ EFI in place of the conventional carburetor. Two types of fuel injection are used. Throttle Body Injection (TBI) and Multi-port Fuel Injection (MFI). Fuel injection provides optimum mixture ratios at all stages of combustion. Combined with its immediate response characteristics, EFI permits the engine to run on the leanest possible air/fuel mixture, which greatly reduces exhaust gas emissions.

The EFI system is controlled directly by the vehicle's Electronic Control Module (ECM), which automatically adjusts the air/fuel mixture in accordance with engine load and performance.

The main component of the TBI system is the Throttle Body Injector (TBI), which is mounted on the intake manifold just like a carburetor. The TBI is made up of two major assemblies: the throttle body and the fuel metering assembly.

The throttle body contains a single throttle valve, controlled by the accelerator pedal, similar to a carburetor. Attached to the exterior of the body are the throttle position sensor (TPS), which sends throttle position information to the ECM, and the idle air control assembly (IAC), which is used by the ECM to maintain a constant idle speed during normal engine operation.

The fuel metering assembly contains the fuel pressure regulator and the single fuel injector. The regulator dampens the pulsations of the fuel pump and maintains a steady pressure at the injector. The fuel injector is controlled by the ECM through an electrically operated solenoid. The amount of fuel injected into the intake manifold is varied by the length of time the injector plunger is held open.

Multi-port Fuel Injection (MFI) consists of an air intake manifold, the throttle body, the injectors, the fuel rail assembly, an electric fuel pump and attendant plumbing.

Air is drawn through the air cleaner and throttle body. A mass air flow sensor mounted between the air cleaner and the throttle measures the mass of air passing through the manifold and compensates for temperature and pressure variations. The air is drawn into the cylinders where the fuel is injected above the intake valves.

While the engine is running, the fuel constantly circulates through the fuel rail, which removes vapors and keeps the fuel cool while maintaining a constant pressure at the injectors of 36 psi.

As with TBI, the operation of the MFI injection system is controlled by the ECM so that it works in conjunction with the rest of the vehicle functions to provide improved driveability and emissions control.

Because the MFI system meters fuel and air precisely, it is important to the proper operation of the vehicle that the fuel and air filters be changed at the specified intervals.

The ECM controlling both types of EFI systems has a learning capability for certain performance conditions. If the battery is disconnected, part of the ECM memory is erased, which makes it necessary

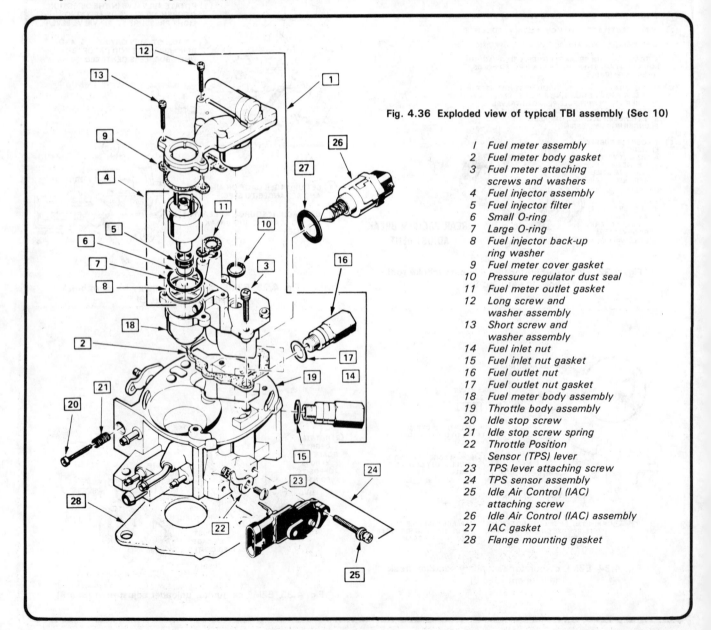

**Fig. 4.36  Exploded view of typical TBI assembly (Sec 10)**

1   Fuel meter assembly
2   Fuel meter body gasket
3   Fuel meter attaching
    screws and washers
4   Fuel injector assembly
5   Fuel injector filter
6   Small O-ring
7   Large O-ring
8   Fuel injector back-up
    ring washer
9   Fuel meter cover gasket
10  Pressure regulator dust seal
11  Fuel meter outlet gasket
12  Long screw and
    washer assembly
13  Short screw and
    washer assembly
14  Fuel inlet nut
15  Fuel inlet nut gasket
16  Fuel outlet nut
17  Fuel outlet nut gasket
18  Fuel meter body assembly
19  Throttle body assembly
20  Idle stop screw
21  Idle stop screw spring
22  Throttle Position
    Sensor (TPS) lever
23  TPS lever attaching screw
24  TPS sensor assembly
25  Idle Air Control (IAC)
    attaching screw
26  Idle Air Control (IAC) assembly
27  IAC gasket
28  Flange mounting gasket

to reteach the computer. This is done by thoroughly warming up the engine and operating the vehicle at part throttle, stop and go and idle conditions.

No mechanical fuel pump is employed in either fuel injection system. Rather, an electric pump, located in the fuel tank, is used.

A fuel pump relay is used to control the electric fuel pump operation. When the ignition is turned on, the fuel pump relay immediately supplies current to the fuel pump to pressurize the fuel system. If the engine doesn't start after two seconds, the fuel pump will automatically shut off. If the fuel pump relay fails, the fuel pump will still operate after the ECM receives pulses from the distributor or about four pounds of oil pressure has built up, depending on the model.

The throttle stop screw, used to regulate the minimum idle speed, is adjusted at the factory and sealed with a plug to discourage unnecessary readjustment. For this reason, this adjustment, if necessary, should be left to a dealer or other qualified mechanic.

The complexity of the EFI system prevents many problems from being accurately diagnosed by the home mechanic. Therefore, if a problem should develop in the system, take the vehicle to a dealer to locate the fault. **Caution:** *Prior to any operation in which a fuel line will be disconnected, the high pressure in the system must first be relieved as described in Section 11. Also, disconnect the negative battery cable to eliminate the possibility of sparks occurring when fuel vapors are present.*

## 11  Fuel injection pressure relief procedure

**Warning:** *To reduce the risk of fire and personal injury, relieve the pressure in the fuel system before servicing any fuel injection components.*
1    Remove the fuel pump fuse from the fuse block located in the passenger compartment under the dash (Chapter 10).
2    Start the engine and let it run until lack of fuel causes it to stop.
3    Engage the starter again for about three seconds to ensure that all pressure has been relieved.
4    Turn the ignition off, disconnect the negative cable from the battery and remove the fuel tank cap to relieve the pressure in the tank.
5    After servicing the fuel system, reinstall the fuel pump fuse, reconnect the battery cable and install the fuel tank filler cap.

## 12  Fuel pump (fuel injected models) — removal and installation

**Note:** *Before starting this procedure, the fuel system pressure must be relieved as outlined in Section 11.*

1    On fuel injected models, the electric fuel pump is an integral part of the fuel gauge tank unit, but it may be replaced separately after the fuel gauge/fuel pump assembly has been removed from the fuel tank.
2    Remove the fuel tank (refer to Section 5).
3    Unbolt and remove the fuel pump/gauge assembly from the fuel tank.
4    Installation is the reverse of the removal procedure.
5    When the installation is complete, carefully check all lines, hoses and fittings for leaks.

## 13  Idle Air Control assembly (IAC) — removal and installation

1    Relieve the pressure in the fuel system (refer to Section 11).
2    Disconnect the cable from the negative battery terminal.
3    Remove the air cleaner.
4    Disconnect the wire from the Idle Air Control (IAC) assembly.
5    Use a wrench to unscrew the assembly from the throttle body injection unit.
6    Before installing the IAC, measure the distance between the end of the motor assembly housing and the tip of the conical valve. The valve should be extended from the housing no more than 1.260-inch (32 mm) on 1982 models or 1.125-inch (28.6 mm) on later models or damage may occur to the motor when it is installed. If the distance is excessive, first determine if the assembly is a Type 1, with a collar at the end of the motor, or Type 2, without a collar. The pintle on a Type 1 assembly can be retracted simply by pushing on the end of the cone until it's in position. For a Type 2, push the pintle in and attempt to turn it clockwise. If it turns, continue turning until it is properly set. If it will not turn, exert firm hand pressure to retract it. **Note:** *If the pintle was turned, be sure the spring is in its original position with the straight portion of the spring end aligned with the flat surface under the pintle head.*
7    Installation of the IAC assembly is the reverse of removal. Be sure to install the gasket with the assembly.
8    Following installation, start the engine and allow it to reach normal operating temperature. On manual transmission-equipped vehicles, the idle speed will automatically be controlled when operating temperature is reached. On automatic transmission-equipped vehicles, the assembly will begin controlling idle speed when the engine is at operating temperature and the transmission is shifted into Drive.
9    If the idle speed is abnormally high and does not regulate back to normal after a few moments, operate the vehicle at a speed of 45 mph (72 kph). At that speed the ECM will command the IAC pintle to extend fully to the mating seat in the throttle body and allow the ECM to establish an accurate reference with respect to the pintle position. Proper idle regulation will result.

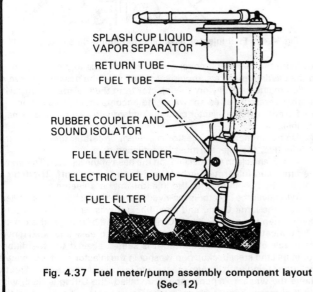

Fig. 4.37  Fuel meter/pump assembly component layout (Sec 12)

SPLASH CUP LIQUID VAPOR SEPARATOR
RETURN TUBE
FUEL TUBE
RUBBER COUPLER AND SOUND ISOLATOR
FUEL LEVEL SENDER
ELECTRIC FUEL PUMP
FUEL FILTER

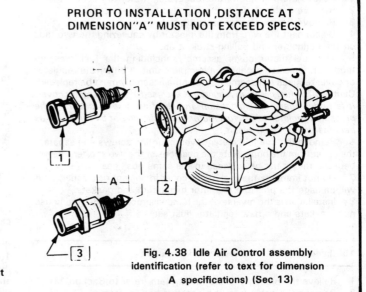

PRIOR TO INSTALLATION, DISTANCE AT DIMENSION "A" MUST NOT EXCEED SPECS.

Fig. 4.38  Idle Air Control assembly identification (refer to text for dimension A specifications) (Sec 13)

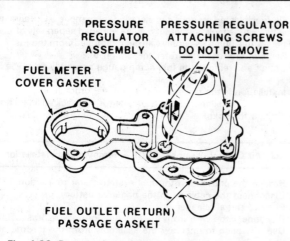

Fig. 4.39 Bottom view of the fuel meter body, showing the fuel pressure regulator (Sec 14)

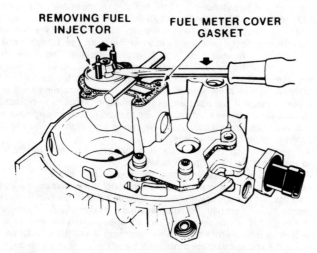

Fig. 4.41 Correct procedure for removing the fuel injector assembly from the fuel meter body (Sec 15)

## 14   Fuel pressure regulator — removal and installation

1   Relieve the pressure in the fuel system (refer to Section 11).
2   Remove the cable from the negative battery terminal.
3   Remove the air cleaner assembly.
4   Disconnect the wire from the injector by squeezing the two tabs on the connector and pulling straight up.
5   The fuel meter cover assembly, including the fuel pressure regulator, is serviced only as a complete unit. If either the regulator or cover requires replacement, the entire assembly must be replaced. **Caution:** *The fuel pressure regulator is enclosed in the fuel meter cover. It is under heavy spring tension and the four screws securing the pressure regulator to the fuel meter cover should not be removed, as personal injury could result.*
6   Remove the five fuel meter cover mounting screws and separate the cover from the body. Note the positions of the two shorter screws, because they must be replaced in the same positions.
7   Do not immerse the fuel meter cover in solvent or cleaner, as it will damage the pressure regulator diaphragm and gaskets.
8   Installation is the reverse of the removal procedure. Be sure to use new gaskets and a new regulator dust seal.

## 15   Injector (TBI) — removal and installation

1   Relieve the pressure in the fuel system (refer to Section 11).
2   Remove the cable from the negative battery terminal.
3   Remove the fuel meter cover as described in Section 14.

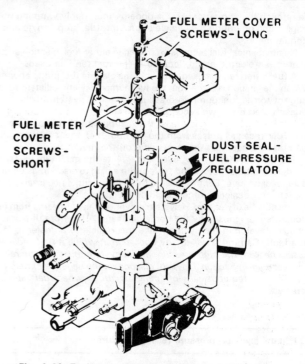

Fig. 4.40 Fuel meter cover-to-fuel meter body screw locations (Sec 14)

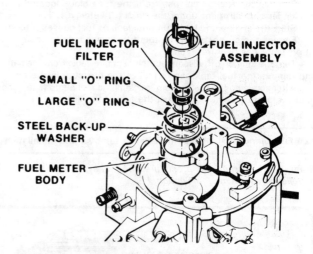

Fig. 4.42 Fuel injector assembly mounting details (Sec 15)

4   With the fuel meter cover gasket still in place to prevent damage to the casting, place a screwdriver shank atop the gasket to serve as a fulcrum and carefully pry the injector from the fuel meter body with another screwdriver as shown in the accompanying illustration.
5   Do not push the injector out from underneath as this could damage the injector tip.
6   Do not immerse the injector in solvent or carburetor cleaner. If it is defective, the injector must be replaced as a unit.
7   Check and clean the fuel filter on the base of the injector. To remove the filter, carefully rotate it back-and-forth to pull it off. The filter is installed by pushing it into the injector until it's seated.
8   Whenever the injector is removed, new O-rings should be installed. Remove the large O-ring and steel backup washer from the injector cavity, then remove the small O-ring from the bottom of the cavity.
9   Lubricate a new small O-ring with lithium grease and push it over the nozzle end of the injector so it is seated against the fuel filter.
10  Install the steel backup ring washer in the injector cavity. Lubricate the large O-ring with lithium grease and install it in the cavity, directly above the washer. When properly installed, the O-ring is flush with the fuel meter body surface. **Note:** *Do not attempt to reverse this procedure by installing the backup washer and O-ring after the injector*

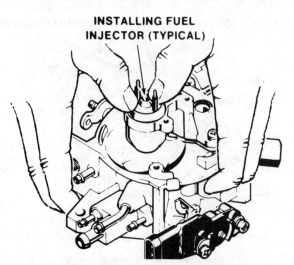

**INSTALLING FUEL INJECTOR (TYPICAL)**

Fig. 4.43 Correct procedure for attaching the fuel injector assembly to the fuel meter body (Sec 15)

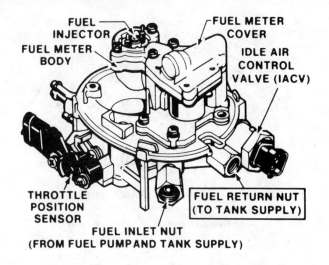

Fig. 4.44 TBI assembly (Sec 16)

*is located in the cavity, as this would prevent proper seating of the O-ring.*
11 Use a pushing and twisting motion to install the injector into the cavity. Be sure it is fully seated and that the raised lug in the injector base is aligned with the notch in the fuel meter body.
12 The remainder of the installation is the reverse of removal.

### 16 Throttle Body Injection (TBI) assembly — removal and installation

1 Relieve the pressure in the fuel system (refer to Section 11).
2 Remove the cable from the negative battery terminal.
3 Remove the air cleaner.
4 Disconnect the wires leading to the Idle Air Control (IAC), throttle position sensor and injector included in the TBI assembly.
5 Disconnect the throttle linkage and return spring from the TBI.
6 If so equipped, disconnect the cruise control linkage from the TBI.
7 Use tape to label the installed locations of all vacuum hoses leading to the TBI, then disconnect them.
8 Disconnect the fuel lines from the TBI.
9 Remove the three TBI mounting bolts and lift it off, along with the gasket.
10 Prior to installing the TBI, be sure the intake manifold mating surface is clean and that all old gasket material has been scraped off.
11 Using a new gasket, place the TBI into position on the intake manifold. Connect the fuel lines to the assembly. **Note:** *Be sure the fuel line O-rings are not nicked, cut or damaged before connecting the lines.*
12 Install the TBI mounting bolts and tighten them to the specified torque.
13 The remainder of the installation procedure is the reverse of removal.
14 Following installation, start the engine and check for fuel leaks.

### 17 Throttle Body Injection (TBI) assembly — overhaul

**Note:** *The following procedures cover the complete disassembly, cleaning, inspection and reassembly of the TBI assembly after it has been removed from the engine. Refer to the illustrations throughout this chapter for location and identification of parts. In many cases, service and repair of individual TBI systems may be completed without removing the TBI unit from the engine. If such service is indicated, refer to the appropriate Section in this Chapter.*
1 The TBI assembly must be supported on a fixture to prevent damage to the throttle valve.

#### Disassembly

2 Refer to the appropriate Steps in Section 13 and remove the fuel meter cover.

3 Refer to the appropriate Steps in Section 14 and remove the fuel injector assembly.
4 If not previously done, remove the air cleaner stud.
5 Remove the fuel inlet and outlet nuts and gaskets from the fuel meter body.
6 Remove the three screws and washers retaining the fuel meter body to the throttle body assembly and separate them.
7 Remove the fuel meter body insulator gasket.
8 Invert the throttle body and place it on a clean, level surface.
9 Remove the two Throttle Position Sensor (TPS) retaining screws and separate the TPS from the throttle body.
10 Remove the Idle Air Control (IAC) valve and gasket from the throttle body and discard the gasket.
11 Further disassembly of the throttle body is not required for cleaning and inspection purposes. The throttle valve retaining screws are welded in place and should not be removed. If defective, the throttle body must be replaced as a unit.

#### Cleaning and inspection

12 Clean all metal parts in a cold immersion-type cleaner and blow them dry. **Note:** *The TPS, IAC assembly, fuel meter cover (with the fuel pressure regulator), fuel injector, fuel injector filter and all diaphragms and other rubber parts should not be immersed in cleaner, as it will cause swelling, hardening and distortion. Clean these parts by hand with clean shop rags.* Make sure all air and fuel passages are clear. **Note:** *Any thread locking compound on the IAC mounting threads should be allowed to remain.*

#### Reassembly

13 Refer to the appropriate Steps in Section 13, check the pintle position in the IAC and install the IAC in the throttle body.
14 Place the throttle body assembly on the holding fixture to avoid damage to the throttle valve.
15 Install a new fuel meter body insulator gasket on the throttle body. Make sure the cutout portions of the gasket match the openings in the throttle body.
16 Attach the fuel meter body to the throttle body.
17 Apply thread locking compound, supplied in the service kit, to the threads on the three fuel meter body mounting screws. If locking compound is not provided, Threadlock Adhesive 262 or its equivalent may be substituted. Do not use a compound of higher strength than recommended, as it may promote screwhead breakage or prevent removal of the screws when service is again required.
18 Install the fuel meter body mounting screws and lockwashers and tighten the screws to the specified torque.
19 Install the fuel feed and return nuts (with new gaskets) in the fuel meter body and tighten them to the specified torque.
20 Refer to the appropriate Steps in Section 15 and reassemble and install the injector in the injector cavity in the fuel meter body.
21 Refer to the appropriate Steps in Section 14 and install the fuel meter cover.

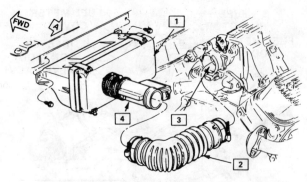

**Fig. 4.45  Multi-port Fuel Injection (MFI) air system component layout (Sec 18)**

1  Air cleaner assembly    3  Throttle body
2  Duct                    4  Mass air flow sensor

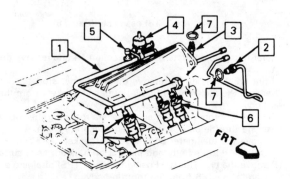

**Fig. 4.47  MFI fuel rail components (Sec 18)**

1  Fuel rail assembly      5  Fuel pressure tap
2  Fuel inlet              6  Fuel injector
3  Fuel return             7  O-ring
4  Fuel pressure regulator

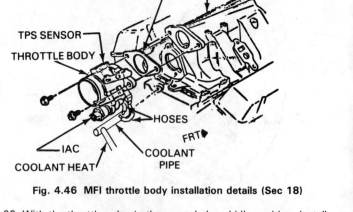

**Fig. 4.46  MFI throttle body installation details (Sec 18)**

22  With the throttle valve in the normal closed idle position, install the TPS on the throttle body assembly, making sure the TPS pick-up lever is located above the tang on the throttle actuator lever.

23  Install two new screws, retainers and lockwashers to secure the TPS to the throttle body. Use thread locking compound on the screw threads.

---

**18   Multi-port Fuel Injection (MFI) — check and repair**

Refer to Chapter 13 for Multi-Port Fuel Injection system checks and component replacement procedures.

---

**19   Exhaust system components — removal and installation**

---

**Caution:** *The vehicle's exhaust system generates very high temperatures and should be allowed to cool down completely before any of the components are touched. Be especially careful around the catalytic converter, where the highest temperatures are generated.*

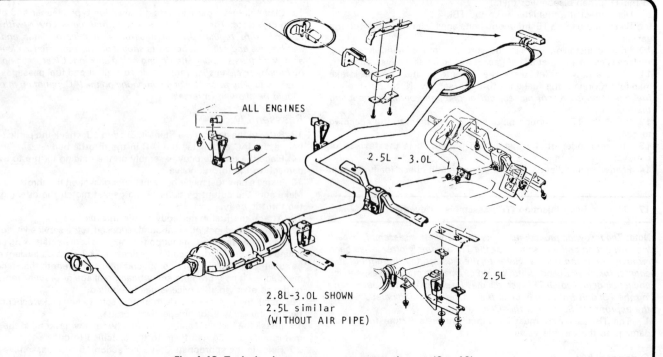

**Fig. 4.48  Typical exhaust system component layout  (Sec 19)**

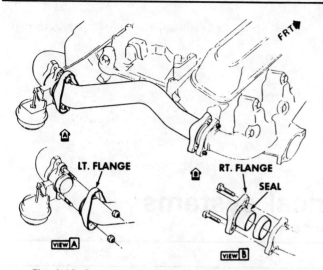

LT. FLANGE

RT. FLANGE

SEAL

VIEW A

VIEW b

FRT

Fig. 4.49 Crossover pipe installation details (Sec 19)

1    Replacement of exhaust system components is basically a matter of removing the heat shields, disconnecting the component and install-ing a new one. The heat shields and exhaust system hangers must be reinstalled in the original locations or damage could result. Due to the high temperatures and exposed locations of the exhaust system components, rust and corrosion can freeze parts together. Penetrating oils are available to help loosen frozen fasteners. However, in some cases it may be necessary to cut the pieces apart with a hacksaw or cutting torch. The latter method should be employed only by persons experienced in this work.

## Crossover pipe

### Removal
2    The following procedure must be used for removing and installing the crossover pipe or broken manifold flanges could result.
3    Raise the vehicle and support it securely on jackstands.
4    Remove the bolts or nuts securing the crossover pipe to the exhaust manifolds.

### Installation
5    Insert the right side crossover pipe slip fit joint in the right rear manifold and install the nuts finger tight.
6    Insert the right side crossover pipe in the right manifold.
7    Install the upper nut and tighten it to approximately half of the threaded distance.
8    Install the lower nut and tighten it to the specified torque.
9    Tighten first the lower and then the right nut to the specified torque.
10   Lower the vehicle.

# Chapter 5   Engine electrical systems

*Refer to Chapter 13 for information applicable to 1986 and later models*

## Contents

Alternator — removal and installation .................. 15
Alternator brushes — replacement .................... 16
Battery cables — check and replacement .............. 4
Battery — emergency jump starting ................... 3
Battery — removal and installation ................... 2
Charging system — check .......................... 14
Charging system — general information and precautions .... 13
Check Engine light...................... See Chapter 6
Distributor (4-cylinder engine) — removal and
  installation ................................. 7
Distributor (V6 engine) — removal and installation ........ 6
Hall Effect switch — testing and replacement ........... 12
Ignition coil — removal and installation ............... 10
Ignition key lock — removal and installation .... See Chapter 10

Ignition module — removal and installation ............. 9
Ignition module — testing......................... 11
Ignition pick-up coil — check and replacement .......... 8
Ignition switch — replacement............. See Chapter 10
Ignition system — check .......................... 5
Ignition system — general information and precautions ..... 1
Ignition timing — check and adjustment ....... See Chapter 1
Spark plug wires, distributor cap and rotor —
  check and replacement................... See Chapter 1
Starter motor — removal and installation.............. 19
Starter motor — testing in vehicle.................. 18
Starter motor brushes — replacement ................ 21
Starter solenoid — removal and installation ............ 20
Starting system — general information ................ 17

## Specifications

| Torque specifications | Ft-lbs |
| --- | --- |
| Alternator adjustment bolt ....................... | 20 to 25 |
| Alternator bracket-to-engine bolt ................... | 30 to 40 |
| Alternator pivot bolt ........................... | 20 to 30 |
| Distributor clamp bolt .......................... | 20 to 30 |
| Starter motor bolts............................ | 26 to 37 |

## 1   Ignition system — general information and precautions

The ignition system on most models is composed of the battery, distributor, coil, ignition switch, spark plugs and the primary (low tension) and secondary (high tension) wiring circuits.

A high energy ignition (HEI) distributor is used on these vehicles. Some models use a coil mounted integrally with the distributor, while others use a separately mounted coil.

Multi-port Fuel Injection (MFI) models are equipped with Computer Controlled Coil Ignition (CCCI), which does not use a distributor. The CCCI system consists of the battery, coilpack, ignition module, crankshaft sensor and camshaft sensor. It works in conjunction with the Electronic Control Module (ECM) to control the spark in accordance with engine operation.

The HEI works in conjunction with the Electronic Spark Timing (EST) system and uses a magnetic pickup assembly located inside the distributor, which contains a permanent magnet, a pole piece with internal teeth, a Hall-effect switch (some four-cylinder models) and a pickup coil.

All ignition timing changes in the HEI-ESC distributor are accomplished by the ECM, which monitors data from various engine sensors, computes the desired spark timing and signals the distributor to change the timing accordingly. The Electronic Spark Control (ESC) used on some engines retards the spark advance when detonation occurs. This retard mode is held for approximately 20 seconds, after which the spark control will revert to the ESC.

There are three basic components involved in the ESC system. The sensor, the controller and the distributor. The ESC sensor detects the presence (or absence) and intensity of detonation through vibrations in the engine and sends the data to the controller. The ESC controller changes the sensor signal into a command signal to the distributor, which then adjusts the spark timing accordingly.

The distributor is modified to respond to the controller signal. This command is delayed when detonation occurs, thus providing the level of retard required. The degree of retard is based on the detonation.

The secondary (spark plug) wire used with the HEI system is a carbon impregnated cord conductor encased in an 8 mm (5/16-inch) diameter rubber jacket with an outer silicone jacket. This type of wire will withstand very high temperatures and still provide insulation for the HEI's high voltage. For more information on spark plug wiring refer to Chapter 1. **Note:** *Because of the very high voltage generated by the HEI and CCCI systems, extreme care should be taken whenever an operation involving ignition components is performed. This not only includes the distributor, coil, control module and spark plug wires, but related items that are connected to the systems as well, such as the plug connections, tachometer, and testing equipment. Consequently, before any work is performed, the ignition should be turned off and the negative battery cable disconnected.*

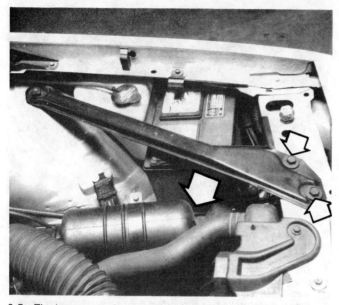

2.5 The battery can be removed after first removing the two brace bolts (arrows) and swinging the brace in the direction shown

## 2 Battery — removal and installation

1 The battery is located at the front of the engine compartment. It is held in place by a hold-down clamp near the bottom of the battery case.
2 Hydrogen gas is produced by the battery, so keep open flames and lighted cigarettes away from it at all times.
3 Always keep the battery in an upright position. Spilled electrolyte should be rinsed off immediately with large quantities of water. Always wear eye protection when working around a battery.
4 Always disconnect the negative (-) battery cable first, followed by the positive (+) cable.
5 Remove the chassis brace bolts and swing the brace out of the way (photo).
6 After the cables are disconnected from the battery, remove the hold-down clamp.
7 Carefully lift the battery out of the engine compartment.
8 Installation is the reverse of removal. The cable clamps should be tight, but do not overtighten them as damage to the battery case could occur. The battery posts and cable ends should be cleaned prior to connection (see Chapter 1).

## 3 Battery — emergency jump starting

Refer to the booster battery (jump) starting procedure at the front of this manual.

## 4 Battery cables — check and replacement

1 Periodically inspect the entire length of each battery cable for damage, cracked or burned insulation and corrosion. Poor battery cable connections can cause starting problems and decreased engine performance.
2 Check the cable-to-terminal connections at the ends of the cables for cracks, loose wire strands and corrosion. The presence of white, fluffy deposits under the insulation at the cable terminal connection is a sign the cable is corroded and should be replaced. Check the terminals for distortion, missing mounting bolts or nuts and corrosion.
3 If only the positive cable is to be replaced, be sure to disconnect the negative cable from the battery first.
4 Disconnect and remove the cable from the vehicle. Make sure the replacement cable is the same length and diameter.

5 Clean the threads of the starter or ground connection with a wire brush to remove rust and corrosion. Apply a light coat of petroleum jelly to the threads to ease installation and prevent future corrosion. Inspect the connections frequently to make sure they are clean and tight.
6 Attach the cable to the starter or ground connection and tighten the mounting nut securely.
7 Before connecting the new cable to the battery, make sure it reaches the terminals without having to be stretched.
8 Connect the positive cable first, followed by the negative cable. Tighten the nuts and apply a thin coat of petroleum jelly to the terminal and cable connection.

## 5 Ignition system — check

**Caution:** *Because of the very high voltage generated by the High Energy Ignition (HEI) and Computer Controlled Coil Ignition (CCCI) systems, extreme care should be taken whenever an operation is performed involving ignition components. This not only includes the distributor, coil, control module and spark plug wires, but related items that are connected to the system as well, such as the plug connections, tachometer and any test equipment. Consequently, before any work is performed, the ignition should be turned off or the battery ground cable disconnected.*

### CCCI system
1 Due to the special tools and techniques required, checking the CCCI system is confined to inspecting for loose or damaged components and wires.

### HEI system
2 If the engine turns over but will not start, remove the spark plug wire from a spark plug and, using an insulated tool, hold the wire about 1/4-inch from a good ground and have an assistant crank the engine. **Note:** *A special tool, ST-125, is available for making the above test. It is available from your dealer and auto parts stores.*
3 If there is no spark, check another wire in the same manner. A few sparks, then no spark, should be considered as no spark.
4 If there is good spark, check the spark plugs (refer to Chapter 1) and/or the fuel system (refer to Chapter 4).
5 If there is a weak spark or no spark, unplug the coil lead from the distributor, hold it about 1/4-inch from a good ground and check for spark as described above.
6 If there is no spark, have the system checked by a dealer or repair shop.

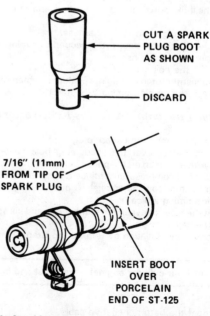

**Fig. 5.1 An old spark plug boot and the ST-125 tool are used for testing the ignition system (Sec 5)**

7   If there is a spark, check the distributor cap and/or rotor (refer to Chapter 1).
8   Further checks of the HEI ignition system must be done by a dealer or repair shop.

## 6   Distributor (V6 engine) — removal and installation

### Removal

1   Disconnect the ignition switch/battery feed wire (BAT) and the tachometer lead (TACH), if so equipped, from the distributor cap.
2   Release the coil connectors from the cap. Depress the locking tabs by hand. Do not use a screwdriver or other tool.
3   Turn the distributor cap locking latches counterclockwise, remove the cap and position it out of the way.
4   Disconnect the four-terminal ECM wiring harness connector from the distributor.
5   If necessary for clearance, on distributor caps with a secondary wiring harness attached to the cap, release the wiring harness latches and remove the wiring harness retainer. Note that the spark plug wire numbers are indicated on the retainer.
6   Remove the distributor hold-down clamp bolt and the hold-down clamp.
7   Make matching marks on the base of the distributor and the engine block to insure that you will be able to put the distributor back in the same position.
8   Make a mark on the distributor housing to show the direction the rotor is pointing. Lift the distributor slowly. As you lift it the rotor will turn slightly. When it stops turning make another mark on the distributor body to show where it is pointing when the gear on the distributor is disengaged. This is the position the rotor should be in when you begin reinstallation.
9   Remove the distributor. Avoid turning the crankshaft with the distributor removed, as this will change the timing position of rotor and require retiming the engine.

### Installation if the crankshaft was not turned after distributor removal

10   Position the rotor in the exact location (second mark on the housing) it was in when the distributor was removed.
11   Lower the distributor into the engine. To mesh the gears at the bottom of the distributor it may be necessary to turn the rotor slightly.
12   With the base of the distributor seated against the engine block turn the distributor housing to align the marks made on the distributor base and the engine block.
13   With the distributor all the way down and the marks aligned the rotor should point to the first mark made on the distributor housing.
14   Place the hold-down clamp in position and loosely install the hold-down bolt.
15   Reconnect the ignition wiring harness.
16   Install the distributor cap. If the secondary wiring harness was removed from the cap, reinstall it.
17   Reconnect the coil connector.
18   With the distributor in its original position, tighten the hold-down bolt and check the ignition timing (Chapter 1).

### Installation if the crankshaft was turned after distributor removal

19   Remove the number one spark plug.
20   Place your finger over the spark plug hole while turning the crankshaft with a wrench on the pulley bolt at the front of the engine.
21   When you feel compression continue turning the crankshaft slowly until the timing mark on the crankshaft pulley is aligned with the 0 on the engine timing indicator.
22   Position the rotor between the number one and six spark plug terminals on the cap.
23   Complete the installation by referring to Steps 11 through 18.

## 7   Distributor (four-cylinder engine) — removal and installation

### Removal

1   Disconnect the battery negative cable.
2   Raise the vehicle, support it securely on jackstands and remove the right front wheel.

7.3   The four-cylinder engine distributor is accessible through the right wheel well

3   On automatic transaxle models, remove the two rear cradle attaching bolts and lower the cradle sufficiently to provide access to the distributor (photo).
4   Remove the brake line support-to-floor pan attaching screws.
5   Remove the coil wire from the distributor cap.
6   Remove the distributor cap.
7   Note the position of the rotor and the distributor-to-block alignment mark.
8   Loosen the distributor clamp screws, slide the clamp out of the way and remove the distributor from the engine.

### Installation if the crankshaft was not turned after distributor removal

9   With the rotor and distributor-to-block alignment in the relationship noted in Step 7, insert the distributor into the engine.
10   Slide the clamp into position and install the screws.
11   Install the distributor cap and coil wire.
12   Raise the cradle into position and install the bolts.
13   Install the brake line support screws.
14   Lower the vehicle.

### Installation if the crankshaft was turned after distributor removal

15   Remove the number one spark plug.
16   Place your finger over the spark plug hole while turning the crankshaft with a wrench on the pulley bolt at the front of the engine.
17   When you feel compression, continue turning the crankshaft slowly until the timing mark on the crankshaft pulley is aligned with the 0 on the engine timing indicator.
18   Position the rotor to point to between the number one and number three distributor terminals.
19   Complete the installation by referring to Steps 11 through 14.

## 8   Ignition pickup coil — replacement

1   Remove the distributor from the engine as previously described (Section 6 or 7).
2   Remove the two rotor mounting screws and remove the rotor.
3   Disconnect the pickup coil leads from the module.
4   On models with a separately mounted coil and a Hall-effect switch, remove the switch retaining screws and the switch.
5   Mark the distributor gear and shaft so they can be reassembled in the same position.
6   Carefully mount the distributor in a soft-jawed vice and, using a hammer and punch, remove the roll pin from the distributor shaft and gear.
7   Remove the gear and washers from the shaft.
8   Carefully pull the shaft out through the top of the distributor.
9   On distributors with coil-in-cap construction, remove the three mounting screws and the magnetic shield.
10   Remove the C washer retaining ring at the center of the distributor and remove the pickup coil.
11   Installation is the reverse of the removal procedure.

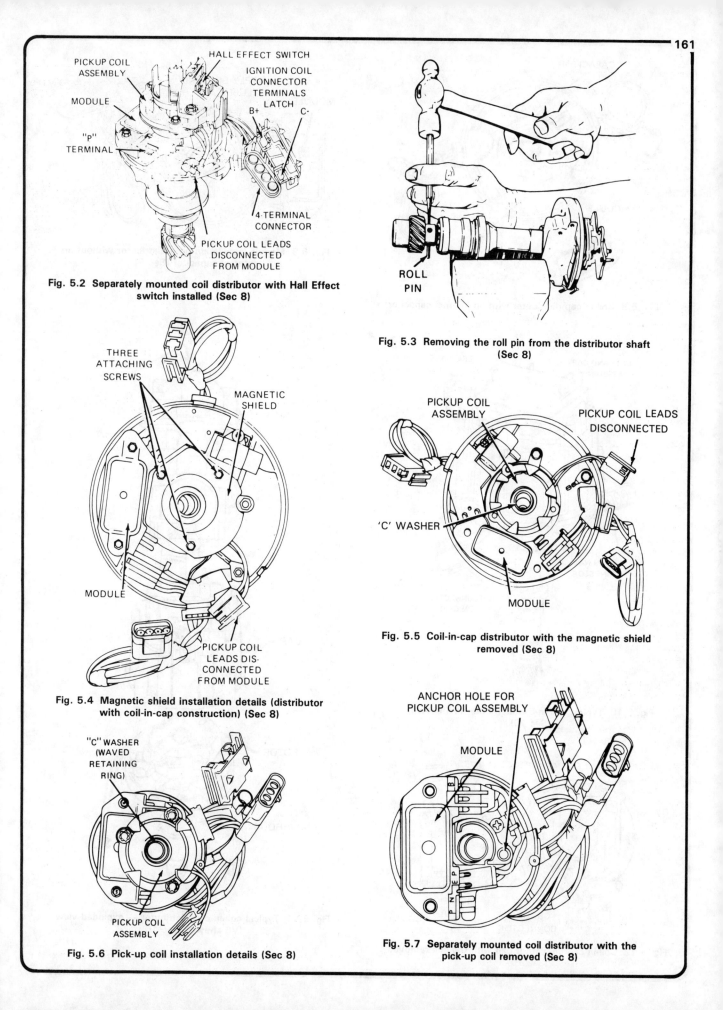

PICKUP COIL ASSEMBLY

MODULE

"P" TERMINAL

HALL EFFECT SWITCH

IGNITION COIL CONNECTOR TERMINALS LATCH

B+     C-

4-TERMINAL CONNECTOR

PICKUP COIL LEADS DISCONNECTED FROM MODULE

Fig. 5.2  Separately mounted coil distributor with Hall Effect switch installed (Sec 8)

ROLL PIN

Fig. 5.3  Removing the roll pin from the distributor shaft (Sec 8)

THREE ATTACHING SCREWS

MAGNETIC SHIELD

MODULE

PICKUP COIL LEADS DIS-CONNECTED FROM MODULE

Fig. 5.4  Magnetic shield installation details (distributor with coil-in-cap construction) (Sec 8)

PICKUP COIL ASSEMBLY

PICKUP COIL LEADS DISCONNECTED

'C' WASHER

MODULE

Fig. 5.5  Coil-in-cap distributor with the magnetic shield removed (Sec 8)

"C" WASHER (WAVED RETAINING RING)

PICKUP COIL ASSEMBLY

Fig. 5.6  Pick-up coil installation details (Sec 8)

ANCHOR HOLE FOR PICKUP COIL ASSEMBLY

MODULE

Fig. 5.7  Separately mounted coil distributor with the pick-up coil removed (Sec 8)

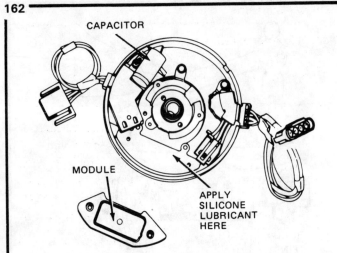

CAPACITOR

MODULE

APPLY SILICONE LUBRICANT HERE

Fig. 5.8  Coil-in-cap distributor with an internal capacitor (Sec 9)

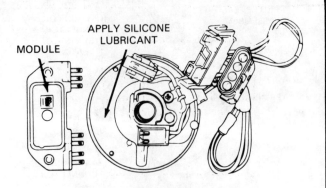

MODULE

APPLY SILICONE LUBRICANT

Fig. 5.9  Module installation on a distributor without an internal capacitor (Sec 9)

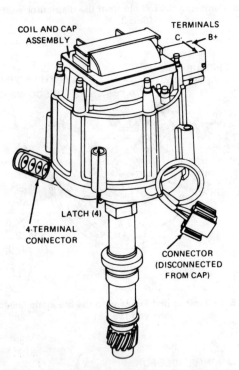

COIL AND CAP ASSEMBLY

TERMINALS
C.      B+

LATCH (4)

4-TERMINAL CONNECTOR

CONNECTOR (DISCONNECTED FROM CAP)

Fig. 5.10  Typical coil-in-cap distributor (V6 shown) (Sec 10)

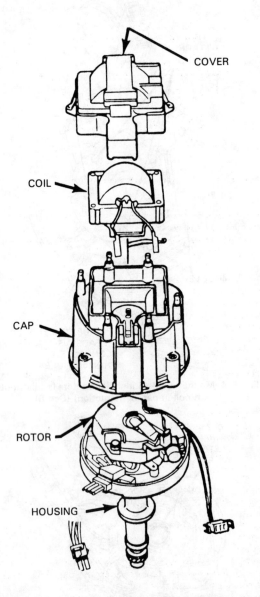

COVER

COIL

CAP

ROTOR

HOUSING

Fig. 5.11  Typical coil-in-cap distributor — exploded view (V6 shown) (Sec 10)

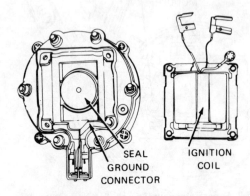

SEAL
GROUND
CONNECTOR

IGNITION COIL

Fig. 5.12  Coil-in-cap distributor cap with the coil removed (Sec 10)

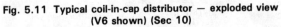

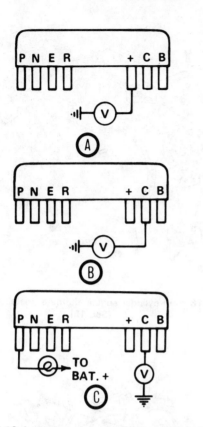

**Fig. 5.13 Ignition module test (see text) (Sec 11)**

## 9  Ignition module — removal and replacement

1    Remove the distributor (Section 6 or 7).
2    Remove the pick-up coil assembly (Section 8).
3    On distributors with an internal capacitor, remove the module mounting screws and the capacitor mounting screw, then separate the module, capacitor and harness assembly from the distributor base and disconnect the wiring harness from the module.
4    On distributors without an internal capacitor, disconnect the wiring harness from the module, remove the two mounting screws and remove the module.
5    Installation is the reverse of the removal procedure. Before installing the module apply silicone lubricant to the housing on which the module mounts.

## 10  Ignition coil — removal and installation

### Coil-in-cap models

1    Disconnect the ignition switch/battery feed wire (BAT) from the distributor cap.
2    Disconnect the coil connector from the distributor cap.
3    Disconnect the four-terminal ECM wiring harness connector from the distributor.
4    Release the spark plug wiring retainers from the distributor cap and remove the wiring retainer. To simplify installation, note that the spark plug wire numbers are indicated on the retainer.
5    If necessary for working clearance, turn the distributor cap locking latches counterclockwise, remove the cap from the distributor and position it so that the coil cover and coil may be removed.
6    Remove the coil cover mounting screws and lift the cover off.
7    Remove the coil mounting screws and separate the coil and leads from the cap.
8    Before installing the coil, remove the arc seal and clean it with a soft cloth.
9    Installation is the reverse of the removal procedure.

### Models with separately mounted coil

10   Disconnect the secondary wire from the coil.
11   Loosen the coil bracket mounting nuts and remove the coil.
12   Installation is the reverse of the removal procedure.

## 11  Ignition module — testing

1    Disconnect the tachometer (if so equipped) at the distributor.
2    Check for a spark at the coil and spark plug wires (Section 5).
3    If there is no spark, remove the distributor cap. Remove the ignition module from the distributor but leave the connector plugged in.
4    With the ignition switch turned On, check for voltage at the module positive terminal (A in the accompanying illustration).
5    If the reading is less than ten volts, there is a fault in the wire between the module positive (+) terminal and the ignition coil positive connector or the ignition coil and primary circuit-to-ignition switch.
6    If the reading is ten volts or more, check the C terminal on the module (C in the accompanying illustration).
7    If the reading is less than one volt, there is an open or grounded lead in the distributor-to-coil C terminal connection or ignition coil or an open primary circuit in the coil itself.
8    If the reading is one to ten volts, replace the module with a new one and check for a spark (Section 5). If there is a spark the module was faulty and the system is now operating properly. If there is no spark, there is a fault in the ignition coil.
9    If the reading in Step 4 is ten volts or more, unplug the pickup coil connector from the module. Check the C terminal voltage with the ignition switch On and watch the voltage reading as a test light is momentarily (five seconds or less) connected between the battery positive (+) terminal and the module P terminal (C in the illustration).
10   If there is no drop in voltage, check the module ground and, if it is good, replace the module with a new one.
11   If the voltage drops, check for spark at the coil wire as the test light is removed from the module terminal. If there is no spark, the module is faulty and should be replaced with a new one. If there is a spark, the pick-up coil or connections are faulty or not grounded.

## 12  Hall-effect switch — testing and replacement

1    Some four-cylinder models are equipped with a Hall-effect switch which is located above the pickup coil assembly. The Hall-effect switch is used in place of the R terminal of the HEI distributor to send engine RPM information to the ECM.
2    Test the switch by connecting a 12-volt power supply and voltmeter as shown in the accompanying illustration. Check the polarity markings carefully before making any connections.
3    When the knife blade is *not* inserted as shown, the voltmeter should read less than 0.5 volts. If the reading is more, the Hall effect switch is faulty and must be replaced by a new one.
4    With the knife blade inserted, the voltmeter should read within 0.5 volts of battery voltage. Replace the switch with a new one if the reading is more.
5    Remove the Hall-effect switch by unplugging the connector and removing the retaining screws.
6    Installation is the reverse of removal.

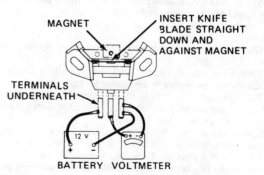

**Fig. 5.14 Hall Effect switch test (Sec 12)**

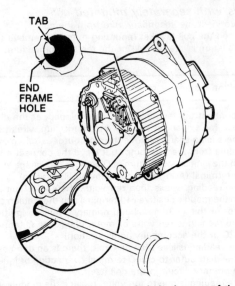

**Fig. 5.15 Location of the test hole in the rear of the alternator (inset shows grounding procedure) (Sec 14)**

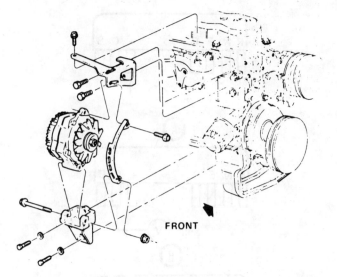

**Fig. 5.16 Four-cylinder engine alternator installation details (Sec 15)**

## 13  Charging system — general information and precautions

The charging system is made up of the alternator, voltage regulator and battery. These components work together to supply electrical power for the engine ignition, lights, radio, etc.

The alternator is turned by a drivebelt at the front of the engine. When the engine is operating, voltage is generated by the internal components of the alternator to be sent to the battery for storage.

The purpose of the voltage regulator is to limit the alternator voltage to a preset value. This prevents power surges, circuit overloads, etc., during peak voltage output. On all models with which this manual is concerned, the voltage regulator is contained within the alternator housing.

The charging system does not ordinarily require periodic maintenance. The drivebelts, electrical wiring and connections should, however, be inspected at the intervals suggested in Chapter 1.

Take extreme care when making circuit connections to a vehicle equipped with an alternator and note the following. When making connections to the alternator from a battery, always match correct polarity. Before using arc welding equipment to repair any part of the vehicle, disconnect the wires from the alternator and the battery terminal. Never start the engine with a battery charger connected. Always disconnect both battery leads before using a battery charger.

## 14  Charging system — check

1   If a malfunction occurs in the charging circuit, do not immediately assume that the alternator is causing the problem. First check the following items:
   a) The battery cables where they connect to the battery. Make sure the connections are clean and tight.
   b) The battery electrolyte specific gravity. If it is low, charge the battery.
   c) Check the external alternator wiring and connections. They must be in good condition.
   d) Check the drivebelt condition and tension (see Chapter 1).
   e) Check the alternator mount bolts for tightness.
   f) Run the engine and check the alternator for abnormal noise.
2   Using a voltmeter, check the battery voltage with the engine off. It should be approximately 12 volts.
3   Start the engine and check the battery voltage again. It should now be approximately 14 to 15 volts. If it does not rise when the engine is started, or if it exceeds 15 volts, proceed to Step 4.
4   Locate the test hole in the back of the alternator and ground the tab that is located inside the hole by inserting a screwdriver blade into the hole and touching the tab and the case at the same time. **Note:**

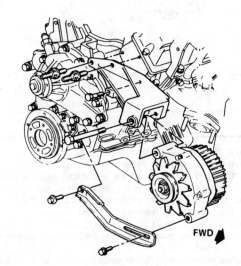

**Fig. 5.17  2.8 liter V6 engine alternator installation details (Sec 15)**

*Do not run the engine with the tab grounded any longer than necessary to obtain a voltmeter reading. The alternator, if it is charging, is running unregulated at this point. This condition may overload the electrical system and cause damage to the components.*
5   The reading on the voltmeter should be 15 volts or higher with the tab grounded in the test hole.
6   If the voltmeter indicates low battery voltage, the alternator is faulty and should be replaced with a new one (refer to Section 15).
7   If the voltage reading is 15 volts or higher and a no charge condition is present, the regulator or field circuit is the problem. Remove the alternator and have it checked further by an auto electric shop.

## 15  Alternator — removal and installation

### Removal
1   Disconnect the battery negative cable.
2   On some models it will be necessary to raise the vehicle, support

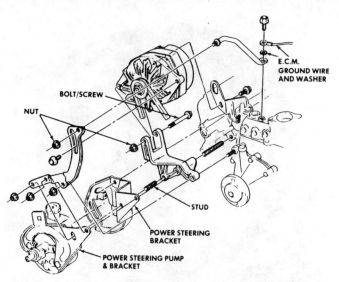

Fig. 5.18 3.0 and 3.8 liter alternator installation details
(Sec 15)

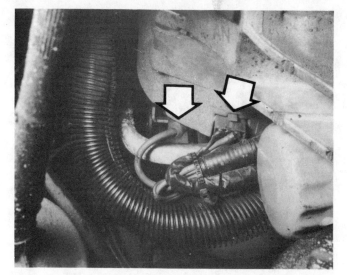

15.3 Alternator electrical connectors (arrows)

16.3 A paper clip is inserted from the rear of the alternator to
hold the brushes in place during disassembly and reassembly

16.4A Separate the alternator front and rear end frames

it securely and remove the right front wheel for access to the alternator.
3    Unplug the two terminal plug and battery leads from the back of
the alternator (photo).
4    Loosen the adjusting bolts and remove the drive belt.
5    Remove the through-bolt and nut and the adjusting bolt. Lift or
lower the alternator from the engine.

*Installation*
6    Place the alternator in position and install the through-bolt and nut.
Install the adjusting bolt.
7    Install the drivebelt and adjust the tension (Chapter 1).
8    Plug in the alternator connectors.
9    Connect the battery negative cable.

---

**16    Alternator brushes — replacement**

1    Remove the alternator from the vehicle (refer to Section 15).
2    Scribe a match mark on the front and rear end frame housings of
the alternator to facilitate reassembly.
3    From the rear of the alternator, insert a paper clip through the rear
end frame to hold the brushes in place (photo).
4    Remove the four through-bolts holding the front and rear end
frames together, then separate the end frames with the paper clip still
in place (photos).

16.4B  Details of the alternator rear end frame

A    Brush holder                D    Resistor (not all models)
B    Paper clip retaining brushes E    Diode trio
C    Regulator                   F    Rectifier bridge

16.5   Separate the stator from the rear end frame

16.6   Remove the diode trio from the rectifier bridge

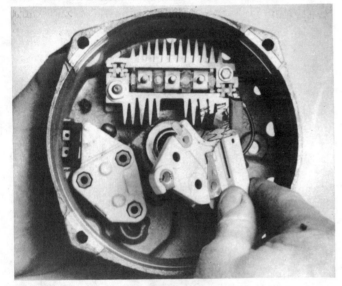

16.8   Remove the regulator from the rear end frame

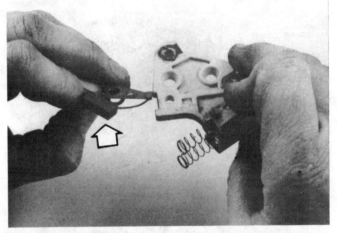

16.9   Remove the brush assembly (arrow) from the regulator

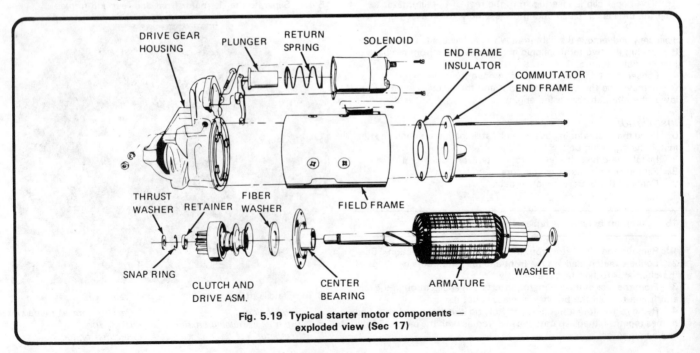

Fig. 5.19 Typical starter motor components —
exploded view (Sec 17)

5    Remove the bolts holding the stator to the rear end frame and separate the stator from the end frame (photo).
6    Remove the nuts attaching the diode trio to the rectifier bridge and remove the trio (photo).
7    Remove the paper clip from the rear of the end frame while holding your hand over the end of the brush holder to catch the brushes as they are released.
8    Remove the screws retaining the regulator and resistor (if equipped) to the end frame and remove the regulator (photo).
9    Remove the brushes from the regulator by slipping the brush retainer off the regulator (photo).
10   Remove the springs from the brush holder.
11   Installation is the reverse of the removal procedure, noting the following:
12   When installing the brushes in the brush holder, install the brush closest to the end frame first. Slip the paper clip through the rear of the end frame to hold the brush, then insert the second brush and push the paper clip in to hold both brushes while reassembly is completed. The paper clip should not be removed until the front and rear end frames have been bolted together.

## 17   Starting system — general information

The function of the starting system is to crank the engine. This system is composed of a starting motor, solenoid and battery. The battery supplies the electrical energy to the solenoid, which then completes the circuit to the starting motor, which does the actual work of cranking the engine.

The solenoid and starting motor are mounted together at the lower right side of the engine. No periodic lubrication or maintenance is required.

The electrical circuitry of the vehicle is arranged so that the starter motor can only be operated when the clutch pedal is depressed (manual transmission) or the transmission selector lever is in Park or Neutral (automatic transmission).

Never operate the starter motor for more than 30 seconds at a time without pausing to allow it to cool for at least two minutes. Excessive cranking can cause overheating, which can seriously damage the starter.

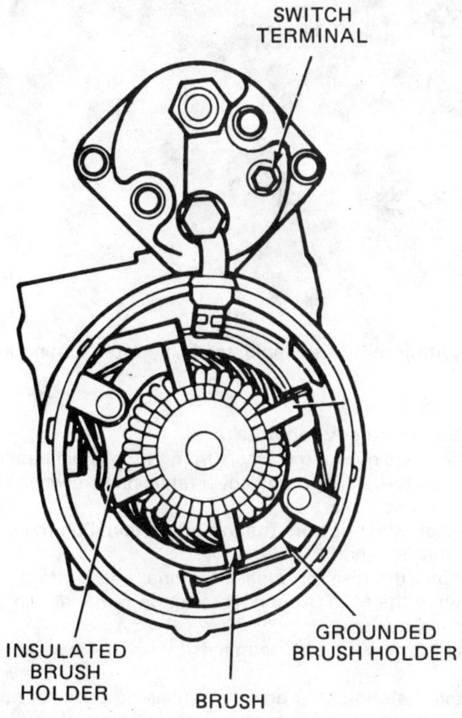

## 18   Starter motor — testing in vehicle

1    If the starter motor does not turn at all when the switch is operated, make sure that the shift lever is in Neutral or Park (automatic transmission) or that the clutch pedal is depressed (manual transmission).
2    Make sure that the battery is charged and that all cables, both at the battery and starter solenoid terminals, are secure.
3    If the starter motor spins but the engine is not being cranked, then the overrunning clutch in the starter motor is slipping and the motor must be removed from the engine and disassembled.
4    If, when the switch is actuated, the starter motor does not operate at all but the solenoid clicks, then the problem is in the main solenoid contacts or the starter motor itself. This assumes that the battery has been checked and it is fully charged.
5    If the solenoid plunger cannot be heard when the switch is actuated, the solenoid itself is defective or the solenoid circuit is open.
6    To check the solenoid, connect a jumper lead between the battery (+) and the S terminal on the solenoid. If the starter motor now operates, the solenoid is OK and the problem is in the ignition switch, neutral start switch or in the wiring.
7    If the starter motor still does not operate, remove the starter/solenoid assembly for disassembly, testing and repair.
8    If the starter motor cranks the engine at an abnormally slow speed, first make sure that the battery is charged and that all terminal connections are tight. If the engine is partially seized, or has the wrong viscosity oil in it, it will crank slowly.
9    Run the engine until normal operating temperature is reached, then disconnect the coil wire from the distributor cap and ground it on the engine.
10   Connect a voltmeter positive lead to the starter motor terminal of the solenoid and then connect the negative lead to ground.
11   Actuate the ignition switch and take the voltmeter readings as soon as a steady figure is indicated. Do not allow the starter motor to turn for more than 30 seconds at a time. A reading of 9 volts or more, with the starter motor turning at normal cranking speed, is normal. If the reading is 9 volts or more but the cranking speed is slow, the motor is faulty. If the reading is less than 9 volts and the cranking speed is slow, the solenoid contacts are probably burned (refer to Section 22).

## 19   Starter motor — removal and installation

1    Disconnect the negative battery cable.
2    Raise the front of the vehicle and support it securely on jackstands.

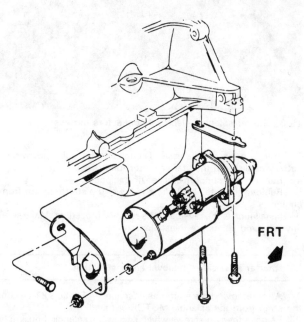

Fig. 5.21 Details of four-cylinder engine starter motor installation (Sec 19)

Fig. 5.20 View of the starter and solenoid showing the S (switch) terminal on the solenoid and detail of the brush installation in the starter field frame housing (Sec 18)

SWITCH TERMINAL

INSULATED BRUSH HOLDER

BRUSH

GROUNDED BRUSH HOLDER

FRT

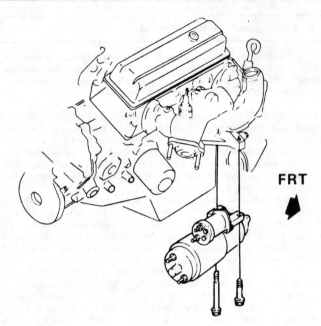

**Fig. 5.22  2.8 liter V6 engine starter motor installation (Sec 19)**

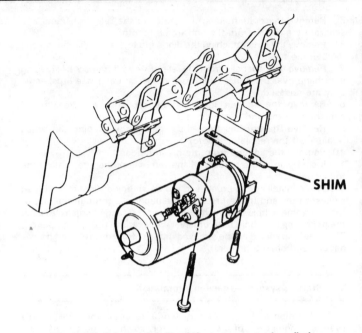

**Fig. 5.23  3.0 and 3.8 liter V6 starter motor installation (Sec 19)**

19.3   Starter solenoid electrical connectors (arrows)

20.3   Withdraw the solenoid assembly after turning it clockwise (arrows)

3   From under the vehicle, disconnect the solenoid wires and battery cable from the starter motor (photo).
4   Remove the support bracket (if equipped).
5   Remove the retaining bolts and lower the starter motor from the engine.
6   Installation is the reverse of the removal procedure. Make sure that any removed shims are reinstalled.

**20   Starter solenoid — removal and installation**

1   After removing the starter as described in Section 21 disconnect the strap from the solenoid MOTOR terminal.
2   Remove the two screws which secure the solenoid housing to the starter end frame.
3   Twist the solenoid in a clockwise direction to disengage the flange

from the starter body (photo).
4   Remove the nuts and washers from the solenoid terminals and then unscrew the two solenoid end cover retaining screws and washers and pull off the end cover.
5   Unscrew the nut from the battery terminal on the end cover and remove the terminal.
6   Remove the resistor bypass terminal and contact.
7   Remove the MOTOR connector strap terminal and solder a new terminal in position.
8   Install a new battery terminal. Install the bypass terminal and contact.
9   Install the end cover and the remaining terminal nuts.
10  To install, first make sure the return spring is in position on the plunger, then insert the solenoid body into the starter housing and turn the solenoid counterclockwise to engage the flange.
11  Install the two solenoid screws and connect the MOTOR strap.

## 21  Starter motor brushes — replacement

1   Remove the starter and solenoid assembly from the vehicle.

2   Remove the solenoid from the starter housing (refer to Section 20).

3   Remove the starter motor through bolts after marking the relationship of the commutator end frame to the field frame housing to simplify reassembly.

4   Remove the end frame from the field frame housing (photo).

5   Mark the relationship of the field frame housing to the drive end housing. Pull the field frame housing away from the drive end housing and over the armature.

6   Unbolt the brushes and brush supports from the brush holders in the field frame housing (photo).

7   To install new brushes, attach the brushes to the brush supports, making sure they are flush with the bottom of the supports, and bolt the brushes/supports to the brush holders.

8   Install the field frame over the armature, with the brushes resting on the first step of the armature collar at this point (photo).

9   Make sure the field frame is properly aligned with the drive end housing, then push the brushes off the collar and into place on the armature.

10  The remaining installation steps are the reverse of those for removal.

21.4   Remove the end frame from the field frame housing

21.6   Unbolt the brush and brush support from the brush holder

21.8   Install the field frame over the armature (note the position of the brushes on the armature collar)

# Chapter 6  Emissions control systems

*Refer to Chapter 13 for information applicable to 1986 and later models*

## Contents

| | |
|---|---|
| Air Injection Reactor AIR/PULSAIR reactor systems . . . . . . . . | 5 |
| Computer Command Control System (CCCS) . . . . . . . . . . . . . | 2 |
| Early Fuel Evaporation (EFE) system . . . . . . . . . . . . . . . . . | 6 |
| Electronic Spark Timing (EST) . . . . . . . . . . . . . . . . . . . . | 4 |
| Evaporative Emissions Control (EEC) system . . . . . . . . . . . | 8 |
| Exhaust Gas Recirculation (EGR) system . . . . . . . . . . . . . | 7 |

| | |
|---|---|
| Fuel control system . . . . . . . . . . . . . . . . . . . . . . . . . . . . | 3 |
| General information . . . . . . . . . . . . . . . . . . . . . . . . . . . . | 1 |
| Positive Crankcase Ventilation (PCV) system . . . . . . . . . . . | 9 |
| Thermostatic Air Cleaner (THERMAC) . . . . . . . . . . . . . . . | 10 |
| Transmission Converter Clutch (TCC) . . . . . . . . . . . . . . . . | 11 |

## Specifications

| Torque specifications | Ft-lbs |
|---|---|
| EGR valve . . . . . . . . . . . . . . . . . . . . . . . . . . . . . . . . . . | 10 to 20 |
| EFE heater relay . . . . . . . . . . . . . . . . . . . . . . . . . . . . . . | 3 |
| AIR pump pulley . . . . . . . . . . . . . . . . . . . . . . . . . . . . . . . | 24 |
| AIR pump through-bolt . . . . . . . . . . . . . . . . . . . . . . . . . . | 23 |
| AIR management valve bolt . . . . . . . . . . . . . . . . . . . . . . . | 12 |
| Oxygen sensor . . . . . . . . . . . . . . . . . . . . . . . . . . . . . . . . | 30 |
| Servo-type EFE valve-to-exhaust manifold nuts . . . . . . . . . . | 15 |

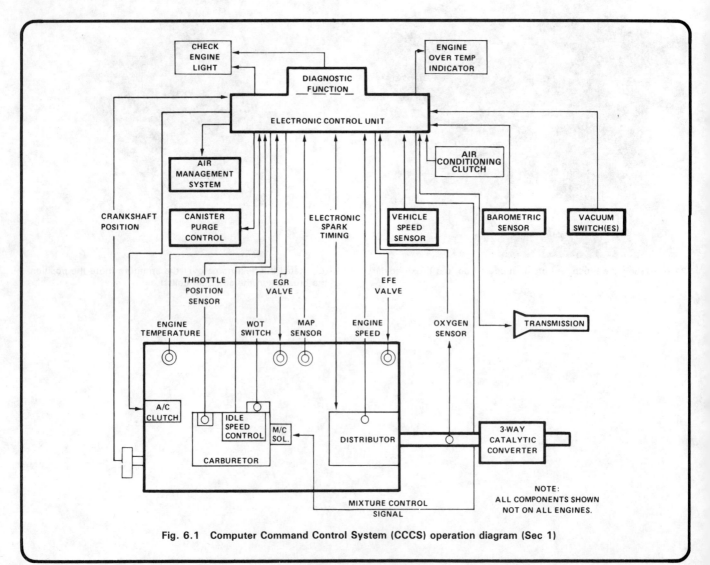

**Fig. 6.1  Computer Command Control System (CCCS) operation diagram (Sec 1)**

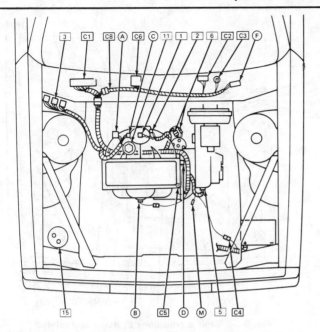

**Fig. 6.2  Typical locations of emissions system and related components (4-cylinder engine) (1985 engine shown, others similar) (Sec 1)**

*Computer system*
  *CI Electronic Control*
    *Module (ECM)*
  *C2 Diagnostic connector*
  *C3 Check Engine light*
  *C4 System power*
  *C5 System ground*
  *C6 Fuse panel*
  *C8 Computer control*
    *electrical harness*

*Air/fuel system*
  *1 Throttle body injection*
  *2 Idle air control*
  *3 Fuel pump relay*

*Transmission Converter clutch*
*(TCC) connector*
  *5 Transmission converter*
    *clutch connector*

*Ignition system*
  *6 Electronic spark*
    *timing connector*

*Exhaust Gas Recirculation*
*(EGR) control system*
  *11 EGR valve*

*Evaporative Emissions Control*
*(EEC) system*
  *15 Vapor canister*

*Sensors/switches*
  *A Manifold pressure sensor*
  *B Exhaust gas sensor*
  *C Throttle position sensor*
  *D Coolant sensor*
  *F Vehicle speed sensor*
  *M Fuel pump test connector*

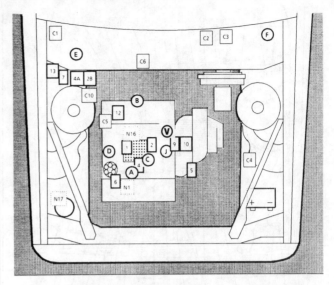

**Fig. 6.3  Typical locations of emissions system and related components (3.0 liter V6 engine) (1985 engine shown, others similar) (Sec 1)**

*Computer harness*
  *C1 Electronic Contol*
    *Module (ECM)*
  *C2 Diagnostic connector*
  *C3 Check Engine light*
  *C4 ECM power*
  *C5 ECM harness ground*
  *C6 Fuse panel*
  *C10 Air/fuel dwell connector*

*Non-ECM connected*
  *N1 PCV valve*
  *N16 Vapor canister valve*
  *N17 Vapor canister*

*CM controlled devices*
  *1 Mixture control solenoid*
  *2 Idle speed control motor*
  *2B Air conditioner wide-open*
    *throttle cutout relay*
  *4 Heated EFE grid*
  *4A Heated EFE grid relay*

*5 TCC connector*
*6 EST connector*
*7 Electronic Spark*
  *Control (ESC)*
*9 Air diverter solenoid*
*10 Air switching solenoid*
*12 EGR vacuum solenoid*
*13 Air conditioner*
  *compressor relay*

*Exhaust Gas Recirculation*
*(EGR) system*
  *V EGR valve*

*Sensors*
  *A Manifold Absolute Pressure*
    *(MAPS)*
  *B Exhaust sensor*
  *C Throttle position sensor*
  *D Coolant temperature sensor*
  *E Barometric pressure sensor*
  *F Vehicle speed sensor*
  *J Detonation sensor*

## 1  General information

To prevent pollution of the atmosphere from burned and evaporating gases, a number of emissions control systems are incorporated on the vehicles covered by this manual. The combination of systems used depends on the year in which the vehicle was manufactured, the locality to which it was originally delivered and the engine type. The major systems incorporated on the vehicles with which this manual is concerned include the:

  *Air Injection Reactor (AIR)*
  *Fuel Control System*
  *Electronic Spark Timing (EST)*
  *Early Fuel Evaporation (EFE)*
  *Exhaust Gas Recirculation (EGR)*
  *Evaporative Emissions Control (EECS)*
  *Transmission Converter Clutch (TCC)*
  *Positive Crankcase Ventilation (PCV)*
  *Thermostatic Air Cleaner (THERMAC)*

All of these systems are linked, directly or indirectly, to the Computer Command Control System (CCCS).

The Sections in this Chapter include general descriptions, checking procedures (where possible) and component replacement procedures (where applicable) for each of the systems listed above.

Before assuming that an emissions control system is malfunctioning, check the fuel and ignition systems carefully. In some cases special tools and equipment, as well as specialized training, are required to accurately diagnose the causes of a rough running or difficult to start engine. If checking and servicing become too difficult, or if a procedure is beyond the scope of the home mechanic, consult your dealer service department. This does not necessarily mean, however, that the emissions control systems are particularly difficult to maintain and repair. You can quickly and easily perform many checks and do most (if not all) of the regular maintenance at home with common tune-up and hand tools. **Note:** *The most frequent cause of emissions system problems is simply a loose or broken vacuum hose or wiring connection. Therefore, always check the hose and wiring connections first.*

Pay close attention to any special precautions outlined in this Chapter. It should be noted that the illustrations of the various systems may not exactly match the system installed on your particular vehicle due to changes made by the manufacturer during production or from year to year.

A Vehicle Emissions Control Information label is located in the engine compartment of all vehicles with which this manual is concerned. This label contains important emissions specifications and setting procedures, as well as a vacuum hose schematic with emissions components identified. When servicing the engine or emissions systems, the VECI label in your particular vehicle should always be checked for up-to-date information.

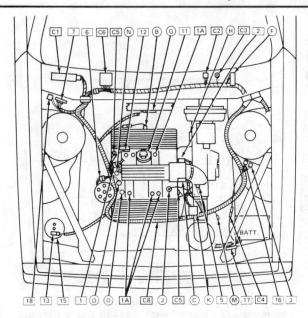

**Fig. 6.4   Typical locations of emissions system and related components (1985 3.8 liter Multi-port Fuel Injection (MFI) engine) (Sec 1)**

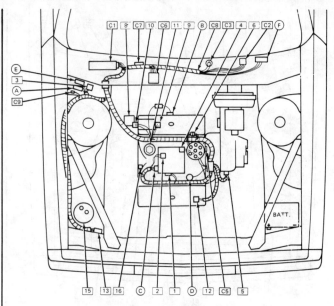

**Fig. 6.5   Typical emissions systems and related components (2.8 liter carbureted V6) (Sec 6)**

*Computer system*
  CI Electronic control
     module (ECM)
  C2 Diagnostic connector
  C3 Check Engine light
  C4 System power
  C5 System ground
  C6 Fuse panel
  C8 Computer control
     electrical harness

*Air/fuel system*
   1 Fuel injector connector
  1A Fuel injectors
   2 Idle air control (IAC) valve
   3 Fuel pump relay

*Transmission Converter
Clutch (TCC) system*
   5  TCC connector

*Ignition system*
   5 TCC connector
   6 EST connector
   7 Electronic Spark
     Control (ESC)

*Exhaust Gas Recirculation
(EGR) system*
  11 EGR valve
  12 EGR solenoid valve

*Evaporative Emissions Control
System (EECS)*
  13 Vapor canister purge
     solenoid valve
  15 Vapor canister

*Fan control*
  16 Timer relay
  17 Fan control relay
  18 Air conditioner control relay

*Sensors/relays*
  B Oxygen sensor
  C Throttle position sensor
  D Coolant sensor connector
  F Vehicle Speed Sensor (VSS)
  G Pressure Switch
  H P/N switch
  J Detonation sensor
  K Mass air flow sensor
  M Fuel pump test connector
  N Temperature sending unit
  O Coolant temperature
     override switch

*Computer system*
  C1 ECM
  C2 Diagnostic connector
  C3 Check Engine light
  C5 System ground
  C6 Fuse panel
  C7 Lamp driver
  C8 Computer control
     electrical harness
  C9 Dwell connector

*Air/fuel system*
   1 Mixture control
   2 Idle Speed Control (ISC)
   3 EFE relay
   4 Heated grid EFE

*Transmission Converter
Clutch (TCC) system*
   5 TCC connector

*Ignition system*
   6 EST connector

*Air Injection (AIR) system*
   8 AIR pump
   9 AIR control solenoid valve
  10 AIR switching solenoid valve

*Exhaust Gas Recirculation
(EGR) system*
  11 EGR valve
  12 EGR solenoid valve

*Evaporative Emissions
Control System (EECS)*
  13 Solenoid purge valve
  15 Vapor canister
  16 Fuel bowl vent solenoid

*Sensors/switches*
  A Differential pressure sensor
  B Oxygen sensor
  C Throttle position sensor
  D Coolant sensor
  E Barometric pressure sensor
  F Vehicle speed sensor (VSS)

In many ways, this system can be compared to the central nervous system in the human body. The sensors (nerves) constantly gather information and send this data to the ECM (brain), which processes the data and, if necessary, sends out a command for some type of vehicle (body) change.

Here's a specific example of how one portion of this system operates. An oxygen sensor, mounted in the exhaust manifold and protruding into the exhaust gas stream, constantly monitors the oxygen content of the exhaust gas as it travels through the exhaust pipe. If the percentage of oxygen in the exhaust gas is incorrect, an electrical signal is sent to the ECM. The ECM takes this information, processes it and then sends a command to the carburetor Mixture Control (M/C) solenoid, telling it to change the fuel/air mixture. To be effective, all this happens in a fraction of a second, and it goes on continuously while the engine is running. The end result is a fuel/air ratio which is constantly kept at a predetermined proportion, regardless of driving conditions.

Unless otherwise noted, procedures in this Chapter referring to carbureted models also apply to fuel injected models. Because of their more precise fuel/air management, fuel injected engines use simpler emissions systems which do not use all of the systems described above.

## 2   Computer Command Control System (CCCS)

### General description

This electronically controlled emissions system is linked with as many as nine other related emissions systems. It consists mainly of sensors (as many as 15) and an Electronic Control Module (ECM). Completing the system are various engine components which respond to commands from the ECM.

### Testing

One might think that a system which uses exotic electrical sensors and is controlled by an on-board computer would be difficult to diagnose. This is not necessarily the case.

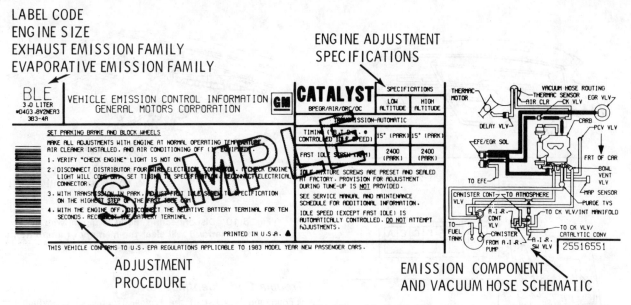

LABEL CODE
ENGINE SIZE
EXHAUST EMISSION FAMILY
EVAPORATIVE EMISSION FAMILY

ENGINE ADJUSTMENT
SPECIFICATIONS

ADJUSTMENT
PROCEDURE

EMISSION COMPONENT
AND VACUUM HOSE SCHEMATIC

**Fig. 6.6 A Vehicle Emissions Control Information label will be found in the engine compartment of all vehicles (Sec 1)**

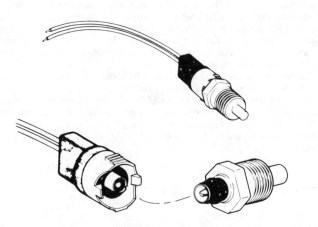

**Fig. 6.7 The engine coolant sensor (right), shown with its ECM harness, is located in a coolant passage (Sec 2)**

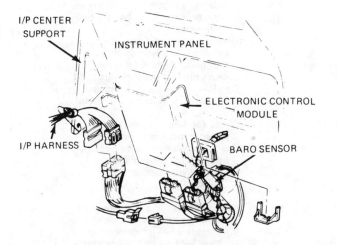

**Fig. 6.8 Typical Electronic Control Module (ECM) installation (Sec 2)**

The Computer Command Control System has a built-in diagnostic system which indicates a problem by flashing a *CHECK ENGINE* light on the instrument panel. When this light comes on during normal vehicle operation, a fault has been detected.

Perhaps more importantly, the ECM will recognize this fault in a particular system monitored by one of the various information sensors and store it in its memory in the form of a trouble code. Although the trouble code cannot reveal the exact cause of the malfunction, it greatly facilitates diagnosis as you or a dealer mechanic can "tap into" the ECM's memory and be directed to the problem area.

To extract this information from the ECM memory, you must use a short jumper wire to ground a *TEST* terminal. This terminal is part of a wiring connector located just behind the dashboard, next to the steering column. A small, rectangular plate is used to cover the connector and must be pried out of place to provide access to the terminals.

With the connector exposed to view, push one end of the jumper wire into the *TEST* terminal and the other end into the *GROUND* terminal. **Note:** *Do not start the engine with the TEST terminal grounded.*

Turn the ignition to the On position — not the Start position. The *CHECK ENGINE* light should flash *Trouble Code 12*, indicating that the diagnostic system is working. Code 12 will consist of one flash, followed by a short pause, and then two flashes in quick succession. After a longer pause, the code will repeat itself two more times.

If no other codes have been stored, Code 12 will continue to repeat itself until the jumper wire is disconnected. If additional Trouble Codes have been stored, they will follow Code 12. Again, each Trouble Code will flash three times before moving on.

The ECM can also be checked for stored codes on carbureted models with the engine running. Completely remove the jumper wire from the *TEST* and *GROUND* terminals, start the engine, and then plug the jumper wire back in. With the engine running, all stored Trouble Codes will flash. However, Code 12 will flash only if there is a fault in the distributor reference circuit.

Once the code(s) have been noted, use the Trouble Code Identification information which follows to locate the source of the fault. **Note:** *Whenever the positive battery cable is disconnected, all stored Trouble Codes in the ECM are erased. Be aware of this before you disconnect the battery for servicing or replacement of electrical components, engine removal, etc.*

It should be noted that the self-diagnosis feature built into this system does not detect all possible faults. If you suspect a problem with the Computer Command Control System, but a *CHECK ENGINE* light has not come on, have your local dealer perform a *System Performance Check.*

Furthermore, when diagnosing an engine performance, fuel economy or exhaust emissions problem (which is not accompanied by a *CHECK ENGINE* light) do not automatically assume the fault lies in this system. Perform all standard troubleshooting procedures, as indicated elsewhere

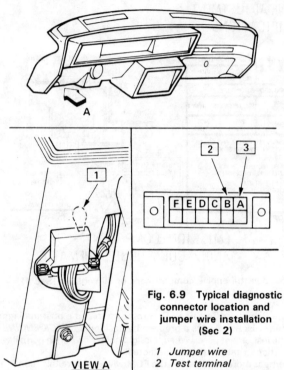

**Fig. 6.9 Typical diagnostic connector location and jumper wire installation (Sec 2)**

1 Jumper wire
2 Test terminal
3 Ground terminal

VIEW A

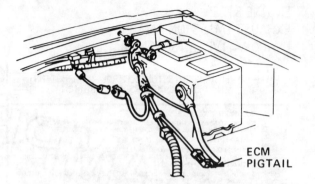

**Fig. 6.10 Disconnecting the ECM pigtail wire at the connector (arrow) will clear the memory of intermittent trouble codes (Sec 2)**

in this manual, before turning to the Computer Command Control System.

Finally, since this is an electronic system, you should have a basic knowledge of automotive electronics before attempting any diagnosis. Damage to the ECM, Programmable Read Only Memory Calibration Unit (PROM) or related components can easily occur if care is not exercised.

## Trouble Code Identification

Following is a list of the typical Trouble Codes which may be encountered while diagnosing the Computer Command Control System. Also included are simplified troubleshooting procedures. If the problem persists after these checks have been made, the vehicle must be diagnosed by a professional mechanic who can use specialized diagnostic tools and advanced troubleshooting methods to check the system. Procedures marked with an asterisk (*) indicate component replacements which may *not* cure the problem in all cases. For this reason, you may want to seek professional advice before purchasing replacement parts.

To clear the Trouble Code(s) from the ECM memory, unplug the ECM electrical pigtail at the positive (+) battery cable.

Disconnecting the power to the ECM to clear the memory can be an important diagnostic tool, especially on intermittent problems. On later models it is a simple matter to unplug the ECM harness positive battery cable pigtail for ten seconds to clear all the stored Trouble Codes.

| Trouble Code | Circuit or system | Probable cause |
|---|---|---|
| 12 (one flash, pause, two flashes) | No reference pulses to ECM | This code should flash whenever the 'Test' terminal is grounded with the ignition On and the engine not running. If additional Trouble Codes are stored (indicating a problem), they will appear after this code has flashed three times<br>With the engine running, the appearance of this code indicates that no references from the distributor are reaching the ECM.<br>Carefully check the four-terminal EST connector at the distributor |
| 13 (one flash, pause, three flashes) | Oxygen sensor circuit | Check for a sticking or misadjusted throttle position sensor<br>Check the wiring and connectors from the oxygen sensor<br>Replace oxygen sensor (see Chapter 1) |
| 14 (one flash, pause, four flashes) | Coolant sensor circuit | **Note:** *If the engine is experiencing overheating problems (as indicated by high temperature gauge readings or the 'hot' light coming on), rectify by referring to Chapters 1 and 3 before continuing.* |

| Trouble Code | Circuit or system | Probable cause |
| --- | --- | --- |
| 14 (one flash, pause, four flashes) | Coolant sensor circuit (high temperature indicated) | Check all wiring and connectors from the coolant sensor *Replace coolant sensor (located at front of left-hand cylinder head on V6; front of engine block on four-cylinder) |
| 15 (one flash, pause, five flashes) | Coolant sensor circuit (low temperature indicated) | See above, plus: Check the wiring connections at the ECM |
| 21 (two flashes, pause, one flash) | TPS circuit (signal voltage high) | Check for sticking or misadjusted TPS plunger Check all wiring and connections at the TPS and at the ECM *Adjust or replace TPS (see Chapter 4) |
| 22 (two flashes, pause, two flashes) | TPS circuit (signal voltage low) | Check TPS adjustment (Chapter 4) Check ECM connector *Replace TPS (Chapter 4) |
| 23 (two flashes, pause, three flashes) | M/C solenoid circuit | Check the electrical connections at the M/C solenoid (see Chapter 4). If OK, clear the ECM memory and recheck for code(s) after driving the vehicle Check wiring connections at the ECM Check wiring from M/C solenoid (Chapter 4) |
| 24 (two flashes, pause, four flashes) | Vehicle speed sensor (VSS) circuit | **Note:** *A fault in this circuit should be indicated only while the vehicle is in motion. Disregard code 24 if set when drive wheels are not turning.* Check connections at the ECM Check the TPS setting (Chapter 4) |
| 32 (three flashes, pause, two flashes) | Baro sensor circuit | Check for a short between sensor terminals B and C or the wires leading to these terminals Check the wire leading to ECM terminal 1 Check the ECM connections Check the wires leading to ECM terminals 21 and 22 *Replace Baro sensor (located in the engine compartment, attached to the firewall) |
| 33 (three flashes, pause, three flashes) | MAP sensor | Check vacuum hose(s) from MAP sensor Check electrical connections at ECM *Replace MAP sensor |
| 34 (three flashes, pause, four flashes) | Vacuum sensor circuit | Check the wiring leading to terminals 20, 21 and 22 of the ECM Check the connections at the ECM Check the vacuum sensor wiring and connections *Replace vacuum sensor (located in the engine compartment) |
| 41 (four flashes, pause, one flash) | No distributor signals | Check all wires and connections at the distributor Check distributor pick-up coil connections (Chapter 5) Check vacuum sensor circuit (see above) |
| 42 (four flashes, pause, two flashes) | Bypass or EST problem | **Note:** *If the vehicle will not start and run, check the wire leading to ECM terminal 12.* |

| Trouble Code | Circuit or system | Probable cause |
|---|---|---|
| 42 (four flashes, pause, two flashes) | Bypass or EST problem | **Note:** *An improper HEI module can cause this trouble code.* Check the EST wire leading to the HEI module E terminal; Check all distributor wires; Check the wire leading from EST terminal A to ECM terminal 12 and the wire from EST terminal C to ECM terminal 11; Check all ECM connections; *Replace HEI module |
| 43 (four flashes, pause, three flashes) | Electronic Spark Control (ESC) system | Check wire leading to ECM terminal L; Check the wiring connector at the ESC controller and at the ECM; Check wire from knock sensor to ESC controller; if necessary, reroute it away from other wires such as spark plug, etc. |
| 44 (four flashes, pause, four flashes) | Lean exhaust | Check for a sticking M/C solenoid (Chapter 4); Check ECM wiring connections, particularly terminals 14 and 9; Check for vacuum leakage at carburetor base gasket, vacuum hoses or intake manifold gasket; Check for air leakage at air management system-to-exhaust ports and at decel valve; *Replace oxygen sensor |
| 45 (four flashes, pause, five flashes) | Rich exhaust | Check for a sticking M/C solenoid (Chapter 4); Check wiring at M/C solenoid connector; Check the evaporative charcoal canister and its components for the presence of fuel (Chapters 1, 6); *Replace oxygen sensor |
| 51 (five flashes, pause, one flash) | PROM problem | The PROM is located inside the ECM and is very delicate and easily broken. All diagnostic procedures should be done by a dealer mechanic. |
| 54 (five flashes, pause, four flashes) | M/C solenoid | Check all M/C solenoid and ECM wires and connections; *Replace the M/C solenoid (see Chapter 4) |
| 55 (five flashes, pause, five flashes) | Oxygen sensor circuit | Check for corrosion on the ECM connectors and terminals; Make sure that the four-terminal EST wiring harness is not too close to electrical signals such as spark plug wires, distributor housing, alternator, etc.; Check the wiring of the various sensors; *Replace the oxygen sensor |

### 3   Fuel Control System

#### General description

1    The function of this system is to control the flow of fuel through the carburetor idle and main metering circuits. The major components of the system are the mixture control (M/C) solenoid and the oxygen sensor.

2    The M/C solenoid changes the fuel/air mixture by allowing more or less fuel to flow through the carburetor. The M/C solenoid, located in the carburetor air horn, is in turn controlled by the Electronic Control Module (ECM), which provides a ground for the solenoid. When the solenoid is energized, the fuel flow through the carburetor is reduced, providing a leaner mixture. When the ECM removes the ground path, the solenoid de-energizes and allows more fuel flow.

3    The ECM determines the proper fuel mixture required by monitoring a signal sent by the oxygen sensor, located in the exhaust stream. When the mixture is lean, the oxygen sensor voltage is low and the ECM commands a richer mixture. Conversely, when the mixture is rich, the oxygen sensor voltage is higher and the ECM commands a leaner mixture.

#### Checking

**Oxygen sensor**

4    Make sure that the oxygen sensor has been replaced at the proper maintenance interval (refer to Chapter 1).

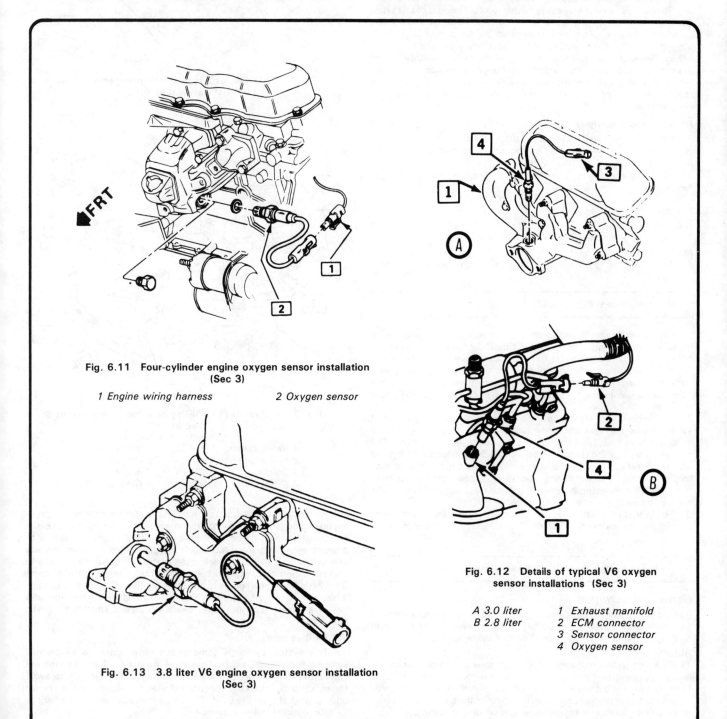

Fig. 6.11   Four-cylinder engine oxygen sensor installation (Sec 3)

1 Engine wiring harness          2 Oxygen sensor

Fig. 6.13   3.8 liter V6 engine oxygen sensor installation (Sec 3)

Fig. 6.12   Details of typical V6 oxygen sensor installations  (Sec 3)

A 3.0 liter          1  Exhaust manifold
B 2.8 liter          2  ECM connector
                     3  Sensor connector
                     4  Oxygen sensor

5   The proper operation of the sensor depends on the four conditions which follow:

6   *Electrical conditions:* The low voltages and low currents generated by the sensor depend upon good, clean connections which should be checked whenever a malfunction of the sensor is suspected or indicated.

7   *Outside air supply:* The sensor is designed to allow air circulation to the internal portion of the sensor. Whenever the sensor is removed and installed or replaced, make sure the air passages are not restricted.

8   *Proper operating temperature:* The ECM will not react to the sensor signal until the sensor reaches approximately 600°F (315°C). This factor must be taken into consideration when evaluating the performance of the sensor.

9   *Unleaded fuel:* The use of unleaded fuel is essential for proper operation of the sensor. Make sure the fuel you are using is of this type.

10  In addition to observing the above conditions, special care must be taken whenever the sensor is handled, as directed in Chapter 1. Violation of any of these cautionary procedures may lead to sensor failure. **Note:** *Do not attempt to measure the voltage output of the oxygen sensor, because the current drain from a conventional voltmeter would be enough to permanently damage the sensor. For the same reason, never hook up test leads, jumpers or other electrical connections.*

**Mixture control solenoid**

11  Check the wiring connectors and wires leading to the mixture control solenoid for looseness, fraying and other damage. Repair or replace any damaged wiring as necessary.

12  Check the mixture control solenoid for apparent physical damage. Replace it if damage is found.

## Component replacement

**Oxygen sensor**

13  To replace the sensor, refer to Chapter 1.

**Mixture control solenoid**

14  For E2SE and E2ME carburetors, refer to Chapter 4.

---

### 4  Electronic Spark Timing (EST)

1   Electronic Spark Timing is used on all engines with which this manual is concerned. The EST distributor contains no vacuum or centrifugal advance, depending on commands from the ECM instead. The ECM receives a reference pulse from the distributor, indicating both engine rpm and crankshaft position, determines the proper spark advance for the engine operating conditions and sends an EST pulse to the distributor.

2   Under normal operating conditions, the ECM will always control the spark advance. However, under certain conditions, such as cranking or setting base timing, the distributor can operate independent of ECM control. This condition is called *Bypass* and is determined by the bypass lead from the ECM to the distributor. When the bypass lead is over two volts, the ECM will control the spark. Disconnecting the four-terminal EST connector, or grounding the bypass lead, will cause the engine to operate in the bypass mode.

3   For further information (and checking and component replacement procedures) regarding the EST distributor, refer to Chapter 5.

---

### 5  Air Injection Reactor (AIR/PULSAIR) system

## General description

**Note:** *If your engine is equipped with an air pump, your concern in this Section will be with the AIR system. If no air pump is present, refer to the procedures involving the PULSAIR system.*

**AIR system**

1   The AIR system helps reduce hydrocarbons and carbon monoxide levels in the exhaust by injecting air into the exhaust ports of each cylinder during cold engine operation, or directly into the catalytic converter during normal operation. It also helps the catalytic converter reach proper operating temperature quickly during warm-up.

2   The AIR system uses an air pump to force the air into the exhaust stream. An air management valve, controlled by the vehicle's electronic

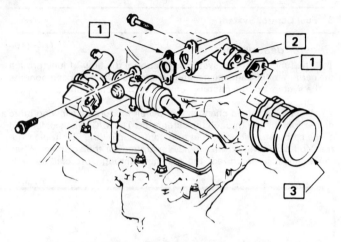

**Fig. 6.14  Details of a typical AIR management valve installation (Sec 5)**

| 1 Seal | 2 Adapter | 3 Air pump |
|---|---|---|

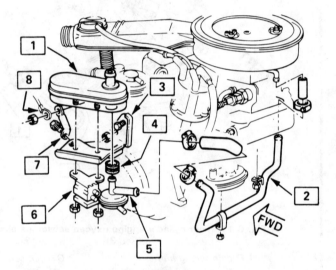

**Fig. 6.15  Typical PULSAIR system component layout (Sec 5)**

| 1 Valve assembly | 5 Valve |
|---|---|
| 2 Pipe assembly | 6 Actuator |
| 3 Bracket | 7 Brace |
| 4 Grommet | 8 Ground strap |

control module (ECM) directs the air to the correct location, depending on engine temperature and driving conditions. During certain situations, such as deceleration, the air is diverted to the air cleaner to prevent backfiring from too much oxygen in the exhaust stream. One-way check valves are also used in the AIR system's air lines to prevent exhaust gases from being forced back through the system.

3   The following components are utilized in the AIR system: an engine driven air pump; air control, air switching and divert management valves; air flow and control hoses; check valves; and a dual bed catalytic converter.

**PULSAIR system**

4   This system performs some of the same functions as the AIR system, but utilizes exhaust pressure pulses to draw air into the exhaust system. Fresh air that is filtered by the air cleaner, to avoid the build-up of dirt on the check valve seat, is supplied to the system on a command from the ECM. The air cleaner also serves as a muffler to reduce noise in the system.

5   Components utilized in the system include the PULSAIR valve and external tubes and hoses.

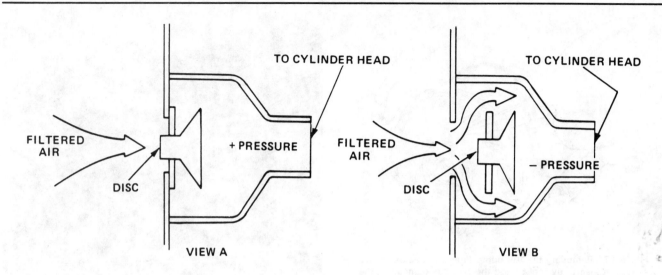

**Fig. 6.16  With positive pressure present in the PULSAIR valve (left), the valve disc remains closed and no air enters the valve; when a vacuum is present in the valve (right), the disc opens and air mixes with the exhaust gases (Sec 5)**

6   The PULSAIR system's operation begins with the engine's firing, creating a pulsating flow of exhaust gases which are of positive or negative pressure. The pressure or vacuum is transmitted through the external tubes to the PULSAIR valve, which reacts as follows:

7   If the pressure is positive, the disc in the valve is forced to the closed position and no exhaust gas is allowed to flow past the valve and into the air supply.

8   If there is negative pressure (vacuum) present in the exhaust system at the valve, the disc will open, allowing fresh air to mix with the exhaust gases.

9   The disc, due to the inertia of the system, ceases to follow the pressure pulsations at high engine rpm. At this point the disc remains closed, preventing any further flow of fresh air.

## Checking

### AIR system

10   Because of the complexity of this system it is difficult for the home mechanic to make a proper diagnosis. If the system is suspected of not operating properly, individual components can be checked.

11   Begin any inspection by carefully checking all hoses, vacuum lines and wires. Be sure they are in good condition and that all connections are tight and clean. Also make sure that the pump drivebelt is in good condition and properly adjusted.

12   To check the pump allow the engine to reach normal operating temperature and run it at about 1500 rpm. Locate the hose running from the air pump and squeeze it to feel the pulsations. Have an assistant increase the engine speed and check for a parallel increase in air flow. If this is observed as described, the pump is functioning properly. If it is not operating in this manner, a faulty pump is indicated.

13   The check valve can be inspected by first removing it from the air line. Attempt to blow through it from both directions. Air should only pass through it in the direction of normal air flow. If it is either stuck open or stuck closed the valve should be replaced.

14   To check the air management valve disconnect the vacuum signal line at the valve. With the engine running see if vacuum is present in the line. If not, the line is clogged.

15   To check the deceleration valve plug the air cleaner vacuum source. With the engine running at the specified idle speed remove the small deceleration valve signal hose from the manifold vacuum source, then reconnect the signal hose and listen for air flow through the ventilation pipe and into the deceleration valve. There should also be a noticeable engine speed drop when the signal hose is reconnected. If the air flow does not continue for at least one second, or the engine speed does not drop noticeably, check the deceleration valve hoses for restrictions and leaks. If no restrictions or leaks are found replace the deceleration valve.

### PULSAIR system

16   A simple, functional test of this system can be performed with the engine running. Disconnect the rubber hose from the air valve and hold your hand over the valve's inlet hole. With the engine idling there should be a steady stream of air being sucked into the valve. Have an assistant apply throttle, and as the engine gains speed, see if the suction increases. If this does not occur, the lines are leaking or restricted or the check valves are sticking. Also make sure that air is not being blown out of the air valve, as this is also an indication that the check valves are sticking open. Service or replace the components as necessary. If other PULSAIR problems are suspected, have a dealer or repair shop diagnose the problems, as they might relate to the ECM/Computer Command Control System.

## Component replacement (AIR system)

### Drivebelt

17   Loosen the pump mounting bolt and the pump adjustment bracket bolt.

18   Move the pump inboard until the belt can be removed.

19   Install the new belt and adjust it (refer to Chapter 1).

### AIR pump pulley and filter

20   Compress the drivebelt to keep the pulley from turning and loosen the pulley bolts.

21   Remove the drivebelt as described above.

22   Remove the mounting bolts and lift off the pulley (photo).

5.22  Removing the air pump pulley (note that the drivebelt has previously been removed

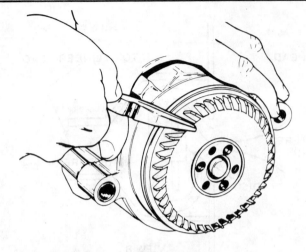

**Fig. 6.17  Removing the AIR pump filter (remove as shown — do not insert any tool behind the filter, as damage to the pump may occur) (Sec 5)**

5.29  Removing the hose from the AIR system check valve

5.33  Removing a hose from the AIR management valve

5.42  AIR system deceleration valve (arrow) (some V6 engines)

23  If the fan-like filter must be removed, grasp it firmly with needle-nose pliers, as shown in the accompanying illustration, and pull it from the pump. **Note:** *Do not insert a screwdriver between the filter and pump housing as the edge of the housing could be damaged. The filter will usually be distorted when pulled off. Be sure no fragments fall into the air intake hose.*

24  The new filter is installed by placing it in position on the pump, placing the pulley over it and tightening the pulley bolts evenly to draw the filter into the pump. Do not attempt to install a filter by pressing or hammering it into place. **Note:** *It is normal for the new filter to have an interference fit with the pump housing and, upon initial operation, it may squeal until worn in.*

25  Install the drivebelt and, while compressing the belt, tighten the pulley bolts to the specified torque.

26  Adjust the drivebelt tension.

**Hoses and tubes**

27  To replace any tube or hose always note how it is routed first, either with a sketch or with numbered pieces of tape.

28  Remove the defective hose or tube and replace it with a new one of the same material and size and tighten all connections.

**Check valve**

29  Disconnect the pump outlet hose at the check valve (photo).

30  Remove the check valve from the pipe assembly, making sure not to bend or twist the assembly.

31  Install a new valve after making sure that it is a duplicate of the part removed, then tighten all connections.

**Air management valve**

32  Disconnect the negative battery cable at the battery.

33  Disconnect the vacuum signal line from the valve (photo). Also disconnect the air hoses and wiring connectors.

34  If the mounting bolts are retained by tabbed lock washers, bend the tabs back, then remove the mounting bolts and lift the valve off the adaptor or bracket.

35  Installation is the reverse of the removal procedure. Be sure to use a new gasket when installing the valve.

**Air pump**

36  Remove the air management valve and adapter, if so equipped.

37  If the pulley must be removed from the pump it should be done prior to removing the drivebelt.

38  If the pulley is not being removed, remove the drivebelt.

39  Remove the pump mounting bolts and separate the pump from the engine.

40  Installation is the reverse of the removal procedure. **Note:** *Do not tighten the pump mounting bolts until all components are installed.*

41  Following installation adjust the drivebelt tension as described in Chapter 1.

**Deceleration valve**

42  Disconnect the vacuum hoses from the valve (photo).

43  Remove the screws retaining the valve to the engine bracket (if present) and remove the valve.

44  Install a new valve and reconnect all hoses.

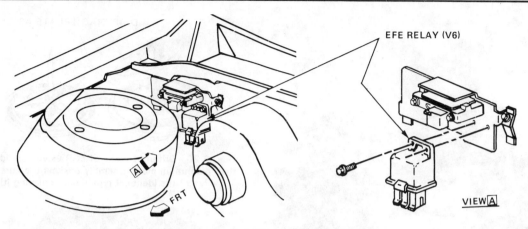

Fig. 6.18   Typical EFE relay location (Sec 6)

## Component replacement (PULSAIR system)

45  Remove the air cleaner and disconnect the negative cable from the battery.
46  Disconnect the rubber hose from the PULSAIR valve.
47  Disconnect the support bracket.
48  Remove the PULSAIR solenoid and bracket from the PULSAIR unit.
49  Loosen the nuts that secure the air tubes to the cylinder head and remove the assembly. Due to the high temperature at this area, these connections may be difficult to loosen. Penetrating oil applied to the threads of the nuts may help.
50  Before installing, apply a light coat of oil to the ends of the air tubes and anti-seize compound to the threads of the attaching nuts.
51  Installation is the reverse of the removal procedure.

## 6   Early Fuel Evaporation (EFE) system

### General description

**Servo type**
If your vehicle is equipped with vacuum servo type EFE system, refer to Chapter 1 for a general description of the system and system checking procedures.

**Electrically heated type**
1  This unit provides rapid heat to the intake air supply on carbureted and some throttle body injection engines by means of a ceramic heater grid. The grid is integral with the carburetor/TBI base gasket and located under the primary bore.
2  The components involved in the EFE's operation include the heater grid, a relay, electrical wires and connectors and the ECM.
3  The EFE heater unit is controlled by the vehicle's Electronic Control Module (ECM) through a relay. The ECM senses the coolant temperature level and applies voltage to the heater unit only when the engine temperature is below a predetermined level. At normal operating temperatures the heater unit is off.
4  If the EFE heater is not coming on poor cold engine performance will be experienced. If the heater unit is not shutting off when the engine is warmed up the engine will run as if it is out of tune due to the constant flow of hot air through the carburetor or TBI.

### Checking

**Servo type**
5  To check the operation of the EFE/TVS, allow the engine temperature to fall below 80°F (26°C).
6  Drain the coolant from the engine until the level is below the level of the switch.
7  Disconnect and label the vacuum lines, then remove the switch.
8  Blow into either of the TVS ports. Air should flow through the valve.
9  Heat the TVS in hot water until the temperature of the valve is above 90°F (32°C).
10  Blow into either port of the TVS. No air should flow through the valve.
11  If the condition in either Step 9 or 10 is not met, replace the valve with a new one.

12  For other checking procedures for the servo type EFE system, refer to Chapter 1.

**Electrically heated type**
13  If the EFE system is suspected of malfunctioning while the engine is cold, first check all electrical wires and connectors to be sure they are clean, tight and in good condition.
14  With the ignition switch in the On position, use a circuit tester or voltmeter to check that current is reaching the relay. If not, there is a problem in the wiring leading to the relay, in the ECM's thermo switch or the ECM itself.
15  With the engine cold and the ignition switch On, disconnect the heater unit wiring connector and use a circuit tester or voltmeter to see if current is reaching the heater unit. If so, use a continuity tester to check for continuity in the wiring connector attached to the heater unit. If continuity exists, the system is operating correctly in the cold engine mode.
16  If current is not reaching the heater unit, but is reaching the relay, replace the relay.
17  To check that the system turns off at normal engine operating temperature, first allow the engine to warm up thoroughly. With the engine idling, disconnect the heater unit wiring connector and use a circuit tester or voltmeter to check for current at the heater unit.
18  If current is reaching the heater unit a faulty ECM is indicated.
19  For confirmation of the ECM's condition, refer to Section 2 or have the system checked by a dealer or automotive repair shop.

### Component replacement

**Heater relay**
20  Disconnect the battery negative cable.
21  Remove the relay bracket from the fender skirt.
22  Unplug the electrical connectors, remove the retaining bolts and lift the relay from the vehicle.
23  Installation is the reverse of removal.

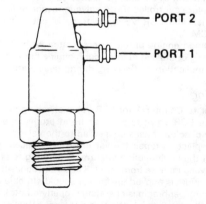

Fig. 6.19   A typical EFE/TVS switch employed in servo-type EFE systems, typically located in the intake manifold (Sec 6)

6.27   Removing the EFE system under-carburetor heater element

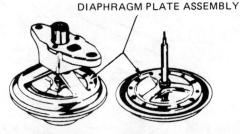

Fig. 6.20   Different types of EGR valves are identified by their diaphragm plate assembly designs (be sure to obtain a valve of the identical type when replacing it) (Sec 7)

### Heater element

24  Remove the air cleaner and disconnect all electrical, vacuum and fuel connections from the carburetor.
25  Unplug the EFE heater electrical connector.
26  Remove the carburetor (Chapter 4).
27  Remove the EFE heater assembly (photo).
28  Installation is the reverse of removal.

### Component replacement — TBI engines

#### Heater

29  Release the fuel system pressure (Chapter 1).
30  Remove the air cleaner assembly.
31  Disconnect the electrical, vacuum and fuel connections from the throttle body.
32  Unplug the EFE heater electrical connector.
33  Remove the throttle body assembly (Chapter 4).
34  Remove the heater insulator assembly.
35  Installation is the reverse of removal.

---

### 7  Exhaust Gas Recirculation (EGR) system

### General description

1   An EGR system is used on all engines with which this manual is concerned. The system meters exhaust gases into the engine induction system through passages cast into the intake manifold. From there the exhaust gases pass into the fuel/air mixture for the purpose of lowering combustion temperatures, thereby reducing the amount of oxides of nitrogen (NOX) formed.
2   The amount of exhaust gas admitted is regulated by a vacuum or backpressure controlled (EGR) valve in response to engine operating conditions. The EGR valve, in turn, is under the control of the CCCS/ECM.
3   Common engine problems associated with the EGR system are rough idling or stalling at idle, rough engine performance during light throttle application and stalling during deceleration.

### Checking

4   Refer to Chapter 1 for EGR valve checking procedures.
5   If the EGR valve appears to be in proper operating condition, carefully check all hoses connected to the valve for breaks, leaks or kinks. Replace or repair the valve/hoses as necessary.
6   With the engine idling at normal operating temperature, disconnect the vacuum hose from the EGR valve and connect a vacuum pump. When vacuum is applied the engine should stumble or die, indicating the vacuum diaphragm is operating properly (photo). Replace the EGR valve with a new one if the test does not affect the idle.
7   Due to the interrelationship of the EGR system and the ECM, further checks of the system should be made by referring to Section 2 or having the system checked by a dealer or repair shop.

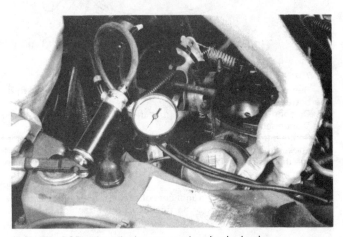

7.6   The EGR valve diaphragm can be checked using a vacuum pump

### Component replacement

#### EGR valve

8   Disconnect the vacuum hose at the EGR valve.
9   Remove the nuts or bolts which secure the valve to the intake manifold or adapter.
10  Lift the EGR valve from the engine.
11  Clean the mounting surfaces of the EGR valve. Remove all traces of gasket material.
12  Place the new EGR valve, with a new lithium-base grease coated gasket, on the intake manifold or adapter and tighten the attaching nuts or bolts (photo).
13  Connect the vacuum signal hose.

#### TVS (some V6 engines)

14  Drain sufficient coolant from the radiator to bring the level below the bottom of the TVS. The TVS is usually located at the front of the intake manifold.
15  Remove the hoses from the valve, labeling them to ensure proper installation.
16  Remove the TVS and replace it with a new one (photo).

### Cleaning

#### EGR valve

17  3.0 and 3.8 liter V6 engines use an EGR valve which can be disassembled for cleaning at the specified intervals. This valve can be identified by two alignment punch marks and wrench slots on the pintle seat.
18  Clean the seat, base and threads and note the location of the punch marks for reassembly to the same position.
19  Measure and record the distance from the base surface to the shoulder of the seat as shown in the accompanying illustration.
20  Place the valve securely in a vise and unscrew the seat. Because the pintle seat is staked in place, it may be necessary work it back and forth to remove it. A suitable thread penetrant will also help ease removal.
21  With the valve in an upright position, use a pair of pliers to remove the pintle, taking care not to contact the sealing surface, as shown in the accompanying illustration.

7.12    Installing the EGR valve on the manifold

7.16    Removing the EGR TVS from the manifold
(some V6 engines)

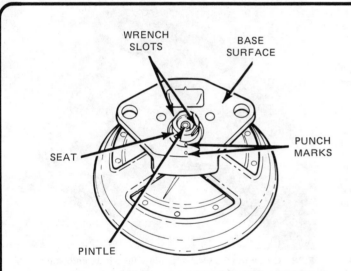

Fig. 6.21    EGR valves which can be disassembled for
cleaning are identified by wrench slots on the pintle and
punch marks on the seat (Sec 7)

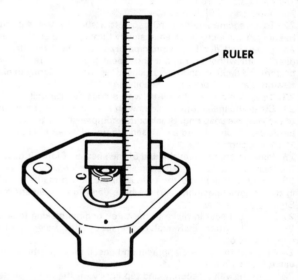

Fig. 6.22    Measuring the EGR valve seat height (Sec 7)

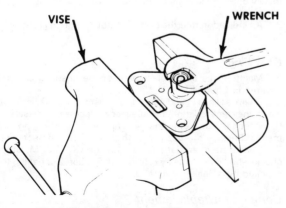

Fig. 6.23    Removing the EGR valve seat (Sec 7)

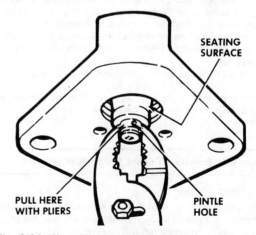

Fig. 6.24    Use pliers to work the pintle out of the valve
(Sec 7)

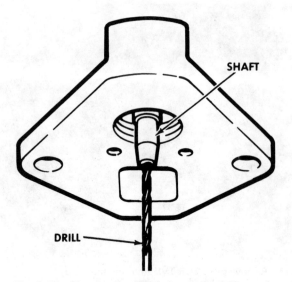

Fig. 6.25    Cleaning the EGR valve pintle shaft opening
with a drill bit (Sec 7)

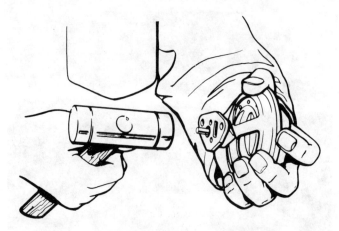

Fig. 6.26    Deposits can be removed from the EGR pintle
seating area by tapping the end of the pintle lightly with a
plastic hammer (Sec 7)

22  To clean the shaft opening, insert a suitable size drill into the
opening in one inch increments, slowly turning it in a clockwise direction. The shaft depth is approximately two inches. Pull the drill bit
directly out without turning it and repeat the procedure. The bit will
bottom at a depth of about two inches. Tap the valve lightly to dislodge
foreign material from the shaft opening.
23  Clean the hole in the pintle with a suitable size drill bit.
24  Clean the inside of the pintle with a suitable tool. Take care not
to damage the snap ring. Brush or use compressed air to blow out the
particles. If compressed air is used, do not blow air directly into the
shaft opening.
25  Place the pintle over the end of the shaft and force it down until
the locking ring can be felt snapping into position.
26  Screw the seat into the base until the punch marks are aligned
in their original positions and the base depth measurement made in
Step 19 is reached.
27  Stake the seat in place at the three original staking locations.
28  On all other EGR valves, inspect the valve pintle for
deposits (photo).
29  Depress the valve diaphragm and check for deposits around the
valve seating area.
30  Hold the valve securely and tap lightly on the round pintle with
a plastic hammer, using a light snapping action, to remove any deposits
from the valve seat. Make sure to empty any loose particles from the
valve. Depress the valve diaphragm again and inspect the valve seating
area, repeating the cleaning operation as necessary.
31  Use a wire brush to carefully clean deposits from the pintle.
32  Remove any deposits from the valve outlet using a screwdriver.

**EGR passages**

33  With the EGR valve removed, inspect the passages for excessive
deposits.
34  It is a good idea to place a rag securely in the passage opening
to keep debris from entering. Clean the passages by hand, using
a drill bit.

## 8  Evaporative Emissions Control System (EECS)

### General description

1    This system is designed to trap and store fuel that evaporates from
the carburetor and fuel tank which would normally enter the atmosphere
and contribute to hydrocarbon (HC) emissions.
2    The system consists of a charcoal-filled canister and lines
running to and from the canister. These lines include a vent line from
the gas tank, a vent line from the carburetor float bowl or injection
unit, an idle purge line into the vehicle's induction system and a vacuum

7.28    Check the EGR valve pintle where it extends into the
exhaust passage for free movement and clean this
area of deposits (arrow)

line to the manifold. In addition, there is a purge valve in the canister.
The CCCS/ECM controls the vacuum to the purge valve with an electrically operated solenoid. The fuel tank cap is also an integral part of
the system.
3    An indication that the system is not operating properly is a strong
fuel odor.

### Checking

4    Maintenance and replacement of the charcoal canister filter is
covered in Chapter 1.
5    Check all lines in and out of the canister for kinks, leaks and breaks
along their entire lengths. Repair or replace as necessary.
6    Check the gasket in the gas cap for signs of drying, cracking or
breaks. Replace the gas cap with a new one if defects are found.
7    Due to its interrelationship with the CCCS/ECM, other system
checks should be made by referring to Section 2 or having the system
checked by a dealer or repair shop.

### Component replacement

8    Replacement of the canister filter is covered in Chapter 1.
9    When replacing any line running to or from the canister, make sure
the replacement line is a duplicate of the one you are replacing. These
lines are often color coded to denote their particular usage.

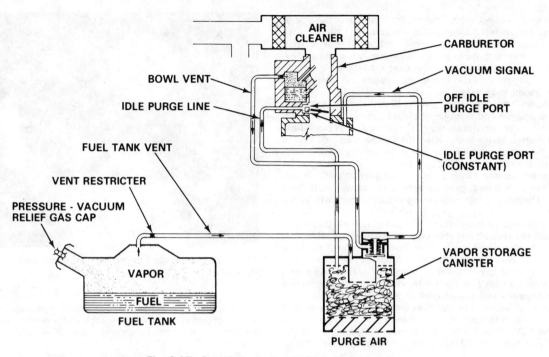

Fig. 6.27  Detail of a typical EECS system (Sec 8)

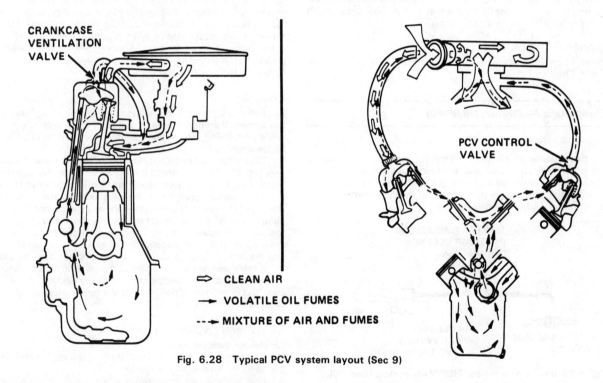

⇨ CLEAN AIR

→ VOLATILE OIL FUMES

--→ MIXTURE OF AIR AND FUMES

Fig. 6.28  Typical PCV system layout (Sec 9)

## 9  Positive Crankcase Ventilation (PCV) system

### General description

1    The positive crankcase ventilation system reduces hydrocarbon emissions by circulating fresh air through the crankcase to pick up blow-by gases, which are then rerouted through the carburetor to be burned in the engine.

2    The main components of this system are vacuum hoses and a PCV valve, which regulates the flow of gases according to engine speed and manifold vacuum.

### Checking

3    The PCV system can be checked quickly and easily for proper operation. This system should be checked regularly, as carbon and gunk deposited by the blow-by gases will eventually clog the PCV valve and system hoses. When the flow of the PCV system is reduced or stopped, common symptoms are rough idling or reduced engine speed at idle.

4    To check for proper vacuum in the system, remove the top plate of the air cleaner and locate the small PCV filter on the inside of the air cleaner housing.

5    Disconnect the hose leading to this filter. Be careful not to break

the molded fitting on the filter.

6    With the engine idling, place your thumb lightly over the end of the hose. You should feel a slight pull or vacuum. The suction may be heard as your thumb is released. This will indicate that air is being drawn all the way through the system. If a vacuum is felt, the system is functioning properly. Check that the filter inside the air cleaner housing is not clogged or dirty. If in doubt, replace the filter with a new one, an inexpensive safeguard (refer to Chapter 1).

7    If there is very little vacuum or none at all at the end of the hose, the system is clogged and must be inspected further.

8    Shut off the engine and locate the PCV valve. Carefully pull it from its rubber grommet. Shake it and listen for a clicking sound. That is the rattle of the valve's check ball. If the valve does not click freely, replace it with a new one.

9    Start the engine and run it at idle speed with the PCV valve removed. Place your thumb over the end of the valve and feel for suction. This should be a relatively strong vacuum which will be felt immediately.

10   If little or no vacuum is felt at the PCV valve, turn off the engine and disconnect the vacuum hose from the other end of the valve. Run the engine at idle speed and check for vacuum at the end of the hose just disconnected. No vacuum at this point indicates that the vacuum hose or inlet fitting at the engine is plugged. If it is the hose which is blocked, replace it with a new one or remove it from the engine and blow it out sufficiently with compressed air. A clogged passage at the carburetor or manifold requires that the component be removed and thoroughly cleaned to remove carbon build-up. A strong vacuum felt going into the PCV valve, but little or no vacuum coming out of the valve, indicates a failure of the PCV valve requiring replacement with a new one.

11   When purchasing a new PCV valve, make sure it is the correct one for your engine. An incorrect PCV valve may pull too little or too much vacuum, possibly leading to engine damage.

### Component replacement

12   The replacement procedures for both the PCV valve and filter are covered in Chapter 1.

---

## 10   Thermostatic Air Cleaner (THERMAC)

### General description

1    The thermostatic air cleaner (THERMAC) system is provided to improve engine efficiency and reduce hydrocarbon emissions during the initial warm-up period by maintaining a controlled air temperature at the carburetor. This temperature control of the incoming air allows leaner carburetor and choke calibrations.

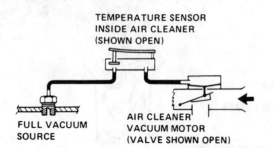

TEMPERATURE SENSOR
INSIDE AIR CLEANER
(SHOWN OPEN)

FULL VACUUM
SOURCE

AIR CLEANER
VACUUM MOTOR
(VALVE SHOWN OPEN)

**Fig. 6.29 Details of a typical THERMAC system (Sec 10)**

2    The system uses a damper assembly, located in the snorkel of the air cleaner housing, to control the ratio of cold and warm air directed into the carburetor. This damper is controlled by a vacuum motor which is, in turn, modulated by a temperature sensor in the air cleaner. On some engines a check valve is used in the sensor, which delays the opening of the damper flap when the engine is cold and the vacuum signal is low.

3    It is during the first few miles of driving, depending on outside temperature, that this system has its greatest effect on engine performance and emissions output. When the engine is cold, the damper flap blocks off the air cleaner inlet snorkel, allowing only warm air from around the exhaust manifold to enter the carburetor. Gradually, as the

10.6   Vacuum applied to the vacuum motor should actuate the damper door

engine warms up, the flap opens the snorkel passage, increasing the amount of cold air allowed in. Once the engine reaches normal operating temperature, the flap opens completely, allowing only cold, fresh air to enter.

4    Because of this cold-engine-only function, it is important to periodically check this system to prevent poor engine performance when cold or overheating of the fuel mixture once the engine has reached operating temperatures. If the air cleaner valve sticks in the no heat position, the engine will run poorly, stall and waste gas until it has warmed up on its own. A valve sticking in the heat position causes the engine to run as if it is out of tune due to the constant flow of hot air to the carburetor.

### Checking

5    Refer to Chapter 1 for maintenance and checking procedures for this system. If problems were encountered in the system's performance while performing the routine maintenance checks, refer to the procedures which follow.

6    If the damper door did not close off snorkel air when the cold engine was first started, disconnect the vacuum hose at the snorkel vacuum motor and place your thumb over the hose end, checking for vacuum. If there is vacuum going to the motor, check that the damper door and link are not frozen or binding within the air cleaner snorkel. If a vacuum pump is available, disconnect the vacuum hose and apply vacuum to the motor to make sure the damper door actuates (photo). Replace the vacuum motor if the application of vacuum does not open the door and the hose routing is correct but the damper door moves freely.

7    If there was no vacuum going to the motor in the above test, check the hoses for cracks, crimps and proper connection. If the hoses are clear and in good condition, replace the temperature sensor inside the air cleaner housing.

### Component replacement

**Air cleaner vacuum motor**

8    Remove the air cleaner assembly from the engine and disconnect the vacuum hose from the motor.

9    Drill out the two spot welds which secure the vacuum motor retaining strap to the snorkel tube.

10   Remove the motor attaching strap.

11   Lift up the motor, cocking it to one side to unhook the motor linkage at the control damper assembly.

12   To install, drill a 7/64-inch hole in the snorkel tube at the center of the retaining strap.

13   Insert the vacuum motor linkage into the control damper assembly.

14   Using the sheet metal screw supplied with the motor service kit, attach the motor and retaining strap to the snorkel. Make sure the sheet metal screw does not interfere with the operation of the damper door. Shorten the screw if necessary.

15   Connect the vacuum hose to the motor and install the air cleaner assembly.

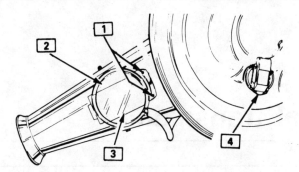

**Fig. 6.30   Components involved in removing the THERMAC vacuum motor on a typical carbureted vehicle (Sec 10)**

1 Spot welds          3 Retaining strap
2 Motor assembly      4 Sensor

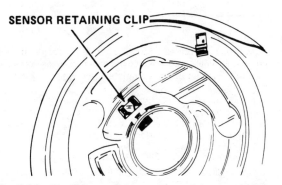

**Fig. 6.32   Carefully note the position of the sensor before removing the retaining clip (Sec 10)**

**Air cleaner temperature sensor**

16  Remove the air cleaner from the engine and disconnect the vacuum hoses at the sensor.

17  Carefully note the position of the sensor. The new sensor must be installed in exactly the same position.

18  Pry up the tabs on the sensor retaining clip and remove the sensor and clip from the air cleaner.

19  Install the new sensor with a new gasket in the same position as the old one.

20  Press the retaining clip onto the sensor. Do not damage the control mechanism in the center of the sensor.

21  Connect the vacuum hoses and attach the air cleaner to the engine.

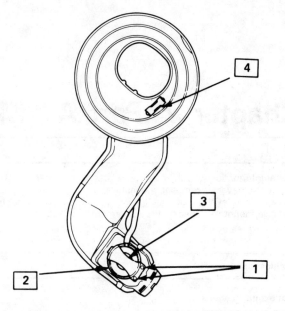

**Fig. 6.31   Components involved in removing the THERMAC vacuum motor on a typical fuel injected vehicle (Sec 10)**

1 Spot welds          3 Retaining strap
2 Motor assembly      4 Sensor

**11   Transmission Converter Clutch (TCC)**

1  Toward optimizing the efficiency of the emissions control network, the ECM controls an electrical solenoid mounted in the automatic transmission of vehicles so equipped. When the vehicle reaches a specified speed, the ECM energizes the solenoid and allows the torque converter to mechanically couple the engine to the transmission, under which conditions emissions are at their minimum. However, because of other operating condition demands (deceleration, passing, idle, etc.), the transmission must also function in its normal, fluid-coupled mode. When such latter conditions exist, the solenoid de-energizes, returning the transmission to fluid coupling. The transmission also returns to fluid-coupling operation whenever the brake pedal is depressed.

2  Due to the requirement of special diagnostic equipment for the testing of this system, and the possible requirement for dismantling of the automatic transmission to replace components of this system, checking and replacing of the components should be handled by a dealer or automotive repair shop.

# Chapter 7 Part A Manual transaxle

**Contents**

General information ................................ 1
Shift control lever — removal and installation ........... 4
Transaxle fluid level check ................ See Chapter 1
Transaxle mounts — check and replacement ............. 2
Transaxle — removal and installation .................. 6
Transaxle shift cables — removal and installation ......... 3
Transaxle shift linkage (4-speed) — adjustment .......... 5

---

**Specifications**

| Torque specifications | Ft-lb |
| --- | --- |
| Clutch cover housing bolts ........................... | 10 |
| Shift control retaining nuts ......................... | 20 |
| Strut bracket-to-transxle bolts ...................... | 35 |
| Strut bracket mounting stud nut ..................... | 30 |
| Strut bolts ........................................ | 30 |
| Suspension support bolts ........................... | 75 |
| Transaxle ground cable stud nut ..................... | 30 |
| Transaxle-to-engine bolts .......................... | 55 |
| Transaxle mount-to-engine bolts ..................... | 40 |
| Transaxle mount-to-side frame | |
|     Bolts ..................................... | 40 |
|     Nuts ...................................... | 23 |

---

## 1 General information

The manual transaxle combines the transmission and differential assemblies into one compact unit. These models are equipped with four-speed transaxles.

Shifting is accomplished by a floor mounted shifter, which is connected to the transaxle shift levers by cable assemblies.

2.1 A pry bar should be used to check the transaxle mounts

## 2 Transaxle mounts — check and replacement

### Checking

1 Watch the mount as an assistant pulls up and pushes down on the transaxle. If the rubber separates from the plate or the case moves up but not down, indicating the mount is bottomed out, replace the mount with a new one (photo).

### Replacement

2 Disconnect the battery negative cable.
3 Support the transaxle with a jack.
4 Remove the transaxle mount through-bolt.

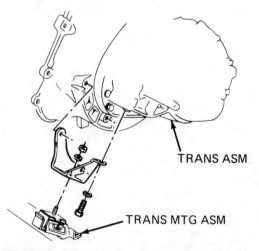

TRANS ASM

TRANS MTG ASM

Fig. 7A.1 Manual transaxle front mount (Sec 2)

5   Remove the retaining bolts and remove the mount.
6   Place the new mount in position and install the mount-to-side frame bolts.
7   Install the through-bolt and tighten the nut to the specified torque.
8   Loosen the two nuts at the top of the mount and lower the jack supporting the transaxle so the weight will center the mount. Tighten the nuts to the specified torque.
9   Connect the battery negative cable.

### 3   Transaxle shift cables — removal and installation

*Removal*

1   Disconnect the battery negative cable.
2   Disconnect the retaining clips and cables at the transaxle.
3   Remove the console and shift boot (Chapter 12).
4   Disconnect the cables and remove the shift control lever assembly (Section 4).
5   Remove the left front sill plate and pull the carpet back sufficiently to gain access to the cables.
6   Remove the shift cable cover screws from the floor pan and remove the cables from the vehicle.

*Installation*

7   Route the cables into position and install the cable cover and attaching screws.
8   Place the carpet in position and install the sill plate.
9   From under the vehicle, route the cables to the transaxle.
10  In the engine compartment, connect the cables and retainers to the transaxle levers.
11  In the passenger compartment, connect the cables to the shift lever

and install the console and shifter boot.
12  Adjust the shift linkage (Section 5).
13  Connect the battery negative cable.

### 4   Shift control lever — removal and installation

*Removal*

1   Disconnect the battery negative cable.
2   In the engine compartment, loosen the shift cables at the transaxle levers.
3   Remove the console and shifter boot.
4   Disconnect the cables from the control lever.
5   Unbolt and remove the control lever.

*Installation*

6   Place the control lever in position and install the attaching nuts, tightening to the specified torque.
7   Connect the cables to the control assembly and follow the adjustment procedure in Sections 5 or 6.
8   Install the console and shifter boot.
9   Connect the battery negative cable.

### 5   Transaxle shift linkage — adjustment

1   Disconnect the battery negative cable.
2   Place the transaxle in first gear.
3   Referring to the accompanying illustration, loosen the cable attaching nuts (E) at the transaxle levers (D and F).

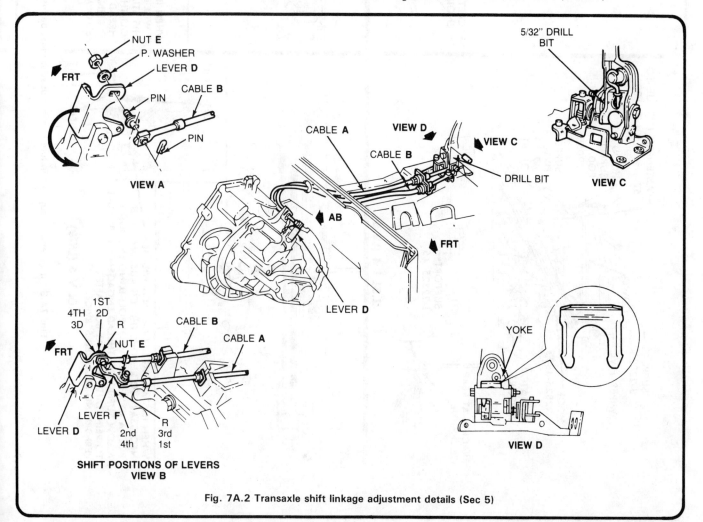

Fig. 7A.2 Transaxle shift linkage adjustment details (Sec 5)

190

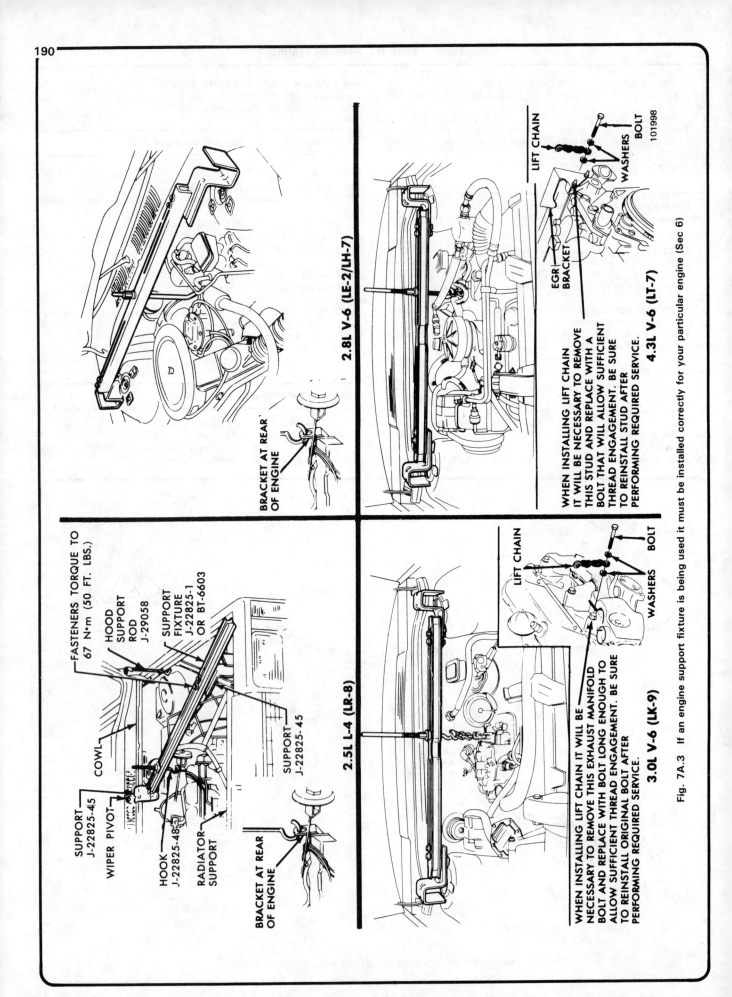

**2.8L V-6 (LE-2/LH-7)**

BRACKET AT REAR OF ENGINE

**4.3L V-6 (LT-7)**

LIFT CHAIN

WASHERS

BOLT

EGR BRACKET

101998

WHEN INSTALLING LIFT CHAIN IT WILL BE NECESSARY TO REMOVE THIS STUD AND REPLACE WITH A BOLT THAT WILL ALLOW SUFFICIENT THREAD ENGAGEMENT. BE SURE TO REINSTALL STUD AFTER PERFORMING REQUIRED SERVICE.

FASTENERS TORQUE TO 67 N•m (50 FT. LBS.)

HOOD SUPPORT ROD J-29058

SUPPORT FIXTURE J-22825-1 OR BT-6603

SUPPORT J-22825-45

WIPER PIVOT

COWL

HOOK J-22825-48

RADIATOR SUPPORT

SUPPORT J-22825-45

**2.5L L-4 (LR-8)**

BRACKET AT REAR OF ENGINE

**3.0L V-6 (LK-9)**

LIFT CHAIN

WASHERS

BOLT

WHEN INSTALLING LIFT CHAIN IT WILL BE NECESSARY TO REMOVE THIS EXHAUST MANIFOLD BOLT AND REPLACE WITH BOLT LONG ENOUGH TO ALLOW SUFFICIENT THREAD ENGAGEMENT. BE SURE TO REINSTALL ORIGINAL BOLT AFTER PERFORMING REQUIRED SERVICE.

Fig. 7A.3  If an engine support fixture is being used it must be installed correctly for your particular engine (Sec 6)

4   Remove the console trim plate, slide the shifter boot up the handle and then remove the console.

5   With the shifter pulled to the left and held against the stop (first gear position), insert a yoke clip or suitable shim so that it is snug enough to hold the lever as shown in View D.

6   Insert a 5/32 inch or No. 22 drill bit into the alignment hole at the side of the shifter assembly as shown in View C.

7   Install a yoke clip or suitable shim between the tower and carrier as shown in view D.

8   To remove any lash from the transaxle, rotate lever D in the direction of the arrow while tightening nut E (View B)

9   Remove the drill bit or yoke clip from the shifter assembly and install the shifter boot and retainer.

10  Lubricate the moving parts of the shift mechanism with white lithium base grease, using a stiff bristle brush.

11  Connect the battery negative cable and road test the vehicle to check the shifting operation. It may be necessary to repeat the adjustment procedure to completely remove looseness or misalignment from the linkage.

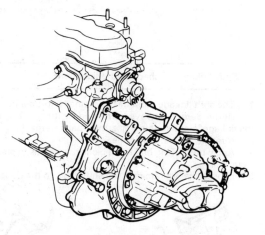

**Fig. 7A.4   Transaxle to engine bolt locations (Sec 6)**

## 6   Transaxle — removal and installation

### Removal

1   Disconnect the battery negative cable from the transaxle case and secure it out of the way.

2   Disconnect and remove the horn from the engine compartment.

3   Remove the air cleaner assembly.

4   Disconnect the clutch cable as outlined in chapter 8.

5   On V6 engines, disconnect the fuel lines and clamps at the clutch cable bracket.

6   Remove the clutch cable bracket.

7   Loosen, but do not remove, the left front wheel lug nuts.

8   Raise the vehicle to provide sufficient clearance for lowering the transaxle and support it securely on jackstands. Drain the transaxle fluid into a suitable container.

9   On V6 engines, remove the exhaust crossover pipe.

10  Disconnect the shift cables and speedometer cable from the transaxle (Section 4).

11  There are two principal ways of supporting the weight of the engine during the removal of the cradle and transaxle. A special support fixture can be obtained which rests on the cowl and radiator support (Fig 7A.4), or an engine hoist can be used. If the engine support fixture is being used, install it at this time. If the engine hoist is being used to support the engine, the hood must be removed to gain sufficient clearance (Chapter 12).

12  Remove the five top transaxle-to-engine mounting bolts.

13  Remove the left front wheel.

14  Remove left side cradle and crossmember assembly. See Chapter 11.

15  Disconnect both driveaxles from the transaxle. See Chapter 8. **Caution:** *Care must be taken not to overextend the CV joints and boots whenever the suspension is disconnected.* After disconnecting the driveaxles, the left axle can be removed from the transaxle and supported with a wire. The right axle can be removed as the transaxle is lowered from the vehicle.

16  Remove the shield from around the starter and flywheel.

17  Firmly support the transaxle on a jack and remove the last transaxle-to-engine bolt.

18  Remove the transaxle from the vehicle by sliding the transaxle toward the left side to clear the clutch, then lower it out of the vehicle.

### Installation

19  Raise the transaxle into position and carefully guide the right driveaxle into the bore.

20  With the transaxle in position, install two four-inch long bolts with the same threads as the mounting bolts in the top transaxle-to-engine bolt holes to use as guide pins when drawing the transaxle into place. Insert the input shaft and slide the transaxle toward the engine. If it does not move easily, have an assistant turn the engine over using a socket on the front pulley bolt as the transaxle is moved into position.

21  Install the transaxle-to-engine mounting bolts, tightening to the specified torque.

22  Refer to Chapter 11 for the installation procedure of the partial cradle.

23  The rest of the installation procedure is the reverse of the removal procedure, making sure all nuts and bolts are torqued to the proper specification.

# Chapter 7 Part B  Automatic transaxle

## Contents

Automatic transaxle fluid and filter change . . . . .   See Chapter 1
Diagnosis — general . . . . . . . . . . . . . . . . . . . . . . . . . . . . .   2
Fluid level check . . . . . . . . . . . . . . . . . . . . . .   See Chapter 1
General information . . . . . . . . . . . . . . . . . . . . . . . . . . . .   1
Neutral safety and back up light switch — adjustment . . . . . .   5
Shift linkage — check and adjustment . . . . . . . . . . . . . . . . .   3
Throttle valve (TV) cable — description and adjustment . . . . .   4
Transaxle — removal and installation . . . . . . . . . . . . . . . . .   6
Transaxle mounts — check and replacement  . . .  See Chapter 7A

## Specifications

| Torque specifications | Ft-lbs |
| --- | --- |
| Shifter assembly retaining nuts . . . . . . . . . . . . . . . . . . . . . | 18 |
| Shifter cover screws . . . . . . . . . . . . . . . . . . . . . . . . . . . . | 12 in-lb |
| Shifter cable bracket-to-transaxle bolt . . . . . . . . . . . . . . . . | 18 |
| Shifter cable-to-transaxle lever pin nut . . . . . . . . . . . . . . . | 15 |
| Shifter lever-to-transaxle nut . . . . . . . . . . . . . . . . . . . . . . | 20 |
| Strut mount through-bolt . . . . . . . . . . . . . . . . . . . . . . . . . | 31 |
| Transaxle-to-engine bolts . . . . . . . . . . . . . . . . . . . . . . . . | 55 |
| TV cable-to-transaxle bolt . . . . . . . . . . . . . . . . . . . . . . . . | 9 |

## 1  General information

Due to the complexity of the clutches and the hydraulic control system, and because of the special tools and expertise required to perform an automatic transmission overhaul, it should not be undertaken by the home mechanic. Therefore, the procedures in this Chapter are limited to general diagnosis, routine maintenance and adjustment and transmission removal and installation.

If the transmission requires major repair work it should be left to a dealer service department or an automotive or transmission repair shop. You can, however, remove and install the transmission yourself and save the expense, even if the repair work is done by a transmission specialist.

Adjustments that the home mechanic may perform include those involving the throttle valve cable, the shift linkage and the neutral safety switch. **Caution:** *Never tow a disabled vehicle at speeds greater than 30 mph or distances over 50 miles unless the front wheels are off the ground. Failure to observe this precaution may result in severe transmission damage caused by lack of lubrication.*

## 2  Diagnosis — general

1   Automatic transmission malfunctions may be caused by four general conditions: poor engine performance, improper adjustments, hydraulic malfunctions and mechanical malfunctions. Diagnosis of these problems should always begin with a check of the easily repaired items: fluid level and condition, shift linkage adjustment and throttle linkage adjustment. Next, perform a road test to determine if the problem has been corrected or if more diagnosis is necessary. If the problem persists after the preliminary tests and corrections are completed, additional diagnosis should be done by a dealer service department or an automotive or transmission repair shop.

## 3  Shift linkage — check and adjustment

1   The shift linkage must be maintained in proper adjustment so that the shifter detents always correspond with the transaxle detents. If the linkage is not kept in adjustment, an internal leak in the transaxle could result, causing slippage.
2   Apply the parking brake and block the wheels to prevent the vehicle from rolling.
3   Loosen the nut retaining the shift cable to the transaxle shift lever.

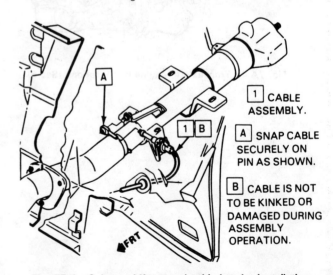

1 CABLE ASSEMBLY.

A SNAP CABLE SECURELY ON PIN AS SHOWN.

B CABLE IS NOT TO BE KINKED OR DAMAGED DURING ASSEMBLY OPERATION.

**Fig. 7B.1  Column shift control cable interior installation details (Sec 3)**

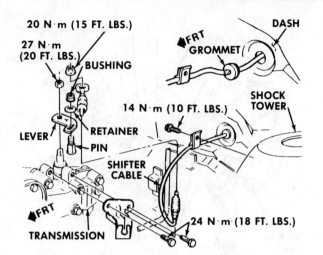

Fig. 7B.2   Column shift control cable engine compartment installation details (Sec 3)

4    Place the console shift lever in Neutral.
5    Place the transaxle lever in the Neutral position. This is accomplished by rotating the lever clockwise from the Park position, through Park, Reverse and into Neutral, or counterclockwise through 1, 2 and Drive into Neutral.
6    Tighten the attaching nut to the specified torque. The shift lever must be held out of the Park position during tightening.
7    Make sure the engine will start in the Park and Neutral positions only.
8    If the engine can be started in any of the drive positions, as indicated by the shifter inside the vehicle, see Section 5 for the neutral safety switch adjustment procedure or have the vehicle examined by a dealer.

## 4   Throttle valve (TV) cable — description and adjustment

1    The throttle valve cable controls the transaxle line pressure and consequently the shift feel and timing, as well as the part throttle and detent downshifts.
2    The TV cable is attached to the link at the throttle lever and bracket at the transaxle and to the throttle lever on the carburetor or TBI on the engine.

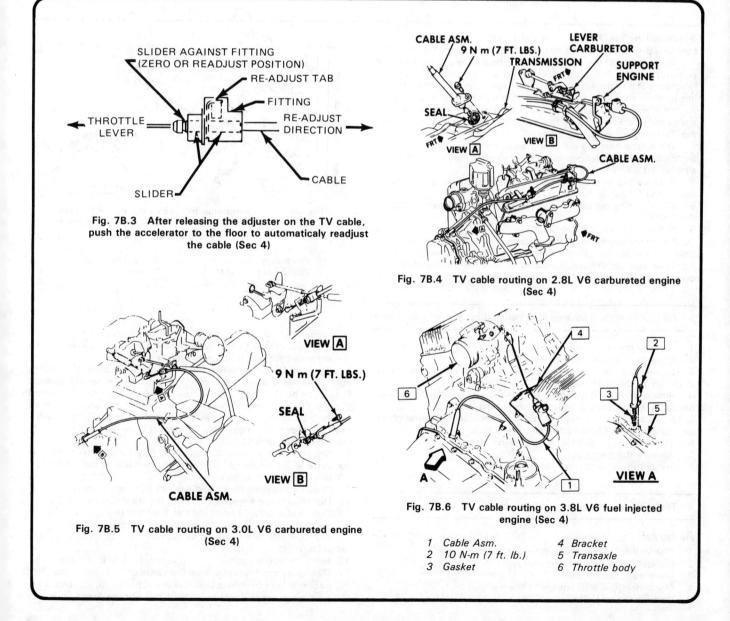

Fig. 7B.3   After releasing the adjuster on the TV cable, push the accelerator to the floor to automaticaly readjust the cable (Sec 4)

Fig. 7B.4   TV cable routing on 2.8L V6 carbureted engine (Sec 4)

Fig. 7B.5   TV cable routing on 3.0L V6 carbureted engine (Sec 4)

Fig. 7B.6   TV cable routing on 3.8L V6 fuel injected engine (Sec 4)

1   Cable Asm.               4   Bracket
2   10 N-m (7 ft. lb.)       5   Transaxle
3   Gasket                   6   Throttle body

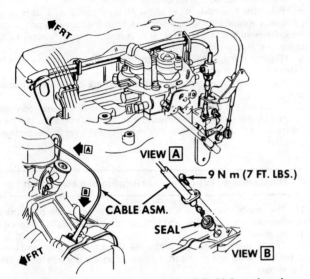

Fig. 7B.7   TV cable routing on 2.5L L4 fuel injected engine
(Sec 4)

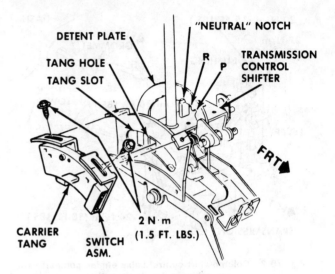

Fig. 7B.8   Floorshift neutral switch assembly (Sec 5)

3    Whenever the TV cable has been disconnected from the car-
buretor/TBI unit, it must be adjusted after installation.
4    The freeness of the TV cable can be checked by pulling the upper
end of the cable. The cable should travel a short distance with light
resistance due to the small coiled return spring. Pull the cable farther
out to move the lever into contact with the plunger, thus compressing the heavier TV spring. When released the cable should return to
the closed position, verifying that the cable, TV lever and bracket and
the TV plunger are moving freely.
5    The engine must be off during adjustment.
6    Remove the air cleaner, labeling all hoses as they are removed to
simplify installation.
7    Depress and hold down the metal readjusting tab at the engine
end of the TV cable.
8    While holding the tab down, move the slider until it stops against
the fitting.
9    Release the readjustment tab.
10   Rotate the throttle lever to the maximum travel stop position. The
cable will ratchet through the slider and automatically readjust itself.
11   Road test the vehicle. If delayed or only full-throttle shifts still
occur, have the vehicle checked by a dealer.

**5   Neutral safety and back-up light switch (floor shifter) adjustment**

1    Remove the shift indicator plate.
2    Place the transaxle shifter lever in Neutral.
3    Loosen but do not remove the screws retaining the switch
assembly to the shifter assembly.
4    Rotate the switch assembly so that the service adjustment hole
on the switch is aligned with the carrier tang hole.
5    Insert a 3/32-inch gauge pin (a drill bit will work fine) through the
service adjustment hole to a depth of 5/8 inch.
6    Tighten the switch assembly retaining screws.
7    Remove the gauge pin.
8    Install the shift indicator plate.

**6   Transaxle — removal and installation**

*Removal*

1    Disconnect the battery negative cable.
2    Remove the air cleaner assembly.
3    Disconnect the TV cable.
4    Disconnect the shift linkage at the transaxle.
5    Remove the shift linkage bracket.

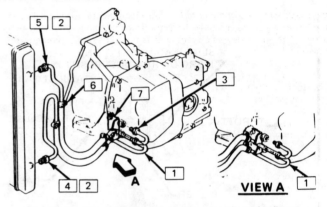

Fig. 7B.9   On automatic transaxles the oil cooler lines
must be disconnected before the transaxle mount can be
removed (Sec 6)

| | |
|---|---|
| *1  Hose asm.* | *5  Pipe asm. upper* |
| *2  Nut 27 N-m  (20 ft. lb.)* | *6  Clamp* |
| *3  Nut 22 N-m  (16 ft. lb.)* | *7  Guide* |
| *4  Pipe asm. lower* | |

6    Loosen but do not remove the left front wheel lug nuts.
7    Raise the vehicle to provide sufficient clearance for lowering the
transaxle and support it securely on jackstands.
8    There are two principal ways of supporting the weight of the engine
during the removal of the cradle and transaxle. A special support
fixture can be obtained which rests on the cowl and radiator support
(Fig 7A.4), or an engine hoist can be used. If the engine support
fixture is being used, install it at this time. If the engine hoist is being
used to support the engine, the hood must be removed to gain sufficient clearance (see Chapter 11.)
9    Disconnect any vacuum or electrical connectors attached to the
transaxle which might interfere with the removal of the transaxle.
10   Remove the left front wheel.
11   Remove the strut shock and bracket from the transaxle.
12   Disconnect the speedometer from the transaxle.
13   Disconnect the oil cooler lines at the transaxle.
14   Remove the starter and torque converter splash shields.
15   Mark the relationship of the torque converter to the driveplate to
aid in installation.
16   Remove the bolts securing the torque converter to the driveplate.
17   Disengage the driveaxles from the transaxle and insert a plug into
the transaxle bore to reduce fluid leakage (Chapter 8). **Caution:** *Care
must be taken not to overextend the CV joints and boots whenever*

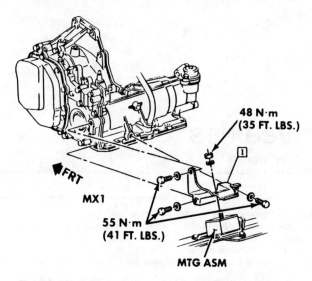

**Fig. 7B.10   Rear mount on automatic transaxles (Sec 6)**

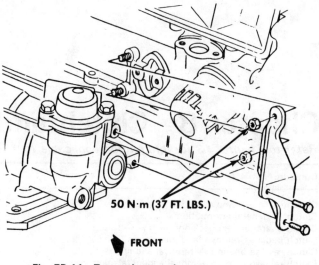

**Fig. 7B.11   Transaxle to engine mount on automatic transaxle (Sec 6)**

*the suspension is disconnected.* After disconnecting the driveaxles, the left axle can be removed from the transaxle and supported with a wire. The right axle can be removed as the transaxle is lowered from the vehicle.

18  Remove the front left cradle assembly (Chapter 11).

19  Firmly support the transaxle on a jack.

20  Remove the transaxle-to-engine supports and transaxle mounts. It may be necessary to lift the transaxle slightly to remove the rear support.

21  Remove the transaxle-to-engine bolts and remove the transaxle by sliding it away from the engine and lowering it from the vehicle.

## Installation

22  Raise the transaxle into position and carefully guide the right driveaxle into the bore.

23  With the transaxle in position, install two four inch long bolts in the top transaxle-to-engine bolt holes to use as guide pins when drawing the transaxle into place. Align the torque converter to the driveplate and slide the transaxle toward the engine.

24  Install the transaxle-to-engine mounting bolts, tightening to the specified torque.

25  Refer to Chapter 11 for the installation procedure of the partial cradle.

26  The rest of the installation procedure is the reverse of the removal procedure with the following notes:

    a) Make sure all nuts and bolts are torqued to the proper specification.

    b) The suspension alignment should be checked by a dealer or automotive alignment shop.

    c) Adjust the TV cable (Section 4).

    d) Check the transaxle fluid level (Chapter 1).

# Chapter 8  Clutch and driveaxles

*Refer to Chapter 13 for information applicable to 1986 and later models*

## Contents

| | |
|---|---|
| Clutch cable — removal and installation . . . . . . . . . . . . . . . 5 | Clutch — removal, inspection and installation . . . . . . . . . . . 6 |
| Clutch — general information . . . . . . . . . . . . . . . . . . . . . . . 1 | Driveaxle boot — replacement (driveaxle removed) . . . . . . . . 10 |
| Clutch operation — checking . . . . . . . . . . . . . . . . . . . . . . 2 | Driveaxle — general information . . . . . . . . . . . . . . . . . . . . . 8 |
| Clutch pedal — removal and installation . . . . . . . . . . . . . . 4 | Driveaxle — removal and installation . . . . . . . . . . . . . . . . . . 9 |
| Clutch release bearing — removal and installation . . . . . . . . 7 | Outer driveaxle boot — replacement (driveaxle installed) . . . . 11 |
| Clutch release lever — removal and installation . . . . . . . . . . 3 | |

## Specifications

| Torque specifications | Ft-lbs |
|---|---|
| Clutch release lever bolt . . . . . . . . . . . . . . . . . . . . . . . . . . . | 20 |
| Clutch pedal-to-mounting bracket bolt . . . . . . . . . . . . . . . . . | 25 |
| Clutch pedal-to-locking pawl bolt . . . . . . . . . . . . . . . . . . . . | 3.7 |
| Clutch pressure plate-to-flywheel bolt . . . . . . . . . . . . . . . . . | 15 |
| Flywheel bolt . . . . . . . . . . . . . . . . . . . . . . . . . . . . . . . . . . . | 50 |
| Neutral start switch screw . . . . . . . . . . . . . . . . . . . . . . . . . | 2.2 |
| Axleshaft nut . . . . . . . . . . . . . . . . . . . . . . . . . . . . . . . . . . . | 191 |

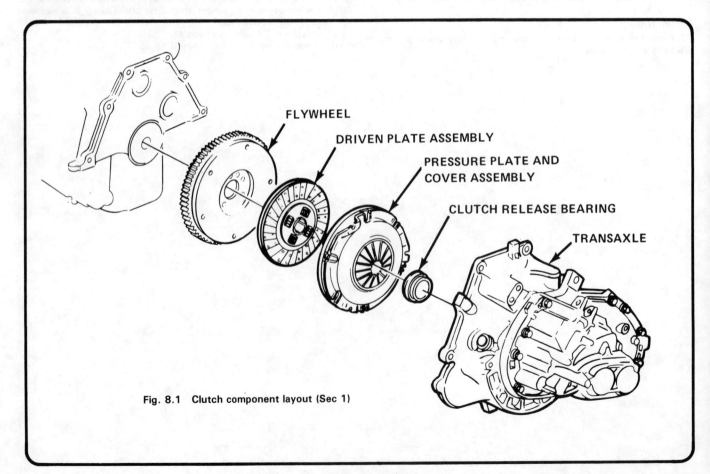

Fig. 8.1  Clutch component layout (Sec 1)

FLYWHEEL

DRIVEN PLATE ASSEMBLY

PRESSURE PLATE AND
COVER ASSEMBLY

CLUTCH RELEASE BEARING

TRANSAXLE

## 1  Clutch — general information

All manual transaxle-equipped vehicles use a single dry plate, diaphragm spring-type clutch. Operation is through a foot pedal incorporating a self-adjusting mechanism, cable, fork lever, clutch shaft and fork assembly and a release bearing.

The adjusting mechanism is integral to the pedal and bracket assembly and has a fixed length cable. The cable position can be changed by adjusting the position of the detent relative to the clutch pedal. By lifting the pedal up against the rubber stop (Chapter 1), the pawl is forced against the metal stop, which rotates it out of mesh with the detent teeth. This allows the cable to play out until the detent spring load is balanced against the load applied by the clutch release bearing.

## 2  Clutch operation — checking

1    Before performing any operations on the clutch, several checks should be made to determine if there is actually a fault in the clutch itself.
2    With the engine running and the brake applied, hold the clutch pedal 1/2-inch from the floor and shift back and forth between first and second several times. If the shifts are smooth, the clutch is releasing properly. If it is not the clutch is not releasing fully and the linkage should be checked.
3    Inspect the clutch pedal bushings for wear or binding.
4    Observe the clutch fork lever travel at the transaxle while an assistant depresses the pedal fully to the floor. The end of the fork should travel a total of between 1.5 and 1.7 inches.
5    If the fork travel is not within specifications, check the adjusting mechanism by depressing the clutch pedal and watching the pawl to make sure it engages firmly with the detent teeth.

## 3  Clutch release lever — removal and installation

*Refer to Fig. 8.2*

### Removal

1    Support the clutch pedal upward against the bumper stop so the pawl is released.
2    Disconnect the clutch cable from the release lever at the transaxle, taking care not to let it snap rearward, which could damage the adjusting mechanism.
3    Remove the attaching bolt and lift the lever from the clutch fork shaft.

### Installation

4    Place the release lever in position on the fork shaft and install the bolt and washers, tightening to the specified torque.
5    Attach the clutch cable to the release lever.
6    Check the clutch operation by lifting the pedal up to allow the mechanism to adjust the cable length, then depress it slowly several times to mesh the pawl with the detent teeth.

## 4  Clutch pedal — removal and installation

### Removal

1    Perform the operations described in Steps 1 and 2 of Section 3.
2    Remove the under dash hush panel and remove the neutral start switch from the pedal and bracket.
3    Disconnect the clutch cable from the tangs of the detent, lift the pawl away and slide the cable between the detent and pawl.
4    Remove the pivot bolt. Remove the spring, pawl and spacer from the pedal assembly.

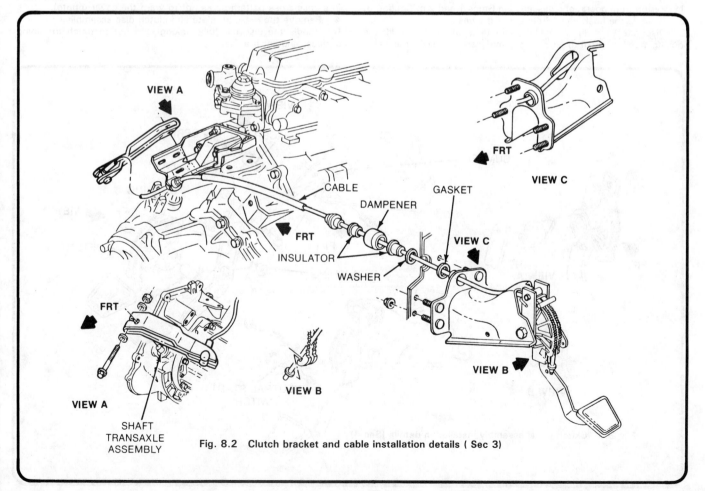

Fig. 8.2  Clutch bracket and cable installation details ( Sec 3)

5   Remove the detent spacer, bushings, spring and pawl.
6   Clean the parts and inspect for wear or damage. Replace both the pawl and detent if the teeth on either are damaged or worn.

## Installation

7   Position the detent spring in the side of the detent and install the detent into the clutch pedal opening, hooking the spring onto the pedal.
8   Install the bushings onto the pedal assembly.
9   Install the pawl, spring, spacer and pivot mounting bolt, tightening to the specified torque.
10  Attach the clutch pedal to the mounting bracket and install the pivot bolt and nut. Both the pivot and pawl bolts must be installed as shown in the accompanying illustration and tightened to the specified torque.
11  Check the pawl and detent for proper operation to make sure the pawl disengages when pulled to the upper position and the detent rotates freely in both directions.
12  Attach the cable end to the pawl, making sure to route the cable underneath the pawl and into the detent cable groove.
13  Install the neutral start switch.
14  Hold the clutch pedal up against the bumper stop and release the pawl from the detent.
15  Check the clutch pedal mechanism for proper operation and adjust the cable length by lifting the pedal (Chapter 1). Depress the pedal slowly several times so the pawl meshes properly with the detent teeth.
16  Install the hush panel.

## 5   Clutch cable — removal and installation

*Refer to Fig.8.2*

## Removal

1   Perform the operations described in Steps 1 and 2 of Section 3.
2   Remove the hush panel from under the dash.
3   Disconnect the clutch cable from the tangs of the detent, lift the locking pawl away from the detent and carefully slide the cable forward between the detent and pawl.
4   Remove the windshield washer reservoir.
5   In the engine compartment, pull the clutch cable out to disengage it from the clutch pedal mounting bracket. Be prepared to retrieve the insulators, dampener and washers, which may separate during removal.
6   Disconnect the cable from the mounting bracket on the transaxle and remove it from the vehicle.
7   Inspect the cable and replace it is frayed, worn, damaged or kinked.

## Installation

8   Connect the cable into both of the insulators and the damper and washers. Lubricating the rear insulator with a small amount of light oil will ease the installation into the pedal mounting bracket.
9   Inside the passenger compartment, route the liner on the cable into the rubber isolator on the pedal bracket and then attach the cable end to the detent. Make sure the cable is routed underneath the pawl and into the detent cable groove.
10  Install the hush panel.
11  Hold the clutch pedal upward against the bumper stop to release the pawl from the detent and install the other end of the cable to the release lever and transaxle mount bracket.
12  Install the windshield washer reservoir.
13  Lift the clutch pedal up several times to allow the mechanism to adjust the cable length, then depress it several times to mesh the pawl with the detent teeth.

## 6   Clutch — removal, inspection and installation

## Removal

1   Remove the transaxle (Chapter 7).
2   If the pressure plate is to be reinstalled, mark the pressure plate-to-flywheel relationship so that it can be installed in the same position.
3   Loosen the pressure plate retaining bolts evenly, one turn at a time, in a criss-cross pattern so as not to warp the cover (photo).
4   Remove the pressure plate and clutch disc assemblies.
5   Handle the disc carefully, taking care not to touch the lining surface, and set it aside.

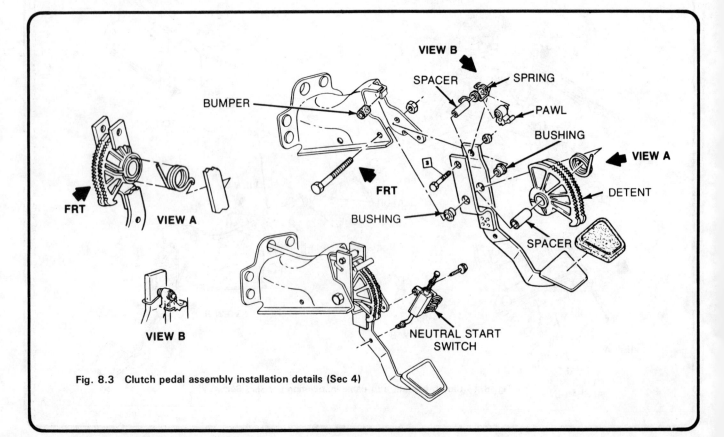

**Fig. 8.3   Clutch pedal assembly installation details (Sec 4)**

**6.3  Use the numbered sequence to remove or install the clutch pressure plate**

## Inspection

6    Inspect the clutch release bearing for damage or wear (Section 7).

7    Clean the dust out of the clutch housing, using a vacuum cleaner or clean cloth. Do not use compressed air as the dust can endanger your health if inhaled.

8    Inspect the friction surfaces of the clutch disc and flywheel for signs of uneven contact, indicating improper mounting or damaged

clutch springs. Check the surfaces for burned areas, grooves, cracks or other signs of wear. It may be necessary to remove a badly grooved flywheel and have it machined to restore the surface. Light glazing of the flywheel surface can be removed with fine sandpaper. Inspect the clutch lining for contamination by oil, grease or any other substance and replace the disc with a new one if any is present. Slide the disc onto the input shaft temporarily to make sure the fit is snug and the splines are not burred or worn.

## Installation

9    Place the clutch disc in position on the flywheel, centering it with an alignment tool. The disc spring offset and the stamped *Flywheel Side* letters must face the flywheel.

10   With the disc held in place by the alignment tool, place the pressure plate assembly in position and align it with any marks made prior to removal.

11   Install the bolts and tighten them in a criss-cross pattern, two turns at a time, until they are tightened to the specified torque.

12   Install the clutch release bearing (Section 7).

13   Remove the alignment tool and install the transaxle.

## 7  Clutch release bearing — removal and installation

### Removal

1    Remove the transaxle (Chapter 7).

2    Remove the clutch release bearing from the clutch fork.

3    Hold the center of the bearing and spin the outer portion. If the bearing doesn't turn smoothly or if it is noisy, replace it with a new one. Wipe the bearing with a clean rag and inspect it for damage, wear or cracks.

### Installation

4    Lightly lubricate the clutch fork ends with white lithium base grease where they contact the bearing (photo). Pack the inner diameter of

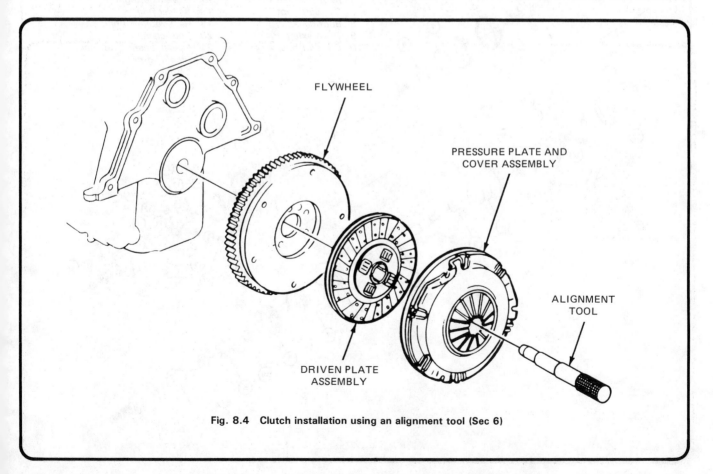

**Fig. 8.4   Clutch installation using an alignment tool (Sec 6)**

7.4   Lightly lubricate the clutch fork prior to installing the release bearing (arrows)

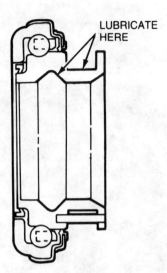

Fig. 8.5   Clutch release bearing lubrication (Sec 7)

LUBRICATE HERE

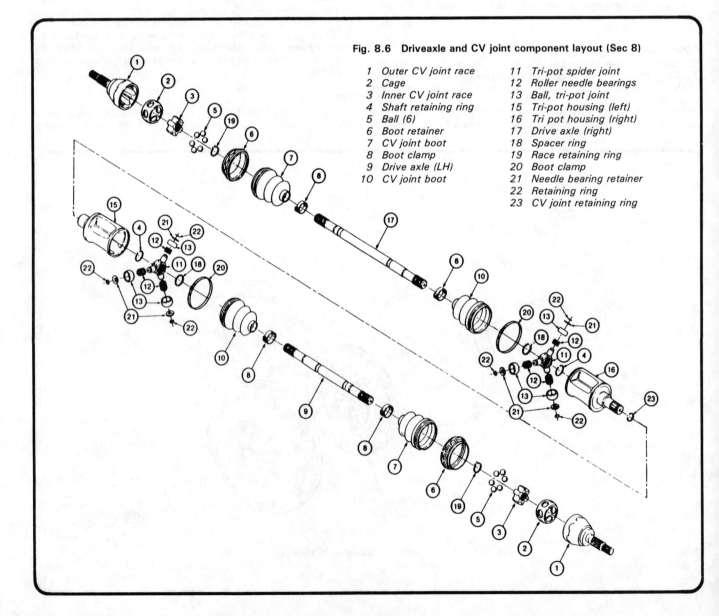

Fig. 8.6   Driveaxle and CV joint component layout (Sec 8)

| | | | |
|---|---|---|---|
| 1 | Outer CV joint race | 11 | Tri-pot spider joint |
| 2 | Cage | 12 | Roller needle bearings |
| 3 | Inner CV joint race | 13 | Ball, tri-pot joint |
| 4 | Shaft retaining ring | 15 | Tri-pot housing (left) |
| 5 | Ball (6) | 16 | Tri pot housing (right) |
| 6 | Boot retainer | 17 | Drive axle (right) |
| 7 | CV joint boot | 18 | Spacer ring |
| 8 | Boot clamp | 19 | Race retaining ring |
| 9 | Drive axle (LH) | 20 | Boot clamp |
| 10 | CV joint boot | 21 | Needle bearing retainer |
| | | 22 | Retaining ring |
| | | 23 | CV joint retaining ring |

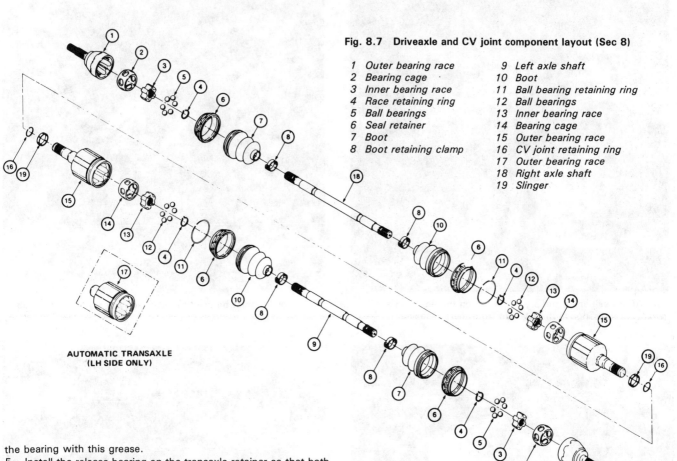

**Fig. 8.7   Driveaxle and CV joint component layout (Sec 8)**

| | |
|---|---|
| 1  Outer bearing race | 9  Left axle shaft |
| 2  Bearing cage | 10  Boot |
| 3  Inner bearing race | 11  Ball bearing retaining ring |
| 4  Race retaining ring | 12  Ball bearings |
| 5  Ball bearings | 13  Inner bearing race |
| 6  Seal retainer | 14  Bearing cage |
| 7  Boot | 15  Outer bearing race |
| 8  Boot retaining clamp | 16  CV joint retaining ring |
| | 17  Outer bearing race |
| | 18  Right axle shaft |
| | 19  Slinger |

**AUTOMATIC TRANSAXLE
(LH SIDE ONLY)**

the bearing with this grease.

5   Install the release bearing on the transaxle retainer so that both of the fork tangs fit into the outer diameter of the bearing groove.

6   Install the transaxle, making sure that the clutch lever does not move toward the flywheel until the transaxle is bolted to the engine.

7   Check the clutch operation, adjust the clutch cable and depress the pedal slowly several times to mesh the pawl with the detent teeth.

## 8   Driveaxle — general information

1   Power is transmitted from the transaxle to the front wheels by two driveaxles, which consist of splined solid axles with constant velocity (CV) joints at each end. There are two types of inner CV joints used. On certain models a double-offset design using ball bearings with an inner and outer race is used to allow angular movement. The other CV joint used is a tri-pot design, using a spider bearing assembly and tri-pot housing to allow angular movement. To determine which CV joint is used on your vehicle, simply look at the housing while it is still installed on the vehicle and compare it to the accompanying illustration, noting that the tri-pot housing will have three major indentations in it and a very thin retaining clamp holding the boot in position. All outer CV joints are the double-offset design. The CV joints are protected by rubber boots, which are retained by straps so that the joints are not contaminated by water or dirt.

2   The boots should be inspected periodically (Chapter 1) for damage, leaking lubricant or cuts. The inner boots have very small breather holes which may leak a small amount of lubricant under some circumstances, such as when the joint is compressed during removal.

3   Damaged CV joint boots must be replaced immediately or the joints can be damaged. Boot replacement involves removing the driveaxles (Section 10). The outer boots can be replaced with the driveaxles in the vehicle, using an aftermarket boot kit featuring split boots (Section 11).

4   The most common symptom of worn or damaged CV joints, besides lubricant leaks, are a clicking noise in turns, a clunk when accelerating from a coasting condition or vibration at highway speeds.

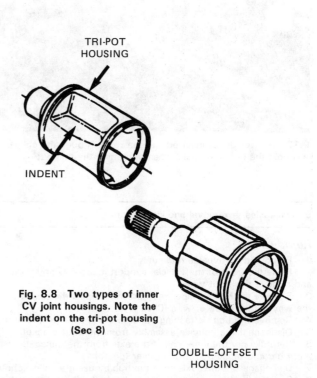

TRI-POT
HOUSING

INDENT

**Fig. 8.8   Two types of inner CV joint housings. Note the indent on the tri-pot housing (Sec 8)**

DOUBLE-OFFSET
HOUSING

9.6   After positioning the pry bar, a tap on the end with a hammer will disengage the CV joint from the transaxle

9.7   A puller must be used to disengage the axle from the hub

9.12   A screwdriver inserted into the rotor through the caliper will hold the hub stationary when tightening the hub nut

9.13   A large screwdriver or punch can be used to install the CV joint into the transaxle

## 9   Driveaxles — removal and installation

### Removal

1   Remove the driveaxle hub nut.
2   Raise the front of the vehicle, support it securely on jackstands and remove the front wheel.
3   Remove the brake caliper and disc and support the caliper out of the way with a piece of wire (Chapter 9).
4   Remove the bolts attaching the steering knuckle to the strut.
5   Disconnect the knuckle assembly from the strut bracket.
6   Carefully pry the inner end of the axle from the transaxle, using a pry bar and tapping with a hammer (photo).
7   Disengage the driveaxle from the hub by using a puller (photo).
8   Support the CV joints and remove the driveaxle from the vehicle.

### Installation

9   Raise the driveaxle into position while supporting the CV joints and insert the splined ends into the hub and transaxle. Place the steering knuckle in position in the strut bracket and install the bolts (Chapter 10).
10  Install the brake disc and caliper.
11  Install the hub nut.
12  Lock the disc so that it cannot turn, using a screwdriver or punch inserted through the caliper into a disc cooling vane, and tighten the hub nut (Chapter 10) (photo).
13  Seat the driveaxle into the transaxle by inserting a screwdriver into the groove in the CV joint and tapping it into position with a hammer (photo).
14  Grasp the CV housing (not the driveaxle) and pull out to make sure that the axle has seated securely in the transaxle.
15  Install the wheel and lower the vehicle.

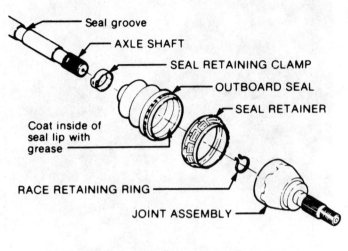

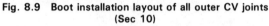

**Fig. 8.9 Boot installation layout of all outer CV joints (Sec 10)**

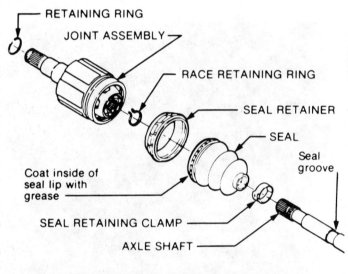

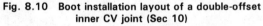

**Fig. 8.10 Boot installation layout of a double-offset inner CV joint (Sec 10)**

10.3 Carefully tap around the circumference of the retaining ring to remove it from the housing

10.4 Wire cutters can be used to cut the inner boot clamp from the axle shaft

10.5 Use snap-ring pliers to remove the inner retaining ring

---

**10 Driveaxle boot — replacement (driveaxle removed)**

1 Remove the driveaxle (Section 9)
2 Place the driveaxle in a vise.

*Double-offset design*

3 Tap lightly around the outer circumference of the seal retainer with a hammer and drift to dislodge and remove it. Take care not to deform the retainer, as this would destroy its ability to seal properly (photo).
4 Cut off the band retaining the boot to the shaft (photo).
5 Remove the snap-ring and slide the joint assembly off (photo).
6 Slide the old boot off the driveaxle.
7 Clean the old grease from the joint.
8 Repack the CV joint with half the grease supplied with the new boot and put the remaining half in the boot.
9 Slide the retainer and boot into position on the driveaxle.
10 Install the joint and snap-ring.

10.12   Carefully tap around the circumference of the retaining ring to install it on the housing

10.14   Snap-ring pliers should be used to remove both the inner and outer retaining rings

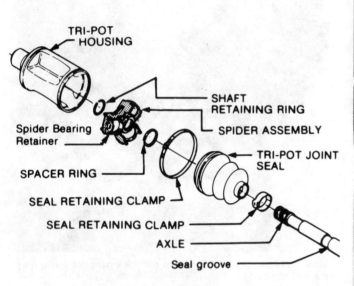

Fig. 8.11   Boot installation layout of a tri-pot inner CV joint. Note the tape around the spider assembly to prevent it from coming apart (Sec 10)

Labels:
TRI-POT HOUSING
Spider Bearing Retainer
SPACER RING
SEAL RETAINING CLAMP
SEAL RETAINING CLAMP
AXLE
Seal groove
SHAFT RETAINING RING
SPIDER ASSEMBLY
TRI-POT JOINT SEAL

10.21   When installing the spider assembly onto the axleshaft, make sure the recess in the counterbore is facing away from the axleshaft

11  Seat the inner end of the boot in the seal groove and install the retaining clamp.

12  Install the seal retainer securely in place by tapping evenly around the outer circumference with a hammer and punch (photo).

### Tri-pot design

13  Cut off the boot seal retaining clamps.

14  Remove the joint housing from the axle by first removing the inner retaining ring and sliding the spider assembly back to expose the front retaining ring. Remove the front retaining ring and slide the joint off the axle shaft (photo).

15  Use tape or a cloth wrapped around the spider bearing assembly to retain the bearings during removal and installation.

16  Remove the assembly from the axle.

17  Slide the boot off the axle.

18  Clean old grease from the housing and spider assembly.

19  Pack the housing with half of the grease furnished with the new boot and place the remainder in the boot.

20  Slide the boot onto the axle.

21  Install the spider bearing with the recess in the counterbore facing out (photo).

22  Install the housing.

23  Seat the boot in the housing and axle seal grooves and install the retaining clamps.

## 11 Outer driveaxle boot — replacement (driveaxle installed)

1    The outer boot can be replaced with the axle installed, using an aftermarket boot replacement kit. These boots are split so they can be installed with the driveaxle in place.

2    Raise the vehicle, support it securely on jackstands and remove the front wheel. Raise the suspension arm with a jack so that the axle shaft is level.

3    Remove the brake caliper and rotor and wire the caliper out of the way.

4    Using a chisel and hammer, cut the boot retainer off the joint housing (photo).

5    Remove the remaining boot retaining strap.

6    Cut the old boot and remove it.

7    Inspect the CV joint to determine if the damaged boot has allowed the grease to become contaminated with dirt or water. If it has, wipe the old grease off and apply new grease from the replacement boot kit, working it in with your fingers. **Note:** *The following steps describe a typical installation. Follow the instructions included with the replacement boot kit.*

8    Place the new boot in position over the axle. Typically these kits use a special fluid, which when applied to the sealing grooves, ''welds'' the boot into one piece. The retaining straps included are installed to hold the body in place until the glue has set (photo).

9    Install the boot in the sealing grooves on the driveaxle shaft and joint and securely install the retaining straps, following the included instructions.

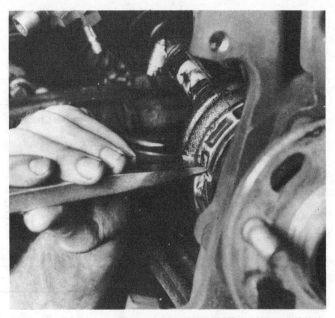

11.4   A chisel should be used to cut the retaining clamp off the housing

11.8a   Applying glue to the boot grove

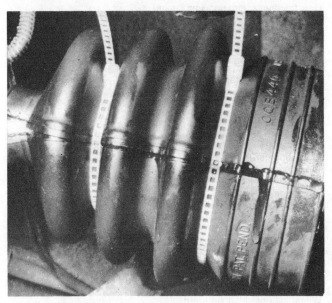

11.8b   The supplied straps should be used to hold the boot together while the glue is drying

# Chapter 9 Brakes

*Refer to Chapter 13 for Specifications applicable to 1986 and later models*

## Contents

Brake check .......................... See Chapter 1
Disc brake rotor — inspection, removal and installation ..... 8
Drum brake shoes — inspection and replacement ......... 9
Drum brake wheel cylinder — removal, overhaul
  and installation ................................ 10
Fluid level check ...................... See Chapter 1
Front disc brake caliper — overhaul .................. 4
Front disc brake caliper — removal and installation ........ 3
Front disc brake pads — replacement ................. 2
General information .............................. 1

Hydraulic brake hoses and lines — inspection
  and replacement ............................... 12
Hydraulic system — bleeding ...................... 15
Master cylinder — removal, overhaul and installation ....... 11
Parking brake — adjustment ....................... 13
Power brake booster — inspection, removal and installation .. 14
Rear disc brake caliper — overhaul .................. 7
Rear disc brake caliper — removal and installation ........ 5
Rear disc brake pads — replacement ................. 6
Stop light switch — removal, installation and adjustment .... 16

## Specifications

### Disc brakes

| | |
|---|---|
| Rotor thickness after resurfacing (minimum) ............. | 0.830 in |
| Discard thickness ................................ | 0.815 in |
| Disc runout (maximum) ........................... | 0.005 in |
| Disc thickness variation (maximum) .................. | 0.0005 in |

### Rear drum brakes

| | |
|---|---|
| Drum diameter | |
|   Standard ..................................... | 7.88 in |
|   Service limit .................................. | 7.90 in |
|   Discard diameter ............................... | 7.93 in |
| Drum taper (maximum) ............................ | 0.003 in |
| Out-of-round (maximum) ........................... | 0.002 in |

| Torque specifications | Ft-lbs |
|---|---|
| Brake pedal-to-bracket ............................ | 25 |
| Brake booster-to-pedal bracket ..................... | 20 |
| Brake booster-to-firewall .......................... | 22 to 33 |
| Caliper mounting bolts ............................ | 25 to 28 |
| Caliper fluid inlet fitting .......................... | 18 to 30 |
| Caliper bleeder screw ............................ | 9 to 16 |
| Failure switch-to-master cylinder .................... | 2 to 4 |
| Master cylinder-to-booster ......................... | 16 |
| Master cylinder tube nuts .......................... | 11 to 14 |
| Proportioner valve-to-master cylinder ................. | 18 to 30 |
| Parking brake lever-to-body ........................ | 13 |
| Parking brake front cable nut ...................... | 24 |
| Switch piston-to-master cylinder .................... | 2 to 4 |
| Wheel cylinder bleeder screw ...................... | 3 to 6 |
| Wheel cylinder inlet tube nut ....................... | 11 to 14 |
| Wheel lug nuts................................... | 100 |

## 1  General information

All vehicles covered by this manual are equipped with hydraulically operated front and rear brake systems. All front brake systems are disc type, while the rear brakes are either disc or drum type.

All brakes are self-adjusting. The front and rear disc brakes automatically compensate for pad wear, while the rear drum brakes incorporate an adjustment mechanism which is activated as the brakes are applied when the vehicle is driven in reverse.

The hydraulic system consists of separate front and rear circuits. The master cylinder has separate reservoirs for the two circuits, and in the event of a leak or failure in one hydraulic circuit, the other circuit will remain operative. A visual warning of circuit failure, air in the system, or other pressure differential conditions in the brake system is given by a warning light activated by a failure warning switch in the master cylinder.

The parking brake mechanically operates the rear brakes only. It is activated by a pull-handle in the center console between the front seats.

The power brake booster, located in the engine compartment on the firewall, uses engine manifold vacuum and atmospheric pressure to provide assistance to the hydraulically operated brakes.

After completing any operation involving the disassembly of any part of the brake system, always test drive the vehicle to check for proper braking performance before resuming normal driving. Test the brakes while driving on a clean, dry, flat surface. Conditions other than these can lead to inaccurate test results. Test the brakes at various speeds with both light and heavy pedal pressure. The vehicle should stop evenly without pulling to one side or the other. Avoid locking the brakes because this slides the tires and diminishes braking efficiency and control.

Tires, vehicle load and front end alignment are factors which also affect braking performance.

Torque values given in the Specifications section are for dry, unlubricated fasteners.

## 2  Disc brake pads (front) — replacement

**Note:** *Disc brake pads should be replaced on both wheels at the same time.*

1    Whenever you are working on the brake system, be aware that asbestos dust is present and be careful not to inhale any of it as this could be harmful to your health.

2    Remove the cover from the brake fluid reservoir and siphon off about two ounces of the fluid into a container and discard it.

3    Raise the front of the vehicle and support it securely on jackstands.

4    Remove the front wheel, then reinstall two wheel lugs (flat side toward the rotor) to hold the rotor in place. Work on one brake assembly at a time, using the assembled brake for reference if necessary.

5    Push the piston back into its bore. If necessary, a C-clamp can be used, but a flat bar will usually do the job (photo). As the piston is depressed to the bottom of the caliper bore, the fluid in the master cylinder will rise. Make sure that it does not overflow. If necessary, siphon off more of the fluid as directed in Step 2.

6    Refer to the accompanying photographs and perform the procedure illustrated. Start with photograph 2.6/1.

2.5   A large C-clamp can be used to compress the caliper for removal.

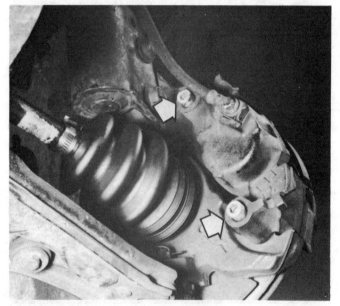

2.6/1 Brake caliper mounting bolts (arrows) (early models have Allen head bolts, later models have Torx head bolts)

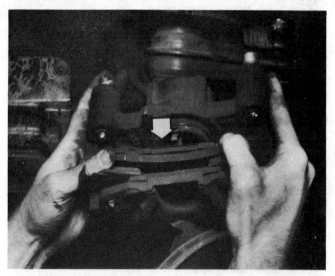

2.6/2 Remove the inner pad by snapping it out of the piston in the direction shown (arrow)

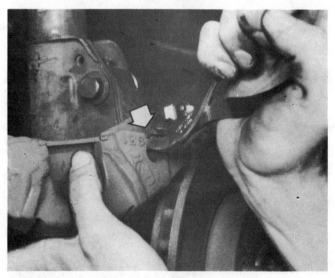

2.6/3 Remove the outboard pad by bending the tabs (arrow) straight out with channel lock pliers

2.6/4 After bending the tabs straight the outboard pad can be removed using a hammer to dislodge it from the caliper.

2.6/5 Inspect the caliper bolts and bushings (A) for damage and the contact surfaces (B) for corrosion

2.6/6 Carefully peel back the edge of the piston boot and check for corrosion and leaking fluid

2.6/7 Snap the inner pad retainer spring into the new pad in the direction shown (arrow)

2.6/8 Lubricate the lower steering knuckle contact surface lightly with white lithium base grease

2.6/9 Apply a light coat of white lithium base grease to the upper steering knuckle-to-caliper contact surface

2.6/10 Place the pads in position and snap the inner pad into place in the piston (arrow)

2.6/11 After installing the caliper, insert a large screwdriver between the outer pad flange and the disc hat to seat the pad and then bend the tabs over with a hammer

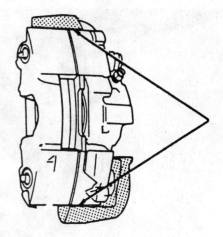

Fig. 9.1  Measure the clearance between the caliper and bracket stops at the points indicated (Sec 3)

## 3  Front disc brake caliper — removal and installation

Refer to photos 2.5 through 2.6/6

### Removal

1    Remove the cover from the brake fluid reservoir and siphon off two thirds of the fluid into a container and discard it.

2    Raise the front of the vehicle, support it securely on jackstands and remove the front wheels.

3    Reinstall two lug nuts, flat side against the disc, to hold the disc rotor in place.

4    Bottom the piston in the caliper bore. This is accomplished by pushing on the caliper, although it may be necessary to carefully use a flat pry bar or a C-clamp.

5    If the caliper is to be removed from the vehicle, remove the brake line hose inlet fitting bolt and disconnect the fitting.

6    Remove the two mounting bolts and lift the caliper from the vehicle. If the caliper is not to be removed from the vehicle, hang it out of the way with a piece of wire so the brake hose will not be damaged.

### Installation

7    Inspect the mounting bolts for excessive corrosion.

8    Place the caliper in position over the rotor and mounting bracket, install the bolts and tighten to the specified torque.

9    Check to make sure the clearance between the caliper and the bracket stops at the points shown in the accompanying illustration is between 0.005 and 0.012 in.

10  Connect the inlet fitting (if removed) and install the retaining bolt. It will be necessary to bleed the brakes (Section 12) if the fitting was disconnected.

11  Install the wheels and lower the vehicle.

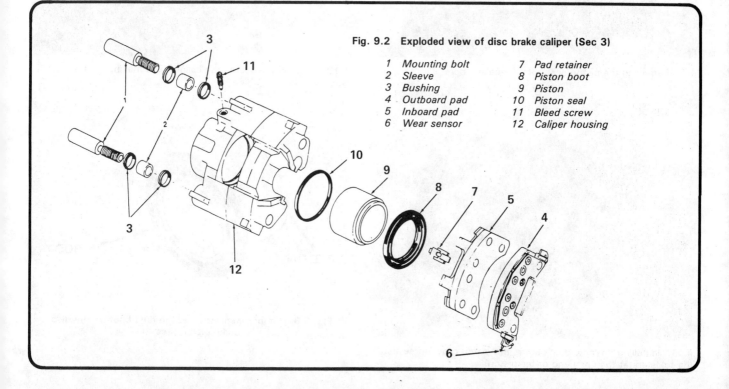

Fig. 9.2  Exploded view of disc brake caliper (Sec 3)

| 1 | Mounting bolt | 7 | Pad retainer |
|---|---|---|---|
| 2 | Sleeve | 8 | Piston boot |
| 3 | Bushing | 9 | Piston |
| 4 | Outboard pad | 10 | Piston seal |
| 5 | Inboard pad | 11 | Bleed screw |
| 6 | Wear sensor | 12 | Caliper housing |

4.4   With the caliper padded to catch the piston, use compressed air to force the piston out of its bore. Make sure your hands or fingers are not between the piston and caliper.

4.5   Carefully pry the dust boot out of the housing, taking care not to scratch the bore surface

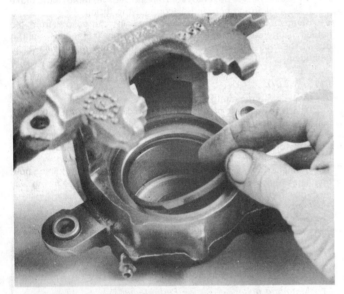

4.6   Removing the piston seal from the caliper bore

4.10   Position the seal in the caliper bore making sure it is not twisted.

4.11   Installing the new dust boot in the piston grove (note that the folds are at the open end of the piston)

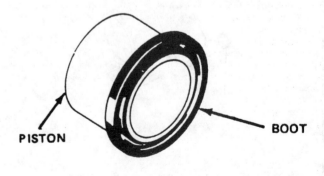

Fig. 9.3   Proper installation of the dust boot on the disc brake piston (Sec 4)

4.12 Installing the piston squarely in the caliper bore

## 4 Front disc brake caliper — overhaul

**Note:** *Purchase a brake caliper overhaul kit for your particular vehicle before beginning this procedure.*

1    Refer to Section 3 and remove the caliper.
2    Refer to Section 2 and remove the brake pad and plate assemblies.
3    Clean the exterior of the brake caliper with brake fluid. Never use gasoline, kerosene or cleaning solvents. Place the caliper on a clean workbench.
4    Place a wooden block or shop rag in the caliper as a cushion, then use compressed air to remove the piston from the caliper (photo). Use only enough air pressure to ease the piston out of the bore. If the piston is blown out, even with the cushion in place, it may be damaged.
**Caution:** *Never place your fingers in front of the piston in an attempt to catch or protect it when applying compressed air, as serious injury could occur.*
5    Carefully pry the dust boot out of the caliper bore (photo).
6    Using a wood or plastic tool, remove the piston seal from the groove in the caliper bore (photo). Metal tools may cause bore damage.
7    Remove the caliper bleeder valve, then remove and discard the sleeves and bushings from the caliper ears. Discard all rubber parts.
8    Clean the remaining parts with brake fluid. Allow them to drain and then shake them vigorously to remove as much fluid as possible.
9    Carefully examine the piston for nicks and burrs and loss of plating. If surface defects are present, parts must be replaced. Check the caliper bore in a similar way, but light polishing with crocus cloth is permissible to remove light corrosion and stains. Discard the mounting bolts if they are corroded or damaged.
10  When assembling, lubricate the piston bores and seal with clean brake fluid. Position the seal in the caliper bore groove (photo).
11  Lubricate the piston with clean brake fluid, then install a new boot in the piston groove with the fold toward the open end of the piston (photo).
12  Insert the piston squarely into the caliper bore, then apply force to bottom the piston in the bore (photo).
13  Position the dust boot in the caliper counterbore, then use a drift to drive it into position (photo). Make sure that the boot is evenly installed below the caliper face.
14  Install the bleeder valve.
15  The remainder of the installation procedure is the reverse of the removal procedure. Always use new copper gaskets when connecting the brake hose and bleed the system as described in Section 15.

## 5 Rear disc brake caliper — removal and installation

1    Whenever you are working on the brake system, be aware that asbestos dust is present and be careful not to inhale any of it, as it has been proven to be harmful to your health.
2    Remove the cover from the brake fluid reservoir and siphon off

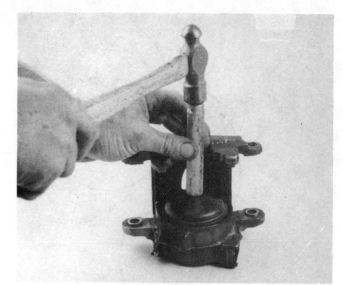

4.13 Using a hammer to seat the boot into the caliper housing counter bore

two-thirds of the fluid into a container and discard it.
3    Raise the rear of the vehicle and place it securely on jackstands, then release the parking brake handle.
4    Remove the wheel, then reinstall one wheel lug, flat side toward the rotor, to hold the rotor in place. Work on one brake assembly at a time, using the assembled brake for reference, if necessary.
5    Loosen the tension on the parking brake cable by loosening the nuts at the equalizer.
6    Remove the cable, damper and spring from the cable lever.
7    Hold the lever and remove the nut, then remove the lever, lever seal and anti-friction washer from the caliper actuator screw.
8    Refer to the accompanying illustration and position a C-clamp on the caliper housing. **Note:** *Make sure the C-clamp does not contact the actuator screw.*

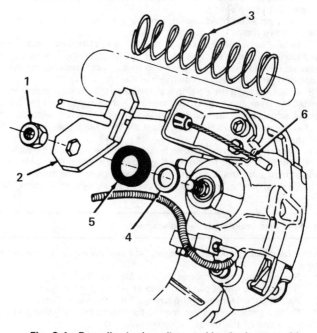

Fig. 9.4  Rear disc brake caliper parking brake assembly
(Sec 5)

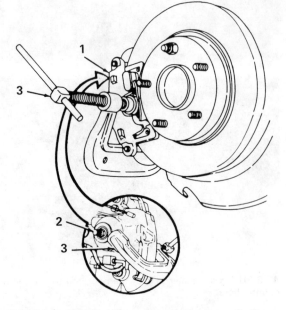

Fig. 9.5   Bottoming the caliper piston with a large C-clamp
(make sure the caliper does not contact the
actuator screw (Sec 5)

1   Caliper housing          3   C-clamp
2   Actuator screw

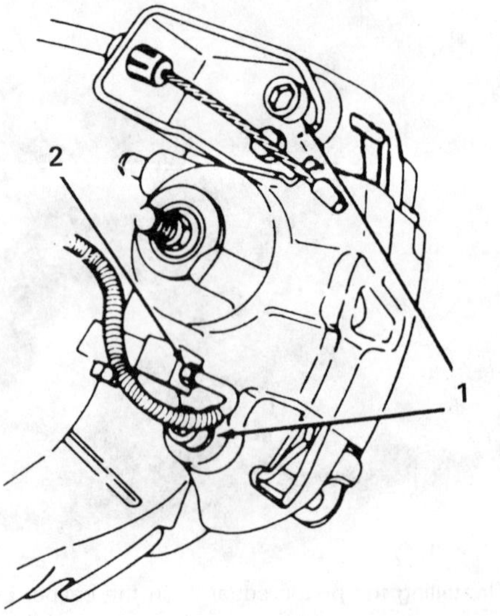

9   Tighten the C-clamp until the piston bottoms in the cylinder bore,
then remove the clamp.
10  Reinstall the anti-friction washer, lever seal (with the sealing bead
against the housing), lever and nut on the actuating screw.
11  Loosen the brake line nut, then disconnect the brake line from the
caliper. **Note:** *If the brake line is seized, remove the banjo fitting bolt,
banjo fitting and copper washers in order to free the line.*
12  To prevent fluid loss and contamination, plug the openings in the
caliper and brake line.
13  Using an Allen head socket, remove the caliper mounting bolts.
14  Remove the caliper from the vehicle.
15  Installation is the reverse of removal. Always use a new lever seal
and lubricate it with silicone lubricant before installing it. Also use a
new anti-friction washer. If the banjo fitting was removed, use new
copper washers when reinstalling it.
16  When installing the parking brake lever on the actuator screw hex,
install the lever pointing down, then rotate the lever toward the front
of the vehicle and hold it while installing the retaining nut. Tighten the
nut to the specified torque, then rotate the lever back against the stop
on the caliper.
17  After connecting the parking brake cable, tighten it at the equalizer
until the lever starts to move off the caliper stop, then loosen the
adjustment until the lever just moves back against the stop.
18  Fill the master cylinder and bleed the hydraulic system (Section 15).

## 6   Rear disc brake pads — replacement

**Note:** *Disc brake pads should be replaced on both wheels at the same
time.*
1   Remove the brake caliper (refer to Section 5).
2   Remove the brake pad and plate assemblies from the caliper.
3   Remove the sleeves and bushings from the caliper ears.
4   Using a small screwdriver, remove the flexible two-way check valve
from the end of the caliper piston.
5   If leakage is noted at the caliper assembly, refer to Section 7 and
overhaul the caliper.
6   Lubricate the new sleeves and bushings with silicone grease and
install them in the caliper ears.
7   Lubricate a new two-way check valve with silicone grease and
install it in the caliper piston end.
8   Position the inboard pad and plate assembly in the caliper. Make

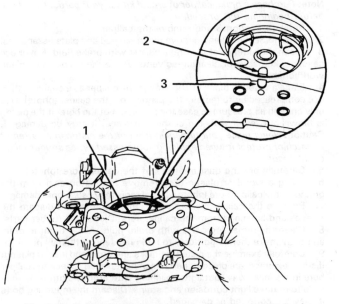

Fig. 9.6   Brake line and caliper mounting details (Sec 5)

1   Caliper mounting bolts          2   Brake line nut

Fig. 9.7   Pad and plate assembly installation details (make
sure the D-notch and D-tab engage) (Sec 6)

1   Shoe dampening spring          3   D-tab on shoe
2   D-notch in piston

sure that the D-shaped tab on the shoe engages the D-shaped notch
in the piston. If the tab and notch do not line up, use a spanner wrench
to turn the piston until they do.
9   With the tab and notch properly aligned, install the inboard pad
and plate assembly in the caliper, with the wear sensor positioned so
that it is at the leading edge. Slide the edge of the plate under the ends
of the dampening spring and snap the assembly into place against the
piston, making sure that the plate lies flat against the piston. **Note:**
*If the assembly fails to lie flat, recheck the alignment of the D-shaped
notch and tab.*
10  Install the outboard pad and plate assembly in the caliper.
11  Reinstall the caliper (refer to Section 5).
12  Set the caliper by applying the brake pedal firmly.
13  Using channel lock pliers, bend the ears on the upper edge of the
plate assembly until they are flush with the caliper housing, with no
radial clearance.

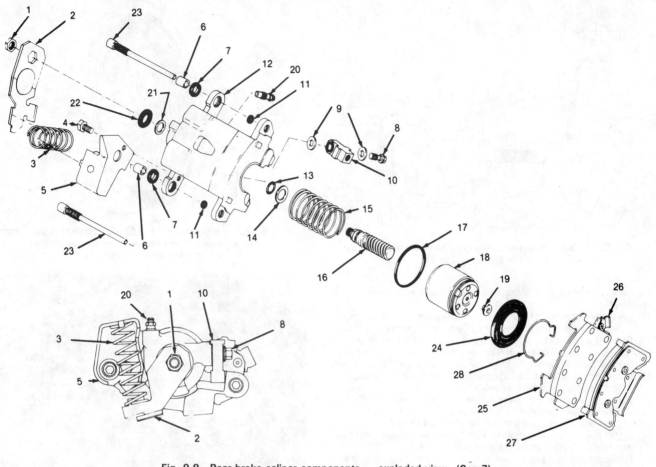

**Fig. 9.8   Rear brake caliper components — exploded view   (Sec 7)**

| | |
|---|---|
| 1  Parking brake lever retaining nut | 8  Banjo fitting bolt |
| 2  Parking brake lever | 9  Copper washers |
| 3  Return spring | 10  Banjo fitting |
| 4  Bolt | 11  Bushing |
| 5  Bracket | 12  Caliper housing |
| 6  Sleeve | 13  Seal |
| 7  Bushing | 14  Thrust washer |
| 15  Balance spring | 22  Lever seal |
| 16  Actuator screw | 23  Caliper mounting bolts |
| 17  Piston seal | 24  Dust boot |
| 18  Piston | 25  Inboard pad |
| 19  Two-way check valve | 26  Wear sensor |
| 20  Bleeder valve | 27  Outboard pad |
| 21  Anti-friction washer | 28  Shoe dampening spring |

**Fig. 9.9   Working the piston out of the caliper bore with the parking brake lever (Sec 7)**

## 7   Rear disc brake caliper — overhaul

**Note:** *Purchase a brake caliper overhaul kit for your particular vehicle before beginning this procedure.*

1   Remove the caliper (refer to Section 5) and place it on a workbench.
2   Remove the pad and plate assemblies from the caliper (refer to Section 6).
3   Remove the shoe dampening spring from the end of the caliper piston.
4   Place the caliper in a vise equipped with soft jaws and cushion the interior with a piece of wood or shop towels.
5   Move the parking brake lever back and forth to work the piston out of the caliper bore. If the piston will not come out, remove the lever retaining nut and lever and use a wrench to rotate the actuator screw in the same direction as the parking brake is applied until the piston comes out of the cylinder.
6   Remove the balance spring.
7   If not previously removed, remove the retaining nut and lever, then remove the lever seal and anti-friction washer.
8   Press on the threaded end of the actuator screw to remove it from the housing.
9   Remove the dust boot from the caliper.
10  Use a wood or plastic tool to remove the piston seal from the bore.
11  If not previously removed, remove the banjo fitting bolt, banjo fitting and copper washers.

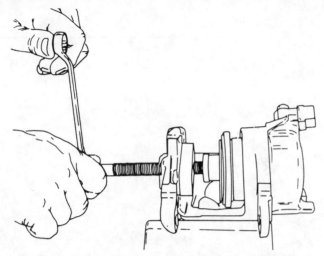

Fig. 9.10   Using a piston compressor to bottom the caliper
piston in the bore (Sec 7)

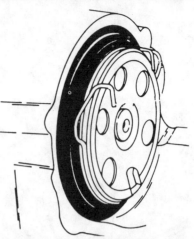

Fig. 9.11 The shoe dampening spring installed in the piston
end groove (arrows indicate correct position of
the spring ends) (Sec 7)

12   Remove the parking brake lever mounting bracket only if it is
damaged.
13   Carefully check the caliper bore for score marks, nicks, corrosion
and excessive wear. Light corrosion may be removed with crocus cloth.
14   Clean all parts not included in the caliper repair kit with denatured
alcohol, clean brake fluid or brake system cleaner. Never use gasoline,
kerosene or cleaning solvents. Place the caliper on a clean workbench.
15   Use compressed air to dry the parts and blow out all passages in
the caliper housing and bleeder valve.
16   Install the bleeder valve and tighten it to the specified torque.
17   If removed for replacement, install the parking brake lever mounting bracket and tighten the bolt to the specified torque.
18   Install the banjo fitting, making sure to use new copper washers.
Tighten the retaining bolt to the specified torque.
19   Lubricate the new piston seal with clean brake fluid and install it
in the caliper bore groove. Make sure the seal is not twisted.
20   Attach the boot to the piston with the inside lip of the boot in the
piston groove and the boot fold toward the end of the piston that contacts the inboard brake pad.
21   Install the thrust washer on the actuator screw with the bearing
surface toward the caliper housing.
22   Lubricate the shaft seal with brake fluid and install it on the
actuator screw.
23   Lubricate the actuator screw with brake fluid and install it in the
piston.
24   Install the balance spring in the piston recess.
25   Lubricate the piston and caliper bore with brake fluid and start the
piston assembly into the caliper bore.
26   Using a piston compressor or other suitable tool, push the piston
in until it bottoms in the caliper bore. Before removing the tool, lubricate
the anti-friction washer and lever seal with silicone lubricant and
install them over the end of the actuating screw, making sure that the
sealing bead on the lever seal is against the housing. Install the lever
over the actuating screw, then rotate the lever slightly away from the
stop on the housing and hold it while installing the lever retaining nut.
Tighten the nut to the specified torque, then rotate the lever back to
the stop.
27   Position the outside of the boot in the caliper recess. Using a driver
and hammer, seat the boot in the recess.
28   Install the dampening spring in the groove in the piston end. **Note:**
*It may be necessary to move the parking brake lever off its stop so
that the piston may be extended slightly, making the spring groove
accessible. If this is necessary, push the piston back into the bottom
of the caliper bore before installing the caliper.*
29   Install the caliper on the vehicle (refer to Section 5).

---

**8   Disc brake rotor — inspection, removal and installation**

1   Raise the vehicle and place it securely on jackstands.
2   Remove the wheel and tire.

8.5   Checking the disc pad surface runout with a dial indicator

8.6   Using a micrometer to check the disc brake rotor thickness

3   Remove the brake caliper assembly (refer to Section 3 or 5). **Note:**
*On front disc brakes, it is not necessary to disconnect the brake hose.*
After removing the caliper mounting bolts, hang the caliper out of the
way on a piece of wire. Never hang the caliper by the brake hose
because damage to the hose will occur.
4   Inspect the rotor surfaces. Light scoring or grooving is normal, but
deep grooves or severe erosion is not. If pulsating has been noticed
during application of the brakes, suspect disc runout.

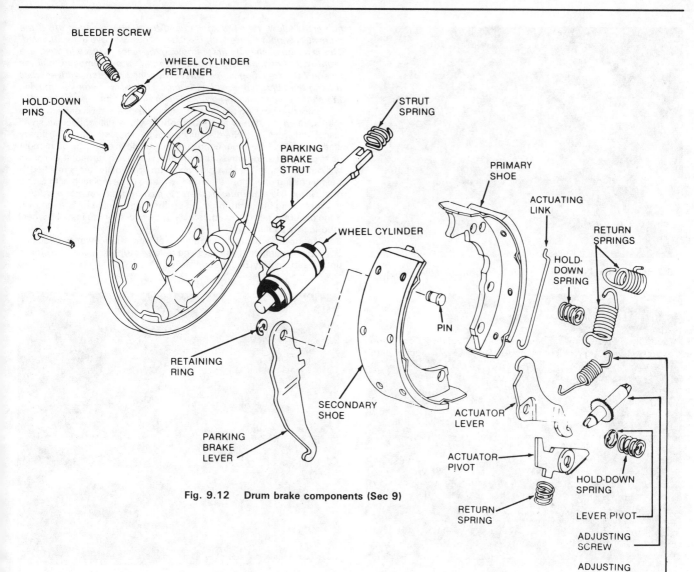

Fig. 9.12   Drum brake components (Sec 9)

5    Attach a dial indicator to the caliper mounting bracket, turn the rotor and note the amount of runout. Check both inboard and outboard surfaces (photo). If the runout is more than the maximum allowable, the rotor must be removed from the vehicle and taken to an automotive machine shop for resurfacing.
6    Using a micrometer, measure the thickness of the rotor (photo). If it is less than the minimum specified, replace the rotor with a new one. Also measure the thickness at several points to determine variations in the surface. Any variation over 0.0005-inch may cause pedal pulsations during brake application. If this condition exists and the thickness is not below the minimum, the rotor can be removed and taken to an automotive machine shop for resurfacing.
7    To remove and install the front rotor, remove the caliper (Section 3) and pull the rotor off the hub.
8    The rotor on the rear wheel disc brake models can also be pulled off after the caliper is removed.

## 9   Drum brake shoes — inspection and replacement

1    Whenever working on the brake system, be aware that asbestos dust is present. It has been proven to be harmful to your health, so be careful not to inhale it.
2    Raise the vehicle and support it securely on jackstands.
3    Release the parking brake handle.
4    Remove the wheel. **Note:** *All four rear shoes should be replaced at the same time, but to avoid mixing up parts, work on only one brake assembly at a time.*

9.5/1 Remove and discard the brake drum retaining clip

5    Refer to the accompanying photographs and perform the brake shoe inspection and, if necessary, the replacement procedure. Start with photo 9.5/1. **Note:** *If the brake drum cannot be easily pulled off the axle and shoe assembly, make sure that the parking brake is completely released, then squirt some penetrating oil around the center*

9.5/2 Remove the brake drum

hub area. Allow the oil to soak in and try to pull the drum off. If the drum still cannot be pulled off, the brake shoes will have to be retracted. This is accomplished by first removing the lanced cutout in the brake drum with a hammer and chisel. With the cutout removed, pull the lever off the adjusting screw wheel with one small screwdriver while turning the adjusting wheel with another small screwdriver, moving the shoes away from the drum. The drum may now be pulled off.

6    Before reinstalling the drum it should be checked for cracks, score marks, deep scratches and hard spots, which will appear as small discolored areas. If the hard spots cannot be removed with a fine emery cloth or if any of the other conditions listed above exist, the drum must be taken to an automotive machine shop to have it turned. If the drum will not ''clean up'' before the maximum drum diameter is reached in the machining operation, the drum will have to be replaced with a new one. **Note:** *The maximum diameter is cast into the each brake drum.*

7    Install the brake drum, lining up the marks made before removal if the old brake drum is used. It will not be necessary to install a wheel stud lock washer.

8    Mount the wheel, install the wheel lugs, then lower the vehicle.

9    Make a number of forward and reverse stops to adjust the brakes until a satisfactory pedal action is obtained.

9.5/3 Remove the return springs using brake spring pliers

9.5/4 Remove the hold down springs and pins by pushing in with pliers and turning (arrows)

9.5/5 Lift up on the actuator lever and remove the actuating link from the anchor pin pivot along with the actuator lever and return spring (arrow)

9.5/6 Spread the shoes apart and remove the parking brake strut

9.5/7 With the shoe assembly spread to clear the hub flange, lift it from the backing plate

9.5/8 Disconnect the parking brake lever from the cable in the direction shown (arrow) and remove the shoe assembly

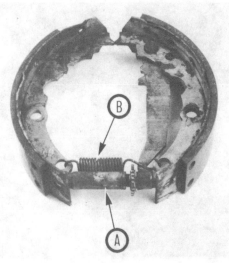

9.5/9 Remove the adjusting screw (A) and spring (B) from the shoe assembly, making sure to note the direction in which they are installed

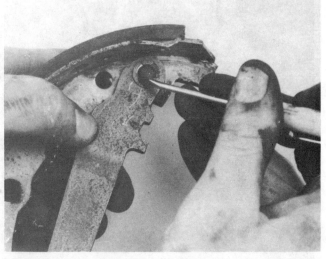

9.5/10 Remove the parking brake lever by prying the C-clip off

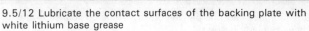

9.5/11 Install the parking brake lever on the new brake shoe by pressing the C-clip into place with needle nose pliers

9.5/12 Lubricate the contact surfaces of the backing plate with white lithium base grease

9.5/13 Lubricate the adjuster screw with white lithium base grease prior to installation

9.5/14 Connect the parking brake lever to the cable

9.5/15 Spread the brake assembly apart sufficiently to clear the hub flange and raise it into position

9.5/16 Install the parking brake strut

9.5/17 Make sure the parking brake strut is positioned in the shoes properly (arrows)

9.5/18 Install the hold-down pin and spring on the primary brake shoe.

9.5/19 Install the anchor link

9.5/20 Install the actuator pivot, lever and return spring

9.5/21 Install the hold-down spring assembly

9.5/22 Install the return springs

9.5/23 Center the brake shoe assembly so the drum will slide over it

9.5/24 Adjust the star wheel so the drum fits snugly over the shoes

9.5/25 The drum has a maximum permissible diameter cast into it which must not be exceeded when removing scoring or other service imperfections in the friction surface

10.4 A flare-nut wrench should be used to disconnect the brake line

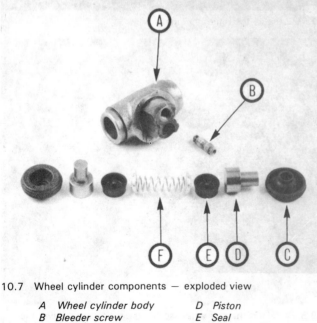

10.7   Wheel cylinder components — exploded view

    A  *Wheel cylinder body*     D  *Piston*
    B  *Bleeder screw*          E  *Seal*
    C  *Boot*                F  *Spring*

## 10   Drum brake wheel cylinder — removal, overhaul and installation

### *Removal*

1    Raise the rear of the vehicle and support it securely on jackstands.
2    Remove the brake shoe assembly (Section 9).
3    Carefully clean all dirt and foreign material from around the wheel cylinder.
4    Disconnect and plug the brake fluid inlet tube (photo).
5    Remove the wheel cylinder retainer by using a screwdriver to release the clips (photo).
6    Remove the wheel cylinder from the brake backing plate and place it on a clean workbench.
7    Remove the bleeder valve, seals, pistons, boots and spring assembly from the cylinder body (photo).
8    Clean the wheel cylinder with brake fluid, denatured alcohol or brake system cleaner. Do not, under any circumstances, use petroleum based solvents to clean brake parts.
9    Use compressed air to remove excess fluid from the wheel cylinder and to blow out the passages.
10    Check the cylinder bore for corrosion and scoring. Crocus cloth may be used to remove light corrosion and stains, but the cylinder must be replaced with a new one if the defects cannot be removed easily, or if the bore is scored.
11    Lubricate the new seals with brake fluid.
12    Assemble the brake cylinder, making sure the boots are properly seated.

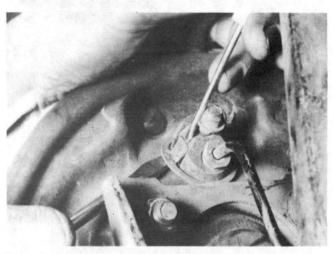

10.5   A pair of screwdrivers should be used to remove the wheel cylinder retainer

10.13   A wood block should be used to hold the wheel cylinder in position

## Installation

13  Place the wheel cylinder in position and use a wooden block wedged against the axle flange to hold it in place (photo).

14  Install the retainer over the wheel cylinder using a 1-1/8 inch 12 point socket to press it into place.

15  Connect the brake tube and install brake shoe assembly.

---

## 11  Master cylinder — removal, overhaul and installation

1  A master cylinder overhaul kit should be purchased before beginning this procedure. The kit will include all the replacement parts necessary for the overhaul procedure. The rubber replacement parts, particularly the seals, are the key to fluid control within the master cylinder. As such, it is very important that they be installed securely and facing in the proper direction. Be careful during the rebuild procedure that no grease or mineral-based solvents come in contact with the rubber parts.

2  Completely cover the front fender and cowling area of the vehicle, as brake fluid can ruin painted surfaces if it is spilled.

3  Disconnect the brake line connections. Rags or newspapers should be placed under the master cylinder to soak up the fluid that will drain out.

4  Remove the two master cylinder mounting nuts (photo), move the bracket retaining the combination valve forward slightly, taking care not to bend the hydraulic lines running to the combination valve, and remove the master cylinder from the vehicle.

5  Remove the reservoir cover and reservoir diaphragm, then discard any remaining fluid in the reservoir.

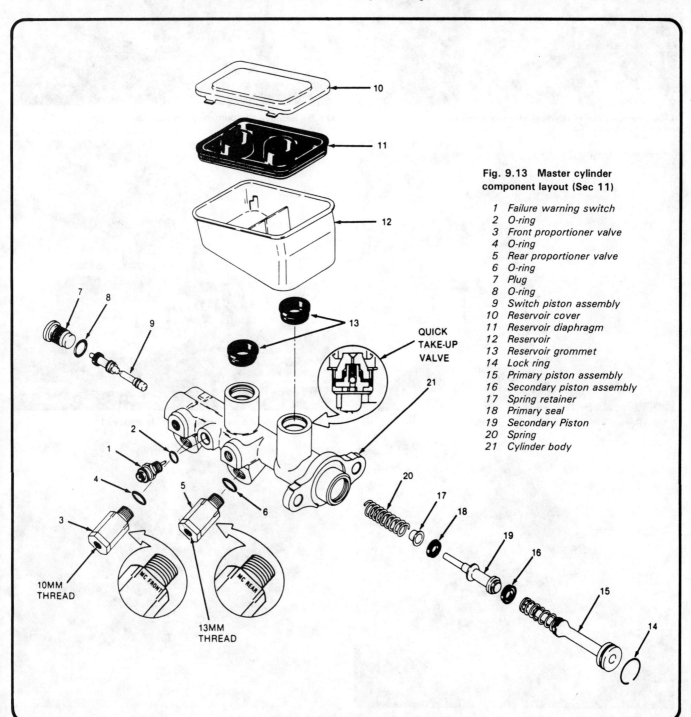

**Fig. 9.13  Master cylinder component layout (Sec 11)**

1   Failure warning switch
2   O-ring
3   Front proportioner valve
4   O-ring
5   Rear proportioner valve
6   O-ring
7   Plug
8   O-ring
9   Switch piston assembly
10  Reservoir cover
11  Reservoir diaphragm
12  Reservoir
13  Reservoir grommet
14  Lock ring
15  Primary piston assembly
16  Secondary piston assembly
17  Spring retainer
18  Primary seal
19  Secondary Piston
20  Spring
21  Cylinder body

QUICK TAKE-UP VALVE

10MM THREAD

13MM THREAD

11.4   Remove the master cylinder mounting nuts

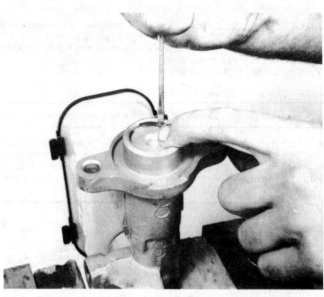

11.6   Remove the primary piston circlip

11.7   Remove the primary piston assembly

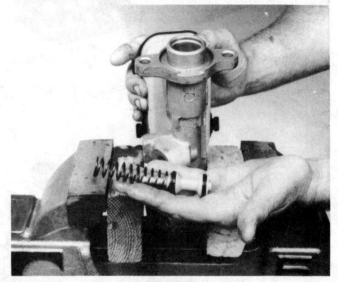

11.8   The secondary piston assembly removed

11.9a   Pry the plastic reservoir from the cylinder body

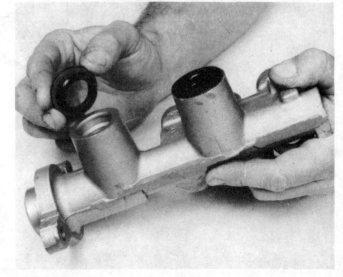

11.9b   Remove the reservoir grommets

6 Remove the primary piston lock ring by depressing the piston and prying the ring out with a screwdriver (photo).

7 Remove the primary piston assembly with a wire hook, being careful not to scratch the bore surface (photo).

8 Remove the secondary piston assembly in the same manner (photo).

9 Place the master cylinder in a vise and pry the reservoir from the cylinder body with a pry bar. Remove the reservoir grommets. (photo).

10 Do not attempt to remove the quick take-up valve from the cylinder body, as this valve is not serviceable.

11 With an Allen wrench, remove the switch piston plug and the switch piston assembly (photos). It may be necessary to lightly tap the master cylinder to remove the piston.

12 Inspect the cylinder bore for corrosion and damage. If any corrosion or damage is found, replace the master cylinder body with a new one, as abrasives cannot be used on the bore.

13 Lubricate the new reservoir grommets with silicone lubricant and press the grommets into the master cylinder body, making sure they are properly seated.

14 Lay the reservoir on a hard surface and press the master cylinder body onto the reservoir, using a rocking motion (photo).

15 Remove the old seals from the secondary piston assembly and install the new seals so that the cups face out (photo).

16 Attach the spring retainer to the secondary piston assembly.

17 Lubricate the cylinder bore with clean brake fluid and install the spring and secondary piston assembly in the cylinder (photo).

11.11a   Remove the switch piston plug

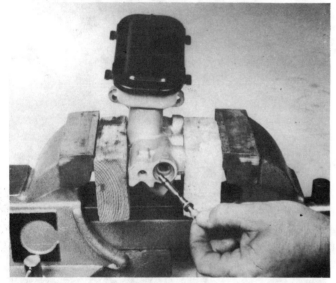

11.11b   Remove the switch piston assembly

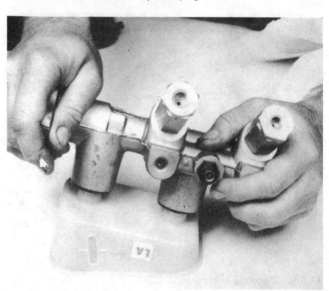

11.14   Use a rocking motion when pressing the reservoir onto the master cylinder

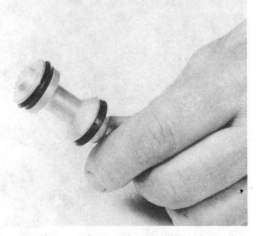

11.15   The secondary piston seals must be installed with the lips facing outwards as shown

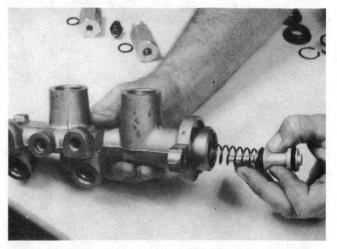

11.17   Install the secondary piston assembly

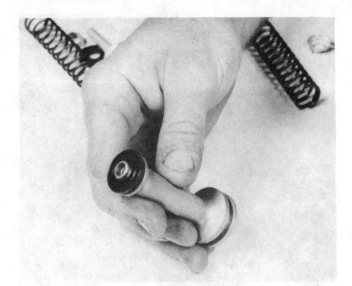

11.18a   The primary piston seal must be installed with the lip facing away from the piston

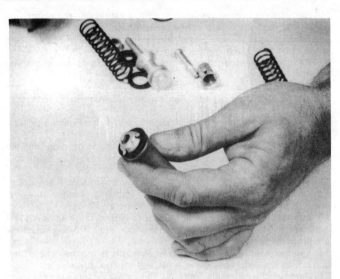

11.18b   Install the seal guard over the seal

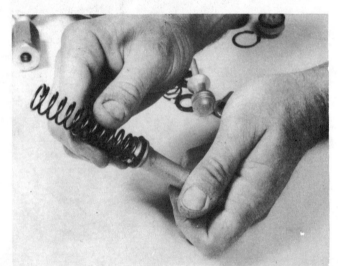

11.18c   Place the primary piston spring in position

11.18d   Insert the spring retainer into the spring

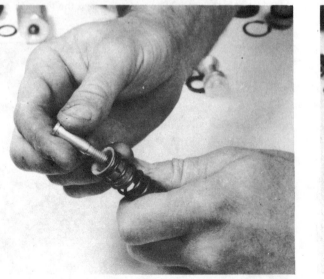

11.18e   Insert the spring retaining bolt through the retainer and spring and thread it into the piston

11.18f   Install the O-ring on the piston

18  Disassemble the primary piston assembly, noting the position of the parts, then lubricate the new seals with clean brake fluid and install them on the piston (photos).

19  Install the primary piston assembly in the cylinder bore, depress it and install the lock ring (photo).

20  Install the new O-rings on the switch piston and carefully insert it back into the master cylinder (photos).

21  Install a new O-ring on the piston plug and install the plug.

22  Inspect the reservoir cover and diaphragm for cracks and deformation. Replace any damaged parts with new ones and attach the diaphragm to the cover (photo).

23  **Note:** *Whenever the master cylinder is removed, the complete hydraulic system must be bled.* The time required to bleed the system can be reduced if the master cylinder is filled with fluid and bench bled (refer to Steps 24 through 27) before the master cylinder is installed on the vehicle.

24  Insert threaded plugs of the correct size into the cylinder outlet holes and fill the reservoirs with brake fluid. The master cylinder should be supported in such a manner that brake fluid will not spill during the bench bleeding procedure.

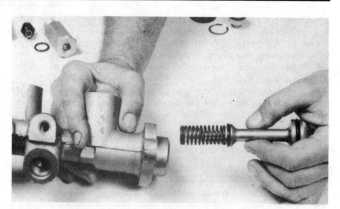

11.19  Install the primary piston assembly in the body

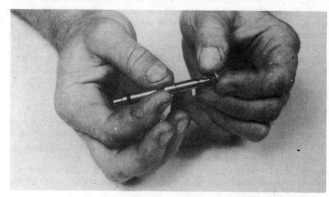

11.20b  Install the metal retainer on the switch piston

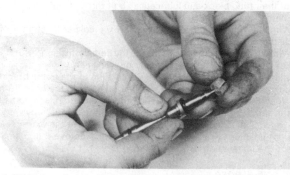

11.20d  Install the plastic retainer on the switch piston

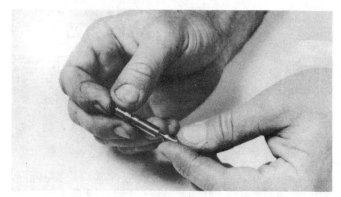

11.20a  Install the small O-ring on the switch piston

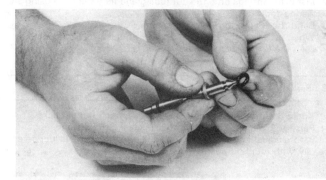

11.20c  Install the large O-ring on the switch piston

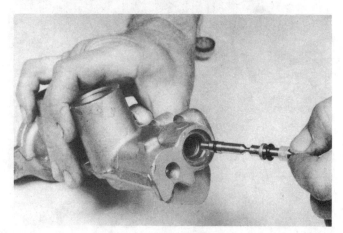

11.20e  Install the switch piston assembly into the cylinder body

11.22  Install the reservoir diaphragm into the cover

25  Loosen one plug at a time and push the piston assembly into the bore to force air from the master cylinder. To prevent air from being drawn back into the cylinder, the appropriate plug must be replaced before allowing the piston to return to its original position.
26  Stroke the piston three or four times for each outlet to assure that all air has been expelled.
27  Refill the master cylinder reservoirs and install the diaphragm and cover assembly. **Note:** *The reservoirs should only be filled to the top of the reservoir divider to prevent overflowing when the cover is installed.*
28  Carefully install the master cylinder by reversing the removal steps, then bleed the brakes at the wheel bleed valves (refer to Section 15).

## 12  Hydraulic brake hoses and lines — inspection and replacement

1    Every six months, with the vehicle raised and placed securely on jackstands, the flexible hoses which connect the steel brake lines with the front and rear brake assemblies should be inspected for cracks, chafing of the outer cover, leaks, blisters and other damage. These are important and vulnerable parts of the brake system and inspection should be complete. A light and mirror will prove helpful for a thorough check. If a hose exhibits any of the above conditions, replace it with a new one.

### Front brake hose

2    Using a back-up wrench, disconnect the brake line from the hose fitting, being careful not to bend the frame bracket or brake line.
3    Use pliers to remove the U-clip from the female fitting at the bracket, then remove the hose from the bracket.
4    At the caliper end of the hose, remove the bolt from the fitting block, then remove the hose and the copper gaskets on either side of the fitting block.
5    When installing the hose, always use new copper gaskets on either side of the fitting block and lubricate all bolt threads with clean brake fluid before installation.
6    With the fitting flange engaged with the caliper locating ledge, attach the hose to the caliper.
7    Without twisting the hose, install the female fitting in the hose bracket. It will fit the bracket in only one position.
8    Install the U-clip retaining the female fitting to the frame bracket.
9    Using a back-up wrench, attach the brake line to the hose fitting.
10  When the brake hose installation is complete, there should be no kinks in the hose. Make sure the hose does not contact any part of the suspension. Check this by turning the wheels to the extreme left and right positions. If the hose makes contact, remove the hose and correct the installation as necessary.

### Rear brake hose

11  Using a back-up wrench, disconnect the hose at both ends, being careful not to bend the bracket or steel lines.
12  Remove the two U-clips with pliers and separate the female fittings from the brackets.
13  Unbolt the hose retaining clip and remove the hose.
14  Without twisting the hose, install the female ends of the hose in the frame brackets. It will fit the bracket in only one position.
15  Install the U-clips retaining the female end to the bracket.
16  Using a back-up wrench, attach the steel line fittings to the female fittings. Again, be careful not to bend the bracket or steel line.
17  Check that the hose installation did not loosen the frame bracket. Tighten the bracket if necessary.
18  Fill the master cylinder reservoir and bleed the system (refer to Section 15).

### Steel brake lines

19  When it becomes necessary to replace steel lines, use only double-walled steel tubing. Never substitute copper tubing because copper is subject to fatigue cracking and corrosion. The outside diameter of the tubing is used for sizing.
20  Auto parts stores and brake supply houses carry various lengths of prefabricated brake line. These sections can either be bent by hand into the desired shape or can be bent in a tubing bender.
21  If prefabricated lengths are not available, obtain the recommended steel tubing and fittings to match the line to be replaced. Deter-

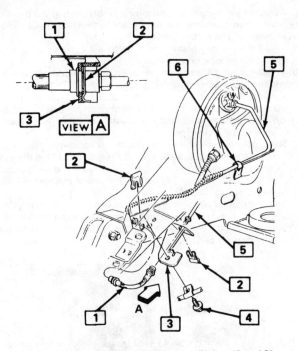

**Fig. 9.14  Rear brake hose installation (Sec 12)**

| | |
|---|---|
| 1  Hose | 4  Retainer bolt |
| 2  U-clip | 5  Brake tube |
| 3  Bracket | 6  Clip |

mine the correct length by measuring the old brake line, and cut the new tubing to length, leaving about 1/2-inch extra at each end for flaring.
22  Install the fittings onto the cut tubing and flare the ends using an ISO flaring tool.
23  Bend the tubing to match the shape of the old brake line.
24  When installing the brake line, leave at least 3/4-inch clearance between the line and any moving parts.

## 13  Parking brake — adjustment

1    Apply the parking brake pedal exactly three ratchet clicks.
2    Raise the vehicle and support it securely on jackstands.
3    Before adjusting, make sure the equalizer nut groove is lubricated liberally with multi-purpose lithium base grease (photo).

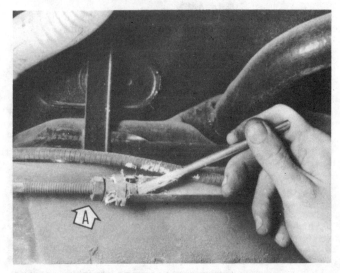

13.3  Lubricate the parking brake equalizer nut

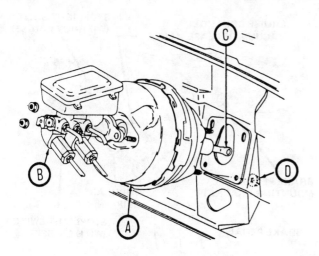

**Fig. 9.15  Brake booster installation details (Sec 14)**

A  *Booster*          C  *Pushrod*
B  *Master cylinder*  D  *Retaining nut*

4   Tighten the adjusting nut (A) until the right rear wheel can just be turned rearward with two hands, but locks when forward motion is attempted.
5   Release the parking brake lever and check to make sure the rear wheels turn freely in both directions with no drag.
6   Lower the vehicle.

## 14  Power brake booster — removal, inspection and installation

1   The power brake unit requires no special maintenance apart from periodic inspection of the hoses and inspection of the air filter beneath the boot at the pedal pushrod end.
2   Dismantling of the power brake unit requires special tools. If a problem develops, it is recommended that a new or factory-exchange unit be installed rather than trying to overhaul the original booster.
3   Remove the mounting nuts which hold the master cylinder to the power brake unit. Position the master cylinder out of the way, being careful not to strain the lines leading to the master cylinder. If there is any doubt as to the flexibility of the lines, disconnect them at the cylinder and plug the ends.
4   Disconnect the vacuum hose leading to the front of the power brake booster. Cover the end of the hose.
5   Loosen the four nuts that secure the booster to the firewall. Do not remove these nuts at this time.
6   Inside the vehicle, disconnect the power brake pushrod from the brake pedal. Do not force the pushrod to the side when disconnecting it.
7   Remove the four booster mounting nuts and carefully lift the unit out of the engine compartment (photo).
8   When installing, loosely install the four mounting nuts and connect the pushrod to the brake pedal. Tighten the nuts to the specified torque and reconnect the vacuum hose and master cylinder. If the hydraulic brake lines were disconnected, the entire brake system should be bled to eliminate any air which has entered the system (refer to Section 15).

## 15  Hydraulic system — bleeding

1   Bleeding the hydraulic system is necessary to remove air whenever it is introduced into the brake system.
2   It may be necessary to bleed the system at all four brakes if air has entered the system due to low fluid level, or if the brake lines have been disconnected at the master cylinder.
3   If a brake line was disconnected only at a wheel, then only that wheel cylinder or caliper must be bled.
4   If a brake line is disconnected at a fitting located between the

**14.7  Removing the power brake booster from the engine compartment**

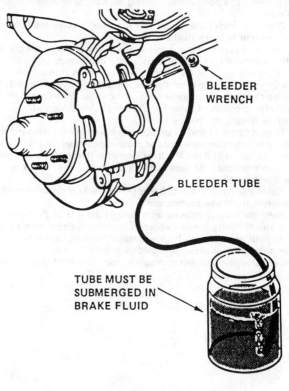

**Fig. 9.16  Details of the brake bleeding procedure (Sec 15)**

BLEEDER WRENCH
BLEEDER TUBE
TUBE MUST BE SUBMERGED IN BRAKE FLUID

master cylinder and any of the brakes, that part of the system served by the disconnected line must be bled.
5   If the master cylinder has been removed from the vehicle, refer to Section 11, Step 23 before proceeding.
6   If the master cylinder is installed on the vehicle but is known to have, or is suspected of having, air in the bore, the master cylinder must be bled before any wheel cylinder or caliper is bled. Follow Steps 7 through 16 to bleed the master cylinder while it is installed on the vehicle.
7   Remove the vacuum reserve from the brake power booster by

applying the brake several times with the engine off.

8   Remove the master cylinder reservoir cover and fill the reservoir with brake fluid. Keep checking the fluid level often during the bleeding operation, adding fluid as necessary to keep the reservoir full. Reinstall the cover.

9   Disconnect the forward brake line connection at the master cylinder.

10   Fill the master cylinder with brake fluid until it begins to flow from the forward line connector port. Have a container and shop rags handy to catch and clean up spilled fluid.

11   Reconnect the forward brake line to the master cylinder.

12   Have an assistant depress the brake pedal very slowly, one time only, and hold it down.

13   Loosen the forward brake line at the master cylinder to purge the air from the bore, retighten the connection, then have the brake pedal released slowly.

14   Wait 15 seconds (important).

15   Repeat the sequence, including the 15 second wait, until all air is removed from the bore.

16   After the forward port has been completely purged of air, bleed the rear port in the same manner.

17   To bleed the individual wheel cylinders or calipers, first refer to Steps 7 and 8.

18   Have an assistant on hand, as well as a supply of new brake fluid, an empty clear plastic container, a length of 3/16-inch plastic, rubber or vinyl tubing to fit over the bleeder valve and a wrench to open and close the bleeder valve. The vehicle may have to be raised and placed on jackstands for clearance.

19   Beginning at the right rear wheel, loosen the bleeder valve slightly, then tighten it to a point where it is snug but can still be loosened quickly and easily.

20   Place one end of the tubing over the bleeder valve and submerge the other end in brake fluid in the container.

21   Have the assistant pump the brakes a few times to get pressure in the system, then hold the pedal firmly depressed.

22   While the pedal is held depressed, open the bleeder valve just enough to allow a flow of fluid to leave the valve. Watch for air bubbles to exit the submerged end of the tube. When the fluid flow slows after a couple of seconds, close the valve again and have your assistant release the pedal.

23   Repeat Steps 21 and 22 until no more air is seen leaving the tube, then tighten the bleeder valve and proceed to the left rear wheel, the right front wheel and the left front wheel, in that order, and perform the same procedure. Be sure to check the fluid in the master cylinder reservoir frequently.

24   Never use old brake fluid because it attracts moisture which will deteriorate the brake system components.

25   Refill the master cylinder with fluid at the end of the operation.

26   If any difficulty is experienced in bleeding the hydraulic system, or if an assistant is not available, a pressure bleeding kit is a worthwhile investment. If connected in accordance with the instructions, each bleeder valve can be opened in turn to allow the fluid to be pressure

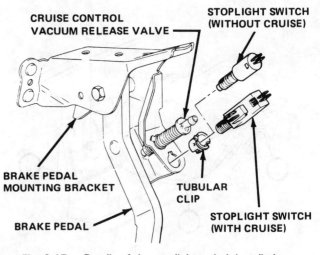

Fig. 9.17   Details of the stoplight switch installation (Sec 16)

ejected until it is clear of air bubbles without the need to replenish the master cylinder reservoir during the process.

---

## 16   Stop light switch — removal, installation and adjustment

1   The switch is located on a flange or bracket protruding from the brake pedal support.

2   With the brake pedal in the fully released position, the plunger on the body of the switch should be completely pressed in. When the pedal is pushed in, the plunger releases and sends electrical current to the stop lights.

3   If the stop lights are inoperative and it has been determined that the bulbs are not burned out, push the stop light switch into the tubular clip, noting that audible clicks can be heard as the threaded portion of the switch is pushed through the clip toward the brake pedal.

4   Pull the brake pedal all the way to the rear against the pedal stop until no further clicks can be heard. This will seat the switch in the tubular clip and provide the correct adjustment.

5   Release the brake pedal and repeat Step 4 to ensure that no further clicks can be heard.

6   Make sure that the stop lights are working.

7   If the lights are not working, disconnect the electrical connectors at the stop light switch and remove the switch from the clip.

8   Install a new switch and adjust it by performing Steps 3 through 6, making sure the electrical connectors are hooked up.

# Chapter 10 Suspension and steering systems

*Refer to Chapter 13 for Specifications and information applicable to 1986 and later models*

## Contents

Bleeding the power steering system .................. 32
Control arm bushing — removal and installation .......... 18
Front end alignment ................................ 3
Front hub and bearing assembly — removal and installation .. 13
Front shock absorbers — general information ........... 12
Front wheel stud — removal and installation ........... 14
Lower control arm balljoint — removal and installation ...... 8
Lower control arm — removal and installation ........... 7
Outer tie rod — removal and installation .............. 26
Power steering pump belt — adjustment ........ See Chapter 1
Power steering pump belt — removal
  and installation ........................ See Chapter 1
Power steering pump (L-4 engine) — removal
  and installation .............................. 29
Power steering pump (2.8 L V6 engine) — removal
  and installation .............................. 30
Power steering pump (3.0L and 3.8 L V6 engine) — removal
  and installation .............................. 31
Rack and pinion boot seal — removal and installation ...... 27
Rack and pinion — removal and installation ............. 28

Rear axle assembly — removal and installation ........... 19
Rear hub and bearing assembly — removal and installation .. 20
Rear shock absorber — removal, inspection
  and installation .............................. 15
Rear springs and insulators — removal and installation ..... 17
Rear wheel stud — removal and installation ............. 21
Stabilizer bar — removal and installation .............. 6
Steering column — removal and installation ............ 24
Steering knuckle — removal and installation ............ 25
Steering system — general information ................ 22
Steering wheel — removal and installation ............. 23
Strut damper assembly ............................. 11
Strut damper assembly — removal and installation ........ 9
Strut service preparation ........................... 10
Suspension system — general information .............. 4
Suspension system — inspection ..................... 5
Track bar — removal and installation ................. 16
Wheels and tires — general information ................ 1
Wheels and tires — removal and installation ............ 2

---

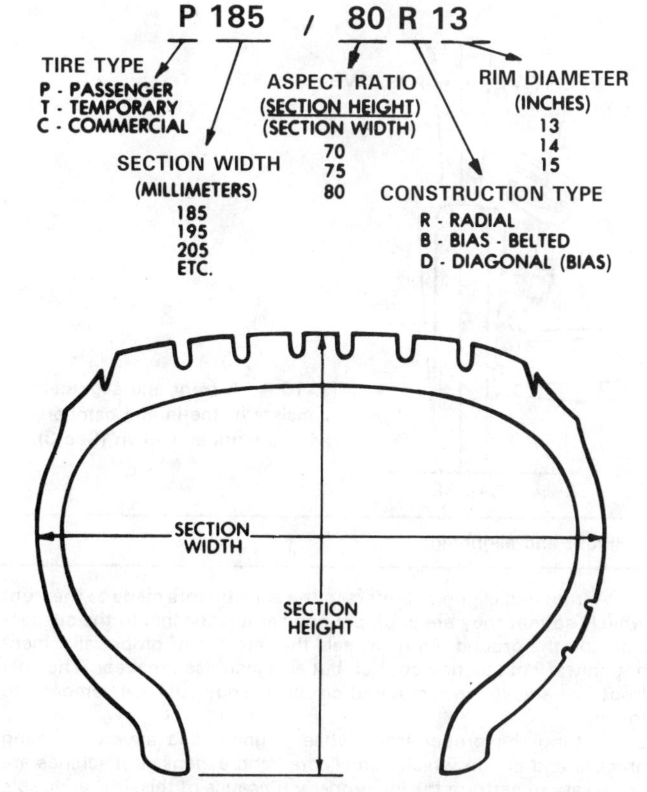

Fig. 10.1 Metric tire size code (Sec 1)

## 1  Wheels and tires — general information

1    All A-body cars are equipped with metric-sized fiberglass or steel belted radial tires. The metric tire size code is shown in Fig. 10.1. Use of other size or type of tires may affect the ride and handling of the car. Do not mix different types of tires, such as radials and bias belted, on the same car as handling may be seriously affected.

2    It is recommended that tires be replaced in pairs on the same axle, but if only one tire is being replaced, be sure it is of the same size, structure and tread design as the other.

3    Because tire pressure has a substantial effect on handling and wear, the pressure on all tires should be checked at least once a month or before any extended trips and set to the correct pressure. Tire pressure should be checked and adjusted with the tires cold.

4    To achieve the maximum life of your tires they should be rotated at 7500 miles and then again at every 15,000-mile interval.

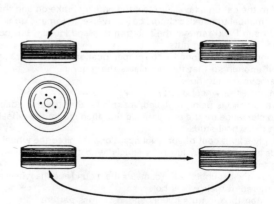

Fig. 10.2  Tires should be rotated as shown at recommended intervals (Sec 1)

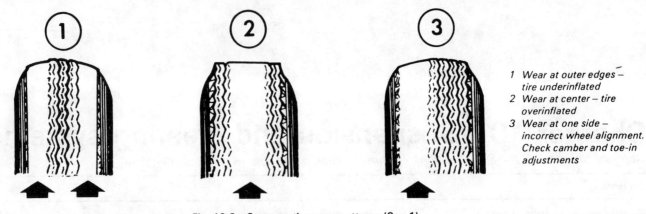

1 Wear at outer edges –
  tire underinflated
2 Wear at center – tire
  overinflated
3 Wear at one side –
  incorrect wheel alignment.
  Check camber and toe-in
  adjustments

Fig. 10.3   Common tire wear patterns (Sec 1)

5   The tires should be replaced when the depth of the tread is a minimum of 1/16-in (1.5 mm). Correct tire pressures and driving techniques have an important influence on tire life. Heavy cornering, excessively rapid acceleration and sharp braking increase tire wear. Extremely worn tires are not only very susceptible to going flat but are especially dangerous in wet weather conditions.

6   The tire tread pattern can give a good indication of problems in the maintenance or adjustment of tires, suspension and front end components. Fig. 10.3 gives some common examples of tire wear patterns and their usual causes. If a tire exhibits a wear pattern caused by incorrect front end alignment, refer to Section 3.

7   Wheels must be replaced if they are bent, dented, leak air, have elongated bolt holes, are heavily rusted, out of vertical symmetry or if the lug nuts won't stay tight. Wheel repairs that use welding or peening are not recommended, as this can weaken the metal.

8   Tire and wheel balance is important in the overall handling, braking and performance of the car. Unbalanced wheels can adversely affect handling and ride characteristics as well as tire life. Whenever a tire is installed on a wheel, the tire and wheel should be balanced by a shop with the proper equipment.

9   All A-body cars are equipped with a compact spare tire, which is designed to save space in the trunk as well as being easier to handle due to its lighter weight. The spare tire pressure should be checked at least once a month, and maintained at 70 psi (412 kPa).

10  The compact spare tire and wheel are designed for use with each other only, and neither the tire nor the wheel should be coupled with other types or size of wheels and tires.

11  Because the compact spare is designed as a temporary replacement for an out-of-service standard wheel and tire, the compact spare should be used on the car only until the standard wheel and tire are repaired or replaced. Continuous use of the compact spare at speeds of over 50 mph (80 kph) is not recommended. In addition, the expected tread life of the compact spare is only 3000 miles (4800 kilometers).

## 2   Wheels and tires — removal and installation

1   With the car on a level surface, the parking brake on and the car in gear (manual transaxles should be in Reverse, automatic transaxles should be in Park) remove the hub trim ring and loosen, but do not remove, the wheel lug nuts.

2   Using a jack positioned in the proper location on the car, raise the car just enough so that the tire clears the ground.

3   Remove the lug nuts.

4   Remove the wheel and tire.

5   If a flat tire is being replaced, make sure that there is adequate ground clearance for the new inflated tire, then mount the wheel and tire on the wheel studs.

6   Apply a light coat of spray lubricant or light oil to the wheel stud threads and install the lug nuts snugly with the cone-shaped end facing the wheel.

7   Lower the car until the tire contacts the ground and the wheel studs are centered in their wheel holes.

8   Tighten the lug nuts evenly and in a cross pattern.

9   Lower the car and remove the jack.

10  Replace the hub trim ring.

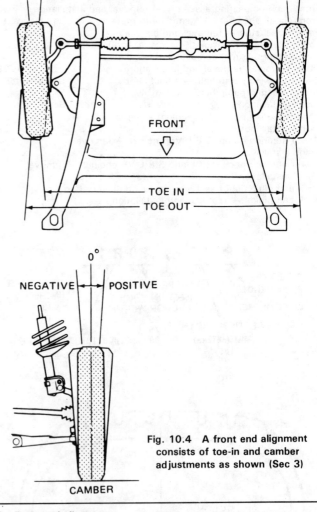

Fig. 10.4   A front end alignment
consists of toe-in and camber
adjustments as shown (Sec 3)

## 3   Front end alignment

1   A front end alignment refers to the adjustments made to the front wheels so that they are in proper angular relationship to the suspension and the ground. Front wheels that are out of proper alignment not only affect steering control, but also increase tire wear. The only front end adjustments required on the A-Body cars are camber and toe-in.

2   Getting the proper front wheel alignment is a very exacting process and one in which complicated and expensive machines are necessary to perform the job properly. Because of this, it is advisable to have a specialist with the proper equipment perform these tasks.

3   We will, however, use this space to give you a basic idea of what

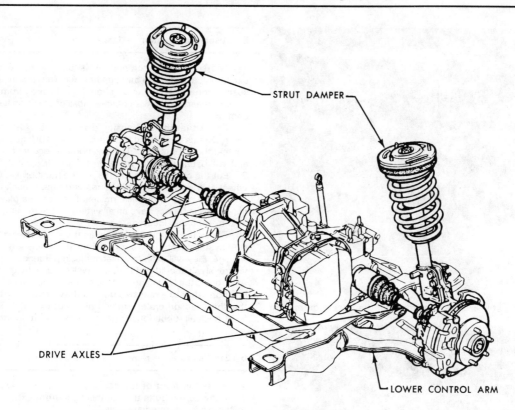

STRUT DAMPER

DRIVE AXLES

LOWER CONTROL ARM

**Fig. 10.5 The front suspension and driveaxle assemblies (Sec 4)**

is involved with front end alignment so you can better understand the process and deal intelligently with shops which do this work.

4   Toe-in is the turning in of the front wheels. The purpose of a toe specification is to ensure parallel rolling of the front wheels. In a car with zero toe-in, the distance between the front edges of the wheels will be the same as the distance between the rear edges of the wheels. The actual amount of toe in is normally only a fraction of an inch. The A-Body cars have a static toe-in of 2.5 mm per wheel. Thus the distance between the front edges of the wheels should be 5 mm less than the distance between the rear edges of the wheels when the car is standing. This is because even when the wheels are set to toe-in slightly when the vehicle is standing still, they tend to roll parallel on the road when the car is moving.

5   Toe-in adjustment is controlled by the outer tie rod's position on the inner tie rod. Incorrect toe-in will cause the tires to wear improperly by making them scrub against the road surface.

6   Camber is the tilting of the front wheels from the vertical when viewed from the front of the vehicle. When the wheels tilt outward at the top, the camber is said to be positive (+). When the wheels tilt inward at the top the camber is negative (-). The amount of tilt is measured in degrees from the vertical and this measurement is called the camber angle. This angle affects the amount of tire tread which contacts the road and compensates for changes in the suspension geometry when the car is cornering or travelling over undulating surface.

7   The camber is adjusted by rotating the cam bolts located where the strut damper assemblies are attached to the steering knuckles. The correct camber angle for the A-Body cars is $0.00° + 0.25°$.

## 4   Suspension system — general information

1   The A-Bodies feature an independent front suspension of the MacPherson Strut design. This design uses a combination strut and shock absorber assembly which is mounted directly to the steering knuckle. A lower control arm, which pivots on the engine cradle, is also attached to the steering knuckle by way of a balljoint.

2   To minimize the transmission of vibration to the body, rubber bushings are used in the lower control arm pivots in the engine cradle. The cradle also uses rubber bushings for isolation from the body. The

upper end of the strut is isolated by a rubber mount which contains the bearing for wheel turning.

3   The rear suspension consists of a rear axle assembly, two coil springs, two shock absorbers and a track bar. The rear axle has two control arms welded to it, which are used to mount the axle assembly to the body. These control arms, together with the track bar and shock absorbers, maintain the proper geometric relationship of the axle assembly to the body under the forces created by accelerating, braking and cornering. In addition, a non-serviceable stabilizer bar is welded to the inside of the axle housing.

4   The two coil springs support the weight of the car in the rear and are retained between seats in the underbody and rear axle housing. A rubber insulator is used to isolate the spring from the underbody seat.

5   The shock absorbers are conventional sealed hydraulic units. They are non-adjustable, non-refillable and cannot be disassembled. They are mounted at the bottom to a bracket on the axle housing and at the top to the body.

6   The track bar attaches to the left side of the axle housing and to the right side of the underbody to control side movement of the the axle assembly. Non-replaceable rubber bushings are used for mounting both ends of the bar.

7   The rear hub and bearing assemblies, mounted to either end of the rear axle, are single, sealed units and the bearing is not replaceable separate from the hub assembly.

8   An option to the conventional rear shock absorbers is GM's Superlift system. This system gives the car greater loading carrying flexibility by maintaining a level ride under heavy loads. The system consists of normal hydraulic shock absorbers with a pliable neoprene boot and an air cylinder, and is adjusted for different loads by varying the air pressure. Both Superlift shocks are filled by flexible air lines connected to one air valve located inside the fuel fill door. They are mounted in the same location as conventional shocks and are designed so that the shock absorber function is not impaired in the event of accidental air loss.

9   While the air lines used in the Superlift system are flexible, care should be taken not to kink them and to keep them a safe distance from all exhaust system parts.

10  To maintain the best ride characteristics with an empty car, the air pressure within the Superlift system should be kept at a minimum of 10 psi (70 kPa). To adjust for loads, the air pressure may be increased up to a maximum of 90 psi (620 kPa).

6.4   Remove the stabilizer bar bracket from the lower control arm

## 5   Suspension system — inspection

1   The suspension components should normally last a long time, except in cases where damage has occurred due to an accident. The suspension parts, however, should be checked from time to time for signs of wear, which will result in a loss of precision handling and riding comfort.

2   Check that the suspension components have not sagged due to wear. Do this by parking the car on a level surface and visually checking that the car sits level. This will normally occur only after many miles and will usually appear more on the driver's side of the vehicle.

3   Put the car in gear and take off the hand brake. Grip the steering wheel at the top with both hands and rock it back and forth. Listen for any squeaks or metallic noises. Feel for free play. If any of these conditions is found, have an assistant do the rocking while the source of the trouble is located.

4   Check the shock absorbers, as these are the parts of the suspension system likely to wear out first. If there is any evidence of fluid leakage, they will definitely need replacing. Bounce the car up and down vigorously. It should feel stiff, and well damped by the shock absorbers. As soon as the bouncing is stopped the car should return to its normal position without excessive up and down movement. Do not replace the shock absorbers as single units, but rather in pairs.

5   Check all rubber bushings for signs of deterioration and cracking.

## 6   Stabilizer bar — removal and installation

1   Raise the front of the car and support it on jackstands.

2   Remove the bolts that connect the front exhaust crossover pipe to the front intermediate pipe.

3   Disconnect the front crossover pipe from the exhaust manifold and remove.

4   Remove the bolts that secure the stabilizer brackets to the lower control arm and remove the brackets (photo).

5   Remove the bolts that secure the stabilizer mounting plates to the engine cradle and remove both plates (photo).

6   Remove the stabilizer bar from its recesses in the engine cradle, complete with bushings and center brackets. The bushings need not be removed from the stabilizer bar unless either the bushings or the bar are being replaced (photo).

7   Inspect the bushings to be sure they are not hardened, cracked or excessively worn, and replace if necessary.

8   Installation is the reverse of the removal procedure.

6.5   Remove the stabilizer bar mounting plate from the engine cradle

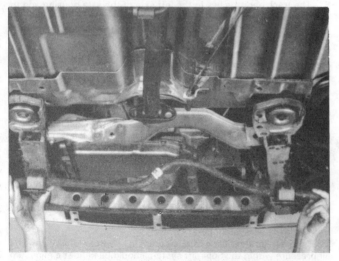

6.6   Remove the stabilizer bar complete with bushings and brackets

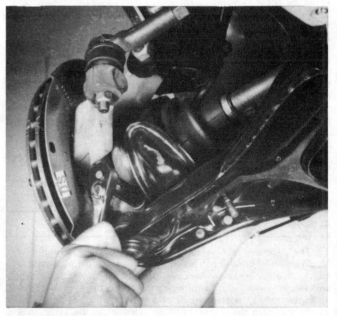

7.4   Remove the pinch bolt that secures the balljoint to the steering knuckle

## 7   Lower control arm — removal and installation

1   Raise the front of the car and support it on jackstands.
2   If only one lower control arm is being removed, disconnect only that end of the stabilizer bar. If both lower control arms are being removed, remove the stabilizer bar completely. Refer to Section 6.
3   Remove the wheel.
4   Remove the bolt that retains the balljoint to the steering knuckle (photo).
5   Remove the balljoint from the steering knuckle (photo).
6   Remove the control arm bushing bolts that secure the control arm to the engine cradle.
7   Remove the control arm. The balljoint does not have to be removed from the control arm unless it needs replacing (photo).
8   Inspect the control arm bushings for hardening, cracking or excessive wear and replace if necessary.
9   Installation of the lower control arm is the reverse of the removal procedure. **Note:** *Do not tighten the bushing bolts to their specified torque until the car has been lowered to the ground and its full weight is on the suspension.*

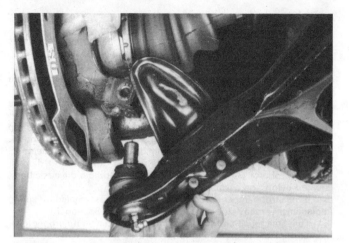

7.5   Remove the lower balljoint from the steering knuckle

## 8   Lower control arm balljoint — removal and installation

1   Raise the front of the car and support it on jackstands.
2   Remove the wheel.
3   Remove the bolt that retains the balljoint to the brake caliper bracket and disconnect the balljoint from the bracket.
4   Using a 1/8-inch drill bit, drill approximately 1/4-inch deep into the center of the rivets that secure the balljoint to the lower control arm.
5   Using a 1/2-inch drill bit, drill just deep enough to remove the rivet heads.
6   Punch out the remainder of the rivets and remove the balljoint.
7   When reinstalling the balljoint to the lower control arm, use nuts and bolts to replace the rivets.
8   Install the balljoint into the steering knuckle, tightening the bolt and nut to the proper torque.
9   Mount the wheel and lower the car to the ground.

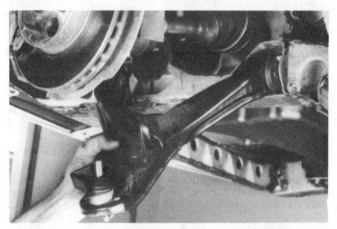

7.7   Remove the lower control arm from the engine cradle

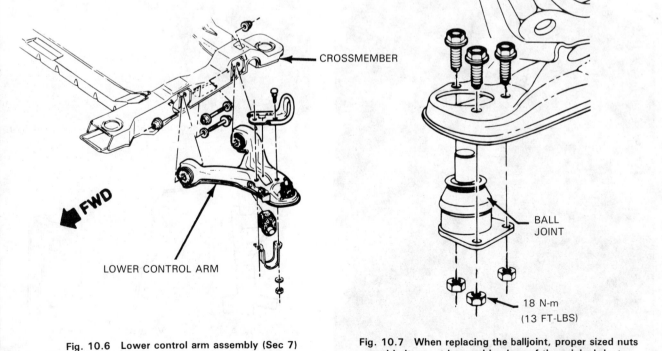

CROSSMEMBER

FWD

LOWER CONTROL ARM

BALL JOINT

18 N-m
(13 FT-LBS)

Fig. 10.6   Lower control arm assembly (Sec 7)

Fig. 10.7   When replacing the balljoint, proper sized nuts and bolts must be used in place of the original rivets (Sec 8)

## 9   Strut damper assembly — removal and installation

1    Raise the front of the car and support it on jackstands.
2    Remove the wheel.
3    Refer to Section 10 and scribe the strut assembly to retain the same camber adjustment upon reinstallation.
4    Loosen, but do not yet remove, the two strut-to-steering knuckle bolts (photo).
5    Loosen, but do not yet remove, the three nuts securing the top of the strut assembly to the shock well, underneath the hood (photo).
6    Disconnect the brake line clip from its mounting tab on the strut.
7    Remove all of the loosened bolts and lift out the strut damper assembly (photo). Be careful not to damage the rubber driveaxle boot, located below the assembly, during removal.
8    If the strut damper assembly needs to be disassembled for spring replacement, follow the procedure described in Section 11.
9    To install, position the strut damper assembly in its proper location and install its upper and lower mounting bolts.
10   Place a jack under the hub and disc brake rotor assembly to hold it in position.
11   Lower the car enough to set the cam adjuster in its position as marked in Step 3.
12   Install the brake line clip to its mounting tab on the front strut.
13   Tighten all the strut damper assembly mounting nuts to the specified torque.
14   Install the wheel and lower the car.
15   If the strut damper assembly has been replaced, a front end alignment check is necessary. See Section 3.

## 10   Strut service preparation

*Refer to Fig. 10.8*

1    To eliminate the need to readjust the camber setting when servicing the strut mount, jounce bumper, strut shield, spring seat or spring insulator, or when removing the driveaxles, the following marking pro-

9.4   Break loose the two strut-to-steering knuckle nuts and bolts

9.5   Loosen the three strut damper assembly upper mounting nuts

9.7   Carefully remove the strut damper assembly

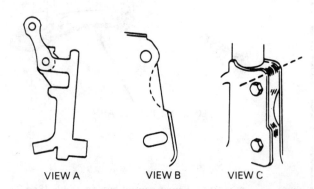

VIEW A              VIEW B              VIEW C

Fig. 10.8   Prior to certain front end operations listed in the text, the positioning of the strut to the knuckle must be carefully marked as shown (Sec 10)

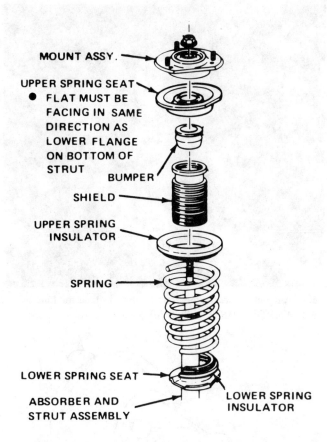

MOUNT ASSY.

UPPER SPRING SEAT
● FLAT MUST BE
FACING IN SAME
DIRECTION AS
LOWER FLANGE
ON BOTTOM OF
STRUT
BUMPER

SHIELD

UPPER SPRING
INSULATOR

SPRING

LOWER SPRING SEAT

ABSORBER AND
STRUT ASSEMBLY

LOWER SPRING
INSULATOR

**Fig. 10.9  The strut damper assembly (Sec 11)**

cedure should be preformed prior to such operations. **Note:** *This procedure is only to return the camber to its approximate setting. The camber setting as well as the toe-in setting should be checked and adjusted after any major service to the front suspension.*

2    Use a sharp tool to scribe a line on the knuckle marking the position of the lower part of the strut mount. Refer to view A of the accompanying illustration.

3    Scribe a line on the inner side of the strut flange, along the curve of the knuckle. Refer to view B of the accompanying illustration.

4    Make matching marks on the knuckle and strut mount at the upper corner of the mount as shown in view C of the accompanying illustration.

5    After completing the required service, be sure that these marks are properly aligned.

## 11  Strut damper assembly — disassembly and reassembly

1    The spring on the front shock absorber is under considerable pressure, requiring that a spring compressor be used to compress the spring and disengage its components. Do not attempt to disassemble the spring without a compressor, as serious injury can occur.

2    A strut spring compressor can either be purchased through GM dealers or through most auto parts stores. Compressors can also be rented on a daily basis from rental agencies and some auto parts stores.

3    Hold the shock in a vise, using wood blocks to cushion the jaws, preventing damage to the shock.

4    Follow the manufacturer's instructions for the particular spring compressor being used. Slightly compress the spring, making sure that the jaws of the compressor are firmly seated around the coils and cannot slip off (photo).

5    Tighten the compressor from side to side, a little at a time, until the spring seat is clear of the uppermost coil.

6    With the spring firmly compressed and clear of its seat, remove the top locknut and washer (photo).

7    Pull the mounting off the top of the shock absorber assembly.

8    Remove the spring seat, bumper, shield and insulator.

9    Relieve the tension on the spring and remove it from the shock absorber. Loosen the compressor a little at a time until it is free to be lifted off the shock absorber body. Although some compressors allow you to lift the spring off the shock absorber in its compressed state, this could prove dangerous should the compressor and spring be jostled and accidentally disengaged from each other.

10   The spring should be checked for cracking or deformation of any kind. If the vehicle was sagging in the front, this is an indication that the springs are in need of replacement.

11   Test the front shock absorbers as described in Section 12.

12   Using the spring compressor, compress the spring approximately 2-inch (50.8 mm). With the shock absorber main body mounted in a

11.4   A spring compressor must be used to disassemble the strut damper assembly

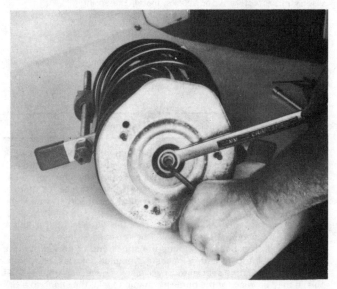

11.6   With the spring compressed remove the strut assembly upper retaining nut

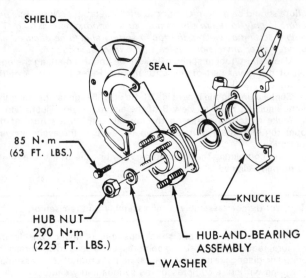

Fig. 10.10   The front hub and bearing assembly and related components (Sec 13)

13.3   A punch or screwdriver can be used to hold the hub stationary while removing the hub nut

13.6   Remove the front hub and bearing retaining bolts

vise with protective wood blocks, install the spring.
13   Install the insulator, shield and bumper to the shock body.
14   Install the spring seat.
15   Install the mounting assembly.
16   Install the lockwasher and locknut to the top of the piston rod.
17   Carefully relieve tension on the spring by loosening the compressor from side to side, a little at a time. Check to be sure the top of the spring is raised properly into its seat.

## 12   Front shock absorbers — general information

1   To test the shock absorber, hold it in an upright position and work the piston rod up and down its full length of travel. If you can feel a strong resistance because of hydraulic pressure, the shock absorber is functioning properly. If you feel no marked resistance, or there is a sudden free movement in travel, the shock absorber should be replaced.
2   If there is fluid leakage evident on the outside of the shock absorber, the shock absorber should be replaced.
3   Although it is possible to strip the shock and fit new parts, the work is very intricate and demands extreme cleanliness. Numerous small parts and some special tools will also be necessary. Because of this, it may be wise for the home mechanic to take the shock to a GM dealer or repair shop specializing in MacPherson strut shock absorbers to install a replacement cartridge.

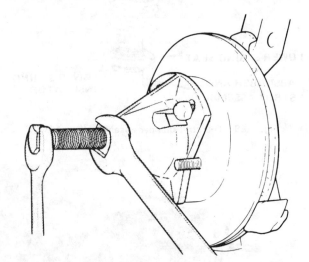

Fig. 10.11   A puller must be used to remove the front hub and bearing assembly from the driveaxle (Sec 13)

## 13   Front hub and bearing assembly — removal and installation

*Refer to Fig. 10.10*
1   Break loose the hub nut.
2   Raise the front of the car and support it on jackstands.
3   Remove the front wheel. Insert a punch through the caliper and into the rotor to allow removal of the hub nut (photo).
4   Remove the disc brake caliper as described in Chapter 9. **Note:** *It is not necessary to disconnect the brake line.*
5   Remove the the brake rotor.
6   Remove the hub and bearing assembly attaching bolts (photo). If the old assembly is to be reinstalled, mark the attaching bolts so they can be installed in the same holes from which they were removed.
7   Using a GM special tool or equivalent puller as shown, remove the hub and bearing assembly from the drive axle.
8   Spin the bearing with your finger and check for any roughness or noise. Check the bearing mating surfaces and steering knuckle bore for dirt or nicks. This assembly is a sealed unit and if the bearing needs replacing, the entire hub and bearing assembly must be replaced.
9   If the hub and bearing assembly is being replaced, a new steering knuckle seal must be installed in the steering knuckle prior to installation of the hub and bearing assembly. This is done by applying grease

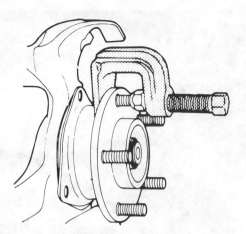

**Fig. 10.12  Pressing out a wheel stud from the hub and bearing assembly (Sec 14)**

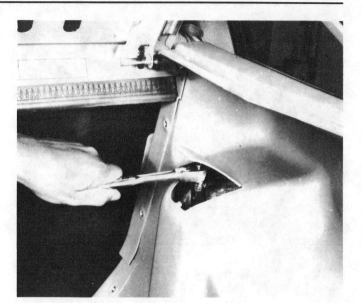

15.1  On hatchback models the trim cover access panel must be lifted to expose the top shock mount

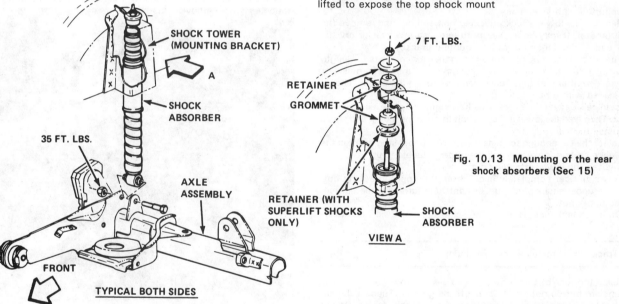

SHOCK TOWER (MOUNTING BRACKET)

A

SHOCK ABSORBER

35 FT. LBS.

AXLE ASSEMBLY

FRONT

**TYPICAL BOTH SIDES**

7 FT. LBS.

RETAINER

GROMMET

RETAINER (WITH SUPERLIFT SHOCKS ONLY)

SHOCK ABSORBER

**VIEW A**

**Fig. 10.13  Mounting of the rear shock absorbers (Sec 15)**

to the seal and its bore in the steering knuckle and then taping the seal into place using a hammer and a socket.

10  Install the hub and bearing assembly onto the axleshaft. Install the hub nut onto the axleshaft and tighten it until the hub and bearing assembly is seated.

11  Install the shield and hub assembly attaching bolts.

12  Remove the hub nut, install the rotor on the axleshaft and replace the hub nut on the shaft.

13  Install the brake caliper.

14  Install the wheel and lower the car to the ground.

15  Tighten the hub nut to the specified torque (see Chapter 8).

## 14  Front wheel stud — removal and installation

1  Raise the front of the car and support it on jackstands.

2  Remove the wheel.

3  Remove the brake caliper as described in Chapter 9.

4  Remove the rotor as described in Chapter 9.

5  Remove the splash shield.

6  Position the stud to be replaced at either the 5 or 7 o'clock position. Install a lug nut onto the end of the stud and, using a GM special tool or equivalent, press the stud from its seat.

7  Remove the lug nut, then the stud.

8  With the stud hole at either the 5 or 7 o'clock position, insert the new stud in the hole, making sure the serrations are aligned with those made by the original bolt.

9  Place four flat washers over the outside end of the stud, then thread a lug nut onto the stud.

10  Tighten the lug nut until the stud head seats against the rear of the hub. Remove the lug nut and washers.

11  Reinstall the splash shield, rotor and caliper.

12  Mount the wheel and lower the car to the ground.

## 15  Rear shock absorber — removal, inspection and installation

1  In the rear compartment of the car, open the upper shock nut access panel in the trim cover (hatchbacks only) and remove the upper shock nut (photo). The upper shock stud must be kept from turning while the nut is loosened.

2  Raise the rear of the car enough to take the weight off of the suspension, but do not lift the tires off the ground. Support the car with jackstands placed at suitable locations under the car's frame. Do not place them under the rear axle. If more clearance is needed under the car, the car can be raised higher, but then the rear axle must also

15.3   Remove the lower shock mounting bolt

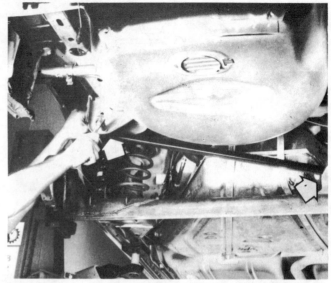

16.2   Remove both mounting nuts and bolts on the track bar

be supported with jackstands.

3    Remove the lower shock attaching bolt and nut and remove the shock (photo). It may be necessary to use a screwdriver to pry the lower end of the shock out of its mounting bracket.

4    The shock should be compressed and then extended its full length a few times to check for any free movement of the shaft, noise, or fluid leakage. If any of these conditions are found the shocks should be replaced with a new set.

5    To install, extend the shock to its full length and place it in its lower mount. Then feed the lower attaching bolt through the mount and shock and install the nut loosely.

6    Lower the car enough to guide the shock's upper stud through the body opening and loosely install the upper attaching nut.

7    Tighten the lower attaching nut.

8    Lower the car completely and tighten the upper attaching nut. Again the upper shock stud must be kept from turning while tightening the upper nut.

9    On hatchback models, close the access panel in the trim cover.

## 16   Track bar — removal and installation

1    Raise the rear of the car enough to take the weight off of the suspension, but do not lift the tires off the ground. Support the car with jackstands placed at suitable locations under the frame. Do not place them under the rear axle. If more clearance is needed under the car, the car can be raised higher, but then the rear axle must also be supported with jackstands.

2    Remove the nuts and bolts securing the track bar at both ends (photo).

3    Remove the track bar.

4    Inspect the bushings for hardening, cracking or excessive wear. If they exhibit any of these conditions, the track bar must be replaced.

5    To install, place the left end of the track bar in the body mount and loosely install the bolt and nut. The open side of the bar must face to the rear.

6    Place the other end of the bar in the axle mount and loosely install the bolt and nut. Both nuts must face the rear of the car.

7    Lower the car to the ground.

8    Tighten both nuts to the specified torque.

## 17   Rear springs and insulators — removal and installation

1    Raise the rear of the car and support it with jackstands placed at suitable locations under the frame.

2    Support the rear axle with a floor jack. Such jacks can be rented on a daily basis from rental agencies and some auto parts stores.

3    Remove the wheels and brake drums.

17.9   After lowering the rear axle, remove the rear springs

4    Disconnect the parking brake cable by loosening the adjustment nut and prying forward on the parking brake equalizer lever to disconnect the forward cable from the equalizer lever.

5    Twist the equalizer lever and disengage it from the pivot mount on the body.

6    Remove the bolts attaching the brake line brackets to the chassis on both the left and right sides.

7    Remove the track bar as described in Section 16.

8    Remove the lower shock attaching nuts and bolts from both shock absorbers.

9    Lower the rear axle enough to remove the springs and insulators (photo). Do not suspend the rear axle by the brake hoses, as this could damage the hoses.

10   If the insulators are worn, cracked or damaged, they should be replaced.

11   Inspect the springs for cracks or other damage. If they exhibit any of these conditions, or if the car has been sagging in the rear, the springs should be replaced. The rear springs should always be replaced as a pair.

12   Installation is the reverse of the removal procedure. **Note:** *When installing the springs, be sure they are in the proper position as shown in the accompanying illustration.*

13   Adjust the parking brake as described in Chapter 9.

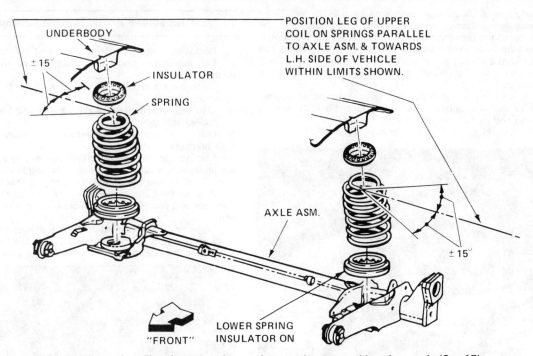

Fig. 10.14  When reinstalling the rear springs make sure they are positioned correctly (Sec 17)

18.8  Remove the four rear axle control arm mounting bolts

### 18  Control arm bushing — removal and installation

1   Raise the rear of the car and support it with jackstands positioned at suitable locations under the frame.
2   Support the rear axle with a floor jack. A jack such as this can be rented on a daily basis from a rental agency or some auto parts stores.
3   Remove the wheels and brake drums.
4   If the right control arm bushing is being replaced, loosen the parking brake adjustment nut and disconnect the forward cable from the parking brake equalizer lever by prying forward on the equalizer lever. Twist the equalizer lever to disengage it from the pivot mount on the body.
5   Remove the bolts attaching the brake line brackets to the chassis.
6   Remove the lower shock attaching nuts and bolts.
7   Remove the springs.
8   Remove the bolts securing the control arm bracket to the underbody (photo) and allow the control arm to rotate downward.
9   Remove the control arm bracket from the control arm.
10  Removal of the old bushing and installation of the new one must

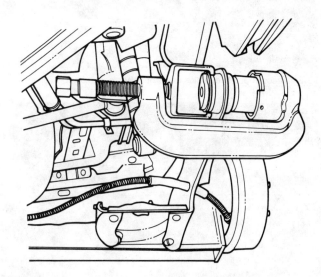

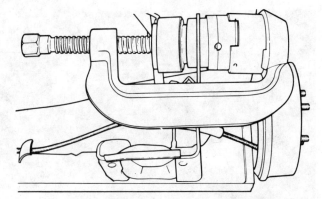

Fig. 10.15  Removing and installing the control arm bushing (Sec 18)

be done using special GM tools or equivalents, such as the one shown in the accompanying illustration. When installing, the cutouts on the rubber portion of the bushing must face toward the front and rear.

11  Remount the control arm bracket to the control arm and check that it is positioned at a 45 degree angle to the lower edge of the control arm. When the proper angle is set, tighten the nut and torque it to the specified torque.

12  Install the various components by reversing the removal procedure. Do not tighten the lower shock nuts to specifications until the car has been lowered and its full weight is on the suspension.

13  Adjust the parking brake as described in Chapter 9.

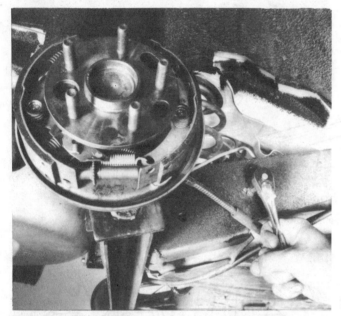

19.2   Disconnect the brake line from the rear axle control arm

19.6   Allow the parking brake assembly to hang from the right backing plate

## 19   Rear axle assembly — removal and installation

1    Remove the rear springs as described in Section 17.

2    Disconnect the brake lines from the control arm attachment (photo).

3    Disconnect and cap the rigid brake lines from both rear brake cylinders.

4    Disconnect the right rear parking brake cable from the left rear parking brake cable (photo).

5    Disconnect the right rear and left rear parking brake cables from their brackets on the rear axle.

6    Remove the bolts securing the rear parking brake cable guide to the underbody and allow the entire parking brake assembly to hang from the right rear backing plate as shown (photo).

7    Remove the bolts securing the hub and bearing assembly to the rear axle and remove the assemblies along with the brake backing plates.

8    While an assistant steadies the rear axle on the jack, remove the bolts securing the control arm brackets to the body.

9    Lower the rear axle and remove it from under the car (photo).

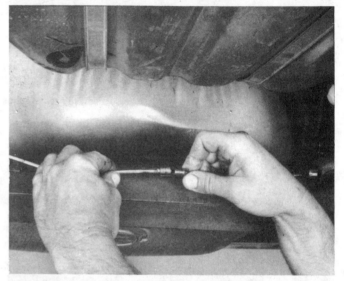

19.4   Disconnect the right rear parking brake cable from the left rear cable

19.9   Carefully remove the rear axle

10 If the rear axle is being replaced, remove the control arm brackets from the control arms and install them on the new axle.
11 Inspect the control arm bushings for cracking, hardening or other damage and replace if necessary as described in Section 18.
12 Prior to installation, lay the axle on a flat surface and, using an angle measuring instrument, make sure the lower edge of the control arms are on a horizontal plane (photo). Measure the control arm brackets. These should be on an angle of 45 degrees to the horizontal plane or the lower edge of the control arm (photo). If they are at a different angle, loosen the bracket nuts and adjust them to a 45 degree angle.
13 Installation of the rear axle is the reverse of the removal procedure. Do not tighten the lower shock nuts and track arm nuts to specification until after the car has been lowered and the full weight of the car is on the suspension.
14 Bleed the brake system as described in Chapter 9.
15 Adjust the parking brake as described in Chapter 9.

## 20 Rear hub and bearing assembly — removal and installation

1 Raise the rear of the car and support it on jackstands.
2 Remove the wheel and brake drum.
3 Remove the brake shoes as described in Chapter 9.
4 Remove the bolts securing the hub and bearing assembly to the rear axle and remove the assembly.
5 Spin the bearing with your fingers and check for any roughness or noise. This assembly is a sealed unit and if the bearing needs replacing the entire hub and bearing assembly must be replaced.
6 Installation is the reverse of the removal procedure.

## 21 Rear wheel stud — removal and installation

1 Raise the rear of the car and support it on jackstands.
2 Remove the wheel and brake drum.
3 Install a lug nut on the end of the stud and, using a GM tool or equivalent as shown in the accompanying illustration, press the stud from its seat.
4 Remove the lug nut and remove the stud.
5 Insert the new stud in the hole, making sure the serrations are aligned with those made by the original bolt.
6 Place four flat washers over the stud and thread a lug nut onto the stud.
7 Tighten the lug nut until the stud head seats against the rear of the hub. Remove the lug nut and washers.
8 Install the brake drum and wheel and lower the car to the ground.

## 22 Steering system — general information

1 All models of the A-Body cars use a rack and pinion steering system. The components making up the system are the steering wheel, steering column, intermediate shaft, rack and pinion assembly, tie rods and steering knuckles. The power steering system uses a belt-driven pump to provide hydraulic pressure.
2 In a manual system, the motion of turning the steering wheel is transferred through the column and intermediate shaft to the pinion shaft in the rack and pinion assembly. Teeth on the pinion shaft are meshed with teeth on the rack, so when the shaft is turned, the rack is moved left or right in the housing. Attached to each end of the rack are tie rods which, in turn, are attached to the steering knuckles on the front wheels. This left and right movement of the rack is the direct force which turns the wheels.
3 The power steering system operates in essentially the same way as the manual system, except that the power rack and pinion system uses hydraulic pressure to boost the manual steering force. A rotary control valve in the rack and pinion assembly directs hydraulic fluid from the power steering pump to either side of the integral rack piston, which is attached to the rack. Depending on which side of the piston this hydraulic pressure is applied to, the rack will be forced either left or right, which moves the tie rods, etc.
4 If the power steering system loses its hydraulic pressure it will still

19.12a  Support the rear axle so that the lower edge of the control arm is on a horizontal line

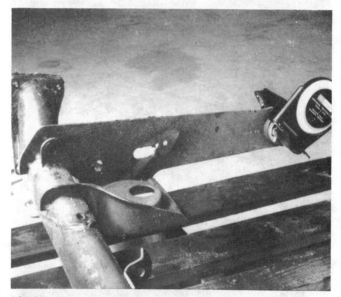

19.12b  The angle of the control arm bracket to lower edge of the control arm should be 45 degrees

function manually, though with increased effort.
5 The steering column is of the collapsible, energy-absorbing type, designed to compress in the event of a front end collision to minimize injury to the driver. The column also houses the ignition switch lock, key warning buzzer, turn signal controls, headlight dimmer control and windshield wiper controls. The ignition and steering wheel can both be locked while the car is parked to inhibit theft.
6 Due to the column's collapsible design, it is important that only specified screws, bolts and nuts can be used as designated and that they be tightened to the specified torque. Other precautions particular to this design are noted in appropriate Sections.
7 In addition to the standard steering column, optional tilt and key-release versions are also offered. The tilt model can be set in five different positions, while with the key release model the ignition key is locked in the column until a lever is depressed to extract it.
8 Because disassembly of the steering column is more often performed to repair a switch or other electrical part than to correct a problem in the steering functioning, the steering column disassembly and reassembly procedure is included in Chapter 12.

## 23 Steering wheel — removal and installation

1 Disconnect the negative battery cable.
2 On standard steering wheels remove the two screws securing the

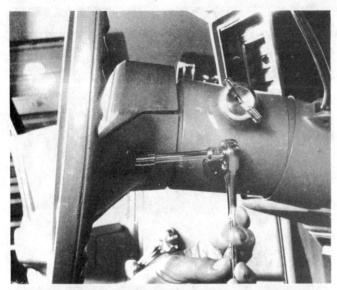

23.2a   Remove the two horn cover screws from the steering wheel

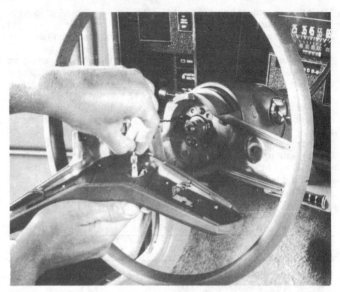

23.2b   After removing the horn cover disconnect the horn wire

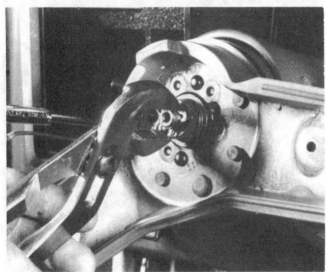

23.4   Remove the steering wheel nut retainer

23.6   Mark the relationship of the steering wheel to the steering shaft

23.7   A steering wheel puller can be used to remove the steering wheel

23.8   A slight twist will disengage the horn lead from the steering column

24.4 Remove the steering column trim cover from the dash and disconnect the vent tube if equipped

horn cover to the steering wheel (photo). Lift off the horn cover and disconnect the horn wire (photo).
3 On sport steering wheels pry off the center cap.
4 Using slip joint pliers, remove the steering wheel nut retainer (photo).
5 Be sure the steering wheel is unlocked, then remove the steering wheel nut.
6 Mark the position of the steering wheel in relation to the steering shaft. (photo).
7 Using a GM special tool or equivalent steering wheel puller, remove the steering wheel. **Note:** *Under no circumstances should the end of the shaft be hammered on, as impact of this nature could loosen the plastic injections which maintain the column's rigidity (photo).*
8 Remove the horn lead, complete with spring from the steering column (photo).
9 Installation is the reverse of the removal procedure with the following note: When installing the steering wheel on the shaft be sure the alignment marks on the steering wheel and shaft match.

## 24 Steering column — removal and installation

1 Although it is not mandatory, the steering column removal operation can be made much easier by first removing the front seat.
2 Disconnect the negative cable at the battery terminal.
3 If the column is to be disassembled after it is removed from the vehicle, the steering wheel should be removed as described in Section 23. If the column is to be kept as one piece, removal of the steering wheel is not necessary.
4 Remove the screws securing the steering column trim cover to the dash and lift off the cover. On cars with air conditioning, disconnect the vent hose when you remove the cover (photo).
5 Disconnect all electrical connections from the steering column, including those from the dimmer switch, windshield wiper switch, ignition switch, back-up light switch and turn signal switch.
6 Disconnect the shift indicator cable by prying the clip from the shaft bowl.
7 Disconnect the shift cable from the column by removing the clip, pin retainer and washer.
8 Use a screwdriver to pry back the plastic cover over the intermediate shaft so the U-joint is exposed. Remove the locking bolt and nut.
9 Remove the three bolts and one nut securing the steering column to the support (photo) and remove the column.
10 Because of its collapsible design, the steering column is very susceptible to damage when removed from the car. Be careful not to lean on or drop the column, as this could weaken the column structure and impair its performance.
11 If the car has been in an accident which resulted in frame damage, major body damage or in which the steering column was impacted, the column could be damaged or misaligned and should be checked by a qualified shop.

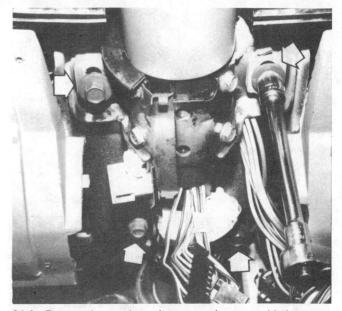

24.9 Remove the steering column mounting nut and bolts

12 The steering column is installed by reversing the sequence of the removal operation with the following note: When reattaching the shift indicator cable clip to the shift bowl, place the shift lever in the Neutral position, then position the clip on the edge of the bowl so that the shift indicator pointer is pointing to the N. Push the clip onto the bowl to secure it.

## 25 Steering knuckle — removal and installation

1 Remove the hub and bearing assembly as described in Section 13.
2 Mark the cam bolt so the proper camber alignment can be maintained upon installation.
3 Remove the cam bolt and the upper strut-to-steering knuckle mounting bolt.
4 Remove the nut securing the tie rod to the steering knuckle.

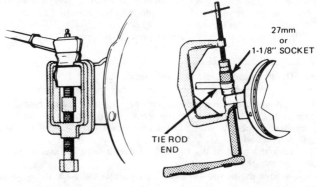

REMOVE TIE ROD END          INSTALL TIE ROD END

Fig. 10.16 engaging and disengaging the outer tie rod from the steering knuckle (Sec 25)

5 Using a GM special tool or equivalent as shown in the accompanying illustration, disengage the tie rod from the steering knuckle.
6 Remove the bolt securing the lower balljoint in the lower control arm to the steering knuckle and disengage the balljoint.
7 Remove the steering knuckle from the axleshaft.
8 If the steering knuckle is being replaced, install a new steering knuckle seal into the new knuckle. This is done by greasing both the seal and the knuckle bore and then tapping the seal into place using a hammer and socket.
9 Install the steering knuckle onto the axleshaft.
10 Insert the balljoint stud into the steering knuckle, then insert the

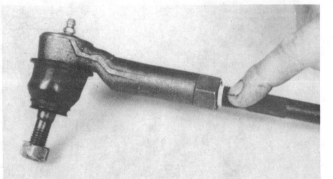

26.6   Mark the position of the jam nut on the inner tie rod

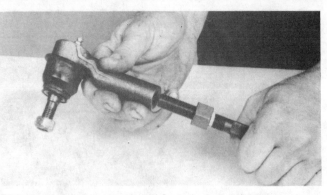

26.8   Unscrew the outer tie rod from the inner tie rod

27.4   Use a pair of pliers to remove the outer retaining clip from the rack and pinion boot

27.5   Use wire cutters to remove the inner tie rod clamp from the rack and pinion boot

27.6   Slide the boot off the inner tie rod

bolt and nut and tighten the nut.

11   Loosely install the strut to the steering knuckle by installing the cam bolt and upper strut-to-steering knuckle mounting bolt.

12   Install the hub and bearing assembly, shield and rotor.

13   Place a jackstand under the hub and bearing assembly and rotor to support it. Lower the car enough to align the cam with its mark made during the removal procedure, and tighten the bolts to the specified torque.

14   Engage the tie rod with the steering knuckle using a C-clamp and a 1-1/8 inch (27 mm) socket as shown in the accompanying illustration.

15   Install the tie rod nut and tighten it to the specified torque.

16   Install the brake caliper.

17   Install the wheel and lower the car to the ground.

## 26   Outer tie rod — removal and installation

1   In most cases when one or both tie rods must be replaced, the operation can be done with the rack and pinion in the car. For photographic clarity, we performed the operation with the rack and pinion removed.

2   Raise the front of the car and support it with jackstands.

3   Remove the front wheel.

4   Remove the tie rod nut securing the outer tie rod to the steering knuckle.

5   Using a GM special tool or equivalent as shown in the accompanying illustration, disengage the tie rod from the steering knuckle.

6   Mark the relationship of the jam nut to the inner tie rod threads so front end alignment can be maintained upon installation (photo).

7   Back off the jam nut from the outer tie rod.

8   Unscrew the outer tie rod from the inner tie rod (photo).

9   To install, position the jam nut at its mark on the threads. Screw the outer tie rod onto the inner tie rod until it's snug against the jam nut.

10   Using a C-clamp and a 1-1/8 inch (27 mm) socket as shown in the accompanying illustration, install the tie rod into the steering knuckle.

11   Install the tie rod nut and tighten it to the specified torque.

12   Torque the jam nut to specs.

13   Mount the front wheel and lower the car to the ground.

14   A front end alignment must now be performed.

## 27   Rack and pinion boot seals — removal and installation

1   Since the rack and pinion boot seals protect the assembly's internals from dirt and water, they should be checked periodically for holes, cracking and other damage or deterioration. If the boots exhibit such conditions they should be replaced immediately to prevent having to overhaul the entire rack and pinion assembly. The seal boots can be removed and installed with the rack and pinion still in the car, through for photographic clarity we performed the operation with the rack and pinion removed.

2   Remove the outer tie rod as described in Section 26.

3   Remove the jam nut from the inner tie rod.

4   Use pliers to spread the outer boot clamp and remove it from the inner tie rod (photo).

5   Cut off the inner boot clamp and remove (photo).

6   Only if the same boot is to be reinstalled, mark the rack and pinion breather tube location on the boot and remove the boot (photo).

7   Install a new inner boot clamp or appropriate size hose clamp over the inner tie rod.

8   Install the seal boot so the large end is over the rack and pinion housing lip and the hole in the boot is aligned with the breather tube. If the old boot is being installed, simply line up the marks made during removal.

9   Install the inner boot clamp over the large end of the boot and tighten.

10   Install the outer boot clamp over the small end of the boot and tighten.

11   Install the jam nut onto the inner tie rod.

12   Install the outer tie rod and engage it in the steering knuckle.

13   Mount the front wheel and lower the car to the ground.

14   Have a front end alignment performed.

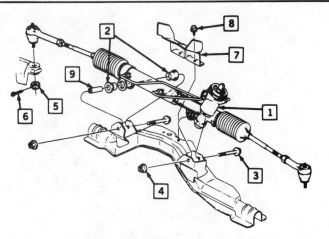

Fig. 10.17   Power rack and pinion mounting (manual rack
and pinion similar) (Sec 28)

1  Steering gear
2  Bushing
3  Bolt
4  Nut
5  Nut
6  Cotter pin
7  Shield
8  Bolt — fully driven, seated
   and not stripped
9  Sleeve

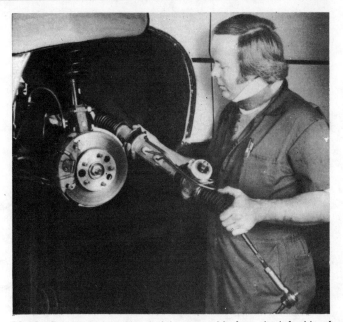

28.10   Remove the rack and pinion assembly from the left side of
the vehicle

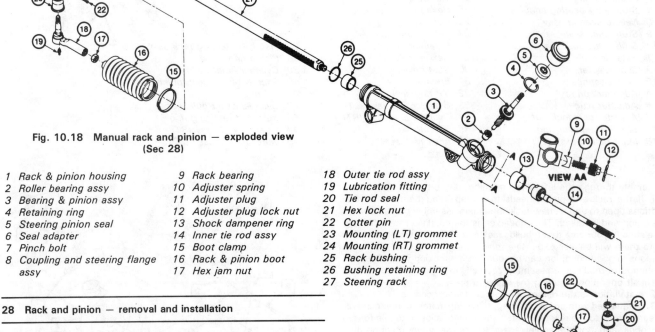

Fig. 10.18   Manual rack and pinion — exploded view
(Sec 28)

1  Rack & pinion housing
2  Roller bearing assy
3  Bearing & pinion assy
4  Retaining ring
5  Steering pinion seal
6  Seal adapter
7  Pinch bolt
8  Coupling and steering flange
   assy
9  Rack bearing
10  Adjuster spring
11  Adjuster plug
12  Adjuster plug lock nut
13  Shock dampener ring
14  Inner tie rod assy
15  Boot clamp
16  Rack & pinion boot
17  Hex jam nut
18  Outer tie rod assy
19  Lubrication fitting
20  Tie rod seal
21  Hex lock nut
22  Cotter pin
23  Mounting (LT) grommet
24  Mounting (RT) grommet
25  Rack bushing
26  Bushing retaining ring
27  Steering rack

## 28   Rack and pinion — removal and installation

*Refer to Fig. 10.17*

1   Move the steering column intermediate shaft seal upwards and
remove the pinch bolt attaching the intermediate shaft to the rack and
pinion stub shaft.
2   On power steering equipped models, remove the air cleaner for
clearance.
3   On power steering equipped models, place newspapers and a drain
pan under the rack and pinion.
4   Raise the front of the car and support it with jackstands placed
under the body, not under the cradle.
5   Remove both front wheels.
6   Remove the cotter pins and nuts from both tie rod ends at the steering knuckles.

7   If equipped, remove the air management pipe bracket bolt from
the crossmember.
8   Place a jack under the rear cradle crossmember to support it and
remove the two rear cradle mounting bolts. Lower the rear of the cradle
five inches. **Note:** *Lowering more than this may damage engine components near the cowl.*
9   If equipped, remove the rack and pinion heat shield.
10  Remove the two rack and pinion mounting bolts and remove the

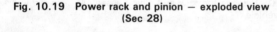

**Fig. 10.19  Power rack and pinion — exploded view (Sec 28)**

| | | | |
|---|---|---|---|
| 1 | Rack & pinion housing assy | 19 | Boot clamp |
| 2 | Upper pinion bushing | 20 | Rack & pinion boot |
| 3 | Rack & pinion seal | 21 | Hex jam nut |
| 4 | Pinion & valve aay | 22 | Outer tie rod assy (LT) |
| 5 | Valve body ring (4) | 23 | Lubrication fitting |
| 6 | Retaining ring | 24 | Tie rod seal |
| 7 | Stub shaft bearing annulus | 25 | Hexagon slotted nut |
| 8 | Needle bearing assy | 26 | Cotter pin |
| 9 | Stub shaft seal | 27 | Ball bearing ssy |
| 10 | Stub shaft dust seal | 28 | Retaining ring |
| 11 | Retaining ring | 29 | Hex lock nut |
| 12 | Seal adapter | 30 | Dust cover |
| 13 | Rack bearing | 31 | Breather tube |
| 14 | Adjuster spring | 32 | 'O' ring seal |
| 15 | Adjuster plug | 33 | Cylinder line assy (LT) |
| 16 | Adjuster plug lock nut | 34 | Cylinder line assy (RT) |
| 17 | Shock dampener ring | 35 | 'O' ring seal |
| 18 | Inner tie rod assy (LT) | 36 | Inner rack seal |

| | |
|---|---|
| 37 | Piston & steering rack assy |
| 38 | Piston ring |
| 39 | Cylinder inner bulkhead |
| 40 | Rack & pinion seal (bulkhead) |
| 41 | 'O' ring seal |
| 42 | Cylinder outer bulkhead |
| 43 | Bulkhead retaining ring |
| 44 | Inner tie rod assy (RT) |
| 45 | Outer tie rod assy (RT) |

assembly through the left wheel opening (photo).

11  If the rack and pinion needs to be repaired, there are several options open to you. A new rack and pinion assembly can be bought as a unit and installed. This, however, is the costliest route. If there is a shop in your area that rebuilds rack and pinion assemblies, taking it to them will be less expensive than buying a new unit. Rack and pinions in good condition can be found at a wrecking yard. The final option is to rebuild the assembly yourself, though it is a somewhat difficult operation requiring the use of a press.

12  Installation is the reverse of the removal procedure.

13  If equipped with power steering, following installation add power steering fluid to the reservoir. Start the engine, allow it to idle for ten seconds, and stop the engine again. Check the power steering fluid level and add more as necessary.

14  On all models, following installation have the toe-in checked, and if necessary, adjusted.

## 29  Power steering pump (L4 engine) — removal and installation

*Refer to Fig. 10.20*

1  Raise the front of the car and support it with jackstands.

2  Remove the radiator hose clamp bolt.

3  Disconnect the pressure hose from its fitting on the rear of the pump.

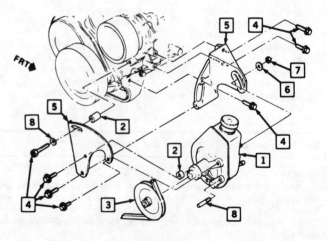

**Fig. 10.20  The power steering pump arrangement on the L4 engine (Sec 31)**

| | | | |
|---|---|---|---|
| 1 | Power steering pump | 5 | Bracket |
| 2 | Spacer | 6 | Washer |
| 3 | Pulley | 7 | Nut — 50 N-m (38 ft. lb.) |
| 4 | Bolt — 50 N-m (38 ft. lb.) | 8 | Pin — 25 N-m (18 ft. lb.) |

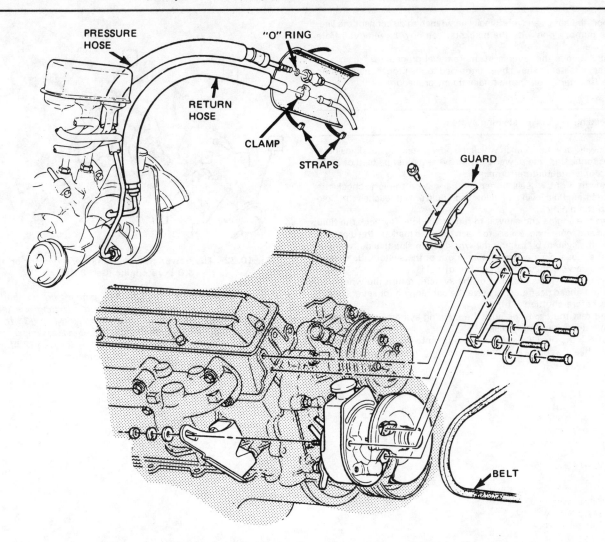

**Fig. 10.21  The power steering pump arrangement on the 2.8 L V6 engine (Sec 30)**

4  Remove the clamp securing the flexible hose to the rigid steel line and disconnect the hose from the line.
5  Loosen the pump attaching bolts and nuts, move the pump toward the engine and remove the belt from the pulley.
6  Remove the bolt and spacer used in the upper rear mounting of the pump.
7  Remove the three bolts holding the left pump bracket to the engine block.
8  Remove the pump and left pump bracket.
9  Remove the pump from the pump bracket.
10  Remove the three bolts securing the right pump bracket to the pump.
11  If the power steering pump needs replacing, a rebuilt unit can be obtained.
12  Install the pump by reversing the removal procedure.
13  Adjust the belt tension as described in Chapter 1.

---

**30  Power steering pump (2.8L V6 engine) — removal and installation**

*Refer to Fig. 11.21*
1  Disconnect the negative cable at the battery terminal.
2  Disconnect the electrical connector from the blower motor.
3  Remove the blower motor.
4  Drain the radiator and disconnect the heater hose at the water pump.
5  Disconnect the pressure and return hoses at the connection shown in the accompanying illustration.
6  Loosen the pump mounting bolts, move the pump toward the

engine and remove the belt from the pulley.
7  Remove the five bolts securing the right pump bracket to the pump and rear engine head.
8  Remove the pump from the left pump bracket and remove from the engine compartment.
9  If the power steering pump needs replacing, a rebuilt unit can be obtained.
10  Install the pump by reversing the removal procedure.
11  Adjust the belt tension as described in Chapter 1.

---

**31  Power steering pump (3.0L and 3.8L engine) — removal and installation**

1  Disconnect the negative battery cable.
2  Remove the air cleaner for working clearance.
3  Loosen the alternator belt and remove belt and the alternator (refer to Chapter 5 for alternator removal).
4  Jack the vehicle up and support it on jackstands.
5  Remove the rear adjustment nut from the pump.
6  Remove the alternator adjustment bracket.
7  Remove the pump belt.
8  Remove the two studs retaining the alternator mounting bracket by using two nuts tightened against each other on the end of the stud to act as a bolt head. After the studs have been removed, lift out the alternator bracket.
9  Using a 15 mm box end wrench, remove the two bolts attaching the pump rear adjusting bracket to the engine block.
10  Disconnect the pump pressure hose by using a thin 1-inch wrench

to support the flange and a 5/8-inch line wrench to disconnect the line.
11  The pump, along with the brackets, can now be removed from the vehicle.
12  Installation is the reverse of the removal procedure.
13  After all fasteners have been tightened to the proper specification refer to Chapter 1 for the belt adjustment procedure.

## 32  Bleeding the power steering system

1  Following any operation in which the power steering fluid lines have been disconnected, the power steering system must be bled of air to obtain proper steering performance.
2  With the front wheels turned all the way to the left, check the power steering fluid level and, if low, add fluid until it reaches the Cold mark on the dipstick.
3  Start the engine and allow it to run at fast idle. Recheck the fluid level and add more if necessary to reach the Cold mark on the dipstick.
4  Bled the system by turning the wheels from side to side, without hitting the stops. This will work the air out of the system. Be careful that the reservoir does not run empty of fluid.
5  When the air is worked out of the system, return the wheels to the straight ahead position and leave the car running for several more minutes before shutting it off.
6  Road test the car to be sure the steering system is functioning normally and is free from noise.
7  Recheck the fluid level to be sure it is up to the Hot mark on the dipstick while the engine is at normal operating temperature. Add fluid if necessary.

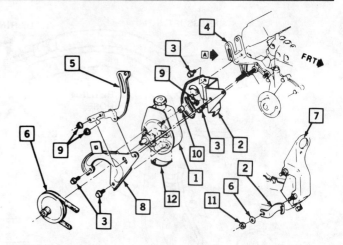

**Fig. 10.22  The power steering pump arrangement on the 3.8 L V6 engine (Sec 31)**

| | |
|---|---|
| 1  *Power steering pump* | 7  *Engine lift bracket and shield* |
| 2  *Rear adjusting bracket* | 8  *Front adjusting bracket* |
| 3  *Bolt — 50 N-m (38 ft. lb.)* | 9  *Nut — 50 N-m (38 ft. lb.)* |
| 4  *Generator mounting bracket* | 10  *Rear bracket spacer* |
| 5  *Generator adjusting bracket* | 11  *Nut — 27 N-m (20 ft. lb.)* |
| 6  *Pulley* | 12  *Protector* |

# Chapter 11  Body

## Contents

Body — maintenance ........................................ 2
Body repair — major damage ............................ 7
Complete cradle — removal and installation ............. 26
Body repair — minor damage ........................... 6
Console — removal and installation ..................... 23
Door lock assembly — removal and installation .......... 16
Door lock knob — removal and installation ............. 12
Door trim panel — removal and installation ............ 13
Door outside handle — removal and installation ......... 17
Door window regulator handle — removal and installation ... 14
Door window glass replacement ........................ 18
Exterior mirror — removal and installation .............. 21
Fixed glass replacement ............................... 22
Front door lock cylinder — removal and installation ....... 15

General information ................................... 1
Hinges and locks — maintenance ....................... 5
Hood latch release cable — replacement ............... 9
Hood — removal and installation ...................... 8
Instrument panel trim plates — removal and installation ..... 24
Partial cradle — removal and installation ............... 25
Rear compartment lid lock cylinder — removal
 and installation .................................... 19
Rear compartment lid lock assembly — removal
 and installation .................................... 20
Rear hatch damper — removal and installation ......... 10
Rear hatch — removal, installation and adjustment ........ 11
Upholstery and carpets — maintenance ................. 3
Vinyl trim — maintenance ............................. 4

## Specifications

### Torque specifications

| | ft-lbs | Nm |
|---|---|---|
| Frame-to-body bolts ........................................ | 103 | 140 |

## 1  General information

The GM A-car, for the years covered by this manual, was available in three models: Two-door coupe, four-door sedan and a four-door wagon. Differences between the various models are noted where appropriate in the service procedures within this Chapter.

A-car bodies are of unitized construction, in which the body is designed to provide vehicle rigidity so that a separate frame is not necessary. Front and rear frame side rails, integral with the body, support the front end sheet metal, front and rear suspension systems and other mechanical components. Due to this type of construction, it is very important that, in the event of collision damage, the underbody be thoroughly checked by a facility with the proper equipment to do so.

Component replacement and repairs possible for the home mechanic are included in this Chapter.

## 2  Body — maintenance

1    The condition of your vehicle's body is very important, because it is on this that the second hand value will mainly depend. It is much more difficult to repair a neglected or damaged body than it is to repair mechanical components. The hidden areas of the body, such as the fender wells, the frame and the engine compartment, are equally important, although obviously do not require as frequent attention as the rest of the body.

2    Once a year, or every 12 000 miles, it is a good idea to have the underside of the body and the frame steam cleaned. All traces of dirt and oil will be removed and the underside can then be inspected carefully for rust, damaged brake lines, frayed electrical wiring, damaged cables, and other problems. The front suspension components should be greased after completion of this job.

3    At the same time, clean the engine and the engine compartment using either a steam cleaner or a water soluble degreaser.

4    The fender wells should be given particular attention, as undercoating can peel away and stones and dirt thrown up by the tires can cause the paint to chip and flake, allowing rust to set in. If rust is found,

clean down to the bare metal and apply an anti-rust paint.

5    The body should be washed once a week (or when dirty). Wet the vehicle thoroughly to soften the dirt, then wash it down with a soft sponge and plenty of clean, soapy water. If the surplus dirt is not washed off very carefully, it will in time wear down the paint.

6    Spots of tar or asphalt coating thrown up from the road should be removed with a cloth soaked in solvent.

7    Once every six months, give the body and chrome trim a thorough waxing. If a chrome cleaner is used to remove rust from any of the vehicle's plated parts, remember that the cleaner also removes part of the chrome, so use it sparingly.

## 3  Upholstery and carpets — maintenance

1    Every three months remove the carpets or mats and clean the interior of the vehicle (more frequently if necessary). Vacuum the upholstery and carpets to remove loose dirt and dust.

2    If the upholstery is soiled, apply upholstery cleaner with a damp sponge and wipe it off with a clean, dry cloth.

## 4  Vinyl trim — maintenance

1    Vinyl trim should not be cleaned with detergents, caustic soaps or petroleum-based cleaners. Plain soap and water or a mild vinyl cleaner is best for stains. Test a small area for color fastness. Bubbles under the vinyl can be corrected by piercing them with a pin and then working the air out.

## 5  Hinges and locks — maintenance

1    Every 3000 miles or three months, the door, hood and rear hatch hinges and locks should be lubricated with a few drops of oil. The door and rear hatch striker plates should also be given a thin coat of grease to reduce wear and ensure free movement.

### 6  Body repair — minor damage

*Repair of minor scratches — see color photo sequence*

1   If the scratch is very superficial and does not penetrate to the metal of the body, repair is very simple. Lightly rub the scratched area with a fine rubbing compound to remove loose paint and built-up wax. Rinse the area with clean water.

2   Apply touch-up paint to the scratch, using a small brush. Continue to apply thin layers of paint until the surface of the paint in the scratch is level with the surrounding paint. Allow the new paint at least two weeks to harden, then blend it into the surrounding paint by rubbing with a very fine rubbing compound. Finally, apply a coat of wax to the scratch area.

3   If the scratch has penetrated the paint and exposed the metal of the body, causing the metal to rust, a different repair technique is required. Remove all loose rust from the bottom of the scratch with a pocket knife, then apply rust inhibiting paint to prevent the formation of rust in the future. Using a rubber or nylon applicator, coat the scratched area with glaze-type filler. If required, the filler can be mixed with thinner to provide a very thin paste, which is ideal for filling narrow scratches. Before the glaze filler in the scratch hardens, wrap a piece of smooth cotton cloth around the tip of a finger. Dip the cloth in thinner and then quickly wipe it along the surface of the scratch. This will ensure that the surface of the filler is slightly hollow. The scratch can now be painted over as described earlier in this section.

*Repair of dents*

4   When repairing dents, the first job is to pull the dent out until the affected area is as close as possible to its original shape. There is no point in trying to restore the original shape completely as the metal in the damaged area will have stretched on impact and cannot be restored to its original contours. It is better to bring the level of the dent up to a point which is about 1/8-inch below the level of the surrounding metal. In cases where the dent is very shallow, it is not worth trying to pull it out at all.

5   If the back side of the dent is accessible, it can be hammered out gently from behind using a soft-face hammer. While doing this, hold a block of wood firmly against the opposite side of the metal to absorb the hammer blows and prevent the metal from being stretched.

6   If the dent is in a section of the body which has double layers, or some other factor that makes it inaccessible from behind, a different technique is required. Drill several small holes through the metal inside the damaged area, particularly in the deeper sections. Screw long, self-tapping screws into the holes just enough for them to get a good grip in the metal. Now the dent can be pulled out by pulling on the protruding heads of the screws with locking pliers.

7   The next stage of repair is the removal of paint from the damaged area and from an inch or so of the surrounding metal. This is easily done with a wire brush or sanding disk in a drill motor, although it can be done just as effectively by hand with sandpaper. To complete the preparation for filling, score the surface of the bare metal with a screwdriver or the tang of a file (or drill small holes in the affected area). This will provide a good grip for the filler material. To complete the repair, see the Section on filling and painting.

*Repair of rust holes or gashes*

8   Remove all paint from the affected area and from an inch or so of the surrounding metal, using a sanding disk or wire brush mounted in a drill motor. If these are not available, a few sheets of sandpaper will do the job just as effectively.

9   With the paint removed you will be able to determine the severity of the corrosion and decide whether to replace the whole panel, if possible, or repair the affected area. New body panels are not as expensive as most people think and it is often quicker to install a new panel than to repair large areas of rust.

10  Remove all trim pieces from the affected area except those which will act as a guide to the original shape of the damaged body, such as headlight shells, etc. Using metal snips or a hacksaw blade, remove all loose metal and any other metal that is badly affected by rust. Hammer the edges of the hole in to create a slight depression for the filler material.

11  Wire brush the affected area to remove the powdery rust from the surface of the metal. If the back of the rusted area is accessible, treat it with rust inhibiting paint.

12  Before filling is done, block the hole in some way. This can be done with sheet metal riveted or screwed into place, or by stuffing the hole with wire mesh.

13  Once the hole is blocked off, the affected area can be filled and painted.

*Filling and painting*

14  Many types of body fillers are available, but generally speaking, body repair kits which contain filler paste and a tube of resin hardener are best for this type of repair work. A wide, flexible plastic or nylon applicator will be necessary for imparting a smooth and contoured finish to the surface of the filler material. Mix up a small amount of filler on a clean piece of wood or cardboard (use the hardener sparingly). Follow the manufacturer's instructions on the package, otherwise the filler will set incorrectly.

15  Using the applicator, apply the filler paste to the prepared area. Draw the applicator across the surface of the filler to achieve the desired contour and to level the filler surface. As soon as a contour that approximates the original one is achieved, stop working the paste. If you continue, the paste will begin to stick to the applicator. Continue to add thin layers of paste at 20-minute intervals until the level of the filler is just above the surrounding metal.

16  Once the filler has hardened, the excess can be removed with a body file. From then on, progressively finer grades of sandpaper should be used, starting with a 180-grit paper and finishing with 600-grit wet-or-dry paper. Always wrap the sandpaper around a flat rubber or wooden block, otherwise the surface of the filler will not be completely flat. During the sanding of the filler surface, the wet-or-dry paper should be periodically rinsed in water. This will ensure that a very smooth finish is produced in the final stage.

17  At this point the repair area should be surrounded by a ring of bare metal, which in turn should be encircled by the finely feathered edge of good paint. Rinse the repair area with clean water until all of the dust produced by the sanding operation is gone.

18  Spray the entire area with a light coat of primer. This will reveal any imperfections in the surface of the filler. Repair the imperfections with fresh filler paste or glaze filler and once more smooth the surface with sandpaper. Repeat this spray-and-repair procedure until you are satisfied that the surface of the filler and the feathered edge of the paint are perfect. Rinse the area with clean water and allow it to dry completely.

19  The repair area is now ready for painting. Spray painting must be carried out in a warm, dry, windless and dust free atmosphere. These conditions can be created if you have access to a large indoor work area, but if you are forced to work in the open, you will have to pick the day very carefully. If you are working indoors, dousing the floor in the work area with water will help settle the dust which would otherwise be in the air.

20  If the repair area is confined to one body panel, mask off the surrounding panels. This will help minimize the effects of a slight mismatch in paint color. Trim pieces such as chrome strips, door handles, etc., will also need to be masked off or removed. Use masking tape and several thicknesses of newspaper for the masking operations.

21  Before spraying, shake the paint can thoroughly, then spray a test area until the spray painting technique is mastered. Cover the repair area with a thick coat of primer. The thickness should be built up using several thin layers of primer, rather than one thick one. Using 600-grit wet-or-dry sandpaper, rub down the surface of the primer until it is very smooth. While doing this, the work area should be thoroughly rinsed with water and the wet-or-dry sandpaper periodically rinsed as well. Allow the primer to dry before spraying additional coats.

22  Spray on the top coat, again building up the thickness by using several thin layers of paint. Begin spraying in the center of the repair area and then, using a circular motion, work out until the whole repair area and about two inches of the surrounding original paint is covered. Remove all masking material 10 to 15 minutes after spraying on the final coat of paint. Allow the new paint at least two weeks to harden, then use a very fine rubbing compound to blend the edges of the new paint into the existing paint. Finally, apply a coat of wax.

### 7  Body repair — major damage

1   Major damage must be repaired by an auto body shop specifically

9.1   A pair of screwdrivers should be used to remove the hood latch release cable from the locking mechanism

9.2   Prying the cable out of the retaining bracket

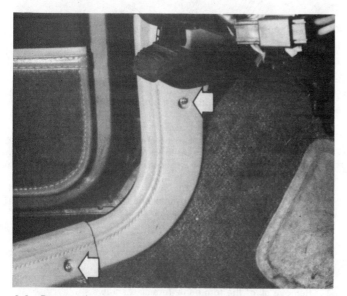

9.3   Remove the two screws to remove the trim panel

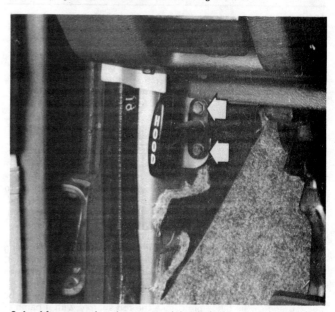

9.4   After removing the two retaining bolts the entire cable assembly can be removed from the vehicle

equipped to perform unibody repairs. These shops have available the specialized equipment required to do the job properly.

2    If the damage is extensive, the underbody must be checked for proper alignment or the vehicle's handling characteristics may be adversely affected and other components may wear at an accelerated rate.

3    Due to the fact that all of the major body components (hood, fenders, etc.) are separate and replaceable units, any seriously damaged components should be replaced rather than repaired. Sometimes these components can be found in a wrecking yard that specializes in used vehicle components, often at considerable savings over the cost of new parts.

## 8   Hood — removal and installation

1    Raise the hood.

2    Place protective pads along the edges of the engine compartment to prevent damage to the painted surfaces.

3    Scribe or paint lines around the mounting bracket, so the hood can be installed in the same position.

4    Apply white paint around the bracket-to-hood bolts so they can be aligned quickly and accurately during installation.

5    With an assistant supporting the weight, remove the bracket bolts and remove the hood from the vehicle.

6    Installation is the reverse of removal, taking care to align the brackets and bolts with the markings made prior to removal.

## 9   Hood latch release cable — replacement

1    In the engine compartment, disconnect the release cable from the latch mechanism (photo).

2    Pry the cable from the retaining bracket with a screwdriver (photo).

3    In the passenger compartment, remove the left trim panel (photo).

4    Remove the two screws holding the T-handle to the shroud panel (photo).

5    Connect string or thin wire to the end of the cable and remove it by pulling it through into the passenger compartment.

6    Installation is the reverse of removal after connecting the string or wire to the new cable and pulling it into position.

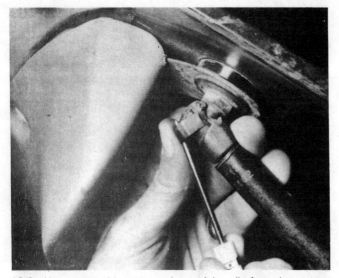

10.2  Use a screwdriver to pry the retaining clip from the support

---

**10  Rear hatch damper — removal and installation**

1    Support the hatch in the fully open position.
2    Use a flat blade screwdriver to remove the clips from the ends
(photo) and remove the damper.
3    Installation is the reverse of removal, taking care to replace the
damper with one having the same color coded lettering.

---

**11  Rear hatch — removal, installation and adjustment**

*Removal*
1    Open the rear hatch and support it with a prop.
2    Place protective pads along the edges of the hatch opening to
prevent damage to the painted surfaces while work is being performed.
3    On hatchback models, remove the trim panel covering the hatch-
to-body bolts.
4    On all models, remove the damper struts (Section 10).
5    On hatchback models, remove the nuts from the hinge retaining
bolts and lift the hatch from the vehicle with the help of an assistant.
6    Disconnect any wiring harnesses which would interfere with hatch
removal.
7    On station wagon models, place a 5/32 inch metal rod on the
pointed end of the hinge pin. Strike the rod sharply with a hammer
to shear off the retaining clip tabs and drive the pin out of the hinge.
With the help of an assistant, lift the hatch from the vehicle.

*Installation*
8    Installation is the reverse of removal except that on station wagon
models, new retaining clips must be installed with their tabs toward
the head of the pins before the pins are driven into place.

*Adjustment*
9    The rear hatch on hatchback models can be adjusted, but the
station wagon hatch cannot.
10  The hatch attachment bolt holes are oversize and with the hatch
propped open, the dampers disconnected and the bolts loose, the hatch
fore-and-aft and side-to-side position can be adjusted.
11  Hatch height may be adjusted by adding or subtracting the number
of shims at the hinge-to-body locations. Height adjustment can also
be made at the rubber bumpers on the lower panel.

---

**12  Door lock knob — removal and installation**

1    Remove the control handle bezel screws to gain access to the back
side of the lock knob.

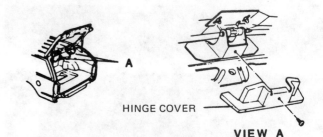

HINGE COVER

**VIEW A**

Fig. 11.1  To access the lift gate hinge bolts the trim
cover must first be removed (Sec 11)

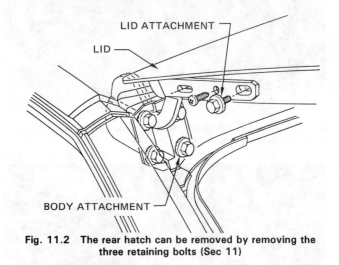

LID ATTACHMENT
LID
BODY ATTACHMENT

Fig. 11.2  The rear hatch can be removed by removing the
three retaining bolts (Sec 11)

2    Insert a small flat blade screwdriver behind the leading end of the
lock knob and pry it away from the locking rod, located behind the knob.
3    After the end of the rod is free from the knob, slide the knob
forward and remove it.
4    To install the knob, place the bezel in position with the lock rod
through the hole, and insert the small end of the knob rearward into
place until the end of the rod engages the depression in the front end
of the knob.

---

**13  Door trim panel — removal and installation**

1    Remove all of the trim panel retaining screws.
2    Remove the inside door locking knob (Section 12).
3    On models with remote control mirrors, remove the escutcheon
and disengage the control cable end from the escutcheon.
4    On power window equipped models, disconnect the wiring harness
from the switch assembly.
5    Remove the window regulator crank handle (Section 14).
6    Pry the trim panel loose by working around the outer circumference,
using a large screwdriver or pry bar to disengage the plastic retainers.
These retainers fit very tightly and care must be taken not to destroy
them during removal (photo).
7    On models with courtesy lights in the door panels, disconnect the
wire harness.
8    Remove the panel by pushing up and outward to disengage it from
the top of the door.
9    Carefully peel back the water deflector for access to the inner door
panel.
10  Installation is the reverse of removal, noting the following:
11  Before attaching the trim panel to the door, make sure that all the
plastic trim retainers are undamaged and installed tightly in the panel.
12  If the retainer is to be replaced with a new one, start the retainer
flange into the cutout attachment hole in the trim panel, then rotate
the retainer until the flange is fully engaged.
13  When attaching the door trim panel to the door, locate the top of
the panel over the upper flange of the inner door panel and press down

13.6 A screwdriver or pry bar should be used to pry the door panel off

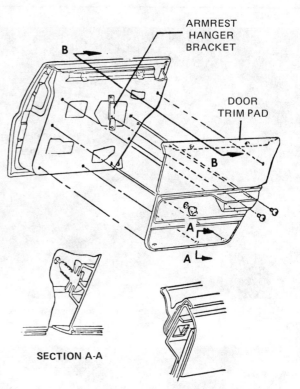

ARMREST HANGER BRACKET

DOOR TRIM PAD

SECTION A-A

SECTION B-B

Fig. 11.3 Door trim attachment points (Sec 13)

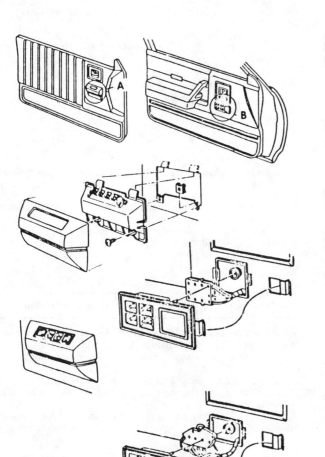

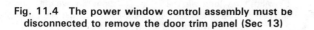

Fig. 11.4 The power window control assembly must be disconnected to remove the door trim panel (Sec 13)

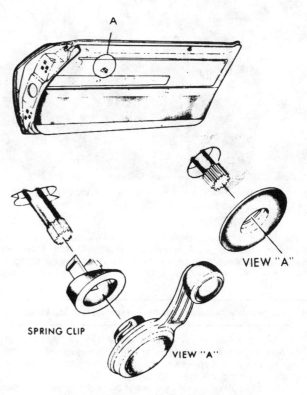

SPRING CLIP

VIEW "A"

VIEW "A"

Fig. 11.5 Window regulator handle installation (Sec 13)

14.2  A special tool can be used to remove the window crank
easily

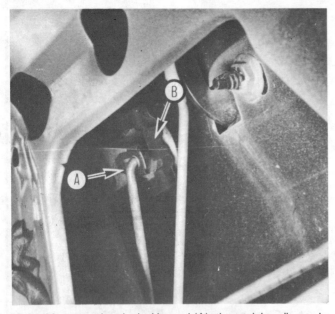

15.3  After removing the locking rod (A), the retaining clip can be
pried off to remove the lock cylinder (B)

on the trim panel to engage the upper retaining clips.
14  Position the trim panel on the inner door panel so that the panel
retainers are aligned with the holes in the door panel and tap the
retainers into the holes with the palm of your hand or a rubber mallet.

## 14  Door window regulator handle — removal and installation

1   Push the trim panel away from the handle to expose the spring clip.
2   Insert two small screwdrivers or a special forked tool (available
at auto parts stores) between the handle and the plastic washer and
push the spring clip off the shaft (photo).
3   To install, replace the spring clip and press the handle into place.

## 15  Door lock cylinder — removal and installation

1   Raise the door window, remove the trim panel and peel back the

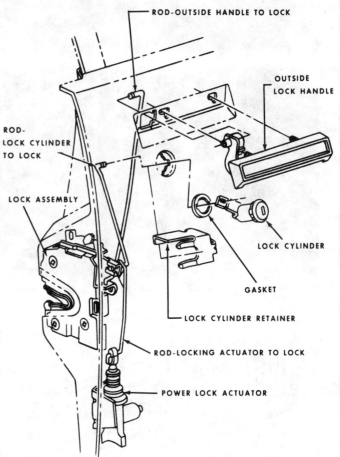

Fig. 11.7  A typical front door locking mechanism (Sec 15)

water deflector sufficiently to gain access to the lock cylinder.
2   Disconnect the lock cylinder actuating rod from the cylinder.
3   Use a screwdriver to slide the lock cylinder retainer forward until
it is disengaged and the lock cylinder can be removed (photo).
4   Installation is the reverse of removal, making sure the gasket is
correctly installed.

## 16  Front door lock assembly — removal and installation

1   Raise the door glass, remove the door trim panel and peel back
the water deflector for access to locking rods.
2   Disconnect the inside locking rod, the inside handle and lock
cylinder lock rods.
3   Remove the retaining screws, lower the lock assembly and
disengage the outside handle from the lock rod. Remove the assembly
from the door.
4   After installing the spring clips to the lock assembly, installation
is the reverse of removal. Tighten the retaining screws to the specified
torque.

## 17  Door outside handle — removal and installation

1   With the window in the full up position, remove the door trim panel
and peel the water deflector back sufficiently to expose the access hole.
2   Disengage the lock rod from the outside handle.
3   Remove the two attaching nuts from the handle studs.
4   Remove the handle by sliding it forward while rotating it up to
disengage it from the attaching nut holes.
5   Installation is the reverse of removal.

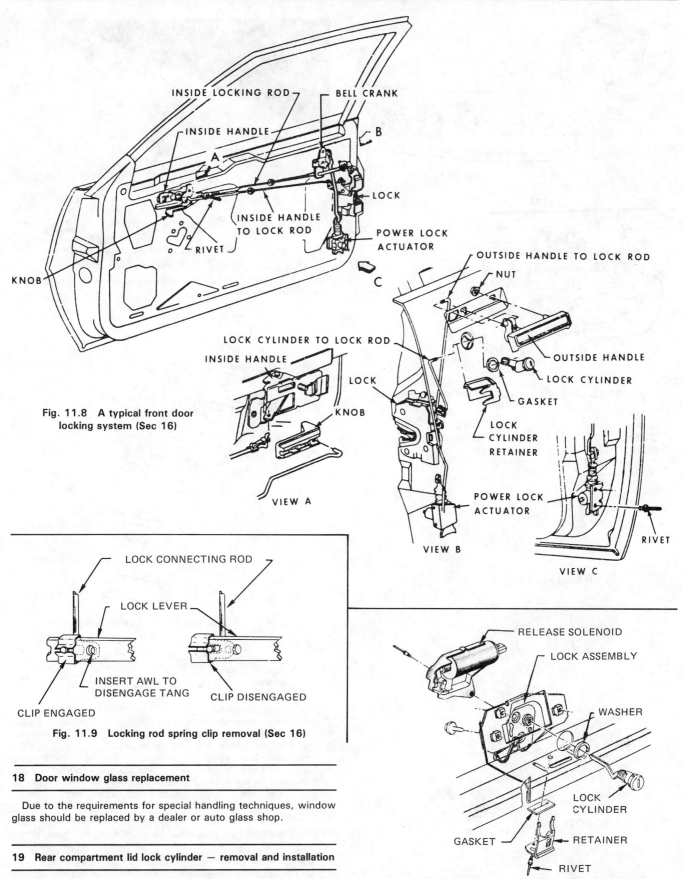

Fig. 11.8  A typical front door locking system (Sec 16)

VIEW A

VIEW B

VIEW C

Fig. 11.9  Locking rod spring clip removal (Sec 16)

## 18  Door window glass replacement

Due to the requirements for special handling techniques, window glass should be replaced by a dealer or auto glass shop.

## 19  Rear compartment lid lock cylinder — removal and installation

1   Open the rear compartment and remove the lock cylinder emblem (if equipped).
2   Using a 5/32-inch drill bit, drill out the rivet holding the lock cylinder

Fig. 11.10  The rivet must be drilled out of the retainer clip to remove the lock cylinder (Sec 19)

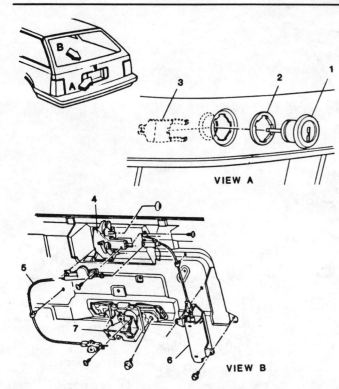

19.2   A 5/32-inch drill bit is used to remove the rivet holding the lock cylinder retaining clip

Fig. 11.11   Rear lift gate lock cylinder and assembly (Sec 19)

1   Lock cylinder
2   Gasket
3   Retainer
4   Lock and cam assembly lift gate glass
5   Actuator assembly lift gate lock to lock cylinder
6   Lift gate release solenoid
7   Lift gate lock assembly

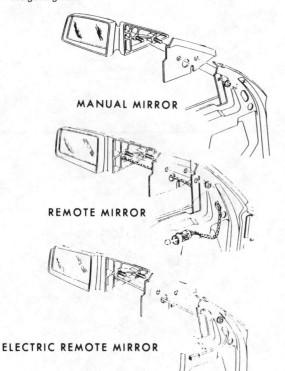

Fig. 11.13   Rear view mirror installation, remote and manual (Sec 21)

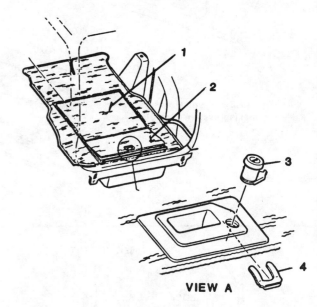

Fig. 11.12   Rear luggage compartment lock cylinder (Sec 20)

1   Front luggage compartment panel
2   Rear luggage compartment panel
3   Lock cylinder
4   Lock cylinder retainer

retainer to the lid (photo).
3   Use a flat blade screwdriver to slide the lock cylinder retainer forward until it is disengaged and the lock cylinder can be removed.
4   Remove the cylinder from the vehicle.
5   Installation is the reverse of removal, making sure that the lock cylinder shaft engages with the lock and the gasket mates with the outer panel to form a watertight seal. Check the lock cylinder with the key for proper operation then install a new rivet or screw.

## 20   Rear compartment lock assembly — removal and installation

1   Open the compartment lid.
2   Use a flat blade screwdriver to slide the lock cylinder retainer forward until it is disengaged and the lock cylinder can be removed.
3   Remove the cylinder from the vehicle.
4   Installation is the reverse of removal.

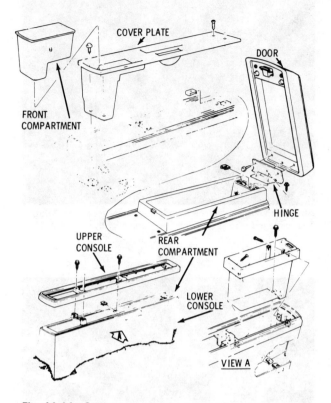

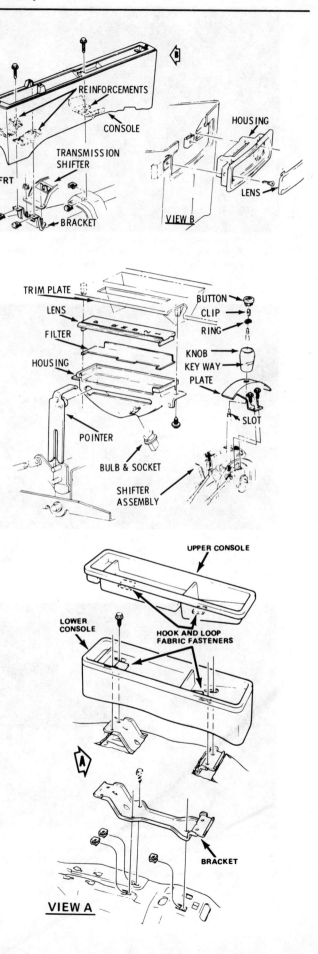

Fig. 11.14   Center console removal and installation details
(Sec 23)

## 21   Exterior mirror — removal and installation

1    Remove the trim panel or bezel. On some models it may be necessary to remove the door trim panel and peel the water deflector back for access to the retaining nuts.
2    Remove the retaining nuts and lift the mirror from the vehicle. On remote control mirrors, detach the cable clip and remove the mirror and cable as an assembly.
3    Installation is the reverse of removal, making sure the mirror gasket is properly aligned.

## 22   Fixed glass replacement

Due to the requirements for special handling techniques, the fixed glass, such as the windshield, rear and side glass, should be replaced by a dealer or auto glass shop.

## 23   Console — removal and installation

1    Disconnect the negative cable at the battery.
2    Remove the front compartment by pulling up on it.
3    Remove the shift knob button by inserting a screwdriver in the notch and prying upward.
4    Remove the snap-ring in the recess of the knob and remove the shift knob.
5    Remove the four retaining screws holding the cover plate and lift the cover plate up enough to disconnect the indicator bulb. Remove the cover plate.
6    Separate the upper console from the lower console by removing the three attaching screws. Remove the upper console.
7    Remove the four screws holding the lower console to the floor and disconnect the rear courtesy light.
8    Lift the lower console from the vehicle.

This photo sequence illustrates the repair of a dent and damaged paintwork. The procedure for the repair of a hole is similar. Refer to the text for more complete instructions

After removing any adjacent body trim, hammer the dent out. The damaged area should then be made slightly concave

Use coarse sandpaper or a sanding disc on a drill motor to remove all paint from the damaged area. Feather the sanded area into the edges of the surrounding paint, using progressively finer grades of sandpaper

The damaged area should be treated with rust remover prior to application of the body filler. In the case of a rust hole, all rusted sheet metal should be cut away

Carefully follow manufacturer's instructions when mixing the body filler so as to have the longest possible working time during application. Rust holes should be covered with fiberglass screen held in place with dabs of body filler prior to repair

Apply the filler with a flexible applicator in thin layers at 20 minute intervals. Use an applicator such as a wood spatula for confined areas. The filler should protrude slightly above the surrounding area

Shape the filler with a surform-type plane. Then, use water and progressively finer grades of sandpaper and a sanding block to wet-sand the area until it is smooth. Feather the edges of the repair area into the surrounding paint.

Use spray or brush applied primer to cover the entire repair area so that slight imperfections in the surface will be filled in. Prime at least one inch into the area surrounding the repair. Be careful of over-spray when using spray-type primer

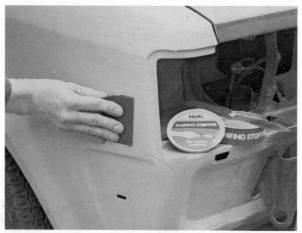

Wet-sand the primer with fine (approximately 400 grade) sandpaper until the area is smooth to the touch and blended into the surrounding paint. Use filler paste on minor imperfections

After the filler paste has dried, use rubbing compound to ensure that the surface of the primer is smooth. Prior to painting, the surface should be wiped down with a tack rag or lint-free cloth soaked in lacquer thinner

Choose a dry, warm, breeze-free area in which to paint and make sure that adjacent areas are protected from over-spray. Shake the spray paint can thoroughly and apply the top coat to the repair area, building it up by applying several coats, working from the center

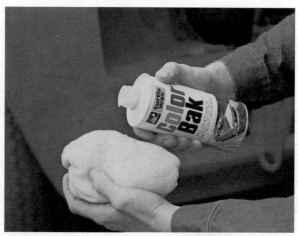

After allowing at least two weeks for the paint to harden, use fine rubbing compound to blend the area into the original paint. Wax can now be applied

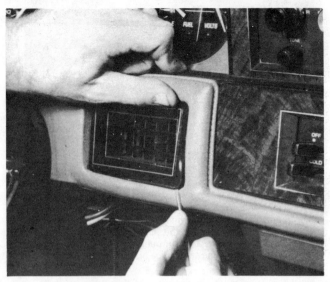

24.1   Be very careful when removing the vents from the trim pad to avoid tearing the pad

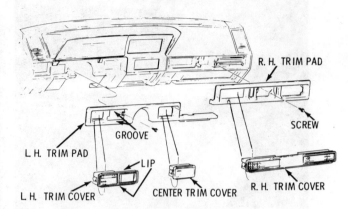

Fig. 11.15   Instrument panel trim pads and covers (Sec 24)

24.4   Location of the trim pad retaining screws

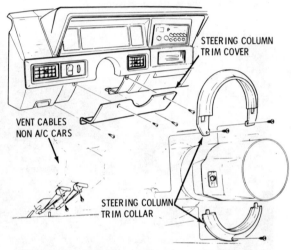

Fig. 11.16   Steering column trim covers (Sec 24)

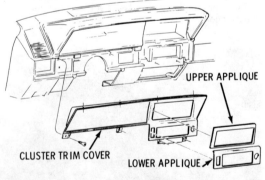

Fig. 11.17   Instrument cluster trim panel (Sec 24)

## 24   Instrument panel trim plates — removal and installation

1   Insert a screwdriver or putty knife between air vent and the trim pad and gently pry the vent out (photo).

2   Remove the remaining vents the same way.

3   Remove the three screws retaining the steering column trim collar and remove the collar.

4   With the ashtray open, remove the six screws retaining the trim pad (photo)

5   To remove the cluster trim cover remove the eight screws holding the cover to the instrument panel.

6   Installation is the reverse of the removal procedure.

24.6   To install the vent insert one end and push

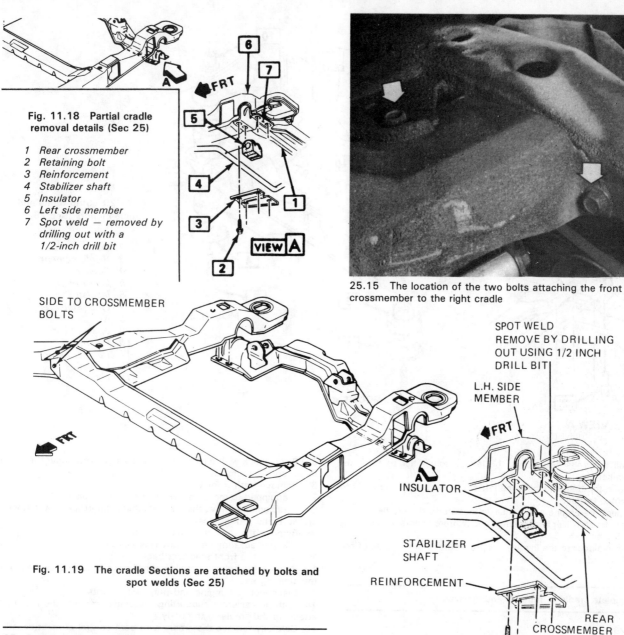

Fig. 11.18   Partial cradle removal details (Sec 25)

1  Rear crossmember
2  Retaining bolt
3  Reinforcement
4  Stabilizer shaft
5  Insulator
6  Left side member
7  Spot weld — removed by drilling out with a 1/2-inch drill bit

VIEW A

25.15   The location of the two bolts attaching the front crossmember to the right cradle

SIDE TO CROSSMEMBER BOLTS

FRT

Fig. 11.19   The cradle Sections are attached by bolts and spot welds (Sec 25)

SPOT WELD
REMOVE BY DRILLING
OUT USING 1/2 INCH
DRILL BIT

L.H. SIDE
MEMBER

FRT

INSULATOR

STABILIZER
SHAFT

REINFORCEMENT

REAR
CROSSMEMBER

VIEW A

## 25   Partial cradle — removal and installation

**Warning:** *Whenever frame-to-body bolts are loosened or removed, they should be replaced with new parts and torqued to 103 ft-lbs. Failure to replace frame-to-body bolts may result in damage to the frame, powertrain or suspension.*

1   Disconnect the negative cable at the battery.
2   Raise the vehicle and support it securely on jackstands.
3   Connect an engine hoist to the engine lifting brackets and raise the hoist until the lifting chain is taut. An alternative method of supporting the engine is with an engine support bracket. Types especially designed for GM A-cars are available from your local dealer, although more general types can be rented on an daily basis. If using an engine support bracket, hook it up according to the instructions accompanying the bracket.
4   Turn the steering wheel until the bolt attaching the steering column intermediate shaft to the rack and pinion stub shaft is facing up. Remove the bolt.
5   Place a jack with a block of wood as a cushion under the oil pan to support the engine.
6   Remove the left front wheel.
7   If equipped, remove the bracket supporting the power steering pressure and return lines.

8   Remove the rack and pinion mounting bolts.
9   If equipped, remove the driveline vibration damper.
10  Remove the bolts attaching the stabilizer bar to the left lower control arm.
11  Disconnect the left lower balljoint from the steering knuckle.
12  Remove the stabilizer bar reinforcements and bushings from the right and left sidemembers.
13  Use a 1/2-inch drill bit to drill though the spot weld located between left rear mounting holes of the stabilizer bar.
14  Disconnect the engine and transaxle mounts from the cradle.
15  Remove the bolts connecting the front crossmember to the right sidemember (photo).
16  Remove the bolts securing the left cradle section to the body.
17  Carefully lower the left cradle section from the vehicle. It may be necessary to pull or carefully pry the section loose.
18  Raise the cradle section into position and loosely install the body mounting bolts.
19  Insert a 1/2-inch bolt though the hole drilled at the spot weld to maintain correct alignment.

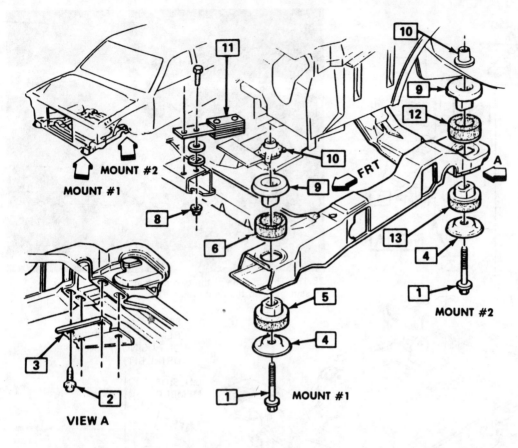

Fig. 11.20  Stub frame and cradle mounts (Sec 26)

1  Bolt
2  Bolt
3  Reinforcement
4  Retainer
5  Insulator
6  Insulator
7  Front stabilizer
8  Nut
9  Spacer
10  Cage nut
11  Damper assembly
12  Insulator
13  Insulator

20  Install the bolts connecting the left crossmember to the right crossmember.
21  Tighten the bolt attaching the left cradle section to the body to the specified torque.
22  Connect the engine and transaxle mounts to the cradle.
23  Install the stabilizer bar bushings and reinforcements, and remove the drill bit.
24  The remainder of the installation procedure is the reverse of the removal procedure.

## 26  Complete cradle — removal and installation

### Removal

1  Disconnect the negative cable at the battery.
2  Raise the vehicle and support it securely on jackstands.
3  Connect an engine hoist to the engine lifting brackets and raise the hoist until the lifting chain is taut. An alternative method of supporting the engine is with an engine support bracket. Types especially designed for GM A-cars are available from your local dealer, although more general types can be rented on an daily basis. If using an engine support bracket, hook it up according to the instructions accompanying the bracket.
4  Turn the steering wheel until the bolt attaching the steering column intermediate shaft to the rack and pinion stub shaft is facing up. Remove the bolt.

5  Place a jack with a block of wood as a cushion under the oil pan to support the engine.
6  Remove both front wheels.
7  If equipped, remove the exhaust crossover pipe.
8  If equipped, remove the brackets that support the power steering pressure and return lines.
9  Remove the rack and pinion mounting bolts.
10  If equipped, remove the driveline vibration damper.
11  Remove the front stabilizer bar.
12  Remove the bolts at both lower balljoints and separate them from the steering knuckles.
13  Disconnect all engine and transaxle mounts.
14  With an assistant supporting the cradle, remove the four bolts attaching the cradle to the body.
15  Carefully remove the cradle with both control arms attached.
16  If a new cradle is being installed, transfer the control arms, frame reinforcements and damper assembly, as equipped, to the new cradle.

### Installation

17  With the help of an assistant, raise the cradle into position and loosely install the four body mounting bolts.
18  Tighten the cradle-to-body bolts in the following order: right rear, right front, left rear, left front. This sequence is necessary to assure correct body alignment.
19  The rest of the installation is the reverse of the removal procedure.
20  Following installation have the toe-in checked and adjusted.

# Chapter 12   Chassis electrical system

*Refer to Chapter 13 for information applicable to 1986 and later models*

## Contents

Bulb replacement . . . . . . . . . . . . . . . . . . . . . . . . . . . . . 10
Check Engine light . . . . . . . . . . . . . . . . . . . . . . See Chapter 6
Circuit breakers — general information . . . . . . . . . . . . . . . . 5
Cluster panel instruments (except
   speedometer) — removal and installation . . . . . . . . . . . 16
Cruise control — general information and servicing . . . . . . . 22
Electrical troubleshooting — general information . . . . . . . . . 2
Fuses — general information . . . . . . . . . . . . . . . . . . . . . . . 3
Fusible links — general information . . . . . . . . . . . . . . . . . . 4
General information . . . . . . . . . . . . . . . . . . . . . . . . . . . . . 1
Headlight — adjustment . . . . . . . . . . . . . . . . . . . . . . . . . . 9
Headlight — removal and installation . . . . . . . . . . . . . . . . . 8
Headlight switch — removal and installation . . . . . . . . . . . 17
Instrument panel cluster — removal and installation . . . . . . . 15
Neutral safety and back up light switch (AT)
   adjustment . . . . . . . . . . . . . . . . . . . . . . . . See Chapter 7B

Neutral start switch — replacement
   and adjustment . . . . . . . . . . . . . . . . . . . . . See Chapter 7A
Parking brake switch — replacement . . . . . . . . . . . . . . . . . 21
Radio antenna — removal and installation . . . . . . . . . . . . . 12
Radio and speakers — removal and installation . . . . . . . . . . 11
Rear defogger (electric grid type) — check and repair . . . . . . 23
Rear window washer/wiper and rear window
   defogger switches — removal and installation . . . . . . . . . 18
Speedometer cable — replacement . . . . . . . . . . . . . . . . . . 14
Speedometer — removal and installation . . . . . . . . . . . . . . 13
Steering column switches — removal and installation . . . . . . 7
Stoplight switch — removal, installation and
   adjustment . . . . . . . . . . . . . . . . . . . . . . . . . See Chapter 9
Turn signal and hazard flashers — check and replacement . . . 6
Wiper motor — removal and installation . . . . . . . . . . . . . . . 20
Windshield wiper arm — removal and installation . . . . . . . . . 19

## Specifications

### Bulb application
**Front**
Headlight
| | |
|---|---|
| Dual — high and low beam . . . . . . . . . . . . . . . . . . . . . . . | 4652 |
| Dual — high beam (except halogen) . . . . . . . . . . . . . . . | 4651 |
| Dual — halogen high beam . . . . . . . . . . . . . . . . . . . . | H46561 |
| Park and turn lamp . . . . . . . . . . . . . . . . . . . . . . . . . . . . | 1157NA |
| Sidemarker . . . . . . . . . . . . . . . . . . . . . . . . . . . . . . . . . . . | 194 |
| Underhood lamp . . . . . . . . . . . . . . . . . . . . . . . . . . . . . . . | 94 |

**Interior**
| | |
|---|---|
| Dome lamp . . . . . . . . . . . . . . . . . . . . . . . . . . . . . . . . . . | 561 |
| Dome lamp with reading lamp . . . . . . . . . . . . . . . . . . . . | 562 |
| Reading lamp . . . . . . . . . . . . . . . . . . . . . . . . . . . . . . . . | 90 |
| Courtesy lamp . . . . . . . . . . . . . . . . . . . . . . . . . . . . . . . | 906 |
| Instrument cluster illumination | |
|    Standard . . . . . . . . . . . . . . . . . . . . . . . . . . . . . . . | 194 |
|    Gauges . . . . . . . . . . . . . . . . . . . . . . . . . . . . . . . . . | 168 |
| Clock, heater control, brake, Check Engine, | |
| Fasten Belt, choke, radio dial, ash tray lamps . . . . . . . . . | 168 |
| Radio dial . . . . . . . . . . . . . . . . . . . . . . . . . . . . . . . . . . . | 194 |

**Rear**
| | |
|---|---|
| Tail, stop and directional signal . . . . . . . . . . . . . . . . . . . | 1157 |
| Directional signal . . . . . . . . . . . . . . . . . . . . . . . . . . . . . | 1157A |
| Sidemarker . . . . . . . . . . . . . . . . . . . . . . . . . . . . . . . . . . | 1157 |
| License plate light . . . . . . . . . . . . . . . . . . . . . . . . . . . . . | 194 |
| Back up lamp . . . . . . . . . . . . . . . . . . . . . . . . . . . . . . . . | 1156 |

## 1   General information

The electrical system is a 12-volt, negative ground type. Power for the lights and all electrical accessories is supplied by a lead/acid-type battery which is charged by the alternator.

This chapter covers repair and service procedures for the various electrical components not associated with the engine. Information on the battery, alternator, distributor and starter motor can be found in Chapter 5.

It should be noted that whenever portions of the electrical system are worked on, the negative battery cable should be disconnected to prevent electrical shorts and/or fires.

**Note:** *Information concerning digital instrumentation and dash-related accessories is not included in this manual. Problems involving these components should be referred to your dealer.*

## 2   Electrical troubleshooting — general information

A typical electrical circuit consists of an electrical component, any switches, relays, motors, etc. related to that component and the wiring and connectors that connect the component to both the battery and the chassis. To aid in locating a problem in any electrical circuit, wiring diagrams are included at the end of this book.

Before tackling any troublesome electrical circuit, first study the appropriate diagrams to get a complete understanding of what makes up that individual circuit. Trouble spots, for instance, can often be narrowed down by noting if other components related to that circuit are operating properly or not. If several components or circuits fail at one time, chances are the problem lies in the fuse or ground connection, as several circuits often are routed through the same fuse and ground connections.

Electrical problems often stem from simple causes, such as loose or corroded connections, a blown fuse or melted fusible link. Prior to any electrical troubleshooting, always visually check the condition of the fuse, wires and connections in the problem circuit.

If testing instruments are going to be utilized, use the diagrams to plan ahead of time where you will make the necessary connections in order to accurately pinpoint the trouble spot.

The basic tools needed for electrical troubleshooting include a circuit tester or voltmeter (a 12-volt bulb with a set of test leads can also be used), a continuity tester, which includes a bulb, battery and set of test leads, and a jumper wire, preferably with a circuit breaker incorporated, which can be used to bypass electrical components.

Voltage checks should be performed if a circuit is not functioning properly.

Connect one lead of a circuit tester to either the negative battery terminal or a known good ground. Connect the other lead to a connector in the circuit being tested, preferably nearest to the battery or fuse. If the bulb of the tester goes on, voltage is reaching that point, which means the part of the circuit between that connector and the battery is problem free. Continue checking along the entire circuit in the same fashion. When you reach a point where no voltage is present, the problem lies between there and the last good test point. Most of the time the problem is due to a loose connection. **Note:** *Keep in mind that some circuits receive voltage only when the ignition key is in the Accessory or Run position.*

A method of finding shorts in a circuit is to remove the fuse and connect a test light or voltmeter in its place to the fuse terminals. There should be no load in the circuit. Move the wiring harness from side-to-side while watching the test light. If the bulb goes on, there is a short to ground somewhere in that area, probably where insulation has rubbed off of a wire. The same test can be performed on other components of the circuit, including the switch.

A ground check should be done to see if a component is grounded properly. Disconnect the battery and connect one lead of a self-powered test light, such as a continuity tester, to a known good ground. Connect the other lead to the wire or ground connection being tested. If the bulb goes on, the ground is good. If the bulb does not go on, the ground is not good.

A continuity check is performed to see if a circuit, section of circuit or individual component is passing electricity properly. Disconnect the battery and connect one lead of a self-powered test light, such as a continuity tester, to one end of the circuit. If the bulb goes on, there is continuity, which means the circuit is passing electricity properly. Switches can be checked in the same way.

Remember that all electrical circuits are composed basically of electricity running from the battery, through the wires, switches, relays, etc. to the electrical component (light bulb, motor, etc.). From there it is run to the body (ground), where it is passed back to the battery. Any electrical problem is basically an interruption in the flow of electricity to and from the battery.

## 3   Fuses — general information

The electrical circuits of the vehicle are protected by a combination of fuses, circuit breakers and fusible links. The fuse block is located in one of three locations. On the underside of the instrument panel on the driver's side, under the radio in the center of the dash or in the glove box. Check your owners manual for the location of the fuse box in your particular vehicle.

Each of the fuses is designed to protect a specific circuit, and the various circuits are identified on the fuse panel itself. Miniaturized fuses are employed in the fuse block. These compact fuses, with blade terminal design, allow fingertip removal and replacement.

If an electrical component fails, your first check should be the fuse. A fuse which has blown is easily identified by inspecting the element inside the clear plastic body. Also, the blade terminal tips are exposed in the fuse body, allowing for continuity checks.

It is important that the correct fuse be installed. The different electrical circuits need varying amounts of protection, indicated by the amperage rating molded in bold, color coded numbers on the fuse body. **Caution:** *At no time should the fuse be bypassed with pieces of metal or foil. Serious damage to the electrical system could result.*

If the replacement fuse immediately fails, do not replace it again until the cause of the problem is isolated and corrected. In most cases, this will be a short circuit in the wiring caused by a broken or deteriorated wire.

## 4   Fusible links — general information

In addition to fuses, the wiring is protected by fusible links. These links are used in circuits which are not ordinarily fused, such as the ignition circuit.

Although the fusible links appear to be a heavier gauge than the wire they are protecting, the appearance is due to the thick insulation. All fusible links are four wire gauges smaller than the wire they are designed to protect. The location of the fusible links on your particular vehicle may be determined by referring to the wiring diagrams at the end of this book.

The fusible links cannot be repaired, but a new link of the same size wire can be put in its place. The procedure is as follows:

a) Disconnect the negative cable at the battery.

b) Disconnect the fusible link from the starter solenoid.

c) Cut the damaged fusible link out of the wiring just behind the connector.

d) Strip the insulation approximately 1/2-inch.

e) Position the connector on the new fusible link and crimp it into place.

f) Use rosin core solder at each end of the new link to obtain a good solder joint.

g) Use plenty of electrical tape around the soldered joint. No wires should be exposed.

h) Connect the fusible link at the starter solenoid. Connect the battery ground cable. Test the circuit for proper operation.

4.1   The fusible links are attached to the starter and can be easily reached

## 5   Circuit breakers — general information

A circuit breaker is used to protect the headlight wiring and is located in the light switch. An electrical overload in the system will cause the lights to go on and off, or in some cases to remain off. If this happens, check the entire headlight circuit immediately. Once the overload condition is corrected, the circuit breaker will function normally. Circuit breakers are also used with accessories such as power windows, power door locks and the rear window defogger.

The circuit breakers in your particular vehicle may be found by referring to the wiring diagrams at the end of this book.

## 6   Turn signal and hazard flashers — check and replacement

1   Small canister-shaped flasher units are incorporated into the electrical circuits for the directional signals and hazard warning lights.
2   When the units are functioning properly, an audible click can be heard with the circuit in operation. If the turn signals fail on one side only and the flasher unit cannot be heard, a faulty bulb is indicated.
3   If the turn signal fails on both sides, the problem many be due to a blown fuse, faulty flasher unit or switch, or a broken or loose connection. If the fuse has blown, check the wiring for a short before installing a new fuse.
4   The hazard warning lights are checked as described in paragraph 3 above.

5   The hazard warning flasher is located in the convenience center adjacent to the fuse block. The fuse block could be in one of three places, Under the dash in the far left corner, in the glove box, in a swing panel under the radio. Your owners manual will give you the exact location of the fuse box.
6   The turn signal flasher is mounted on right side of the steering column and retained by a spring clip.
7   When replacing either of the flasher units, be sure to buy a replacement of the same capacity. Compare the new flasher to the old one before installing it.

## 7   Steering column switches — removal and installation

### *Turn signal switch*
1   Disconnect the negative cable at the battery.
2   Remove the steering wheel.
3   Pry the lock ring cover off, using two screwdrivers (photo).
4   Push the lock ring in sufficiently to allow removal of the ring retainer with two screwdrivers (photo).
5   Remove the lock ring.
6   Remove the retaining screw and remove the turn signal actuator lever.
7   Remove the three retaining screws and the hazard switch button (photos).

7.3   Screwdrivers can be used to remove the cover plate

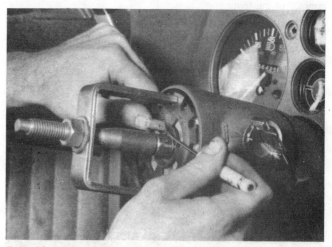

7.4   After relieving the tension on the locking ring screwdrivers should be used to remove it

7.7a   After removing the retaining screw (A) from the turn signal actuating lever, the three turn signal retaining screws (B) can be removed

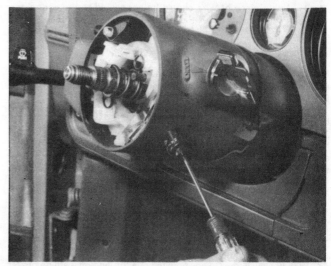

7.7b   A small Phillips screwdriver should be used to remove the hazard flasher knob

7.9   The turn signal electrical connector can be unplugged after removal of the trim panel

7.10   Remove the four retaining bolts to lower the steering column bracket

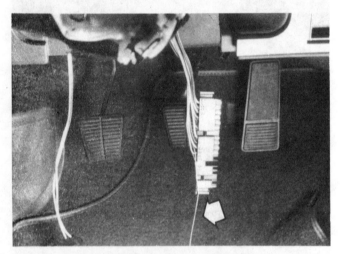

7.11   A thin piece of wire should be connected to the connector to aid in the installation of the new connector

7.15   Needle-nose pliers should be used to remove the ignition buzzer switch (A), then remove the ignition switch retaining screw (B)

8    Remove the trim panel from beneath the steering column to gain access to the turn signal switch harness.
9    Unplug the switch connector (photo).
10  Remove the steering column retaining bracket bolts and lower the bracket (photo).
11  Remove the switch assembly and harness, carefully guiding the harness and connector out of the column. For ease of reassembly, tie a string or fasten a thin wire to the harness connector to use in pulling the connector back into the narrow confines of the steering column (photo).
12  Installation is the reverse of removal.

### Ignition switch

13  Perform Steps 1 through 9 and pull the turn signal switch up sufficiently to provide access to the ignition switch.
14  With the key in the On position, remove the ignition warning buzzer switch contacts with needle-nose pliers.
15  Remove the switch retaining screw (photo).
16  Withdraw the switch from the steering column.

17  Installation is the reverse of removal, paying attention to the following points:
    a) Assemble the ignition warning buzzer contacts before inserting them (photos).
    b) When installing the turn signal actuator arm, make sure it is securely engaged in the lever mechanism before tightening the screw.

## 8   Headlight — removal and installation

### Removal

1    When replacing the headlight, do not turn the spring-loaded adjusting screws or the headlight aim will be changed.
2    Remove the five Torx head headlight bezel retaining screws and the decorative bezel (photo).
3    Remove the four screws which secure the retaining ring and withdraw the ring. Support the light as this is done (photo).
4    Pull the light away, unplug the connector and remove it from the vehicle (photo).

7.17a  The proper relationship of the ignition switch buzzer pieces

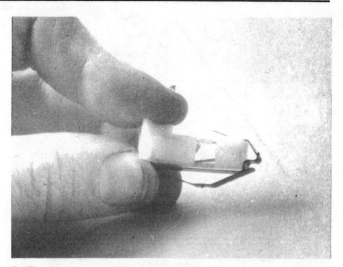

7.17b  Ignition switch buzzer assembled

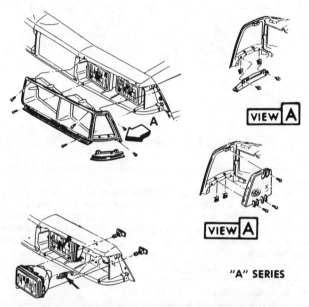

VIEW A

VIEW A

"A" SERIES

Fig. 12.1  Headlight installation details (Sec 8)

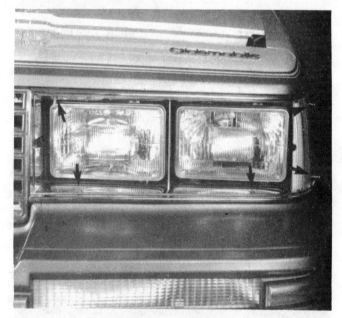

8.2  Location of the five retaining screws on the headlight bezel

8.3  Remove the four retaining screws to change the light bulb

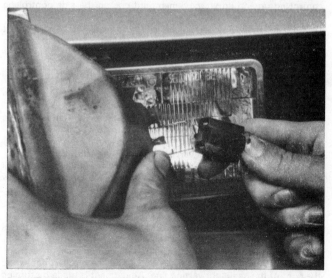

8.4  The light bulb can be unplugged by pulling on the connector to disengage it

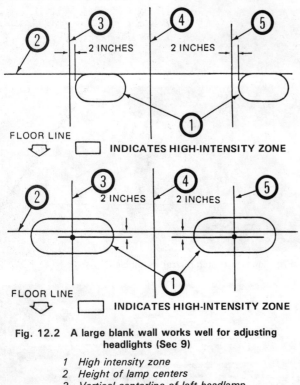

**Fig. 12.2   A large blank wall works well for adjusting headlights (Sec 9)**

1   *High intensity zone*
2   *Height of lamp centers*
3   *Vertical centerline of left headlamp*
4   *Vertical centerline of vehicle*
5   *Vertical centerline of right headlamp*

## Installation

5   Position the new unit close enough to connect the wires. Make sure the numbers molded into the lens are at the top.
6   Install the retaining ring and mounting screws.
7   Install the bezel and check for proper operation. If the adjusting screws were not turned, the headlight should not require adjustment.

## 9   Headlight — adjustment

**Note:** *It is important that the headlights are aimed correctly. If adjusted incorrectly they could blind an oncoming car and cause a serious accident or seriously reduce the your ability to see the road.*

Headlights have two spring loaded adjusting screws, one on the top controlling up and down movement and one on the side controlling left and right movement.

There are several methods of adjusting the headlights. The simplest method uses a screen or empty wall set at 25 feet in front of the vehicle and a level floor.

### Preparation

1   Park the vehicle on a known level floor 25 feet from the screen or light colored wall.
2   Position masking tape vertically on the screen in reference to the vehicle centerline and the centerlines of both headlights (see the accompanying illustration. **Note:** *If the vehicle has a four headlight system, four vertical lines plus the vehicle centerline will be used.*
3   Position a horizontal tape line in reference to the centerline of all the headlights. **Note:** *It may be easier to position the tape on the screen with the vehicle parked only a few inches away.*

### Adjustment

4   Adjustment should be made with the vehicle sitting level, the gas tank half-full and no unusually heavy load in the vehicle.
5   Starting with the low beam adjustment, position the high-intensity zone so it is two inches below the horizontal line and two inches to the right of the headlight vertical line. Adjustment is made by turning the top adjusting screw clockwise to raise the beam and counterclockwise to lower the beam. The adjusting screw on the side should be

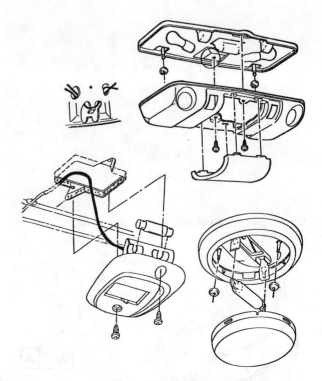

**Fig. 12.3   Typical dome lamps**

used in the same manner to move the beam left or right (see the accompanying illustration).
6   With the high beams on, the high-intensity zone should be vertically centered with the exact center just below the horizontal line. **Note:** *It may not be possible to position the headlight aim exactly for both high and low beams. If a compromise must be used, keep in mind that the low beams are the most used and have the greatest effect on driver safety.*

## 10   Bulb replacement

### Front end
**Parking and turn signal**
1   The turn signal and side marker light bulb can be replaced from outside the engine compartment after removing the five Torx screws and removing the fascia panel. The side marker bulb is located at the end of the fascia panel. The front turn signal bulb can be reached through the slot in the front bumper (photos). Turn the bulbs to remove them from the housings.

### Interior
**Courtesy lights**
2   The lower courtesy light bulbs are replaced by pushing up and turning to the left to unlatch the bulb from the socket.
**Dome light**
3   On some models screws retain the dome lamp lens, on others grasp the lens to remove it. Remove the bulb by pulling it straight down (photo).
**Instrument panel lights**
4   Most instrument panel bulbs can be replaced after removal of the instrument cluster (Section 16). If a bulb is located in a recess and cannot be grasped with the fingers, push a suitable piece of tubing, such as vacuum hose, over the bulb and pull straight out to remove it.
**Ashtray**
5   Remove the ashtray and remove the console cover for access to the bulb.
**Glove box**
6   Open the glove box, remove the striker assembly and remove the bulb.

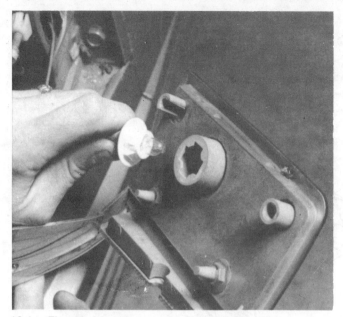

10.1a   The side lamp is removed by twisting it...

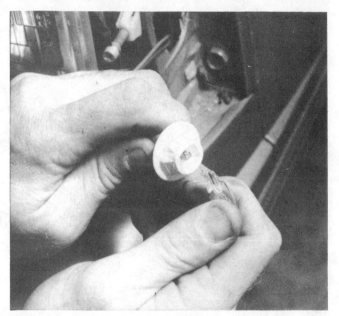

10.1b...then the bulb can be replaced by pulling it out and pushing it in

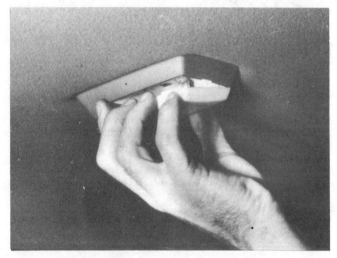

10.3   If there are no screws retaining the dome lamp cover in position, it can be removed by simply pulling it down

10.13   The tail lamp assembly is held in place by four wing nuts

**Heater and air conditioner control**

7    Remove the left side trim pad and instrument panel trim cover. Remove the screws retaining the control to the instrument panel.

8    Pull the control out sufficiently to gain access to the bulb socket and remove it. Remove the bulb from the socket.

**Radio bulb**

9    Remove the radio.

10   Remove the top cover from the radio, grasp the bulb and pull straight out.

**Console**

11   Remove the console cover retaining screws and pull the cover up sufficiently to gain access to the bulb socket. Twist the socket counterclockwise to remove it and then remove the bulb.

*Rear end*

**Courtesy light**

12   The rear compartment courtesy light bulb is contained in a plastic housing. Use a screwdriver to pry the housing out of the panel for access to the bulb.

**Tail and backup lights**

13   On hatchback models, remove the interior panel to gain access to the tail and back up lights. Remove the four plastic wing nuts and

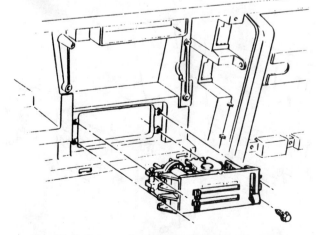

Fig. 12.4   Remove the four retaining screws to gain access to the heater control lamp (Sec 10)

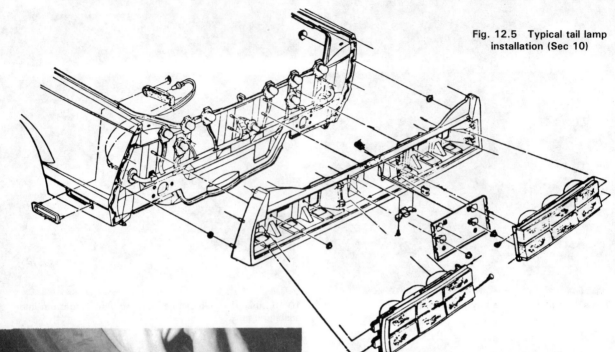

Fig. 12.5  Typical tail lamp installation (Sec 10)

10.15a  The back up lamp can be changed be first removing the retaining screw...

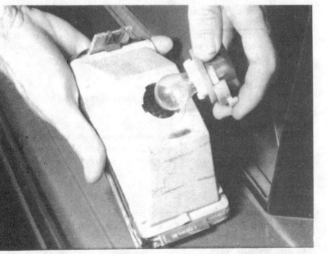

10.15b...and twisting the bulb socket to remove it from the lamp assembly

remove the tail light assembly. Turn the bulb socket assembly to remove and then push the bulb in and turn to remove (photo).

14  The tail light bulbs on sedan models can be replaced after removing the four wing nuts retaining the lamp housing and removing the housing.

15  The back up light bulb is replaced by removing the retaining screw and carefully prying out the lamp assembly (photos). The bulb is removed in the same manner as the tail lights.

### License plate

16  Access to the license plate lamp is gained by removing the two screws and removing the lamp assembly. Turn and pull the bulb to remove it.

---

## 11  Radio and speakers — removal and installation

### Radio

1  Remove the instrument panel trim plate.
2  Remove the radio retaining bolts.

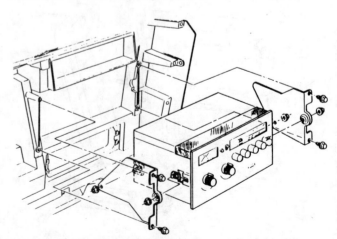

Fig. 12.6  Remove the four retaining bolts to remove the radio (Sec 11)

11.9   The front speakers are held in by two retaining bolts

3   Pull the radio out sufficiently for access to the antenna wire.
4   Use a screwdriver to disconnect the antenna wire.
5   Unplug the wiring connectors from the radio by depressing the tabs.
6   Lift the radio from the dash.
7   Installation is the reverse of removal.

## Speakers

### Front

8   Remove the speaker grille by carefully prying up on it, and lift the grille from the instrument panel.
9   Remove the two screws attaching the speaker to the instrument panel (photo) and lift the speaker sufficiently to disconnect the wiring.
10   Remove the speaker.
11   Installation is the reverse of removal.

### Rear

*Hatchback*

12   Remove the two plastic retaining screws and remove the speaker cover trim panel.
13   Pull the carpet back sufficiently for clearance and swing the speaker and cover assembly into the rear compartment.
14   Disconnect the wires and remove the speaker.
15   Installation is the reverse of removal.

*Sedan*

16   The speakers are accessible after opening the trunk. Refer to the accompanying illustration for removal and installation procedures.

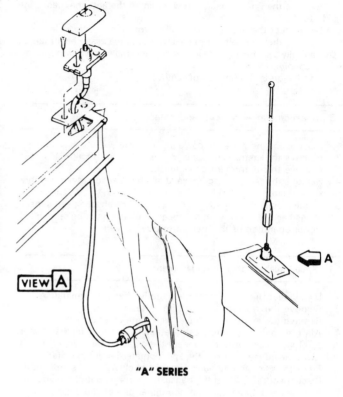

"A" SERIES

Fig. 12.7   Manual antenna installation (Sec 12)

## 12   Radio antenna — removal and installation

### Standard

1   The antenna mast can be removed by loosening the retaining nut and unscrewing the antenna as shown in the accompanying illustration.
2   The antenna body and cable assembly can be removed after the mast has been removed by unbolting it from the fender.
3   Installation is the reverse of removal, taking care to locate the studs securely in the fender.

### Power

4   Turn the steering wheel to the far left position.
5   Disconnect the negative cable at the battery.

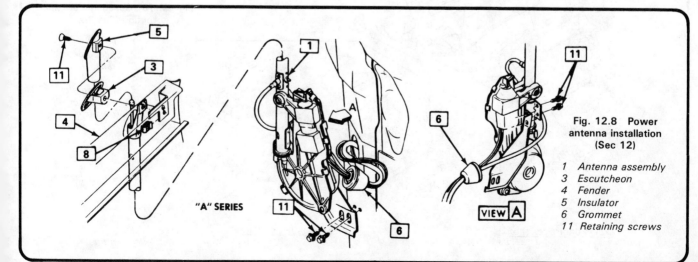

"A" SERIES

Fig. 12.8   Power antenna installation (Sec 12)

1   Antenna assembly
3   Escutcheon
4   Fender
5   Insulator
6   Grommet
11   Retaining screws

6    Remove the right inner fender splash shield, which is held in place
by four plastic studs and three screws.
7    Remove the Phillips head screw retaining the antenna mast trim
guide to the fender.
8    Disconnect the antenna lead and motor wires.
9    Remove the two bolts from the lower antenna assembly bracket.
10   Carefully pull the antenna and wiring assembly down through the
wheel opening.
11   Installation is the reverse of removal.

## 13   Speedometer — removal and installation

1    Disconnect the negative cable at the battery.
2    Remove the instrument panel cluster housing (Section 15).
3    Remove the instrument panel mask.
4    Remove the retaining screws and lift the speedometer assembly
from the cluster.
5    Installation is the reverse of removal. If the vehicle speed sensor
(VSS) has been removed with the speedometer, it must be reinstalled
for proper operation of the lock-up torque converter.

## 14   Speedometer cable — replacement

1    Disconnect the cable from the negative battery terminal.
2    Remove the steering column trim plate.
3    Remove the instrument cluster trim plate and pad.
4    After removing the four cluster retaining screws, pull the cluster
out carefully so as not to disconnect the cluster wiring until there is
sufficient clearance to reach the speedometer retaining collar.
5    Press the clip directly back toward the cluster to disconnect it.
6    Disconnect the cable at the transaxle or cruise control transducer.
7    Slide the old cable out from the upper end of the casing, or, if
broken, from both ends of the casing.
8    If the speedometer operation has been noisy, but the speedometer
cable appears to be in good condition, take a short piece of speedometer
cable with a tip to fit the speedometer and insert it in the speedometer
socket. Spin the piece of cable between your fingers. If binding is noted,
the speedometer is faulty and should be replaced with a new one.
9    Inspect the speedometer cable casing for sharp bends and breaks,
especially at the transaxle end. If breaks are noted, replace the casing
with a new one.
10   When installing the cable, perform the following operations to
ensure quiet operation.
11   Wipe the cable clean with a lint-free cloth.

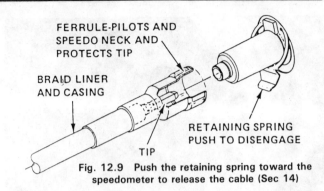

Fig. 12.9   Push the retaining spring toward the
speedometer to release the cable (Sec 14)

12   Flush the bore of the casing with solvent and blow it dry with compressed air.
13   Place some speedometer cable lubricant in the palm of one hand.
14   Feed the cable through the lubricant and into the casing until lubricant has been applied to the lower two-thirds of the cable. Do not
overlubricate.
15   Seat the upper cable tip in the speedometer and snap the retainer
onto the housing.
16   The remaining installation steps are the reverse of removal.

## 15   Instrument panel cluster — removal and installation

1    Disconnect the negative cable at the battery.
2    Remove the left side trim panels.
3    Remove the cluster retaining screws.
4    Disconnect the speedometer cable.
5    Pull the cluster out, disconnect the wiring and remove it from the
instrument panel.
6    Installation is the reverse of removal.

## 16   Cluster panel instruments (except speedometer) — removal and installation

1    Disconnect the negative cable at the battery.
2    Remove the instrument panel cluster.
3    Remove the cluster mask.
4    Remove the retaining bolts and lift the instruments from the cluster.
5    Installation is the reverse of removal.

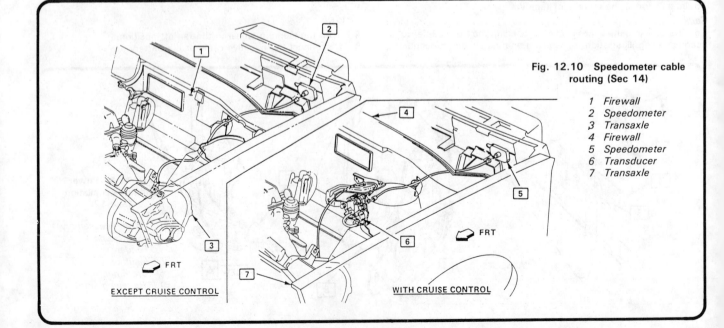

Fig. 12.10   Speedometer cable
routing (Sec 14)

1   Firewall
2   Speedometer
3   Transaxle
4   Firewall
5   Speedometer
6   Transducer
7   Transaxle

19.1  If the special tool required for wiper arm removal is unavailable, a rag and screwdriver can be used to remove it

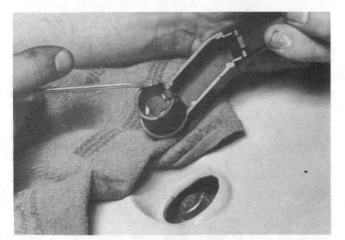

19.2  To reinstall the wiper arm, first align the slot with the notch on the shaft and press it on until it seats into position

## 17  Headlight switch — removal and installation

1  Disconnect the negative cable at the battery.
2  Remove the left side instrument panel trim panel.
3  Remove the retaining screws and lift the switch from the instrument panel.
4  Installation is the reverse of removal, taking care not to press on the switch buttons when placing the switch in position.

## 18  Rear window washer/wiper and rear window defogger switches — removal and installation

1  Disconnect the negative cable at the battery.
2  Remove the right side instrument panel trim cover.
3  Remove the retaining screws and lift the appropriate switch from the trim cover.
4  Installation is a reversal of removal.

## 19  Windshield wiper arm — removal and installation

1  Using rags to protect the paint and wiper arm, carefully pry up

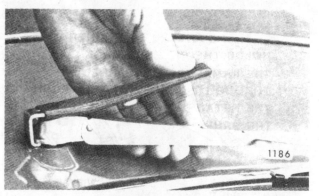

Fig. 12.11  A special tool being used to remove the windshield wiper arm (Sec 19)

20.3a  To gain access to the wiper transmission first remove all the top retaining bolts...

20.3b...then remove the retaining bolt inside under the cover at each end

on the arm to release it from the shaft (photo).
2  To reinstall the wiper arm, align the slot in the arm with the ridge on the wiper shaft and firmly push it into place (photo).

## 20  Windshield wiper motor — removal and installation

1  Disconnect the negative cable at the battery.
2  Remove the wiper arms.
3  Remove the eleven retaining screws holding the shroud grille panel. A #15 Torx bit will be needed to remove two of the eleven screws (photos).

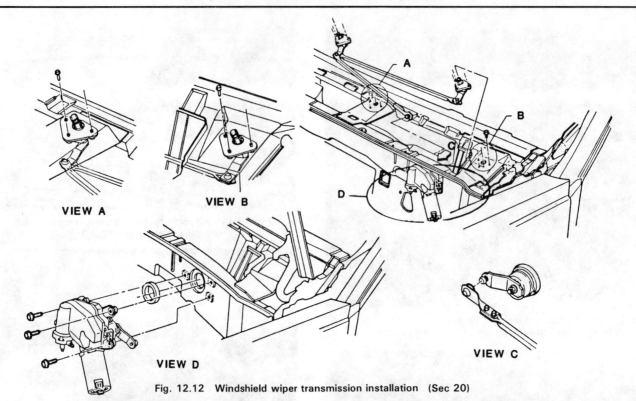

**Fig. 12.12  Windshield wiper transmission installation  (Sec 20)**

VIEW A

VIEW B

VIEW C

VIEW D

20.4   To help on reinstallation, first apply some paint to the wiper arm

20.7   The three wiper motor mounting bolts

4   To avoid problems on reinstallation, use paint to mark the position of the motor crank arm to the wiper linkage (photo).
5   Disconnect the motor crank arm from the wiper linkage.
6   Disconnect the wiring and washer hoses from the wiper motor.
7   Remove the three motor to body attaching screws (photo) and carefully remove the wiper motor from the vehicle.
8   Installation is the reverse of the removal procedure, noting that the paint marks on the wiper linkage should be aligned for proper operation.

## 21  Parking brake switch — replacement

1   Remove the console cover.
2   Unplug the electrical connector from the switch.

3   Remove the screw retaining the switch to the parking brake and remove the switch.

## 22  Cruise Control — general information and servicing

### 1982 and 1983

The Cruise Control with Resume system is an option which maintains a desired vehicle speed under normal driving conditions. The system also has the capability of resuming a preset speed upon driver demand after the system has been disengaged. This is accomplished by moving a slide on the Cruise Control lever handle to the Resume position. Steep grades, up or down, may cause variations in the selected

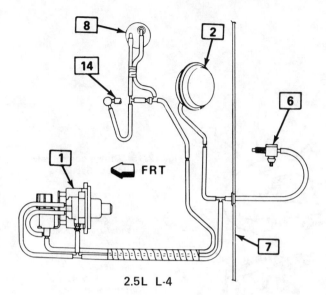

2.5L  L-4

2.8L  V6

VIEW A
WITHOUT A/C

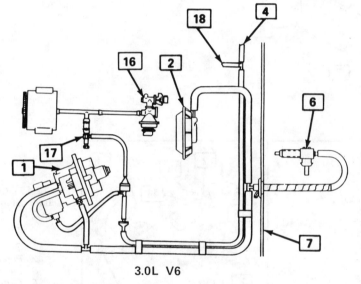

3.0L  V6

Fig. 12.13  Cruise control
vacuum schematic (Sec 22)

1   Transducer
2   Servo
4   A/C vacuum
6   Vacuum release valve
7   Front of dash panel
8   Vacuum pump
13  Vacuum regulator
14  Brake booster hose
16  Air management valve
17  Aspirator
18  Manifold vacuum
19  Vacuum tank

speed, which is considered normal.

The main components of the cruise control system are a transducer assembly, a resume solenoid valve, a vacuum servo with linkage, an engagement switch button and an On/Off/Resume switch on the turn signal lever, and vacuum and electric release switches attached to the brake pedal (automatic) or clutch pedal (manual).

Because of the variations in installations, it is not possible to include all the service procedures in this manual. However, those elements of the system most often requiring service or adjustment are covered.

If the servo unit requires replacement or adjustment, refer to the appropriate diagram and instructions accompanying this Section.

The transducer is calibrated in such a manner during production that overhaul operations are impractical. A defective transducer must be replaced with a new one. However, one adjustment is possible. If there is a difference between the engagement speed selected and the actual cruising speed, proceed as follows:

a) Check all hoses for kinks and cracks. If there is still a difference between the engagement and cruising speeds, proceed to b.

b) If the cruising speed is lower than the engagement speed, loosen the orifice tube locknut and turn the tube out.

c) If the cruising speed is higher than the engagement speed, loosen the orifice tube locknut and turn the tube in.

d) Each 90-degree (1/4-turn) rotation will alter the engagement/cruising speed one mph.

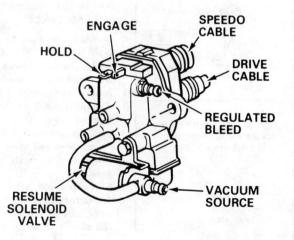

Fig. 12.14  Cruise control transducer (Sec 22)

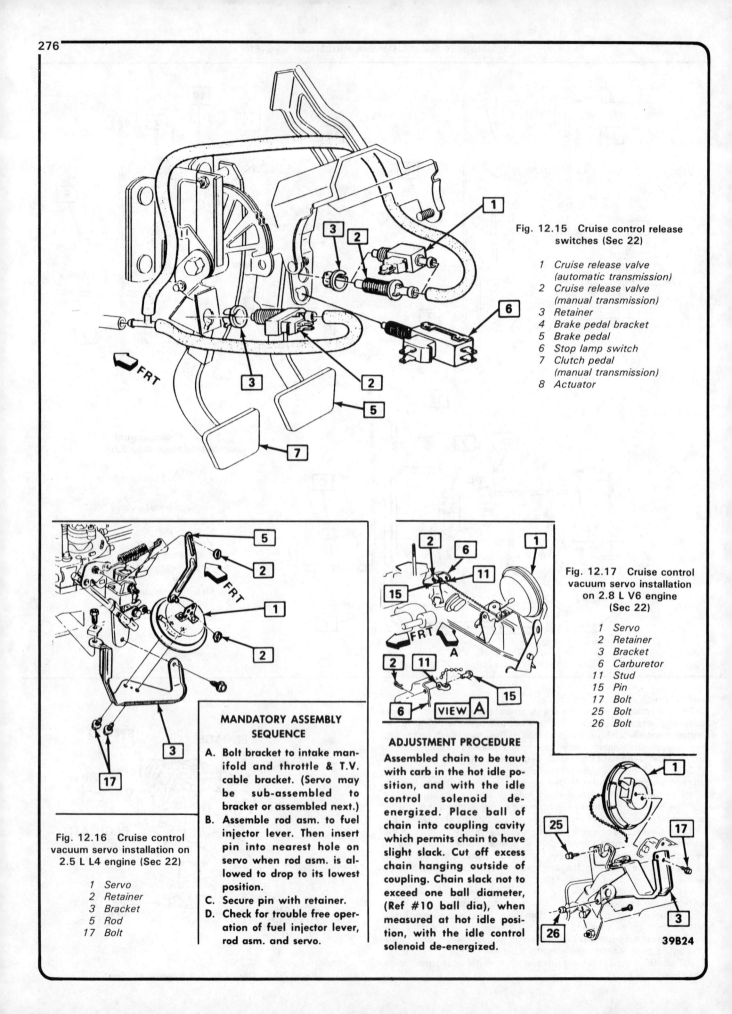

**Fig. 12.15 Cruise control release switches (Sec 22)**

1 Cruise release valve (automatic transmission)
2 Cruise release valve (manual transmission)
3 Retainer
4 Brake pedal bracket
5 Brake pedal
6 Stop lamp switch
7 Clutch pedal (manual transmission)
8 Actuator

**Fig. 12.16 Cruise control vacuum servo installation on 2.5 L L4 engine (Sec 22)**

1 Servo
2 Retainer
3 Bracket
5 Rod
17 Bolt

**MANDATORY ASSEMBLY SEQUENCE**

A. Bolt bracket to intake manifold and throttle & T.V. cable bracket. (Servo may be sub-assembled to bracket or assembled next.)
B. Assemble rod asm. to fuel injector lever. Then insert pin into nearest hole on servo when rod asm. is allowed to drop to its lowest position.
C. Secure pin with retainer.
D. Check for trouble free operation of fuel injector lever, rod asm. and servo.

**ADJUSTMENT PROCEDURE**

Assembled chain to be taut with carb in the hot idle position, and with the idle control solenoid de-energized. Place ball of chain into coupling cavity which permits chain to have slight slack. Cut off excess chain hanging outside of coupling. Chain slack not to exceed one ball diameter, (Ref #10 ball dia), when measured at hot idle position, with the idle control solenoid de-energized.

**Fig. 12.17 Cruise control vacuum servo installation on 2.8 L V6 engine (Sec 22)**

1 Servo
2 Retainer
3 Bracket
6 Carburetor
11 Stud
15 Pin
17 Bolt
25 Bolt
26 Bolt

39B24

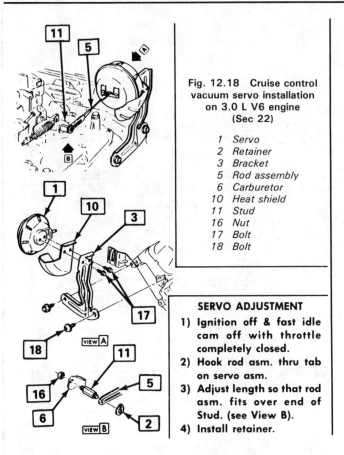

**Fig. 12.18  Cruise control vacuum servo installation on 3.0 L V6 engine (Sec 22)**

1 *Servo*
2 *Retainer*
3 *Bracket*
5 *Rod assembly*
6 *Carburetor*
10 *Heat shield*
11 *Stud*
16 *Nut*
17 *Bolt*
18 *Bolt*

### SERVO ADJUSTMENT

1) **Ignition off & fast idle cam off with throttle completely closed.**
2) **Hook rod asm. thru tab on servo asm.**
3) **Adjust length so that rod asm. fits over end of Stud. (see View B).**
4) **Install retainer.**

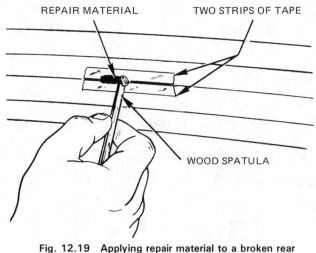

**Fig. 12.19  Applying repair material to a broken rear defogger grid (Sec 23)**

e) Tighten the locknut after adjustment has been made and check the system operation at 55 mph.

1    To remove, install and adjust the brake and clutch release switches and valves, refer to the accompanying illustration.

2    To remove the cruise control switch, vacuum valve assembly/TCC switch (automatic transmission) or vacuum release valve (manual transmission), pull the component from the bracket under the dash, then disconnect the wiring and/or vacuum connector and discard the faulty component and the retainer.

3    Install a new retainer in the bracket.

4    With the brake or clutch pedal depressed, install the new component in the retainer and make sure it is seated. Note that audible clicks can be heard as the component is pressed into the retainer.

5    Pull the brake or clutch pedal all the way up against the stop until the clicks can no longer be heard.

6    Reconnect the wiring and/or vacuum connectors.

7    Other servicing of the cruise control system components should be done by your dealer.

## 1984 and 1985

The Cruise III system is an option which maintains a desired vehicle speed under normal driving conditions. The system also has the capability of resuming a preset speed upon driver demand after the system has been disengaged. This is accomplished by moving a slide on the cruise control lever handle to the R/A position momentarily, if the lever is held longer than a second the system reverts to the accel mode. Steep grades, up or down, may cause variations in the selected speed, which is considered normal.

The main components of the Cruise III system are an electronic control assembly, a two valve servo unit containing two solenoids, a vacuum supply, an engagement switch button and an On-Off/Resume/accel switch on the turn signal lever, and vacuum and electric release switches attached to the brake pedal (automatic) or clutch pedal (manual).

Because of the solid state design of this system, there are no adjustments and diagnosis is a complicated procedure. Any service of the system should be done by a qualified technician.

## 23  Rear defogger (electric grid type) — check and repair

1    This option consists of a rear window with a number of horizontal elements baked into the glass surface during the glass forming operation.

2    Small breaks in the element can be successfully repaired without removing the rear window.

3    To test the grids for proper operation, start the engine and turn on the system.

4    Ground one lead of a test light and carefully touch the other lead to each element line.

5    The brilliance of the test light should increase as the lead is moved across the element from right to left. If the test light glows brightly at both ends of the lines, check for a loose ground wire. All of the lines should be checked in at least two places.

6    To repair a break in a line, it is recommended that a repair kit specifically for this purpose be purchased from a GM dealer. Included in the repair kit will be a decal, a container of silver plastic and hardener, a mixing stick and instructions.

7    To repair a break, first turn off the system and allow it to de-energize for a few minutes.

8    Lightly buff the element area with fine steel wool then clean it thoroughly with alcohol.

9    Use the decal supplied in the repair kit or apply strips of electrician's tape above and below the area to be repaired. The space between the pieces of tape should be the same width as the existing lines. This can be checked from outside the vehicle. Press the tape tightly against the glass to prevent seepage.

10  Mix the hardener and silver plastic thoroughly.

11  Using the wood spatula, apply the silver plastic mixture between the pieces of tape, overlapping the undamaged area slightly on either end.

12  Carefully remove the decal or tape and apply a constant stream of hot air directly to the repaired area. A heat gun set at 500 to 700 degrees Fahrenheit is recommended. Hold the gun one inch from the glass for two minutes.

13  If the new element appears off color, tincture of iodine can be used to clean the repair and bring it back to the proper color. This mixture should not remain on the repair for more than 30 seconds.

14  Although the defogger is now fully operational, the repaired area should not be disturbed for at least 24 hours.

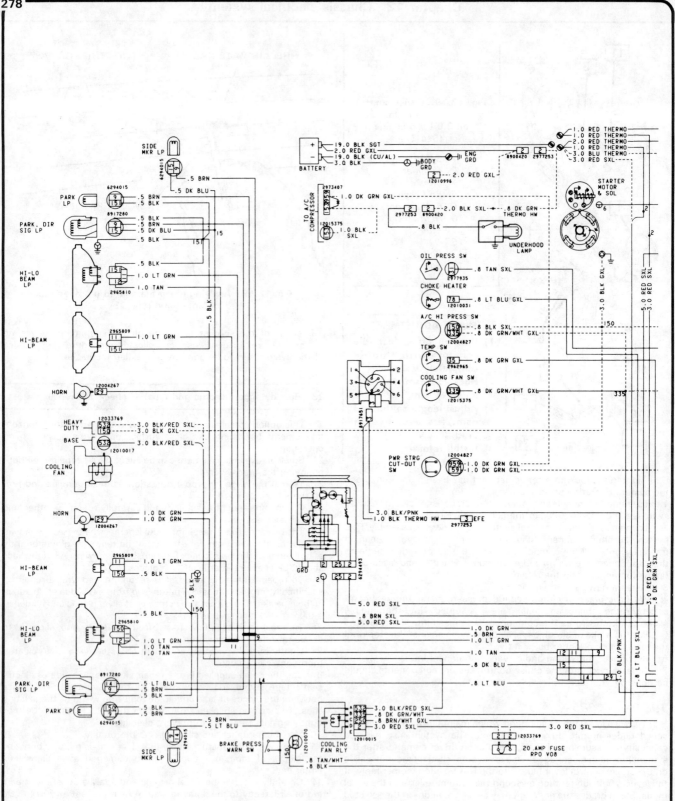

Wiring diagram — front end and engine compartment

279

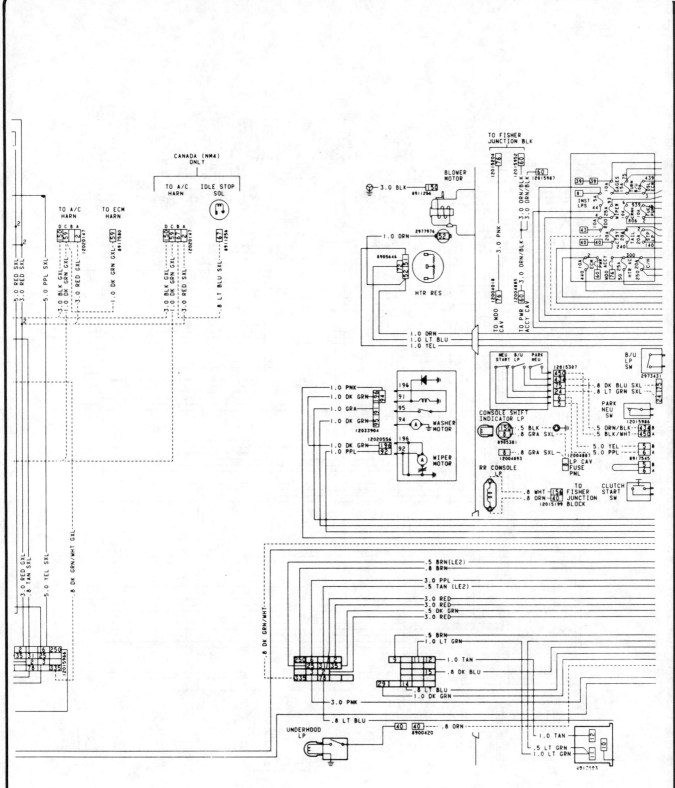

Wiring diagram — front end and engine compartment

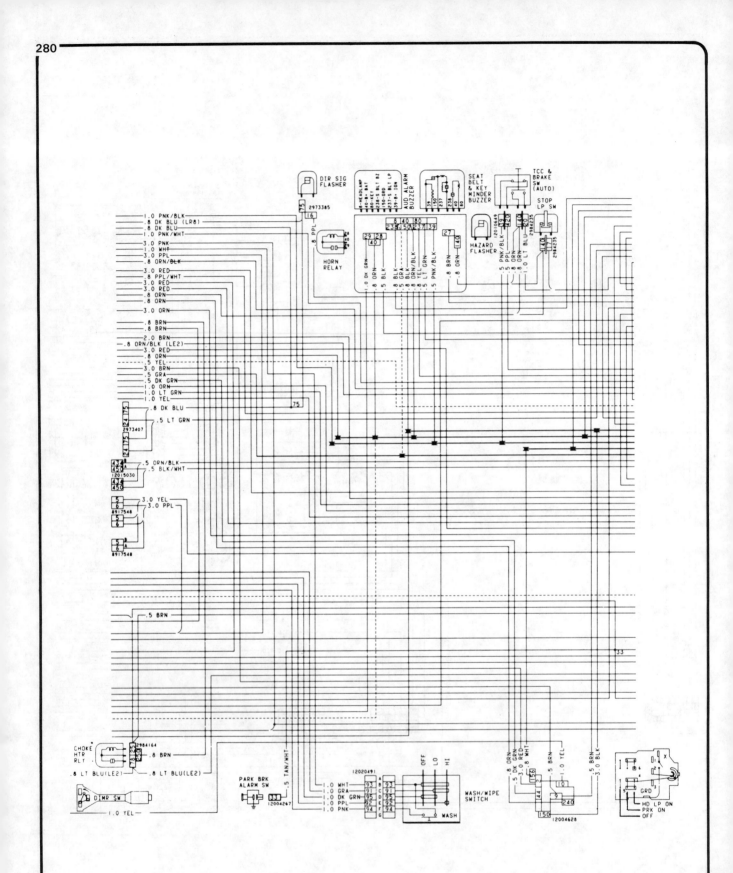

Wiring diagram — instrument panel and interior

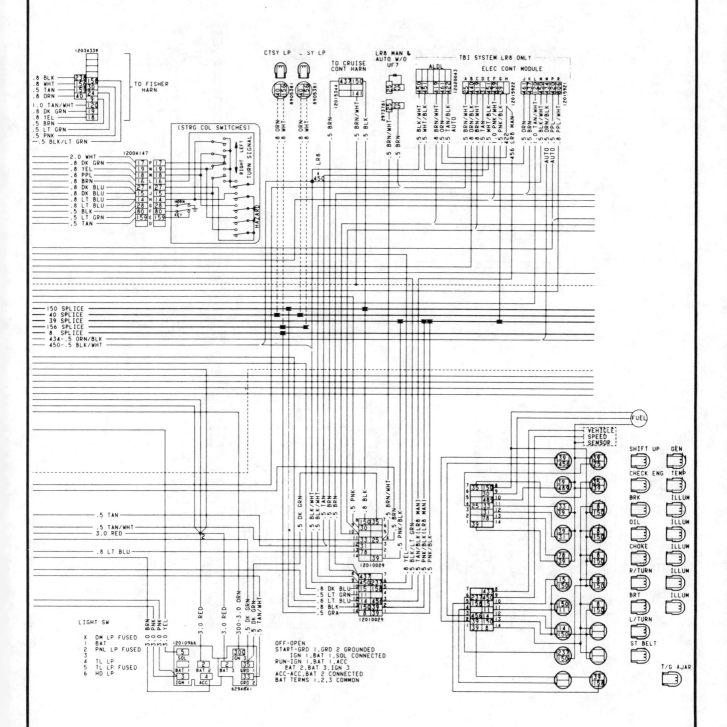

**Wiring diagram — instrument panel and interior (continued)**

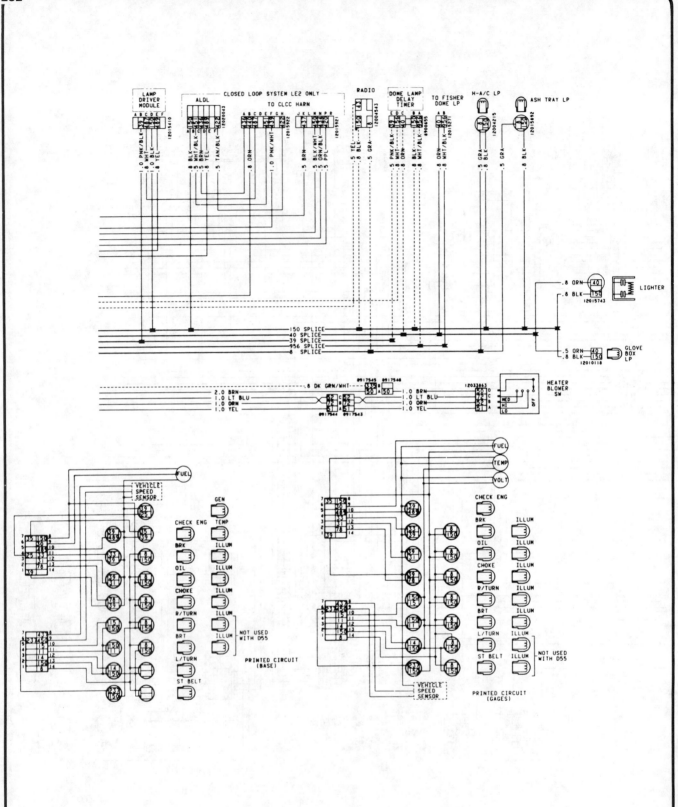

Wiring diagram — instrument panel and interior (continued)

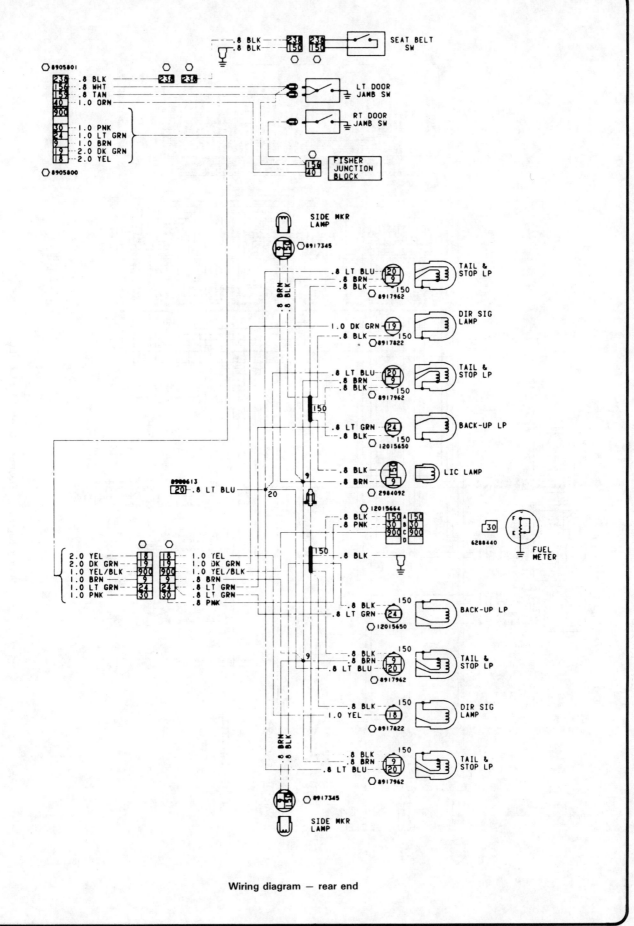

**Wiring diagram — rear end**

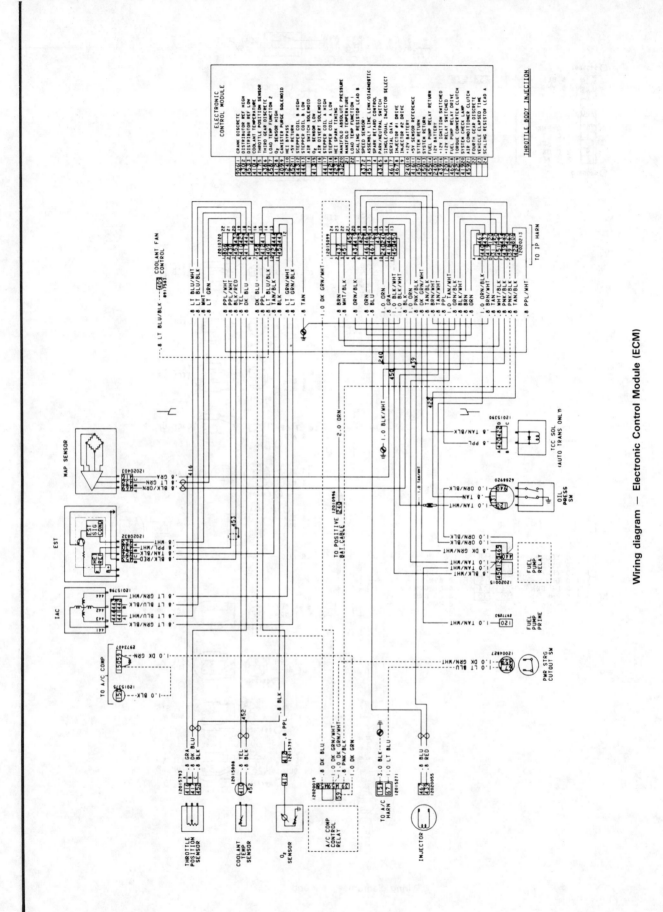

**Wiring diagram — Electronic Control Module (ECM)**

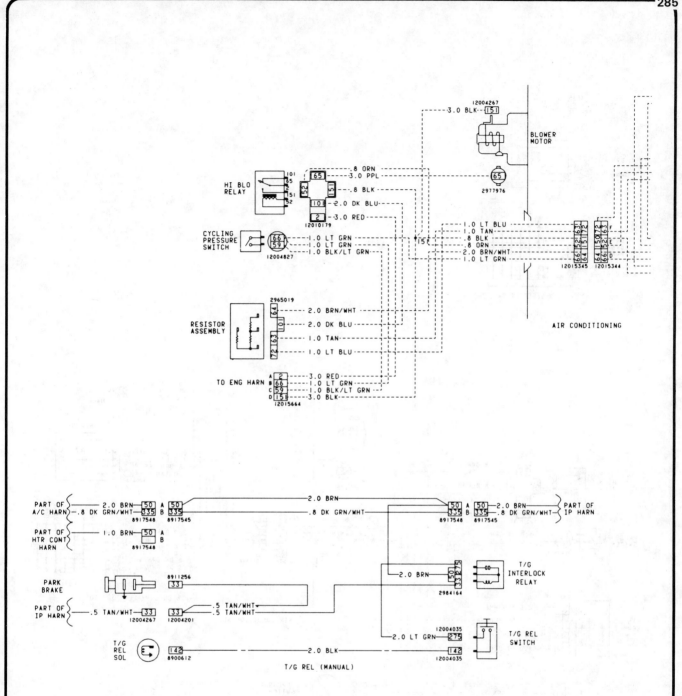

**Wiring diagram — optional circuits**

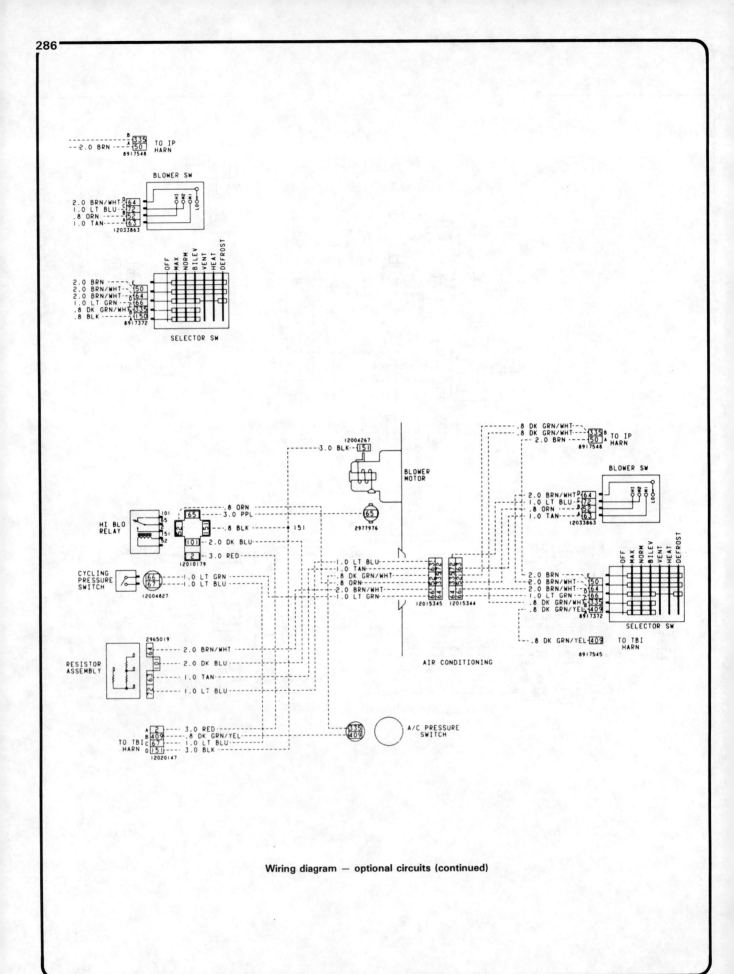

**Wiring diagram — optional circuits (continued)**

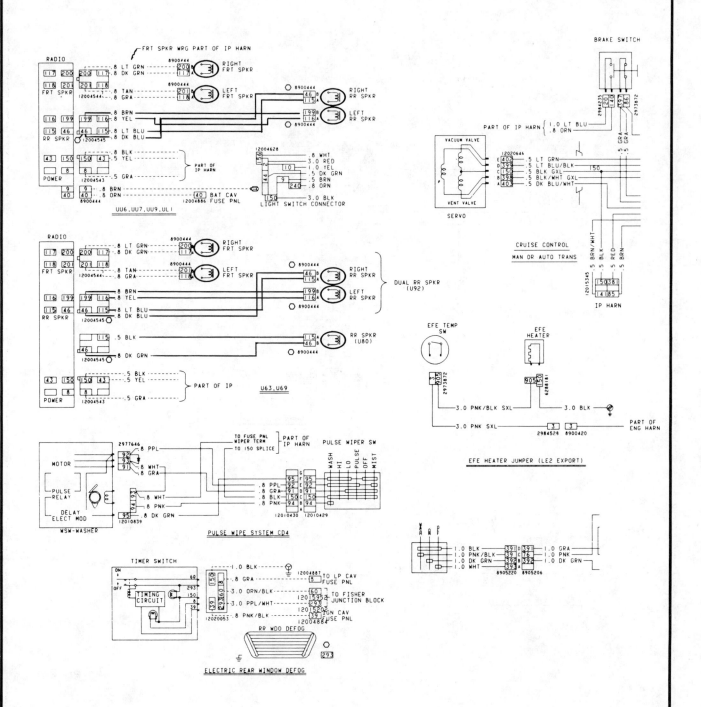

**Wiring diagram — optional circuits (continued)**

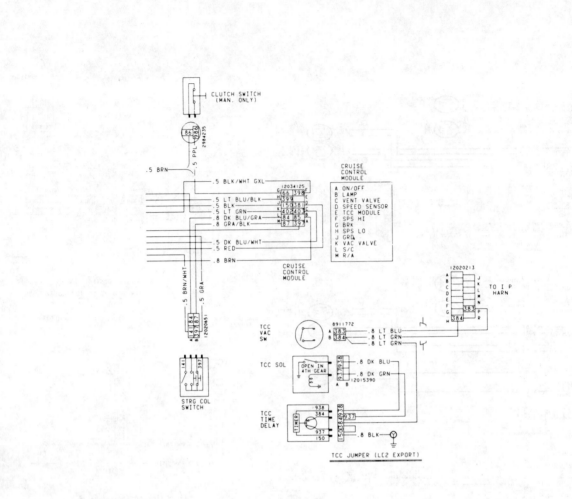

CLUTCH SWITCH
(MAN. ONLY)

2984235

CRUISE
CONTROL
MODULE

A ON/OFF
B LAMP
C VENT VALVE
D SPEED SENSOR
E TCC MODULE
F SPS HI
G BRK
H SPS LO
J GRD
K VAC VALVE
L S/C
M R/A

.5 BRN
.5 PPL

.5 BLK/WHT GXL
.5 LT BLU/BLK
.5 BLK
.5 LT GRN
.8 DK BLU/GRA
.8 GRA/BLK

.5 DK BLU/WHT
.5 RED
.8 BRN

CRUISE
CONTROL
MODULE

.5 BRN/WHT
.5 GRA
12020651

STRG COL
SWITCH

12020213

TO I P
HARN

TCC
VAC
SW

8911772

.8 LT BLU
.8 LT GRN
.8 LT GRN

TCC SOL

OPEN IN
4TH GEAR

.8 DK BLU
.8 DK GRN
12015390

TCC
TIME
DELAY

TIMER

.8 BLK

TCC JUMPER (LC2 EXPORT)

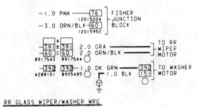

—1.0 PNK — 76    FISHER
12015204   JUNCTION
—3.0 ORN/BLK—60   BLOCK
12015952

391 B 391  2.0 GRA        TO RR
60 C 60    2.0 ORN/BLK     WIPER
8917543 8917544            MOTOR

392 392 —1.0 DK GRN— 392  TO WASHER
6288101 8905485  1.0 BLK 151  MOTOR

RR GLASS WIPER/WASHER WRG

**Wiring diagram — optional circuits (continued)**

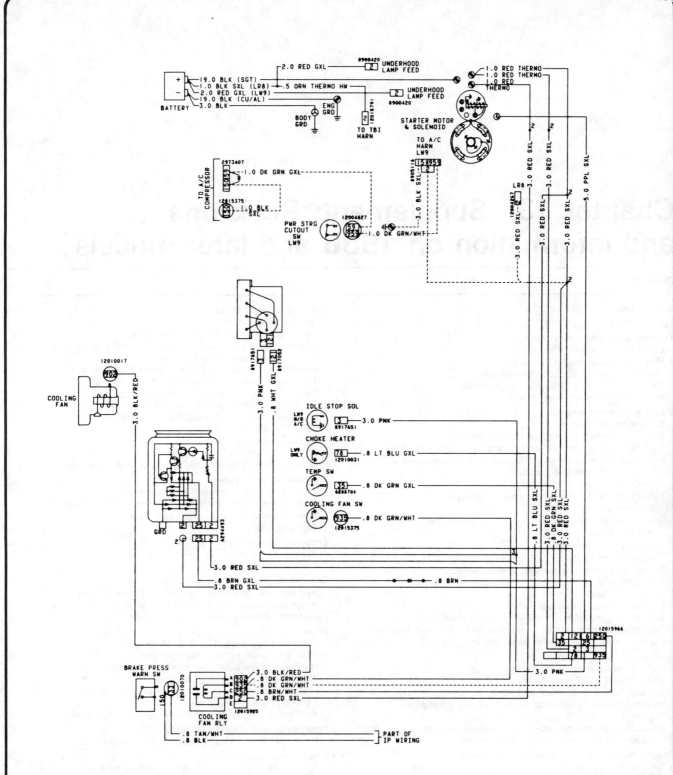

Wiring diagram — engine and alternator wiring four-cylinder engine only

# Chapter 13   Supplement: Revisions and information on 1986 and later models

## Contents

| | |
|---|---|
| Introduction | 1 |
| Specifications | 2 |
| Tune-up and routine maintenance | 3 |
| Drivebelt check and adjustment | |
| Hydraulic clutch fluid level check | |
| Manual transaxle lubricant level check | |
| Engine oil and filter change (2.5L four-cylinder engine) | |
| Automatic transaxle fluid change | |
| 2.5L four-cylinder engine | 4 |
| General information | |
| Exhaust manifold — removal and installation | |
| Cylinder head — removal and installation (1987 models) | |
| Hydraulic lifters — removal, inspection and installation | |
| Oil pan — removal and installation | |
| Timing gear cover — removal and installation | |
| Force balancer/oil pump assembly — removal and installation | |
| Oil pump/pressure regulator valve — removal, inspection and installation | |
| 2.8L and 3.1L V6 engines | 5 |
| General information | |
| Rocker arm covers — removal and installation | |
| Intake manifold (multi-port fuel injection) — removal and installation | |
| Cylinder heads — removal and installation | |
| Oil pan — removal and installation (1987 models) | |
| Rear main bearing oil seal — replacement (engine in vehicle) | |
| Crankcase front cover — removal and installation | |
| 3.3L and 3.8L V6 engines | 6 |
| General information | |
| Intake manifold — removal and installation | |
| Cylinder heads — removal and installation | |
| Hydraulic lifters — removal, inspection and installation | |
| Oil pump — removal and installation | |
| Piston/connecting rod assembly — installation and bearing oil clearance check (3.3L engine) | |
| Cooling, heating and air conditioning systems | 7 |
| General information | |
| Water pump — removal and installation | |
| Fuel and exhaust systems | 8 |
| General information | |
| Fuel injection pressure relief procedure | |
| Quick-connect fuel line fittings — removal and installation | |
| Electric fuel pump — replacement | |
| Throttle body injection (TBI) — general information | |
| TBI components — removal and installation | |
| TBI assembly — removal, overhaul and installation | |
| TBI minimum idle speed — adjustment | |
| Multi-port fuel injection (MPFI) — general information | |
| MPFI fuel pump — check | |
| MPFI fuel pressure test | |
| MPFI fuel flow test | |
| MPFI system components — removal and installation | |
| Engine electrical systems | 9 |
| Ignition system — general information | |
| Ignition system components — removal and installation | |
| Charging system — general information | |
| Charging system — check | |
| Emissions control systems | 10 |
| General information | |
| Trouble codes | |
| Clutch and driveaxles | 11 |
| Hydraulic clutch release system — general information | |
| Hydraulic clutch release system — removal and installation | |
| Hydraulic clutch release system — bleeding | |
| Brakes | 12 |
| Front disc brake pads — replacement | |
| Rear disc brake pads — replacement | |
| Rear disc brake caliper — removal and installation | |
| Rear disc brake caliper — overhaul | |
| Master cylinder — removal, overhaul and installation | |
| Parking brake — adjustment | |
| Anti-lock brake system (ABS) — general information | |
| Suspension and steering systems | 13 |
| Power steering pump — removal and installation | |
| Chassis electrical system | 14 |
| Composite headlights — removal and installation | |
| Wiring diagrams | |

## 1   Introduction

This Supplement contains specifications and service procedure changes that apply to the General Motors A-cars (Chevrolet Celebrity, Pontiac 6000, Buick Century and Oldsmobile Ciera) manufactured from 1986 on. Also included is information related to previous models that was not available at the time of original publication of this manual.

Where no differences (or very minor differences) exist between 1985 models and later models, no information is given; the original material

included in Chapters 1 through 12, pertaining to 1985 models, should be used.

Before beginning any service or repair procedure, check this Supplement for new specifications and procedure changes. Note the supplementary information and be sure to include it while following the original procedure(s) in Chapters 1 through 12.

## 2 Specifications

**Note:** *The following specifications are revisions of or supplementary to those listed at the beginning of each Chapter of this manual. The original specifications also apply to later models unless alternative figures are included here.*

### Tune-up and routine maintenance
*Recommended lubricants, fluids and capacities*

| | |
|---|---|
| Engine oil viscosity | See accompanying chart |
| Engine oil capacity * | |
|   2.5L four-cylinder engine | 3 qts |
|   All V6 engines | 4 qts |

\* *When changing the oil filter, one additional quart of oil may be needed*

| | |
|---|---|
| Cooling system capacity | |
|   2.5L four-cylinder engine | 10.0 qts |
|   All V6 engines | 12.75 qts |
| Manual transaxle lubricant | |
|   Type | |
|     1986 and 1987 | SAE 5W-30 manual transaxle fluid (GM part No. 1052931) or equivalent |
|     1988 on | Synchromesh Transmission Fluid (GM part No. 12345349) |
|   Capacity | 2 qts (approximate) |
| Automatic transaxle capacity ** | |
|   Without overdrive | 4 qts |
|   With overdrive | 6.5 qts |
| Power steering fluid type | GM power steering fluid (GM part No. 1052884) or equivalent |
| Hydraulic clutch fluid type | Delco Supreme 11 brake fluid (GM part No. 1052535) or DOT 3 brake fluid |

\*\* *Capacity is approximate for refill after draining for routine maintenance. Actual capacity should be measured on the transaxle dipstick as discussed in Chapter 1.*

| Torque specifications | Ft-lbs | Nm |
|---|---|---|
| Spark plugs (3.8L V6 engine only) | 20 | 27 |
| M12 x 1.5 wheel lug nuts | 100 | 136 |

### 2.5L four-cylinder engine
*General*

| | |
|---|---|
| Oil pressure (1988 on) | 50 psi at 2000 rpm |

*Valves and related components*

| | |
|---|---|
| Valve stem diameter | |
|   Intake | 0.313 to 0.314 in (7.95 to 7.98 mm) |
|   Exhaust | 0.312 to 0.313 in (7.92 to 7.95 mm) |
| Stem-to-guide clearance (1988 and later exhaust valve) | 0.0012 to 0.003 in (0.030 to 0.078 mm) |
| Valve seat width | |
|   Intake | 0.035 to 0.075 in (0.889 to 1.905 mm) |
|   Exhaust | 0.058 to 0.105 in (1.473 to 2.667 mm) |
| Valve spring installed height | |
|   1986 and 1987 | 1.440 in (36.58 mm) |
|   1988 on | 1.679 in (42.65 mm) |
| Valve spring pressure and length (intake and exhaust) | |
|   1986 and 1987 | |
|     Valve closed | 1.440 in at 71 to 78 lbs. |
|     Valve open | 1.040 in at 158 to 170 lbs. |

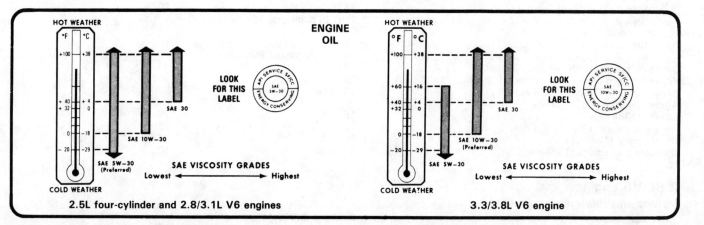

2.5L four-cylinder and 2.8/3.1L V6 engines            3.3/3.8L V6 engine

Valve spring pressure and length (intake and exhaust) (continued)
 1988 on
  Valve closed ............................................. 1.68 in at 70 to 78 lbs.
  Valve open ............................................... 1.239 in at 169 to 181 lbs.
 Pushrod length ............................................. 8.299 in (210.80 mm)

## Pistons and rings
Piston-to-bore clearance ..................................... 0.0014 to 0.0022 in (0.035 to 0.055 mm) (measured 1-1/8 inch down from piston top)
Pin-to-piston clearance ...................................... Loose; 0.002 to 0.004 in (0.050 to 0.101 mm)
Piston ring end gap
 Top ring .................................................. 0.010 to 0.020 in (0.254 to 0.508 mm)
 Second ring ............................................... 0.010 to 0.020 in (0.254 to 0.508 mm)
 Oil ring .................................................. 0.020 to 0.060 in (0.508 to 1.524 mm)

## Camshaft
Lobe lift (intake and exhaust) ............................... 0.398 in (10.109 mm)

## Engine block
Cylinder out-of-round limits
 1988 ..................................................... 0.001 in (0.025 mm)
 1989 ..................................................... 0.002 in (0.051 mm)

## Oil pump (1988 on)
Gear pocket depth
 Minimum .................................................. 0.514 in (13.056 mm)
 Maximum .................................................. 0.516 in (13.106 mm)
Gear thickness ............................................. 0.511 to 0.512 in (12.98 to 13.00 mm)

| **Torque specifications** | **Ft-lbs** *(unless otherwise indicated)* | **Nm** |
|---|---|---|
| Exhaust manifold bolts | See Fig. 13.9 | |
| Intake manifold bolts | 25 | 34 |
| Cylinder head bolts (1986 and 1987) | | |
| Step 1 | 18 | 25 |
| Step 2 | | |
| All but bolt 9 | 22 | 30 |
| Bolt 9 | 29 | 40 |
| Step 3 | | |
| All but bolt 9 | Turn an additional 120° | |
| Bolt 9 | Turn an additional 90° | |
| Cylinder head bolts (1988 on) | | |
| Step one | 18 | 24 |
| Step two | | |
| All but bolt 9 | 26 | 35 |
| Bolt 9 | 18 | 24 |
| Step three (all bolts) | Turn an additional 90° | |
| Balancer-to-block bolts | | |
| 1988 | | |
| Short bolts | | |
| Step 1 | 9 | 12 |
| Step 2 | Turn an additional 75° | |
| Long bolts | | |
| Step 1 | 9 | 12 |
| Step 2 | Turn an additional 90° | |
| 1989 | | |
| Short bolts | | |
| Step 1 | 15 | 20 |
| Step 2 | Turn an additional 60° | |
| Long bolts | | |
| Step 1 | 11 | 15 |
| Step 2 | Turn an additional 90° | |
| Rocker arm bolt (1988 on) | 24 | 33 |
| Water pump-to-engine block bolts (1988 on) | 25 | 34 |
| Rocker arm cover bolts (1988 on) | 45 in-lbs | 5 |
| Automatic transaxle driveplate-to-crankshaft bolts (1988 on) | 55 | 75 |
| Harmonic balancer bolt (1988 on) | 162 | 220 |
| Oil pan bolts (1988 on) | 20 | 27 |
| Oil pump cover bolts (1988 on) | 90 in-lbs | 10 |

# 2.8L V6 engine
## Valves and related components
Valve seat runout ............................................. 0.001 in (0.025 mm) maximum

| | |
|---|---|
| Valve seat width | |
| Intake . . . . . . . . . . . . . . . . . . . . . . . . . . . . . . . . . . . . . | 0.061 to 0.073 in (1.55 to 1.85 mm) |
| Exhaust . . . . . . . . . . . . . . . . . . . . . . . . . . . . . . . . . . . . | 0.067 to 0.079 in (1.70 to 2.0 mm) |
| Valve spring pressure and length (intake and exhaust) | |
| Valve closed . . . . . . . . . . . . . . . . . . . . . . . . . . . . . . . . . | 1.701 in at 90 lbs. |
| Valve open . . . . . . . . . . . . . . . . . . . . . . . . . . . . . . . . . . | 1.291 in at 215 lbs. |
| Stem-to-guide clearance (1938 on) . . . . . . . . . . . . . . . | 0.001 to 0.0027 in (0.025 to 0.069 mm) |

## Crankshaft and connecting rods

| | |
|---|---|
| Crankshaft end play | |
| 1986 and 1987 . . . . . . . . . . . . . . . . . . . . . . . . . . . . . | 0.0024 to 0.0083 in (0.06 to 0.21 mm) |
| 1988 on . . . . . . . . . . . . . . . . . . . . . . . . . . . . . . . . . . | 0.0016 to 0.0031 in (0.041 to 0.079 mm) |
| Main bearing journal diameter . . . . . . . . . . . . . . . . . . . | 2.6473 to 2.6483 in (67.241 to 67.265 mm) |
| Main bearing oil clearance | |
| (1986 and 1987) . . . . . . . . . . . . . . . . . . . . . . . . . . . | 0.0016 to 0.0032 in (0.041 to 0.081 mm) |
| 1988 on . . . . . . . . . . . . . . . . . . . . . . . . . . . . . . . . . . | 0.0012 to 0.0027 in (0.030 to 0.069 mm) |
| Connecting rod bearing journal diameter . . . . . . . . . . . . . | 1.9983 to 1.9994 in (50.758 to 50.784 mm) |
| Connecting rod bearing oil clearance | |
| 1986 and 1987 . . . . . . . . . . . . . . . . . . . . . . . . . . . . . | 0.0013 to 0.0026 in (0.033 to 0.066 mm) |
| 1988 on . . . . . . . . . . . . . . . . . . . . . . . . . . . . . . . . . . | 0.0015 to 0.0036 in (0.038 to 0.091 mm) |
| Connecting rod end play (side clearance) (1988 on) . . . . . . . . | 0.014 to 0.027 in (0.356 to 0.686 mm) |

## Engine block

| | |
|---|---|
| Cylinder diameter (1988 on) . . . . . . . . . . . . . . . . . . . . | 3.5033 to 3.546 in (88.98 to 90.07 mm) |
| Cylinder bore | |
| Out-of-round limit . . . . . . . . . . . . . . . . . . . . . . . . . . | 0.0005 in (0.013 mm) |
| Taper limit . . . . . . . . . . . . . . . . . . . . . . . . . . . . . . . | 0.0005 in (0.013 mm) |

## Pistons and rings

| | |
|---|---|
| Compression ring side clearance | |
| Top ring . . . . . . . . . . . . . . . . . . . . . . . . . . . . . . . . . | 0.001 to 0.003 in (0.025 to 0.08 mm) |
| Second ring . . . . . . . . . . . . . . . . . . . . . . . . . . . . . . . | 0.001 to 0.003 in (0.025 to 0.08 mm) |
| Oil ring . . . . . . . . . . . . . . . . . . . . . . . . . . . . . . . . . . | 0.008 in (0.20 mm) |
| Piston-to-bore clearance | |
| 1986 | |
| Carburetor equipped models . . . . . . . . . . . . . . . . . | 0.0006 to 0.0016 in (0.017 to 0.043 mm) |
| Fuel injected models . . . . . . . . . . . . . . . . . . . . . . . | 0.001 to 0.002 in (0.025 to 0.055 mm) |
| 1987 on (all) . . . . . . . . . . . . . . . . . . . . . . . . . . . . . | 0.002 to 0.0028 in (0.050 to 0.073 mm |
| Piston pin diameter . . . . . . . . . . . . . . . . . . . . . . . . . . | 0.9052 to 0.9056 in (22.937 to 23.0015 mm) |
| Pin-to-piston clearance . . . . . . . . . . . . . . . . . . . . . . . | 0.00025 to 0.0007 in (0.0065 to 0.018 mm) |
| Pin-to-rod clearance . . . . . . . . . . . . . . . . . . . . . . . . . | 0.00078 to 0.0021 in (0.020 to 0.0515 mm) |
| Piston ring end gap | |
| Top ring . . . . . . . . . . . . . . . . . . . . . . . . . . . . . . . . . | 0.010 to 0.020 in (0.25 to 0.50 mm) |
| Second ring . . . . . . . . . . . . . . . . . . . . . . . . . . . . . . . | 0.010 to 0.020 in (0.25 to 0.50 mm) |
| Oil ring . . . . . . . . . . . . . . . . . . . . . . . . . . . . . . . . . . | 0.020 to 0.055 in (0.50 to 1.40 mm) |

## Camshaft

| | |
|---|---|
| Lobe lift | |
| Intake . . . . . . . . . . . . . . . . . . . . . . . . . . . . . . . . . . . | 0.2626 in (6.67 mm) |
| Exhaust . . . . . . . . . . . . . . . . . . . . . . . . . . . . . . . . . . | 0.2732 in (6.94 mm) |
| Bearing journal diameter . . . . . . . . . . . . . . . . . . . . . . . | 1.86798 to 1.8815 in (47.44 to 47.79 mm) |

| **Torque specifications** | **Ft-lbs** | **Nm** |
|---|---|---|
| Main bearing cap bolts . . . . . . . . . . . . . . . . . . . . . . . . . | 83 | 112 |
| Cylinder head bolts | | |
| Step 1 . . . . . . . . . . . . . . . . . . . . . . . . . . . . . . . . . . . | 33 | 45 |
| Step 2 . . . . . . . . . . . . . . . . . . . . . . . . . . . . . . . . . . . | Turn an additional 90° | |

# 3.1L V6 engine

**Note:** *The 3.1L V6 engine is nearly identical to the 2.8L engine, so the following specifications are only those which differ from the equivalent specifications for the 2.8L engine. For specifications not included here, refer to the 2.8L engine section.*

## General

| | |
|---|---|
| Stroke . . . . . . . . . . . . . . . . . . . . . . . . . . . . . . . . . . . . | 3.3122 in (84.13 mm) |

## Pistons and rings

| | |
|---|---|
| Piston-to-bore clearance . . . . . . . . . . . . . . . . . . . . . . . | 0.0022 to 0.0028 in (0.056 to 0.071 mm) |
| Compression ring side clearance . . . . . . . . . . . . . . . . . . | 0.002 to 0.0035 in (0.051 to 0.089 mm) |
| Oil ring end gap . . . . . . . . . . . . . . . . . . . . . . . . . . . . . | 0.010 to 0.050 in (0.254 to 0.1.27 mm) |
| Piston pin | |
| Diameter . . . . . . . . . . . . . . . . . . . . . . . . . . . . . . . . | 0.9052 to 0.9054 in (22.992 to 22.997 mm) |
| Pin-to-rod clearance . . . . . . . . . . . . . . . . . . . . . . . . | 0.0004 to 0.0008 in (0.010 to 0.020 mm) |

## Crankshaft and connecting rods

| | |
|---|---|
| Main journal taper limit | 0.0003 in (0.008 mm) |
| Crankshaft end play at thrust bearing | 0.0012 to 0.0027 in (0.030 to 0.069 mm) |
| Connecting rod journal taper limit | 0.003 in (0.076 mm) |
| Connecting rod bearing oil clearance | 0.0013 to 0.0031 in (0.033 to 0.079 mm) |

# 3.3L V6 engine

Note: *The 3.3L V6 engine is nearly identical to the 3.8L engine, so the following specifications are only those which differ from the equivalent specifications for the 3.8L engine. For specifications not included here, refer to the 3.8L engine section.*

## Valves and related conponents

Intake valve
| | |
|---|---|
| Stem height | 1.935 to 1.975 in (49.149 to 50.165 mm) |
| Seat angle | 45° |
| Seat width | 0.060 to 0.080 in (1.524 to 2.032 mm) |

Exhaust valve
| | |
|---|---|
| Stem height | 1.935 to 1.975 in (49.149 to 50.165 mm) |
| Stem-to-guide clearance | 0.0032 to 0.0035 in (0.081 to 0.089 mm) |
| Seat angle | 45° |
| Seat width | 0.090 to 0.110 in (2.286 to 2.794 mm) |

Valve springs
| | |
|---|---|
| Free length | 1.981 in (50.32 mm) |
| Installed height | 1.690 to 1.750 in (42.93 to 44.45 mm) |

Load
| | |
|---|---|
| Valve closed | 1.750 in (44.45 mm) at 76 to 84 lbs. |
| Valve open | 1.315 in (33.40 mm) at 200 to 220 lbs. |

## Camshaft

Lobe lift
| | |
|---|---|
| Intake | 0.250 in (6.35 mm) |
| Exhaust | 0.255 in (6.48 mm) |

## Engine block

Cylinder bore
| | |
|---|---|
| Diameter | 3.700 in (93.98 mm) |
| Out-of-round limit | 0.0004 in (0.010 mm) |

## Pistons and connecting rods

| | |
|---|---|
| Piston diameter measuring point | 1.65 in (41.91 mm) down from top of piston |

Piston pin
| | |
|---|---|
| Diameter | 0.9053 to 0.9055 in (22.995 to 22.999 mm) |
| Pin-to-piston clearance | 0.0004 to 0.0008 in (0.010 to 0.020 mm) |
| Connecting rod bearing oil clearance | 0.0003 to 0.0026 in (0.0076 to 0.066 mm) |

Piston ring end gap
| | |
|---|---|
| Compression rings | 0.0013 to 0.0031 in (0.033 to 0.079 mm) |
| Oil control ring | 0.010 to 0.040 in (0.254 to 1.0 mm) |

Piston ring side clearance
| | |
|---|---|
| Compression rings | 0.0013 to 0.0031 in (0.033 to 0.079 mm) |
| Oil control ring | 0.0011 to 0.0081 in (0.028 to 0.206 mm) |

| Torque specifications | Ft-lbs | Nm |
|---|---|---|
| Camshaft sprocket bolts | 26 | 35 |
| Connecting rod cap bolts | | |
| Step 1 | 20 | 27 |
| Step 2 | Turn an additional 50° | |
| Main bearing cap bolts | 90 | 122 |
| Cylinder head bolts | | |
| Step 1 | 35 | 47 |
| Step 2 | Turn an additional 130° | |
| Step 3 (FOUR CENTER BOLTS ONLY) | Turn an additional 30° | |
| Flywheel-to-crankshaft bolts | 61 | 83 |
| Oil pan bolts | 10 | 13.5 |
| Rocker arm pedestal bolts | 28 | 38 |

# 3.8L V6 engine

## Valves and related components

Valve spring load
| | |
|---|---|
| Valve closed | 1.727 in (43.87 mm) at 90 lbs. |
| Valve open | 1.340 in (34.04 mm) at 185 lbs. |

## Crankshaft and connecting rods

| | |
|---|---|
| Connecting rod bearing journal | |
| Taper/runout limit | 0.0003 in (0.0076 mm) |
| Oil clearance | 0.0003 to 0.0028 in (0.0076 to 0.071 mm) |
| Connecting rod end play (side clearance) | 0.003 to 0.015 in (0.076 to 0.381 mm) |
| Main bearing journal diameter | 2.4988 to 2.4998 in (63.47 to 63.49 mm) |

## Engine block

| | |
|---|---|
| Cylinder bore out-of-round limit | 0.00039 in (0.009 mm) |

## Pistons and connecting rods

| | |
|---|---|
| Piston ring end gap | |
| Compression rings | 0.010 to 0.020 in (0.254 to 0.508 mm) |
| Oil control ring | 0.015 to 0.055 in (0.381 to 0.1.397 mm) |
| Piston ring side clearance | |
| Compression rings | 0.001 to 0.003 in (0.025 to 0.076 mm) |
| Oil control ring | 0.005 to 0.0065 in (0.127 to 0.165 mm) |

| Torque specifications | Ft-lbs | Nm |
|---|---|---|
| Timing chain cover-to-block bolts | 22 | 30 |
| Connecting rod bolts | 45 | 61 |
| Cylinder head bolts | | |
| Step 1 | 25 | 34 |
| Step 2 | Turn an additional 90° **(Caution:** *If a torque value of 60 ft-lbs is attained, do not continue to tighten the bolt.)* | |
| Step 3 | Repeat Step 2 | |
| Rocker arm pivot bolts | 45 | 61 |
| Spark plug | 20 | 27 |

# Fuel and exhaust systems

## Carburetor specifications — 1986 models

| | |
|---|---|
| Float adjustment | |
| 17084534 | 5/32 in |
| 17084535 | |
| 17084540 | |
| 17084542 | 1/8 in |
| Fast idle cam (choke rod) (all) | 28° |
| Primary vacuum break adjustment (all) | 25° |
| Air valve link rod (all) | 1° |
| Secondary vacuum break adjustment (all) | 35° |
| Unloader adjustment (all) | 45° |
| Lean mixture screw adjustment (all) | 2-1/2 turns |
| Idle air bleed valve (all) | 1/2 turn |
| Idle mixture needle (all) | 4 turns (preset) |

## Multi-port fuel injection (MPFI)

| Torque specifications | Ft-lbs | Nm |
|---|---|---|
| Plenum-to-intake manifold bolts | 19 | 25 |
| Throttle body-to-plenum bolts | 15 | 20 |
| Fuel rail-to-intake manifold bolts | 15 | 20 |
| IAC valve (1986) | 13 | 17 |

# Brakes

## Rear drum brakes

| | |
|---|---|
| Drum diameter | |
| Standard | 8.86 in |
| Service limit | |
| Wagon | 8.88 in |
| Coupe/Sedan | 8.92 in |

## Rear disc brakes (Pontiac 6000 only)

| | |
|---|---|
| Rotor diameter | |
| 1988 | 10.43 in |
| 1989 | 10.334 in |
| Disc runout | |
| 1988 | 0.003 in |
| 1989 | 0.004 in |
| Disc thickness variation limit | 0.0005 in |
| Discard thickness | |
| 1988 | 0.681 in |
| 1989 | 0.429 in |

## Rear disc brakes *(Pontiac 6000 only)* (continued)

Minimum thickness after resurfacing

| | |
|---|---|
| 1988 . . . . . . . . . . . . . . . . . . . . . . . . . . . . . . . . . . | 0.702 in |
| 1989 . . . . . . . . . . . . . . . . . . . . . . . . . . . . . . . . . . | 0.444 in |

| Torque specifications (1989 Pontiac 6000 only) | Ft-lbs | Nm |
|---|---|---|
| Rear caliper bleeder valve . . . . . . . . . . . . . . . . . . . . . . . . . | 9.5 | 13 |
| Rear caliper bridge bolts . . . . . . . . . . . . . . . . . . . . . . . . | 74 | 100 |
| Parking brake lever nut . . . . . . . . . . . . . . . . . . . . . . . . | 35 | 47 |
| Rear caliper mounting bolts . . . . . . . . . . . . . . . . . . . | 74 | 100 |

## Suspension and steering systems

| Torque specifications | Ft-lbs | Nm |
|---|---|---|
| Front suspension | | |
| Plate-to-frame bolts . . . . . . . . . . . . . . . . . . . . . . | 40 | 54 |
| Insulator clamp nuts . . . . . . . . . . . . . . . . . . . . . | 33 | 45 |
| Strut assembly-to-body nuts . . . . . . . . . . . . . . . | 18 | 25 |
| Steering knuckle-to-strut assembly bolts . . . . . . . . . . . . | 140 | 190 |
| Brake line bracket bolt . . . . . . . . . . . . . . . . . . . . . . | 13 | 18 |
| Stabilizer shaft bushing clamp nuts . . . . . . . . . . . | 33 | 45 |
| Control arm pivot bolt nut . . . . . . . . . . . . . . . . . . . | 61 | 83 |
| Balljoint pinch bolt nut . . . . . . . . . . . . . . . . . . . . | 33 | 45 |
| Hub and bearing retaining bolt | | |
| With JA2 . . . . . . . . . . . . . . . . . . . . . . . . . . . . | 70 | 95 |
| Without JA2 . . . . . . . . . . . . . . . . . . . . . . . | 63 | 85 |
| Hub nut . . . . . . . . . . . . . . . . . . . . . . . . . . . . | 185 | 251 |
| Strut dampener shaft nut . . . . . . . . . . . . . . . . . . | 65 | 88 |
| Rear suspension | | |
| Shock absorber mount-to-body . . . . . . . . . . . . . . . . . | 16 | 22 |
| Shock absorber-to-mount. . . . . . . . . . . . . . . . . . | 28 | 38 |
| Shock absorber nut at axle . . . . . . . . . . . . . . . . | 44 | 60 |
| Track bar bolt at axle . . . . . . . . . . . . . . . . . . . . | 44 | 60 |
| Track bar nut at brace or underbody bracket . . . . . . . . . . | 35 | 48 |
| Control arm-to-bracket nut . . . . . . . . . . . . . . . . . | 84 | 116 |
| Control arm bracket-to-underbody . . . . . . . . . . . . . . . | 28 | 38 |
| Hub and bearing assembly bolts . . . . . . . . . . . . . . . | 44 | 60 |

---

### 3   Tune-up and routine maintenance

## Drivebelt check and adjustment

Later models are equipped with a single ''serpentine'' drivebelt, which powers all engine accessories. This style belt requires no adjustment; it is handled by a spring-loaded tensioner pulley.

The belt should be inspected regularly for missing ribs and frayed plies. Cracks in the belt ribs do not necessarily indicate a faulty or damaged belt, since they will not impair belt performance.

1   To replace the belt, insert a half-inch drive breaker bar (some models require a 15 mm socket) into the tensioner and rotate the pulley counterclockwise, releasing belt tension.

2   Remove the drivebelt from the pulleys.

3   Install the new belt, starting with the bottom pulleys, then release the tensioner. Make sure the belt is properly centered on each pulley.

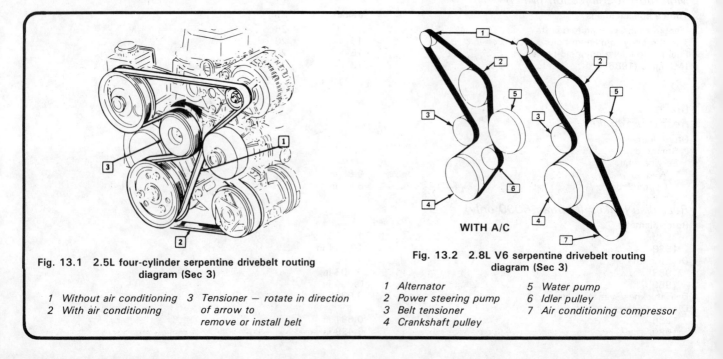

Fig. 13.1   2.5L four-cylinder serpentine drivebelt routing diagram (Sec 3)

Fig. 13.2   2.8L V6 serpentine drivebelt routing diagram (Sec 3)

| | | | |
|---|---|---|---|
| 1 | Without air conditioning | 3 | Tensioner — rotate in direction of arrow to remove or install belt |
| 2 | With air conditioning | | |

| | | | |
|---|---|---|---|
| 1 | Alternator | 5 | Water pump |
| 2 | Power steering pump | 6 | Idler pulley |
| 3 | Belt tensioner | 7 | Air conditioning compressor |
| 4 | Crankshaft pulley | | |

WITH A/C

## Hydraulic clutch fluid level check

4    Check the fluid level in the reservoir at least once every month and add more fluid as required. The proper level is indicated by a step on the reservoir. **Caution:** *Be sure to clean the top and sides of the reservoir before removing the cover.*

## Manual transaxle lubricant level check

5    All 1988 and later model manual transaxles are equipped with a dipstick for checking the lubricant level.
6    Check the lubricant level only when the engine is off, the vehicle is on a level surface and the transaxle is cool enough to touch without burning your fingers.
7    Remove the dipstick (see Fig. 13.5) and wipe it off with a rag, then reinsert it and remove it again. Read the indicated level.

    a )    If the dipstick indicates FULL, and the transaxle is warm, the lubricant is correct.

    b )    If the dipstick indicates C (cold) and the transaxle is cold, the lubricant level is correct.

    c )    If the dipstick indicates ADD, or below, add lubricant. Use Synchromesh Transmission Fluid (12345349) or equivalent lubricant to fill the transaxle. Be sure the lubricant level is between the FULL and C (cold) marks on the dipstick.

## Engine oil and filter change (2.5L four-cylinder engine)

8    Some 1987 and all 1988 and later model four-cylinder engines are equipped with a force balancer, which necessitates a different location for the oil filter. On these models, an element-type filter in the oil pan replaces the spin-on type filter on the side of the engine block. Some of these engines have a separate drain plug to make draining the oil easier.
9    If the engine has this type of filter (see Fig. 13.6), complete Steps 1 through 8 in Section 16 of Chapter 1, then proceed to the next Step.

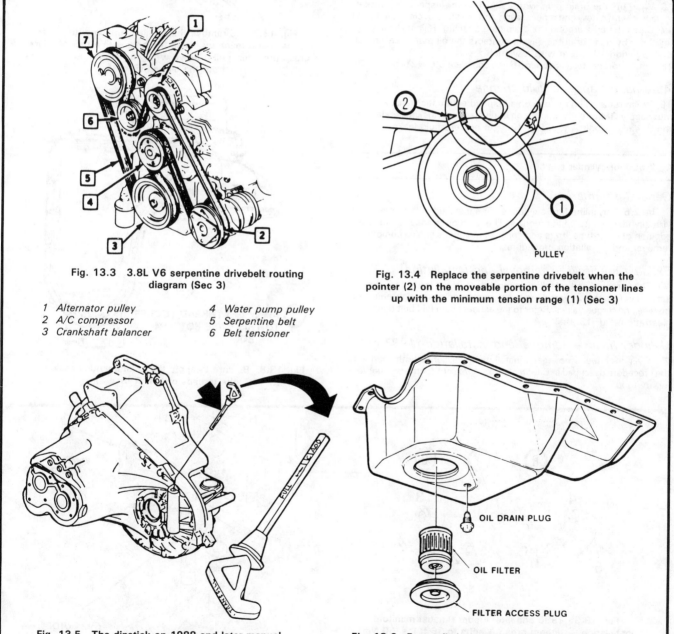

**Fig. 13.3    3.8L V6 serpentine drivebelt routing diagram (Sec 3)**

1    *Alternator pulley*
2    *A/C compressor*
3    *Crankshaft balancer*
4    *Water pump pulley*
5    *Serpentine belt*
6    *Belt tensioner*

**Fig. 13.4    Replace the serpentine drivebelt when the pointer (2) on the moveable portion of the tensioner lines up with the minimum tension range (1) (Sec 3)**

PULLEY

OIL DRAIN PLUG

OIL FILTER

FILTER ACCESS PLUG

**Fig. 13.5    The dipstick on 1988 and later manual transaxles is located as shown here (arrow) (Sec 3)**

**Fig. 13.6    Four-cylinder engines with a force balancer assembly have the oil filter mounted in the oil pan (Sec 3)**

10   To avoid burns from hot engine oil it's a good idea to wear gloves when removing the drain plug(s). Being careful not to touch any of the hot exhaust components, unscrew and remove the large oil filter access plug from the center of the oil pan (see Fig. 13.7). Some models are equipped with a smaller drain plug next to the large one. In this case, unscrew and remove the smaller drain plug and allow all the oil to drain. Replace and tighten the smaller drain plug, then unscrew and remove the filter access plug.

11   Reach up inside the oil drain plug hole with a pair of pliers, grasp the filter securely, pull it down using a twisting motion and remove it from the oil pan (see Fig. 13.7).

12   Check the filter to make sure the rubber O-ring has come out with it. If it hasn't, reach up inside the pan opening and remove it.

13   Coat the new O-ring (included with the new filter) with clean engine oil and then slide it into position, all the way up in the filter opening.

14   Coat the inside of the grommet on the top of the new filter with clean engine oil.

15   Slide the new oil filter up into the oil pan opening as far as possible without forcing it.

16   Wipe off the drain plug with a clean cloth. Inspect the gasket, replace it with a new one if necessary, and coat it with clean engine oil.

17   Clean the area around the drain plug opening. Reinstall the plug, tighten it by hand until the gasket contacts the oil pan, then tighten it an additional 1/4-turn with a wrench.

18   Return to Chapter 1, Section 16 and complete Steps 21 through 28.

### Automatic transaxle fluid change

19   When reinstalling the pan on a 3-speed automatic transaxle, you must apply GM threadlocker, or an equivalent non-locking sealant, to the threads of bolt A (see Fig. 13.8) to prevent fluid leaks.

---

### 4   2.5L four-cylinder engine

### General information

The 2.5 liter, inline four-cylinder engine installed in later models is virtually identical to earlier models. The main differences include the addition of roller-type lifters and changes to various engine component removal and installation procedures.

### Exhaust manifold — removal and installation

1   The removal and installation procedure is similar to the one described in Chapter 2, Part A, with the exception of the tightening sequence and torque values. Refer to the exhaust manifold bolt tightening illustration (Fig. 13.9).

### Cylinder head — removal and installation (1987 on)

2   Cylinder head removal and installation is essentially the same as the procedure described in Chapter 2, Part A, except for the bolt tightening method.

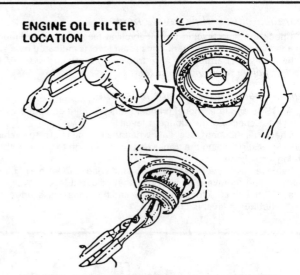

**ENGINE OIL FILTER LOCATION**

Fig. 13.7   To remove the oil filter, unscrew the filter access plug, reach up inside the hole with a pair of pliers, grasp the filter, pull it down while turning it and remove it from the oil pan (Sec 3)

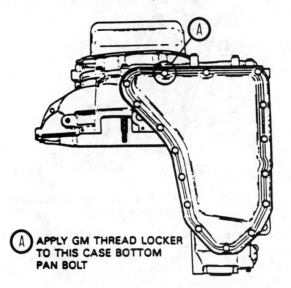

APPLY GM THREAD LOCKER TO THIS CASE BOTTOM PAN BOLT

Fig. 13.8   Be sure to apply the recommended sealant to the threads of bolt A (Sec 3)

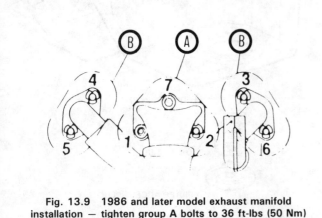

Fig. 13.9   1986 and later model exhaust manifold installation — tighten group A bolts to 36 ft-lbs (50 Nm) and group B bolts to 36 ft-lbs (43 Nm) in the sequence shown (Sec 4)

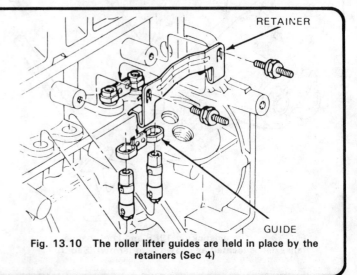

RETAINER

GUIDE

Fig. 13.10   The roller lifter guides are held in place by the retainers (Sec 4)

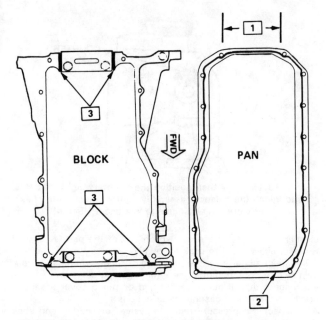

Fig. 13.11   2.5L four-cylinder engine oil pan sealant
application details (Sec 4)

1   3/8-inch wide by 3/16-inch thick        3   1/8-inch bead at
2   3/16-inch wide by 1/8-inch thick              points indicated

3    Gradually tighten the cylinder head bolts in the sequence shown
in Chapter 2, Part A (Fig. 2A.7), to the Step 1 torque figure outlined
in the Specifications in this Supplement.
4    Repeat the sequence, bringing them to the Step 2 specified torque
figure on all bolts except number 9. Tighten number 9 to the separate
specified torque.
5    Repeat the sequence. Turn all bolts, except number 9, an additional
120-degrees (1/3-turn). Turn bolt number 9 an additional 90-degrees
(1/4 turn).
6    The remaining steps are the reverse of the removal procedure.

## Hydraulic lifters — removal, inspection and installation

7    Roller-type hydraulic lifters are installed on 1985 and later models.
Lifter retainers and guides are installed in the block, behind the pushrod
cover, to prevent the lifters from rotating on the camshaft lobes. Consequently, the camshaft lobes are ground with no front-to-rear taper.
Follow the removal procedures in Chapter 2, Part A, but note that before
the lifters are removed, the retainers and guides must first be removed.
Operation, disassembly and inspection are similar to a standard hydraulic lifter. However, the roller must be inspected for freedom of movement, excessive looseness of the roller bearings, flat spots and pitting.
The camshaft must also be inspected if any abnormal roller wear is
indicated.
8    During installation, position the lifter guides and retainers and
tighten the studs before installing the pushrods. The remaining reassembly sequence is identical to the procedure described in Chapter 2,
Part A, Section 8.

## Oil pan — removal and installation

9    Follow the removal procedures outlined in Chapter 2, Part A, Section 10, Paragraphs 1 through 9.
10   Clean the sealing surfaces on the oil pan, engine block and the
exposed portion of the front cover.
11   Apply a continous bead of RTV sealant to the oil pan as shown
in the accompanying illustration.
12   Install the oil pan and bolts while the sealant is still wet, then tighten
the bolts to the specified torque.
13   The remainder of the installation procedure is the reverse of removal.

## Timing gear cover — removal and installation

14   Refer to Chapter 2, Part A, Section 13 for the removal procedure.
15   On 1985 and later models, RTV sealant is used in place of a gasket.
16   Clean the mating surfaces on the cover and block, removing all

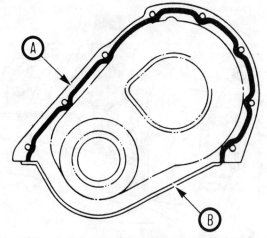

Fig. 13.12   2.5L four-cylinder engine timing gear cover
sealant application details (Sec 4)

A   3/8-inch by 3/16-inch bead        B   1/4-inch by 1/8-inch bead
of RTV sealant                            of RTV sealant

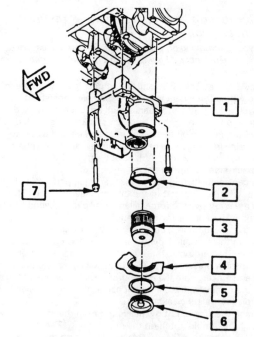

Fig. 13.13   Force balancer assembly and related
components — exploded view (Sec 4)

1   Balancer assembly        5   Gasket
2   Restrictor               6   Drain plug/access plug
3   Oil filter               7   Mounting bolt
4   Oil pan

traces of old sealing material.
17   If the pulley hub seal is to be replaced, refer to Chapter 2, Part A,
Section 13.
18   Apply a 3/8-inch (wide) by 3/16-inch (thick) bead of RTV sealant
to the joint at the oil pan and timing gear cover.
19   Apply a 1/4-inch (wide) by 1/8-inch (thick) bead of RTV sealant
to the timing gear cover at the block mating surfaces.
20   Lubricate the pulley hub seal with clean engine oil.
21   Insert the hub through the cover seal and place the cover in position
on the block as the hub slides onto the crankshaft. This will ensure
that the seal is centered evenly around the hub.
22   Install the oil pan-to-cover bolts and partially tighten them.
23   Install the timing gear cover-to-block bolts, then tighten all of the
mounting bolts to the specified torque.
24   The remaining steps are the reverse of removal.

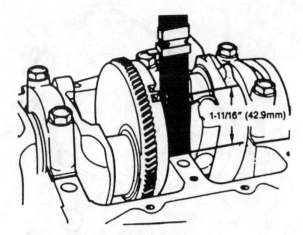

Fig. 13.14   Position the crankshaft by measuring from the engine block to the first cut of the double notch on the reluctor ring (the distance should be 1-11/16 inches), . . .

Fig. 13.15   . . . then position the counterweights like this and install the balancer assembly — they must be in phase or vibration and damage will occur! (Sec 4)

### Force balancer/oil pump assembly — removal and installation

**Note:** *If you're removing only the oil pump, it's not necessary to remove the entire force balancer/oil pump assembly. The oil pump removal procedure begins at Step 35.*

25   Some 1987 and all 1988 and later model four-cylinder engines are equipped with a force balancer. The assembly consists of two eccentrically weighted shafts and gears which are counter-rotated by a concentric gear on the crankshaft at twice crankshaft speed, dampening engine vibration. The oil filter, a pick-up screen and a gerotor type oil pump are also integral parts of the assembly, so the oil pump removal procedure in Chapter 2, Part A does not apply. The oil pump is driven off the back side of one of the balance shafts.
26   You can easily distinguish a balancer-equipped engine by the element-type oil filter located in the oil pan (see Fig. 13.13).
27   You must remove the force balancer/oil pump assembly when you disassemble the engine for overhaul.
28   Remove the oil pan (see Section 10 in Chapter 2A).
29   Position the number 1 piston at TDC on the compression stroke. This is done by removing the number 1 cylinder spark plug, feeling for compression pressure at the plug hole while turning the crankshaft by hand and making sure the distributor rotor is pointing at the number 1 plug wire terminal in the distributor cap as the compression builds up.
30   Unbolt the balancer assembly.
31   Position the crankshaft by measuring from the engine block to the first cut of the double notch on the reluctor ring. The distance should be 1-11/16-inches (see Fig. 13.14). If it isn't, turn the crankshaft until it is.
32   Mount the balancer with the counterweights parallel and pointing AWAY from the crankshaft. Tighten the bolts to the specified torque.
33   Install the oil pan.
34   Install a new filter and add oil (see Section 3). Run the engine and check for leaks.

### Oil pump/pressure regulator valve — removal, inspection and installation

**Note:** *It isn't necessary to remove the force balancer assembly to service the oil pump or pressure regulator valve.*

**Removal**
35   Remove the oil pan (see Chapter 2A, Section 10).
36   Remove the restrictor (if equipped) and filter (see Fig. 13.15).
37   Remove the oil pump cover assembly and oil pump gears.
38   **Warning:** *The pressure regulator valve spring is under pressure. Exercise caution when unscrewing the plug or removing the pin, as bodily injury may result.* Remove the pressure regulator valve plug (or pin) and spring, then remove the valve itself. If the valve is stuck, clean the valve and pump housing with carburetor cleaner or solvent.

**Inspection**
39   Remove any sludge, oil or varnish from the parts with carburetor

cleaner or solvent. If the varnish on any of the parts is difficult to remove, allow them to soak for awhile.
40   Inspect all parts for the presence of foreign material. If you find evidence of contamination, determine its source.
41   Inspect the oil pump pocket and oil pump cover assembly for cracks, scoring and casting imperfections.
42   Inspect the pressure regulator valve for scoring and sticking. Remove burrs with a fine oil stone.
43   Inspect the pressure regulator valve spring for distortion and loss of tension. If you have any doubt regarding the condition of the spring, replace it.
44   Clean the screen assembly and inspect it for damage.
45   Inspect the pump gears for chipping, galling and wear.
46   Measure the oil pump pocket depth and gear thickness and compare your measurements to the specified depth and thickness. If in doubt about the condition of the oil pump, replace it.

**Installation**
47   Lubricate all internal parts with engine oil.
48   To assure priming and avoid engine damage, pack all pump cavities with petroleum jelly.
49   Install the oil pump gears.
50   Install the oil pump cover assembly.
51   Install the pressure regulator valve and spring.
52   Install the pressure regulator plug or pin. Make sure it's properly secured.
53   Install the oil pump cover assembly and tighten the bolts to the specified torque.
54   Install the restrictor (if equipped) and a new filter.
55   Install the oil pan.
56   Fill the crankcase to the correct level with clean engine oil.
57   Remove the oil pressure sending unit and install an oil pressure gauge in its place.
58   Start the engine and note the oil pressure. If it doesn't build up quickly, remove the oil pan and examine the pump. If necessary, disassemble the pump and repack all cavities with petroleum jelly. Running the engine without oil pressure will cause extensive damage.

---

### 5   2.8L and 3.1L V6 engines

### General information

Although the 2.8 liter V6 engine installed in later vehicles is similar to the 1985 and earlier V6 engines, some component removal and replacement procedures differ from those described in Chapter 2, Part B. These differences are mainly due to changes in the air induction system and the elimination of the conventional HEI distributor on 1987 and later models.

### Rocker arm covers — removal and installation

**Left side (radiator)**
1   Disconnect the cable from the negative terminal of the battery.
2   Remove any fuel injection (air induction) parts necessary to gain access to the rocker arm cover bolts and cover (refer to Section 7 of this Supplement).
3   Drain the coolant from the radiator (see Chapter 1).

4   Loosen the coolant tube hose clamp below the thermostat housing, then disconnect the other end of the hose at the water pump.
5   Unbolt the coolant tube bracket and move it aside.
6   Remove the vent tube from the rocker arm cover to the air inlet hose.
7   Mark the three spark plug wires with pieces of numbered tape, disconnect them from the spark plugs and reposition them out of the way with the plastic spark plug wire guide.
8   Unbolt the engine strut from the bracket on the cylinder head, loosen but do not remove the through bolt on the opposite end at the radiator support, then swing the bracket up and forward, out of the way.
9   Remove the strut bracket from the cylinder head.
10  Remove the rocker arm cover bolts.
11  Detach the rocker arm cover. **Note:** *If the cover sticks to the cylinder head, use a soft-face hammer and a block of wood to dislodge it. If it still will not come loose, pry on it carefully, but do not distort or scratch the sealing flange surface.*
12  Clean the rocker arm cover and cylinder head mating surfaces with solvent or degreaser. Be sure to remove all traces of old gasket material and sealant.
13  Apply a 3 mm dab of RTV sealant to the intake manifold-to-cylinder head notch.
14  Install a new rocker arm cover gasket. It may be helpful to ''glue'' the gasket to the rocker arm cover using a small amount of RTV sealant. Make sure the bolt holes in the gasket line up with the holes in the cover.
15  Place the cover on the cylinder head, install the bolts and tighten them to the specified torque.
16  Complete the job by reversing the removal procedure.

**Right side (firewall)**

17  Follow the procedures in Paragraphs 1 and 2 above.
18  Undo the brake booster vacuum line from the bracket.
19  Remove the serpentine drivebelt (refer to Section 3 of this Supplement).
20  Mark the wires to the alternator with pieces of numbered tape, then disconnect the wires. Remove the rear alternator brace and detach the alternator.
21  Remove the alternator bracket.
22  Pull the PCV valve from the rocker arm cover and remove it, along with the PCV hose.
23  Mark the spark plug wires with tape to facilitate reassembly, then disconnect the wires and lay them out of the way.
24  Move aside any wires and hoses that may interfere with rocker arm cover removal.
25  Follow the procedures in Paragraphs 10 through 16 of this Section.

## Intake manifold (multi-port fuel injection) — removal and installation

**Warning:** *Gasoline is extremely flammable, so extra precautions must be taken when working on any part of the fuel system. Do not smoke or allow open flames or bare light bulbs near the work area. Also, do not work in a garage if a natural gas-type appliance with a pilot light is present.*

26  Relieve the fuel system pressure (refer to Section 7 of this Supplement).
27  Disconnect the cable from the negative battery terminal.
28  Drain the cooling system (Chapter 1).
29  Remove the accelerator cable, transmission downshift cable and cruise control cable (if so equipped) from the throttle body, then unbolt the cable bracket from the plenum, positioning the cables aside.
30  Remove the throttle body. (Refer to Section 7 of this Supplement).
31  Remove the serpentine belt (refer to Section 3 of this Supplement).
32  Remove the AIR pump and bracket, if so equipped (refer to Chapter 6).
33  On vehicles with distributors, remove the distributor cap. Mark the relationship of the rotor to the distributor housing and the distributor housing to the intake manifold.
34  Remove the distributor clamp bolt and detach the distributor.
35  Remove the coolant hoses from the manifold.
36  Remove the power brake vacuum booster pipe and bracket (1986 on).
37  Remove the EGR valve from the plenum (1987 on).
38  Remove the plenum (see Section 7 of this Supplement).
39  Disconnect the fuel inlet and return lines at the fuel rail.

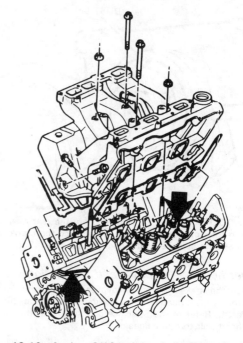

**Fig. 13.16   Apply a 3/16-inch bead of RTV sealant (arrows) to the front and rear ridges of the engine block (Sec 5)**

40  Unbolt the power steering pump and position it aside.
41  Remove the alternator from the bracket and lay it aside, without straining the wires.
42  Remove the alternator bracket.
43  Carefully mark and remove all wires and vacuum hoses from the intake manifold and fuel rail.
44  Remove the fuel rail (refer to Section 7 of this Supplement).
45  Remove both rocker arm covers (refer to the beginning of this Section).
46  Remove the coolant temperature sensor.
47  Remove the intake manifold bolts, then detach the intake manifold. If the manifold is stuck, follow the procedure described in Chapter 2, Part B, Section 4.
48  On 1987 and later models, loosen the rocker arms and withdraw the pushrods. Store the pushrods separately to ensure reinstallation in their original positions (see photo 8.8B in Chapter 2, Part B, Section 8 for the preferred storage method).
49  Before installing the intake manifold, place clean, lint-free rags in the engine cavity and clean the engine block, cylinder head and manifold gasket surfaces. All gasket material and sealant must be removed prior to installation. Remove all dirt and gasket remnants from the engine cavity.
50  Clean the gasket sealing surfaces with degreaser, then apply a 5 mm diameter bead of RTV sealant to the front and rear ridges of the engine block. Extend the bead of sealant 1/4-inch up onto the cylinder heads to help hold the gasket in place.
51  Place the new gaskets on the cylinder heads. If the gaskets are designated *right* and *left*, be sure they are installed in their correct positions.
52  On 1987 and later models, install the pushrods in their original locations and reposition the rocker arms on the pushrods. Refer to Chapter 2, Part B, for valve lash adjustment.
53  Gently lower the intake manifold into position, taking care not to disturb the gaskets.
54  Install the intake manifold mounting bolts and tighten them a little at a time to the specified torque in the sequence illustrated in Chapter 2, Part B, Section 4 (Fig. 2B.3 — 1986 vehicles). On 1987 and later models, tighten the bolts a little at a time, working from the inner bolts out, until the specified torque value is reached.
55  Install the remaining components in the reverse order of removal.
56  Fill the radiator with coolant, start the engine and check for leaks. Adjust the ignition timing (distributor ignition systems). Refer to Chapter 1 and the *Vehicle Emission Control Information label* under the hood.

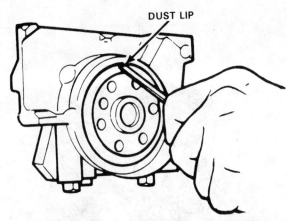

Fig. 13.17  Using a screwdriver, pry the rear main seal from the bore (be careful not to scratch the crankshaft sealing surface or the edge of the bore) (Sec 5)

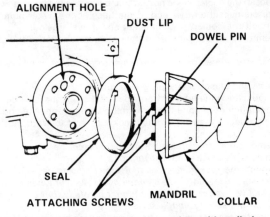

Fig. 13.18  2.8L V6 engine rear main seal installation details (Sec 5)

## Cylinder heads — removal and installation

57  Follow the intake manifold removal procedure in this Section, then refer to the cylinder head removal and installation procedure in Chapter 2, Part B. Refer to the Specificatons section in this Supplement for the head bolt torque values.

## Oil pan — removal and installation (1987 on)

58  Disconnect the cable from the negative battery terminal.
59  If the vehicle is equipped with an AIR pump, remove the serpentine belt and tensioner, then remove the AIR pump and bracket.
60  Follow Paragraphs 2 through 10 in Chapter 2, Part B, Section 9.
61  Clean the oil pan, front cover, bolt holes and block mating surfaces with solvent or degreaser, then wipe them dry with a clean rag. It is imperative that all mating surfaces are absolutely free of oil or grit, or leaks will develop.
62  A new design one-piece neoprene gasket is utilized. No gasket sealant is required. Attach the gasket to the oil pan, raise the pan into position on the block and install the bolts finger tight.
63  There is no specific sequence for tightening the bolts, but it is a good idea to tighten the end bolts first, then tighten the rest of them a little at a time in a criss-cross pattern across the width of the oil pan.
64  To complete the operation, reverse the removal procedure.

## Rear main bearing oil seal — replacement (engine in vehicle)

Note: *Special tools, as noted in the steps which follow, are required for this procedure. They are available from your dealer or may in some cases be rented from an auto parts store or tool rental shop.*

65  Beginning in 1986, a 360-degree lip-type seal is utilized, which allows the oil pan to remain in place when performing this operation.
66  Remove the transmission (refer to Chapter 7).
67  Remove the flywheel or driveplate.
68  Pry out the old seal, taking care not to mar the crankshaft surface. Inspect the crankshaft for scratches, burrs and nicks on the sealing surface.
69  A special seal installation tool (GM tool J-34686) is required to properly seat the seal in the bore without damaging it. Lubricate the seal bore, seal lip and sealing surface on the crankshaft with engine oil. Slide the seal over the mandril on the tool until the dust lip on the seal bottoms squarely against the collar on the tool.
70  Position the dowel pin on the tool in the dowel pin hole in the crankshaft and secure the tool to the crankshaft.
71  Turn the T-handle of the tool until the collar pushes the seal completely into the bore. Make sure the seal is installed squarely.
72  To complete the operation, install the flywheel (or driveplate) and transmission, then start the engine and check for leaks.

## Crankcase front cover — removal and installation

73  Disconnect the cable from the negative battery terminal.
74  Open the drain valve at the bottom of the radiator and drain the cooling system (see Chapter 1).
75  Remove the serpentine belt and tensioner (refer to Section 3 of

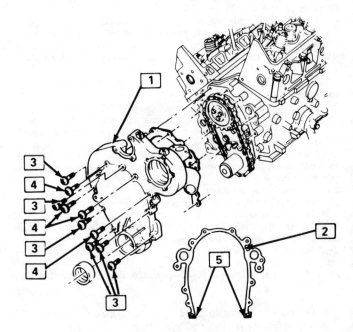

Fig. 13.19  2.8L V6 engine crankcase front cover installation details (Sec 5)

| | |
|---|---|
| 1  Front cover | 4  20 to 35 Ft-lbs |
| 2  Gasket | (27 to 48 Nm) |
| 3  13 to 26 Ft-lbs | 5  Sealer (GM part No. 1052080 or |
| (18 to 36 Nm) | equivalent) |

this Supplement.
76  Unbolt the alternator and position it aside.
77  Unbolt the power steering pump and move it aside. It is not necessary to disconnect the power steering hoses.
78  Raise the vehicle and support it on jackstands.
79  Remove the inner fender splash shield for access.
80  Remove the vibration damper (refer to Chapter 2, Part B).
81  Drain the crankcase oil and remove the oil pan (refer to the oil pan removal procedure in this Section).
82  Remove the lower front cover bolts.
83  Lower the vehicle.
84  Disconnect the radiator hose at the water pump.
85  Disconnect the heater hose, bypass and overflow hoses and position them aside.
86  Remove the remaining front cover bolts and separate the cover from the engine block. If the cover sticks, break it loose with a soft-face hammer, but do not pry between the sealing surfaces.
87  Clean all traces of old gasket material from the front cover and engine block mating surfaces. To replace the front cover oil seal, pry

the old seal out of the cover with a large screwdriver.

88 With the front of the cover facing up, place the new seal in position with the sealing lip facing down.

89 Using a large socket or block of wood and a hammer, drive the seal into the cover until it is completely seated.

90 Install a new front cover gasket and apply RTV-type sealant to the areas indicated in the accompanying illustration.

91 Place the front cover in position and install the upper mounting bolts.

92 Once again, raise the vehicle and support it on jackstands.

93 Install the lower cover mounting bolts and tighten them to the specified torque.

94 Tighten the upper bolts to the specified torque.

95 Install the crankshaft damper pulley.

96 Lower the vehicle.

97 Reconnect the heater hose, radiator hose and bypass and overflow hoses.

98 Install the power steering pump.

99 Install the alternator.

100 Install the belt tensioner and serpentine belt.

101 Fill the cooling system with the proper antifreeze solution (refer to Chapter 1). Do not install the cooling system pressure cap at this time.

102 Reconnect the battery cable and start the engine. Allow it to run until the upper radiator hose becomes warm to the touch, indicating that the thermostat has opened.

103 Stop the engine and check the coolant level. Add coolant as necessary, install the pressure cap and check for leaks.

## 6  3.3L and 3.8L V6 engines

### General information

The 3.3 liter V6 engine installed in 1989 models is a smaller version of the 3.8 liter V6 engine, the main differences being in torquing procedures and the addition of a pushrod guide plate. Cylinder head and connecting rod cap installation procedures differ slightly from the 3.8 liter engine — they're covered later in this Section.

### Intake manifold — removal and installation

**Warning:** *Gasoline is extremely flammable, so extra precautions must be taken when working on any part of the fuel system. Do not smoke or allow open flames or bare light bulbs near the work area. Also, do not work in a garage if a natural gas-type appliance with a pilot light is present.*

1 Depressurize the fuel system (refer to Chapter 4).

2 Disconnect the cable from the negative battery terminal.

3 Drain the cooling system (refer to Chapter 1).

4 Loosen the hose clamp on the intake duct to the throttle body, disconnect the breather tube from the duct and separate the duct from

the throttle body. Disconnect the other end of the duct at the MAF sensor and remove it.

5 Unplug the Idle Air Control and Throttle Position Sensor electrical connectors from the throttle body.

6 Disconnect the throttle linkage, transmission downshift cable and cruise control cable (if equipped) from the throttle lever.

7 Unbolt the vacuum line cluster connector from the throttle body, disconnect the PCV hose, the brake booster vacuum hose and the EGR solenoid vacuum hoses, then move the vacuum line assembly aside. Be sure to mark the hoses with pieces of numbered or colored tape to simplify reassembly.

8 Disconnect the fuel feed and return lines from the fuel rail, using a backup wrench to avoid damaging the fuel lines or rail. Place rags under the fittings to catch the spilled fuel.

9 Mark and remove the vacuum control hose to the fuel pressure regulator.

10 Unplug the injector wiring harness at the multi-wire connector.

11 Remove the fuel rail mounting bolts and carefully lift the fuel rail from the intake manifold. Store it in a clean location with the injectors pointing up to avoid damage to the injector nozzles.

12 Remove the serpentine belt.

13 Remove the power steering/belt tensioner rear support bracket.

14 Mark and unplug the electrical connectors to the alternator, then remove the alternator and rear bracket.

15 Unplug the spark plug wires from cylinders 1, 3 and 5 (the forward facing cylinder head). Remove the plastic spark plug wire harness protector from the forward rocker arm cover and position the harness and protector out of the way.

16 Mark and remove the electrical connectors from the sensors on the front of the intake manifold.

17 Unbolt the coil-pack/ignition module bracket from the intake manifold and from the exhaust manifold studs, then lay the unit aside.

18 Remove the upper radiator hose and heater hoses from the intake manifold. Remove the small coolant hose from the underside of the throttle body.

19 Remove the intake manifold mounting bolts and separate the manifold from the cylinder heads. **Caution:** *Do not pry between the manifold and head, as damage to the gasket sealing surfaces may result.*

20 Clean all traces of old gasket material and sealant from the cylinder head and manifold mating surfaces. It is a good idea to place rags in the engine cavity to prevent foreign matter from entering the engine.

21 Apply gasket sealer (GM part No. 1050026 or *Gaskacinch*) to the intake manifold gasket. Place the gasket and new engine block ridge seals in position. Apply RTV-type sealant to the ends of the ridge seals. Apply anti-seize compound to all pipe thread fittings (if a new manifold is being installed and parts are being transferred).

22 Carefully lower the manifold onto the engine and install the bolts. Tighten the bolts a little at a time in the sequence shown in the accompanying illustration until the specified torque is reached.

23 Install the remaining components in the reverse order of removal.

24 Fill the cooling system, start the engine and check for leaks.

### Cylinder heads — removal and installation

25 Follow the procedure described in Chapter 2, Part C, Section 7, but note that the serpentine belt must be detached for removal of either head. Right side (rear) head removal requires the removal of the alternator, power steering pump and mounting bracket. Left side (front) head removal necessitates unbolting and carefully repositioning the dipstick tube.

26 Upon installation, coat the threads of the head bolts with a sealing compound (GM part No. 1052080 is recommended). Install the bolts finger tight at this time.

**3.8L engine only**

27 Tighten the bolts, in the sequence shown in Chapter 2, Part C (Fig. 2C.8) to the initial torque value.

28 Tighten each bolt in sequence 1/4-turn (90-degrees). **Caution:** *If at any time during this step a torque of 60 ft-lbs is reached, do not continue to turn the bolt being tightened; stop at this point and move on to the next bolt.*

29 Repeat the procedure described in Paragraph 28, again using caution not to exceed the maximum allowable torque of 60 ft-lbs or head gasket failure and possible engine damage may result.

**3.3L engine only**

**Note:** *GM special tool no. J-36660 (torque angle meter) is needed to correctly tighten the cylinder head bolts on this engine.*

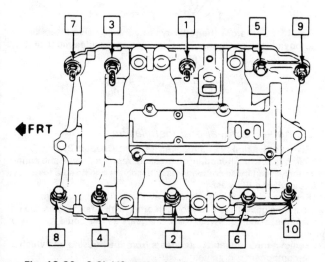

Fig. 13.20  3.8L V6 engine intake manifold bolt tightening sequence (Sec 6)

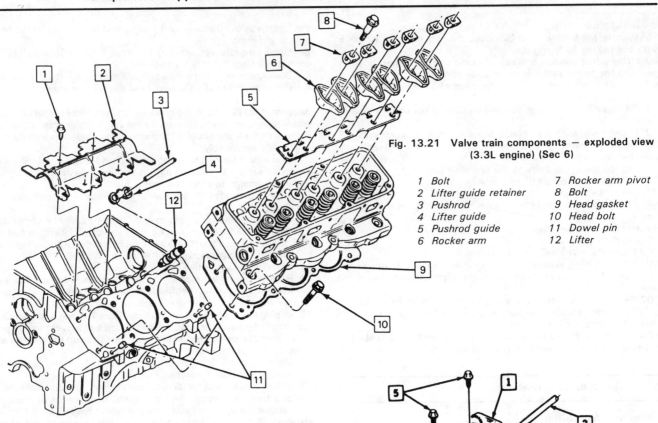

**Fig. 13.21  Valve train components — exploded view (3.3L engine) (Sec 6)**

| | | | |
|---|---|---|---|
| 1 | Bolt | 7 | Rocker arm pivot |
| 2 | Lifter guide retainer | 8 | Bolt |
| 3 | Pushrod | 9 | Head gasket |
| 4 | Lifter guide | 10 | Head bolt |
| 5 | Pushrod guide | 11 | Dowel pin |
| 6 | Rocker arm | 12 | Lifter |

30  Tighten the cylinder head bolts to 35 ft-lbs in sequence (Fig. 2C.8 in Chapter 2, Part C).

31  Using a torque angle meter, turn each head bolt in sequence an additional 130°.

32  Rotate only the four center bolts an additional 30°, in sequence, using a torque angle meter.

33  Install the pushrods.

34  Install the pushrod guide plate (Fig. 13.21).

35  Install the rocker arms and pivots.

36  Apply GM sealant (P/N 1052624) to the rocker arm pedestal bolts before installation and tighten them to 38 ft-lbs.

### Hydraulic lifters — removal, inspection and installation

37  Late model 3.8 liter V6 engines are equipped with roller-type hydraulic valve lifters. Lifter guides and retainers are used to prevent the lifters from rotating on the camshaft lobes. Consequently, the cam lobes are ground with no front-to-rear taper.

38  Remove the rocker arm covers.

39  Remove the intake manifold as outlined in this Chapter.

40  Loosen the rocker arm nuts and rotate the rocker arms away from the pushrods.

41  Remove the pushrods and store them in order so they can be installed in their original positions.

42  Remove the valve lifter retainer (refer to the accompanying illustration).

43  Remove the lifter guides.

44  Remove the lifters. A special lifter removal tool is available, or a scribe can be positioned at the top of the lifter and used to pull the lifter up. Do not use pliers or other tools on the outside of the lifter body, as they will damage the finished surface and render the lifter useless.

45  The lifters should be kept separate for reinstallation in their original positions.

46  Inspection and disassembly are similar to the standard hydraulic lifter (Chapter 2, Part C, Section 7). However, the roller must be inspected for freedom of movement, excessive looseness, flat spots or pitting. The camshaft must also be inspected if any signs of abnormal wear are indicated.

47  When reinstalling the lifters, coat them with moly-base grease or engine assembly lube and make sure they are returned to their original bores.

48  The remaining installation steps are the reverse of removal.

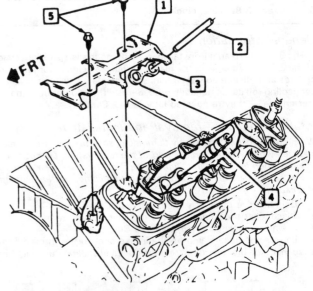

**Fig. 13.22  Before the roller-type hydraulic valve lifters are removed, the pushrods, lifter retainer and guides must first be removed (Sec 6)**

| | | | |
|---|---|---|---|
| 1 | Retainer | 4 | Lifter |
| 2 | Pushrod | 5 | Bolts |
| 3 | Guide | | |

### Oil pump — removal and installation

49  Remove the timing chain cover (refer to Chapter 2, Part C).

50  Remove the oil filter adapter, pressure regulator valve and spring. Thoroughly clean these components with solvent and be sure to remove all traces of the old gasket.

51  Remove the oil pump cover screws and lift off the cover.

52  Mark the gears in relation to each other with a felt-tip pen. Do not use a scribe, punch or awl to mark the gears as this could ruin the oil pump.

53  Remove the inner and outer gears from the housing and wash all of the components in solvent.

54  During reassembly, lubricate the gears with petroleum jelly and install them in the housing. Pack the gear housing with petroleum jelly

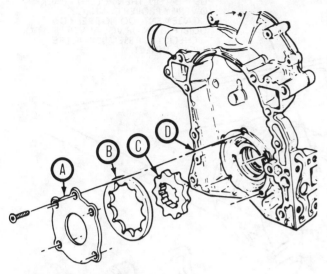

**Fig. 13.23   Details of the 3.8L engine oil pump (Sec 6)**

A   Oil pump cover        C   Inner gear
B   Outer gear            D   Timing chain cover

also, to insure adequate priming of the oil pump.
55  The remaining steps are the reverse of removal.

## Piston/connecting rod assembly — installation and bearing oil clearance check (3.3L engine)

**Note:** *GM special tool no. J-36660 (torque angle meter) is needed to correctly tighten the connecting rod bolts on this engine.*

56  Follow the piston/connecting rod installation procedure in Chapter 2, but note that the bolt tightening procedure is different when working on a 3.3L V6 engine.
57  Tighten the connecting rod bolts to 20 ft-lbs.
58  Using a torque angle meter, turn each connecting rod bolt an additional 50° rotation.

---

## 7   Cooling, heating and air conditioning systems

---

## General information

Radiators used on some 1987 models and all later models are aluminum and plastic (an aluminum core with plastic side tanks). The drain fitting is located on the lower part of one of the tanks and can be repaired. Radiator repairs should be done by a dealer service department or radiator repair shop.

## Water pump — removal and installation

### 2.5 liter four-cylinder engine
1  When replacing the water pump, you'll have to transfer the old pulley to the new water pump. If special tools aren't available, take the pump to a GM dealer or a repair shop to have the pulley pressed on and off. **Caution:** *Do not pry or hammer on the pulley as damage may occur.*

### 2.8 liter and 3.1 liter V6 engines
2  When replacing the water pump on these engines, be sure the locators on the pump and gasket are vertical (Fig. 13.24).

---

## 8   Fuel and exhaust systems

---

## General information

Some 1986 models with a 2.8 liter V6 engine were equipped with a carburetor, but carburetors were not used on any other 1986 models or any later models. All other 1986 models and all later models were equipped with either throttle body injection (TBI) (2.5 liter four-cylinder engines only) or multi-port fuel injection (MPFI) (all V6 engines).

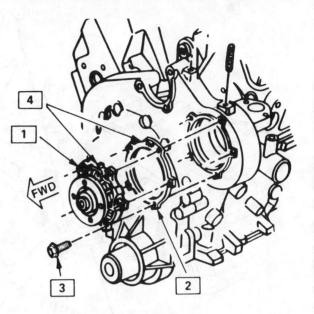

**Fig. 13.24   Water pump mounting details — 2.8/3.1L V6 engines (Sec 7)**

1   Water pump         3   Bolts
2   Gasket             4   Locator — must be VERTICAL

## Fuel injection pressure relief procedure

**Warning:** *To reduce the risk of fire and personal injury, relieve the pressure in the fuel system before loosening any fuel line fittings or servicing any fuel injection components.*

1  Disable the fuel pump by removing the fuel pump fuse from the fuse block, located in the glove box or under the dash, or by unplugging the fuel pump harness at the fuel tank. Start the engine and let it run until lack of fuel causes it to stop. Engage the starter again for about three seconds to ensure that all pressure has been relieved. Remove the fuel tank cap to relieve the pressure in the tank.
2  Turn the ignition off and disconnect the negative battery cable. After servicing the fuel system, reinstall the fuel pump fuse (or reconnect the fuel pump wire harness) and the negative battery cable.

## Quick-connect fuel line fittings — removal and installation

3  New quick-connect fuel line fittings were introduced on 1989 models. A special tool (GM no. J-37008 — fuel line separator) is required to disconnect them.
4  To separate the fuel lines, relieve the fuel system pressure and

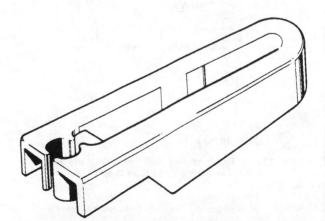

**Fig. 13.25   A special tool is required to detach quick-connect fuel line fittings (Sec 8)**

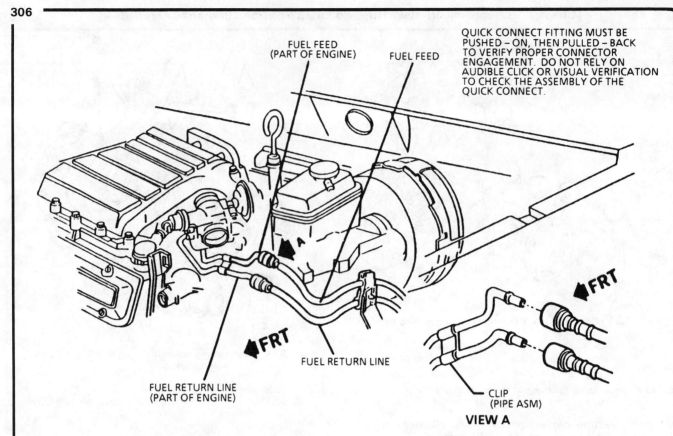

FUEL FEED
(PART OF ENGINE)

FUEL FEED

QUICK CONNECT FITTING MUST BE
PUSHED – ON, THEN PULLED – BACK
TO VERIFY PROPER CONNECTOR
ENGAGEMENT. DO NOT RELY ON
AUDIBLE CLICK OR VISUAL VERIFICATION
TO CHECK THE ASSEMBLY OF THE
QUICK CONNECT.

FRT

FUEL RETURN LINE

FUEL RETURN LINE
(PART OF ENGINE)

FRT

CLIP
(PIPE ASM)

VIEW A

Fig. 13.26   Quick-connect fuel line fitting locations — 2.8L/3.1L V6 engine shown (Sec 8)

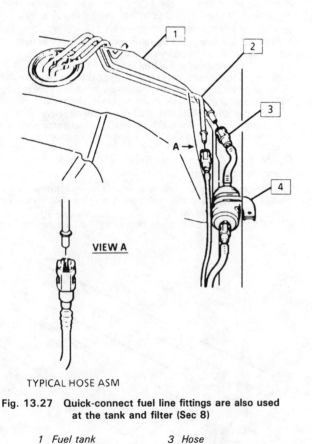

VIEW A

TYPICAL HOSE ASM

Fig. 13.27   Quick-connect fuel line fittings are also used
at the tank and filter (Sec 8)

| 1 Fuel tank | 3 Hose |
|---|---|
| 2 Fuel line | 4 Filter bracket |

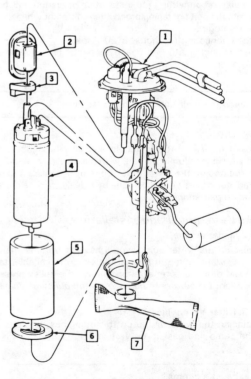

Fig. 13.28   Later model electric fuel pump mounting
details (Sec 8)

| 1 Sending unit | 5 Sound isolator sleeve |
|---|---|
| 2 Pulsator (port injection only) | 6 Sound isolator |
| 3 Bumper | 7 Strainer |
| 4 Fuel pump | |

remove the gas tank cap to relieve the tank pressure. Insert the fuel line separator tool into the fitting and pull the lines apart.

5    To reattach quick-connect fittings, push the line into the fitting as far as possible, then pull back on it to verify that the connection is secure. **Warning:** *The line must be pushed in and pulled back to verify proper connector engagement — DO NOT rely on an audible click or visual verification to check the assembly of the quick-connect fittings.*

### Electric fuel pump — replacement

6    Refer to Chapter 4 to remove the pump from the gas tank. To remove the pump from the sending unit assembly (later models only), pull it up into the attaching hose or pulsator while pulling out, away from the bottom support. Be careful not to damage the rubber insulator

and strainer during removal. Inspect all rubber parts for deterioration and replace as necessary.

7    Installation is the reverse of removal. Care should be taken not to fold over or twist the fuel strainer when inserting the fuel pump into the tank (this might restrict fuel flow).

### Throttle body injection (TBI) — general information

All 1987 and later 2.5 liter four-cylinder engines are equipped with a different throttle body injection unit called the Model 700 TBI. It is similar in operation to the TBI system described in Chapter 4, but some service procedures are slightly different due to the redesigned components.

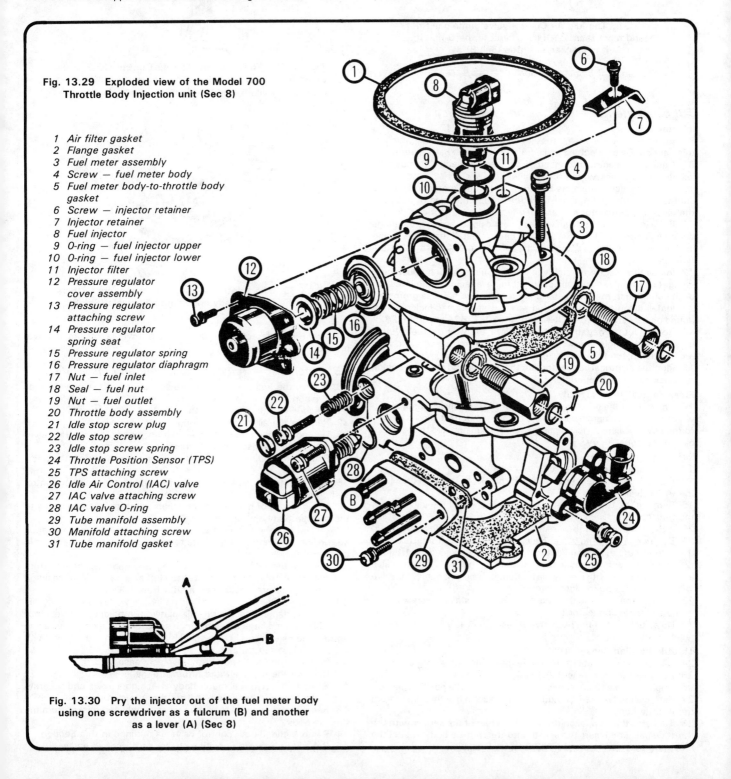

Fig. 13.29   Exploded view of the Model 700 Throttle Body Injection unit (Sec 8)

1   Air filter gasket
2   Flange gasket
3   Fuel meter assembly
4   Screw — fuel meter body
5   Fuel meter body-to-throttle body gasket
6   Screw — injector retainer
7   Injector retainer
8   Fuel injector
9   O-ring — fuel injector upper
10  O-ring — fuel injector lower
11  Injector filter
12  Pressure regulator cover assembly
13  Pressure regulator attaching screw
14  Pressure regulator spring seat
15  Pressure regulator spring
16  Pressure regulator diaphragm
17  Nut — fuel inlet
18  Seal — fuel nut
19  Nut — fuel outlet
20  Throttle body assembly
21  Idle stop screw plug
22  Idle stop screw
23  Idle stop screw spring
24  Throttle Position Sensor (TPS)
25  TPS attaching screw
26  Idle Air Control (IAC) valve
27  IAC valve attaching screw
28  IAC valve O-ring
29  Tube manifold assembly
30  Manifold attaching screw
31  Tube manifold gasket

Fig. 13.30   Pry the injector out of the fuel meter body using one screwdriver as a fulcrum (B) and another as a lever (A) (Sec 8)

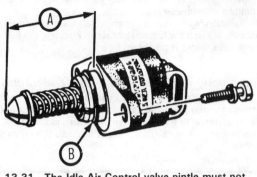

**Fig. 13.31  The Idle Air Control valve pintle must not extend more than 1-1/8 inch; replace the O-ring if it is cracked or brittle (Sec 8)**

A  Distance of pintle extension          B  O-ring

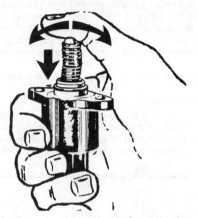

**Fig. 13.32  To reduce the Idle Air Control valve pintle extension, grasp the valve and depress the pintle using a slight side-to-side motion (Sec 8)**

## TBI components — removal and installation

### Injector

8  Relieve the fuel system pressure as decribed at the beginning of this Section. Disconnect the cable from the negative battery terminal.
9  Unplug the electrical connector from the fuel injector. Remove the injector retainer screw and the retainer.
10  Using one screwdriver as a fulcrum on the fuel meter body, place another screwdriver tip under the ridge on the fuel injector opposite the electrical connector end and gently pry the injector out.
11  If the injector is to be reused, replace the upper and lower O-rings on the injector and in the fuel injector cavity. Install the upper O-ring in the groove on the injector and the lower O-ring flush against the filter element.
12  Install the injector assembly in the fuel meter body by pushing it straight down. Make sure the connector end is facing in the direction of the opening in the fuel meter body for the wire harness grommet.
13  Install the injector retainer and screw. Use a thread locking compound on the retainer screw (GM part No. 10522624 or *Loctite 262*).
14  Reconnect the negative battery cable. Pressurize the fuel system by turning the ignition key to the On position and inspect the area around the injector for leaks.
15  Plug the electrical connector into the injector and start the engine to check for correct operation.

### Pressure regulator assembly

16  Underneath the pressure regulator cover assembly is a large spring which is highly compressed. Repairs to this component should be performed by a dealer service department or repair shop due to the possibilty of personal injury.

### Idle Air Control valve

17  Disconnect the negative battery cable.
18  Remove the air cleaner and unplug the electrical connector from the IAC valve.
19  Remove the two valve retaining screws and pull the valve out of the throttle body.
20  If the same valve is to be reinstalled, be sure to use a new O-ring.
21  Before installing the valve, measure the distance from the end of the pintle to the mounting flange. If the distance exceeds 1-1/8 inch (28 mm), reduce that measurement by pushing the pintle into the valve assembly with a slight side-to-side motion. If this is not done, the valve will be damaged during installation.
22  Position the valve on the throttle body and install the screws. Plug in the electrical connector to the valve.
23  No adjustment of the IAC valve is necessary, as it is automatically reset by the ECM.

### Throttle Position Sensor (TPS)

24  Disconnect the cable from the negative battery terminal.
25  Remove the air cleaner housing.
26  Unplug the electrical connector from the throttle position sensor.
27  Remove the two sensor mounting screws and pull the sensor from the throttle body.
28  To install the TPS, align the slot in the rear of the sensor with the throttle shaft and insert the sensor into the throttle body. Install the mounting screws. This style TPS is not adjustable.

**Fig. 13.33  The throttle position sensor mounts to the side of the throttle body and is not adjustable (Sec 8)**

29  The remainder of installation is the reverse of the removal procedure.

## TBI assembly — removal, overhaul and installation

30  Relieve the fuel system pressure as outlined at the beginning of this Section.
31  Disconnect the cable from the negative battery terminal.
32  Remove the air cleaner housing.
33  Unplug the electrical connectors from the idle air control valve, throttle position sensor and fuel injector.
34  Remove the wiring harness and insulating grommet from the throttle body.
35  Remove the throttle linkage and return spring, transmission control and cruise control cables (if applicable).
36  Using pieces of numbered tape, mark all of the vacuum hoses to the throttle body and disconnect them.
37  Disconnect the fuel inlet and return lines. Use a backup wrench on the inlet and return fitting nuts to prevent damage to the throttle body and fuel lines.
38  Remove the TBI assembly mounting studs and lift the unit from the intake manifold. It is a good idea to stuff a rag into the intake manifold opening to prevent foreign matter from falling in.
39  Place the TBI assembly in a holding fixture while servicing it. This will prevent damage to the throttle plates. If a holding fixture is not available, insert a large tapered punch upright in the jaws of a vise and tighten the vise securely. Set the TBI assembly on the punch, with the punch inserted through one of the TBI mounting holes.
40  Remove the fuel injector as pre, ouisly described.
41  Remove the fuel inlet and return fittings.
42  Remove the two fuel meter body attaching screws and separate the fuel meter body and gasket from the throttle body.
43  Remove the vacuum tube module assembly and gasket from the throttle body.
44  Remove the idle air control valve as outlined in this Section.
45  Remove the throttle position sensor as described earlier.

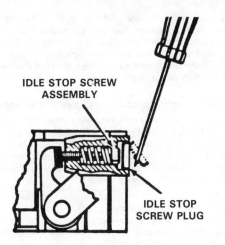

**Fig. 13.34  To gain access to the TBI idle stop screw, pierce the metal plug with a sharp object and pry it from the throttle body (this is not a routine tune-up adjustment and should only be performed when the TBI unit is replaced and the idle speed is then incorrect) (Sec 8)**

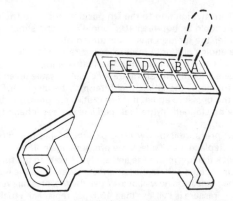

**Fig. 13.35  When adjusting the TBI minimum idle speed, ground the diagnostic test terminal with a jumper wire (Sec 8)**

46  Further disassembly of the throttle body unit is not recommended. *Do not immerse the throttle body or fuel meter cover in solvent or carburetor cleaner.* Use an aerosol cleaner to remove any dirt or varnish deposits.

47  During reassembly, replace all gaskets and seals to ensure against fuel, air and vacuum leaks.

48  Reassembly is the reverse of disassembly.

49  Installation of the throttle body is the reverse of removal.

### TBI minimum idle speed — adjustment

50  This adjustment should be performed only when the throttle body has been replaced. The engine must be at normal operating temperature for correct adjustment.

51  Remove the air cleaner housing.

52  Locate the idle stop screw plug and pierce it with a sharp object. Pry the plug from the hole.

53  Connect a tachometer to the engine.

54  Ground the diagnostic terminal (terminal B of the ALCL connector) with a jumper lead.

55  Turn the ignition to the On postion, but do not start the engine. Wait for 30 seconds, then disconnect the IAC valve electrical connector.

56  Remove the ground wire from the diagnostic terminal and start the engine.

57  Adjust the idle stop screw to obtain the specified minimum idle RPM.

58  Turn the ignition to the Off position and plug in the IAC valve electrical connector.

59  Cover the idle adjustment screw hole with RTV sealant.

60  Install the air cleaner housing.

### Multi-port fuel injection (MPFI) — general information

The multi-port fuel injection system used on the later model V6 engine incorporates a throttle body, plenum chamber, manifold and an injector solenoid at each intake port. The Electronic Control Module (ECM) controls the opening time of the injectors, which determines the amount of fuel delivered to the engine.

The throttle body, plenum chamber and intake manifold are unique in the fact that they only regulate and carry air, unlike the throttle body injection or carburetor.

All of the injectors operate simultaneously. Half of the fuel required by each cylinder is injected with each injector pulse. The pulses occur once every crankshaft revolution. Therefore, the full charge needed is available in the intake port for induction into the cylinder when the intake valve opens every other revolution.

#### Electronic control module

In determining how much fuel is required at any given moment, the Electronic Control Module (ECM) processes signals from sensors recording engine coolant temperature, exhaust oxygen content, throttle position, intake air mass, engine rpm, vehicle speed and accessory load.

#### Mass Air Flow (MAF) sensor

The Mass Air Flow (MAF) sensor measures the mass (weight) of the air entering the intake manifold, rather than the volume, which gives better control of the fuel/air mixture. The mass of any given volume of air is dependent upon the temperature of the air. Cold air weighs more than warm or hot air, and therefore the colder the air is, the more fuel is required to maintain the proper fuel/air ratio.

Within the body of the Mass Air Flow sensor, a heated film is used to measure the intake air mass. The temperature of the incoming air is constantly monitored and the air mass sensor plate is maintained at exactly 75 degrees above the temperature of the air. Since the incoming air, passing over the plate, acts to cool the plate, the measurement of the amount of electrical energy needed to maintain that 75 degree temperature differential accurately indicates the mass of air entering the engine, and therefore the amount of fuel necessary to mix with that mass to provide the proper fuel/air ratio.

#### Idle air control

The idle speed on the Multi-port injection system is also controlled by the electronic control module, through an idle air control bypass channel. When the engine is cold or when accessory loads, such as air conditioning, necessitate a higher idle speed, the ECM, through a stepper motor, opens the bypass valve to provide more air into the system. At the same time, the ECM increases the fuel injector open time to maintain the proper fuel/air ratio.

#### Fuel pump

While the open time of the injectors is controlled by the electronic control module, the actual fuel delivery is determined by the fuel pressure, which must be maintained at an adequate level, depending on manifold vacuum (engine load). This is done by a positive displacement roller vane pump mounted in the fuel tank. The pump intake is mounted in a special sump in the fuel tank so that a low fuel level, combined with hard cornering, acceleration or deceleration, cannot uncover the pump inlet, causing a pressure drop.

#### Fuel pressure regulator

A fuel pressure regulator maintains the required pressure in the system by returning unneeded fuel to the tank. A fuel accumulator is used to dampen the pulses which would otherwise be set up in the fuel rail and fuel line when the injectors open and close.

### MPFI fuel pump — check

61  Before testing the fuel pump, check the fuel pump fuse (FP on the fuse block in the glove box). If the fuse is blown, replace it before proceeding.

62  Energize the fuel pump by applying battery voltage to the fuel pump test terminal, located behind the left shock tower. If the pump does not come on, there is a loose connection, defective relay, an open in the fuel pump circuit or the fuel pump is faulty. Check the entire fuel pump electrical circuit (see *Wiring Diagrams*) before diagnosing the fuel pump as faulty. If the circuit checks out, replace the pump.

63  If the pump runs, check the fuel pressure.

### MPFI fuel pressure test

64  Remove the cap from the Schrader valve on the fuel rail and install a pressure gauge. The gauge must be capable of reading between 30

and 50 psi. Turn the ignition to the On position and read the gauge. The pressure should be between 40.5 and 47 psi and should remain there even after the ignition has been turned off.

65  Start the engine and note the fuel pressure reading. It should be approximately 3 to 10 psi less than the first reading.

66  If the engine does not run and there is no fuel pressure (even though the pump is running), the in-line fuel filter may be clogged. Replace it and check the pressure again. If there is still zero pressure, the fuel feed line may be clogged. If the fuel feed line is clear, check the fuel pump inlet filter.

67  If the fuel pressure is below 40.5 psi, the in-line fuel filter may be restricted. Replace it and check the pressure again. If the pressure is still low, block the fuel return line and apply 12-volts to the fuel pump test connector, located behind the left shock tower. Note the indicated pressure. If the pressure is now above 47 psi, the fuel pressure regulator is faulty. If the pressure is still less than 40.5 psi, replace the fuel pump. If it is still low, check for a loose fuel line fitting or a punctured fuel line. Also inspect the pressure regulator, fuel rail, cold start valve (if so equipped) and injectors for a leak. This is accomplished by removing the plenum and fuel rail without disconnecting the fuel feed and return lines, energizing the fuel pump and watching the injector nozzles for squirting or dripping fuel.

68  If the fuel pressure is above 47 psi, disconnect the fuel return line flexible hose and attach a 5/16-inch ID rubber hose to the pressure regulator side of the return line. Insert the other end into an approved gasoline container. Note the fuel pressure within two seconds after the ignition is turned to the On position. If pressure is still above 47 psi, replace the regulator. If the fuel pressure is now between 40.5 and 47 psi, the return line is restricted. Locate and remove the restriction.

### MPFI fuel flow test

69  Disconnect the fuel feed line from the fuel rail and connect a hose to the feed line. Run the other end of the hose into an unbreakable container.

70  If you have an assistant to monitor the hose and container, the easiest way to activate the fuel pump is to apply battery voltage to the fuel pump test connector near the left shock tower.

71  The fuel pump should supply 1/2-pint or more in 15 seconds. If the fuel system flow is below the minimum, inspect the fuel system for a restriction between the pump and the fuel rail. If there is no restriction, check the fuel pump pressure.

### MPFI system components — removal and installation

**Warning:** *Before servicing an injector, fuel pump, fuel line, fuel rail or pressure regulator, relieve the pressure in the fuel system to minimize the risk of fire and injury (refer to the fuel pressure relief procedure described in this Section). After servicing the fuel system, cycle the ignition between On and Off several times (wait 10 seconds between cycles) and check the system for leaks.*

**Throttle Body**

72  Disconnect the cable from the negative terminal of the battery.

73  Unplug the IAC and TPS connectors.

74  Mark and disconnect any vacuum hoses to the throttle body.

75  Disconnect the coolant lines.

76  Disconnect the throttle linkage.

77  Detach the air inlet duct.

78  Remove the throttle body bolts and detach the throttle body.

79  Install the throttle body and gasket and tighten the bolts to the specified torque.

80  Reconnect the air inlet duct.

81  Reconnect the throttle linkage.

82  Reconnect the coolant lines.

83  Reconnect the vacuum hoses.

84  Plug in the TPS and IAC electrical connectors.

85  Reconnect the cable to the negative terminal of the battery.

**Idle Air Control (IAC) valve**

86  Unplug the electrical connector from the Idle Air Control (IAC) valve assembly.

87  On 2.8 liter engines, remove the two IAC valve attaching screws and withdraw the valve.

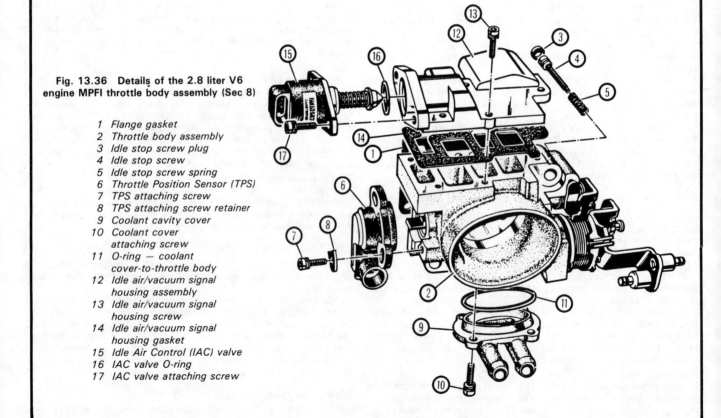

**Fig. 13.36  Details of the 2.8 liter V6 engine MPFI throttle body assembly (Sec 8)**

1  *Flange gasket*
2  *Throttle body assembly*
3  *Idle stop screw plug*
4  *Idle stop screw*
5  *Idle stop screw spring*
6  *Throttle Position Sensor (TPS)*
7  *TPS attaching screw*
8  *TPS attaching screw retainer*
9  *Coolant cavity cover*
10  *Coolant cover attaching screw*
11  *O-ring — coolant cover-to-throttle body*
12  *Idle air/vacuum signal housing assembly*
13  *Idle air/vacuum signal housing screw*
14  *Idle air/vacuum signal housing gasket*
15  *Idle Air Control (IAC) valve*
16  *IAC valve O-ring*
17  *IAC valve attaching screw*

88 On 3.8 liter engines, unscrew the IAC valve assembly from the idle air/vacuum signal housing assembly. **Caution:** *Do not remove any thread locking compound from the threads.*

89 Remove the IAC valve assembly gasket and discard it (3.8 liter engines) or replace the rubber O-ring (2.8 liter engines).

90 Clean the sealing surface and the bore of the idle air/vacuum signal housing assembly to ensure a good seal. **Caution:** *The IAC valve assembly itself is an electrical component and must not be soaked in any liquid cleaner or solvent or damage may result.*

*91 Before installing the IAC valve assembly, the position of the pintle must be checked. If the pintle is extended too far, damage to the assembly may occur.*

92 Measure the distance from the gasket mounting surface (the mounting flange on 2.8L engines) of the IAC valve assembly to the tip of the pintle

93 If the distance is greater than 1-1/8 inch, reduce it as follows:

   a) If the IAC valve assembly has a collar around the electrical connector end, apply firm hand pressure on the pintle to retract it (a slight side-to-side motion may help).

   b) If the IAC valve assembly has no collar, compress the pintle retaining spring toward the body of the IAC and try to turn the pintle *clockwise*. If the pintle will turn, continue turning it until the 1-1/8-inch dimension is reached. Return the spring to its original position with the straight part of the spring end lined up with the flat surface under the pintle head. If the pintle will not turn, apply firm hand pressure to retract it.

94 Position the new gasket or O-ring seal on the IAC valve assembly. Lubricate the O-ring with engine oil.

95 Install the IAC valve in the idle air/vacuum signal housing assembly and tighten to the specified torque.

96 Plug in the electrical connector at the IAC valve assembly. **Note:** *No adjustment is made to the IAC assembly after reinstallation. IAC resetting is controlled by the ECM when the engine is started.*

**Plenum**

97 Remove the cable from the negative terminal of the battery.

98 Mark and remove all of the vacuum lines that may interfere, then remove the throttle cable bracket bolts.

99 Remove the EGR pipe-to-EGR valve base bolts.

100 Remove the throttle body.

101 Remove the plastic spark plug wire shield bolts.

102 Remove the plenum bolts.

103 Remove the plenum and gaskets. If the plenum sticks, use a block of wood and a rubber mallet to dislodge it. Do not pry between the sealing flanges, as this will damage the machined surfaces and vacuum leaks may develop.

104 Remove all traces of old gasket material from the plenum and intake manifold mating surfaces. It is a good idea to stuff rags into the intake manifold openings to prevent debris and old gasket material from falling in.

105 Install the new gaskets and set the plenum into position.

106 Install the plenum bolts and tighten them to the specified torque.

107 Install the throttle body. Tighten the throttle body bolts to the

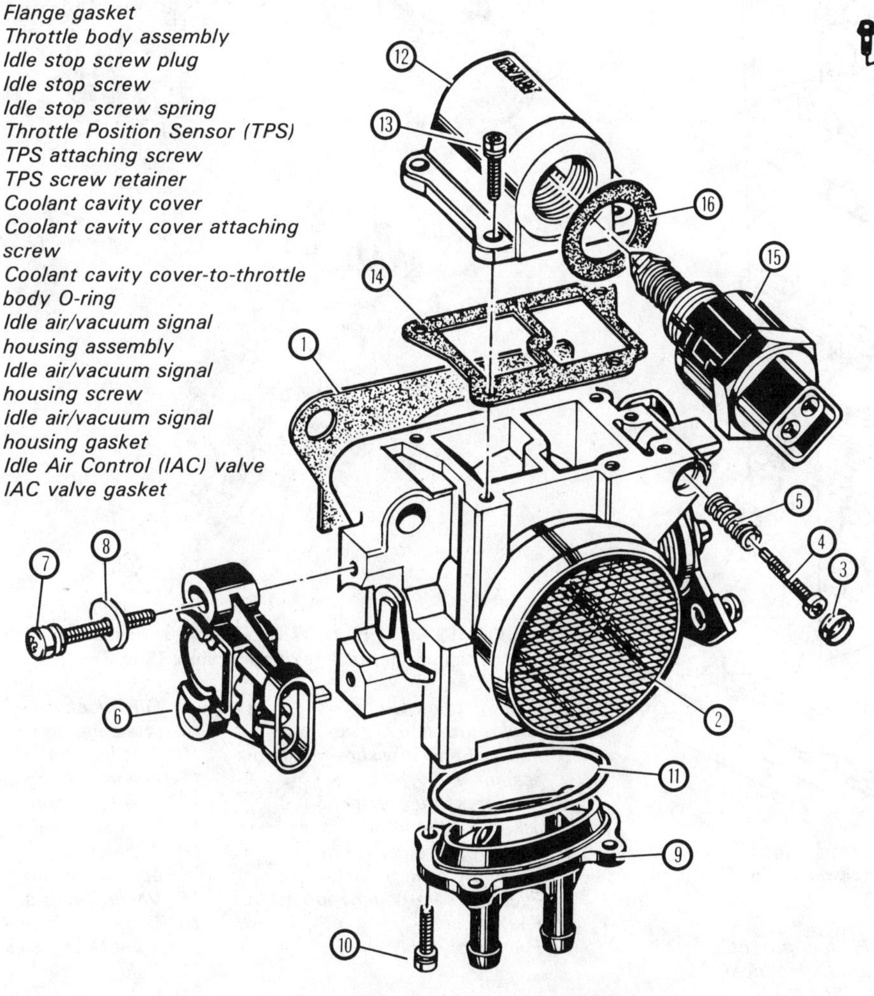

Fig. 13.37  Details of the 3.8L V6 engine MPFI throttle body assembly (Sec 8)

1  Flange gasket
2  Throttle body assembly
3  Idle stop screw plug
4  Idle stop screw
5  Idle stop screw spring
6  Throttle Position Sensor (TPS)
7  TPS attaching screw
8  TPS screw retainer
9  Coolant cavity cover
10  Coolant cavity cover attaching screw
11  Coolant cavity cover-to-throttle body O-ring
12  Idle air/vacuum signal housing assembly
13  Idle air/vacuum signal housing screw
14  Idle air/vacuum signal housing gasket
15  Idle Air Control (IAC) valve
16  IAC valve gasket

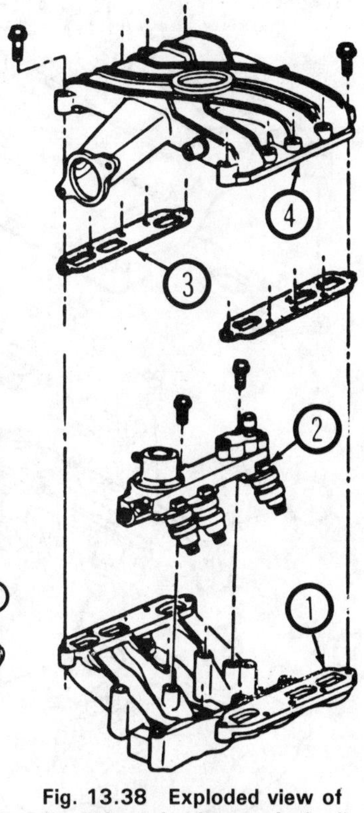

Fig. 13.38  Exploded view of the early style plenum, fuel rail and intake manifold components (Sec 8)

1  Intake manifold
2  Fuel rail assembly
3  Gasket
4  Plenum

specified torque.
108 Install the EGR pipe.
109 Install the throttle cable bracket bolts.
110 Install the vacuum lines, replacing any that are cracked or otherwise deteriorated.
111 Attach the negative battery cable to the battery.

### Fuel rail and related components

**Warning:** *Before any work is performed on the fuel lines, fuel rail or injectors, the fuel system pressure must be relieved (refer to the fuel pressure relief procedure in this Section).*

112 There are two styles of fuel rails used on the 2.8 liter V6 engine; one for 1985 and 1986 and a new type for 1987 on. The latter does not incorporate a cold start valve. Note that 3.3 liter and 3.8 liter V6 engines have a slightly different fuel rail, but the design doesn't really affect the procedures included here.
113 Detach the negative battery cable from the battery.
114 Remove the plenum (2.8L/3.1L engines only).
115 Remove the cold start valve line at the fuel rail (pre-1987 only).
116 Using a backup wrench, remove the fuel lines at the fuel rail.
117 Remove the vacuum line at the regulator.
118 On the 2.8L/3.1L engines, unplug the injector electrical connectors.

119 On the 3.3L/3.8L engines, unplug the single injector harness electrical connector.
120 Remove the fuel rail retaining bolts.
121 Carefully remove the fuel rail with the injectors. **Caution:** *Use care when handling the fuel rail assembly to avoid damaging the injectors.*

**Cold start valve**
122 On 1985 and 1986 models, to remove the cold start valve, disconnect the electrical connector and remove the cold start valve retaining bolt. Disconnect the valve from the tube and body assembly by bending the tab back to permit unscrewing of the valve.
123 Install a new cold start valve O-ring seal and body O-ring seal on the cold start valve. **Note:** *An eight digit identification number is stamped on the side of the fuel rail assembly. Refer to this number if servicing or part replacement is required.*
124 Install a new O-ring seal on the tube and body assembly.
125 Turn the valve completely into the body assembly.
126 Turn the valve back one full turn, until the electrical connector is at the top position.
127 Bend the tang of the body forward to limit rotation of the valve to less than one full turn.
128 Before reinstalling the valve assembly, coat the O-ring seals with engine oil.

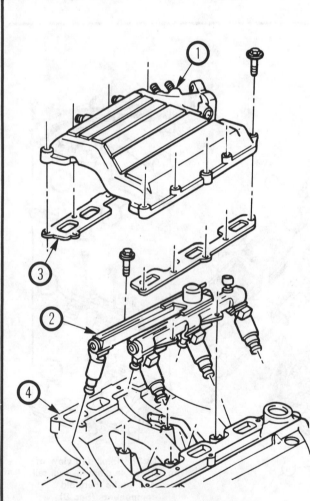

**Fig. 13.39 Exploded view of the later style plenum, fuel rail and intake manifold components (Sec 8)**

| 1 | Plenum | 3 | Plenum gasket |
| 2 | Fuel rail assembly | 4 | Intake manifold |

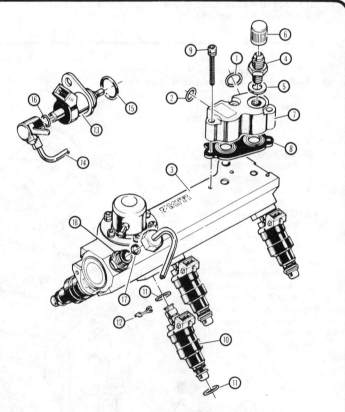

**Fig. 13.40 Pre-1987 MPFI fuel rail assembly components — exploded view (Sec 8)**

| 1 | Fuel inlet line O-ring | 9 | Fuel block |
|---|---|---|---|
| 2 | Fuel return line O-ring | | attaching screw |
| 3 | Fuel rail and pressure regulator | 10 | Port injector |
| | assembly | 11 | Injector O-ring seal |
| 4 | Fuel pressure connection | 12 | Injector retainer clip |
| | assembly (Schrader valve) | 13 | Cold start valve |
| 5 | Fuel pressure connection | 14 | Tube and |
| | assembly seal | | body assembly |
| 6 | Fuel pressure connection cap | 15 | Valve O-ring seal |
| 7 | Fuel block | 16 | Body O-ring seal |
| 8 | Fuel block seal | 17 | Tube O-ring seal |
| | | 18 | Cold start fitting |

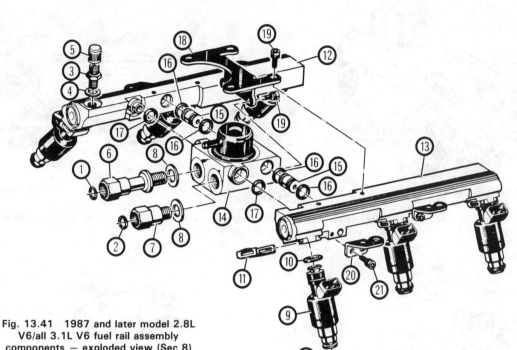

**Fig. 13.41  1987 and later model 2.8L V6/all 3.1L V6 fuel rail assembly components — exploded view (Sec 8)**

1  Fuel inlet line O-ring
2  Fuel return line O-ring
3  Fuel pressure connection assembly (Schrader valve)
4  Fuel pressure connection seal
5  Fuel pressure connection cap
6  Fuel inlet fitting
7  Fuel outlet fitting
8  Fuel fitting gasket
9  Port injector

10  Injector O-ring seal
11  Injector retainer clip
12  Fuel rail and plug assembly — left hand
13  Fuel rail and plug assembly — right hand
14  Pressure regulator assembly
15  Base-to-rail connector

16  Connector O-ring seal
17  Fuel return O-ring
18  Pressure regulator mounting bracket
19  Pressure regulator mounting bracket attaching screw
20  Rail mouting bracket
21  Bracket attaching screw

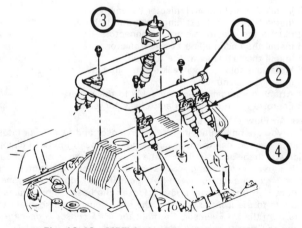

**Fig. 13.42  MPFI fuel rail, pressure regulator and injectors — 3.8L V6 engine (Sec 8)**

1  Fuel rail assembly
2  Injector

3  Pressure regulator
4  Intake manifold

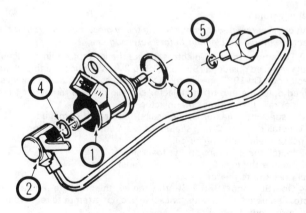

**Fig. 13.43  Pre-1987 2.8L V6 MPFI system cold start valve components (Sec 8)**

1  Cold start valve
2  Tube and body assembly
3  Valve O-ring seal

4  Body O-ring seal
5  Tube O-ring seal

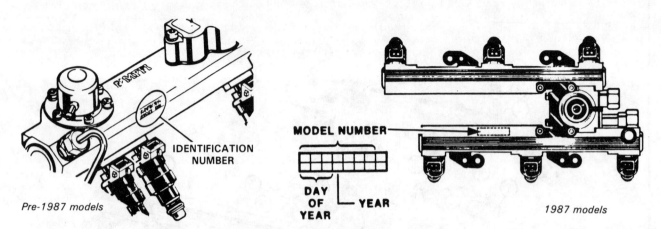

Fig. 13.44    The fuel rail assembly has an identification number stamped on the side — refer to it every time you buy a part for the fuel rail (Sec 8)

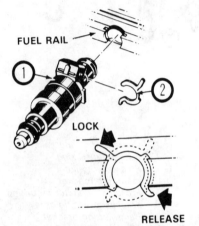

Fig. 13.45    A pre-1987 injector with an injector retaining clip is removed by rotating the clip clockwise to the release position (Sec 8)

1  Injector            2  Retaining clip

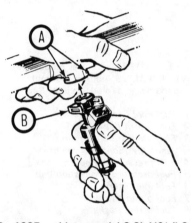

Fig. 13.46    1987 and later model 2.8L V6/all 3.1L V6 port fuel injectors and all 3.3L V6/3.8L V6 injectors are retained by a spring steel clip (B) which slides into the machined slots (A) on the fuel rail (Sec 8)

### Fuel injectors

**Caution:** *To prevent dirt from entering the engine, the area around the injectors should be cleaned before servicing.*

129 To remove the fuel injectors, rotate the injector retaining clip(s) to the released position (1985 and 1986 2.8L V6 models) and pull the injector out. On 1987 and later 2.8L/3.1L and all 3.3L/3.8L V6 engines, spread open the end of the injector clip slightly and remove it from the fuel rail, then extract the injector.
130 Inspect the injector O-ring seal(s). Replace if damaged.
131 Install the new O-ring seal(s), as required, on the injector(s) and lubricate them with engine oil.
132 Install the injectors on the fuel rail.
133 Secure the injectors with the retainer clips.

### Fuel pressure regulator

134 On 1985 and 1986 2.8L V6 engines, the pressure regulator is factory adjusted and is not serviceable. Do not attempt to remove the regulator from the fuel rail.
135 On 1987 and later 2.8L/3.1L V6 models, to remove the fuel pressure regulator from the fuel rail, remove the two fuel line fittings and gaskets.
136 Remove the pressure regulator mounting bracket screws and lift off the mounting bracket.
137 Separate the two fuel rails from the pressure regulator assembly and remove the base-to-rail connectors from the regulator.
138 Reassembly is the reverse of disassembly. Be sure to replace all gaskets and seals, otherwise a dangerous fuel leak may develop.
139 Before installing the fuel rail, lubricate all injector O-ring seals with engine oil.

140 Install the fuel rail and injector assembly.
141 Install the fuel rail retaining bolts and tighten.
142 Plug in the injector electrical connectors.
143 Install the vacuum line at the regulator.
144 Install the fuel lines at the fuel rail.
145 Install the cold start valve line at the fuel rail (pre-1987 models).
146 Install the plenum.
147 Attach the negative battery cable to the battery.
148 Energize the fuel system and check for leaks.

### Mass Air Flow (MAF) sensor

149 If you are only removing the MAF sensor and flexible air intake ducts to gain access to other components, loosen the hose clamps which attach the ducts to the throttle body and to the air cleaner housing. Remove the mounting screws and disconnect the electrical connector. If you are replacing the MAF sensor itself, do not disconnect the duct from the throttle body — loosen the hose clamp attaching the ducts to the front and rear of the MAF sensor and separate the ducts from the MAF sensor. **Caution:** *the MAF sensor is delicate — if you are going to reinstall the existing unit, handle it carefully.*
150 Installation is the reverse of the removal procedure.

---

**9    Engine electrical systems**

*Ignition system — general information*

The highly efficient distributorless ignition systems, designated the Computer Controlled Coil Ignition (3.3L/3.8L V6 engines) or Direct

Ignition System (2.5 liter four-cylinder and 2.8L/3.1L V6 engines) incorporate a coil pack, ignition module, a magnetic crankshaft sensor, a camshaft sensor (3.8L engine), interrupter (3.3L/3.8L) or reluctor (2.8L/3.1L) rings and the Electronic Control Module (ECM).

The coil pack consists of separate ignition coils, one for every two cylinders, mounted on the ignition module. The ignition module is ECM controlled and regulates the primary coil circuits, turning them on and off, as well as the spark timing when the engine speed is less then 400 RPM. The coil pack/ignition module assembly is located on the backside of the cylinder block on 2.5 liter four cylinder engines, at the front side of the cylinder block on 2.8/3.1 liter V6 engines, atop the rear rocker arm cover on 3.8 liter V6 engines and on 3.3L V6 engines, it's mounted atop the front rocker arm cover.

The crankshaft reluctor ring (2.5 and 2.8/3.1 liter engines) or interrupter rings (3.3/3.8 liter engines) and magnetic pickup sensor provide a reference pulse to the ECM, which in turn signals the ignition module to fire the proper coil at the proper time. On the Direct Ignition System the sensor also provides a cam signal for the ECM to synchronize the system to the engine's firing sequence. The DIS system reluctor ring is an integral part of the crankshaft and cannot be serviced separately. Early production Computer Controlled Coil Ignition systems also have a combined crankshaft/cam sensor, triggered by an interrupter ring on the crankshaft vibration damper. Later models use a separate cam sensor, excited by a magnet mounted on the camshaft sprocket. The crankshaft sensor on 2.5 liter engines is located under the coil pack/ignition module unit. On 2.8/3.1 liter engines it is in the rear bank of the cylinder block, and on 3.3/3.8 liter V6 engines it is mounted to the front cover behind the vibration damper. The cam sensor is located on the front cover as well, partially obscured by the water pump.

### Ignition system components -- removal and installation

**Ignition coil(s)/ignition module/crankshaft**
**sensor assembly — 2.5 liter four-cylinder engine**
1   Disconnect the cable from the negative terminal of the battery.
2   Mark the spark plug wire leads and remove them from the coil high tension towers.
3   Unplug the wiring harness connectors from the ignition module assembly.
4   Remove the three securing bolts and pull the assembly straight back from the engine block so as not to damage the crankshaft sensor.
5   To replace the coil(s), remove the coil mounting nuts and separate the coil(s) from the module.
6   To replace the crankshaft sensor, remove the two sensor retaining screws from the underside of the module assembly. Pull the sensor from the module and install the new one, taking care to engage the sensor and module terminals without bending them. Inspect the sensor O-ring and replace it if it is cracked or signs of leakage are apparent.
7   To replace the ignition module, remove the coils, shield and crank-

shaft sensor, then separate the module from the base plate. Installation is the reverse of the removal procedure.
8   Before installing the coil pack/ignition module assembly, lubricate the crankshaft sensor O-ring with clean engine oil. Position the assembly with the sensor directly above the hole in the crankcase, then push the unit straight in all the way. Install the mounting bolts, wiring harness connectors and spark plug leads.
9   Reconnect the negative battery cable.

**Ignition coil(s)/ignition module — 2.8/3.1 liter V6 engines**
10   Follow Paragraphs 1 through 3 in this Section.
11   Remove the three ignition coil/module assembly-to-block bolts and remove the unit from the vehicle.
12   To remove the coil(s), remove the coil retaining screws and separate the coil(s) from the module.
13   To replace the module, remove all three coils and the shield between the module and coils. Position the coils on the new module, place the assembly on the mounting bracket and install the screws through the coils and module into the bracket.

**Ignition coil(s)/ignition module — 3.3/3.8 liter V6 engines**
14   There are two styles of coils in use with this engine. With the Type I style, all three coils are integrated into one unit and are not serviceable separately. The Type II coil is similar to the coils used on the 2.5L and 2.8/3.1L engines, in that they are each replaceable.
15   Disconnect the cable from the negative terminal of the battery.
16   Mark and remove the spark plug wires from the coil high tension towers.

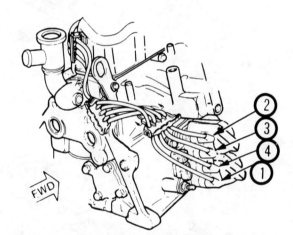

**Fig. 13.47  Four-cylinder engine Direct Ignition System (DIS) mounting location and spark plug wire positions (Sec 9)**

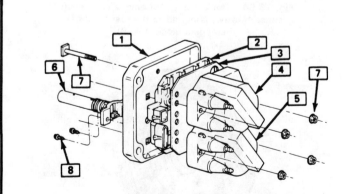

**Fig. 13.48  Exploded view of the 2.5L four-cylinder engine coil/ignition module/crankshaft sensor assembly (Sec 9)**

| | |
|---|---|
| 1  Base plate | 4  Coil for cylinders 2 and 3 |
| 2  Ignition module | 5  Coil for cylinders 1 and 4 |
| 3  Shield | 6  Crankshaft sensor |

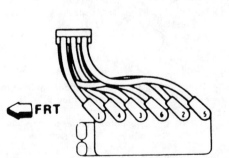

**Fig. 13.49  Positions of the spark plug leads on the coil high tension towers — 2.8/3.1L V6 engines (Sec 9)**

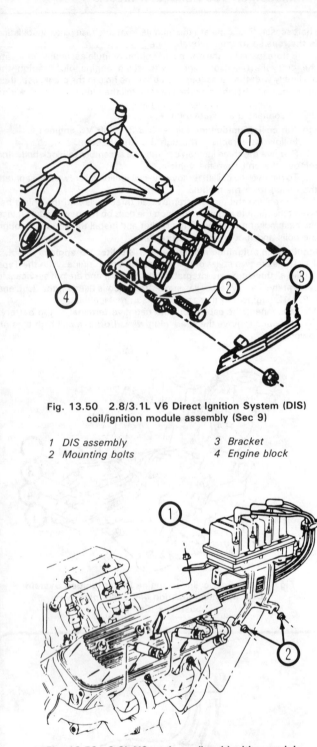

Fig. 13.50   2.8/3.1L V6 Direct Ignition System (DIS)
coil/ignition module assembly (Sec 9)

1  DIS assembly            3  Bracket
2  Mounting bolts          4  Engine block

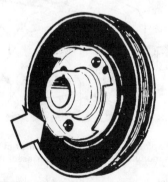

Fig. 13.53   3.8L V6 engine coil and ignition module
mounting details (Sec 9)

1  Coil/ignition module assembly
2  Securing nuts — the two rear
   nuts fasten to the exhaust
   manifold studs

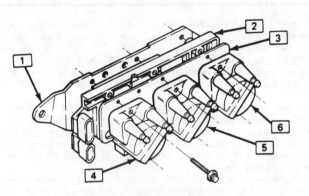

Fig. 13.51   Exploded view of the 2.8/3.1L V6 engine
coil/ignition module assembly (Sec 9)

1  Bracket            4  Coil for cylinders 1 and 4
2  Ignition module    5  Coil for cylinders 6 and 3
3  Shield             6  Coil for cylinders 5 and 2

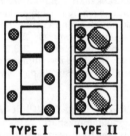

TYPE I      TYPE II

Fig. 13.52   The two different styles of ignition coils used
on the 3.3/3.8L V6 engine can be identified by the
placement of the coil high tension towers (Sec 9)

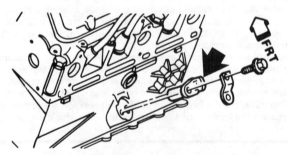

Fig. 13.54   The 2.8/3.1L V6 engine crankshaft
sensor (arrow) is bolted to the rear bank of
the engine block (Sec 9)

Fig. 13.55   The interrupter ring (arrow) is mounted on the
crankshaft vibration damper (Sec 9)

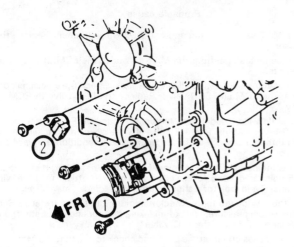

**Fig. 13.56 Details of the crankshaft (1) and camshaft (2) sensors — 3.8L V6 engine (Sec 9)**

17 To remove the Type I coil, remove the six Torx head screws securing the coil to the ignition module. Separate the coil from the module by tilting it back to gain access to the electrical connectors underneath. Mark the wires to avoid possible confusion, unplug the connectors and remove the coil from the module.

18 Installation is the reverse of the removal procedure.

19 To remove the Type II coil(s), remove the two retaining nuts for the particular coil(s) to be replaced and lift the coil from the module. Installation is the reverse of removal.

20 To remove the ignition module, undo the screw securing the 14-way connector to the module and pull the connector away from the module.

21 Mark and remove the spark plug wires from the coil high tension towers.

22 Remove the four nuts and washers securing the module to the support bracket and lift the coil/ignition module unit from the vehicle.

23 Follow Paragraph 17 or 19, depending on the style coil, to remove the ignition coil(s) from the module.

24 Installation is the reverse of the removal procedure.

25 If it is necessary to remove the coil/module assembly from the engine complete with the mounting bracket, follow Paragraphs 20 and 21, then remove the two rear bracket mounting nuts, located on the rear center exhaust manifold studs, and remove the front bracket mounting bolt on the intake manifold. The assembly can now be detached from the engine.

26 Installation is the reverse of the removal procedure.

**Crankshaft sensor — 2.8/3.1 liter V6 engines**

27 Disconnect the cable from the negative battery terminal.

28 Unplug the electrical connector from the sensor.

29 Remove the sensor to engine block bolt and pull the sensor from the bore.

30 Inspect the sealing O-ring for signs of damage and leakage. It is a good idea to replace it as a matter of course, just to be safe.

31 Installation is the reverse of the removal procedure.

**Crankshaft sensor — 3.3/3.8 liter V6 engines**

**Note:** *A special tool is required to replace the crankshaft sensor on the 3.3L engine.*

32 Disconnect the negative battery cable.

33 Raise the vehicle and support it on jackstands.

34 Using a socket and breaker bar, turn the crankshaft vibration damper until one of the windows (openings) in the interrupter ring is aligned with the sensor. On 3.3L engines, remove the vibration damper (see Chapter 2C).

35 Loosen the clamp bolt on the sensor mounting bracket, then remove the two bracket-to-front cover bolts. On the 3.8L engine, carefully withdraw the sensor and bracket through the interrupter ring window.

36 Unplug the electrical connector from the sensor and plug it into the new one. On the 3.3L engine, GM special tool J-37089 is needed to align the sensor with the vibration damper.

37 On the 3.8L engine, loosen the clamp bolt on the new assembly

and insert the sensor into the interrupter ring window. Install the two sensor mounting bracket bolts and tighten them.

38 On the 3.8L engine, align the groove on the sensor with the interrupter ring so that the ring passes exactly through the center of the sensor groove. There should be approximately 0.030-inch clearance on each side of the interrupter ring. This clearance is critical because the sensor and the interrupter ring will be damaged if they come in contact with each other.

39 When the desired clearance is attained, tighten the sensor clamp bolt and recheck the clearance at three points around the interrupter ring (120-degree intervals). Rotate the crankshaft using a wrench on the vibration damper bolt to ensure that the sensor does not rub or come in contact with the interrupter ring. On the 3.3L engine, if the vibration damper touches the special tool, the damper must be replaced.

40 Install the vibration damper (3.3L engine only), lower the vehicle and reconnect the negative battery cable.

**Camshaft sensor — 3.8 liter V6 engine**

41 Disconnect the cable from the negative battery terminal.

42 Remove the sensor retaining bolt and pull the sensor from the front cover.

43 Disconnect the electrical connector and plug it into the new sensor.

44 Position the new sensor and install the retaining bolt.

*Charging system — general information*

Later model vehicles are equipped with new style alternators, designated the CS-121 and CS-130. These alternators have no test hole in the end frame and are not serviceable.

*Charging system — check*

45 Check to make sure the drivebelt is tensioned and not slipping.

46 Verify that the battery is in good condition and is fully charged and that the battery and alternator connections are clean and tight.

47 With the ignition switch turned to the On postion and the engine stopped, the charge indicator light on the dash should be glowing brightly.

48 If your vehicle does not have a charge indicator light, proceed to Step 53.

49 If the light is not on, disconnect the wiring harness at the rear of the alternator and ground the L terminal wire. If the light now glows, replace the alternator.

50 If the light does not glow, check the bulb. If the bulb is not burned out, locate and repair the open circuit between the grounded terminal and the ignition switch.

51 With the engine running, the light should be off. If if is on, detach the wiring harness at the alternator. If the light goes out, replace the alternator.

52 If the light stays on, trace the L terminal wire, looking for a short to ground.

53 On vehicles without a charge indicator light, detach the connector from the alternator and probe terminal L and terminal I (if used) on the wiring harness side with a voltmeter connected to ground.

54 With the ignition switch On and the engine not running, a reading of 12 to 14-volts should be attained.

55 If the voltmeter reads zero, an open circuit exists between the battery and the circuit being tested. Locate and repair the open circuit condition.

56 Reattach the harness connector and run the engine at moderate speed with all accessories turned off.

57 Using a voltmeter, measure the voltage across the battery terminals. If the voltage indicated is above 16-volts, replace the alternator.

58 Additional checks should be performed by a dealer service department or a repair shop.

---

**10 Emissions control systems**

*General information*

The number of emissions control system components on later model fuel injected vehicles has actually decreased due to the high efficiency of the new fuel injection and ignition systems. No longer needed are the AIR pump (most models), early fuel evaporation (EFE) system, dual bed catalytic converter (although a single bed or monolithic converter is still used) and many of the confusing thermal vacuum switches, valves and hoses as installed on the carbureted versions.

| Trouble codes | Circuit or system | Probable cause |
|---|---|---|
| Code 23 . . . . . . . . . . . . . .<br>(2 flashes, pause, 3 flashes) | Manifold air temperature . . . . . .<br>sensor circuit | Check the MAT sensor, wiring and connectors for an open. Replace the MAT sensor.* |
| Code 25 . . . . . . . . . . . . . .<br>(2 flashes, pause, 5 flashes) | Manifold air temperature sensor | Check the voltage signal from the MAT sensor to the ECM. It should be above 4-volts. |
| Code 32 . . . . . . . . . . . . . .<br>(3 flashes, pause, 2 flashes | EGR failure . . . . . . . . . . . . . . . | Check the vacuum source and all vacuum lines. Check the electrical connections at the ECM and EGR valve. Replace the EGR valve or ECM as necessary.* |
| Code 33 . . . . . . . . . . . . . .<br>(3 flashes, pause, 3 flashes) | (MPFI) MAF sensor . . . . . . . . . | Excessive airflow indicated. Check terminal C on the MAF sensor; it should be about 0.5-volts at idle and 4.7-volts at wide open throttle. Trace the wire from terminal C and look for an open circuit condition. Replace the MAF sensor.* |
| Code 34 . . . . . . . . . . . . . .<br>(3 flashes, pause, 4 flashes) | (MPFI) MAF sensor | Low airflow indicated. Check terminal C on the MAF sensor; it should be about 0.5-volts at idle and 4.7-volts at wide open throttle. Trace the wire from terminal C and look for a short to ground. Replace the MAF sensor.* |
| Code 35 . . . . . . . . . . . . . .<br>(3 flashes, pause, 5 flashes) | Idle speed control circuit . . . . . .<br>(IAC valve) | Idle RPM too low or too high. Check minimum idle speed (refer to Section 7), check fuel pressure, check for leaking injector and for obstructions in throttle body. Replace the IAC valve* |
| Code 41 . . . . . . . . . . . . . .<br>(4 flashes, pause, 1 flash) | Cylinder select error . . . . . . . . | Remove the access cover on the ECM and check to see that the Mem-Cal (prom) is installed properly. Clear the trouble code and see if the code resets. If so, replace the Mem-Cal.* |
| Code 42 . . . . . . . . . . . . . .<br>(4 flashes, pause, 2 flashes) | Electronic Spark Timing. . . . . . . | Check the wiring between the ignition module and the ECM. Replace the ignition module.* Replace the ECM.* |
| Code 43 . . . . . . . . . . . . . .<br>(4 flashes, pause, 3 flashes) | Electronic Spark Control . . . . . . | Check the wire (circuit 496) from the knock sensor to the ECM. Replace the knock (ESC) sensor.* Replace the Mem-Cal.* Replace the ECM.* |
| Code 44 . . . . . . . . . . . . . .<br>(4 flashes, pause, 4 flashes) | Lean exhaust . . . . . . . . . . . . . | Check the ECM wiring connection terminals E14 and E15. Check the fuel pressure (see Section 7 of this supplement). Check the oxygen sensor wire. Check the throttle body gasket, vacuum hoses and intake manifold gaskets for leaks. Replace the oxygen sensor.* |
| Code 45 . . . . . . . . . . . . . .<br>(4 flashes, pause, 5 flashes) | Rich exhaust. . . . . . . . . . . . . . | Check the evaporative charcoal canister and its components for the presence of fuel. Check the fuel pressure regulator vacuum control hose for the presence of fuel. Check for a sticking EGR valve. Replace the oxygen sensor.* |
| Code 53 . . . . . . . . . . . . . .<br>(5 flashes, pause, 3 flashes) | System over-voltage . . . . . . . . | Code 53 will set if the voltage at ECM terminal B2 is greater than 17.1-volts for 2 seconds. Check the charging system. |
| Code 54 . . . . . . . . . . . . . .<br>(5 flashes, pause, 4 flashes) | Fuel pump circuit . . . . . . . . . . | Code 54 will set if the voltage at terminal B2 is less than 2-volts for 1.5 seconds since last reference pulse was received. Check fuel pump relay, circuit and connections. Check oil pressure switch. Repair/replace faulty components.* |

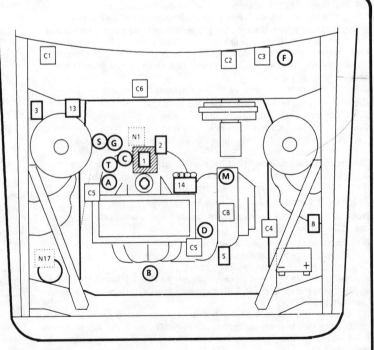

**INFORMATION SENSORS**
A  Manifold pressure (M.A.P.)
B  Exhaust oxygen
C  Throttle position
D  Coolant temperature
F  Vehicle speed Buffer Amplifier (if used)
G  Vehicle Speed PM Generator (if used)
M  P/N switch/neutral start
S  P/S pressure switch
T  Manifold Air Temperature

**CONTROLLED DEVICES**
1  Fuel injector
2  Idle air control valve
3  Fuel pump relay
5  Trans. Converter Clutch connector
8  Engine fan relay
13  A/C compressor relay
14  Direct Ignition System Assembly

**COMPUTER HARNESS**
C1  Electronic Control Module (ECM)
C2  ALCL diagnostic connector
C3  "SERVICE ENGINE SOON" light
C4  ECM power
C5  ECM harness ground
C6  Fuse panel
C8  Fuel pump test connector

**NOT ECM CONNECTED**
N1  Crankcase vent valve (PCV)
N17  Fuel vapor canister

Exhaust Gas Recirculation valve

Fig. 13.57  2.5L four-cylinder engine emissions control system and related component locations (1987 model shown, others similar) (Sec 10)

**Code 55** . . . . . . . . . . . . . . ECM . . . . . . . . . . . . . . . . . . . . Be sure that the ECM ground connections are tight. If they are, replace
(5 flashes, pause, 5 flashes)                                      the ECM.*

**Code 61** . . . . . . . . . . . . . . Contaminated oxygen sensor . . Replace the oxygen sensor. A contaminated sensor can be caused by fuel
(6 flashes, pause, 1 flash)                                        additives containing silicon or non-GM approved sealants or lubricants.

**Code 63** . . . . . . . . . . . . . . MAP sensor circuit . . . . . . . . . . The ECM is reading a low vacuum condition from the Manifold Absolute
(6 flashes, pause, 3 flashes)                                      Pressure sensor. Check wires and connections from the MAP sensor to
                                                                   the ECM. Check the vacuum hose to the sensor for leaks. Replace the
                                                                   MAP sensor.* Replace the ECM.*

**Code 64** . . . . . . . . . . . . . . MAP sensor circuit . . . . . . . . . . High vacuum has been detected by the ECM. Check the wiring and con-
(6 flashes, pause, 4 flashes)                                      nections from the MAP sensor to the ECM. Replace the MAP sensor.*
                                                                   Replace the ECM.*

*\* Component replacement may **not** cure the problem in all cases. For this reason, you may want to seek professional advice before
purchasing replacement parts.*

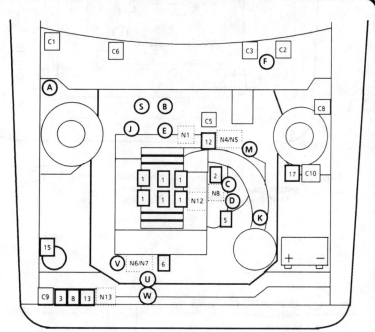

**◯INFORMATION SENSORS**
A  Manifold Pressure (MAP)
B  Exhaust oxygen
C  Throttle position
D  Coolant temperature
E  Crank Shaft Sensor
F  Vehicle speed
J  Knock (ESC)
K  Mass Air Flow & MAT
M  P/N switch
S  P/S pressure switch
U  A/C pressure fan switch (upper switch)
V  A/C Low Press. sw. mounted in Compressor
W  A/C Hi Press cutout sw. (lower switch)

**☐CONTROLLED DEVICES**
1  Fuel injector
2  Idle air control motor
3  Fuel pump relay
5  Trans. Converter Clutch connector
6  Direct Ignition System (DIS)
8  Engine fan relay
12  Exhaust Gas Recirc. valve
13  A/C compressor relay
15  Fuel vapor canister solenoid
17  Mass Air Flow sensor relay

**☐COMPUTER HARNESS**
C1  Electronic Control Module (ECM)
C2  ALDL diagnostic connector
C3  "SERVICE ENGINE SOON" light
C5  ECM harness ground
C6  Fuse panel
C8  Fuel pump test connector
C9  Fuel pump / ECM fuse
C10  Mass Air Flow sensor fuse

**⬚ NOT ECM CONNECTED**
N1  Crankcase vent valve (PCV)
N4  Engine temp. switch (telltale)
N5  Engine temp. sensor (gage)
N6  Oil press. switch (telltale)
N7  Oil press. sensor (gage)
N8  Oil press. switch (fuel pump)
N12  Fuel pressure connector
N13  12 Volt junction block

**Fig. 13.58   2.8L V6 engine emissions control system and related component locations
(1987 model shown, others similar) (Sec 10)**

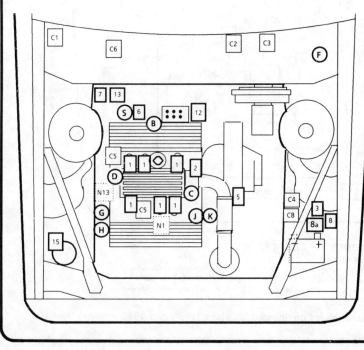

**☐CONTROLLED DEVICES**
1  Fuel injector
2  Idle air control motor (IAC)
3  Fuel pump relay
5  Trans. Conv. Clutch connector (TCC)
6  Comp. Controlled Coil Ignition (C³I)
7  Electronic Spark Control module (ESC)
8  Engine fan relay
8a  Engine fan delay relay
12  Exh. Gas Recirc. vacuum solenoid
13  A/C compressor relay
15  Fuel vapor canister solenoid

◈ Exhaust Gas Recirculation valve

**⬚ NOT ECM CONNECTED**
N1  Crankcase vent valve (PCV)
N13  Coolant fan temp. override switch

**◯INFORMATION SENSORS**
B  Exhaust oxygen (O₂)
C  Throttle position (TPS)
D  Coolant temperature
F  Vehicle speed (VSS)
G  Camshaft Position (C³I)
H  Crankshaft Position (C³I)
J  ESC Knock Sensor
K  Mass Air Flow
S  P/S pressure switch (PSPS)

**☐ COMPUTER HARNESS**
C1  Electronic Control Module (ECM)
C2  ALDL diagnostic connector
C3  "SERVICE ENGINE SOON" light
C4  ECM power
C5  ECM harness ground
C6  Fuse panel
C8  Fuel pump test connector

**Fig. 13.59   3.8L V6 engine emissions control system
and related component locations (1987 model shown,
others similar) (Sec 10)**

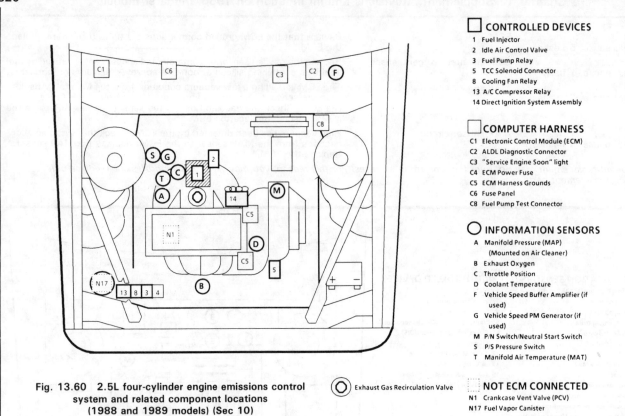

**CONTROLLED DEVICES**

1  Fuel Injector
2  Idle Air Control Valve
3  Fuel Pump Relay
5  TCC Solenoid Connector
8  Cooling Fan Relay
13  A/C Compressor Relay
14  Direct Ignition System Assembly

**COMPUTER HARNESS**

C1  Electronic Control Module (ECM)
C2  ALDL Diagnostic Connector
C3  "Service Engine Soon" light
C4  ECM Power Fuse
C5  ECM Harness Grounds
C6  Fuse Panel
C8  Fuel Pump Test Connector

**INFORMATION SENSORS**

A  Manifold Pressure (MAP)
    (Mounted on Air Cleaner)
B  Exhaust Oxygen
C  Throttle Position
D  Coolant Temperature
F  Vehicle Speed Buffer Amplifier (if used)
G  Vehicle Speed PM Generator (if used)
M  P/N Switch/Neutral Start Switch
S  P/S Pressure Switch
T  Manifold Air Temperature (MAT)

Exhaust Gas Recirculation Valve

**NOT ECM CONNECTED**

N1  Crankcase Vent Valve (PCV)
N17  Fuel Vapor Canister

Fig. 13.60   2.5L four-cylinder engine emissions control system and related component locations (1988 and 1989 models) (Sec 10)

**INFORMATION SENSORS**

A  Manifold Pressure (MAP)
B  Exhaust oxygen
C  Throttle position
D  Coolant temperature
E  Crank Shaft Sensor
F1  Vehicle speed - A/T
J  Knock (ESC)
K  Sensor MAT
M  P/N switch
S  P/S pressure switch
U  A/C pressure fan switch (upper switch)
V  A/C Low Press. sw. mounted in Compressor
W  A/C Hi Press cutout sw. (lower switch)

**COMPUTER HARNESS**

C1  Electronic Control Module (ECM)
C2  ALDL diagnostic connector
C3  "SERVICE ENGINE SOON" light
C5  ECM harness ground
C6  Fuse panel
C8  Fuel pump test connector
C9  Fuel pump / ECM fuse

**NOT ECM CONNECTED**

N1  Crankcase vent valve (PCV)
N4  Engine temp. switch (telltale)
N5  Engine temp. sensor (gage)
N6  Oil press. switch (telltale)
N7  Oil press. sensor (gage)
N8  Oil press. switch (fuel pump)
N12  Fuel pressure connector
N13  12 Volt junction block

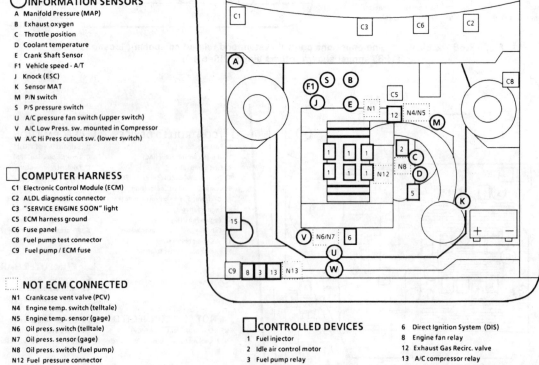

**CONTROLLED DEVICES**

1  Fuel injector
2  Idle air control motor
3  Fuel pump relay
5  Trans. Converter Clutch connector

6  Direct Ignition System (DIS)
8  Engine fan relay
12  Exhaust Gas Recirc. valve
13  A/C compressor relay
15  Fuel vapor canister solenoid

Fig. 13.61   3.1L V6 engine emissions control system and related component locations (1988 and 1989 models) (Sec 10)

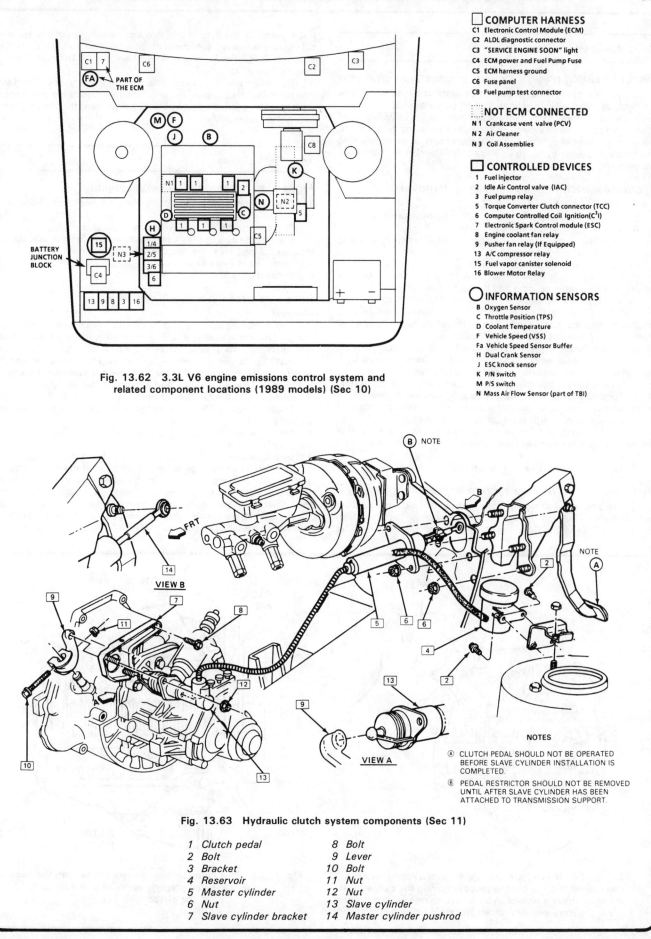

**COMPUTER HARNESS**
C1 Electronic Control Module (ECM)
C2 ALDL diagnostic connector
C3 "SERVICE ENGINE SOON" light
C4 ECM power and Fuel Pump Fuse
C5 ECM harness ground
C6 Fuse panel
C8 Fuel pump test connector

**NOT ECM CONNECTED**
N1 Crankcase vent valve (PCV)
N2 Air Cleaner
N3 Coil Assemblies

**CONTROLLED DEVICES**
1 Fuel injector
2 Idle Air Control valve (IAC)
3 Fuel pump relay
5 Torque Converter Clutch connector (TCC)
6 Computer Controlled Coil Ignition($C^3I$)
7 Electronic Spark Control module (ESC)
8 Engine coolant fan relay
9 Pusher fan relay (If Equipped)
13 A/C compressor relay
15 Fuel vapor canister solenoid
16 Blower Motor Relay

**INFORMATION SENSORS**
B Oxygen Sensor
C Throttle Position (TPS)
D Coolant Temperature
F Vehicle Speed (VSS)
Fa Vehicle Speed Sensor Buffer
H Dual Crank Sensor
J ESC knock sensor
K P/N switch
M P/S switch
N Mass Air Flow Sensor (part of TBI)

PART OF THE ECM

BATTERY JUNCTION BLOCK

Fig. 13.62  3.3L V6 engine emissions control system and
related component locations (1989 models) (Sec 10)

FRT

VIEW B

VIEW A

NOTE

NOTE

**NOTES**

Ⓐ CLUTCH PEDAL SHOULD NOT BE OPERATED
BEFORE SLAVE CYLINDER INSTALLATION IS
COMPLETED.

Ⓑ PEDAL RESTRICTOR SHOULD NOT BE REMOVED
UNTIL AFTER SLAVE CYLINDER HAS BEEN
ATTACHED TO TRANSMISSION SUPPORT.

Fig. 13.63  Hydraulic clutch system components (Sec 11)

| | | | |
|---|---|---|---|
| 1 | Clutch pedal | 8 | Bolt |
| 2 | Bolt | 9 | Lever |
| 3 | Bracket | 10 | Bolt |
| 4 | Reservoir | 11 | Nut |
| 5 | Master cylinder | 12 | Nut |
| 6 | Nut | 13 | Slave cylinder |
| 7 | Slave cylinder bracket | 14 | Master cylinder pushrod |

## 11   Clutch and driveaxles

### Hydraulic clutch release system — general information

The hydraulic clutch release system consists of a master cylinder and fluid reservoir, a slave cylinder and a hydraulic pressure line between the two. The system is serviced as a unit as the individual components are not available separately. Other than replacing the complete system, bleeding the system of air is the only service procedure that may become necessary, due to insufficient fluid level or any time after the hydraulic system has been opened.

### Hydraulic clutch release system — removal and installation

1   Disconnect the cable from the negative battery terminal.
2   Remove the left side under-dash panel.
3   Remove the clutch master cylinder pushrod retaining clip and pushrod from the clutch pedal.
4   Remove the master cylinder mounting nuts (2).
5   Remove the clutch slave cylinder mounting nuts and detach the master cylinder, slave cylinder and hydraulic line.
6   Install the new slave cylinder in the support bracket and insert the pushrod into the cup on the clutch release lever. **Note:** *Do not remove the plastic strap that holds the pushrod in the retracted position. It will break the first time the clutch pedal is depressed.*
7   Mount the clutch master cylinder on the firewall and install the nuts.
8   Remove the pedal restrictor from the master cylinder pushrod. Coat the inside of the pushrod bushing with multi-purpose grease, connect the pushrod to the clutch pedal and install the retaining clip. If the vehicle is equipped with cruise control, check to see that the disengage switch on the clutch pedal bracket is in contact with the clutch pedal with the pedal at rest. If it is not, adjust it accordingly.
9   Pump the clutch pedal several times to break the slave cylinder retaining strap. Leave the remaining plastic button under the pushrod in place.
10  Reconnect the negative battery cable.

### Hydraulic clutch release system — bleeding

11  If it becomes necessary to bleed the clutch hydraulic system, clean and remove the reservoir cap and fill the fluid reservoir to the top with the recommended fluid. Open the bleed screw on the slave cylinder body and allow the fluid to drip into a container. When it is apparent that there are no more bubbles at the bleed screw opening and a steady stream of fluid is flowing out, close the bleed screw. The system should now be free of air.
12  To confirm this, start the engine, depress the clutch pedal and shift into Reverse. There should be no grinding sounds as the gears mesh. If the gears do grind, the system still contains air and the bleeding operation should be repeated.

## 12   Brakes

### Front disc brake pads — replacement

1   Some later models are equipped with a different type of disc brake pad.
2   Remove the caliper as outlined in Chapter 9.
3   Remove the outer pad by using a screwdriver to disengage the buttons on the pad from the holes in the caliper housing.
4   Remove the inner brake pad.
5   Installation is the reverse of removal.

### Rear disc brake pads — replacement

**Removal**
6   The rear brake calipers on 1989 Pontiac 6000 models are a new design. Use the following procedures when working on them. **Note:** *GM specifies two special tools — J-6125-1B (slide hammer) and J-36620 (spring pin remover) — for removing the new style rear disc brake calipers. However, if these tools are not available, try using a hammer and brass drift punch to knock out the spring pins.*
7   Drain 2/3 of the brake fluid from the master cylinder assembly.
8   Loosen the wheel lug nuts, raise the vehicle and place it securely on jackstands.
9   Mark the relationship of the wheel to the axle flange.
10  Remove the wheel.
11  Install two inverted lug nuts to retain the rotor.
12  Position a pair of large adjustable pliers over the caliper housing and flange of the inner brake pad, then squeeze the pliers to compress the piston back into the caliper bore. You must bottom the piston in the caliper bore to provide enough clearance for the new brake pads.
13  If you have the special tools, connnect J-36620 onto J-6125-1B, remove the threaded tip from the rod on J-36620, insert the rod com-

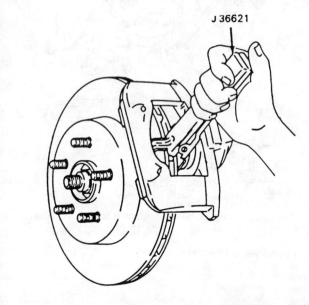

**Fig. 13.64   If you have the special piston rotator wrench, you can retract the pads without removing the caliper — if you don't have a wrench, you'll have to remove the caliper before you can retract the piston (Sec 12)**

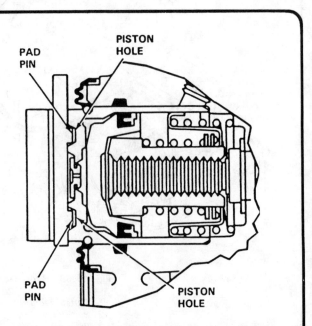

**Fig. 13.65   This cutaway view shows the pins on the back of the brake pad properly engaged in the holes in the piston (Sec 12)**

pletely through the spring pin and install the threaded tip as far as it will go. Slam the weight on J-6125-1B out, against the tool handle, to pull out the pin. **Note:** *If you don't have the special tools, remove the pins with a brass punch and a hammer. Make sure the outside diameter of the punch is the same size as the outside diameter of the pins. If you use a punch that's too small in diameter, it may jam in the end of the hollow pins and flare the ends (making them impossible to remove from the caliper).*

14  Remove the springs from the inner and outer pad flanges. **Warning:** *Wear safety goggles during this procedure — the springs can fly off forcefully when pried loose.*

15  Lift the outer pad through the caliper opening and remove it.

16  Lift the inner pad through the caliper opening and remove it. If necessary, push on the bridge and move the caliper housing toward the center of the vehicle to provide enough clearance for removal.

17  After you have removed the old pads, use a small screwdriver to remove the two-way check valve from the end of the piston assembly.

18  If you note any leakage from the piston hole after you've removed the check valve, remove and overhaul the caliper (begin at Step 33).

**Installation**

**Note:** *GM recommends using a piston rotator wrench (J-36621) to bottom out the pistons prior to installing new pads. If you don't have this special tool, you'll have to unbolt the caliper housing assembly and slide it off the rotor to bottom out the piston.*

19  The piston rotator wrench has pins which engage the holes in the face of the piston assembly. Insert the pins into the holes and rotate the piston assembly until it bottoms in the caliper bore (see Fig. 13.64). **Note:** *The pistons are not threaded the same way: To bottom the pistons, turn the left caliper piston assembly counterclockwise and turn the right caliper assembly clockwise.*

20  If you don't have a rotator wrench, remove the rear caliper assembly (see Steps 33 through 38), stick the tips of a pair of needle-nose pliers into the holes in the face of the piston and rotate the piston until it bottoms in the bore (see the **Note** above in Step 19).

21  After you have bottomed the piston in the caliper bore, lubricate a new two-way check valve and install it in the piston face.

22  Install the inner pad with the wear sensor at the rear of the pad. Make sure the pad pins on the back of the inner pad engage the holes on the front of the piston (see Fig. 13.65). If you have a piston rotator wrench, you can use it to turn the piston until the holes align with the pins; if you don't have a rotator wrench, turn the piston as described above in Step 20 with a pair of needle-nose pliers until the holes are aligned with the pins on the back of the pad.

23  Install the outer pad.

24  Using a small hammer and a brass punch (*not* a steel one), tap in one spring pin until it is through both pads and slightly into the inner section of the caliper housing.

25  Complete pin installation by tapping in both pins until the end of each pin just protrudes from the inner face of the caliper housing.

26  Make sure the springs are centered on the pad flanges with each spring end projecting under the pins an equal amount.

27  If you removed the caliper to bottom the piston, install it now (see Steps 39 through 51).

28  Remove the wheel lug nuts securing the rotor to the hub.

29  Using the alignment marks you made during disassembly, install the wheels. Tighten the lug nuts securely.

30  Lower the vehicle and tighten the lug nuts to the specified torque.

31  Fill the master cylinder to the proper level with clean brake fluid.

32  Depress the brake pedal three or four times to seat the pads.

## *Rear disc brake caliper — removal and installation*

**Removal**

33  Remove the brake pads (see Steps 7 through 18). Detach the parking brake cable (see Fig. 13.66) and return spring (see Fig. 13.67) from the parking brake lever. Loosen the cable adjuster, if necessary.

34  If you're removing the caliper housing for overhaul, remove the bolt which secures the brake hose fitting (if you're removing the caliper to service suspension components, skip this step). Plug the caliper housing and the brake hose to prevent leakage and contamination.

35  Remove the caliper mounting bolts with a no. 55 Torx driver. **Note:** *Don't confuse the mounting bolts with the bridge bolts (see Fig. 13.67).*

36  Detach the caliper housing from the mounting bracket and the rotor. If you're unbolting the caliper to service suspension components, hang

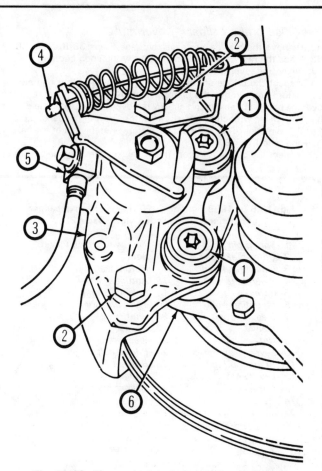

**Fig. 13.66   You must detach the parking brake cable before removing the rear caliper assembly (Sec 12)**

| | |
|---|---|
| 1  *Mounting bolt* | 4  *Parking brake cable* |
| 2  *Bridge bolt* | 5  *Inlet fitting* |
| 3  *Caliper housing* | 6  *Mounting bracket* |

the caliper housing with a wire hook from the suspension. **Warning:** *Don't let it hang by the brake hose.*

37  Remove the sleeves and sleeve boots.

38  Inspect the mounting bolts and sleeves for corrosion. Inspect the sleeve boots for cuts, nicks and deterioration. If you find any corrosion or damage, replace the bolts, sleeves and sleeve boots.

**Installation**

39  Lubricate the outside of the sleeves and the inside of the mounting bolt holes in the caliper housing with silicone grease.

40  Install one sleeve boot in the groove in the mounting bolt hole of the caliper housing.

41  Push the sleeve into the mounting bolt hole, through the installed sleeve boot, about half-way into the hole.

42  Install the second sleeve boot in the groove at the other end of the mounting bolt hole.

43  Push in the sleeve to seat the sleeve boots in the grooves of the sleeve.

44  Repeat steps 40 through 43 for the other sleeve.

45  Slide the caliper housing over the rotor onto the mounting bracket, install the caliper mounting bolts and tighten them to the specified torque.

46  If you detached the brake hose, reattach it and tighten the fitting bolt to the specified torque. Be sure to use new copper crush washers on either side of the fitting.

47  Install the brake pads and linings (see Steps 19 through 32).

48  If you detached the brake hose, bleed the caliper (see Chapter 9).

49  Check the brake fluid level and add fluid, if necessary (see Chapter 1).

50  Attach the parking brake cable and return spring to the parking brake lever.

51  Adjust the parking brake cable as described later in this Section.

## Rear disc brake caliper — overhaul

52  Remove the rear caliper assembly (see Steps 33 through 36).
53  Place the rear caliper assembly on a workbench and remove the nut, lever and lever seal (see Fig. 13.67).
54  Inspect the bridge and bracket for cracks and other damage.
55  Before you remove the piston assembly, place a clean shop rag over the bridge (if you haven't already removed it) and under the caliper housing. Use a wrench to turn the actuator screw in the parking brake "apply" direction. This will work the piston assembly out of the caliper housing (see Fig. 13.68).
56  Inspect the piston for score marks, nicks, corrosion and worn or damaged chrome plating. If damage is evident, replace the piston.
57  Remove the actuator screw by pressing on the threaded end.
58  Remove the balance spring.
59  Remove the shaft seal and thrust washer from the actuator screw. Discard the seal.
60  Inspect the actuator screw for cracks and thread damage. If any wear or damage is evident, replace the screw.
61  Use a screwdriver to pry out the piston boot. Be careful not to scratch the caliper housing.
62  Remove the rubber piston seal with a small wood or plastic tool. Using a metal tool may damage the caliper bore or seal groove.

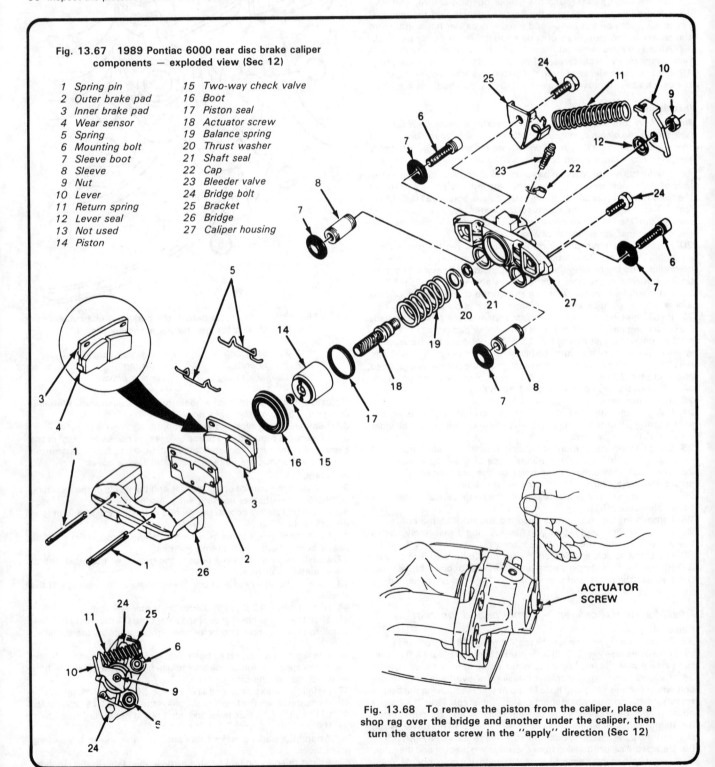

**Fig. 13.67   1989 Pontiac 6000 rear disc brake caliper components — exploded view (Sec 12)**

1   Spring pin
2   Outer brake pad
3   Inner brake pad
4   Wear sensor
5   Spring
6   Mounting bolt
7   Sleeve boot
8   Sleeve
9   Nut
10  Lever
11  Return spring
12  Lever seal
13  Not used
14  Piston
15  Two-way check valve
16  Boot
17  Piston seal
18  Actuator screw
19  Balance spring
20  Thrust washer
21  Shaft seal
22  Cap
23  Bleeder valve
24  Bridge bolt
25  Bracket
26  Bridge
27  Caliper housing

**Fig. 13.68   To remove the piston from the caliper, place a shop rag over the bridge and another under the caliper, then turn the actuator screw in the "apply" direction (Sec 12)**

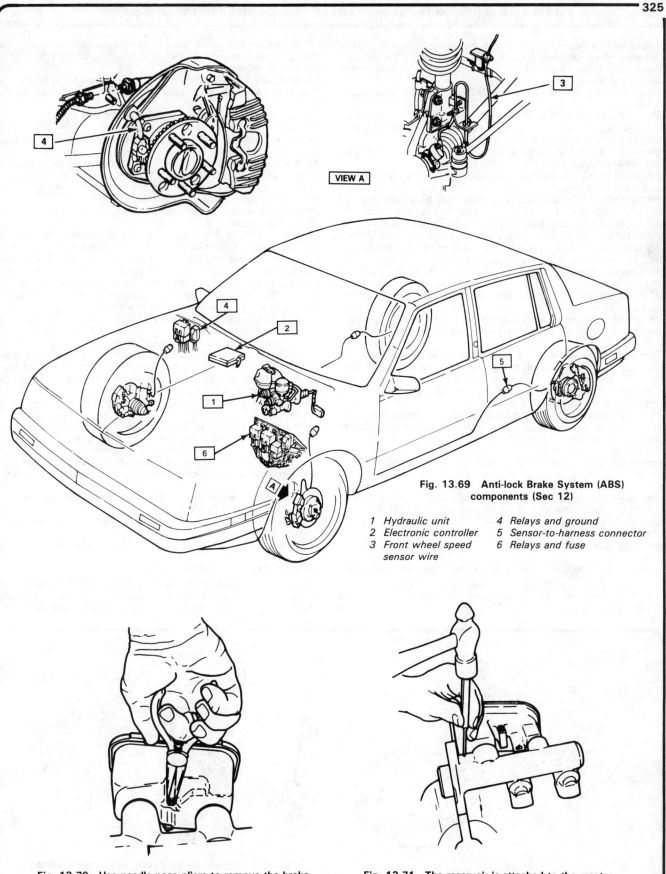

**VIEW A**

**Fig. 13.69   Anti-lock Brake System (ABS) components (Sec 12)**

1  *Hydraulic unit*
2  *Electronic controller*
3  *Front wheel speed sensor wire*
4  *Relays and ground*
5  *Sensor-to-harness connector*
6  *Relays and fuse*

**Fig. 13.70   Use needle-nose pliers to remove the brake fluid level sensor switch from the master cylinder reservoir (Sec 12)**

**Fig. 13.71   The reservoir is attached to the master cylinder body with spring pins that must be driven out with a hammer and punch (Sec 12)**

63  Inspect the caliper bore and piston seal groove for scoring, nicks, corrosion and wear. Use crocus cloth to polish out light corrosion. Replace the caliper housing if you can't clean up the corrosion in and around the seal groove.

64  Remove the bleeder valve cap and bleeder valve from the caliper housing.

65  Wash all parts in clean, denatured alcohol and allow them to air dry. Blow out all pasages in the caliper housing and bleeder valve with unlubricated compressed air.

66  Install the bridge and bridge bolts, if you removed them, and tighten the bolts to the specified torque.

67  Install the bleeder valve and valve cap. Tighten the bleeder valve to the specified torque.

68  Lubricate a new piston seal with clean brake fluid and install it in the piston seal groove. Make sure the seal isn't twisted.

69  Lubricate the piston boot with clean brake fluid and slide it onto the end of the piston. Make sure the boot seats properly in the groove.

70  Install the thrust washer on the actuator screw with the copper side of the washer facing the piston assembly.

71  Lubricate a new shaft seal with clean brake fluid and install it on the actuator screw.

72  Install the actuator screw, shaft seal and thrust washer in the caliper housing.

73  Install the balance spring in the caliper housing bore. Make sure the bottom end of the spring seats in the recess at the bottom of the caliper bore.

74  Lubricate the outside of the piston assembly with clean brake fluid and push the piston assembly toward the bottom of the caliper bore. When the piston contacts the actuator screw, turn the actuator screw to thread it into the piston and continue turning it until the piston is retracted all the way into the caliper bore.

75  Install the lever seal over the end of the actuator screw. The rubber sealing bead on the lever seal should be against the lever and the copper colored side should be facing the caliper housing.

76  Hold the lever against its stop on the caliper housing and tighten the nut (this prevents accidental application of the parking brake mechanism).

77  Install the lever and nut. The hex hole in the lever must engage the hex on the actuator screw. Tighten the nut to the specified torque.

78  Make sure the outer lip of the piston boot seats in its groove in the caliper housing.

79  Install the brake pads (see Steps 19 through 32).

80  Install the caliper (see Steps 39 through 51).

## Master cylinder — removal, overhaul and installation

81  Removal and installation is outlined in Chapter 9.

82  Clamp the master cylinder flange in a vise. Don't apply pressure to the master cylinder body.

83  If equipped, remove the brake fluid level sensor switch. Use needle-nose pliers to compress the switch locking tabs at the inner side of the master cylinder.

84  Drive out the spring pins with a 1/8-inch punch. Be careful not to damage the reservoir or master cylinder body when driving out the pins.

85  Remove the reservoir by pulling it straight up.

86  Remove the O-rings from the reservoir.

87  Inspect the reservoir for cracks and distortion. Replace it if damage is noted.

88  Remove the proportioner valve caps, O-rings and springs. You may have to use needle-nose pliers to remove the proportioner valve pistons — be careful not to scratch or damage the piston stems.

89  Remove the proportioner valve seals.

90  Inspect the proportioner valve pistons for corrosion and deformation and replace them if necessary.

91  Refer to Chapter 9 for removal and installation of the primary and secondary pistons. Be sure to note the installed direction of the old seal lips so the new seals can be installed the same way. The primary piston assembly is serviced as an assembly, while the secondary piston seals can be serviced separately. Clean all parts with denatured alcohol and dry them with unlubricated compressed air. Lubricate all rubber parts with clean brake fluid to ease reassembly.

92  Inspect the master cylinder bore for score marks and corrosion. If any corrosion or damage is found, replace the master cylinder body with a new one (the bore cannot be honed).

93  Lubricate the new O-rings, proportioner valve seals and proportioner valve pistons with silicone grease supplied in the repair kit.

94  Install the new seals on the proportioner valve pistons with the seal lips facing up, towards the cap assembly.

95  Install the proportioner valve pistons and seals in the master cylinder body.

96  Install the springs in the master cylinder body.

97  Install new O-rings in the grooves of the proportioner valve caps and install the caps in the master cylinder. Tighten the caps to 20 ft-lbs.

98  Lubricate the new O-rings with clean brake fluid and install them in the grooves of the reservoir. Make sure the O-rings are properly seated.

99  Install the reservoir on the master cylinder by pressing it straight down by hand into the body.

100 Drive in the spring pins to retain the reservoir, using care not to damage the reservoir or master cylinder body.

101 Install the master cylinder and bleed the brakes (refer to Chapter 9).

## Parking brake — adjustment

**Note:** *This procedure applies to 1989 Pontiac 6000 models only. If the hydraulic system operates with adequate reserve but the parking brake pedal travel exceeds 17 ratchet clicks, the parking brake cable*

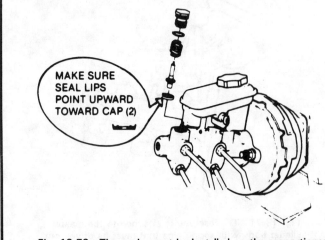

**MAKE SURE SEAL LIPS POINT UPWARD TOWARD CAP (2)**

Fig. 13.72  The seals must be installed on the proportioner valve pistons with the lips facing UP (Sec 12)

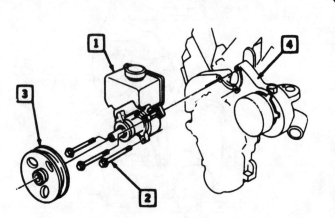

Fig. 13.73  Power steering pump and pulley mounting details — 2.8/3.1L V6 engines (Sec 13)

| | |
|---|---|
| 1  Pump | 3  Pulley |
| 2  Bolt | 4  Cover |

*must be adjusted. It must also be adjusted any time the rear brake cables have been disconnected.*

102 Release the parking brake.

103 Raise the rear of the vehicle and support it securely on jackstands. Block the front wheels.

104 Make sure the equalizer nut groove is lubricated liberally with multi-purpose lithium-base grease.

105 Hold the brake cable stud and tighten the equalizer nut until there is no cable slack.

106 Make sure the caliper levers are against the stops on the caliper housing after tightening the equalizer nut.

107 If the levers are off the stops, loosen the cable until the levers return to the stops.

108 Operate the parking brake several times to check the adjustment. A properly adjusted brake cable will require 14 to 16 notches of movement at the pedal when enough force is applied to lock the rear wheels.

109 Lower the vehicle. The levers must be on the caliper stops after adjustment. Back off the parking brake equalizer if the levers are not against the stops when the vehicle is lowered.

### Anti-lock brake system (ABS) — general information

The anti-lock braking system (ABS) was introduced in 1985 and is designed to maintain vehicle control under severe braking conditions. The system performs this function by monitoring the rotational speed of each wheel and then controlling the brake line pressure to prevent wheel lock-up.

**Operation**

Each time the vehicle is started, the amber "anti-lock" warning light on the dashboard illuminates for a brief time and then goes out. This indicates that the system is operating properly. Additionally, since ABS functions may not be used every day, there is a test which actually runs the modulator valve to ensure that the system is totally functional. This test occurs when the vehicle is first started and when it reaches about four mph. This test can sometimes be heard and felt (if the driver's foot is on the brake pedal). During vehicle operation the system is constantly monitored by the control module. If a fault occurs in any part of the ABS system, the dashboard warning light will illuminate to indicate that repair is necessary. **Note:** *If a fault in the ABS system should occur, the conventional brake system will remain fully operational provided it is not faulty.*

**Components**

The hydraulic unit is located in the passenger compartment under the dash (see Fig. 13.69). The function of the hydraulic unit is to maintain or reduce the brake fluid pressure to the wheel calipers. It cannot increase the pressure above that transmitted to the master cylinder, and can never apply the brakes by itself. The hydraulic unit receives all its instructions from the control unit. If a problem occurs in the hydraulic unit, it must be replaced because it is not serviceable in any way.

The control module is also located in the passenger compartment and is essentially the "brain" for the ABS system. The function of the control module — made up of resistors, diodes, transistors and large integrated circuits — is to accept and process information received from the wheel speed sensors. Wheel acceleration, deceleration and slip values are calculated to produce control commands for the hydraulic unit. If a problem is suspected in the control module, it must be replaced as an assembly.

The wheel speed sensors are located at each wheel and send an electric signal to the control module indicating rotational speed. The wheel speed sensors are installed in the knuckles and have toothed rings pressed onto the front hub and bearing assemblies and the rear spindles. The sensors do not require any adjustment, nor are repairs possible.

**Diagnosis and repair**

If the dashboard warning light comes on and stays on while the vehicle is in operation, the ABS system requires attention. Although a special electronic ABS diagnostic tester is available, the home mechanic can perform a few preliminary checks before taking the vehicle to a dealer who is equipped with this tester.

  a) Check that the control module electrical connector is securely connected.
  b) Follow the wiring harness to each wheel and check that all connections are secure and that the wiring is not damaged.
  c) Check the condition of the *Brake* fuse at the fuse box.
  d) Check the condition of the *Gauge* fuse at the fuse box.

If the above preliminary checks do not rectify the problem, the vehicle should be diagnosed by a dealer service department. Due to the rather complicated nature of this system, all actual repair work must be done by factory authorized technicians.

---

### 13  Suspension and steering systems

### Power steering pump — removal and installation

1   Remove the serpentine drivebelt (see Section 3).

2   Disconnect the power steering lines from the pump. Be careful not to damage the pump as it's made out of plastic.

3   Remove the retaining bolts by inserting a socket and extension through the holes in the pump pulley (see Fig. 13.73).

4   Special tools are needed to transfer the pulley to the new pump. If the tools are not available, take the pump to a dealer service department or repair shop.

5   Installation is the reverse of removal.

---

### 14  Chassis electrical system

### Composite headlights — removal and installation

**Caution:** *The composite headlights have halogen bulbs which contain a gas under pressure. Handling a bulb improperly could cause it to shatter into flying glass fragments. To help avoid personal injury, be sure to turn off the headlights and allow the bulb to cool before changing bulbs. Leave the headlights off until the bulb change is complete. Always wear eye protection when changing a halogen bulb. Handle the bulb only by its base. Avoid touching the glass. Do not drop or scratch the glass. Keep moisture away. Place the used bulb in the new bulb carton and dispose of it properly. Keep halogen bulbs out of the reach of children.*

1   When replacing composite-type bulbs on some models, it may be necessary to remove the grille and the headlight assembly (see Chapter 11). It isn't necessary to replace the entire assembly.

2   Locate the bulb lock ring on the back of the headlight assembly and turn it counterclockwise until it's loose.

3   With a vertical rocking motion, pull the bulb to the rear.

4   With one hand, grip the wire harness end of the bulb. Do not grip the wires. With the other hand, grip the base of the bulb. Do not grip the bulb glass. Pull the bulb and base apart. **Note:** *The bulbs for high and low beams are the same and have two separate filaments. Instead of using a new bulb for a burned out light, low and high beam bulbs can be interchanged.*

5   Installation is the reverse of removal.

### Wiring diagrams

Included in this Supplement are selected wiring diagrams that apply only to those circuits which differ significantly from earlier models. If a particular circuit is not included here, refer to the wiring diagram for the latest model in Chapter 12.

---

**WIRING DIAGRAMS START ON NEXT PAGE**

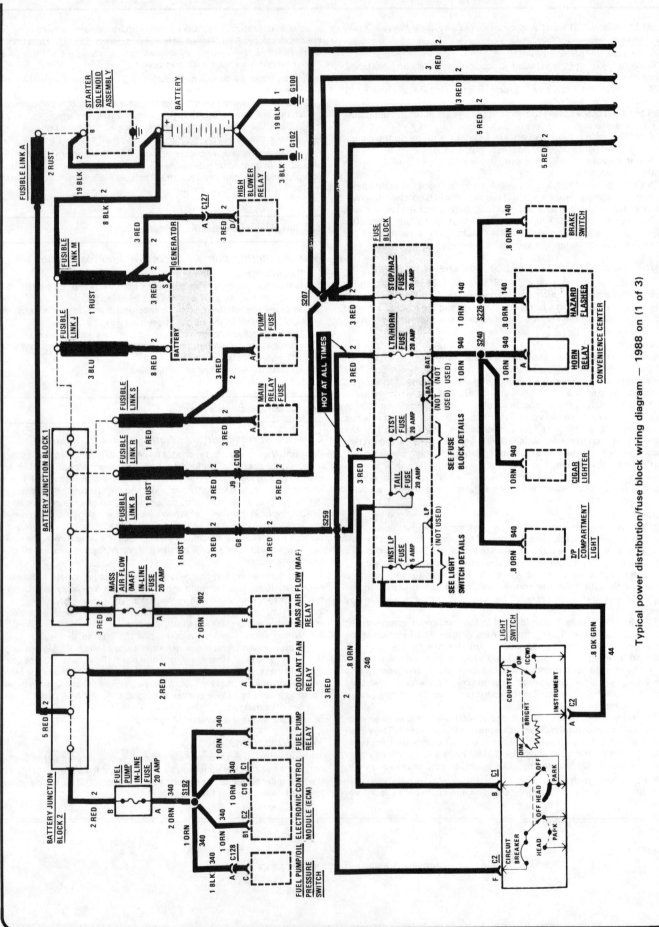

Typical power distribution/fuse block wiring diagram — 1988 on (1 of 3)

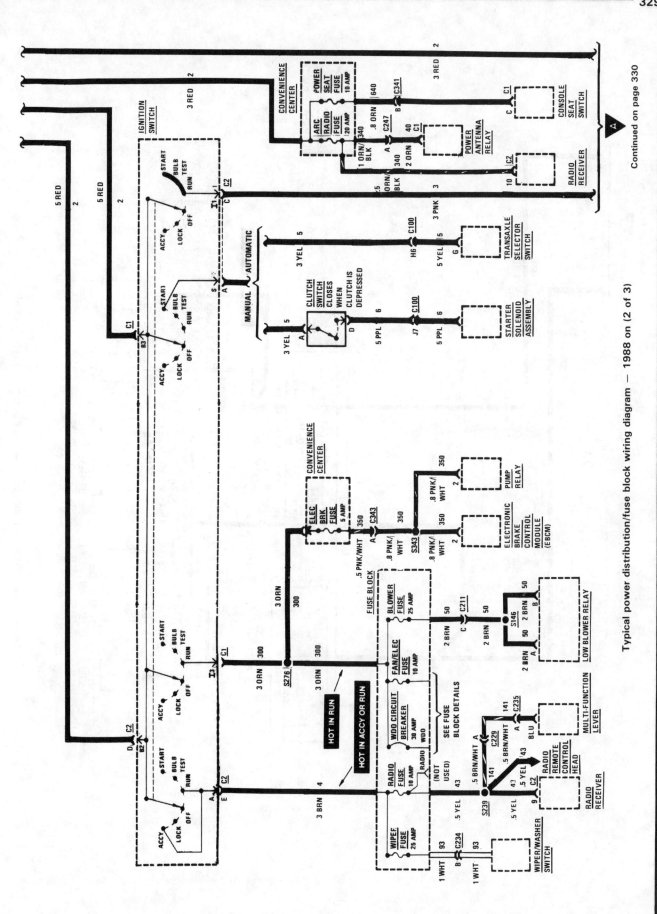

Typical power distribution/fuse block wiring diagram — 1988 on (2 of 3)

Continued on page 330

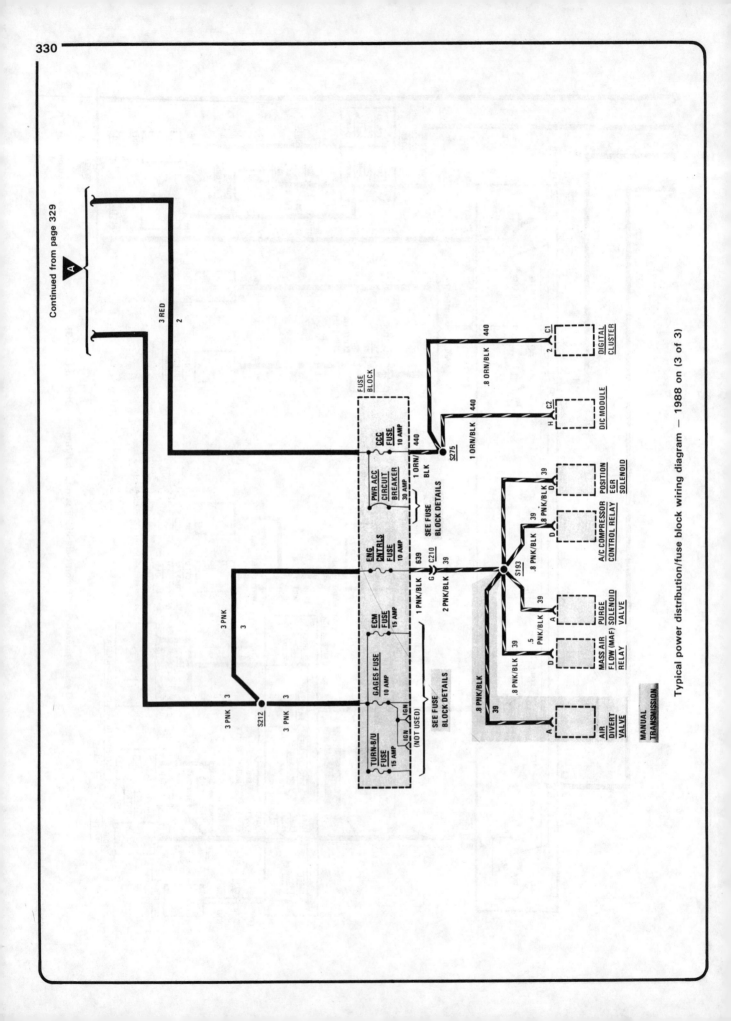

Continued from page 329

Typical power distribution/fuse block wiring diagram — 1988 on (3 of 3)

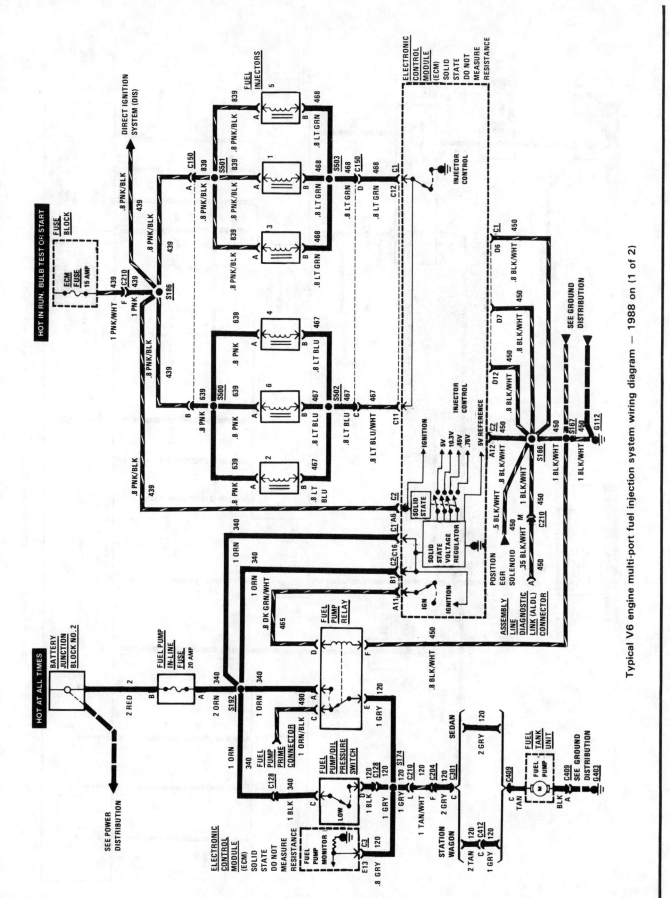

Typical V6 engine multi-port fuel injection system wiring diagram — 1988 on (1 of 2)

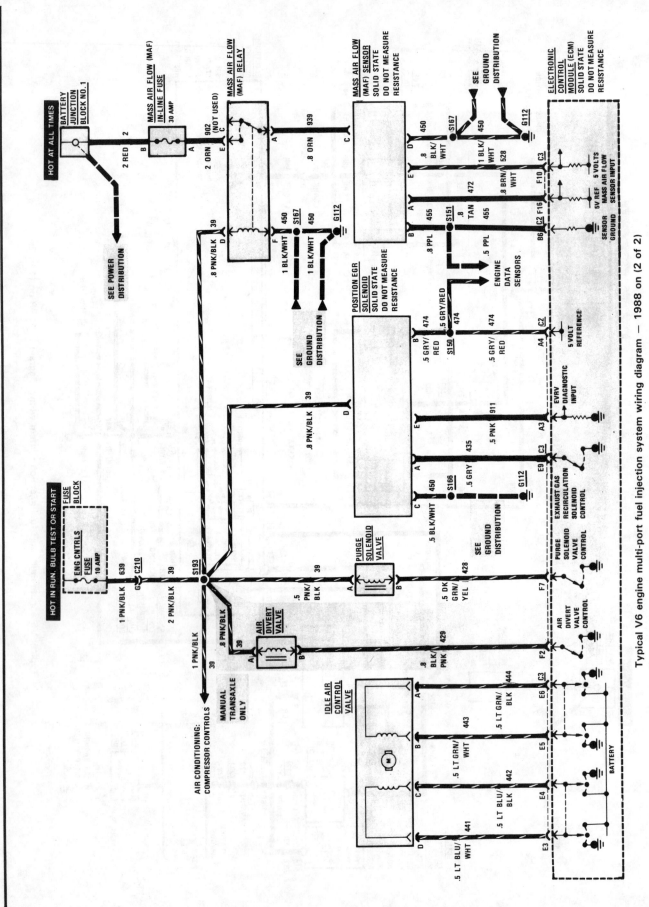

Typical V6 engine multi-port fuel injection system wiring diagram — 1988 on (2 of 2)

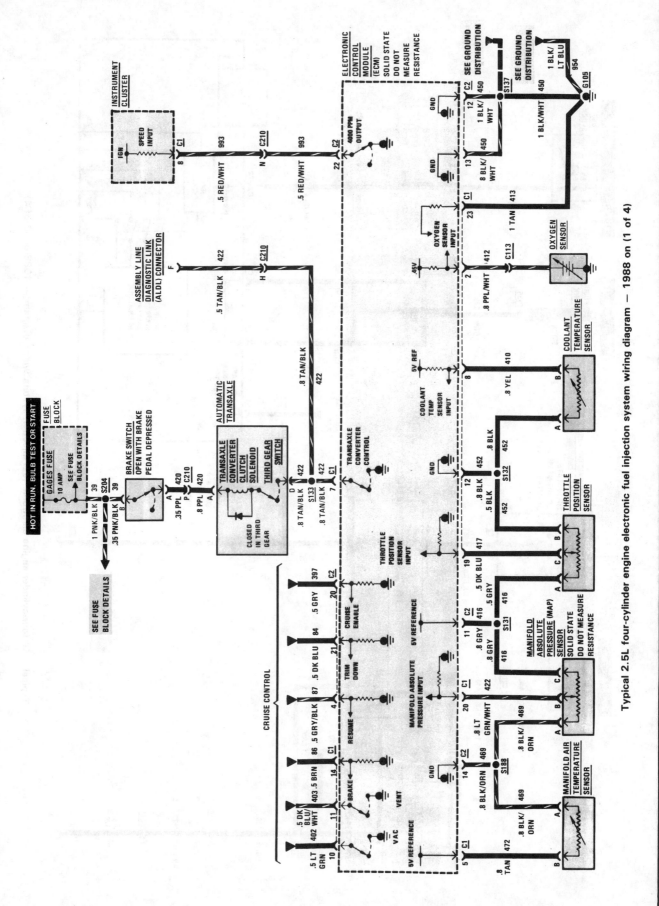

Typical 2.5L four-cylinder engine electronic fuel injection system wiring diagram — 1988 on (1 of 4)

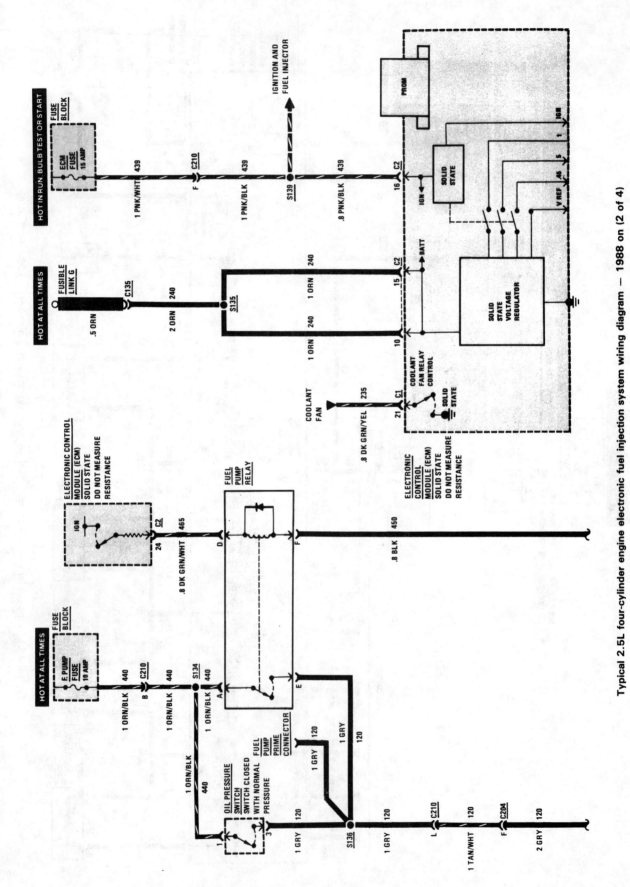

Typical 2.5L four-cylinder engine electronic fuel injection system wiring diagram — 1988 on (2 of 4)

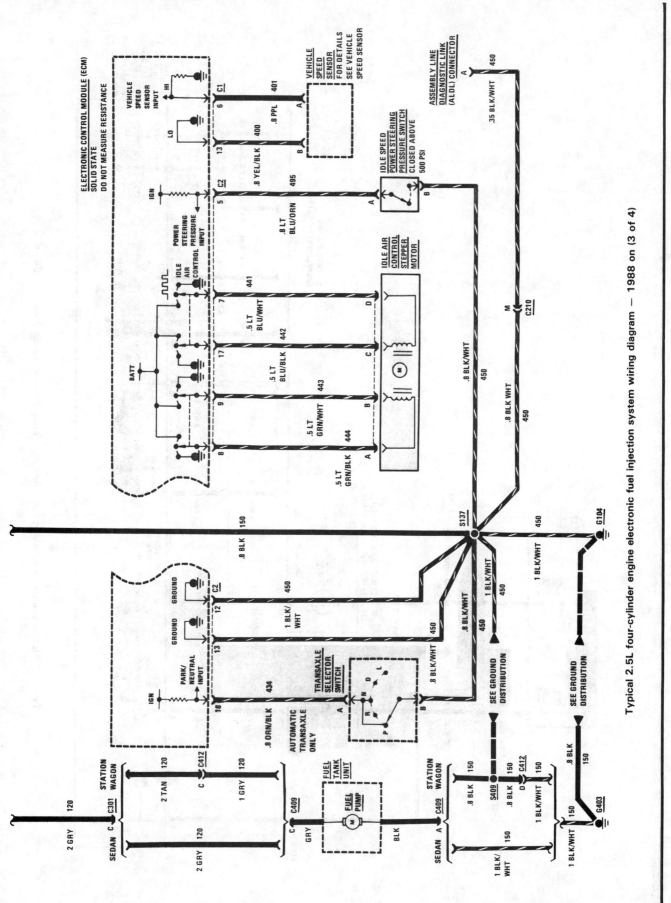

Typical 2.5L four-cylinder engine electronic fuel injection system wiring diagram — 1988 on (3 of 4)

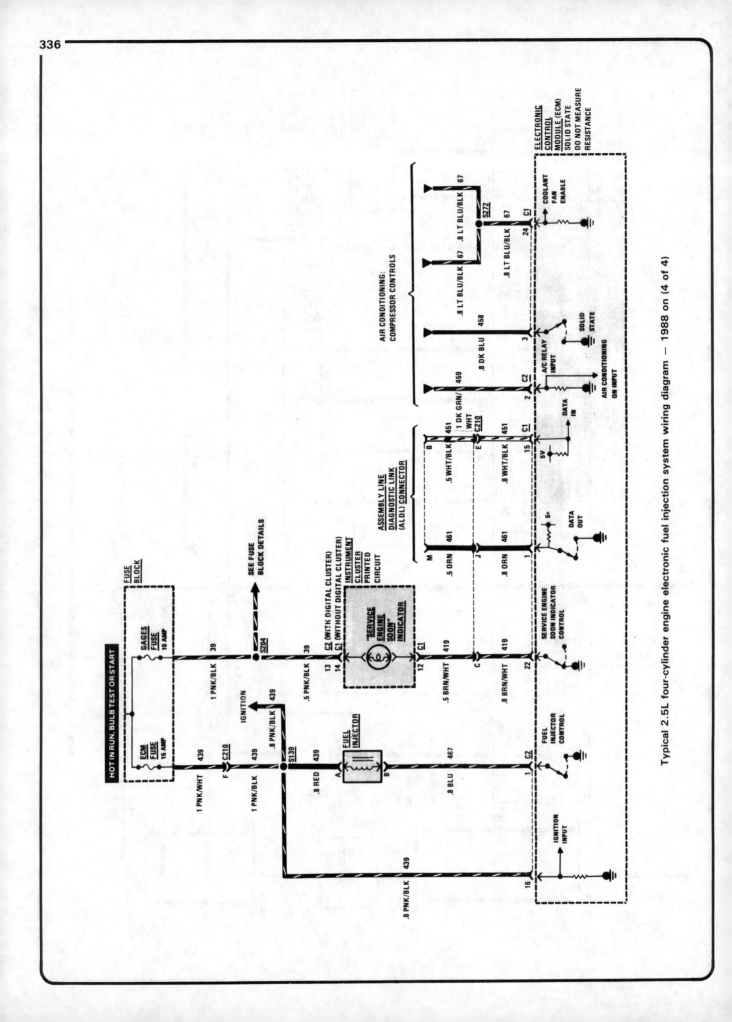

Typical 2.5L four-cylinder engine electronic fuel injection system wiring diagram — 1988 on (4 of 4)

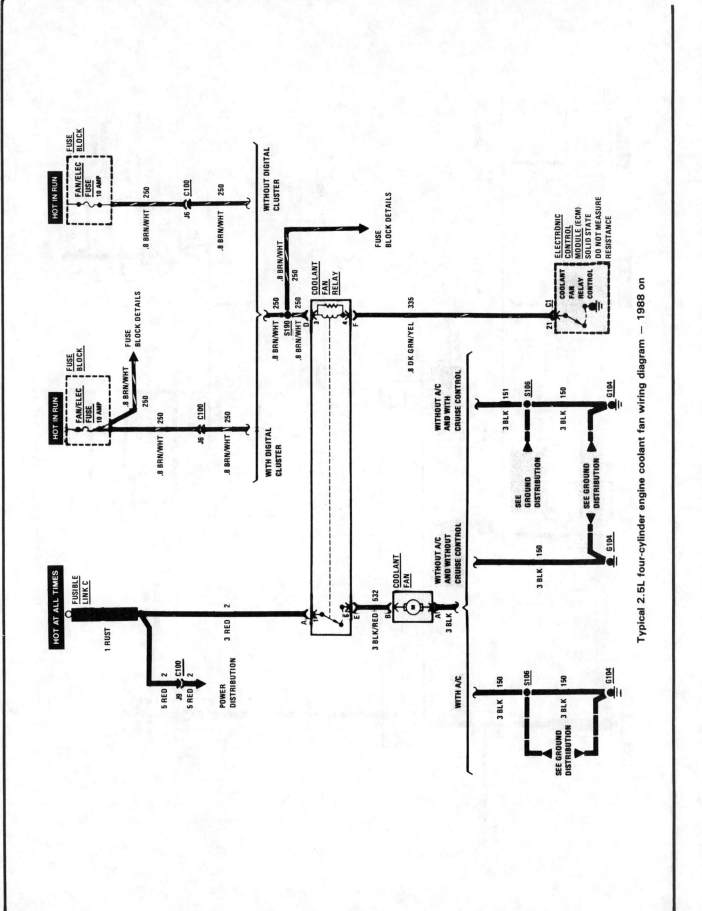

Typical 2.5L four-cylinder engine coolant fan wiring diagram — 1988 on

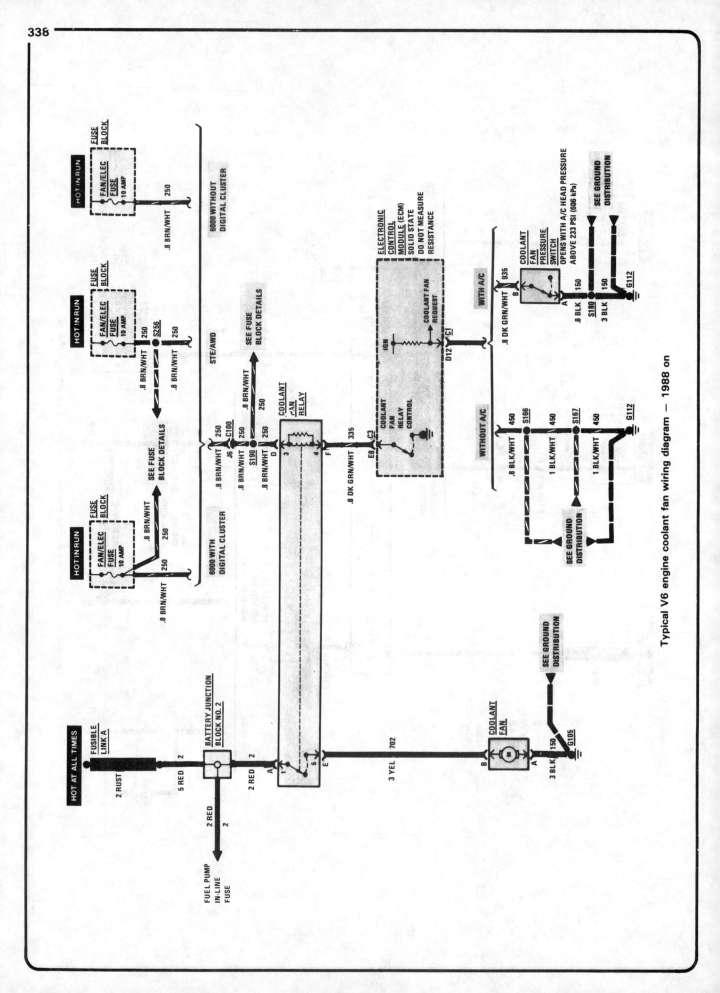

Typical V6 engine coolant fan wiring diagram — 1988 on

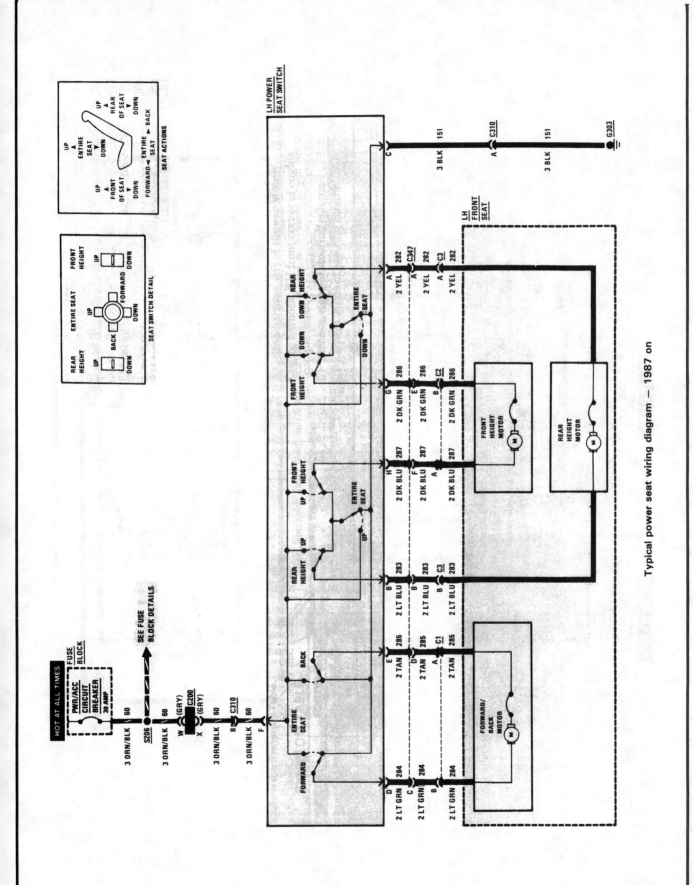

Typical power seat wiring diagram — 1987 on

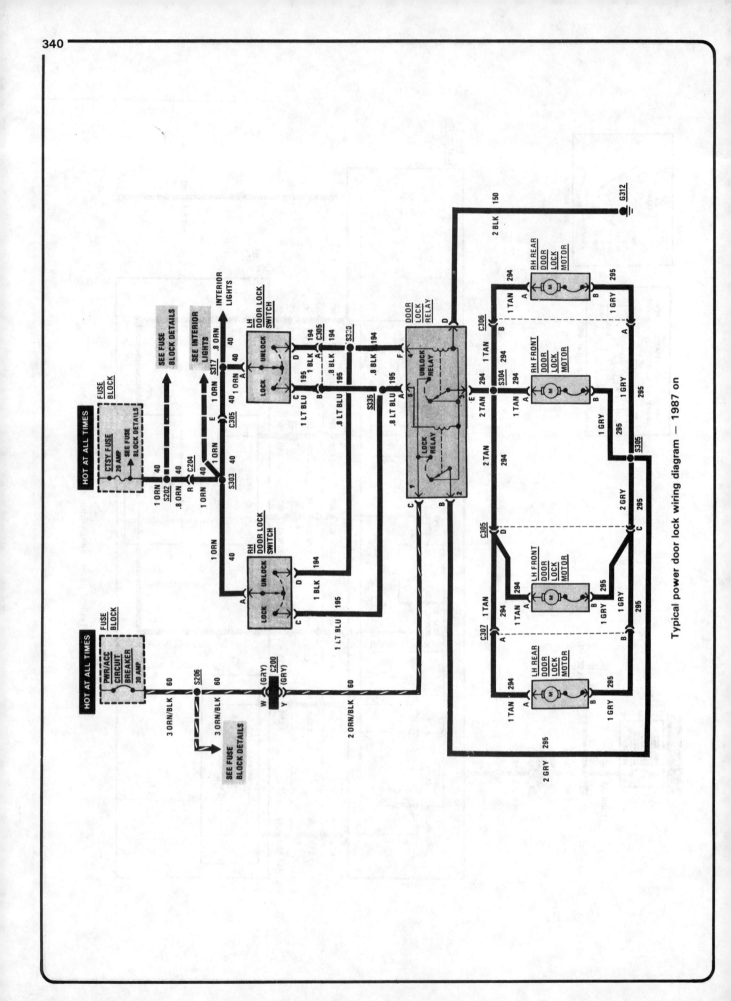

Typical power door lock wiring diagram — 1987 on

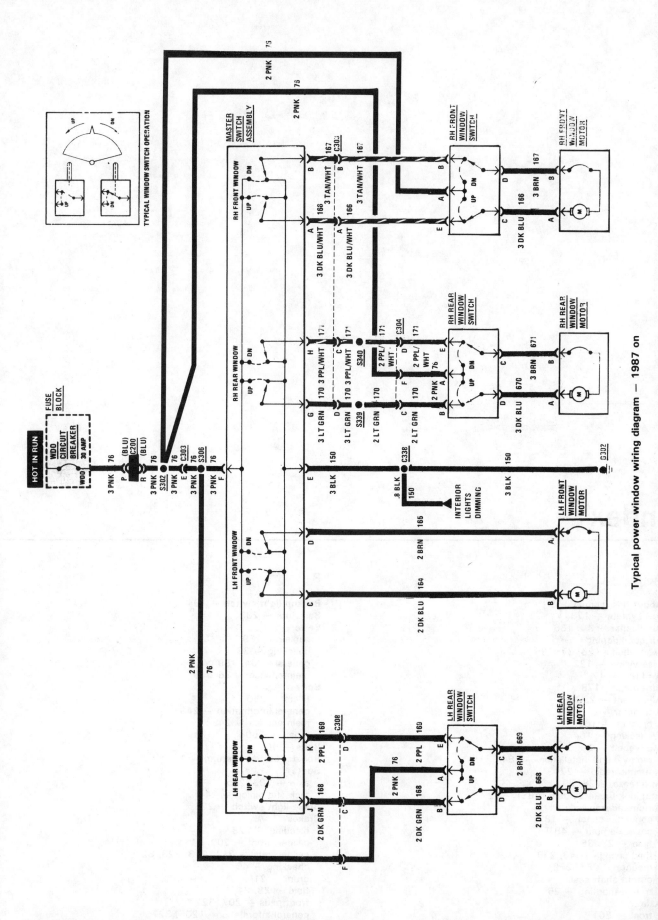

Typical power window wiring diagram — 1987 on

# Index

## A

**About this manual** — 5
**AIR system** — 178
**Air cleaner** — 44, 186
**Air conditioning**
  drivebelt — 29, 37, 296
  servicing — 122
**Air filter** — 47
**Air pump** — 178
**Alignment** — 230
**Alternator**
  brushes — 165
  checking — 164
  drivebelt — 29, 37, 296
  removal and installation — 164
**Antenna, radio** — 271
**Antifreeze** — 28, 33, 117
**Anti-lock Brake System (ABS)** — 327
**Automatic transaxle**
  converter clutch — 187
  driveaxle boot — 45
  fluid — 28, 35
  fluid change — 46, 298
  mounts — 66, 82, 94
  output shaft seal — 45
  troubleshooting — 25
**Axle**
  front — 201
  rear — 240

## B

**Backup light switch** — 194
**Balljoints** — 233
**Battery**
  cables — 159
  checking — 36
  general — 34, 159
  maintenance — 36
**Body**
  fillers — 250
  general information — 249
  maintenance — 249
  repair — 250
**Bolts** — 10
**Booster battery starting** — 17
**Boots**
  axle — 203, 205
  rack and pinion — 244
**Brake light switch** — 228
**Brakes**
  bleeding — 228
  caliper, front — 209, 211
  caliper, rear — 211, 213, 323, 324
  checking — 40
  drum — 215
  fluid — 28, 34
  front pads — 207, 322
  general information — 206, 327
  hoses — 226

lines and hoses — 226
lining thickness — 29
master cylinder — 221, 326
pads — 207, 212, 322
parking — 227, 326
parking switch — 274
power booster — 227
rear drum — 215
rear pads — 212, 322
rear shoes — 215
rotors — 214
shoes — 215
switch — 228
troubleshooting — 26
wheel cylinder — 220
**Bulbs**
replacement — 268
specifications — 263
**Buying parts** — 10

## C

**Caliper**
front brake — 209, 211
rear brake — 211, 213, 323, 324
**Cam bearings** — 107
**Camshaft** — 65, 80, 90, 97, 98, 99, 107
**Capacities** — 28
**Carburetor**
choke check — 41
fuel filter — 43
idle speed — 29, 41
mounting torque — 44
overhaul — 132, 149
throttle linkage — 44
**Carpets, maintenance** — 249
**Charging system** — 164, 317
**Chassis lubrication** — 38
**Chemicals** — 18
**Circuit breakers** — 265
**Cleaners** — 18
**Clutch**
adjustment — 45
bleeding — 322
cable — 198
fluid level check — 297
fluid type — 291
general information — 197, 322
inspection — 198
operation — 197
pedal — 197
release bearing — 199
release lever — 197
removal and installation — 198, 322
troubleshooting — 24
**Coil** — 163, 315
**Composite headlights** — 327
**Compression check** — 55
**Compression pressure** — 29
**Connecting rods** — 96, 97, 98, 104, 108, 114
**Connecting rod bearings** — 110, 114
**Console, removal and installation** — 257
**Control arms** — 233
**Control arm bushings** — 239
**Conversion factors** — 20
**Coolant** — 28
**Cooling system**
antifreeze — 28, 33, 117
capacity — 28, 291
check — 38
coolant — 28, 33, 117
drivebelts — 29, 37, 296
fan — 119
general information — 117, 305

radiator — 119
radiator cap pressure — 29, 117
servicing — 46
temperature sending unit — 122
thermostat — 29, 117, 119
troubleshooting — 24
water pump — 121, 305
**Cradle, removal and installation** — 261, 262
**Crankcase front cover** — 78, 299, 302
**Crankshaft** — 96, 97, 98, 105, 109, 113
**Crankshaft**
balancer — 63, 78, 90
hub — 63, 78, 90
main bearings — 110, 113
oil seals — 63, 66, 76, 79, 90, 93, 111, 302
pulley — 63
**Cruise control** — 274
**Cylinder heads** — 59, 75, 88, 101, 102, 104, 298, 302, 303

## D

**Damper, hatch** — 252
**Defogger** — 277
**Dent repair** — 250
**Dimensions** — 8
**Disc brake pads** — 207
**Distributor** — 29, 160
**Distributor**
cap — 53
rotor — 53
**Door**
glass replacement — 255
handle, outside — 255
lock assembly — 254
lock cylinder — 254
lock knobs — 252
mirror — 257
trim panels — 252
window handle — 254
**Driveaxles**
boots — 45, 203, 205
general information — 201
removal and installation — 202
troubleshooting — 26
**Drivebelts** — 29, 37, 296
**Driveplate** — 66
**Drum brakes** — 215

## E

**Early fuel evaporation system** — 54
**EFI** — 152, 307, 309
**EGR** — 182
**Electronic Fuel Injection (EFI)** — 152, 305 thru 314
**Electrical system**
alternator — 164, 165
battery — 34, 36, 159
bulb replacement — 268
charging system — 164, 317
circuit breakers — 265
cruise control — 274
electrolyte — 34
fuses — 264
fusible links — 264
general information — 263
hazard flasher — 265
headlights — 266, 268, 327
headlight switch — 273
instrument cluster — 272
instruments — 272
parking brake switch — 274
radio and speakers — 270
radio antenna — 271

rear defogger — 277
starter — 167
starter brushes — 169
starting system — 167
steering column switches — 265
solenoid — 168
troubleshooting — 23, 264
turn signal flasher — 265
wiring diagrams — 278 thru 289, 328 thru 341
**Electrolyte** — 34
**Emissions system**
Air Injection Reactor (AIR/PULSAIR) system — 178
Computer Command Control System (CCCS) — 172
Electronic Spark Timing (EST) — 178
evaporative emissions control system — 50, 184
early fuel evaporation system — 54, 181
Exhaust Gas Recirculation (EGR) system — 49, 182
fuel control system — 177
general information — 171, 317
oxygen sensor — 48, 177
Positive Crankcase Ventilation (PCV) system — 47, 49, 185
THERMAC — 44, 186
transmission converter clutch — 187
trouble codes — 174, 318
**Engine**
block — 96, 97, 98, 106
cradle — 261, 262
crankshaft — 96, 97, 98, 105, 109, 113
compression check — 55
compression pressure — 29
connecting rods — 96, 97, 98, 114
connecting rod bearings — 110, 114
disassembly sequence — 100
general information, 2.5L — 56, 298
general information, 2.8/3.1L — 71, 300
general information, 3.0/3.8L — 86
general information, 3.3/3.8L — 303
idle speed — 29
ignition timing — 29, 50
initial start up and break in — 116
main bearings — 110, 113
mounts — 66, 81, 94
oil — 28, 33, 291
oil and filter change — 41, 297
oil seals — 63, 66, 76, 79, 90, 93, 111, 302
overhaul general information — 99
pistons and rings — 97, 98, 104, 108, 110
pre-oiling — 115
pushrod cover — 57
reassembly sequence — 115
rebuilding alternatives — 100
removal and installation — 67, 68, 84, 94
removal methods and precautions — 100
rocker arm cover — 57, 71, 86, 300
timing chain — 80, 90
timing chain cover — 64, 78, 89
troubleshooting — 22
**Evaporative emissions control system** — 50, 184
**Exhaust Gas Recirculation (EGR) system** — 49, 182
**Exhaust system**
check — 40
general information — 131
manifolds — 59, 74, 87, 298
removal and installation — 156
**Exterior mirror** — 257

**F**

**Fan** — 119
**Fasteners** — 10
**Filters**
air — 47
fuel — 43
oil — 41
PCV — 47

**Firing order** — 29
**Flashers** — 265
**Fluid level check** — 33, 297
**Fluids** — 28, 291
**Flywheel** — 66
**Front end alignment** — 230
**Fuel**
line — 131, 305
pump — 131, 153, 307
tank — 131, 132
**Fuel injection**
EFI general information — 152, 307, 309
filter — 43
idle air control — 153, 308
idle speed — 29, 41, 309
injector (TBI) — 154, 308
mounting torque — 44
multiport (MPFI) system — 156, 309 thru 314
overhaul — 155, 308
pressure regulator — 154, 308
pressure relief — 153, 305
pump — 153, 307
quick-connect fuel line fittings — 305
throttle body injection assembly — 155, 308
throttle linkage — 44
**Fuel system**
carburetors — 132, 149
carburetor specifications — 123, 295
checking — 42
choke check — 41
filter — 43
general information — 131, 305
idle speed — 29, 41
intake manifold — 58, 72
throttle linkage — 44
troubleshooting — 24
**Fuses** — 264
**Fusible links** — 264

**G**

**Glass replacement** — 255, 257

**H**

**Hall Effect switch** — 163
**Hatch**
adjustment — 252
damper — 252
removal and installation — 252
**Hazard flasher** — 265
**Headlight**
adjustment — 268
removal and installation — 266, 327
switch — 273
**Hinges, maintenance** — 249
**Hood**
latch cable — 251
removal and installation — 251
**Hoses**
brake — 226
general — 38
removal tips — 13
**Hubs**
front — 236
rear — 241
**Hydraulic clutch** — 291, 321, 322
**Hydraulic lifters** — 61, 73, 88, 107, 299, 304
**Hydraulic system, bleeding** — 228

## I

Identification numbers — 8
Idle speed — 29, 41, 309
Ignition switch — 265
Ignition system
  check — 159
  coil — 163, 315
  distributor — 29, 160
  distributor cap — 53
  firing order — 29
  general information — 158, 314
  Hall Effect switch — 163
  module — 163, 315
  pick-up coil — 160
  precautions — 158
  rotor — 53
  sensors — 315, 317
  spark plugs — 29, 51, 52, 291
  spark plug wires — 53
  switch — 265
  timing — 29, 50
Instrument panel
  removal and installation — 272
  trim plates — 260
Instruments, removal and installation — 272
Intake manifold — 58, 72, 301, 303
Introduction — 5, 290

## J

Jacking — 17
Jumpstarting — 17

## L

Lifters — 61, 73, 88, 107, 299, 304
Light bulbs — 263
Lines, brake — 226
Lock knobs — 252
Lock assembly
  door — 254
  rear lid — 256
Lock cylinder
  door — 254
  rear lid — 255
Locks, maintenance — 249
Lubrication — 38
Lubricants — 18, 28, 291

## M

Maintenance — 10, 29, 296
Maintenance intervals — 29
Master cylinder — 221
Metric conversion — 20
Mirror, door — 257
Multiport fuel injection (MPFI) — 156, 309 thru 314

## N

Neutral safety switch — 194
Numbers — 8
Nuts — 10

## O

Oil — 28, 33, 41, 291, 297
Oil pan — 62, 76, 91, 299, 302
Oil pump — 63, 76, 85, 91, 92, 300, 304
Oil pump driveshaft — 62
Oil seals — 63, 67, 76, 79, 90, 93, 111, 302
Oxygen sensor — 48, 177

## P

Pads, brake — 207, 212, 322
Painting — 250
Parking brake — 227, 326
Parking brake switch — 274
Parts — 10
PCV system — 47, 49, 185
Pistons — 97, 104, 108, 110, 114
Power brake booster — 227
Power steering
  drivebelt — 29, 37, 296
  fluid — 28, 36, 291
  pump — 246, 247, 327
  system bleeding — 248
Pre-oiling — 115
PULSAIR system — 178
Pushrod cover — 57

## R

Rack and pinion
  boots — 244
  removal and installation — 245
Radiator — 119
Radiator cap — 29, 117
Radio
  antenna — 271
  removal and installation — 270
Rear axle — 240
Rear axle, troubleshooting — 26
Rear hatch
  adjustment — 252
  damper — 252
  removal and installation — 252
Rear hub — 241
Rear wheel bearings — 241
Recommended lubricants — 28, 291
Rings — 97, 108, 110
Rocker arm cover — 57, 71, 86, 300
Roll bar — 232
Rotor
  brake — 214
  distributor — 53
Routine maintenance — 29, 296
Rust repairs — 250

## S

Safety — 19
Shift linkage — 189, 192
Shifter — 189, 192
Shock absorbers — 236, 237
Shoes, brake — 215
Spark plugs — 29, 51, 52, 291
Spark plug wires — 53
Speaker, removal and installation — 270
Speedometer cable, replacement — 272
Speedometer, removal and installation — 272
Springs, rear — 238

**Stabilizer bar** — 232
**Starter** — 167
**Starter brushes** — 169
**Starter solenoid** — 168
**Starting system** — 167
**Steering system**
  check — 40
  column — 243
  column switches — 265
  front hub — 236
  knuckle — 243
  pump — 246, 247
  rack and pinion — 245
  rack and pinion boots — 244
  struts — 234
  tie rods — 244
  troubleshooting — 27
  wheel — 241
  wheel bearings — 236
**Stoplight switch** — 228
**Struts** — 234
**Studs, wheel** — 237, 241
**Suspension system**
  balljoints — 233
  bearings — 236
  checking — 40
  control arm bushings — 239
  front bearings — 236
  front hubs — 236
  general information — 231
  inspection — 232
  lower control arm — 233
  rear axle assembly — 240
  rear hub — 241
  rear springs — 238
  shock absorbers — 236, 237
  struts — 234
  track bar — 238
  troubleshooting — 27
**Switches, steering column** — 265


**T**

**Taillight bulb replacement** — 269
**TBI** — 29, 41, 43, 44, 152, 154, 155, 307
**Temperature sending unit** — 122
**THERMAC** — 44, 186
**Thermostat** — 29, 117, 119
**Throttle linkage** — 44
**Throwout bearing** — 199
**Tie rods** — 244
**Tightening sequences** — 12
**Timing** — 29, 50
**Timing chain** — 80, 90
**Timing gear cover** — 64, 78, 89, 299
**Tire pressure** — 32
**Tire rotation** — 45
**Tires** — 32, 45, 229, 230
**Tools** — 13
**Towing** — 17
**Track bar** — 238
**Transaxle, automatic**
  backup light switch — 194
  converter clutch — 187
  diagnosis — 192
  driveaxle boot — 45
  fluid — 28, 35, 291
  fluid change — 46, 298
  general information — 192
  mounts — 66, 82, 94
  neutral safety switch — 194

  output shaft seal — 45
  removal and installation — 194
  shift linkage — 192
  throttle valve (TV) cable — 193
  troubleshooting — 25
**Transaxle, manual**
  driveaxle boots — 45
  general information — 188
  lubricant — 28, 35, 291, 297
  mounts — 66, 82, 94, 188
  oil change — 46
  output shaft seal — 45
  removal and installation — 191
  shift cables — 189
  shift linkage — 189
  troubleshooting — 25
**Trim panel, door** — 252
**Trim plates** — instrument panel — 260
**Trim, vinyl** — 249
**Trouble codes** — 174, 318
**Troubleshooting**
  automatic transaxle — 25
  brakes — 26
  clutch — 24
  cooling system — 24
  driveaxles — 26
  electrical system — 23
  engine — 22
  fuel system — 24
  manual transaxle — 25
  rear axle — 26
  suspension and steering — 27
**Tune up** — 31, 296
**Turn signal flasher** — 265
**Turn signal switch** — 265
**TV cable** — 193


**V**

**Valves** — 96, 97, 98, 103
**Valve clearance** — 29, 73
**Valve lifters** — 61, 73, 88, 107, 299, 304
**Valve springs** — 57, 71, 86
**Valve train components** — 57, 71, 86
**Vehicle identification numbers** — 8
**Vibration damper** — 63, 78, 90


**W**

**Washers** — 10
**Water pump** — 121
**Window glass replacement** — 255
**Window regulator, door** — 254
**Windshield replacement** — 257
**Windshield washer fluid** — 34
**Windshield wiper**
  blades — 38
  motor — 273
  removal and installation — 273
**Wheel bearings** — 46, 236, 241
**Wheel bearing lubricant** — 28
**Wheel cylinder** — 220
**Wheel studs** — 237, 241
**Wheels**
  general information — 229
  removal and installation — 230
**Wiring diagrams** — 278 thru 289, 328 thru 341
**Working facilities** — 16

# HAYNES AUTOMOTIVE MANUALS

## ALFA-ROMEO
531    **Alfa Romeo Sedan & Coupe** '73 thru '80

## AMC
   **Jeep CJ** – see JEEP (412)
694    **Mid-size models,** Concord, Hornet, Gremlin & Spirit '70 thru '83
934    **(Renault) Alliance & Encore** all models '83 thru '87

## AUDI
162    **100** all models '69 thru '77
615    **4000** all models '80 thru '87
428    **5000** all models '77 thru '83
1117    **5000** all models '84 thru '88
207    **Fox** all models '73 thru '79

## AUSTIN
049    **Healey 100/6 & 3000** Roadster '56 thru '68
   **Healey Sprite** – see MG Midget Roadster (265)

## BLMC
260    **1100, 1300 & Austin America** '62 thru '74
527    **Mini** all models '59 thru '69
*646    **Mini** all models '69 thru '88

## BMW
276    **320i** all 4 cyl models '75 thru '83
632    **528i & 530i** all models '75 thru '80
240    **1500 thru 2002** all models except Turbo '59 thru '77
348    **2500, 2800, 3.0 & Bavaria** '69 thru '76

## BUICK
   **Century (front wheel drive)** – see GENERAL MOTORS A-Cars (829)
*1627    **Buick, Oldsmobile & Pontiac Full-size (Front wheel drive)** all models '85 thru '90
   **Buick** Electra, LeSabre and Park Avenue; **Oldsmobile** Delta 88 Royale, Ninety Eight and Regency; **Pontiac** Bonneville
*1551    **Buick Oldsmobile & Pontiac Full-size (Rear wheel drive)**
   **Buick** Electra '70 thru '84, Estate '70 thru '90, LeSabre '70 thru '79
   **Oldsmobile** Custom Cruiser '70 thru '90, Delta 88 '70 thru '85, Ninety-eight '70 thru '84
   **Pontiac** Bonneville '70 thru '86, Catalina '70 thru '81, Grandville '70 thru '75, Parisienne '84 thru '86
627    **Mid-size** all rear-drive **Regal & Century** models with V6, V8 and Turbo '74 thru '87
   **Skyhawk** – see GENERAL MOTORS J-Cars (766)
552    **Skylark** all X-car models '80 thru '85

## CADILLAC
   **Cimarron** – see GENERAL MOTORS J-Cars (766)

## CAPRI
296    **2000 MK I Coupe** all models '71 thru '75
283    **2300 MK II Coupe** all models '74 thru '78
205    **2600 & 2800 V6 Coupe** '71 thru '75
375    **2800 Mk II V6 Coupe** '75 thru '78
   **Mercury in-line engines** – see FORD Mustang (654)
   **Mercury V6 & V8 engines** – see FORD Mustang (558)

## CHEVROLET
*1477    **Astro & GMC Safari Mini-vans** all models '85 thru '90
554    **Camaro** V8 all models '70 thru '81
*866    **Camaro** all models '82 thru '89
   **Cavalier** – see GENERAL MOTORS J-Cars (766)
   **Celebrity** – see GENERAL MOTORS A-Cars (829)

625    **Chevelle, Malibu & El Camino** all V6 & V8 models '69 thru '87
449    **Chevette & Pontiac T1000** all models '76 thru '87
550    **Citation** all models '80 thru '85
*1628    **Corsica/Beretta** all models '87 thru '90
274    **Corvette** all V8 models '68 thru '82
*1336    **Corvette** all models '84 thru '89
704    **Full-size Sedans** Caprice, Impala, Biscayne, Bel Air & Wagons, all V6 & V8 models '69 thru '90
319    **Luv Pick-up** all 2WD & 4WD models '72 thru '82
626    **Monte Carlo** all V6, V8 & Turbo models '70 thru '88
241    **Nova** all V8 models '69 thru '79
*1642    **Nova and Geo Prizm** all front wheel drive models, '85 thru '90
*420    **Pick-ups '67 thru '87** – Chevrolet & GMC, all V8 & in-line 6 cyl 2WD & 4WD models '67 thru '87
*1664    **Pick-ups '88 thru '90** – Chevrolet & GMC all full-size (C and K) models, '88 thru '90
*831    **S-10 & GMC S-15 Pick-ups** all models '82 thru '90
*345    **Vans** – Chevrolet & GMC, V8 & in-line 6 cyl models '68 thru '89
208    **Vega** all models except Cosworth '70 thru '77

## CHRYSLER
*1337    **Chrysler & Plymouth Mid-size** front wheel drive '82 thru '88
   **K-Cars** – see DODGE Aries (723)
   **Laser** – see DODGE Daytona (1140)

## DATSUN
402    **200SX** all models '77 thru '79
647    **200SX** all models '80 thru '83
228    **B-210** all models '73 thru '78
525    **210** all models '78 thru '82
206    **240Z, 260Z & 280Z** Coupe & 2+2 '70 thru '78
563    **280ZX** Coupe & 2+2 '79 thru '83
   **300ZX** – see NISSAN (1137)
679    **310** all models '78 thru '82
123    **510 & PL521 Pick-up** '68 thru '73
430    **510** all models '78 thru '81
372    **610** all models '72 thru '76
277    **620 Series Pick-up** all models '73 thru '79
235    **710** all models '73 thru '77
   **720 Series Pick-up** – see NISSAN Pick-ups (771)
376    **810/Maxima** all gasoline models '77 thru '84
124    **1200** all models '70 thru '73
368    **F10** all models '76 thru '79
   **Pulsar** – see NISSAN (876)
   **Sentra** – see NISSAN (982)
   **Stanza** – see NISSAN (981)

## DODGE
*723    **Aries & Plymouth Reliant** all models '81 thru '88
*1231    **Caravan & Plymouth Voyager Mini-Vans** all models '84 thru '89
699    **Challenger & Plymouth Saporro** all models '78 thru '83
236    **Colt** all models '71 thru '77
419    **Colt (rear wheel drive)** all models '77 thru '80
610    **Colt & Plymouth Champ (front wheel drive)** all models '78 thru '87
*556    **D50 & Plymouth Arrow Pick-ups** '79 thru '88
234    **Dart & Plymouth Valiant** all 6 cyl models '67 thru '76
*1140    **Daytona & Chrysler Laser** all models '84 thru '88
*545    **Omni & Plymouth Horizon** all models '78 thru '89
*912    **Pick-ups** all full-size models '74 thru '90
*349    **Vans** – Dodge & Plymouth V8 & 6 cyl models '71 thru '89

## FIAT
080    **124 Sedan & Wagon** all ohv & dohc models '66 thru '75
094    **124 Sport Coupe & Spider** '68 thru '78
087    **128** all models '72 thru '79
310    **131 & Brava** all models '75 thru '81
038    **850 Sedan, Coupe & Spider** '64 thru '74
479    **Strada** all models '79 thru '82
273    **X1/9** all models '74 thru '80

## FORD
*1476    **Aerostar Mini-vans** all models '86 thru '88
788    **Bronco and Pick-ups** '73 thru '79
*880    **Bronco and Pick-ups** '80 thru '90
014    **Cortina MK II** all models except Lotus '66 thru '70
295    **Cortina MK III** 1600 & 2000 ohc '70 thru '76
268    **Courier Pick-up** all models '72 thru '82
789    **Escort & Mercury Lynx** all models '81 thru '90
560    **Fairmont & Mercury Zephyr** all in-line & V8 models '78 thru '83
334    **Fiesta** all models '77 thru '80
754    **Ford & Mercury Full-size,** Ford LTD & Mercury Marquis ('75 thru '82); Ford Custom 500, Country Squire, Crown Victoria & Mercury Colony Park ('75 thru '87); Ford LTD Crown Victoria & Mercury Gran Marquis ('83 thru '87)
359    **Granada & Mercury Monarch** all in-line, 6 cyl & V8 models '75 thru '80
773    **Ford & Mercury Mid-size,** Ford Thunderbird & Mercury Cougar ('75 thru '82); Ford LTD & Mercury Marquis ('83 thru '86); Ford Torino, Gran Torino, Elite, Ranchero pick-up, LTD II, Mercury Montego, Comet, XR-7 & Lincoln Versailles ('75 thru '86)
*654    **Mustang & Mercury Capri** all in-line models & Turbo '79 thru '90
*558    **Mustang & Mercury Capri** all V6 & V8 models '79 thru '89
357    **Mustang** V8 all models '64-1/2 thru '73
231    **Mustang II** all 4 cyl, V6 & V8 models '74 thru '78
204    **Pinto** all models '70 thru '74
649    **Pinto & Mercury Bobcat** all models '75 thru '80
*1026    **Ranger & Bronco II** all gasoline models '83 thru '89
*1421    **Taurus & Mercury Sable** '86 thru '90
*1418    **Tempo & Mercury Topaz** all gasoline models '84 thru '89
1338    **Thunderbird & Mercury Cougar/XR7** '83 thru '88
*344    **Vans** all V8 Econoline models '69 thru '90

## GENERAL MOTORS
*829    **A-Cars** – Chevrolet Celebrity, Buick Century, Pontiac 6000 & Oldsmobile Cutlass Ciera all models '82 thru '89
*766    **J-Cars** – Chevrolet Cavalier, Pontiac J-2000, Oldsmobile Firenza, Buick Skyhawk & Cadillac Cimarron all models '82 thru '89
*1420    **N-Cars** – Pontiac Grand Am, Buick Somerset and Oldsmobile Calais '85 thru '87; Buick Skylark '86 thru '87

## GEO
   **Tracker** – see SUZUKI Samurai (1626)
   **Prizm** – see CHEVROLET Nova (1642)

## GMC
   **Safari** – see CHEVROLET ASTRO (1477)
   **Vans & Pick-ups** – see CHEVROLET (420, 831, 345, 1664)

(continued on next page)

Haynes Publications Inc., P.O. Box 978, Newbury Park, CA 91320 ● (818) 889-5400 ● (805) 498-6703

NOTE: New manuals are added to this list on a periodic basis. If you do not see a listing for your vehicle, consult your local Haynes dealer for the latest product information.

## HONDA
- **138** 360, 600 & Z Coupe all models '67 thru '75
- **351** Accord CVCC all models '76 thru '83
- *1221 Accord all models '84 thru '89
- **160** Civic 1200 all models '73 thru '79
- **633** Civic 1300 & 1500 CVCC all models '80 thru '83
- **297** Civic 1500 CVCC all models '75 thru '79
- *1227 Civic all models except 16-valve CRX & 4 WD Wagon '84 thru '86
- *601 Prelude CVCC all models '79 thru '89

## HYUNDAI
- *1552 Excel all models '86 thru '89

## ISUZU
- *1641 Trooper & Pick-up, all gasoline models '81 thru '89

## JAGUAR
- **098** MK I & II, 240 & 340 Sedans '55 thru '69
- *242 XJ6 all 6 cyl models '68 thru '86
- *478 XJ12 & XJS all 12 cyl models '72 thru '85
- **140** XK-E 3.8 & 4.2 all 6 cyl models '61 thru '72

## JEEP
- *1553 Cherokee, Comanche & Wagoneer Limited all models '84 thru '89
- **412** CJ all models '49 thru '86

## LADA
- *413 1200, 1300, 1500 & 1600 all models including Riva '74 thru '86

## LANCIA
- **533** Lancia Beta Sedan, Coupe & HPE all models '76 thru '80

## LAND ROVER
- **314** Series II, IIA, & III all 4 cyl gasoline models '58 thru '86
- **529** Diesel all models '58 thru '80

## MAZDA
- **648** 626 Sedan & Coupe (rear wheel drive) all models '79 thru '82
- *1082 626 & MX-6 (front wheel drive) all models '83 thru '90
- *267 B1600, B1800 & B2000 Pick-ups '72 thru '90
- **370** GLC Hatchback (rear wheel drive) all models '77 thru '83
- **757** GLC (front wheel drive) all models '81 thru '86
- **109** RX2 all models '71 thru '75
- **096** RX3 all models '72 thru '76
- **460** RX-7 all models '79 thru '85
- *1419 RX-7 all models '86 thru '89

## MERCEDES-BENZ
- *1643 190 Series all four-cylinder gasoline models, '84 thru '88
- **346** 230, 250 & 280 Sedan, Coupe & Roadster all 6 cyl sohc models '68 thru '72
- **983** 280 123 Series all gasoline models '77 thru '81
- **698** 350 & 450 Sedan, Coupe & Roadster all models '71 thru '80
- **697** Diesel 123 Series 200D, 220D, 240D, 240TD, 300D, 300CD, 300TD, 4- & 5-cyl incl. Turbo '76 thru '85

## MERCURY
*See FORD Listing*

## MG
- **475** MGA all models '56 thru '62
- **111** MGB Roadster & GT Coupe all models '62 thru '80
- **265** MG Midget & Austin Healey Sprite Roadster '58 thru '80

## MITSUBISHI
- Pick-up – see Dodge D-50 (556)

## MORRIS
- **074** (Austin) Marina 1.8 all models '71 thru '80
- **024** Minor 1000 sedan & wagon '56 thru '71

## NISSAN
- *1137 300ZX all Turbo & non-Turbo models '84 thru '86
- *1341 Maxima all models '85 thru '89
- *771 Pick-ups/Pathfinder gas models '80 thru '88
- *876 Pulsar all models '83 thru '86
- *982 Sentra all models '82 thru '90
- *981 Stanza all models '82 thru '90

## OLDSMOBILE
- Custom Cruiser – see BUICK Full-size (1551)
- **658** Cutlass all standard gasoline V6 & V8 models '74 thru '88
- Cutlass Ciera – see GENERAL MOTORS A-Cars (829)
- Firenza – see GENERAL MOTORS J-Cars (766)
- Ninety-eight – see BUICK Full-size (1551)
- Omega – see PONTIAC Phoenix & Omega (551)

## OPEL
- **157** (Buick) Manta Coupe 1900 all models '70 thru '74

## PEUGEOT
- **161** 504 all gasoline models '68 thru '79
- **663** 504 all diesel models '74 thru '83

## PLYMOUTH
- **425** Arrow all models '76 thru '80
- For all other PLYMOUTH titles, see DODGE listing.

## PONTIAC
- T1000 – see CHEVROLET Chevette (449)
- J-2000 – see GENERAL MOTORS J-Cars (766)
- 6000 – see GENERAL MOTORS A-Cars (829)
- **1232** Fiero all models '84 thru '88
- **555** Firebird all V8 models except Turbo '70 thru '81
- *867 Firebird all models '82 thru '89
- Full-size Rear Wheel Drive – see Buick, Oldsmobile, Pontiac Full-size (1551)
- **551** Phoenix & Oldsmobile Omega all X-car models '80 thru '84

## PORSCHE
- *264 911 all Coupe & Targa models except Turbo '65 thru '87
- **239** 914 all 4 cyl models '69 thru '76
- **397** 924 all models including Turbo '76 thru '82
- *1027 944 all models including Turbo '83 thru '89

## RENAULT
- **141** 5 Le Car all models '76 thru '83
- **079** 8 & 10 all models with 58.4 cu in engines '62 thru '72
- **097** 12 Saloon & Estate all models 1289 cc engines '70 thru '80
- **768** 15 & 17 all models '73 thru '79
- **081** 16 all models 89.7 cu in & 95.5 cu in engines '65 thru '72
- **598** 18i & Sportwagon all models '81 thru '86
- Alliance & Encore – see AMC (934)
- **984** Fuego all models '82 thru '85

## ROVER
- **085** 3500 & 3500S Sedan 215 cu in engines '68 thru '76
- *365 3500 SDI V8 all models '76 thru '85

## SAAB
- **198** 95 & 96 V4 all models '66 thru '75
- **247** 99 all models including Turbo '69 thru '80
- *980 900 all models including Turbo '79 thru '88

## SUBARU
- **237** 1100, 1300, 1400 & 1600 all models '71 thru '79
- *681 1600 & 1800 2WD & 4WD all models '80 thru '88

## SUZUKI
- *1626 Samurai/Sidekick and Geo Tracker all models '86 thru '89

## TOYOTA
- *1023 Camry all models '83 thru '90
- **150** Carina Sedan all models '71 thru '74
- **229** Celica ST, GT & liftback all models '71 thru '77
- **437** Celica all models '78 thru '81
- *935 Celica all models except front-wheel drive and Supra '82 thru '85
- **680** Celica Supra all models '79 thru '81
- **1139** Celica Supra all in-line 6-cylinder models '82 thru '86
- **201** Corolla 1100, 1200 & 1600 all models '67 thru '74
- **361** Corolla all models '75 thru '79
- **961** Corolla all models (rear wheel drive) '80 thru '87
- *1025 Corolla all models (front wheel drive) '84 thru '88
- *636 Corolla Tercel all models '80 thru '82
- **230** Corona & MK II all 4 cyl sohc models '69 thru '74
- **360** Corona all models '74 thru '82
- *532 Cressida all models '78 thru '82
- **313** Land Cruiser all models '68 thru '82
- **200** MK II all 6 cyl models '72 thru '76
- *1339 MR2 all models '85 thru '87
- **304** Pick-up all models '69 thru '78
- *656 Pick-up all models '79 thru '90
- **787** Starlet all models '81 thru '84

## TRIUMPH
- **112** GT6 & Vitesse all models '62 thru '74
- **113** Spitfire all models '62 thru '81
- **028** TR2, 3, 3A, & 4A Roadsters '52 thru '67
- **031** TR250 & 6 Roadsters '67 thru '76
- **322** TR7 all models '75 thru '81

## VW
- **091** 411 & 412 all 103 cu in models '68 thru '73
- **036** Bug 1200 all models '54 thru '66
- **039** Bug 1300 & 1500 '65 thru '70
- **159** Bug 1600 all basic, sport & super (curved windshield) models '70 thru '74
- **110** Bug 1600 Super all models (flat windshield) '70 thru '72
- **238** Dasher all gasoline models '74 thru '81
- *884 Rabbit, Jetta, Scirocco, & Pick-up all gasoline models '74 thru '89 & Convertible '80 thru '89
- **451** Rabbit, Jetta & Pick-up all diesel models '77 thru '84
- **082** Transporter 1600 all models '68 thru '79
- **226** Transporter 1700, 1800 & 2000 all models '72 thru '79
- **084** Type 3 1500 & 1600 all models '63 thru '73
- **1029** Vanagon all air-cooled models '80 thru '83

## VOLVO
- **203** 120, 130 Series & 1800 Sports '61 thru '73
- **129** 140 Series all models '66 thru '74
- **244** 164 all models '68 thru '75
- *270 240 Series all models '74 thru '90
- **400** 260 Series all models '75 thru '82
- *1550 740 & 760 Series all models '82 thru '88

## SPECIAL MANUALS
- **1479** Automotive Body Repair & Painting Manual
- **1654** Automotive Electrical Manual
- **1480** Automotive Heating & Air Conditioning Manual
- **482** Fuel Injection Manual
- **299** SU Carburetors thru '88
- **393** Weber Carburetors thru '79
- **300** Zenith/Stromberg CD Carburetors thru '76

*See your dealer for other available titles*

6-1-90

Over 100 Haynes motorcycle manuals also available

* Listings shown with an asterisk (*) indicate model coverage as of this printing. These titles will be periodically updated to include later model years — consult your Haynes dealer for more information.

Haynes Publications Inc., P.O. Box 978, Newbury Park, CA 91320 • (818) 889-5400 • (805) 498-6703